COMMUNICATING IN BUSINESS AND PROFESSIONAL SETTINGS

COMMUNICATING IN BUSINESS AND PROFESSIONAL SETTINGS

FOURTH EDITION

Michael S. Hanna
University of South Alabama

Gerald L. Wilson
University of South Alabama

The McGRAW-HILL Companies, Inc.
New York   St. Louis   San Francisco
Auckland   Bogotá   Caracas   Lisbon   London   Madrid
Mexico City   Milan   Montreal   New Delhi   San Juan   Singapore
Sydney   Tokyo   Toronto

McGraw-Hill Higher Education

A Division of The **McGraw-Hill** Companies

COMMUNICATING IN BUSINESS AND PROFESSIONAL SETTINGS

Copyright © 1998, 1991, 1988, 1984 by The McGraw-Hill Companies, Inc. All rights reserved. Printed in the United States of America. Except as permitted under the United States Copyright Act of 1976, no part of this publication may be reproduced or distributed in any form or by any means, or stored in a data base or retrieval system, without the prior written permission of the publisher.

This book is printed on acid-free paper.

11 12 13 14 15 DOC/DOC 0 9 8 7

ISBN-13: 978-0-07-026022-1
ISBN-10: 0-07-026022-2

This book was set in Sabon by Ruttle, Shaw, and Wetherill.
The editors were Marjorie Byers, Valerie Raymond, and David A. Damstra.
The design manager was Joseph A. Piliero; the cover was designed by Wanda Lubelska.
The production supervisors were Louise Karam and Kathryn Porzio.
The photo editor was Debra Hershkowitz.
Project supervision was done by The Total Book.
R. R. Donnelley & Sons was printer and binder.

Library of Congress Cataloging-in-Publication Data
Hanna, Michael S.,
    Communicating in business and professional settings / Michael S.
Hanna, Gerald L. Wilson. — 4th ed.
        p.   cm
    Includes bibliographical references and index.
    ISBN 0-07-026022-2
    1. Communication in management.   2. Communication in
organizations.   I. Wilson, Gerald L.   II. Title.
HD30.3.H36   1998
658.4'5—dc21   97–122

http://www.mhhe.com

ABOUT THE AUTHORS

Michael S. Hanna is Professor of Communication at the University of South Alabama. He has been teaching at the college and university level for 35 years. He received his A.B., and M.A. from Central Missouri State College and his Ph.D. from the University of Missouri–Columbia.

Professor Hanna is a frequent consultant to business and industry, having worked most recently with such chemical corporations as Courtaulds Fibers, DuPont, Degussa, Olin Corporation and Ciba-Geigy.

Professor Hanna has written or co-authored six books that have, in all, appeared in 17 editions. He has edited five additional books, and has written numerous papers for publication in professional journals and for presentation to academic association meetings. He is currently at work on a new book about interpersonal communication.

Gerald L. Wilson is Professor and Chairman of Communication at the University of South Alabama where he teaches courses in organizational communication. He received his B.S. from Bowling Green State University, his M.A. from Miami University, and his Ph.D. from the University of Wisconsin–Madison. Professor Wilson is an active consultant to business and industry, working over the past ten years with such organizations as RCA Corporation, Jefferson National Life Insurance Company, Scott Paper Company, and International Paper Company.

Professor Wilson has authored numerous articles for journals as well as papers for professional meetings. He is co-author of five books about communication. His most recent books are *Interviewing in Context* (McGraw-Hill, 1991) and *Groups in Context: Participation and Leadership in Small Groups,* 4th ed. (McGraw-Hill, 1996).

DEDICATION

Sons are easy to love, but sometimes difficult to raise. As part of the process of growing up they confront and challenge their fathers. Ours did that in full measure—part of a competition that has characterized the whole history of men. We know we have both been enriched as a result. We proudly dedicate this edition to our grown sons, Paul Russell and Peter Manning Hanna, Shawn David Hall, and Ryan Stewart Wilson, all of whom have taught and continue to teach us much.

CONTENTS

PART II   **Basic Considerations: Foundations for Communication in Organizations**   **95**

CHAPTER 5   **Perception and Listening**   **97**

PREFACE

When we set out to write the first edition of *Communicating in Business and Professional Settings*, our aim was to develop a text for the growing numbers of undergraduate courses that focus attention on communication within organizations. What was needed, we thought, was a lively textbook that would be comprehensive, and that would blend current theory and research with practical skills and applications. We also wanted a book that was richly illustrated with real-life examples from a broad range of business and professional settings. We had become convinced, on the basis of our teaching, research, and consulting experiences, that such a book was much needed.

Many business and managerial concerns—mobility, management of human resources, increased productivity, resolution of client-centered and production problems, contact with the public, creation of a public image, group problem solving, management of conflict, and the like—turn out to be communication activities. The individual who cannot communicate effectively will be unlikely to succeed in these activities. Indeed, some experts have suggested that an organization *is* its communication—that the organization would not exist without the flow of messages that hold it together. What it takes to guide and operate successfully in an organization is an ability to communicate well in a variety of situations. The title of this book, *Communicating in Business and Professional Settings,* conveys our primary focus.

Leadership activity cannot exist independent of communication activity. We also know that the people who make the strongest contributions to their organizations are people who communicate wisely and skillfully. It seems clear to us that there is a direct relationship between a person's verbal ability and how that individual is perceived by others. "Articulate" and "competent" are related perceptions, and they flow directly from a person's communication patterns.

We wrote this book to help our students learn how to communicate better. This means, to us, that they must understand how the communication process works and how they can enter into that process more effectively. They must also understand how organizations work and how people get into, and then function in, their organizations. Clearly, there is a relationship between theory and practice. A book that is only theoretical does not help the student. A book that is only a list of prescribed behaviors cannot help the student, either. Understanding and skill go hand in hand. The first, second and third editions were, therefore, a strong blend of theory and practical applications of that theory. Our aim in this fourth edition is to strengthen and tighten these ties. We think we have done that.

We also carefully reviewed our experiences as teachers and consultants to discover what has helped our students communicate more effectively. The features of this book are designed to respond to student needs based on this careful review.

SPECIAL FEATURES: THE TRIED AND TRUE . . . .

We think that certain features of this book make it stand out as especially useful in business and professional communication courses. We have made every effort to achieve an *appropriate blend of current theory and research with practical explanations, skills, and applications.*

We are convinced that examples can make all the difference between books that are useful in a classroom and books that are not. So *we have filled our book with examples from business and professional settings to show how concepts work in actual organizational contexts.*

Each chapter emphasizes the individual student's own communication behavior, and places that behavior in an organizational context. For example, our book includes an exceptionally thorough coverage of interviewing, including both the interviewer's and the interviewee's roles in selection interviewing and in performance appraisal interviewing.

When we wrote the first edition we pioneered the Troubleshooting Guide that appears at the end of this book. We think students should be able to find answers to questions that are couched in student terms. The guide is organized around the questions most commonly asked by our students and our clients. To use it, a reader need only identify a general category that a question falls into, turn to the questions in that category to find one close to the question at issue, and then identify the page or pages on which the answer may be found. Since the first edition of this book, in all, we have produced six such guides in other works. Our colleagues and our readers have given us good reason to believe students find the Troubleshooting Guide helpful.

Our coverage of material and our sequencing of chapters is designed to fit most courses in oral business and professional communication. Our understanding of the materials in these courses is drawn from a combined teaching, research, and consulting experience of some fifty years.

We have tried to make the book compatible with the way that most of our colleagues approach their courses. Understanding that individual teachers vary in how they approach their courses, however, we have tried to write our chapters so that they are self-contained and well cross-referenced. Instructors can present them in any sequence that meets their particular course requirements.

NEW FEATURES OF THE FOURTH EDITION . . . .

1. Three entirely new chapters provide comprehensive coverage of current "hot topics" in organizational communication (see "Organization of the Book," below, for details):

   - Diversity in the Workplace
   - Communication Technology in the Workplace
   - Conflict Management

2. We found that a single chapter on the subject of ethics isolated this fundamental and permeating concept from the rest of the work. *So we dispersed our discus-*

sion of ethics throughout the text. Our new approach keeps the question of ethics before the student throughout the course.

- In the first chapter students will read a practical discussion of ethical guidelines they can use in all communication contexts. This foundation provides the bases for our discussion of ethical guidelines for interpersonal communication that begins on page 181. Similarly, we present ethical guidelines for small group interaction on page 312.
- *New side-bar questions,* ethical issues that arise from the material under discussion, appear throughout the text.

3. *The entire book has been tightened and updated.* Readers will be satisfied that our coverage of theory, research, and practice are well grounded in both benchmark and current scholarship. Each chapter includes new references that cite current scholarship to assure that students get an up-to-date picture of the field.

4. We have *tied interpersonal perception and listening skills much more closely together* in this edition because we believe this approach has greater utility for the readers.

5. Acknowledging that more and more information is communicated via the Internet, *Internet Exercises* have been added at the back of each chapter.

6. *A guide to written communication* has been added as an appendix. The guide is written in the form of a checklist, giving points for students to review to make sure their written communication is effective and professional.

7. A *Web site* has been established on the *Internet* to support both faculty and students using this book. It has been designed, and continues to evolve, to help students stay up-to-the-minute on what is happening in the world of work. Faculty will find exercises, abstracts and outlines of chapters, and supporting materials for each of the chapters in this text, sample course syllabi for both quarter and semester systems, "hot links" to especially relevant materials on the Internet, and much more. Students will find study guides, chapter outlines, illustrative materials, self-study tests, and of course, "hot links" to materials on the Web they will find both interesting and useful.

In addition, both students and faculty will be able to join Professor Hanna in a weekly "office hour" by logging on. The format is casual, but the subject matter is always valuable because it bears directly on the students' issues and ideas. When a participating student or faculty gets an idea, finds something relevant to share with others, or merely wants to suggest changes in the text or the Web site, all he or she has to do is contact Professor Hanna. Suggestions will be considered carefully, and additions and contributions from students and faculty for the Web site and for the text are very likely to appear!

To access this Web site all a student or faculty member has to do is go to *http://www.mhhe.com* and search under McGraw-Hill college; communications; by either author name, title, or keywords.

We made each of these changes to increase the practical value of our book for faculty and students who use it.

ORGANIZATION OF THE BOOK . . . .

Part 1. Preliminary Considerations: Communication and Organizations

This book is organized deductively. Part I clarifies our focus and provides the theoretical and conceptual foundations for the remainder of the book.

Chapter 1. Communication Perspective

In the first chapter we introduce and explain the idea of a communication perspective—what it is and how it works. We describe the communication process in symbolic interactionist terms—a process of message exchange that molds and creates the worlds in which people work. *An organization is its communication.* The organization's operation and maintenance functions depend on communication. The roles people assume and play emerge from, then inform their communication behavior. It makes sense, then, to examine an organization by examining its communication.

Chapter 2. The Organization—Theoretical Perspectives

Scholars from many fields of inquiry have studied how complex organizations evolve and work. Chapter 2 pulls together a unified perspective from this diverse material. Here we describe organizations as systems, then explain what the communication implications of this perspective actually are. We also describe organizations from a structural perspective for readers who may not have this theoretical underpinning. Thus students will share a common ground of language and concepts such as hierarchy, task and goal focus, organizational decay, and the like.

Organizations can best be described as a system of flows—message flows, work flows, cash flows, and so forth. We explain how such systematic flow gives rise to and is influenced by the organization's structure and by its communication networks.

Chapter 3. Leadership and Communication in Organizations

This chapter presents the four functions of communication in all organizations and describes how organizational leadership is ultimately the result of communication. Leadership can be visionary or reactionary. Leaders can plan for and direct changes or react to them with little planning. However they lead, their primary tool for leadership is their communication skill.

Chapter 4. Diversity in the Workplace

As the society has changed, the roles of women and minority group members have also changed. Moreover, improved communications technology and transportation has shrunk the world. Happily, this evolution has resulted in a more and more diverse workplace. This chapter examines that diversity by looking at both biological and cultural differences and the conclusions these differences sometimes generate among people at work. We show how our use of language can solve the problems that often arise when diverse people work together.

Part II. Basic Considerations: Foundations for Communication in Organizations

The basic foundations of organizational communication turn out to be the fundamental processes that allow it to occur.

Chapter 5. Perception and Listening

From a communication perspective, interpersonal perception and listening walk hand in hand. In this chapter we describe the nature of perception in general and how perception works when we perceive each other. Perceptual problems in work settings can usually be managed by more careful listening and speaking. So, in this chapter, we also describe the listening process and its most common pitfalls, and we explain how to develop listening skills that can make a critical difference.

Chapter 6. Language and Nonverbal Communication

Chapter 6 focuses reader attention on verbal and nonverbal messages. How we communicate controls how we understand and how we are understood. Thus this chapter rounds out the foundations of communication in organizations. Readers will study some of the most interesting current research on nonverbal message exchange, and will learn that they can have some measure of control over the nonverbal message system.

Chapter 7. Technology in the Workplace

Chapter 7 is about how communication technologies have imposed themselves on the world of work. It describes the most current technology available to assist in all kinds of organizational communication, and it predicts the most likely future of the workplace to result from these technologies. Telephone—both cellular and hard-wired   television, computers, etc., are rapidly converging. They will yield a communication device the likes of which many people have not even dreamed of. And they will yield that device before most people in organizations ever become aware that the convergence is happening. Written by Karen Burton, a communications technology professional with graduate education in organizational communication, this chapter offers guidelines for selecting the right technology and some suggestions for using it wisely.

Part III. Organizational Contexts: Interpersonal

The chapters in Part III have been designed to help the reader understand the enormous complexity involved when two or more people interact. Two-person communication events form the core of communication in all organizations. People sometimes believe they "can't give a speech," or they're "not very good in groups," but people take the interpersonal context for granted. That's usually a mistake!

Chapter 8. Interpersonal Communication

Chapter 8 divides a communication event into task and relationship dimensions. It argues that the most difficult interpersonal communication concerns are usually in the relationship dimension. Technology, power, language usage, support-iveness and defensiveness, and conflict management are topics of interest, but the primary goal of this chapter is to show that relationships exist in the observations and inferences that we make as we interact with one another.

Chapter 9. Conflict Management

Chapter 9 defines interpersonal conflict and examines how people in organiza-tions can manage it. The most common strategies for resolving conflict tend to use power to set up a lose-lose situation for the conflict parties, but there is a better way. Managing conflict wisely implies understanding it clearly. This chapter pre-sents several analytical tools designed for that purpose. Finally leaders often have to intervene as third parties in other people's conflicts. We describe how to go about third-party interventions as a sensible last focus for the chapter.

Chapter 10. Interviewing and Interviews: On the Job

Chapter 10 addresses the basics of preparing and carrying out interviews to achieve a variety of goals. It then turns to examine more fully what may be the most problematic interpersonal communication event in a complex organization: the performance ap-praisal. The chapter offers a clear description of the goals that performance appraisal in-terviews seek to achieve, and describes a variety of approaches that have been tried in an effort to accomplish those goals most efficiently and effectively. This treatment leads to specific recommendations about how both supervisors and the employee being ap-praised can prepare for and participate in performance appraisal interviews.

Chapter 11. The Selection Interview: Hiring and Being Hired for the Job

Chapter 11 is about the communication events that take place in hiring and being hired. Students will come to understand how a corporation's culture imposes itself upon the employment process. This groundwork lends sense to the require-ments organizations impose upon application letters, résumés, and employment in-terviews. The analysis yields insights for both the interviewee and the person con-ducting the interview on behalf of the organization.

Part IV. Organizational Contexts: The Group Context

Everything that can be said about the one-to-one context applies, as well, to the small group context. But a group communication event is very much more complex than a one-to-one event.

In these chapters, the reader will study how a balance of power dimension is imposed on a variety of group contexts and events in complex organizations. In ad-dition, since many of the most important decisions of an organization are the result of group discussion, the chapters in this unit present both research findings and sug-gestions for improving the most important communication skills involved before, during, and after a group communication event.

Chapter 12. Small Group Communication Processes

Chapter 12 describes group size, group tasks, cohesiveness, the norms and roles of a group, and the dynamics of the group communication event—both in the topic dimension and in the relationship dimension of communication. The chapter argues that leadership is the responsibility of every group member, and shows the student how to provide that leadership as a function of intelligent group participation.

Chapter 13. Communicating with a Group or Staff

Chapter 13 takes a broader view of group communication contexts in an organization than the one presented in the preceding chapter. Here are described the kinds of group events in a complex organization, and how to prepare and plan for them. The chapter is full of practical, well-grounded suggestions for involvement in routine decision-making meetings, participative management group meetings, regular monthly meetings, and larger conferences, such as an annual sales meeting.

Part V. Organizational Contexts: The One-to-Many Context

We are convinced that individuals who can manage public settings effectively have a far greater chance at success than individuals who cannot. Moreover, public speaking events are often crucial to the organization.

Chapter 14. Thinking about the Ideas and Arguments

This chapter carries the student through the beginning considerations of making a presentation—invention. Students will focus on selecting the topic and purpose, identifying and analyzing the audience, identifying the main lines of analysis and argument, and finding the strongest logical supporting material, and testing it.

Chapter 15. Organizing the Presentation

Chapter 15 is about a presentation's arrangement—making it clear and sensible, and making it apparent to the listeners. Students will learn how to organize introductions, discussions, and conclusions and how to support that organizational structure with visual materials.

Chapter 16. Delivering the Presentation

This chapter is organized along a time line beginning before the presentation and ending with follow-through after the presentation has been delivered. Students will learn how to choose an appropriate method of delivery and how best to practice. The chapter also discusses the most problematic matters of delivery and tells the reader how to avoid those problems. The chapter ends with very specific suggestions about evaluating one's own performance, and about following up with members of the audience.

Troubleshooting the Organization

This guide is a reference tool designed for quick use by the reader. It covers more than 100 communication problems discussed in the book and provides page numbers for easy location of solutions presented in the book.

Appendix: Writing in Business and Professional Settings

This checklist provides students an opportunity to insure that their written business communications meet the best professional standards.

Learning Aids

Each chapter begins with a list of *objectives* that point to the most important themes in the chapter. Our effort has been to make the intent of our book, chapter by chapter, as clear as possible to our readers. *Chapter summaries* at the end of each chapter recast the important ideas of the chapters into overview statements that should leave no doubt in the reader's mind about what are key ideas and what are not.

Over the years we have found that classroom discussion of the materials presented in these chapters is facilitated by certain *discussion questions*. We have included the questions we have found most helpful at the end of each chapter, along with the new *internet exercises*, mentioned above. There, too, may be found a carefully selected and *annotated bibliography*. Our aim has been, in suggesting these materials, to identify the best, and in some cases most influential, works available in our literature. We think students should be made aware of the benchmarks in a discipline. We also think less well-known works, when they are especially relevant, should be brought to reader attention, and so we have mentioned some of them, too.

Resources for Instructors

An Instructor's Manual has been prepared to aid instructors in their teaching. It provides sample syllabi and assignments as well as other teaching materials. Power Point transparencies designed to aid the teaching process by structuring discussions and reinforcing concepts, are new to this edition!

ACKNOWLEDGMENTS ....

We are grateful to all the professors who provided valuable suggestions for this and the previous editions of this book, and would like to express our sincere thanks. We are indebted to: Richard Arthur, University of Wisconsin; C. William Colburn, University of Michigan; Samuel M. Edleman, California State University-Chico; Karen Foss, Humboldt State University; James W. Gibson, University of Missouri-Columbia; Kathryn Greene, East Carolina University; Paul Harper, Oklahoma State University; Carl B. Holmberg, Bowling Green State University; Martha J. Haun, University of Houston; Robert Hirsh, Arizona State University; William E. Holdridge, Southern Illinois University; William E. Jurma, Texas Christian University; Jeff Lambert, University of Texas; Jeffrey K. Lukehart, University of Wisconsin-Platteville; Candy McCormack, The University of Oklahoma; Jerry Mayes, Murray State University; Roger E. Nebergall, University of Illinois; Douglas Pederson, Pennsylvania State University; Marshall Scott Poole, University of Michigan; John Reinard, Arizona State University; Elizabeth Rygh, University of Northern Iowa; David J. Robinson, Youngstown State University; Randall Rose, University of Nebraska-Omaha; Gary Schulman, Miami University, Ohio; Yvette Schwartz, Brooklyn College; Brant Short, Idaho State University-Pocatello; Ritch L. Sorenson, Iowa State University; Robert Vardaman, Indiana Wesleyan University; Ethel Wilcox, University of Toledo; and Charles Wise, El Paso Community College.

No book ever emerges from a single hand. An author writes the manuscript, then editors turn the manuscript into a book. Their essential work goes largely unsung, but it never should. We wish to acknowledge Marjorie Byers, Sponsoring Editor and Valerie Raymond, Associate Editor, whose grace and style and persistence kept us working when we didn't want to. And we thank Annette Bodzin, Project Supervisor, and Linda Biemiller, copy editor, who read every word of this manuscript more carefully, even, than we, and who improved every page in the process.

Michael S. Hanna

Gerald L. Wilson

COMMUNICATING IN BUSINESS AND PROFESSIONAL SETTINGS

PART I
Preliminary Considerations:
Communication and Organizations

Organizational communication is one of the fastest growing areas of academic study. We need to understand how to communicate in business and professional settings because so much human endeavor occurs in and around these organizations. This book has been designed and written with an undergraduate student in mind. The idea was to lay out a text that would help the reader with three things necessary to understanding communication in complex organizations. The first of these is how organizations work.

Complex organizations can be mysterious things. Learning which paths to take and which paths to avoid can be a test of a person's professional acumen. Learning how to set and achieve personal goals within an organization is part of the task. Learning how to manage relationships within a hierarchy can seem overwhelming to a person just starting a career. Thus, one concern of this book is to try to provide an insight into how complex organizations work.

A second concern of this book is how the communication inside complex organizations functions to influence every decision and every outcome of those organizations. An organization is so closely dependent upon the communication behavior of its members that some scholars believe that an organization *is* its communication.

In this book we help you understand this relationship between the organization and its communication, and we show how studying communication can provide insights for success.

The third concern of this book is with the kinds of communication skills individuals need in order to achieve their goals in organizational contexts. Study of both analytical and performance skills are included.

Chapter 1, A Communication Perspective, begins the study by identifying what is meant by a "communication perspective" and then relates organizational communication to the concept of organizations. Here you will find the key terms and concepts for your study of organizational communication defined and explained, as well as an ethical perspective on communication in organizations.

Chapter 2, The Organization—Theoretical Perspectives, takes a closer look at what organizations are, how they work, and how they relate to other organizations in the ever-expanding hierarchy and complexity of our society.

Chapter 3, Leadership and Communication in Organizations, places the question of control in focus. Who makes an organization work, and how? What does it take to reach a position where control of the organization is the focus of the job? What kinds of power must be obtained, and how? What kind of person does it take to manage that power?

Chapter 4, Diversity in the Workplace, asks you to consider how human diversity plays a role in organizational communication behavior. A person can choose how he or she will behave toward individuals and groups who are different from themselves. This chapter asks readers to make intelligent choices.

CHAPTER 1

A Communication Perspective

···**OBJECTIVES**

Upon completion of this chapter, you should be able to:

1. Look at a problem from a communication perspective.
2. Develop and explain a transactional model of the communication process that includes the components discussed in this chapter.
3. Define and explain communication as message exchange.
4. Tell what each of these ideas suggests about the communication process:
   a. communication is intentional,
   b. messages are organized,
   c. communication interactions reflect relational definitions, and
   d. communication within organizations is culturally dependent.
5. Differentiate among interpersonal, group, public, and mass communication.
6. Describe the relationship between ethics and personal character, and describe how this relationship implies an interpersonal ethical contract.
7. Name and describe three fundamental ethical issues each human being must answer.

8. Name and describe three ethical standards that permeate this textbook.
9. Explain how to identify and apply ethical standards when a moral assessment is called for.

Ask anyone who holds a position of authority in any organization—a manager in a business firm, an administrator in a public school, or a director of an institution such as a hospital—what the critical and difficult parts of his or her job are, and among the answers will probably be one that boils down to "communication." We have all known people who have studied theories, have trained themselves in certain techniques, have lots of ideas, but just cannot seem to communicate well.

We believe this book, which is designed to be both practical and workable, will improve *your* ability to communicate—to work things out with others. This book is about communication in business and organizational situations that have been shown to be troublesome for individual employees, managers, and supervisors. More particularly, it is about communication activity for people at all levels. All the activities that make an organization effective involve communication. Anyone who really communicates effectively, or who encourages others to do so, is contributing to the organization.

Whatever the settings, communication can be effective only to the extent that the people involved in it (yourself and at least one other person) can make sense of it. Therefore, you will have to be able to understand and deal intelligently with problems in communication.

We do not wish to suggest that communication is everything in organizations. To succeed in an organization, people need technical knowledge as well as communication skills. Thus, knowledge of economics, engineering, marketing, and production are obviously important, too. But individuals must communicate in order to coordinate their efforts and implement their decisions. We focus on communication skills in this book.

A COMMUNICATION PERSPECTIVE

Our goal is to look at problems in organizations from a communication perspective—as problems of message exchange. The following example will illustrate what we mean.

Suppose Steve has made a mistake on the job. The mistake has the potential to create a serious problem for the organization. If Steve is to do his job properly, he must tell someone higher up in the company about the mistake. Of course, Steve will then look bad, so he is reluctant to speak of it.[1]

Steve's boss, Jean, has status and clout. She is in a position to help or hinder Steve's growth in the organization, to enhance or diminish his chances of moving up in the company. So whether or not Steve confides in Jean depends on his perception of her management and communication style.

The organizational problem illustrated here is not uncommon. From a communication perspective, the problem is that information does not flow very well from bottom to top. Steve's concern in this case *inhibits* communication. From this perspective, the possibility that when Steve says "This went wrong" his superior may hear "Steve is inept" represents a problem of message exchange.[2] So a *communication perspective* requires those involved to look at the communication event—what is being said and how and to whom—rather than how authority is being used or misused (a management perspective).

> **Is it okay for a person to withhold information from his superior as a way of maintaining his image with his superior?**

We will understand the term *communication* to mean the process of transmitting and interpreting verbal and nonverbal messages. To understand a communication problem and to deal with that problem intelligently, we have to know what to look at. Communication models can help us do that, and so, throughout this book, we will introduce appropriate models of the communication process as we study communication in business and professional settings. Every one of the models we present rests on certain basic assumptions that may be found in the above simple definition of communication.

Since communication is a process, it is dynamic and ever-changing. Since communication involves transmitting and interpreting, we must assume that *how* the transmissions occur and *through which channels* are important considerations. Since communication involves interpretation, we must consider what variables influence interpretations. The study of certain models, or theories, will help us do that.

We can use the model of the communication process illustrated in Exhibit 1.1 to examine many communication problems. We are interested here in the components of the communication process. We will be considering *sources*—those persons who generate communications. Relevant questions about the source might be, Is this person's idea sound? Has he conceptualized the idea correctly? Does he understand? Is he biased? Such questions are about the credibility of a source—the extent to which other people believe in the individual.

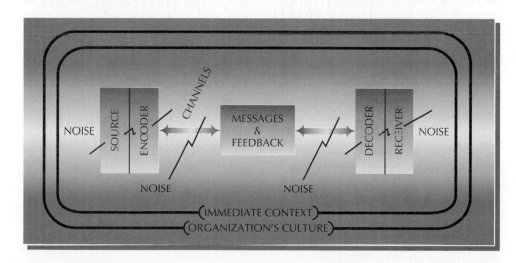

Exhibit 1.1
MODEL OF THE COMMUNICATION PROCESS

Source credibility also involves matters of performance. Does the person encode ideas effectively? That is, does she articulate clearly, with enough force and energy to be heard? Does she spell correctly? Does she construct sentences that are grammatically acceptable? Such questions about the encoder are also part of our concern as we study communicating in business and professional settings. This model helps us to identify that we must be concerned, from a communication perspective, with such questions.

We also will be looking at *channels*—the routes through which the communications are sent. Should the sender have written a memo? Or should he have used a personal talk? Should he make a problem of faulty supplies known through an intermediary? Should he use the public address system to get the foreman's attention? If he now decides to tell his boss about the problem, which channel should he use: a memo, the telephone, or a face-to-face conversation?

We will be concerned with *messages*—the content of the communications. What should the source say first and last? How should he look and act? Is there anything better left unsaid? How much detail would be appropriate or efficient or inefficient? In what order should these details be presented?[3]

Finally we will be focusing on *receivers*—the people for whom the communications are intended. Is the boss the best receiver of the message that the sender wants to send?

So the categories of source, message, channel, and receiver are important for the flow of communication in an organization, on all levels and in all directions.

And there are other key aspects of communication that we will write about in this book. For example, *feedback*—how a receiver responds to a message—can be very important. So can *symbols*—the means by which we transmit and receive messages. *Noise*—those things that impede or distort the message exchange—affects the process.

We will suggest ways to analyze problems intelligently. We will suggest ways to find solutions to problems and criteria by which to select the most effective solution. And finally, we will tell you how you can develop the skills necessary to implement those solutions.

COMMUNICATION: MESSAGE EXCHANGE ·

When we communicate, we are generating, transmitting, receiving, and interpreting messages. To do the job expected of them, our messages must be in some kind of code—such as a language.

As your boss sits at her desk writing, she is generating ideas and then translating them into language. If you and she are sitting in the same room—say, you are in her office in that leather armchair next to her reference table—then your messages will include not only language but also a variety of nonverbal messages. She will use facial expressions, body movements, tone of voice, phrasing, pauses, pitch, and force to communicate her meaning, and so will you.

Consider, for example, the differences in meaning expressed by a sentence when you simply vary the word you stress. Read these sentences out loud, stressing the word in italics.

1. *You* can say that again.
2. You *can* say that again.
3. You can *say* that again.

4. You can say *that* again.
5. You can say that *again*.

We can use a *word* to express our understanding of an *idea*. For example, your boss may use the word *chair* to refer to the leather thing over there—the one you were sitting in a moment ago. We can understand what is being talked about because we have a symbol (*chair*) that allows us to categorize and to make sense of things outside ourselves. But a chair is something that may be touched, felt. It exists as a concrete reality.

Similarly, we can use a word—a symbol—to refer to some idea that has no tangible referent. We can say, for instance, that we appreciate a person's loyalty to the company. There is no physical thing called *loyalty,* and yet we can conceptualize it because we invent symbols to allow us to refer to abstractions.

No symbol—whether one like *chair* or one like *loyalty*—can be said to *have* meaning. Meaning does not exist *in* a symbol; it exists in the minds of people who use the symbol. Each person has to interpret the symbol, to relate to the symbol in some way, and to give the symbol an understandable meaning. By themselves the symbols have no significance. We have to agree with each other that the symbols we use refer to the experiences we share. To illustrate this idea, write down five words that seem to you to characterize the idea of conflict. "Conflict is _____, _____, _____, _____, _____." Now ask a classmate to do the same thing. If you compare the responses, you will discover that each of you has separate images of the concept *conflict*. The word itself does not carry the meaning. You and your classmate carry the meaning, and you attach it to the word.

To illustrate this idea a bit further, consider Exhibit 1.2. The circles represent the personal fields of experience that describe you and someone else. Everything you have experienced is included within that circle. The same is true of the other person's circle. You can see that your personal field of experience includes much that you do not share with the other person. This person's field of experi-

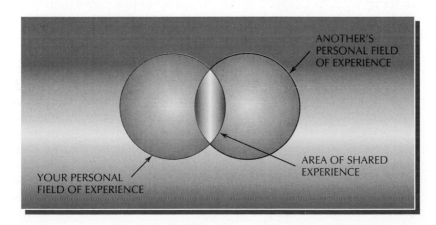

**Exhibit 1.2
PERSONAL
AND SHARED
EXPERIENCE**

ANOTHER'S
PERSONAL FIELD
OF EXPERIENCE

AREA OF SHARED
EXPERIENCE

YOUR PERSONAL
FIELD OF EXPERIENCE

ence includes much that you do not share. The shaded area is the part of your experience that the other person shares. The more you communicate with the other and the more language you use, the greater the expansion of the area of shared experience.

Now, suppose that your idea of conflict is expressed in such words as *growth opportunity, unpleasant,* and *inevitable.* Suppose your classmate's concept of the idea emerges in such words as *battle, hostile, awful,* and *demeaning.* A conflict episode between two people with these orientations in the personal field of experience could be very difficult to manage. Still, you could talk to each other. If you continued to talk over the problem, you might be able to come to some agreement about the understandings and images of conflict that you share.

Communication Is Intentional

Communication refers to a host of *intentional behaviors.*[4] You can group these intentional behaviors into two categories: speaking and acting. When we talk, we employ both verbal and nonverbal messages to represent the way we feel, think, and believe. Taken together, the verbal and nonverbal behaviors are the primary means by which other people can know who we are or what we mean.

When we talk with each other, we are goal-oriented in that we are trying to accomplish some purpose. Thus, our communication behavior is intentional. When the other person listens to us, he uses nonverbal messages to tell us how to interpret the meanings we have tried to express with words, and our intentions, as well. For example, you might say to a friend, "Are you all right?" The friend responds, "Yeah, I'm okay." You consider the whole package of messages to discover how to interpret what your friend means and intends. You might decide that she means that she is okay. You might also decide that she is feeling sad but does not want to talk with you about her feelings or what is causing them.

Communication refers to intentional behaviors, even when the degree of intentionality is questionable.[5] Sometimes we are not as conscious of our purposes as we might be. We usually discover this when the other person gives us feedback that we didn't expect. When caught up in this circumstance, we sometimes try to excuse ourselves by saying something like "Oh, I was just talking. I didn't mean anything by it." Nevertheless, the person who received our communication acted as if we *did* have a reason for saying what we said. This person behaved as if communication is intentional because we expect that people will say what they mean and mean what they say.

Human beings, then, are symbol creators. In communication our intention is to generate, transmit, and receive symbols. Our symbols may be almost anything that we use to suggest the meanings we attach to objects, phenomena, and events either inside ourselves or outside. In order for us to communicate, we have to use symbols in essentially the same ways. Clearly, each of us can never use them in exactly the same ways. Our culture and traditions, society, homes and families, schools, and churches have all had a share in teaching us how to relate the world to ourselves and ourselves to the world. We are each unique in the ways we have learned, so we are each unique in the ways we symbolize. Our uniqueness provides us both satisfaction and frustration: satisfaction in that we are unique, we have personality; frustration because our uniqueness is at the heart of communication breakdowns.

> Is it ethical for a person to organize a sequence of events in order to enhance her own position?

So far, the main ideas of this chapter have been that a communication perspective on business problems places all its attention on the communication events and behavior involved. People use communication models to help understand communication events and behavior. The one we presented in Exhibit 1.1 equates communication with message exchange. Its components are:

Source: the location or origin of an idea—a person
Encoder: the mechanism that translated ideas into codes
Channels: the means by which messages are transmitted
Messages: sense units expressed either verbally or nonverbally
Decoder: the mechanism that translates the message back into a form that can be processed by the brain
Receiver: the individual who processes the messages
Feedback: messages sent by receivers in response to messages they have processed
Noise: anything that impedes or distorts the messages exchanged

Messages Are Organized

In order for the messages to be meaningful to participants in a communication event, the participants must organize them. This means that people organize their experiences in some way—for example, by arbitrarily assigning a beginning and an end—to form a complete message.

Imagine two workers who are engaged in a conflict over which one should be assigned a new truck. Both John and Paul want to drive the new truck rather than the old one. It is air-conditioned and it has power steering and power brakes. Each believes he has a right to drive the new truck because of the way he has organized his experience of previous conversations. Listen to their argument:

JOHN: You told me you really didn't care about the new truck. In fact, you told me that twice—once last Friday and once on Wednesday, I think it was. . . .
PAUL: Yes, I know. But John, that was before I was assigned the new route. You know the new route is twice as long, and it goes over some pretty rough roads. I need the new truck on that route more than you need it for the city route.

John has clearly organized the event by beginning his understanding with what was said last Friday or Wednesday. He believes he has a contract with Paul on the basis of what Paul told him, and so he believes he has a right to the new truck. Paul, for his part, is organizing the event differently. He clearly has organized the talk by beginning the sense unit much later than last Friday. New information—the new route assignment—seems to Paul a sufficient reason to begin the sense unit at a more recent point. Thus they are taking different meanings from the message exchange.

Perhaps a simpler example, one outside the business context, will make the idea clearer. Suppose two little girls, sisters, are caught up in sibling rivalry. You can hear this conversation:

ELLEN: Mom, Susan hit me!
MOTHER: Susan, did you hit Ellen?
SUSAN: Yes, but that's because she kicked me.
ELLEN: Well, she wouldn't give me back my pencil.
SUSAN: I wouldn't give it back because Daddy gave it to me.
ELLEN: He did not, he gave it to me.
SUSAN: He told me I could have it.
ELLEN: But he handed it to me. We were in the car, and. . . .

Each little girl has arbitrarily assigned a beginning to the chain of events, but the two have not assigned the same beginning point. Thus Susan and Ellen have different understandings of the event because they have organized it differently.

Communication Interactions Reflect Relational Definitions

From a communication perspective, every communication event has some definition of the relationship. One common way of describing this is to say it is either symmetrical or complementary, and its symmetry or complementarity is based on power images held by the participants. To understand this idea we need a few definitions.

A *symmetrical relationship* is based on the assumption of equality. No one is "one up" or "one down." Each individual assumes that the other person is OK, just the way he is. Each individual assumes also that he himself is OK. Thus each individual respects the other as a human being.

A *complementary relationship* is based on a different set of assumptions. In a complementary relationship, one person takes a superior position and the other takes an inferior or subordinate position. This arrangement must be negotiated, of course, and the negotiations are based on certain sources of power.

If we imagine a meeting between a sales representative and a buyer, it is easy to see the difference between symmetry and complementarity. Let Cheryl be the sales representative and Henry the buyer. Remember that in a symmetrical relationship, each person assumes his or her equality with the other. Now compare the two conversations below. In the first conversation, Henry takes a superior role and Cheryl allows him to do so. Her response clearly shows that she accepts Henry's definition of their relationship as complementary.

HENRY: You'd better have these items to me on time. I'll need them no later than September 15.
CHERYL: Yes, sir. We'll get them to you. I promise.

In the second conversation, Henry takes the subordinate role and Cheryl takes the superior role. Again their relationship is complementary.

HENRY: I'm awfully worried. I'll need these items delivered to me no later than September 15.
CHERYL: Don't worry about it. It will be all right.

Now compare these two exchanges with some symmetrical interactions. Here each individual assumes a stance of basic equality with the other.

HENRY: How long will it take to deliver these items?
CHERYL: I can get them to you in two weeks.

Notice that neither party puts the other up or down. Each respects the choices of the other. Each assumes that both individuals have adult status. Each preserves the choices of both parties. Suppose, having completed their business, Henry says:

HENRY: How about a game of tennis?
CHERYL: Good idea. Let's leave early and play.

Once again Henry and Cheryl have taken a symmetrical stance. They assume themselves to be equal partners in their negotiations.

Notice that individuals in an organizational context do not define their relationships as complementary or symmetrical out of context. Always they make some assessment of the relative power each has over the other. If, for example, Henry thinks he has power over Cheryl, if he determines to exercise that power, and if he thinks that Cheryl will allow him to do so, Henry may present their relationship to Cheryl as complementary. In this example he clearly believes that he is coming from a position of power, for he presents himself as one-up.

HENRY: The parts were late last time. You'll simply have to do better than that.

Cheryl now has some choices. On the basis of her own assessment of their power relationship, she can choose to accept Henry's definition or to reject it. If she takes the second alternative, then she has two additional choices. She can either assert herself while assuming Henry's equality or assume that she has more power than Henry. If she asserts herself, she will not put him down. If she assumes her power is greater than Henry's, she may put him down.

CHERYL: Who says so?

In this case, Cheryl has decided to put Henry down. She has decided that she has more power than Henry. Had she accepted Henry's definition of their power relationship—he with the power, she without it—she might have said:

CHERYL: Yes, sir. It won't happen again.

Had Cheryl determined to assert herself and at the same time assume Henry's equality with her, she might have answered:

CHERYL: I believe the parts will arrive on time, but of course I can't give you a guarantee.

You can see that the interactions between people depend on how they understand and attach meaning to their life events—how they organize their experiences. In the context you are going to study, complex organizations, the way messages are organized is very often based on the way the individuals perceive power in their relationships. We will have much more to say about power later in this book.

THE ORGANIZATIONAL CONTEXT . . . .

> Are there any circumstances in which it would be unethical for an organization to use hierarchy as a means of legitimizing the roles and decisions of its members?

The context in which business and professional communication events are most likely to occur influences those events greatly. In this book we focus your attention on communication events that occur within the context of complex organizations. Many such events—for example, performance appraisal interviews—do not occur in other contexts. The purposes of these special events, and many of the factors that influence the outcomes, are particular to complex organizations.

Throughout this text we will draw your attention to certain inherent features of complex organizations that do not generally characterize other logical structures. A list of inherent characteristics would include, at least, (1) the organization's recurring cycle of events, (2) the hierarchy that evolves in order that the organization can sustain that cycle of events, and (3) the culture that emerges as a result of the events cycle and the evolution of the hierarchy.

Recurring Cycles

The fiscal year exemplifies an organization's recurring cycle of events. By definition, a fiscal year is the twelve-month period of time between the settlement of the organization's financial accounts. In many corporations, the fiscal year begins on November 1 and ends on the last day of the following October. In addition to the fiscal year, however, there are other recurring cycles, some of which require more than twelve months and some of which require less.

A college or university provides many examples of such events. For example, quarters and semesters begin with opening lectures and end with final examinations. Students are graduated in May or June. New faculty are recruited in early spring. Merit decisions for faculty and staff may be made in February or March.

Such recurring cycles characterize complex organizations. Another such characteristic may be found in the evolution of an organization's hierarchy.

Hierarchy

Every complex organization evolves a hierarchical structure out of the pressures and needs of the organization's members. This hierarchy may be the most apparent of all the defining characteristics of complex organizations. The hierarchy exists to give legitimacy to the roles and decisions of its members. The hierarchy makes formation of subgroups possible. The hierarchy allows the division of labor, task specification, and power and authority relationships. Thus, the hierarchy provides impetus for job instruction, job rationale, procedures and practices of the organization, indoctrination of the organization's goals, and provision of feedback to subordinates.

Still another feature that defines a complex organization—perhaps its most important one—has been called "organizational culture."

···**ORGANIZATIONAL CULTURE**

Culture is the pattern of a group's behavior, including its members' thoughts, speech, actions, and artifacts.[6] In an organization, as elsewhere, a culture develops because of its members' unique ways of viewing their world. Each organization develops a particular "way of doing what it does and its own way of talking about what it is doing." Culture is not something that an organization has; rather, as Michael Pacanowsky and Nick O'Donnell-Trujillo suggest, "a culture is something an organization is."[7]

A short illustration of this idea will help you understand how an organization surrounds itself with messages and artifacts that tell who it is. Look at the slogans that some familiar companies use. Du Pont long described its mission as providing "better things for better living through chemistry." Chevrolet division of General Motors has adopted the slogan, "The heartbeat of America." The implication of Ford's slogan, "Have you driven a Ford lately?" is clearly that the act of driving one will convince the driver that Ford is the vehicle to buy. But, beyond this assumption, the slogan carries a cultural assumption that Ford cars and trucks are superior. It's an idea that Ford has been fostering for a long time. In the 1960s the Ford ads on TV said, "When better ideas are built, Ford will build them." Other organizations adopt the words of one of their prominent members to express the essence of their culture. Procter & Gamble's William Cooper Procter told Richard R. Dupree, the first person to head the company who was neither a Procter nor a Gamble, "Always try to do what's right. If you do that, nobody can really find fault." The most basic value of that company seems to be "do what's right."[8]

Procter & Gamble's management has a long history of listening to its customers—presumably in an effort to do things right. In its early years the company created test kitchens for Crisco, then it hired homemakers to provide feedback on dish detergents, then it instituted door-to-door sampling of Camay. Today Procter & Gamble conducts more than 1.5 million telephone interviews annually. All these activities are viewed by the members as the organization's attempt to "do what's right." One of the organization's heroes demonstrates the lengths to which the firm will go to do things right. In the late 1880s William Cooper Procter worked in the lowest-level job in the organization, loading soap mixers, in order to discover how workers were experiencing the organization. His experiences led him to influence his father and uncle to "do what's right" for the company's employees. Over the course of thirty-five years, his efforts led to the introduction of a variety of plans—profit sharing, putting workers on his board of directors, and the like.

A strong cultural theme at IBM is "IBM means service." Nearly all the organization's members understand this theme, and the IBM service representative is its embodiment. He arrives promptly for a service call, looks crisp and neat,

> Does "always doing what's right" ever present an ethical problem?

seems to have an amazing number of parts at his immediate disposal, and within a short time has the machine repaired.

To understand an organization's culture is to understand how the organization acts on thoughts, actions, and things within its environment. An organization's culture is revealed in its rituals, stories, jokes, language, and fantasies. These help members understand how to perform their roles in that organization effectively.

We can gain a sense of an organization's culture by examining the communication and artifacts (objects, tools, and adornments) used by its members. But such things offer only partial clues to the culture. They tell us only what the culture thinks is important; they don't tell us how their use creates cultural meaning.

A cultural study of an organization is instructive. Gary L. Kreps led a research team to investigate RCA's video disk operations in Indianapolis. They examined annual reports, manuscripts of speeches made by prominent members, employee handbooks, marketing and promotional materials, recruitment handouts and in-house reports. They also observed employees' behavior directly to determine their communication patterns. They looked for repetition of vocabulary and symbols, as well as metaphors and stories that embodied recurring themes. They found stories about RCA's visionary founder/inventor, David Sarnoff, and stories about "the company's history of dynamic growth; development of state-of-the-art technologies; technological excellence; leadership in the field of electronics; corporate strength, diversity, and self-sufficiency; commitment to launching of new industries; and commitment to excellent new products of the future."[9]

For anthropologist Ward J. Goodenough, culture "consists of standards for deciding what is, standards for deciding what can be, standards for deciding how one feels about it, standards for deciding what to do about it, and standards for deciding how to go about doing it."[10] He is suggesting that a culture is revealed in how its members make decisions. We can see how organizational culture suggests standards by examining the way relationships are viewed by members.

Don has greeted Marilyn, a new employee, and is showing her around the office. He stops at the end of a long corridor. "This is the finance department. I'd like to introduce you to Ed. He's the person who really runs this place." He steps through the door and says, "Ed, this is Marilyn—I'm sorry, I'm no good with names, what's your last name again?"

"Thomas." She smiles at Ed.

"Yeah, Thomas. You'll be Marilyn around here, anyway."

Now let's consider how an understanding of organizational culture might affect this transaction. It turns out that Marilyn just left an organization because of the way it treated women employees. One thing she disliked was the fact that women were referred to almost exclusively by first names, whereas men were referred to by last names. Because of this experience and the way the old organizational culture had conditioned her, Don's comment brings Marilyn nearly to the boiling point. Just for a moment, though. Marilyn is competent and understands that things may be done differently here—she understands the concept of organizational culture. She says, "I know it's difficult to remember last names." She smiles at Ed. "I think we all have troubles with them. I'm pleased to meet you, Mr.?"

"Wilson, Ed Wilson, Miss Thomas." Ed offers his hand and she shakes it firmly. "I understand you're the new auditor."

She doesn't know whether people use last names or not in this organization. She wants to know Ed's last name so that she can use it when she needs to. More analysis of this organization's culture will tell her what this communication means.

Marilyn will need to begin an analysis of the attitudes that govern the behavior of the organization's members and of the physical and psychological settings in which these attitudes are acted out. What are the members' attitudes toward women and men? Under what circumstances (physical and psychological) are first names used almost exclusively? How do the attitudes and circumstances interact? The answers to these questions will help her understand the organization's cultural expectations.

Terrence Deal and Allen Kennedy analyzed corporate cultures in an attempt to identify basic types. They looked at values, heroes (prominent members of the organization who are considered role models), rituals and rites (ceremonial and formalized behaviors that members follow, such as Tandem Corporation's company-wide holiday celebrations), and communication as basic elements of an organization's culture. Their examination yielded four basic types of culture. One is the "tough-guy, macho culture," in which individualism, high risks, and quick feedback are valued. Firms engaged in construction, cosmetics, management consulting, advertising, television, movies, publishing, and sports tend to fall into this category. Another culture is characterized by the "work hard/play hard" mystique. Deal and Kennedy place real estate sales, computer companies, automotive distributors, and any door-to-door operation in this category. Success in this world comes from persistence and hard work. A third culture is the "you bet your company" culture. This culture is based on big risks and slow feedback. Oil companies, aircraft manufacturers, mining companies, investment banks, and computer design companies are typical of this culture. Finally, they found a "process" culture, which places less value on what is done than on the way it is done. The important thing is to follow the correct procedure. Here feedback is slow and risk is low. Banks, insurance companies, financial service organizations, much of government, and heavily regulated industries fall into this category.[11] Although organizational cultures are obviously more complex than these categories suggest, the categories help us to see the potential usefulness of viewing organizations as cultures.

Sometimes high-ranking members of the organization deliberately try to alter its culture to change the way the organization is experienced by its members. The assumption is that behavioral changes will result from this new way of viewing things. Pepsi-Cola was successful in persuading its members to adopt a new way of seeing the company. Members initially saw themselves and their organization as second to Coca-Cola. Management undertook a campaign to convince them that they could be the number one company in their industry. Consequently, employees adopted a competitive attitude toward other companies and even toward one another. Attitudes and their consequences are power-

> Is it possible for a naturally evolved culture to be inherently unethical?

ful shapers of behavior. The cultural performance perspective focuses our attention on them.

You might wonder, "So what?" What has all this information about the organization's culture to do with communication in business and professional settings? Our argument is that communication in organizations is *culturally dependent*. We use the term *culture* to mean both the general cultural milieu (e.g., American culture, Italian culture, Indian culture) and the culture of a particular organization (e.g., the way we do things here). Webster's dictionary defines *culture* as "the integrated pattern of human behavior that includes thought, speech, action, and artifacts and depends upon man's capacity for transmitting knowledge to succeeding generations."[12] This definition suggests that the most prominent features of a society—its thought, speech, action—are related to communication.

By *culturally dependent* we mean that:

1. *Our understanding of relationships, and the communication in them, is derived from our culture.* Cultures develop their own standards for behavior. Organizations, as cultures, do the same. They develop standards that regulate relationships among people of various status and power and between the sexes. Behavioral standards develop in regard to communication, too. These standards govern such things as the way communication proceeds, the issues that can be discussed, and the way conflict may be managed. The cultural standards you learn in one organization may be quite different from those you will need to know in another.

2. *Our understanding of appropriateness and inappropriateness is derived from cultural standards.* Communication behavior that is appropriate in one subculture may be inappropriate in another. In some subcultures, such as the federal government, jokes are considered inappropriate. People who tell jokes are revealing a character flaw—they are insufficiently serious. In other subcultures—Toastmasters International, for example—the ability to tell a joke well is an essential skill. Rules of etiquette and appropriateness are communication rules that you need to understand to manage yourself in a particular organizational culture.

The things that make up an organization's culture directly influence its communications. The communication events bind the organization together, give it purpose and direction and degrees of success.

THE IMPORTANCE OF ETHICS AT WORK ....

Each day, every one of us makes countless decisions about how we will run our lives and relationships. These decisions always carry ethical considerations. Indeed, there are so many, and they are so important, that in this book we have decided to point to the ethical decision points that seem obvious to us throughout the text. We have taken a "boxed insert" approach to this task, as you can see by glancing to the top of this page. In all, there are about 60 of these inserts in this text. In them we identify what we believe to be the ethical question, and, based on the three ethical standards which we describe in detail below, we suggest considerations that should help you to come to an appropriate and ethical decision. The three principles are: (1) Tell the truth. (2) Do no harm. (3) Treat people justly.

Ethics, Personal Character, and the Nature of Interpersonal Contracts

Clearly, no one can anticipate every decision point in life. Even when it *is* possible to anticipate them, we are often caught up in the throes and passions of the moment. We face a pressing deadline, and we haven't time or energy to reflect carefully. Further, even with enough time, we may not be able to determine which ethical posture offers the greatest efficacy. Under those circumstances you have to rely upon what kind of a person you are. If you are a good person you are likely to make the right decision, given your understanding of the variables involved and given your cultural biases.

In our relationships with others, too, we must often rely upon what kind of person we are and what kind of person the other individual tries to be. For, as you will see in Chapter 8, the relationship that exists between two people is a function of talk—how they talk to each other, of course, and how they talk to themselves. Put another way, when two people have a relationship, they label it, and in labeling it they define it. They assign roles to each other and they take the roles others assign them. When they do this they have a social contract, each understanding and expecting the other will behave in ways that are consistent with the roles they have agreed to play. To the extent the assigned roles imply trust and goodwill and moral values, we expect each other to behave as trustworthy, well intended, moral people. We have a social contract that binds us just as surely as if we had written all our expectations down on paper.

Still, there is more to say. Behavior, including ethical behavior, becomes habitual in most people. This suggests that your habits of making ethical choices may already be formed. This does not mean, however, that you cannot replace one set of habitual behaviors with another if you choose to do so. Get into the habit, then, of making ethical decisions consistent with the three simple-to-learn standards presented below.

Ethical Standards for Communicating in Business and Professional Settings

Ethical standards are rarely absolute. Instead, they are relative. Decision points may be so complex that absolute honesty, for example, might do more harm than good.

Understanding this problem, Gary Kreps[13] suggested three general principles you can use in a broad range of ethical decision points: (1) tell the truth, (2) do no harm, and (3) treat people justly.

First, tell the truth. As a general principle, people know that honesty is the best policy. Of course, the vicissitudes of daily life can confuse the issue. Organizations do have to keep secrets, for example. And difficult decisions must often be made that place people in ethical dilemmas. For example, an executive group might decide that it must downsize the work force in the company in order to balance the budget and protect the company's investors. So what does this first standard require?

An operational definition of *to lie* may be helpful. If one person attempts to create an image of reality inside another—an image that is different from his own—that person has lied. To tell the truth, then, means to refrain from deceiving others into believing in an image that you do not have in your own head. This does not mean you have to reveal everything you know. You should not, and you could not do that in any case. To follow through on the example of downsizing, you might tell an employee that the company is in difficulty without forecasting the executive group's decision prematurely. This activity would not deceive the employee, although it certainly would withhold information from him.

Second, do no harm. Do not intentionally harm another individual, and do not intentionally harm the organization or its environment. Many decision points, like the executive group's decision to downsize the labor force, occur in the life of any organization. This principle holds that decision makers must take into consideration the nature, extent, and level of harm that will result from decisions. The downsizing decision will inevitably work a harm upon those individuals whose jobs are eliminated. The ethical issue, then, would rest upon *depersonalizing* the choices about which positions to eliminate. Using the ethical approach, the job functions, not the people, would be considered, and the decision made for the good of the company. Done in this way, the decision to eliminate jobs would conform to the "do no harm" ethical standard because the decision makers did not intentionally harm specific individuals and did preserve the organization and its investors from harm.

Third, treat people justly. This third ethical principle recognizes that not all people can be treated equally. For example, some people work more effectively and productively than others, so you would be unlikely to reward them all equally. Some positions are more important to the company than others. Some job functions have a maximum dollar value. A person holding such a job would not expect to be paid above the maximum value of the position.

With this idea in mind—that not all people can be treated equally—the ethical question becomes one of justice. What is just for the people involved in the decisions? What is just treatment following the decisions?

Justice refers to fair play. It suggests that decisions are made rationally and after careful gathering of relevant facts. It calls for conformity to generally accepted standards of right and wrong. So this third principle informs the first and second.

To illustrate, suppose you knew that someone had cheated on her income tax. You would be unlikely to say anything, allowing it to remain a matter between the other person and the Internal Revenue Service. If, however, you knew that someone had cheated on his business travel expense request for reimbursement, you would have an ethical problem much closer to yourself, and therefore much more difficult to manage. In such a situation are you obligated by the first principle ("tell the truth") to report what you know to management? Not to do so conforms to our definition of a lie   to create (or, in this case, allow) a reality in another person's head that you do not have in your own. Moreover, the cheater clearly has violated the first principle. Yet, are you perhaps constrained from reporting the cheater, since you know that doing so would be likely to bring harm to him? Or would the harm to the company be the greater consideration?

Finally, the justice principle comes into play. Your decision to report the cheater, or not, will probably come down to deciding on which side of the question the greater justice rests.

. . . . .COMMUNICATION CONTEXTS

Communication in organizations happens in a wide range of contexts. It is helpful to group communication activities into the four most commonly studied of these contexts. These are the focus of this book. Exhibit 1.3 illustrates these contexts.

One-to-one settings are pervasive in the organization. Your skill in interacting with your superiors, your equals, and your subordinates will mark you for upward mobility. Are you a leader? Can you handle conflict? Do you know how to handle a performance appraisal interview? Can you manage an employment interview in such a way that you identify the best possible candidate? Can you manage your image well enough to persuade an interviewer to hire you? Each of these questions implies a one-to-one communication event in a complex organization.

Groups of all kinds may be found in organizations. There are social groups, decision-making groups, formal and informal *ad hoc* groups. Departments regularly hold meetings for a variety of purposes. Boards meet. People are assigned

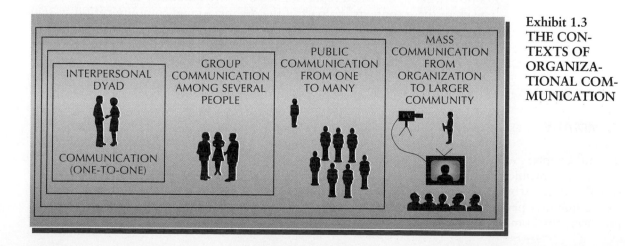

Exhibit 1.3 THE CONTEXTS OF ORGANIZATIONAL COMMUNICATION

to task forces. Groups provide many opportunities for you to demonstrate your business and political skill. Do you have the necessary skills?

Can you tell when and how to help a group accomplish its goals? Can you tell when and how to release tension and when to hold it in? Can you diffuse anger, smooth over ruffled feathers, stimulate creative thinking? Do you know how to help other individuals come to terms with the disappointment of a lost power struggle in a group? Can you provide the kind of communication that will keep a troubled group from disbanding, or from expelling a potentially valuable member? These questions all point to one or more group contexts in a complex organization.

If you spend any time in a business or professional organization, you will inevitably need to make formal presentations in a one-to-many context. Every day people whose interests are far removed from speechmaking are called upon to make presentations. Engineers must describe their activities to management groups. Entrepreneurs and inventors discover that they must ask for financial backing for a business venture. Managers address their colleagues. Supervisors speak to groups of their subordinates. People from one organization are asked to speak to people in other organizations. Executives appear before local civic groups to represent their organizations.

The ability to do these things well is the mark of a successful career. Are your public speaking skills up to the task? Can you organize your thoughts rapidly, clearly, and simply? Can you develop just the right arguments for a particular audience? Do you know how to make or select and use visual materials for a particular audience? Do you know how to make or select and use visual materials for best effect? Can you stand on your own with confidence?

Can you handle the communication problems inherent in group-to-group communication events? Do you know, for example, how to negotiate for the benefit of your own department when the resources of the organization are limited? Are your communication skills sufficient to the task of representing your organization to the community? Could you manage the communication situation if your company accidentally leaked toxic wastes into a local stream? Will you know what to do when reporters begin to fire questions at you?

Each of these contexts is a part of the organizational communication system that you will explore as you read this text. You can see that each is important to the organization, and to your own personal growth. They are the subject matter we will focus on throughout the remainder of this book.

SUMMARY ....

In this chapter we introduced the notion of looking at problems in business and professional settings from a communication perspective. Using that perspective, we can examine the potential for communication error among the various components of the communication process: sources (communication senders), channels, the messages the sources send—both verbal and nonverbal—and the receivers to whom the messages are sent. Effectiveness often involves the intelligent analysis of problems in these areas.

We talked next of communication as the exchange of symbols. Some symbols (such as *chair*) have referents in the tangible world, while others (such as *loyalty*) refer only to internal states. But all symbols have meaning only insofar as we give them meaning. And we communicate only to the extent that we share the same meanings. Meanings we share depend on our agreements about how to organize a message—about where it begins and how it is to be organized. In an organizational context, a message's organization is influenced by the culture—the system of beliefs that its members share, which unifies them and distinguishes that organization from all others.

We said that every communication event is relational—either symmetrical (equal) or complementary (one-up, one-down) and that in an organization people assess the relative power of the participants in a communication event.

We argued that communication in organizations is culturally dependent. This means that each organization develops a unique pattern of behaving—of thinking, speaking, and acting—which is the organization's way of doing things in its world. Thus relationships and communication are derived from the organization's culture. And because the organization's habitual way of doing things seems appropriate to that culture, it has defined the kinds of behavior that are appropriate and inappropriate.

We said that it is important to understand organizational culture. An organization's culture defines its character and its values. Many organizations adopt slogans that present a theme for members to follow. A sense of an organization's culture can be gained by examination of its communications and artifacts (objects, tools, and adornments). Its recurring vocabulary and symbols, along with its metaphors and stories, express its themes. Terrence Deal and Allen Kennedy have categorized organizational cultures as the "tough-guy, macho" culture, the "work hard/play hard" culture, the "you bet your company" culture, and the "process" culture.

Three principles guide organizational members ethically. Members should not intentionally deceive one another. Members should communicate in a way to not purposely harm any other member or members of the organization's environment. Members should treat each other justly.

Finally, we presented four familiar contexts for organizational communication: interpersonal, group, public, and mass communication contexts.

NOTES ....

1. Research suggests that this kind of communication is characterized by increased omissions of information and overall distortions. See Paul D. Krivonos, "Distortion of Subordinate to Superior Communication in Organizational Settings," *Central States Speech Journal,* **33** (1982):345–352.
2. Steve's concern may be well-placed. G. H. Morris, Stasia C. Gaveras, Whitney L. Baker, and Marta L. Coursey found that managers choose faultfinding about half the time when they must face problems of employee performance. See "Aligning Actions at Work: How Managers Confront Problems of Employee Performance," *Management Communication Quarterly,* **3** (1990):303–333.
3. William I. Gorden, Dominic A. Infante, and John Izzo discovered that subordinates seen as possessing constructive, rather than apathetic or complainer, disagreement styles are seen by their supervisors as better job performers than those who don't. See "Variations in Voice Pertaining to Dissatisfaction/Satisfaction with Subordinates," *Management Communication Quarterly,* **2** (1988):6–21.
4. The classic work intentionality is John R. Searle, *Intentionality: An Essay in the Philosophy of Mind* (Cambridge, Cambridge University Press, 1983). Gerald L. Wilson, H. Lloyd Goodall, Jr., and Christopher L. Waagen provide a good discussion of intentionality in *Organizational Communication* (New York, Harper & Row, 1986), Chapter 1.
5. Paul Watzlawick, Janet Helmick Beavin, and Don D. Jackson have argued that we cannot not

communicate because all behaviors have message potential. Thus, "accidental behavior" has message value. We cannot do much to control accidental behavior. We can, however, create intentional messages once we discover them. Thus our focus is on the intentionality of communication. For a discussion of these accidental behaviors, see Watzlawick, Beavin, and Jackson, *Pragmatics of Human Communication: A Study of Interactional Patterns, Pathologies, and Paradoxes* (New York, W. W. Norton, 1967), pp. 48–51.

6. Linda Putnam and Michael Pacanowsky, eds., *Communication and Organizations: An Interpretive Approach* (Beverly Hills, Calif., Sage, 1983); see also Andrew Pettigrew, "On Studying Organizational Cultures," *Administrative Science Quarterly*, 24 (1979):570–581.

7. Quotations are from Michael E. Pacanowsky and Nick O'Donnell-Trujillo, "Organizational Communications as Cultural Performance," *Communication Monographs*, 50 (1983):128–146.

8. Terrence E. Deal and Allen A. Kennedy, *Corporate Cultures* (Reading, Mass., Addison-Wesley, 1982), p. 27.

9. Gary L. Kreps, "Using Interpretive Research: The Development of a Socialization Program at RCA," in Putnam and Pacanowsky, eds., *Communication and Organizations*, p. 251.

10. Ward J. Goodenough, *Culture, Language, and Society* (Reading, Mass., Addison-Wesley, 1971), p. 22.

11. Deal and Kennedy, *Corporate Cultures*, p. 42.

12. *Webster's New Collegiate Dictionary*, 10th ed. (Springfield, Mass., Merriam-Webster, 1973), p. 282.

13. Gary L. Kreps, *Organizational Communication*, 2d ed. (New York, Longman, 1990), pp. 250–251.

RECOMMENDED READINGS . . . .

Eric M. Eisenberg and H. Lloyd Goodall, Jr. "The Changing World of Work," and "Relational Contexts for Organizational Communication." *Organizational Communication: Balancing Creativity and Constraint*. New York, St. Martin's Press, 1993. Chapters 1 and 8. This excellent organizational communication text provides a good illustration of how changing values in lives lead to shifts in how people view work and their relationships.

Richard L. Johannsen. *Ethics in Human Communication*, 3d ed. Prospect Heights, Ill., Waveland Press, 1990. This relatively easy-to-read book on ethics provides a comprehensive treatment of ethical perspectives as they relate to communication in a variety of contexts.

D. Krackhardt and J. R. Hanson. "Informal Networks: The Company Behind the Chart." *Harvard Business Review*, 71 (July 1993): 104–111. The informal networks in an organization are far different from those formal relationships represented by the organizational chart. This essay helps the reader to understand how understanding the informal networks is a key to knowing who actually talks to, advises, and trusts others.

DISCUSSION QUESTIONS . . . .

1. Looking at a situation from a communication perspective, it has been suggested, is different from looking at it from a management perspective. In what ways might the perspectives differ?

2. Why is it important to define communication as symbolic exchange? What difference would it make if communication were defined instead as behavior exchange or message exchange? Why is the word *exchange* necessary to the definition of communication?

3. The text locates the meaning of communication events inside people. What difference would it make if the meaning were located in the channels used to communicate or in the communicative exchange itself, and not in the people? What if the meaning of a sentence actually were in the words? How might that influence our ability to communicate?

4. How many plausible messages can be derived from the sentence, "How are you this evening, buddy?" What did you do to signal the different meanings you had in mind? How is the relationship dimension carried?

INTERNET ACTIVITIES ....

1. Open a search engine such as Yahoo! (http://www.yahoo.com/) or Lycos (http://www.lycos.com/). Perform separate searches using these key words: *communication AND ethics; communication AND theory; communication AND perspective*. Take careful note of your impressions. Prepare to discuss with your classmates what you believe the implications of the Internet and the World Wide Web are for international and interpersonal communication.

2. Locate organizations on the World Wide Web that focus on human communication. Spend enough time at their Web sites so that you can describe their concerns in detail to your classmates. A good place to start is the Southern States Communication Association home page (http://www.uamont.edu/~adams/ssca.htmlx) or the Speech Communication Association home page (http://www.scassn.org/).

CHAPTER 2

The Organization—Theoretical Perspectives

OBJECTIVES ....

Upon completion of this chapter, you should be able to:

1. Talk freely and comfortably about how organizations evolve.
2. Explain and differentiate between systems and structural perspectives.
3. Identify the communication problems that result from the evolution of an organization.
4. Compare and contrast task focus and goal focus, and explain the major leadership problems that arise from the organization's tendency to adopt a task focus.
5. Explain the relationship between job specialization and the evolution of hierarchy.
6. Define and explain *entropy* and *negentropy*.
7. Explain why the simple notion that "there is more than one way to reach a goal" is so very important to management.

Consider an entry-level college graduate named Joe. He is part of a system called a department. Tony, his boss, is head of the department and represents it in the production division, of which the department is a member. The production division, in turn, is part of a still larger organization—also a system—called the corporation. The production division manager represents the division in meetings of officers of the corporation. The corporation is part of a larger system, which is part of a still larger system, and so on.

Similarly, Joe may be part of several systems smaller than the department. For example, he may be a member of a subset called "Ad Hoc Committee on Product Feasibility." Or he may be a member of another subset, the department bowling team.

All this talk about departments, divisions, corporations, and the like may seem a bit confusing. Why not just focus on Joe's department? you may be asking. You reason that you will start out as a member of a department, and departments are what you would most like to understand. You could focus on the department, and sometimes you may want to do so. But it is also important to look at the big picture of organizations. Joe is a member of the entire organization and communicates in various ways within it. His communication affects his department and potentially the entire organization. So it is important to understand organizations more generally. Examination of the structure of the organization is called "structural analysis." We begin by looking at the organization as a whole; then we look at its various parts.

....**THE ORGANIZATION IN PERSPECTIVE**

It may seem like common sense to divide an organization into its natural parts as a means of understanding how it works. In a common-sense analysis we normally look at what we wish to study in order to discover its natural parts. For instance, we might analyze something as having physical components. A person might be analyzed as having torso, arms, legs, and head. Or it would be sensible to divide a person into circulatory system, respiratory system, muscular system, nervous system, and so on. Each of these sets has the common characteristic of appearing to be self-evident, a sensible grouping, in some context.

A common-sense analysis begins with identification of the natural parts or components. To understand organizations, we think it may be more useful to begin with the *goals* of the analysis and then study its parts. In this book, for instance, you will be looking at human beings in an effort to understand how they can receive and send symbols most efficiently and with greatest effect. The goal of the analysis in this case is understanding message exchange. So we need to identify the individual's symbol-using components. These components turn out to be *processes*. Our ability to use symbols depends on such processes as learning, problem solving, perception, and memory. If you look inside a person, you do not find a learning center separate from both a memory center and a problem-solving center. But if you want to increase the effectiveness of your communication, it is useful to think of these processes as separate. If we can understand how these processes work in another person, we can understand how to adapt messages to the other's symbol-using system. The result will surely be increased effectiveness when we talk. Such processes as learning and problem solving and perception are the components to be analyzed.

You will surely notice that those component processes are also interrelated. Learning cannot occur without perception. Problem solving cannot occur without learning. We think, therefore, that the relationships among the component processes are also very important.

You will also notice, we hope, that implied in this description is what we think may be the most important concept in this book—the concept of change. People change. Organizations change. Processes change. We are concerned about change because we are concerned about communication. Communication is almost always an attempt to control change—either by causing it or by preventing it. But before you can understand how to control change, you must understand the organization you want to control.

An Organization as a System

Systems theory suggests that an organization is "a complex set of *interdependent* parts that interact to adapt to a constantly changing environment in order to achieve its goals."[1] This definition suggests that a system has some goal or output in view. It also implies that some process is going on within a system— some interaction with or in regard to something. If processing is going on within the system, something must be taken into it. And change is going on as the system adapts to its environment. So the work of any system can be portrayed as Exhibit 2.1 suggests. This definition also refers to interdependent parts. These parts are commonly termed the system's *subsystems*. In a manufacturing firm, they might be the sales department, the marketing department, the product development department, the production department, and so forth.

One of the easiest ways to understand the concept of a system is to think about a familiar system—the human body. Your body is a system composed of various subsystems. We all have a subsystem called the circulatory system, for example. As a system, your body receives input in the form of food, air, liquids,

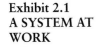

**Exhibit 2.1
A SYSTEM AT
WORK**

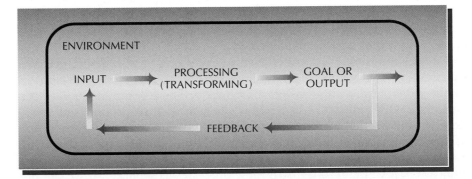

and information. You process this input, and the result of this processing is output. You expel waste products and expend energy in the form of behavior that acts upon and manipulates things within your environment. And finally, you monitor the results of your actions in relation to the environment, and the feedback—information you receive about the impact of your behavior as well as other environment conditions—becomes new input. Such inputs are then used to assess goal achievement, to help you adapt further to your environment, and to set new goals.

Organizations are systems too. They take in resources in the form of people, information, and materials (inputs). These inputs are processed and yield products or services (outputs). The organization monitors the effect of its outputs, in relation to goals and environmental conditions, and produces messages (feedback) about its performance which serve as inputs. Because the inputs are processed, output is never the same as input. The interdependent parts of the system work together (coordinate their activities) to transform the resources into a product or service. So in a manufacturing firm, we have product development, production, marketing, sales, quality control, personnel, and other component parts that work together to produce the product. To assess the firm's productivity, we do not simply add together the individual outputs of each component part. It is necessary to view the output of each part as being the result of interaction and interdependence with other component parts. It is these outputs that combine to produce a result greater than that of each part working independently.

Communication Implications of the Systems Perspective

Here are several important benefits that may come from an efficiently operating system:

1. *The interaction among the system's components can yield creative activity.* When people talk they bring to the communication their unique experiences. The result can be more creative ideas.
2. The creativity fostered by cooperation and coordination of effort leads to a principle of systems theory: *A system can reach a particular goal (output) from a variety of initial conditions and in a variety of ways.* A church, for example, might set the goal of increasing its membership by 10 percent. One way of doing so might be to increase its outreach through a revitalized music program. Another way might be to conduct a weeklong special event. A third option might be to visit potential members. Initial conditions can cover a wide range of possibilities, depending on the differing states of particular church programs at a particular time. So, given a set of initial conditions, the church can effectively pursue its goal of a 10 percent increase in membership by following one or several paths. Thus, this principle suggests that an organization, through interdependent and coordinated efforts, can discover many ways to achieve its goals and can select those judged most likely to produce the desired effect.

3. *Communication enables coordination and cooperation within and among organizational components.* A necessary ingredient in this process, the means by which members and components are able to work together to achieve organizational goals, is communication. Product development, for example, must communicate with production. Marketing must communicate with sales. Without communication, production may not be able to turn out the product in a timely fashion. Marketing may not produce strategies that the sales force can use. Individual members and components of a system must communicate to coordinate their activities.

4. *Communication enables response to the environment.* All systems have some degree of openness to their environment. By *openness* we mean that organizations exert some amount of effort that results in both import and export of information to and from the world around them. So a system is characterized as either open or closed in accordance with the degree to which it takes in and gives out information from the outside environment. Most organizations must be relatively open if they are to receive the information they need to process inputs effectively. An organization, for example, must communicate with those who may purchase its product. Feedback in the form of sales allows the system to adjust its output appropriately.

All organizations are systems, but not all managers of organizations understand and operate from this perspective. An example of a company that has made use of a systems perspective in its operation will help you understand how viewing an organization as a system can be important. General Motors instituted a program that fosters the notion of interdependency among its components and open communication with its environment—its customers, in this case. The Michigan plant, where Pontiacs are built, asks dealers to send them the names and telephone numbers of customers who buy these cars. Names are selected from the list of customers, and a few weeks later the customer receives a call asking how he or she likes the new car. The information received in this way is collected by management and passed on to the various components—styling, production, engineering, marketing—to be used in the decision-making process. This particular plant is viewing its organization as an open system. It is seeking information from its environment to use as an input in order to improve its output. It is involving nearly all its component parts in the process, taking into account the interdependent nature of a system. The result of this involvement should yield greater productivity than would be possible if the individual units worked independently to improve product quality. Working together allows each of the various subsystems to look at product improvement from its particular perspective. The multiple perspectives and their interaction permit insights into product improvement that might never come if the subsystems worked separately.

Exhibit 2.2 represents an organizational structure from a systems perspective. The production division is larger than two other divisions, which are of about equal size. Moreover, Joe's department is about the same size as one other department in the product division, and quite a bit larger than still another.

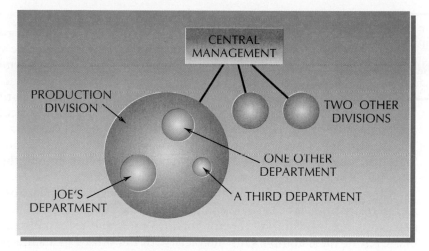

**Exhibit 2.2
THE ORGANI-
ZATION OF
JOE'S WORK-
PLACE**

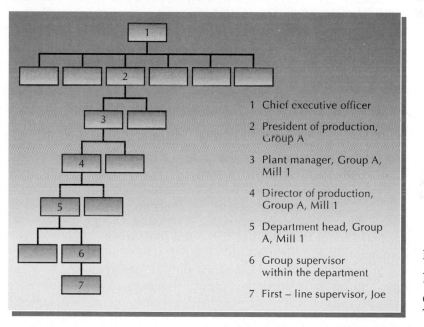

1 Chief executive officer

2 President of production,
Group A

3 Plant manager, Group A,
Mill 1

4 Director of production,
Group A, Mill 1

5 Department head, Group
A, Mill 1

6 Group supervisor
within the department

7 First – line supervisor, Joe

**Exhibit 2.3
A CLASSIC
"TALL"
ORGANIZA-
TION CHART**

A classic organization chart (Exhibit 2.3) of part of Joe's corporation illustrates the divisions and departments and shows relationships among levels and units. Such a chart represents less an organization called the corporation than a *way of thinking about* organizations—a *structural perspective*. It is a common way of conceptualizing a complex organization such as a college, a hospital, or a corporation.

Organizational Structure

> What are the ethical responsibilities implicit when a new manager implements changes in his or her part of the organization?

Organizations evolve structure, by design, in order to provide stability and predictability.[2] This structure recognizes planned power and authority relationships. So when we look at an organization from the structural perspective, we are trying to understand its planned power and authority relationships in order to view and analyze the communication processes within the organization. But often these processes do not reflect actual relationships very closely and so we must also look at the informal communication network. Since for now we want to look at the dynamic interplay among the parts, we must begin by studying the way the parts fit together.[3]

Consider the following example illustrating how components of an organization relate to each other. You could say that the components of a complex organization are its (1) tasks, (2) structure, (3) tools and technology, and (4) people. Each of these components interacts with the others in such a way so that changes in any one of the components works a change in the others.

Suppose, to take a concrete case, you bring in a new manager for a department. The manager's vision and style differ from those of the earlier manager. She may reorganize the department. Perhaps the focus of the department will change somewhat because of the manager's expertise in something her predecessor knew little about. Perhaps, too, the new vision will have implications for the tools and the technology of the department.

In 1995 a man named Patrick took over the communications department of a midsized plastics firm in Chicago. By 1996 the department had grown to twice the number of employees (its people); had significantly broadened its focus to include a vigorous emphasis on research as well as on service to the organization and community (its tasks); had moved into the area of electronic mass communication; had acquired a good deal of video equipment, and several multimedia computers; and had redesigned its own organization (its structure).

Each modification of any one of its components worked changes in all the others. This is the important point: A dynamic change was (and still is) happening that cannot be explained without a look at the whole system. Focus on the community led to the need for a good deal of equipment, which led to broadening of talents, which yielded varied output, which caused new employees to be hired, which broadened the research interests of the members, which yielded more projects, which made possible . . . And so it goes in complex organizations.

Hierarchy

One reasonable definition of the term *hierarchy* is "any system that places persons or objects in rank order, one above the other." When most of us think of complex organizations, we tend to think in terms of people in their hierarchical relationships. Someone is boss. Someone is the chief executive officer (CEO). Someone works at a machine on the production line.

You will recall that the structural perspective recognizes *planned* power and authority relationships. Keep that idea in mind as you consider this discussion of the term *hierarchy*, for it will help you to understand the communication problems discussed in this book.

The Tall Structure and Communication Flow

The tall structure (Exhibit 2.3) includes a hierarchy with many levels. It generally produces close supervision and very careful control. In addition, a tall structure usually implies a very narrow power field—power is held at the top and shared among a limited number of individuals. Individuals at the top are depended on for planning, decision making, and directives. Individuals at the bottom are expected to follow the directives and have very little say in decision making.

Downward communication flow.

Communication that flows from the top of an organization toward the bottom in an expansive fashion has been termed *downward communication*. Communication that flows from the bottom to the top, on the other hand, in a restrictive fashion, is called *upward communication*.[4] The greater the number of levels in the hierarchy, the greater tendency for upward and downward communication flow to be distorted. Communication that flows through several levels of an organization is called *serial communication*.[5]

An illustration of the distorting effects of serial communication: Ted Morris, the CEO of a large corporation, is playing golf one crisp October morning with three subordinates. Just before he makes his shot from the sixteenth tee, he turns to his vice-president for production. "Charlie," he says over his shoulder, "I understand your cost override in the casting plant was two percent above budget last week. Better look into that." Then the chief slices his tee shot into the rough about 180 years off the tee.

Charlie has no idea what the CEO is talking about, but he does know that he is not as well-informed about last week's operations as he ought to be, because his wife was feeling ill and he spent time last week in his role as husband and parent. In short, he thinks that perhaps he messed up. So he interprets the chief's tee shot as evidence that the chief is upset. He makes a mental note to call his division managers together after lunch to get to the bottom of the matter.

By 1:15 P.M. Charlie and his division managers, including not only the casting plant manager but two others as well, are sitting in the small conference room in the casting plant. Charlie is saying: "I don't know what Ted Morris was talking about, but I surely wasn't informed about any budget override last week. Would you please check into it and let me know what happened by noon tomorrow? Can we have lunch to discuss the matter?"

Notice how Charlie has distorted the chief's remark. A supposed cost override in casting has now become a probable budget override. Charlie either has forgotten or did not believe that the CEO was focusing on the casting plant. He has taken his division managers by surprise, and each makes a mental note to call a meeting of department heads just as soon as the conference with Charlie has ended. You can imagine that those three meetings last quite a while. One of the managers has to cancel another luncheon meeting to meet with Charlie tomorrow. Still another has to rearrange his schedule so that he can be in town. Each of those changes works other changes in the part of the company that each division manager controls. Thus downward communication flow in the hierarchy is expanded.

Upward communication flow.

Communication upward through the hierarchy is distorted too, but in a very different manner.[6] Because each superior in the hierarchy has a broader view than the subordinates in his or her span of control, the superior is likely to edit messages based on that view before passing them up the chain. So as we move through the hierarchy, expectations change from one position to another; and as people at these various levels act on the messages, they change too. Someone in the chain may even decide to stop the transmission so that the message never reaches its intended destination. Upward flow tends to be restricted.

To illustrate the restricting nature of upward flow of communication we present another hypothetical situation. Johnny has been working on the same stamping press for four years. He is considered one of the best machine operators in his section, and when new employees are brought into the section, Johnny's supervisor typically places them next to Johnny so that they can learn from him. As a piecework operator, Johnny makes his living on the basis of his efficiency—the more parts he produces, the more money he makes. In other ways Johnny has also been a model employee. He is a high producer, but he does not exceed the culturally acceptable level of output. He is well-respected by his peers and is known for dependability by his own supervisor and by his supervisor's colleagues around the plant. You can imagine his supervisor's surprise, therefore, when Johnny storms into his tiny office and says angrily, "Bill, I'll tell you something. If you ever put a greenhorn next to me on that line again, I'm gonna tell you where you can poke that machine."

Bill's first reaction is to try to calm Johnny down. Clearly something is very wrong. "Sit down, Johnny. What's going on?"

"That kid won't leave me alone. OK, I don't mind his questions, but he keeps getting in the way. Now he's gone and messed up my press. Stuck a piece of sheet into it crooked and the damn thing jammed. Don't send me any more kids to train. I can't afford it."

That afternoon Bill goes to the meeting he had scheduled with his boss last week. The purpose of the meeting is to discuss Johnny's record. Management has been thinking of promoting Johnny. Listen to Bill as he reports his visit with Johnny. He will diminish and restrict the message. He will cut out all of Johnny's emotional tone and all of the strong language, a process called *leveling*. Bill will level Johnny's message, and he will leave out much of what Johnny said. In fact, he will ignore entirely Johnny's remark about not sending him any new kids to train.

"Johnny is one of the best, and he has been for four years," Bill says. "His record is consistent and dependable. Everyone on the line respects and likes him. In fact, he has trained three of them to handle their machines. And the only time in four years I have ever seen him upset was this morning. A new kid was fooling around or something. Anyway, Johnny got miffed because the kid put a sheet of stock into his press wrong and the press jammed. As you know, when Johnny's press is down, he loses money. Anyway, I talked with him for a while, and he went right back to the kid and showed him how to feed the press correctly. I think Johnny would be an excellent 'super.' I don't think there's anyone on the line who could do the job better."

Managing communication flow problems.   Communication fidelity can be enhanced by using multiple channels. In practice this means presenting an important message orally, face-to-face if possible, and in writing. You might make an appointment to see your boss, explain your idea, and leave a written document that makes your argument. The use of multiple channels creates redundancy—the repetition of the ideas. It also provides a "hard copy" of your remarks that may be referred to and passed on when the message is being processed and transmitted. Further, the oral channel, if face-to-face or via telephone, allows for maximum opportunity for feedback and correction.

The Flat Structure and Communication Flow

The hierarchy of a *flat structure* has fewer levels than that of a tall structure, and its power field is broader. Typically, a flat structure tends to be rather loose in terms of control and supervision. More individuals report to a single supervisor, and each individual has more autonomy in decision making. Individuals lower in the hierarchy of a flat structure have more direct responsibility for their success on the job.

Information overload.   The communication problems that derive from a flat structure have to do primarily with information overload and loss of control. Since the individual supervisor's span of control is great, he or she has to process many more messages from subordinates than a manager in a tall structure who has a limited span of control. The supervisor who fails to process all that information risks loss of control.

We do not wish to suggest that either a tall or flat structure is to be preferred, since what is right for an organization depends on a complex set of conditions. Some people work best and some tasks are best accomplished within a tall structure. Other people work better and other kinds of tasks are better accomplished within a flat structure. Moreover, the size of an organization as well as its geographical spread may require taller or less tall organizational structures.[7] Tallness or flatness of organizations tends to evolve out of task and other considerations, and communication problems tend to be related to that evolution. As you will see, such concerns as span of control, division of labor, line and staff functions, and the chains of command, as well as clarity of an individual's role definition and his or her ability to perform that role, are all related to whether or not an appropriate organizational hierarchy has evolved and whether or not the organizational leadership is able and willing to make adaptations when they are necessary.

> At what point, if any, would protecting a manager from information overload begin to present ethical problems?

Managing communication flow problems. The communication flow problem in a flat structure is one of finding ways to reduce overload. If you were a manager who had seventeen departments reporting to you, the overload problem could be considerable. Imagine trying to process seventeen reports each time you asked for information from your departments.

There are two primary ways to manage overload. One strategy is to standardize reporting procedures. This requires creating formats and forms for the information being received. What you are doing is requiring those under you to organize the information for you. Organized material allows easier retrieval, thus simplifying the process. A second strategy is to employ assistants who can sort and sift information and organize it for you. When resources are available, this is a common way of managing information overload.

Appropriateness of Structure

Span of control. *Span of control* refers to the number of subordinates who report to a supervisor. Some authorities believe that no individual's span of control should encompass more than a dozen subordinates. Others believe that a single supervisor can work with many more subordinates, especially if those subordinates are given decision-making autonomy and some degree of responsibility for the success of their activities.

Probably the greatest determinant of what constitutes an appropriate span of control is the kind of decision making that must be accomplished at any given hierarchical level. A production line supervisor can supervise a fairly large number of individuals, for example, if the individuals are involved in the production of a single component. On the other hand, upper-level managers often have to coordinate the broadly diverse activities of entire divisions of an organization. In order to protect upper-level managers from information overload (it would be unrealistic to ask them to carry such complexity in their heads), their span of control may be limited to about five subordinates. In addition, from a communication point of view, a narrower span of control serves to put some distance between upper management and the other workers. As you will see, some distancing is necessary, but it does result in communication problems. One such problem, distortion of messages as they flow both upward and downward, has already been identified.

Division of labor. The meaning of *division of labor* seems self-evident. The term refers to who is responsible for doing what—a key idea in organizational theory. The basic notion is that job specialization creates greater efficiency and higher levels of productivity.

By definition, division of labor tends to separate people. The more it separates them, the more difficult it is for them to communicate. Formalized communication channels emerge in an attempt to resolve the increased difficulty in communication. At the same time, as channels become more cumbersome, political problems may emerge from failure to go through the channels.

In addition, separation tends to cause people to confine their loyalties to their own work groups. Cohesiveness in a work group is necessary to the group's productivity, but it may bring worker commitment to the group's goals rather than to the organization's goals. Such commitment often leads to competition between groups for limited resources—and sometimes to outright hostility.

Finally, dividing labor increases the complexity and changes the nature of the manager's job. At higher levels, jobs become more specialized, and it is more difficult for a manager at this level to keep track of and understand the intricacies of each subordinate's job. Further, there may be a greater number of subordinates within the manager's span of control. Coordination and control become problems, along with the potential for information overload.

Line and staff.   Two primary tasks of a complex organization are to generate units of production and to market those units of production to the organization's constituencies. These two primary tasks are called *line functions*.

The *staff* includes all the individuals involved in supporting the line operations—advising them and generating services that the line officers can use in decision making. Accounting departments, for example, generate data about cash flow through the organization. Legal departments advise the line personnel about compliance with laws and regulations. Personnel departments seek, recruit, and place employees in the organization. Advertising departments include designers, photographers, writers and artists, time and space buyers, and so on, all of whom provide services that support the marketing line.

Typically, although not always, staff personnel relate to line personnel in an advisory capacity only, but sometimes they have authority over the line. The legal department of an organization, for example, may veto the decision of a line officer because of legal considerations. A staff officer may have the authority to shut down the production line if public safety mandates that decision. He would have to explain that decision to the line management very persuasively, of course, and his job might ride on his explanation. As a general rule, the staff advises and the line has responsibility for accepting or rejecting advice from the staff.

Chain of command.   The term *chain of command* refers to the planned power and authority relationships of an organization. As the term is commonly used in most organizations, though, it has come to be equated with "which subordinates are directed by and get to talk with which supervisors."

Consider a supervisor on the production line in an industrial organization. If she were to work through the chain of command, all of her interactions upward would flow through the plant manager. The chain of command requires each subordinate to interact about job-related matters only with those individuals who report to that person and with that person's immediate supervisor. Moreover, any message that flows upward or downward is supposed to pass through every link in the chain. Thus, if this supervisor were to conform to this assumption, she could not interact directly with the vice-president for production—only with the plant production manager, who would then put the supervisor's message into channels along with the messages of several other individuals

What ethical questions influence the decision to stay in the chain of command or to go outside it? For example, would questions of loyalty determine your answer?

at this supervisor's level. Such an expectation is not only unrealistic (this supervisor knows the vice-president personally and sometimes sees her socially as well as for business reasons), it would be unwise.

One reason that strict adherence to chain-of-command assumptions would be unwise is that it can restrict the people to a point where they may not be able to function. A particular manager's span of control may be so great that if all messages are passed according to the "rules," some messages may not flow in a timely manner. This then creates a logjam of stalled messages, frustration and conflict among subordinates, and strangulation of informal information flow which members depend. Even so, the idea that you must "go through channels" is still generally accepted as the rule in most organizations.[8]

Informal Networks and Communication Flow

Alongside the formal chain-of-command network, an *informal network* called "the grapevine" has emerged. Within any organization there is an informal network that is not shown on the chart, and wise leaders will learn to use it.[9] But the literature offers little help in how to go about doing so. We think that the best definition of the term *grapevine* is "who, in fact, talks to whom." That is, the grapevine is the network of interaction that actually occurs in the organization rather than the planned channels that appear on an organization chart.

The importance of cultivating informal networks cannot be overemphasized. Some believe that informal communication is the primary way people communicate in organizations. In fact, respondents in one survey found it so important that 57 percent thought it "the only way to find out what's really happening."[10] Management personnel who understand the importance of informal networks will often encourage them. For example, Andrew S. Grove, president and CEO of Intel Corporation, thinks that encouraging "frank, casual communication" and free flow of information is vital to keeping the organization running smoothly.[11]

How do the formal and informal communication networks relate regarding speed? David Krackhardt and Jeffrey Hanson capture the difference in this metaphor: "If the formal organization is the skeleton of a company, the informal is the central nervous system."[12] The central nervous system in a human is, of course, very fast. This is why organizational decision makers often rely on trusted associates for their information.[13]

Information relayed by the informal network is often quite accurate. In fact, studies in organizational settings put that accuracy at 78 to 90 percent.[14] These informal messages are relatively accurate because their face-to-face nature allows more clarification than the written, one-way, serially transmitted messages that come via formal channels.[15] Gordon Allport and Leo Postman also report that when the information is erroneous and cannot be verified, the results are often dramatic.[16] Imagine that a good friend and fellow classmate tells you he thinks there will be a pop quiz in your history class tomorrow. If you believe your friend, spend your evening studying, and the test does not materialize, you may be quite upset. It appears that people believe in the grapevine and count on its accuracy.

Organizations that recognize the importance of this informal network can make good use of it. Their supervisors are able to feed information into this network through opinion leaders. Supervisors may try to counter negative effects of false rumors by providing some way for people to check the accuracy. Some organizations provide a "hot line" to the personnel office where employees can anonymously check out what they have heard.

The organizations we are concerned with seem a lot like people. They can interact with their environments. In order to understand them we have to examine how the tasks, structures, technologies, and people of the organizations are connected, and how the decision making occurs. Long-range goals drive the business organization we are interested in. The decisions that allow achievement of those goals—management decisions all—are based on the information available. That information, because of a variety of identifiable problems, may be distorted. Thus a most important part of visionary leadership is assuring the quality of information as it flows through the organization.

> **Would it be possible to use the grapevine in a way that would violate ethical principles?**

....TASK FOCUS VERSUS GOAL FOCUS

As organizations mature over time, an interesting thing begins to happen. People move to greater task specialization and sometimes lose sight of overall goals. They take on a *task focus*. We will illustrate what we mean by a task focus versus a goal focus. Then we will address a problem that arises when people lose sight of overall goals.

Creating units of production and marketing them—the line functions—are the most obvious tasks of an organization, easy to identify and easy to describe. The tasks of an individual within the organization are also easy to identify and describe. If you were asked, for example, to identify and describe what you do in your role as student, you would have no difficulty describing what you do.

But if you were asked to talk about your goals—or more specifically, what you want to be doing professionally in ten years—you might have a good deal of difficulty answering. Goals are not usually described in the form of behaviors, as tasks are, and therefore are relatively more difficult to identify and express.

We once asked a department manager who works in the food-canning industry to talk about the goals of his corporation. He said something like "to feed the people" or "to guarantee that people are able to put high-quality, low-priced, nutritious and safe food on their tables." This statement is high-minded and rather vague. No specific behaviors are mentioned.

Because goals tend to be difficult to identify and describe and are usually multiple, and because tasks are usually easy to identify and describe, both organizations and people lose sight of overall goals and focus on immediate tasks.[17] This tendency to focus on what we do rather than on what we want leads to at least four leadership problems. People tend to routinize their tasks. Organizations tend to pigeonhole people in role specializations. People lose their sense of direction. Finally, conflict emerges as opposed goals come into juxtaposition—whether they are organizational goals or individual goals. Because these problems are so common, we think it would be useful to take a closer look at each of them.

Problems Related to Task Focus

Routinization

When people take a new job, they tend to learn it quickly. They polish and hone the relevant skills, develop a routine, and relegate as much of the task as possible to habit. In short, they specialize—become experts. Unless something is done, they may also soon become bored with the job.

Consider a student, Ancel, who had summer employment as a hand assembler in a shoe factory. The job required that a cardboard form be inserted at the heel of the leather "upper" in order to give the back of the shoe shape. This assembly was then attached by two nails to a wooden foot form. At first the job was challenging. The supervisor watched closely and offered instruction. After a couple of weeks, Ancel had learned the job so well that close supervision was unnecessary. Within another week or so, he reached maximum output level. He had exhausted the job's possibilities. The joy and challenge were gone. Remember when you figured out the child's game of tic-tac-toe? You probably do not play it very often any more, and when you do, it is most likely with a child. Since you have figured out how to play the game, the challenge is gone for you—and so is the interest.

Shortly after Ancel achieved maximum output on the hand assembly line, the trouble began. He started to compare his work with that of others. A fellow close by had the position of machine assembler. He did the same thing Ancel did, but he could do it faster because of the machine. Both he and Ancel were paid according to the number of units they produced—and because the other worker had a machine, he could assemble about three times as many units. Ancel knew he was working as hard as his neighbor but with less profitable results, and he complained. The manager said that purchase of a machine for summer help was not cost-effective. Ancel began to air his complaint to other hand assemblers, some of whom had been on the job for years.

Ancel's neighbor with the machine was puzzled at first, and then hostile. From his point of view, Ancel betrayed him. He had, after all, taught Ancel the fine points of the job, thus enabling him to reach maximum capacity quickly. Now it seemed to him that Ancel was trying to get him into trouble with the boss. What had been a friendly working relationship degenerated into silence, and then into open argument. The department supervisor soon had to deal with complaints from the other hand assemblers, and with conflict between the hand assemblers and the machine assemblers. Her way of dealing with the problem was to fire Ancel.

This example is not as farfetched as it may seem. Indeed, it illustrates one of the most fundamental leadership problems in complex organizations. People get caught up in tasks, become specialists, become bored, and lose sight of goals.

> Typically, if employees meet their goals in one cycle, management increases the goals for the next cycle. This is done to encourage and motivate increased productivity. Is there a limit to how far a manager can take this trend before it becomes an ethical issue?

Role Stereotyping

At the same time that individuals are exhausting the possibilities of their jobs, organizations are pigeonholing people into specialized roles. It seems more productive, after all, and usually more economical, to leave people in jobs they clearly do well, rather than transfer them to new positions. But people are not pigeons. Dissatisfaction on the job has been a problem for management since the Industrial Revolution, and most of leadership theory has evolved from attempts to reconcile organizational efficiency and employee satisfaction. People feel trapped, become dissatisfied with the task, and then lose sight of the organization's goal.

Loss of Direction

Greater task specialization can lead to a loss of direction as people focus more and more attention on the daily work. Goals serve as a guide and source of motivation. When we set intermediate and long-range goals, we can see where we are heading and know when we have arrived. Intermediate goals help us chart our course toward our long-range goals. A task focus, in contrast, takes on the current activity as the goal. This focus may be efficient in completing the task but says little about where we will end up tomorrow, or next week, or next month. The more we "buy into" just getting through the task, the more likely that will become our focus. We are in danger of losing the important direction that guides our activity.

Conflict between Organizational and Individual Goals

The third major leadership problem is that organizational goals come into conflict with each other and with individual goals. In the shoe factory the organization wanted to maintain optimum output from the assemblers. Ancel wanted to get status, to earn more money, to develop a new challenge on the job, to move up. Ancel had certain social goals in mind that were not conducive to maintaining balance in the assembly department. Ancel, being summer help, was soon out of a job.

Units of the same organization often come into conflict with each other. Without careful planning, for example, most marketing and production divisions would experience conflict, since marketing will always try to sell the maximum number of units and production will always try to produce the optimum number of units. *Maximum* and *optimum* are not synonymous terms.

We will consider what may be done to alleviate these particular problems in due course, but first let's consider the natural consequence of these three problems: the evolution of a hierarchy.

Evolution of a Hierarchy

A hierarchy develops as people and organizations solve their problems and learn from their mistakes. As problems are solved, tasks can become increasingly complex because each new task must take into account and accommodate the information. A young man with an M.B.A. degree provides an illustration of this point. Say this man reports to work regularly and is a good worker. He makes mistakes and learns from his mistakes. Soon he begins helping others. In time he is promoted. Now he has more problems because he has "direct reports"—people who work for him. He learns from his mistakes on this job, too, then teaches others and is promoted again. Thus a complex hierarchy evolves to manage complex problems. A hierarchy of authority, of power, inevitably emerges to control the variables that result from the problem solving and complexity. Accompanying this evolution is job specialization. The more job specialization, the more hierarchy. The more hierarchy, the more job specialization.[18] The following example illustrates this process of problem solving, complexity, hierarchy, and job specialization.

Suppose a couple of independent truckers, Juan and Sam, are sitting at a lunch counter. Both of them enjoy working with wood and building things. One says to the other, "Let's buy an old house, fix it up, and see if we can sell it for a profit." The idea is accepted, and they shop around for a house that meets their needs. It must be basically sound, in a stable neighborhood, and in need of some tender, loving carpentry. They buy, fix up, and sell the house. Their initial investment of $32,000 returns a handsome profit, say, 50 percent, for easy figuring. They now have $48,000 to invest. Suppose they perform the same cycle again, this time buying in a more expensive neighborhood, and again they increase their initial investment by 50 percent. Now they have $72,000, and they decide to buy two houses.

At this point they have their first real organizational problem. Neither of them has the time to work on two places at once and still operate their trucking business. They need some help, so they decide to hire an employee. What skills should the employee have? Do they need a carpenter? Do they need an agent who will purchase and sell for them?

To carry this illustration just a bit further, suppose that they employ a person who serves a dual function: carpenter and agent. He comes to them one morning and says: "I've been thinking. If you bought most of the materials you use in bulk, you could save about 20 percent on your costs. My figures include rental on one of the little miniwarehouses on Main Street. That would mean a saving of about $5,000, which would allow you to diversify your business a little."

Suddenly, the business is more complex, and this is causing some problems. What they need to do is specialize. As the company continues to grow, increasing specialization will be needed. For the truckers to maintain control over this growing company, they will have to delegate some of their authority. They will also have to focus their interests. Since Jim knows more than Sam does about building, and since he is an expert in such matters as wood quality, hardware use, and transportation, he will probably become the production manager. Sam knows something about the marketplace and so will probably become the marketing director.

There are definite advantages to this ever-increasing job specialization. Production and marketing become more orderly. Staff functions too become easier to fit into the organization. But there are also problems. Job specialization sometimes leads to dehumanization and alienation of the worker narrowness of view, low organizational loyalty, and rigid resistance to change.[19]

Clearly, what is needed to meet these conditions is visionary leadership, especially with regard to organizational planning and goal setting. A *visionary leader* predicts how changes in any of the components of the organization will affect all the other components. Put another way, visionary leadership is communicating in such a way that the quality of information is increased, resulting in power and control that can be intelligently applied. A visionary leader helps individuals maintain a goal focus. We will say more about visionary leadership later in this chapter, but first we want to explore the potential for organizational decay.

....**THE POTENTIAL FOR DECAY**

Every organization has the potential for decay—the potential to disintegrate. The term that has been used to describe this tendency of organizations (and other systems) to disintegrate is *entropy*. If an organization is able to recognize that it is in danger of coming apart and then does something to prevent entropy, it is exerting *negentropy*. An organization that is unable to exert such a countering force will disintegrate much more quickly. Clearly the major task of the leadership of any organization, then, is to counter entropy with negentropy. We think that is a matter of communication. Let us explain.

A stone cannot interact with its environment. It can only exist. Let us say that it exists somewhere above 40 degrees of longitude in North America. The stone gets very cold in winter and warm in summer. This constant heating and cooling expands and contracts its molecular structure. Rain penetrates the stone, however slightly. While the stone is still moist, the temperature drops. The water in the stone freezes and expands. The stone fractures. The wind blows particulate matter into collision with the stone, and with each microscopic impact, bits are chipped away. Over years, over centuries, the stone disintegrates. There is nothing the stone can do to prevent it. The stone becomes a random collection of bits and pieces. In contrast, business organizations have the potential to intervene. Like people, they make decisions about how they will interact with their environment.[20]

Like an organization, you can and do interact with your environment. If you are tired, you sit. If you sit in the same position long enough, you begin to notice that your foot has gone to sleep. You move into a new position in order to take the pressure off the spot where the nerves and blood vessels have been pinched. You have intervened in the process of entropy.

Pretend a different circumstance occurs. You are walking along the street. Suddenly a car screams out of a side road and bumps you as it passes. You are knocked to the street with a broken hip. You are rushed to the hospital, where your fracture is taken care of by the attending physician. You go to a physical therapist, learn the proper exercises, and regain your ability to walk. You have intervened in the process of disintegration.

Now move to a far more complex example involving the major automobile manufacturing companies in the United States. Several years ago, the actions of an international oil cartel dramatically increased gasoline cost. It was clear that American automakers would have no choice but to alter their approach to automobile making. Japanese manufacturers increased their exports of sporty, fuel-efficient cars to the American market. Sales of American cars began to drop in proportion to the increases in Japanese market share. To combat this erosion (entropy), the American automobile industry brought out a variety of smaller cars. However, they were not very fuel-efficient because to make them more economical to run, the industry would have had to retool—a costly operation. Because the change was maladaptive, the Japanese market share increased. Shortly thereafter every major American automobile manufacturer introduced fuel-efficient cars in a variety of models. Thus the American organizations introduced negentropy.

Organizations resist the tendency to disintegrate. Each new factor that tends toward disintegration is met by some adjustment for the purpose of perpetuating the organization. Sometimes the adjustments are effective. Those coping behaviors are admired in our culture. But sometimes coping behaviors generate problems of their own.

VISIONARY LEADERSHIP . . . .

Mischanneling of organizational energy yields many problems for the members of the organization and for the publics they serve. Common sayings reflect this phenomenon: "You can't beat the system"; "You can't fight City Hall"; "You can't cut through the red tape." From our perspective, the problem is that the management of a complex organization loses sight of its original goals, seeks to maintain itself, and so resists needed change.

You could explain this tendency as a failure to understand that there is more than one way for an organization to achieve its goals. But too often people in complex organizations forget that their organizations are tied to their environments and perpetuate rules that no longer serve any useful function in the name of tradition or "the way things are done" or "the system."

Consider the drill sergeant who shouts to his recruits: "There are three ways to do everything—the right way, the wrong way, and the Army way. We're going to do things the Army way." Perhaps also you have heard such statements as "I'm sorry, but I can't help you—we don't make exceptions." In each case there is a clear adherence to the way things are "supposed" to be done. Typically, there are good reasons for the rules. Sometimes, however, the "rules" do not apply to an individual case. Adaptive organizations will take notice if the number of such exceptions is increasing. If it is, then the leadership will adjust the rules. Leadership that is willing to make such adjustments and changes is visionary leadership.

Visionary leaders pay attention to feedback and are able to predict how changes in any of the components of their organizations will affect other components. Furthermore, they communicate in such a way that the quality of the information is improved, and thus they can apply power and control intelligently. Visionary leaders bear in mind that there are many ways to accomplish any particular goal, and that therefore no one way of doing things is always right.

When we talk about visionary leadership, there is a sense in which we are talking about carefully thought-through, long-range plans and goals based on quality information. But we are also talking about decision makers who understand the impact of decisions. No leader can be considered visionary who does not realize that a decision about one component of the organization affects every other component. A visionary leader will understand and take into account the organization's culture. At the same time, visionary leaders must take into account the fact that an organization is an open, living thing: it can and does interact with its environment. Taking the relationship of the organization to the environment into account is a hallmark of the visionary leader.

SUMMARY ....

We have presented two perspectives on complex organizations. A systems approach concentrates on the interaction of the organization's components, whereas a structural approach concentrates on the planned power relationships in the hierarchy. These perspectives are useful, but they must be understood within the framework of the organization's goals and processes (such as learning and problem solving) and the relationships among the components. Such a perspective should help us recognize, initiate, and control change within organizations.

We discussed hierarchy and communication networks. Tall hierarchies have many levels, and those levels affect the communication flow. Communication from top to bottom is fairly unrestricted, but it can be distorted as it flows through the many levels. Upward communication flows less easily and is often distorted because subordinates are concerned about how their messages may be received. Since many messages are being passed upward, such an organization may be subject to information overload. Flat structural hierarchies have fewer levels and broader power fields. The flatness of the organization can lead to overly broad spans of control, resulting in problems of control and information overload.

A hierarchy is characterized by span of control, division of labor, line and staff functions, and chain of command. Span of control refers to the number of subordinates that report to a particular supervisor. Division of labor is the basic notion that organizing people involves specialization of function and the division of people into groups that represent a particular function. The members of an organization who are involved with direct production of the product or service are line personnel. Those who provide services for the organization and for the production personnel are staff. Chain of command refers to planned power and authority relationships of an organization—who reports and talks to whom.

The interaction among the organizational components and between the components and the environment inevitably yields task specialization. We showed that too narrow a focus on tasks, as opposed to goals, leads to organizational problems, including the routinization of tasks, personnel pigeonholing, and conflict between goals.

Task specialization is inevitable, however, and leads to the formation of organizational hierarchies. We noted that well-managed organizations are able to introduce novelty in such a way that they can resist entropy.

Finally, we claimed that there is more than one way to achieve a goal. Visionary leadership needs quality information on which to base decisions about long-range goals.

NOTES ·

1. Gary L. Kreps, *Organizational Communication,* 2d ed. (New York, Longman, 1990), p. 94.

2. James March and Herbert Simon, *Organizations* (New York, Wiley, 1958); Robert McPhee, "Formal Structure and Organizational Communication," in *Organizational Communication,* Robert McPhee and Phillip Tompkins, eds. (Beverly Hills, Calif., Sage, 1985), pp. 149–178.

3. A number of writers emphasize the importance of viewing an organization as a whole, especially systems theorists. See Ludwig van Bertalanffy, *General Systems Theory* (New York, Braziller, 1968), p. 37; Walter Buckley, *Sociology and Modern Systems Theory* (Englewood Cliffs, N.J., Prentice-Hall, 1967), p. 2.

4. An example of a firm structured in this way is provided in Rekha Agarwala-Rogers, "The Structure and Communication of a Manufacturing Company in India," *Indian Journal of Industrial Relations,* 9 (1974):385–396.

5. For a specific analysis of upward influences and message processes, see Cynthia Stohl and W. Charles Redding, "Messages and Message Exchange Processes," in *Handbook of Organizational Communication,* Fredric M. Jablin et al., eds. (Beverly Hills, Calif., Sage, 1987), pp. 451–502.

6. Paul D. Krivonos, "Distortion of Subordinate to Superior Communication in Organizational Settings," *Central States Speech Journal,* 33 (Spring 1982):345–352. Krivonos found that messages concerning unfavorable situations were more distorted than messages concerning favorable situations, especially when they were task-related. Employees were more willing to disclose messages about unfavorable situations if they were not task-related.

7. For an excellent discussion of this "goodness-of-fit" issue, see John J. Morse and Jay W. Lorsch, "Beyond Theory Y," *Harvard Business Review* (May–June 1970):61–68.

8. Rosabeth Moss Kanter, *The Change Masters: Innovation for Productivity in the American Corporation* (New York, Simon & Schuster, 1985), p. 30.

9. Keith Davis, "The Organization That's Not on the Chart," in *Readings in Interpersonal and Organizational Communication,* Richard C. Huseman, Cal M. Logue, and Dwight L. Freshley, eds. (Boston, Holbrook, 1973), p. 228.

10. "Did You Hear It through the Grapevine?" *Training & Development* (October 1994):20.

11. Kreps, op. cit., p. 210.

12. D. Krackhardt and J. R. Hanson, "Informal Networks: The Company Behind the Chart," *Harvard Business Review,* 71 (1993):104–111.

13. E. M. Eisenberg and H. L. Goodall, Jr., *Organizational Communication: Balancing Creativity and Constraint* (New York, St. Martin's, 1993), p. 9.

14. Barbara June Marting, "A Study of Grapevine Communication Patterns in a Manufacturing Organization," Ph.D. diss., Arizona State University, 1969; Evan Edward Rudolph, "A Study of Informal Communication Patterns within a Multi-Shift Utility Organizational Unit," Ph.D. diss., University of Denver, 1971; Keith Davis, *Human Behavior at Work* (New York, McGraw-Hill, 1972).

15. T. J. Murray, "How to Stay Lean and Mean," *Business Month* (August 1987): 29–32, 35.

16. Gordon W. Allport and Leo J. Postman, *The Psychology of Rumor* (New York, Holt, Rinehart & Winston, 1947).

17. This problem of goals is complicated by the question, "Which and whose goals?" David Silverman discusses this issue from the perspective

of a person interested in organizational effectiveness. See David Silverman, *The Theory of Organizations* (New York, Basic Books, 1970), pp. 9–11.

18. David J. Hickson and Arthur F. McCullough, "Power in Organizations," in *Control and Ideology in Organizations,* Graeme Salaman and Kenneth Thompson, eds. (Cambridge, MIT Press, 1980), pp. 27–55.

19. Kenneth Thompson, "The Organizational Society," in *Control and Ideology in Organizations,* Salaman and Thompson, eds., pp. 3–23.

20. Daniel Katz and Robert Kahn, *The Social Psychology of Organizations* (New York, Wiley, 1966), p. 223.

RECOMMENDED READINGS ....

W. Wayland Cummings, Larry W. Long, and Michael L. Lewis. *Managing Communication in Organizations,* 2d ed. Dubuque, Gorsuch Scarisbrick, 1987. This book has an especially worthwhile chapter on selecting organizational communication designs.

Frederic M. Jablin. "Formal Structural Characteristics of Organizations and Superior—Subordinate Communication." *Human Communication Research,* 8 (Summer 1982): 338–347. This research report investigates the relationship of organizational size, organizational level, and span of control on the perception of openness in superior–subordinate communication.

Gary L. Kreps. *Organizational Communication,* 3d ed. New York, Longman, 1996. Part II, "Perspectives on the Organizing Process," is especially relevant to the concerns of this chapter.

Virginia P. Richmond, James C. McCroskey, and Leonard M. Davis. "Individual Differences among Employees, Management Communication Style, and Employee Satisfaction: Replication and Extension." *Human Communication Research,* 8 (Winter 1982): 170–188. This essay explores the relationship between communication and satisfaction and examines how individual differences in supervisors and subordinates affect satisfaction.

Brendt D. Ruben and John Y. Kim. *General Systems Theory and Human Communication.* Rochelle Park, N.J., Hayden, 1975. This fine collection of essays by communication scholars and organization theorists covers systems theory and communication.

Paul Watzlawick, Janet H. Beavin, and Don D. Jackson. *Pragmatics of Human Communication: A Study of Interactional Patterns, Pathologies, and Paradoxes.* New York, W. W. Norton, 1967. This influential book discusses how general systems theory may be applied to the study of human communication. See especially Chapter 4 for a lucid discussion of systems theory.

DISCUSSION QUESTIONS........................

1. Explain some of the major leadership problems your professor might have if students took on a task focus rather than a goal focus.

2. Using the college of which you are a part as a model, explain how job specialization and the evolution of a hierarchy are related.

3. Organizations tend to disintegrate, a process called *entropy.* The process of intervening to resist decay is called *negentropy.* What entropic forces might undermine your class? What negentropic forces might be introduced, and who might introduce them?

4. Explain the idea that there is more than one way to reach a goal, using your class as a model, and relate the discussion to leadership in the class. If your professor understood this concept as well as you do, what kinds of advice might he or she give students as they approach final examinations?

INTERNET ACTIVITIES ....

1. Open a search engine and type these words: *organizations AND systems.* You will get about 250 "hits." Scroll down through the first ten items, then follow one of the "hot links" and notice where it takes you. Now try searching using these words: *communication AND systems.* Where does this search take you? Make

notes so that you can discuss your exploration with class members. Do you think organizations are communication systems?

2. All organizations have to communicate within themselves and outside themselves. See if you can discover at least five consulting firms specializing in public relations and organizational communication that advertise themselves on the World Wide Web. What services do they offer? Prepare a report to share with your classmates.

CHAPTER 3

Leadership and Communication in Organizations

....**OBJECTIVES**

Upon completion of this chapter, you should be able to:

1. List and explain the four functions of organizational communication: information, command and instruction, influence and persuasion, and integration and maintenance.
2. Compare and contrast scientific management, human relations, contingency, and systems schools of organizational theory.
3. Determine appropriate leadership styles for a variety of situations.
4. Use the Michalak and Yager model to determine leadership choices when an employee is causing a problem.
5. Compare and contrast the approaches to change taken by reactionary leaders and visionary leaders.
6. Explain various strategies to avoid dysfunctional subgroup behavior.

This chapter considers some of the most pervasive concerns that individuals who manage organizations have. How does the flow of communication affect productivity? How can communication best be used to motivate the people in the organization? Is there a relationship between our communication and the quality of our problem solving and decision making? And what about change? Can we use the communication systems in our organization to anticipate, plan for, and implement changes?

First we look at the functions that communication serves in an organization. Besides providing information, managers must command and instruct, influence and persuade subordinates, integrate members and maintain the organization—all vital leadership functions.

Next we look at the control of human behavior. Control is actually the primary purpose of all communication activity. When we use the term *control*, it carries no negative connotations. If someone asks you to phone because he or she has enjoyed your company, and you do it, that person will have controlled your behavior. If the manager of a sales group asks an employee to work late, and the person does so, the manager has controlled the employee's behavior.

Control through communication is a key to managing organizational change, the topic we look at next. Changes in organizations are inevitable, but they can be planned or they can be left to accident. We think managing of change implies control. Effective leaders are visionary. They try to anticipate, plan, encourage, and control the changes that occur in their organizations. We call this kind of planning *visionary leadership*.

Visionary leadership is different from reactionary leadership, and we address the differences in this chapter. We do so from a communication perspective. This approach requires us to focus briefly on problem solving and leadership, and also on information management strategies. Control is the primary means by which power may be secured and used. This fact gives rise to much that is dysfunctional about communication in complex organizations. But before we can deal with the possible dysfunctions of some aspects of communication, we must first look at the useful functions that organizational communication can serve.

THE FOUR FUNCTIONS OF ORGANIZATIONAL COMMUNICATION . . . .

Lee Thayer published an unusual and very influential book titled *Communication and Communication Systems in Organization, Management, and Interpersonal Relations*. In it he identified four functions of communication in complex organizations: information, command and instruction, influence and persuasion, and integration and maintenance.[1]

To illustrate these functions, let's suppose you begin working in a company. Juanita is your boss, and John is a recent college graduate—he has been with the company for three years. John works for Juanita. Let's suppose further that you are an entry-level management trainee and that for a few months you will be in Juanita's department. Juanita and John will undoubtedly communicate with you to accomplish all these functions. Juanita might say something like:

"This department is a strong and rapidly growing one. Our main tasks are . . ." and then go on to fill you in on the things her department does. She would obviously be informing you.

If she said, "John, here, will tell you what to do today," she and John would be utilizing the command and instruction function. She would have told you what to expect—and John what to do. John would have told you what to do and how to do it.

There is a close relationship between the command and instruction function and the influence and persuasion function. John, feeling sure of himself, might presume to start to tell you what to do. Far more likely, however, John might work with you differently:

"Well, let's see. I know that Juanita prefers management trainees to get a good look at our operation. There might be lots of ways to do that. What do you think about spending a little time digging around in our files? If you did some filing, you might find out very quickly about the kinds of things we do, and you'd get a flavor of what it is like to work in this section."

John would not be telling you what to do, exactly. He would be trying to persuade you to decide. In addition, he would be offering a benefit: you would learn more quickly. Since the goal of his communication with you would be to integrate you into the department, he would also be practicing the integration and maintenance function. Let's look at these functions more closely.

> At what point, if at all, does persuasion become manipulation? Does this ever produce an ethical issue for managers and for those who are managed?

Information

Remember that human organizations ideally are adapting open systems that intervene against entropy. Remember that organizations are composed of units and parts—divisions, departments, people. Organizations must interact not only with the larger, external environment but also with the units of which they are composed. This is why organizations need and process two kinds of information. *External* information is sent and received by means of marketing, advertising, purchasing, public relations, and the like. *Internal* information provides the basis for determining organizational goals, assessing the performance of the organization's units, and ensuring coordination among interdependent subunits. Internal information is of greater concern to us. Information is the only means an organization has to ensure that the expectations are known to the subunits.

This sharing of information allows for accounting, cross-referencing, coordination, and planning. Consider the accountability system in an electrical appliance firm. If your work is designing small electrical appliances, you will depend on a variety of cross-tabulated data in order to know what features to include. For example, suppose that the company wishes to market a new electric steam iron. A market analysis suggests that it is time for a new model; there is a need "out there" not being served. Once that decision is made, many other questions come to mind. Is there a trend in the market? Is there any standard expectation about the appearance of the iron that might limit design freedom? Is there a cost expectation? Is there a construction limitation? For example, are there limits to the configuration of a handle? What will the retooling costs be if the company decides to change the overall configuration of the handle? You will not be able to answer these questions without cross-referencing data.

To follow through with this example, you could not possibly do your work without examining the blueprints that your company provided of the new heating unit for the steam mechanism. Your design must be shaped to accommodate that unit. In short, you would depend on the sharing of information and cross-referencing that are parts of the integration and maintenance function of organizational communication.

Another reason for sharing information is to relate the various parts of the organization to the whole and to the contexts in which they must work. The classic example of this kind of communication is that which keeps the sales force and the production force synchronized. If the marketing group makes commitments that the production group cannot meet, or if the production group builds more (or fewer) units than the marketing group can sell, then the groups are not well-informed and coordinated.

One of us was present at a business luncheon in Portland, Maine, when the following conversation took place. We offer this paraphrased version in dialog form to illustrate how disconcerting it seems when parts of an organization are not well coordinated. The names have been changed, but the dialog is a faithful rendering of the spirit of that conversation.

NED: Your guys in the sales force don't seem to be paying attention, Jim. Two months ago I wrote to you saying that our mill is at capacity. We're doing everything we can do. I can't get even ten more pounds off the machine, not to mention the ten extra tons you're talking about. Now you tell me that you have to have extra tonnage. Where's it going to come from? I can't make it. I can't run twenty-five hours a day.

JIM: Look, I know I'm asking a lot. But we had a chance to sell paper. That's what we're supposed to do—sell paper. That's what this company is all about—selling paper. I wish you wouldn't get so exercised because my people are selling paper.

Clearly, Ned's production unit and Jim's marketing unit were not adequately coordinated. The problem reflected in this exchange suggests that the leadership of the organization must act to ensure the coordination of its units' activities more carefully. That can happen only as a result of open communication.

Command and Instruction

The command and instruction function of organizational communication is the primary means by which managers keep their units and the individuals in them working toward goals. Determining *what* commands or instructions must be given *to whom* and *how* is no easy task; it requires great care. Commands and instructions ensure compliance with company policy, uniformity in practice and procedure when that is desirable, and accuracy and completeness of job performance. If handled well, commands and instructions keep operational errors to a minimum by training new employees as quickly and cheaply as possible, as we saw with Juanita's and John's practice of this function. Finally, commands and instructions are responsible for keeping the individual working in such a way that his or her efforts mix appropriately with those of another. In this respect, command and instruction serves a coordinating function. Command and instruction is closely related to influence and persuasion.

> Can you name two or more ethical issues involved when a manager determines what commands to deliver to whom? For example, what would be the ethical issue if a manager assigned an unpopular task to an individual because he did not like the individual?

Influence and Persuasion

A third essential need of an organization is to influence and persuade its members. The purpose is to maintain certain kinds of control over the information and behavior of the members. Influence and persuasion are necessary because there are always tasks that need to be accomplished that a manager cannot command a subordinate to do. Beyond mere task completion is the need to motivate subordinates to strive for more than minimal performance.

The closer people get to an organization emotionally—perhaps by achieving recognition, power, increased authority and responsibility, and greater information—the more they will give their energy and loyalty to it. The opposite is also true. The further people get from the center of power and the further they are, emotionally, from the organization, the less their commitment and loyalty, and the less energy they are willing to expend in pursuit of the organization's goals.

Everyone, of course, belongs to many groups and organizations. Thus it is not possible for anyone to commit all his or her energy to an organization. It is not possible to subscribe wholly to the goals, norms, and ideals of a single group, especially since multiple group memberships may mean conflicting goals. So managers must influence and persuade peripheral members to embrace organizational goals.

Consider these two cases. Nancy has been working in her job for nearly a year. She believes she is a valued member of her department, and most of the time she likes doing the tasks that are included in her job description. But from time to time she thinks that she is spinning her wheels. She senses that information is not coming her way, that the boss is diminishing her in some way, that she is isolated from the source of power, that her ideas are not taken into account, and that therefore she is impotent in her day-to-day efforts. At those times she is frustrated and unhappy. She considers three options: she can *do* something to make the organization change (e.g., she can assert herself in her boss's office and perhaps tie into the communication channels again); she can behave in such a way that she damages the organization; or she can withdraw from the organization. At times she wishes to change jobs. At times she marches into the boss's office with a proposal for a solution to problems. At times she fantasizes about "getting them," showing them.

The organization does not worry much that Nancy will choose the "getting them" alternative because management knows that she subscribes to the work

> Under what circumstances would it be unethical for a manager to command a subordinate to accomplish or perform a task?

ethic, that she is marked for promotion (and knows it), and that she receives a good deal of evidence that she is well accepted. Quitting to search for another job would cause her a good deal of inconvenience, loss of income, and the loss of an opportunity to rise in a company that she likes and that, in general, pays her very well for the contributions she makes. Thus there is relatively little risk to the company that Nancy will resign. Every time Nancy marches into the boss's office with a creative solution—her first option—it is good for the company and is precisely the kind of activity the company values.

Herb's frustrations are of a different kind. He is a line worker. His *on* time and *off* time are controlled by the demands of the production schedule and by his own willingness to take time off. He believes there is no place upward for him to go except, perhaps, to the position of supervisor. That promotion requires seniority and a good deal of application beyond the requirements of his present job. Herb has the same choices as Nancy. He can do something positive, such as march into the supervisor's office and suggest a solution to a problem, or negative, such as actively create a hassle for the company; or he can resign his position.

From the company's viewpoint, however, Herb's choices are much different from Nancy's. Therefore the company is far more involved in monitoring Herb's behavior. He is probably unwilling to walk into the supervisor's office with a solution to a problem; more likely he will drop something into the suggestion box. His threat to resign will not be viewed as a big problem: he can easily be replaced; unemployment is high; and his salary is commensurate with his ability—and as high as he's likely to find on another job. So what is his choice when he is feeling alienated? Nancy's fantasy about "getting them" may be his choice of behavior. Herb may toss a wrench into a cogwheel, pull a plug on an electronic robot, or run a piece of material backward in order to gum up the works. These little "gotcha" behaviors become a major source of administrative concern. Alternatively, Herb may believe that he is contributing greatly to the profits of the company—and that he's earned something extra anyway—and so take some small item home with him. In fact, pilfering is a very common problem, one that costs industry enormous sums of money every year.

The law of partial inclusion has worked in both Nancy's and Herb's cases. The law of partial inclusion says that people have 100 percent of their energy available at any given time. They cannot give 100 percent of this energy to every one of their groups or organizations; they must choose among priorities. A person may give 20 percent to one group, 40 percent to another, and so on. Thus, people include themselves "partially." The more energy they devote to a group the more likely they are to conform to its norms and the more likely they are to move toward the center of that group's power structure. The more they move toward the center, the more they give of themselves. The more they give of themselves the more they move toward the center—and so on. For Nancy, who makes a commitment to the organization, rewards seem to come each time she behaves in a way that seems right to her and the company. The more she commits herself to the company, the more the company values her and pays her off; the more it does that, the more Nancy commits herself to it. But note that her continued loyalty and support are directly related to the messages she receives. If she gets the message that she is not valued, she may be willing to suffer the inconvenience of seeking other employment.

> Is awarding cash bonuses to employees a form of bribery? Is there an ethical problem in such rewards? Why or why not?

For Herb, the situation is different. Unlike Nancy, he is not likely to get any closer to the center of the organization. He is as peripheral as almost any member of the organization. He will not subscribe to the company goals, because his loyalty is not to the company but to some other affiliations. He uses his job to sustain his other interests. If he becomes alienated, his behavior is threatening to the organization because he is more likely to choose in favor of what he considers his more important affiliations. One of those affiliations may well be a union, which he may join out of hostility to some of the company's goals. From management's point of view, his understanding and behavior need to be controlled.

The control management exerts over Herb, however, will be different from the control it exerts over Nancy. The organization controls Nancy, who is closer to the center of the organization, by giving her increasing freedom to act. But it controls Herb, a peripheral member, by limiting his alternatives and by giving him sufficient rewards. Influence and persuasion help provide this control in both cases, and so do integration and maintenance.

Integration and Maintenance

Put simply, integration and maintenance communication helps members identify with each other and the organization. It functions to build cohesiveness.

Reconsider Nancy and Herb, in the earlier example. They need what everyone needs: confirmation. People need to believe that what they do is valued. Moreover, they need to believe that their organization is a sensible one that can be relied upon to function accordingly. Thus when they say "I work for XYZ Company," they can know their paychecks will be accepted and cashed.

It is important that the organization's communication system confirm its employees' sense of worth and confirm to them that the organization itself is also worthy. Beyond that, of course, employees need to have confidence that the organization is well managed and has a solid base and a bright future.

Leaders of successful companies look for many ways to confirm their employees and their organizations. For example, managers frequently give certificates to recognize excellence. It is not uncommon to find companies whose employees have received cash awards, shares in the company profits, opportunities to purchase stock at favorable rates, and the like. At a quality-assurance conference of one major national food-packing company, all the employees who attended received lightweight insulated vests with the company logo embroidered on the front. This confirming gesture was not wasted on those employees. In an interview four months later, one reported that he was proud to wear his vest. It was a sign, he said, that the company cares. And besides, he wanted people to know where he works. "I'm a lucky guy," he said. "I work for a great company."

What can an individual do with this information about the functions of organizational communication? What practical value has it for students who are planning their careers? We offer these suggestions.

SUGGESTIONS REGARDING THE COMMUNICATION FUNCTIONS OF AN ORGANIZATION ....

Securing Organizational Commitment

1. *Make a commitment to the organization, then put that commitment into a form that management can understand.* For example, one form of commitment to an organization is your willingness to make suggestions. If you see a problem, suggest a carefully thought out solution.
2. *As far as possible, subscribe to the norms of the organization.* When you cannot subscribe to or support the organization's way of doing things, offer a concrete suggestion for change. Be sure that your suggestion is reasonable, practical, and desirable. You might see how some trusted friend reacts to your suggestion before you offer it to management.
3. *If you are in a position of leadership, determine what you control that is valued by the people you lead, then limit the alternatives of the individuals you lead and reward desired behavior.* When you can count on the employees you lead to meet organizational goals, increase their freedom and allow them more opportunities to act on their own. Monitor their behavior so that you can make appropriate changes.

Confirming People in the Organization

1. *Regardless of your position in the organization, confirm people when what they do is valuable.* This is easy to do, but for some reason is rarely done. Notice what people do, and compliment when they do it well.
2. *Do not disconfirm people whose behavior is counter to your interests.* Rather, try to understand their position. Most people do what they do for what *they* believe is a perfectly good reason. Rejecting the person's ideas or behavior is disconfirming. Use active listening. Once you understand a person's behavior and the reasons for it, you may discover that what the person needs is training. If you are in a position to do so, recommend training. If you are not in such a position, hold your tongue. Everyone makes mistakes. Everyone does what they do because they think they have a good reason for doing so.
3. *Confirm the organization and its people when dealing with others.* Whether you are within the organization or outside of it, this is often called loyalty. But we think it is far more. You *are* the organization when you represent it! Your boss and those higher in the organization know this and therefore count on you. Never diminish the organization or its people.

....**ORGANIZING PERSPECTIVES**

The concern for increased worker satisfaction, increased efficiency in task operation, and cost-effectiveness has been at the very center of organizational theory since before World War I. At least four broad schools of thought about behavior in organizations have emerged: the scientific management school, the human relations school, the contingency school, and the systems school. We will describe these schools briefly, but we choose to take a very practical approach at this point. What matters is not the correctness of any one point of view. A perspective is useful if it allows you to see what you need to see and be effective in what you do, but remember the perspective you assume also limits what can be seen and done.

Scientific Management School

A commonly accepted approach to the study of organizational behavior, the scientific management school is a highly mechanistic one. Its initial ideas were laid out in the writings of Frederick Taylor.[2] People are believed to be economically motivated, and they will respond with their best effort and skill if their economic rewards are tied to their performance. If you can devise ways to achieve more and better performance with less effort and at less per-unit cost, then you will increase the profit margin. Thus the scientific management school makes careful observations of an organization's operations, including time-and-motion studies, carefully written job descriptions, close supervision of workers, and careful control of both cash and material flow through the organization.

Scientific management values written, formal channels of communication and impersonal, work-related communication. It is strongly biased in favor of management, believing that the chain of command is primarily a one-direction phenomenon. The role of communication, per se, is of little interest to the scientific management school. Its primary concern is structure and control. The most prominent advocates of this tradition were Frederick Taylor, Max Weber, and Henri Fayol.[3]

Human Relations School

The human relations school of thought evolved from research of Chester I. Barnard and Elton Mayo of the Harvard Business School.[4] Mayo, prompted by experiments at Western Electric's Hawthorne plant, rejected the views of the scientific management school in favor of a more social view. People who subscribe to this school's tenets believe that attention to workers' needs and job satisfaction increases performance. Thus, workers are encouraged to participate in the decision making.[5] Because workers' motivations may be more social than monetary, such factors as peer relationships are considered important.

Scholars who study the human relations movement conduct surveys and interviews. They ask people to keep diaries. They keep track of leadership and communication patterns. They encourage formation of informal groups, which they believe positively affect production. This school considers informal groups important because it believes workers are motivated by social needs.

The human relations school values informal and formal communication. It places interpersonal relationships high on its priority list and attempts to help employees and employers solve their problems through mutual understanding.

In recent years the human relations school has come under attack for a variety of reasons, but primarily because the basic research on which Mayo and Barnard based their views, the Hawthorne studies, has been challenged.[6] Even so, there is much to be said for its teachings. Common sense and your own experience tell you that recognition and confirmation of the self make an important difference to people. The problem with the approach was excess, but nevertheless, this school became the foundation on which successful management theories were developed.

Contingency School

The proponents of the contingency school of thought reject the idea that there is one best way to manage people. Paul R. Lawrence and Jay W. Lorsch of Harvard Business School were two of the chief proponents of this view.[7] They contended that each situation is unique and that appropriate management depends on the task, the organizational structure, the kinds of employees, and the manager. To be effective, managers need to weigh how these components fit together. That is, they should try to discover the unique characteristics of the contingencies they are facing and base their style of managing on what they discover.

Frederick Fiedler was among the first to argue for this approach.[8] He suggested that managers could discover the appropriate management style by examining the situational contingencies. He believed that managers must look at the degree of task structure, the kind of relationship they have with their employees, and the amount of power they can exercise. Understanding these contingencies allows managers to know whether they should emphasize human relationships or the task.

Gerald M. Goldhaber identified ten contingencies that managers might consider.[9] Five of these are *internal* contingencies, and five are *external*. Internal contingencies include:

1. *The degree of formality* and the *type of structure* that characterize the organization (structural contingencies).
2. The *diversity and quality of products and services* (output contingencies).
3. The *diversity of the people* in the organization (demographic contingencies).
4. The diversity of such *spatial features* of the organization as design, location, distance, and *matters of timing* (spatiotemporal contingencies).
5. The *history* and *traditions* of the organization (traditional contingencies).

Five external contingencies also have an effect on the communication effectiveness of an organization, and give rise to leadership decisions:

1. *Stability of market share and place* and the concomitant influence on the organization's *capital resources* (economic contingencies).
2. *Innovation in research and development* and in the organization's technology (technological contingencies).
3. *Effects of law* (federal, state, and local) on organizational operations (legal contingencies).
4. The *impact of social, political, and cultural factors* on organizational operations (social contingencies).
5. *Effects of climate, geography, population density, and availability of energy* on organizational operations (environmental contingencies).

The central idea of the contingency school is that appropriate leadership depends entirely on the combination of circumstances, both internal and external, that currently bear on the organizational unit in which leadership is being exercised. The leadership style must be tailored to fit the task and the people.

Systems School

Communication is paramount in the systems school. Communication holds the organization together. Communication binds the subsystems. Communication is the means by which systems and subsystems keep up with changes in their world. Communication is the means by which the organization achieves goals. Communication is the means by which the organization affects and is affected by its environment. From this perspective the organization is seen as an open system in continual contact and exchange with its environment.

Systems theorists worry about the organization as a whole and believe that any change anywhere in the system will inevitably influence the rest of the system. Two influential scholars in this area are Daniel Katz and Robert Kahn.[10] Systems theorists conduct network analyses of communication data, computer simulations, systems analysis, and the like to monitor the organization's health. Because they are more concerned with the total organization than with individuals who hold positions in it, they are criticized for ignoring the individual. They are neither pro-management nor pro-labor. They believe that, in the end, individuals merely carry the organization, but the organization exists as a living entity.

LEADERSHIP AND ORGANIZATIONAL CHANGE

We have discussed style of leadership as it relates to a variety of particular situations. But we have not yet talked about leadership in critical situations—such as managing organizational change. We think that circumstances involving change require a special orientation to leadership. We called this "visionary leadership" in Chapter 2. We shall devote the last part of this chapter to that topic.

Change is inevitable, and organizational leadership must be able to manage it. Organizations are continually interacting with and within their environments. A *change* is any modification that occurs in the organization—a new input or an altered process or anything that causes different output. Changes cannot be avoided, and you would not even want to avoid them. Change is often associated in people's minds with risk, but it is not the change itself that creates the risk. Risk tends to accompany changes that are accidental rather than planned, uncontrolled rather than controlled.

You may recall our discussion of visionary leadership in Chapter 2. There we placed a high value on visionary leadership because only leadership of that sort is able to predict how changes in any of the components of the organization will affect other components. Visionary leadership involves communicating in such a way that the quality of information is improved—and therefore power and control can be intelligently applied. You might wish to review our discussion, in which we point out that vision is a matter of predicting the future and planning intelligently for it. That means, in the present context, the planning of change.

Another kind of leadership, *reactionary leadership,* responds to conditions only after they have occurred. Because we think reacting does not often provide for effective decision making, we downplay the value of reactionary leadership—although we recognize that managers often have no other choice.

You will recall that one of the four functions of organizational communication is providing information, and that information is needed by open systems in order to resist entropy. Within an organization this means the information is used to coordinate interdependent units and to help determine goals. Externally, the information systems monitor the environment in order to anticipate the future and to plan to accommodate it. Information use and information control lead to planned change. The opposite leads to unplanned change.

Visionary Leadership and Change

Let us consider what happens in an organization when change is unplanned. A situation is discovered to exist. Leaders evaluate the situation, then determine that it either is or is not OK. If the decision is that the situation is OK, nothing is done. The system continues to flow, although perhaps along a somewhat altered course. If the situation is judged to be problematic, then management energizes itself in order to respond. Sometimes you may hear this called "putting out brush fires." The metaphor refers to the potential of all small problems to become large.

What happens when an organization's leadership is visionary in its approach to change is a different matter. More clearly than ever, the ability of an organization's leadership to anticipate and plan for changes in the environment depends on accurate processing of available information. Thus information control is the primary means by which visionary leadership can be exercised. *Planning for change involves at least three stages,* each of which depends on information control.

First, active monitoring of the organization's outputs yields the information that these outputs are not equal to what is desired. Perhaps the outputs are units of production, profit, or satisfaction. By whatever measure, leadership determines that actual outputs are not equal to desired outputs. That is one of the information functions of organizational communication.

Second, the leadership plans its problem solving. The idea is, always, to find a path that will allow the organization to achieve its desired outputs. This evaluative and problem-solving process will focus on either altering inputs or altering the information processes by which those inputs are manipulated. Thus the problem is carefully identified, defined, delimited, and analyzed. Once it is understood, a number of alternative paths that might yield the desired outputs are suggested. Communicating is involved in gathering and analyzing information for problem solving, and effective communication depends on information control. (Chapters 12 and 13 describe this planning stage in detail.)

> How much of this planning for change can an organization's management initiate, accept, or tolerate? Can you see any potential for such behavior to produce ethical issues for management? Explain.

Decision making is the third and final stage. Informed management, having discovered a number of alternative paths, selects those paths that seem to have the greatest promise of achieving the goal. Having selected, management formulates a program and a plan to implement it. These aspects of decision making depend on information control, which is part of an organization's communication strategy.

Imagine for a moment this particular situation that Juanita experienced soon after John had been given supervisory responsibility. She discovered that her directives were not being acted upon by people in line positions. Reactionary leadership would suggest that she "call John in" and "straighten him out." She chose not to do this, but instead engaged in visionary leadership. She carefully sent messages through the chain of command. Then she monitored by checking with John and those below him to see how accurately the messages got through at each level. She measured the degree to which inputs and outputs differed. Next, she sat down to evaluate and do some problem solving. She discovered that the problem seemed to lie between John and those below him. She talked with John about how he typically conveys information. This information enabled her, with John's help, of course, to generate alternatives for delivering information in the future. Finally, she and John made a decision about which of the methods (paths) would be the best for dealing with the problem. She planned how to make the change and how to check to see that it was working. Juanita understood visionary leadership, and it paid off. Instead of merely reacting, she took the situation into account and planned for a future that would be free of the problem.

Here is an outline for you to follow in your effort to provide visionary leadership:

1. *Monitor organizational output regularly against all relevant variables.* Some important variables would be cost per unit, quality of unit, and time required to produce unit.
2. *Compare established goals and actual output.* If output meets goals, then evaluate the need for new goals. Establish new goals if the analysis indicates a need. If output does not meet goals, then make adjustments.
3. *In developing appropriate goal paths, consider how these resources work together to influence your planning:*
   a. People.

      b. Plant and facilities.
      c. Materials and energy.
      d. Money.
      e. Information.
  4. *In developing adjustments, ask yourself these critical questions:*
      a. *Who* will be involved?
      b. *What* will they do?
      c. *Where* will adjustments be made?
      d. *When* will they be begun? Completed?
      e. *How* will you monitor what is done and how effective it is?
  5. *In developing either goal paths or adjustments in existing goal paths, consider these questions:*
      a. Are all the elements technologically feasible?
      b. Are all the elements operationally viable?

Helping the Individual Employee to Change

Often a supervisor will discover a behavior discrepancy in an employee but not know how to describe it. For example, the supervisor may point to some *symptom* of the problem, thinking that the symptom is the problem. For example, she might say, "This employee has a bad attitude." On more careful analysis she might say, "This employee consistently has a high scrap rate." Or she might claim, "This employee's record shows a high rate of absenteeism." Because the term *bad attitude* is so abstract, it would be virtually impossible to know how to work with the employee. The behavior implied in the terms *high scrap rate* and *high rate of absenteeism* can be seen, and so it can be addressed. But high rates of scrap production and absenteeism are only symptoms. What gives rise to them?

In response to this question, some supervisors have said that an employee is "deficient." We caution against such language. If something is deficient, it is inadequate or defective. We prefer the word *discrepant*. To be discrepant is to be inconsistent, to differ, to disagree.

When managers say that someone is "deficient," they have already made up their minds that the employee is not doing what he or she is supposed to do, and that he or she is at fault. If managers substitute the word *discrepant*, they are far more likely to conclude that the employee is not doing what *they* want. The problem may be in the way the employee is doing the job, or it may be in the expectations that management holds for the position.

Donald F. Michalak and Edwin G. Yager have developed a useful model, shown in Exhibit 3.1, which managers can use to guide their decision making about situations that occur.[11]

The first question you should ask about apparent discrepancies in the behavior of employees is, "What is the exact nature of the discrepancy?" Your answer would be something like "Our salespeople are supposed to call on at least three new accounts each day, but Peter is reporting only ten new contacts a week," or "The employees in Ellen's department are complaining that we're not

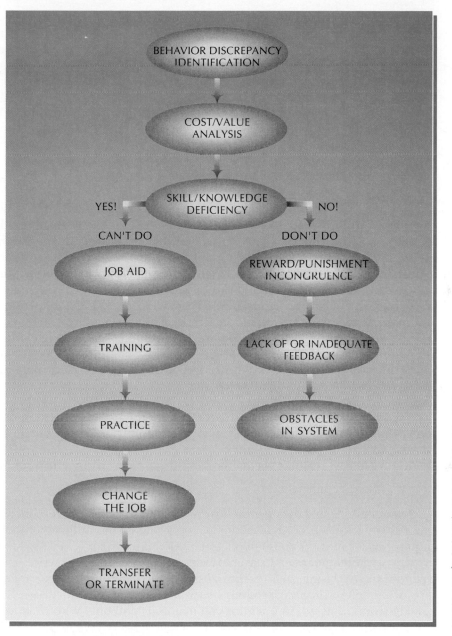

Exhibit 3.1
**TRAINING
NEEDS
ANALYSIS
MODEL**

SOURCE: After Donald F. Michalak and Edwin G. Yager, *Making the Training Process Work: A Practical Guide to Better Training Programs* (New York, Harper & Row, 1979), p. 8. Reprinted by permission of Harper & Row, Publishers, Inc.

giving them accurate information about the changes in the group health insurance plan."

The second question to ask may be answered with a simple yes or no: "Is changing the discrepancy important?" If your answer is yes, then you ask the third question.

The third question you should ask about apparent discrepancies in the behavior of employees is, "Is this problem the result of some deficiency in information or skill?" If your answer to this third question is yes, then you know that the employee is unable to—he cannot—meet your expectation. If your answer to the question is no, then you must conclude that the employee is able to perform as you wish but may have chosen not to do so.

Suppose your response was yes, the problem is the result of some deficiency in information or skill. Your response takes you to the path on the left side of the model in Exhibit 3.1.

Managing Deficiencies in Information or Skill

Job aid.   If the worker cannot perform the task because the task is too complex, a job aid may be more helpful than training. For example, keeping track of the laboratory work and reports and incorporating them into the medical records of all the patients in a major hospital used to be an administrative nightmare. The job is very much easier now, thanks to the widespread use of computers programmed to aid in this task. Software has been developed that is "user friendly." That is, the machine "knows" what it needs, and from whom, and requests that information automatically from the operator in the tech lab.

Something as simple as a plastic overlay with holes cut through at appropriate places may help individual workers to fill out complex forms. A slide-and-sound film strip may allow a worker to complete some very complex project, such as the wiring assembly for a jet liner.

Training.   If an employee cannot do a job because he lacks skill or knowledge, training may seem the most obvious solution. It may also be the most expensive solution, and it may not be very effective. Consider all your options carefully. Then, if training seems the best alternative, arrange to provide it for the worker.

Practice.   Sometimes people lose a skill or knowledge they once had because they lack practice. For example, every one of the military branches that employs pilots requires those pilots to practice. Ability to fly is a skill that fades rapidly without practice. Law-enforcement officers must practice with their weapons or risk losing their marksmanship skill. The computer command structure of complex software programs such as Lotus 1,2,3 and dBase III+ fades quickly from memory. An operator can maintain skill only with practice.

Change the job.   Often a manager will decide that a worker's performance is below standard and therefore that the worker should be changed. Before you make this decision, try to discover if the job can be changed. If a worker cannot do a job because she is not tall enough to reach the machine's controls, for example, you may be able to put a platform at the workstation.

Some complex jobs can be divided into manageable units. For example, some salespeople are good at coming up with possible customers but have difficulty in getting the customer to place the order. This is a common problem in automobile sales. It might be possible to divide the sales job in such a way that the good "prospector" is encouraged to do the prospecting and a good closer is encouraged to do the closing.

Transfer or terminate.   If you have exhausted other possibilities and an employee still cannot perform because of some deficiency in skill or knowledge, it may be sensible to transfer her to a job that allows her to succeed with the knowledge and skills she has. If that is not possible, the final solution is to fire her.

Managing Other Performance Problems

Suppose that when you asked yourself if the problem was the result of some deficiency in information or skill, you answered no. This response takes you to the path on the right side of Michalak and Yager's model. The employee is *able* to do the job but still does not do it properly. In this situation, your analysis should suggest at least three possibilities.

> What are the ethical issues revolving around a decision to terminate an employee? Can you apply the three general principles (don't lie, do no harm, seek justice) to your answer? What ethical issues might revolve around a decision to transfer an employee into another section of the organization? For example, is it ethical to transfer a marginally competent employee because that's the easy way out of a manager's personnel problem?

Reward/punishment incongruence.   Sometimes an individual employee who is known to have the information and skills necessary to do a job refuses to perform because doing so is punishing. For example, a vending machine manufacturer in Kansas City, Missouri, hired a young man who very much wanted to do a good job. He worked hard at first and was strikingly more productive than his coworkers. Soon, however, his performance fell off, until it leveled out at the same production rate as that of the others. His peers did not appreciate his performance, which they believed made their own performance look bad.

Management had not reinforced his above-average performance, or even acknowledged it! So the young man could not see that the payoff for his extra effort was worth the price he had to pay in the disapproval of his coworkers.

Examples are common in any complex organization. People in business and professional organizations tend to do a poor job of performance appraisal because doing it well requires them to take time away from their other duties. The payoff is not worth the price. Or, more often than you might imagine, an employee who works very hard, thus increasing his rate of performance, will be punished by a management decision to increase his quota. The payoff in this case is certainly not worth the price.

If your analysis suggests that there is a discrepancy between the expected level of performance and the reward or punishment the employee receives for performance at that level, bring the reward system into line. Find out from the worker what reward system he or she responds to; salary is only a small part of the total picture.

Lack of or inadequate feedback.   It is not uncommon for an employee who has the essential knowledge and skills to fail to perform as expected simply because he or she has not been told what is expected. "I've always done it this way, and no one ever told me before that I was doing it wrong."

Cleanup at the end of the workday was getting sloppy in one department of a major chemical plant in Alabama. The workers knew that regular cleanup was important, and they had both the knowledge and skills necessary to do the job. Investigation into the problem revealed that one worker, John, had let his responsibility slide one evening because he was in a rush. The following day, his supervisor chatted with John but did not mention the cleanup routine. The second day, John was again lax in his cleanup. Again the supervisor said nothing. Soon Bill too began to take less care in the cleanup at the end of the day. The supervisor still said nothing. Within two months, the day-end cleanup had fallen way off, but the supervisor had not once said anything about it. When management demanded that the supervisor get the situation turned around, the situation changed almost immediately. On Friday the supervisor held a brief meeting with his subordinates and pointed to the problem. "Cleanup will occur every day," he said. "We've got to turn this situation around." That evening things were better but not up to the level expected by management. Monday morning brought a second meeting in the unit. "At the end of this day I want this section clean. If you haven't fulfilled your personal responsibility in the overall cleanup operation, your pay will be docked." The section was spotless on Tuesday morning.

We think our point here is obvious. Give and get feedback often.

Obstacles in the system.　Perhaps the most common reason an employee who has the requisite information and skills does not perform to expectations can be traced to some obstacle in the system. Imagine yourself in a situation in which the boss has asked you to deliver a package of photographic prints to an advertising agency across town. You take the envelope and the car keys and walk to the parking lot. When you try to start the car, you discover a dead battery. When you report the problem to your boss, he says something like "Stop complaining and deliver the photos."

Managers sometimes make a demand that the system simply will not support. One more quick example will illustrate the problem. In one manufacturing plant on the eastern seaboard, management decided that the supervisors should be required to give their new employees orientation on the first day of work. A training program was developed for the supervisors, and all the supervisors participated. But the quality of new employee orientation did not improve. Investigation revealed that the first hour of the supervisor's day was the most important hour. Inventory, personnel absenteeism, equipment operation, and the like had to be verified in that first hour. If the right decisions were made, the day went well. If the wrong decisions were made, or none at all, the day could be difficult. That first hour was full of important duties, and now management was asking that an additional twenty minutes be squeezed into it.

If you discover that an employee who has the information and the skills to perform as expected does not do so, make sure there are no obstacles standing in his or her way. If obstacles exist and you can change them, do so. If they cannot be changed, do not hold the employee to an impossible standard.

....LEADERSHIP AND ORGANIZATIONAL DYSFUNCTION

Occasionally the ways and means by which an organization makes decisions break down. The breakdown occurs because the organization's leadership experiences difficulty in choosing among the paths that promise goal attainment. Subgroups in the organization may perceive things differently or have incompatible goals. Leaders must choose from among a variety of

> Are our suggestions for controlling dysfunctions ethical? How would you test such suggestions?

self-serving proposals put forth by competing subsystems, and they must do so in a way that will serve organizational needs. Solutions tend to fall into one of two groups—those involving structural control and those involving conflict management.

Suggestions for Controlling Structure

1. *Leaders might separate the groups, then control information in such a way that the groups do not learn about what the others are doing.* The design of a typical manufacturing firm provides a good example, and you will quickly spot the parallel in many other complex organizations. The organization will usually have two lines—production and marketing. Marketing may be broken down into several related departments—perhaps sales, advertising, public relations, and marketing research. Each department in the marketing division must compete with the others for limited resources, such as equipment, personnel, dollars, space, and the like. One way to inhibit the conflicts between, say, advertising and public relations is to separate them physically—put them on separate floors of the building. This strategy makes it more difficult for members of one department to communicate directly with members of a competing department, and it fosters a sense of identity *within* each department.

2. *The leaders of an organization can choose to control by arranging group tasks in such a way that the groups do not "bump into" each other.* Although there are obvious differences between advertising and public relations, there are also many similarities. Clearly, these two departments have the potential to bump into each other. Their audiences tend to overlap (Who "owns" the "public" in public relations? Who owns the "market" to which advertising appeals?). They depend on the same supporting structure within the organization: Both must use the services of the art department and the marketing research department. Both must meet the demands of management in coordinating their overall persuasive campaigns. When both departments make a bid for the same tasks, the organization controls the situation by dividing the tasks in such a way that they do not overlap. Public relations departments will focus on generating the image of the organization while the advertising department focuses on generating the images of particular products. This division of tasks helps to prevent possible disagreements.

3. *Leaders can present information to each group in such a way that the attention of each group is directed away from the others.* Suppose that two de-

partments are engaged in conflict. Management might suggest to each, "We must focus our attention on a new demand for more efficiency in production. Each department will be required to show it is striving for excellence. Tell me how you are attempting to meet this demand." This threat from the outside might serve to distract the competing departments, causing each to look inward.

The design of an organization's structure is the principal means by which the leadership uses information control. The structure controls the establishment and evolution of groups and group tasks. It determines both group goals and the evaluation and payoff system to which individuals in the organization must subscribe. The structure is also responsible, more than any other factor, for determining what an individual's working environment is like: who gets promoted, who gets a raise in pay, who gets greater visibility, who gets inclusion, affection, and greater control over their work situation. By controlling the structure, organization leadership can control, in large measure, the competition and conflict.

Suggestions for Managing Conflict

Besides controlling structure, however, there are other means of keeping dissension within bounds. Robert Chin and Kenneth Benne have suggested three strategies for managing change and dysfunctional behavior by subgroups with different goals. The first strategy assumes that people are reasonable and will do what is better for themselves once they know what their options are. The second strategy assumes that people are guided by value systems, social norms, and the like, rather than by reason. The third strategy assumes that people must be coerced through legal means or perhaps through sanctions of some kind in order to get them to change.[12] What is interesting is that all these assumptions are true to some extent in all complex organizations. Thus the leadership of organizations would benefit from a method by which it could select appropriate strategies.

1. *Assuming that people are reasonable and will do what is best for them when they know the options, spell out the options precisely.* Suppose two subunits are in conflict over the matter of video and film equipment purchases. Leadership might bring the managers of the two units together and say something like, "The total budget for equipment purchases for this year is $180,000. There is not a penny more. Your departments have been competing for the lion's share, and you have both made excellent proposals. Now I want you to put your heads together and prepare a joint proposal that will satisfy both departments. If you can't or won't do that, then I'll make the purchase decisions on the basis of my own sense of what's important and what isn't."

2. *If you assume people are guided by value systems and social norms rather than by reason, you may control conflict by appealing to these values.* You

might say something like, "I know that both your departments need more equipment than the budget will afford. Bill, last year your department got 60 percent of the budget and Wilson's got 40 percent. Turnabout is fair play. I know you'll understand the essential rightness of my decision to place a larger percentage of the $180,000 in Wilson's department this year. He's got to play some catch-up ball this year. I expect that if we're all patient during this difficult time, things will balance out next year."

3. *If you assume people must be coerced, sometimes an accurate assumption, then you may wish to make a threat.* You might say something like, "Look, you guys have been bickering over the equipment budget for the past several years. I won't have it again this year. You've made your best arguments in your separate proposals. I'll do my best to allocate the $180,000 wisely for the good of the entire operation. And I don't want to hear of a single unpleasant comment about the equipment budget."

The assumptions of the three strategies provide guidance to the manager. If it is reasonable to suppose that people involved in a change will do what is better for themselves once they know what their options are, and if the proposed change is good for them, then give them the facts and opinions available, and make the proposal. Change strategies, for example, might include specialized and general training programs, development of information diffusion systems, development of idea-gathering systems, and the like.

If, however, in a situation involving change, people are more likely to be guided by their value systems, social norms, and allegiances, then wise leadership will be guided by other principles. Reeducation in order to change norms may require some outside help. Wise leadership could hire new people with new skills and knowledge, or train existing staff in the new skills. Similarly, special groups could be established to study and make recommendations for changes.

Finally, if it seems clear that people will not change unless they are forced, then the leadership will employ still different change strategies. Government agencies, such as the Occupational Safety and Health Administration (OSHA) and the Consumer Product Safety Commission, force changes on organizations that will not change without coercion. The courts of the land impose changes on organizations every day because individual members or subgroups have been assertive enough to sue for change. Within an organization, formal authority that grows out of hierarchical status is sometimes employed. For example, a new manager is sent to a plant to "square it away," with the authority to hire and fire and the prerogative to make the decisions sufficient to work the changes that the leadership wants.

Visionary leadership, communication, and control are intimately linked. We are convinced that your ability to exercise this kind of leadership is important to the productivity of your organization. Visionary leadership requires skill in decision making and thinking. It anticipates and takes steps to manage change. It also adapts the communication to specific requirements. We will have more to say about communication activities in specific contexts in the final part of this book.

SUMMARY . . . .

This chapter sets forth the communication processes involved in managing an organization. We examined first the various functions of organizational communication. We noted that communication serves to provide information, to transmit commands and instructions, to influence and persuade members of an organization, and to integrate the organization and maintain it. These functions of communication in organizations are directly related to managing human behavior.

We turned next to the topic of leadership in an organization as it relates to organizational change. We noted that effective leadership depends on information control. Problem solving, decision making, and the implementation of decisions cannot be conducted successfully without an adequate flow of information to leaders.

Among the most common leadership problems that require expert decision making, the decision whether or not to train an employee may be the most difficult. When someone is not working up to expectation, Michalak and Yager's training needs analysis model can be used to analyze the root cause of the problem.

In the specific situation where change is called for in an organization, the type of leadership we showed to be most effective is visionary leadership. Unlike reactionary leadership, which responds to change only after a problem has occurred, visionary leadership actively anticipates and plans for change.

We concluded the chapter with a look at dysfunctional behavior in organizations. When the subsystems of an organization resist change because of a narrow focus on their particular goals, visionary leadership must redesign the organization's structure to control the flow of information and bring the subsystems into line. Managing change and dysfunctional behavior may also involve other strategies, such as retraining, reeducation, or coercion.

NOTES . . . .

1. Lee Thayer, *Communication and Communication Systems in Organization, Management, and Interpersonal Relations* (Homewood, Ill., Irwin, 1968).
2. Frederick Taylor, *Scientific Management* (New York, Harper, 1911).
3. Max Weber, *The Theory of Social and Economic Organization,* ed. Talcott Parsons, trans. M. Henderson and T. Parsons (New York, Free Press, 1947); Henri Fayol, *General and Industrial Management* (London, Sir Isaac Pitman & Sons, 1949).
4. Chester I. Barnard, *The Functions of the Executive* (Cambridge, Harvard University Press, 1938); F. J. Roethlisberger and W. J. Dickson, *Management and the Worker* (Cambridge, Harvard University Press, 1939).
5. Kurt Lewin, "Group Decision and Social Change," in *Reading in Social Psychology,* G. E. Swanson, T. M. Newcomb, and E. L. Hartley, eds. (New York, Holt, 1952).
6. Richard H. Franke and James D. Kaul, "The Hawthorne Experiments: First Statistical Interpretation," *American Sociological Review,* **43** (October 1978):623–643.
7. Paul R. Lawrence and Jay W. Lorsch, *Organization and Environment: Managing Differentiation and Integration* (Cambridge, Harvard University Press, 1967).
8. Fred E. Fiedler, *A Theory of Leadership Effectiveness* (New York, McGraw-Hill, 1967).
9. Gerald M. Goldhaber, *Organizational Communication,* 4th ed. (Dubuque, Brown, 1986), p. 107.
10. Daniel Katz and Robert L. Kahn, *The Social Psychology of Organizations* (New York, Wiley, 1966).
11. Donald F. Michalak and Edwin G. Yager, *Making the Training Process Work: A Practical Guide to Better Training Programs* (New York, Harper & Row, 1979).
12. Robert Chin and Kenneth D. Benne, "General Strategies for Effecting Changes in Human Systems," in *The Planning of Change,* 2d ed., Warren G. Bennis, Kenneth D. Benne, and Robert Chin, eds. (New York, Holt, Rinehart & Winston, 1969), pp. 32–59.

RECOMMENDED READINGS . . . .

Gerald M. Goldhaber. *Organizational Communication,* 6th ed. Dubuque, Brown,

1993. This is a revision of one of the first books on organizational communication. Chapter 2, "The Theory of Organizations," is especially helpful as it provides more detail on some of the ideas in this chapter.

Don Hellriegel, John W. Slocum, Jr., and Richard W. Woodman. *Organizational Behavior,* 7th ed. St. Paul, West, 1994. This is a readable, clear work on organizational behavior and organizational change. You will notice, as we did, that most of the contingencies discussed are communication contingencies.

Stephen W. Littlejohn. *Theories of Human Communication,* 5th ed. Belmont, Calif., Wadsworth, 1996. This well-written and comprehensive text provides quick access into a variety of communication theories. There are shortcomings in some of the explanations but good bibliographical data.

Burt Nanus and Warren Bennis. *Leaders: The Strategy for Taking Charge.* New York, Harper & Row, 1986. This interesting book supplements our presentation of visionary leadership.

R. Wayne Pace and Don F. Faules. *Organizational Communication,* 3d ed. Englewood Cliffs, N.J., Prentice-Hall, 1993. This is an excellent book and the first to bring together organizational communication and human resource development. It is an important book to read for those planning to go into human resource development as a career.

Lee Thayer. *Communication and Communication Systems.* Homewood, Ill., Irwin, 1968. This classic work in organizational communication is full of jargon but also of ideas.

Gerald L. Wilson, H. Lloyd Goodall, Jr., and Christopher L. Waagen. *Organizational Communication.* New York, Harper & Row, 1986. See especially Chapter 9 of this text. It is a comprehensive treatment of communication and organizational change.

DISCUSSION QUESTIONS . . . .

1. Examine the messages you have received from your professor in this course. Give five examples of messages in each of the following categories:
   a. Information.
   b. Command and instruction.
   c. Influence and persuasion.
   d. Integration and maintenance.
   Does your professor seem to use one category more often than others? If so, how do you account for that fact?

2. Can you identify any instances of information control that have occurred in your class? What was the result of such control? Did anyone benefit? If so, who and how?

3. If you wished to have more say than you now have in the kind and number of tests you must take in a course, what strategies for change do you believe would be most effective? Do you have the power, as students, to effect such a change? To what extent can you expect to be successful change agents in this situation? Why do you believe that?

INTERNET ACTIVITIES . . . .

1. Open the search engine named Yahoo! (http://www.yahoo.com/) and type this word: *leadership.* You will find about 450 "hits." Scroll through the entire list (it is alphabetized) to form mental impressions. Does anything stand out for you? If so, write it down and prepare to report back to the class. What do you think the Internet and the World Wide Web will do to the way organizations communicate in the future?

2. If you wanted to study one of the four functions of organizational communication, what key terms would you use to study it on the Internet? Try two of these search engines, make notes, and share your findings with the class.
   Pathfinder (http://pathfinder.com/@@GbAEYAYA0j91qS@H/welcome/)
   All In One (http://www.albany.net/allinone/)
   Lycos (http://www.lycos.com/)

CHAPTER 4

Diversity in the Workplace

OBJECTIVES

Upon completion of this chapter, you should be able to:

1. Define, explain, compare, and contrast the terms *diversity* and *ethnicity*.
2. Name and explain, compare, and contrast how biology and culture make people different.
3. Describe and explain how people learn to make differences important.
4. Name and explain five value orientations that seem to exist in all cultures.
5. Explain how prejudice works.
6. Suggest four things people can do to communicate more effectively with others who are different from themselves.
7. Identify, compare, and contrast the communication styles of five ethnic groups most commonly found in business and professional settings in the United States.
8. Value your own biological and cultural uniqueness.
9. Explain how to adjust when you're working in a dominant culture different from your own.

A society of people is not like a flock of geese or a batch of cookies—its members are not all the same. Americans, for example, are nothing if not diverse. American skin color is so varied that we no longer quite know how to talk and write about it. Are we black—or Black? Are we white—or White? Are we Occidental? Oriental? Euro-American? Are we African American? Are we Asian American? Are we Native American—or American Indian? Are we Latino, Chicano, Cubano—or simply Americans of Hispanic ancestry?

We are first-generation and second-generation and newly arrived Americans. We are native speakers of English and speakers who use English as a second language. To make matters still more complex, many of us are bilingual and bicultural.

According to the *Chronicle of Higher Education* Web site (http://www. chronicle.merit.edu/.almanac/.almdem2.html), citing U.S. Census Bureau information from 1990, America's racial and ethnic distribution is as follows. The numbers do not add up to 100 percent because some people do not give their racial identity at all, while others give more than one response. Indeed, how would an individual born of a racially mixed couple know which category to check?

American Indian	0.8%
Asian	2.9%
Black	12.1%
White	80.3%
Other and unknown	3.9%
Hispanic (may be any race)	9.0%

We use the term *diversity* to refer to difference, or variety. In this sense, racial diversity refers to different races. Ethnic diversity refers to different ethnic groups. It seems sensible to include gender differences in this discussion of diversity, as well as age differences and social class differences. As you consider business and professional organizations throughout this chapter and this text, bear in mind that one of their most obvious features is their human diversity.

Now consider how rapidly populations and population distributions change. U.S. and world cultural and ethnic diversity ratios will undergo tremendous variation in the coming years. Indeed, the United Nations Population Division estimates that by the year 2000, the world population will stand at 6,261,000,000. Twenty-five years later the population will have jumped to 8,504,000,000. Of those 8.5 billion people, only about 1 billion will reside in industrialized countries. Seven billion will live in developing countries.[1] The ethnic mix in the United States will change rapidly, too. To illustrate, in 1980, the Asian-American population was 3.5 million, but by 1987 it had grown to 5.1 million. It is predicted to reach 10 million by the year 2000.[2] At that time, there will be about 35 million Hispanics—about 12 percent of the population. In contrast, the number of Euro-Americans will shrink from 78 percent in 1990 to about 54 percent by 2080. Thus, clearly, the population is shifting and changing in the United States as well as in the world. All this changing will bring people into more and more contact with the world's diversity.

The American Council on Education (ACE) reported that racial minorities outnumber the traditional majority in such large cities as Chicago, Miami, Los Angeles, Dallas, Detroit, Washington, San Francisco, and Albuquerque. The ACE predicted that in more than fifty cities, public schools will draw students primarily from minority populations.[3] Ultimately, the diverse ethnic groups will encounter one another in the work force.

In the context of work, these changes in the ethnic balance of the nation mean that more and more people will encounter greater and greater diversity. Further, many of the men and women in the U.S. labor force will become specialists doing highly technical or managerial jobs, while the emerging nations will "take over" the world's unskilled labor.

Business and professional organizations reflect, but do not always value, the enormous diversity that is part of U.S. society. In this chapter, as in this book, organizations in the United States are our primary focus.

Citizens of the United States often call themselves Americans, and they are. However, so are Canadians, Mexicans, and all the people from all the countries of Central and South America. If a person uses the word *American,* but thinks only of U.S. citizens, the speaker is expressing his or her centrism. Because *American* is the common form of self-reference in the United States, however, we will adopt it in this chapter and throughout this book. We hope our readers will understand that this is a convention adopted for convenience and that we value the people in other American nations.

Many of the illustrations in this chapter may make it appear that Americans (U.S. citizens) are insensitive, but the word *insensitive* does not quite describe the facts. Rather, Americans (and all other people) are highly sensitive but are focused on a particular set of stimuli. Nevertheless, using the language in its grosser sense, we do not hesitate to say that some Americans are insensitive, and others—most others, we think—are not. However, the purpose of this book is to help its readers learn and grow, and to that end, we have included a good many errors Americans (and others) make in cross-cultural encounters. Do not read into this fact any indictment of the American people. Rather, look at your own behavioral tendencies. If you find some insensitivities, make the choices you believe appropriate as you seek to become more cosmopolitan.

THE DIFFICULT SIDE OF DIVERSITY . . . .

Working with people who are different from ourselves may seem difficult and may make us feel uncomfortable. When we work with people who are different from us, who act differently, who look different, who do not share our beliefs and cultural assumptions, problems sometimes arise. We don't quite know what to say or how to act. We find it difficult to read nonverbal messages, so we are uncertain about what others are thinking and feeling. We are uncertain what others expect of us, or, for that matter, if the others know what we expect from them. So we feel uncomfortable and perhaps a bit suspicious. We may be reluctant to speak to people who are different. Perhaps we are afraid we'll give offense. And sometimes, perhaps, we are simply afraid. A general anxiety often occurs when people who are different from each other come into contact.

If only we could learn to tap into the skills and abilities different people bring to the workplace. Imagine the creative impulse we could generate! But learning to use and value diversity is not easy, and misunderstandings occur too often.

Personal Goals

Our objectives for this chapter are to provide ways for you to feel more comfortable and be more skillful when communicating with people who are different. We intend to suggest ways that you can help others feel more comfortable and communicate more skillfully. You probably have additional goals, as well. We hope you want to:

1. Eradicate any prejudice or injustice that may result when you interact with people who are different from yourself.
2. Improve the climate for people from minority cultures and groups where you work.
3. Avoid offending people who are different, and work more efficiently and effectively with them.
4. Find greater comfort when traveling to other countries or among other cultures.

Unfortunately, you cannot achieve these goals merely by reading a book. You have to choose your values wisely and to act in ways that are consistent with those values. You need an open approach, characterized by genuine interest in someone's culture, effective listening, and empathy. Such an approach will help you appreciate the wisdom and beauty of the other person's culture.

Taking the First Step

Learning to think in a new way about other cultures requires, first, that we learn to look objectively at cultures, our own and those of others. If possible, we need to experience cultures other than our own. We need to pull far enough away from our world view to examine its assumptions. When a person is acting spontaneously, that person automatically judges situations—and people—according to the requirements of his or her own culture. This change in thinking (examining one's own cultural assumptions) is the hardest part of making changes in behavior, for it requires us to be fiercely honest with ourselves about some of our most deep-seated assumptions and opinions.

To illustrate, consider your mental map of the universe. If you are like most people, you, personally, are at the center of your universe. Two words describe this point of view: egocentric and ethnocentric. *Egocentric* means regarding the self as the center of all things. *Ethnocentric* refers to the conscious or subconscious belief that one's own group or culture is inherently superior to all others, that it is the central culture. When we place ourselves at the center, then necessarily, other people must revolve around us. When we place our culture at the center of the universe, then necessarily, other cultures must revolve around ours.

Can you remember the first time you discovered you are not at the center of the universe? You may have been a fairly young child sitting alone, watching the traffic flow by. Suddenly it occurred to you that all those cars had people in them. The people all had things to do and places to go, and none of them was aware that you were sitting there watching. Although they were at the periphery of your world, you were also at the periphery of their worlds. Perhaps you began to expand your thinking. All the cars in the world were driven by people who probably didn't know you existed! Not only cars in America, but also cars in Europe and cars in Japan and cars in Africa! If each one of them is the center of the world—even people who have never seen or thought about the United States, much less the child sitting there watching traffic flow by—you could not possibly be the center of the universe. Or does the world have as many centers as there are people?

This idea that there are as many points of view as there are people is *polycentric,* meaning "many-centered." There are as many centers—and as many world views—as there are people. Indeed, there may be as many cultures as there are individuals in the world. And the problem is more complex, even, than that! People—all people—themselves have many different ways of looking at each other and the world. And all people tend to be *egocentric* and also *ethnocentric* as described above.

To illustrate, Exhibit 4.1 shows a map of the world. Can you draw a line through the exact center of the world using this map? Can you place your city on the map? Can you place the city of Athens, Greece? Where is the Slovak Republic? Can you point to the approximate location of the Nile River? The Ti-

**Exhibit 4.1
MAP OF THE
WORLD**

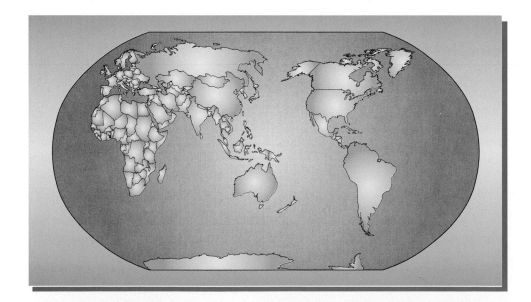

gress? The Thames? Where is Moscow? Peking? Seoul? Hanoi? Where is Sydney? Why is it so easy for you to locate your own city while the rest are more difficult?

Clearly, we have learned to think of ourselves, and our own geographical regions, as central, but we know this is not actually the case. The same thing holds with cultures, too. One's own culture is no more central to the world than is one's city, except in the mind. We have to change our ways of thinking in order to change the problems of egocentrism and ethnocentrism.

. . . . WHAT MAKES PEOPLE DIFFERENT?

Some people are so different from us that we may find them hard to understand and difficult to like, or even accept. To illustrate, bring to mind someone whose differences make it uncomfortable for you to interact with him or her. What makes that person so different from you? What makes you uncomfortable?

Biology

Biology makes people different. Even identical twins are not identical! No one comes close to being exactly like anyone else. Skin, body shape and type, hair texture, eye color, and the like set us apart. Gender sets us apart, too. Not only physical features, but such things as attitudes, beliefs, and values are also influenced by gender.

Differences are important to each of us—they make us unique. But in the broad scheme of things, biological differences do not count for much unless people decide, either consciously or unconsciously, to make them count for something. Still, people in the American business community often do decide to allow biological differences to matter. You hear it in racist jokes; you see it in the lunchroom when people exclude others for no apparent reason. You know it when you examine who occupies the executive suites of many business organizations. With few exceptions (such as a job requirement for a certain height or a certain amount of muscle mass) business organizations should not allow biological differences to matter, and neither should we. There is no need to make a person's physical features an issue in decision-making processes. Doing so diminishes the target of prejudice, the person who exhibits the prejudice, and the organization that allows it.

Gender, in particular, makes us different. Apart from the obvious differences of physique, our identities as men and women, our self-concepts, and our learned responses constitute enormously important perceptual filters in our lives. If you are a man, you see the world from a masculine point of view. If you are part of a male-dominant culture, then your maleness causes you to allow yourself the possibility of dominance. If you are a woman, your view of the world comes through a feminine filtering system. If you are part of a male-dominant culture, your femininity has become a political issue in the world of

> It is easy to see how prejudiced behavior can damage the individual target of prejudice, but how does it damage the person who exhibits the behavior? And how does it damage the organization that allows prejudiced behavior?

work, apparent in such issues as "the glass ceiling"* and broadly publicized cases of sexual harassment (see Chapter 8).

Culture

Culture makes people different. *Culture* means how people are raised to live their lives. Another way to say it is that culture is the way in which people solve problems. Culture tells us what makes sense. It binds us together. It manifests itself in what we do, and what we make, and what events of our lives we celebrate. It provides guidelines for our values, beliefs, and behaviors. It produces a common language, then flows from that language to create tastes, habits, preferences, and needs. In short, culture provides—and is—a frame of reference, a perspective on the world. Thus we see the world through the window of our cultural heritage.

We must learn a culture. For example, if a Japanese woman has a baby in the United States, and she brings up that child in the United States, exposing the youngster to American schools and white society, the child's cultural orientation will be far different from a child born and raised in Japan. Culture is not instinctual; it is learned.

Culture tells us who "we" are and who "they" are. Every cultural group shares a worldview. That is, members share a way of filtering their world through the group's system of beliefs and values. The process leads to *in-groups* and *out-groups*. We are the in-group, and they are the out-group. The words *in-group* and *out-group* may help you think about diversity in the workplace. Whatever group you belong to is your in-group. Anyone who is not in that group is part of the out-group. This dichotomy is true for everyone! If you're not part of their in-group you are a member of their out-group. And consider what belonging to in-groups and out-groups does to your way of thinking about and relating to others.

If you are a member of the majority group you probably think of yourself as someone who treats other people's cultures with respect. Probably, also, you believe you treat everyone fairly and equally. If anyone would tell you that you are insensitive you might very well argue the point. And yet, people in the majority group often are accused of insensitivity and outright prejudice. (*Prejudice* means an unfavorable—often hostile—opinion, formed in advance out of ignorance and inexperience. Thus prejudice is unreasoned and unreasonable. The term includes feelings, opinions, and attitudes and usually concerns religious, ethnic, and national groups.)

It may be that you are a member of a minority out-group at work. If so, you may find it difficult to "read" situations, especially tense situations, accurately and comfortably. Perhaps you feel people don't take you seriously or they "put you down." It may also be that members of your minority group exhibit prejudiced behavior toward the majority. Anger and hostility can flow in more than one direction.

---

*The "glass ceiling" is an intangible barrier within the hierarchy of a company that prevents women or minorities from obtaining upper-level positions.

What gives rise to such behavior and feelings? We think they flow in both directions from *ignorance*. To eradicate prejudice we must reduce ignorance. We can begin by understanding cultures.

A Communication Perspective of Culture

From a communication perspective, a *culture* is best defined as a set of agreed-upon rules that apply when two people are talking to each other.[4] The rules tend to fall into six categories, but the categories overlap and influence each other. They are:

1. Etiquette
2. Values
3. Language
4. Traditions and customs
5. Food, dress, artistic tastes
6. Belief systems/world views

How we think about age, social class, religion, gender, even sexual orientation, and certainly about appropriate behavior at work is a function of our cultural uniqueness, but also how we "fit" into each of these demographic subgroupings constitutes part of our cultural uniqueness. These are the differences that render you an individual. Doing the exercise in Exhibit 4.2 will help you develop a sense of your own uniqueness.

Exhibit 4.2 SOME FACTORS THAT MAKE US INDIVIDUALS	
Fill in details you think may set you apart from others in ways that seem important—either to yourself or to others.	
Demographic Factor	Your Comment
Age	
Sex	
Ethnic identification	
Religious affiliation	
Political affiliation	
Current geographical region	
Geographical region of ancestors	
Family status	
Family type	
Organizations	
Sexual preference	
Social class	
Physical limitations	
Other	

If you become aware of unreasonable negative or hostile feelings toward a person because he or she is different from you, what should you or can you do with those feelings?

Each of us is a blend of many biological and cultural differences. Each of us also has a personal history that no one else shares. But rather than think of ourselves as different from others, we tend to think of others as different from ourselves. As you consider Exhibit 4.1, try to think of your attitudes and beliefs that flow from each of the demographic factors listed. For example, we are said to be born male or female, but we are taught how men and women are supposed to act. What are your attitudes about men and women? What does it mean when you say, "He's a real man" or "She's a real woman"? Are you a single head of a household? If so, how does this fact influence your thinking about yourself and others? If not, how do you feel about single heads of households? Envy? Pity? Worry? Thinking about the workplace, can you imagine how someone else's uniqueness might matter to you or to some of the people you know? Is there anything inherent in the person's uniqueness that could create negative or hostile feelings in you or someone you know?

Evaluating Cultural Differences

Remember that differences aren't important unless people decide they're important. It follows that we must decide to make differences matter when we think they do. Some of us pay more attention to differences than others—and we do this selectively. That is, we choose which differences we make important.

The choices we make are learned choices, and generally we make them without conscious intent. Sometimes we learned from our families and our communities; sometimes we formed our opinions from a combination of influences such as personal experience and family preferences, coupled with religious teaching.

Consider this argument concerning sexual preference: "Our attitudes and beliefs about whom we prefer, if anyone, for sexual partners is not natural, but learned." How you respond to this statement is a learned response. Your agreement or disagreement is learned. How you *feel* about it is also a learned response.

Other examples spring to mind. How do you respond to body shape? Which of the body shapes in Exhibit 4.3 do you prefer? Rank-order your preferences from 1 to 4, most preferred to least preferred. Note that your preference in this regard is *learned*. There is nothing superior or more attractive inherent in a particular body shape.

Social status and education level also influence how we experience each other and what we make of differences. For example, some of us are rich and some are poor. Still others are in the middle range. How would you classify your personal or family wealth? How do others see you? In the workplace as well as in the larger society, some people are illiterate, some have not graduated from high school, and some have completed doctoral degrees. How does your educational level influence your attitudes and beliefs about yourself? How do others see you? How do you see them based upon educational differences?

These few examples help make the point that we are all different from each other in many ways. We ignore most of the differences most of the time, but we choose to make some differences important, and we make these choices, con-

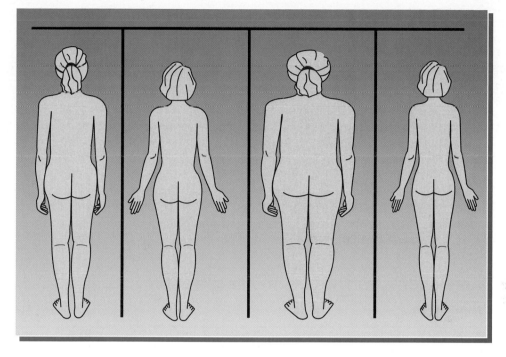

Exhibit 4.3
SEVERAL
BODY SHAPES

sciously or unconsciously, because we have learned to do so. The key point here is that we learn our biases and prejudices. We tend to see other people as different from ourselves, but we rarely think of ourselves as different from other people. Thus, the attitudes and beliefs we hold about these perceptions tend to be supportive of ourselves but not necessarily supportive of people we see as different from ourselves.

Making Sense of the World

We have attitudes and beliefs about nearly everything! Indeed, each time we encounter the world outside our skins we work to make sense out of it. If the encounter is new to us we must put it in perspective. Thus we make sense of the new experience by making it consistent with our own personal, cultural frames of reference. We make the new fit with what we already know and understand by asking, deep in our minds, four questions.

1. Is it one or is it more than one?
2. Is it true or is it false?
3. Is it good or is it evil?
4. Is it beautiful or is it ugly?

The first question, one of many, helps us determine what fits together and what does not. To illustrate, the word *dog* both includes and excludes individual animals. If we say, "That is a dog," we include the animal in the category. This decision is based on the standards of our culture and language. It is *not* an objective truth. You can see how important this decision is to intercultural communication by examining a similar sentence. If we say, "That is an Asian," what shall we include and exclude? Chinese? Japanese? Korean? Indonesian? If we mean Indonesian, then which of the 300 or so different Indonesian ethnic subgroups do we mean? Surely an Indonesian will think her ethnicity marks her as special and important, but will she and you understand its importance in the same way?

For comparison, think of the word WASP (the acronym for *white Anglo-Saxon Protestant*). When we use this word we group people together, then either separate ourselves from them or include ourselves among them. We decide how we are alike or how we are different. Thus we choose to live inclusively or exclusively. We can value our own in-group and devalue others, or we can choose to value all people from all groups, celebrating our enormous diversity and looking for ways to gather strength and power from it. The organizations for which we work benefit when we value our diversity.

INAPPROPRIATE APPROACHES TO THOSE WHO ARE DIFFERENT . . . .

Prejudging

We prejudge others on the basis of similarity and differences. Why do we do this? Why do the people in our workplaces tolerate it? If we choose always to view the world through the in-group perspective we begin to think in prejudicial ways. Prejudice involves self-serving prejudgments: We are good; they are bad. We are beautiful; they are ugly. We are right; they are wrong.

Notice the subjective and objective nature of these thoughts. We are subject; they are object. We are people; they are things having only functions. If we choose language that makes general, absolute, objective facts out of our separate experiences, we create the problem of stereotyping. That is how prejudice starts.

Stereotyping

A *stereotype* is an inflexible statement applied to all the members of a group. Stereotypes are generalizations based on one's own limited experience with members of a group. Our stereotypes are, in a sense, shortcuts. For example, suppose you once heard someone say, "All Russians are Communists." If you identified with the speaker—your parent, perhaps, or a favorite teacher—you might accept this opinion and develop a prejudgment of Russians. That prejudgment, of course, would not be true of every Russian.

Do not misunderstand—we need our stereotypes because they let us know how to behave toward and what to expect from strangers. Within gross limits, when we place people into categories that helps us understand them. However, stereotyping someone is also destructive because it denies individual uniqueness. This limits the person and interferes with our ability to see and understand the person. The result is, too often, that our stereotypes become self-fulfilling prophesy. Consider these statements to illustrate the point:

1. "The auditors are messing around where they're not wanted."
2. "The Hispanics want everything given to them."
3. "The blacks are lazy—they never come to work on time."
4. "Women just aren't cut out for business leadership."
5. "Asians never want you to succeed."
6. "Those Cubans stick too much to themselves."
7. "Women are too emotional."
8. "Americans are all egotists."

> Under what circumstances, if any, is it ethical to ignore opportunities to learn and grow? For example, if you don't understand the principles of some sport, and a friend offers to explain, would ignoring that opportunity be ethical? Would ignoring an opportunity to learn a new culture be ethical?

One way to identify your own biases is to think and talk in the subjective case rather than in the objective case. When you change case you can easily hear your own prejudice in your sentences. Some examples are shown in Exhibit 4.4.

A big part of learning to work successfully in a highly diverse group is to understand our normal tendency to confirm our prejudices. When we're in touch with this normal tendency and realize where it comes from we're better able to make alternative choices.

Now, consider how our prejudices work to create self-fulfilling prophesy. When we resist or change or distort new information about a cultural group in order to make it fit what we already believe, we set up unconscious expectations. We may already think, for example, that members of a certain group are lazy, so we look for evidence to confirm this belief. Since we're looking for behavior of a certain kind (and ignoring behaviors of the opposite kind), we find it. When we find it we confirm in our minds what we already believe.

The tendency to confirm what we already believe can work both positively and negatively. Indeed, when it works positively, this well-known phenomenon is called the *halo effect* (see Chapter 5). We *assume* a person is good at something because we know her to be good at other things. We also *assume* a person is bad at something because we think she's bad at others.

Exhibit 4.4 HEARING PREJUDICE WHEN YOU USE THE SUBJECTIVE CASE	
Instead of saying:	Try saying:
Women are too emotional. They just aren't cut out for business leadership.	I think women are too emotional to be effective business leaders. I don't trust their judgment.
Black people are lazy. They waste time on the job and they're rarely on time.	I think black people waste time. I suspect they are lazy. I wish they would conform to my standards of time usage.
Those Asians stay too much to themselves.	I think those Asians should spend more time with Americans. They should interact with us more.
Those Americans are just too individualistic. They're never part of a group.	I think Americans should subordinate themselves to the greater good of the group.

Prejudging people is a normal and natural thing. It can't be avoided. But we do not have to let our prejudices hurt others. We don't have to allow our prejudices to take charge of our behavior. We don't have to reject people because they are different. When we do so we deny ourselves the opportunity to learn from someone else's knowledge and experience.

Two additional problems seem to underlie most of the cross-cultural difficulties in highly diverse organizations: name-calling and inappropriate use of humor.

Name-calling

Every noun is a name. Each name calls to mind something having particular features. The correct names calls to mind the correct image, but an incorrect name creates an incorrect image. No matter how you classify a mixed-breed dog—cur, mutt, pound puppy, mongrel—the image you raise will be far different from the image you raise with the name of an American Kennel Club purebred dog. For example, think of a Golden Laborador Retriever. Saying "mutt" diminishes the dog, while "Golden Lab" builds the dog's image. *Name-calling* is use of a negative or diminishing word to categorize people.

Some names people give to cultural groups are harmful and disrespectful. Everyone knows many such names. Sometimes people use hurtful names out of ignorance. Others know better, but they use such names because doing so helps them feel better about themselves.

Unfortunately, many of us have grown too tolerant of such name-calling. We "let it go" because we "don't want to make a hassle." But when we allow other people to put us down, or to diminish us—or anyone else—in some way, we encourage their behavior. Thus, allowing name-calling to go unnoticed or unchallenged damages ourselves and others in our organizations.

You can verify these claims from your own experience. Make a list of the disrespectful names people use to refer to your personal group identities. For example, if I am a man, "boy" may be disrespectful. If my ancestors were Italian or Japanese, Jewish or Native American, African or Hispanic, you would have no difficulty finding a slurring name to call me. Now, in your mind's eye, go to work. Can you recall any prejudiced behavior? For example, have you ever seen someone glance about to be sure you are alone before he launches into a racist or sexist story? Have you ever heard someone at work use a slurring name to refer to someone at work? Have you ever heard someone say, "Some of my best friends are ———, but . . .?"

Of course you have. What, if anything, can we or should we do when someone else uses such names? To begin, we can all agree never to call each other such names. Beyond that, we can agree to confront name-calling when we hear it. Tell the offending speaker that you don't use such language and you don't want to hear it. If possible, send this message without putting the other person on the defensive or discounting him or her.

To illustrate, a young man in one of the chemical plants near Mobile used a slurring word to refer to African Americans. "Did you see that Nigger acting like he owned the place?" he asked. Without hesitation another member of the group said, "George, please don't use that word in my presence. I find it offensive." Notice how skillfully this rebuke was delivered. The speaker observed the rules of courtesy, and he talked about himself rather than George. He didn't say, "You're a jerk" or "You offend me." He said, "I find it offensive." George apologized.

Be especially careful not to imply anything negative, such as pity or inability to function. Also, avoid insulting euphemisms. Exhibit 4.5 suggests alternatives to some insensitive language you might hear—or be tempted to use.

> Can you think of any situation that would make telling a racist or sexist joke ethical?

Using Humor Inappropriately

Humor can be used appropriately or inappropriately, too. What a wonderful tool it is when it is used right! When we laugh with each other we grow closer. Laughter makes us well. But humor has a cutting edge, too. All the forms of humor can be used to hurt others, to put them down. Consider Exhibit 4.6. You can see from the descriptions that each of the five broad categories of humor can be used both positively, to build someone up, and negatively, to diminish someone. Why is it ever necessary or useful to use humor inappropriately?

We never have to make fun at another person's expense, and we never should. Just don't do it. Don't tell racist, sexist, or ageist jokes. Don't make fun of someone else's culture. Don't tell sex-loaded jokes or stories; they put down both men and women. Don't make fun of someone's ethnicity. A good rule of thumb about choosing language: If you're in doubt about the appropriateness of a word or expression, don't use it. Rather, focus on the person instead of some irrelevant feature of that person.

What can we do when someone else begins to use humor inappropriately? Just as in the case of name-calling, we can begin by agreeing never to do it our-

Exhibit 4.5 INSENSITIVE EXPRESSIONS AND ALTERNATIVES	
Instead of saying:	Try saying:
The deaf person	The person
The woman doctor	The doctor
The black doctor	The doctor
The doctor, an Iranian guy	The doctor
The blind man	The man
The amputee	The person
The mentally retarded child	The child
Ellen is confined to a wheelchair	Ellen uses a wheelchair.
Ellen is burdened with a disfiguring disease	Ellen has acne.
Ellen is a victim of cancer	Ellen has cancer.
Ellen, an exceptional child	Ellen
Ellen is suffering from	Ellen has

Exhibit 4.6 CATEGORIES OF HUMOR[5]	
1. Exaggeration	Overstatement related to persons, places, sizes, the way people feel or act, and personal experiences.
2. Surprise	Making use of unexpected or unusual feelings, events, or facts.
3. Absurdity	Using ideas and other humor materials that are illogical in thinking or in language.
4. Human problems	Situations in which a person appears foolish or is overcome by events. It includes situations where the speaker or the activity of the speaker appears laughable.
5. Playful ridicule	A sympathetic teasing and acceptance of human faults.

selves. Beyond that, we can agree to confront inappropriate humor when we hear it. Tell the offending speaker how you feel—that you don't use such humor and you don't want to hear it. If possible, send this message in a way that doesn't put the other person on the defensive or discount him or her.

Think clearly about how you will handle a situation in which someone else tells racist or sexist stories. Learn how to confront such a person. But also, if you are from a culture that doesn't tease, learn what a friendly insult is and how to deal with it when it's coming your way. In U.S. society, since there exist some rather strict taboos about expressions of affection, some men express their positive feelings for each other by trading insults. Learn the rules of banter and the value of laughing at yourself.

Recall that we use four questions to decide when differences are important:

1. Is it one or is it more than one?
2. Is it true or is it false?
3. Is it good or is it evil?
4. Is it beautiful or is it ugly?

The third and fourth questions, about whether a thing is good or evil, beautiful or ugly, also help us make sense out of our experiences. When we feel uncomfortable in someone else's presence we tend to avoid them or to reject them. Sometimes, though, we are fascinated by the differences at the same time, which is why many people love to travel—to see the world, to enter strange cultures. We watch the Discovery Channel on television, we read *National Geographic,* and we drive to different states and fly to different nations so we can touch and appreciate different cultures.

The questions "good or evil" and "beautiful or ugly" help us to understand that which is new to us and to know what we should do in its presence. But when we prejudge the new in negative ways (bad, ugly) without first learning about it, we run a great risk. The strange and the new may very well seem, without any rational consideration, bad enough and ugly enough that we reject it. If we do this with people from different cultures we categorize them as out-group; perhaps we isolate them, refusing to share ourselves with them. We lose the opportunities they represent. We experience them as somehow threatening, so we fear them and defend ourselves by holding ourselves away from them, or them from us. In-group members say, "They want what we have." Out-group members say, "They want to keep us out. They want to keep it away from us." These sentences suggest an underlying fear of others based upon ignorance. We fear what we do not understand. Rather than prejudge what we do not understand, we can learn to keep an open mind.

. . . . **CULTURAL VALUES**

We use cultural values to filter objective truth. The values of a culture (good, right, beautiful, should and ought) are the bedrock of the culture. *Values* are ideals, customs, institutions, and the like that arouse an emotional response—either positive or negative—in an individual. Cultural values function for a culture's members as individual values function for individuals. All the observable behaviors of a culture spring from its values. Two anthropologists, Kluckhohn and Strodtbeck,[6] have identified five kinds of problems that must be solved by people from all cultures. They argue, moreover, that all societies are aware of all the possible kinds of solutions but that they prefer different orientations to the problems. Thus, in any culture there exists a set of dominant value orientations. What seems appropriate behavior in a culture springs from this set of orientations or, in other words, the value system. The five kinds of problems and the five value orientations are:

1. What is the relationship of individual to others? (*relationship* orientation)
2. What is the temporal focus of human life? (*time* orientation)
3. What is the mode of human activity? (*activity* orientation)
4. What is a person's relation to nature? (*human nature* orientation)
5. What is the character of innate human nature? (*man-to-nature* orientation)

Kluckhohn and Strodtbeck think that all societies share these problems and that one culture can be distinguished from another according to how it arranges these problems—and by the solutions its members think they have, based upon their value orientations.

For example, if a French woman decides to have a baby, she takes on an obligation to society. In contrast, an American woman takes on an obligation to her baby. This cultural difference explains why so many French people think American children are spoiled, unmannered, and undisciplined, and why Americans can't understand the French parent who will repeatedly tell a child to "stop that," yet let the behavior continue. It is a matter of culture. The French woman's obligation to society requires her to behave politely at all times. To discipline the child *in public* would seem harsh. She will wait until she and the child return home. The American's obligation to the baby is to give him every chance to develop his natural abilities. In the end, the French woman is put to the test, but the American child is put to the test. Has the French woman accepted her appropriate role as teacher, and as spokesperson for her culture? Has the American child proven he hasn't wasted his opportunities?

Lifestyle

A culture's lifestyle comes from its values. Even its language norms and nonverbal behaviors come from the culture's value system. So, for example, matters of etiquette and the rules of protocol are values-based. According to Sandra Thiederman,[7] values control at least four things that affect human interaction in the workplace:

1. Values dictate felt needs.
2. Values dictate what is defined as a problem.
3. Values dictate how a problem is solved.
4. Values dictate expectations of behavior.

Exhibit 4.7 displays comparisons of values among the five most commonly occurring ethnic groups in U.S. society. Consider how differences in cultural values between Whites and Asian Americans, for example, might impose themselves upon a conversation between them.

A WASP architect might be very confused and frustrated that his Asian-American supervisor decided to save an ancient tree by changing the design and making a new building smaller.

To get a sense of the importance of your own cultural values in this regard, how does your native country rank on the values listed in Exhibit 4.8?[9] You might wish to place a mark along each continuum. The first continuum, about time, bears, some explanation. In a *monochronic culture* people experience, and do, one thing at a time. So, for example, a monochronic society values one-on-one conversations, exclusive attention from others, precise and carefully drawn schedules. People are willing to stand in line, waiting their turns—at the supermarket, at the post office, at the ticket window, and so on. In a monochronic

Exhibit 4.7 COMPARISON OF PREFERRED VALUES AMONG FIVE ETHNIC GROUPS[8]				
Native Americans	Asian Americans	African Americans	Hispanics	Whites
Harmony with nature and the environment	Harmony with nature and the environment	Harmony with nature and the environment	Harmony with nature and the environment	Mastery over nature and the environment
Present-tense orientation	Past and present temporal orientation	Present-tense orientation	Past and present temporal orientation	Future temporal orientation
Group/collateral relationship orientation	Group/collateral relationship orientation	Group/collateral relationship orientation	Group/collateral relationship orientation	Individual rather than relational
Being-in-becoming	Doing	Being-in-becoming	Being-in-becoming	Doing
People are basically good	People are basically good	People are both good and bad	People are basically good	People are both good and bad

Exhibit 4.8	SOME CULTURAL VALUES CONTINUA						
Time	monochronic						polychronic
Role of women	subservient						independent
Learning style	memorization						inquiry
Style of dress	formal						informal
Body/social distance	close						distant
Business dealing	formal						informal

culture a sales representative might expect a private, closed-door interview with the potential customer as he makes his presentation and sales pitch.

In a polychronic culture things are far less linear and far more dynamic. People carry out more than one transaction at a time, and they are quite comfortable in social moments that would seem awkward to monochronic people. In a polychronic society the sales representative would not expect a private, one-to-one interview with his potential customer. More likely, the office door would remain open, and people would feel comfortable interrupting the conversation. For another example, in a monochronic society, if someone is waiting on you at a department store counter, you expect him or her to complete the transaction before moving to the next customer. In a polychronic society, you, the salesperson behind the counter, and the new arrival at the counter would all consider it rude if the salesperson did not immediately interrupt his or her transaction with you in order to greet and welcome the new arrival.

Personal and social distance preferences can also figure importantly in cross-cultural encounters. For example, a culture that aspires to be classless, as Americans strive to be, tends also to be wide open. In the United States this striving is so strong that we may accept mere proximity as grounds for a relationship. Neighbors whose houses share a *cul de sac,* for example, may feel obligated to be friendly, to know each other's names, their children's names, and so on. And, while there is no guarantee or requirement, certainly, there is no reason why good neighbors should not also become good friends.

In contrast, in much of the world, and especially in most of Europe and in parts of Asia, people tend to be closed. Mere proximity, such as adjacent houses, does not provide grounds for a social relationship. There must be some basis other than proximity for a closer relationship, or it is not likely to develop beyond simple courtesy. Moreover, Europeans and Asians generally take longer in their move toward intimacy than do Americans. Indeed, one Japanese student explained to her public speaking class that Americans are uncomfortably familiar. She explained her discomfort by drawing Exhibit 4.9 on the chalkboard during her speech. "Americans," she said, "think almost all the people they know are friends. Japanese don't have many friends, although we have just as many acquaintances as Americans." Europeans, in general, share this view with Japanese. Self-disclosure is difficult and rare. A Frenchman, for example, will only allow self-disclosure if he believes the other person is a true intimate.[10]

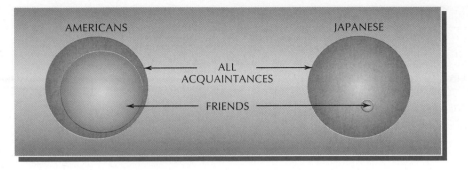

Exhibit 4.9

COMPARISON OF AMERICAN AND JAPANESE FRIENDSHIPS

Communication Style

Exhibit 4.10 compares the communication styles of Native Americans, Asians, African Americans, Hispanics, and the dominant White culture in the United States. In your mind try to explore the impact these differences might make in your conversations at work.

Another example illustrates how communication style differences might affect the workplace. Henry's job is to manage about fifty Hispanic workers, most (but not all) of whom have been in the United States long enough to speak English rather well. Henry doesn't speak Spanish, but he knows that many Spanish and English words sound alike and that many are cognates (that is, they mean

Exhibit 4.10	COMPARISON OF COMMUNICATION STYLES AMONG FIVE ETHNIC GROUPS[11]			
Native Americans	Asian Americans	African Americans	Hispanics	Whites
Speak slowly/ softly	Speak softly	Speak with affect	Speak softly	Speak loud and fast to control listener
Indirect gaze when listening or speaking	Avoid eye contact when listening or speaking to high-status persons	Direct eye contact (prolonged) when speaking, but less when listening	Avoid eye contact when listening or speaking to high-status persons	Greater eye contact when listening than any other group except African Americans
Interject less/ seldom offer encouraging communication		Interrupt (turn taking) when they can		Head nods and other nonverbal markers
Delayed auditory response (silence)	Mild delay	Quickest response of all groups	Mild delay	Quick response
Manner of expression low-key, indirect	Low-key, indirect	Affective, emotional, interpersonal	Low-key, indirect	Objective, task-oriented

almost the same thing in both languages), so he tries to use as many of these words as possible. Examples of such words are *hotel, banco, doctor, complicado, differente,* and *problemo.* Further, Henry is very careful to follow a logical sequence when giving instructions: he tells the workers that he is about to do so, then offers the instructions, then reviews what he told them.

In adapting himself to his employees in these ways Henry is making the right moves. He encourages their use and learning of English, and he boosts workers' confidence in their ability to understand, thus encouraging completion of tasks. And so long as Henry does not diminish anyone by implication with his nonverbal messages or with his tone of voice, his careful attention will be seen as respectful rather than as patronizing.

As we learn more about a new culture our fear of its members gradually fades. Indeed, fear can often become curiosity. As curiosity grows, information increases and anxiety lessons. Thus it makes sense to set a personal goal: Turn your anxiety into a determined effort to learn.

MANAGING DIVERSITY IN THE WORKPLACE

Using Language to Solve the Problem

In the final analysis, the best way to manage cultural diversity in our workplaces is to learn how to use language more wisely and effectively. Basic speech acts such as making requests, agreeing or disagreeing with others, and confirming them or denying their uniqueness all boil down to choices. Language is the fundamental building material of any culture. The greater the diversity of language usage, the greater the cultural diversity. In the United States, people speak as many as 140 languages and dialects other than English.[12] Almost 14 percent of Americans speak a language other than English at home.[13]

Each of us can learn the rules of our own languages, and each of us can learn the rules for communicating with someone whose native language is not our own. Each of us can choose to interpret for others. Each of us can choose to make allowances for others and to remain flexible in doing so. Each of us can choose to give and get feedback and to do that with appropriate frequency. And we must do so or risk some very damaging, wrong-minded thinking. For example, when you hear an accent other than your own, do you make any of these *wrong* assumptions?

1. People with heavy foreign accents are uneducated.
2. People who can't speak much English probably can't understand much English.
3. People who know English grammar and English words can understand English discourse.
4. People who speak with an accent are often rude and demanding.
5. People who use their native language around others who don't understand it are lazy or rude or are trying to exclude others.
6. People with foreign accents who pretend to understand when they don't, are being deceitful.

If you make any of these false assumptions your ethnocentrism may be showing!

From the other person's point of view, working in an English-speaking environment may sometimes seem like a no-win situation. For example, many cultures don't allow direct refusal. Saying no to anyone is taboo in some cultures. In other cultures it's not okay to say no to people in authority. Within some cultures only selected people can say no, while others cannot. "No" can result in very serious loss of face, so some people don't ever say it. Of course, people can communicate disagreement even in these cultures, but they do so very subtly and indirectly. They send these messages in ways that people from outside their cultures may not even notice.

In contrast, some people "won't take no for an answer." Rather, they hear "no" as an invitation to negotiate. To illustrate, one of us watched with amusement during an open registration period at our university. A student with a rather heavy accent—probably from the Middle East—approached an associate dean asking permission to enroll in a closed course. When the associate dean said no, the student began to make arguments in support of his request.

"I just told you no," said the associate dean.

"Yes," said the student, "but I must take that course this term. I am working on a very tight schedule and I need it for graduation."

"No," said the associate dean.

"But this is extremely important. I would be willing to give up my space in another course in order to take this one."

Finally, the associate dean raised his voice and said, "No. No. No. Not now, not this term"—then turned his back on the student in exasperation. That was the student's signal, in his own culture, that the negotiations were over. He was neither offended nor troubled by the exchange, but the associate dean talked about it often over the next few days.

Etiquette, or the rules of courtesy, can create very difficult communication problems in the workplace. To illustrate, some people find it offensive if you show them the bottom of your foot. Some people will be offended if you eat your meal with the wrong (left) hand. Some people think it is polite to stand very close when doing business; others want much more space. Some people feel quite comfortable with touching; others do not want to be touched at all. In some cultures it is not polite to complain, nor to say, "I don't understand." In some face-sensitive cultures (as in the expression "to lose face") these rules are so severe that feedback can only be sent by a third party or by the most subtle of nonverbal messages. In other cultures the very antithesis seems true. Such indirectness is seen as deceitful or, at best, as waste of time. In such cultures people come to the point directly, saying what they mean and often saying it quite bluntly.

Working in a Culturally Diverse Group

So, what can you do? In all the situations we've just described, six general rules will help you to interact more effectively with people who are different:

1. *Learn everything you can about the other person's culture.* Especially, learn the rules of the other culture. Don't take sides or assume that you're right and the other person is wrong. Delay or defer any decisions and judgments until you know more about the other people. Try very hard not to cause the other person to "lose face." In general, the farther east you travel from the United States, the more face-sensitive is the culture. If you are working with people from a face-sensitive culture (for example, Japanese, Chinese, Malaysians) be indirect and abstract. If you are a member of a face-sensitive group, remain as flexible as you can. Learn the rules, then adapt to those rules as much as possible.

2. *Interpret for others.* It may be that your understanding and insight are just what the other person needs to make sense of a new situation. Interpret the situation and the rules for others if you can, and if you need to, seek out such interpretations from others.

3. *Make allowances and remain flexible.* If you can convince yourself that other people are basically well-intended, and that they may not know the rules of your culture, make allowances for them. Try to get specific information about such questions as where, how, which, when? Verify every argument carefully, and be aware of signs that the other person might be uncomfortable. Above all, try to use language that is descriptive and not judgmental. Be scrupulous in giving criticism.

A simple story makes the point. One of us was working with an international student whose credentials and intelligence were never in question. This young woman speaks excellent, nearly flawless English. English is her fourth fluent language—she reads and writes but does not speak a fifth and a sixth and can "make her way" in yet two more. One evening during a party of graduate students and faculty, she misspoke an English expression. She meant to say "spokesperson," but it came out "spokesaperson"—four syllables rather than three. Without thinking, someone in the crowd quoted her. "Yes, someone has to be the spokes-a-person." Both the student and (later, when he understood what he had done) the speaker were embarrassed by this implied criticism. It never had to happen.

4. *When appropriate, get and give feedback.* Feedback is all about correction and control of error. Keep other people informed about what you think and how you feel. Keep yourself informed about what others think and feel. Try to bring your thinking, your feelings, your uncertainties, and your concerns up to the level of talk. But use your feedback skills carefully. Some people in some cultures might find directness offensive; others may never be comfortable bringing such things as feelings and uncertainties out into the open.

5. *Do not fall back on stereotypes.* What you may have learned from observing a particular culture will not apply to everyone in that culture.

6. *Don't assume you already know another culture because you have read a lot about it.* Personal experience—broad personal experience—is usually required before a person can truly "know" a different culture. Whenever you have a chance to interact with people from another culture, do so. Show

interest, ask appropriate questions, travel. To paraphrase St. Augustine, the world is a great book. If you haven't traveled, you have read only one page of that book.

Working in a Dominant Culture Different from Your Own

When you're part of the out-group working in a dominant culture that's different from yours there are also six things you can do to make life simpler.

First, build self-esteem—your own and the other person's. Remind yourself that both you and the other person are okay. Cultural differences do not mean anything except that you are different in certain ways—but think how much you are the same!

Second, try to identify the constructive contributions you can make to the other person and the organization because of your cultural differences.

Third, adjust and adapt yourself as much as you can in the dominant culture. This does not mean giving up your own identity, but it does mean making every effort to identify and adapt to the norms of the new culture when you can.

Fourth, avoid always clustering with your own kind. Try to mix in with members of the new culture when you can. But do refresh yourself occasionally by spending time speaking your own language, with friends from your own culture. Take care to do this in situations that will not threaten your emerging relationships with members of the dominant culture.

Fifth, work with others, from both the dominant and other nondominant groups, to achieve common goals. This means, of course, identifying what those goals are, agreeing upon them, and trying to make progress toward them. It also means trying to help others make progress toward the goals when you can.

Finally, avoid any personal ethnocentrism. Learn as much as you can, interpret for others, make allowances, and give and get feedback often.

SUMMARY . . . .

In summary, we have argued that the U.S. society and U.S. businesses are characterized by enormous diversity. Differences flow from both biology and culture. All this diversity nearly guarantees that at some time we will have a need to communicate with diverse people.

We can learn to identify our own egocentric and ethnocentric tendencies and to compensate for them. We can heighten our awareness of our own cultural uniqueness, identify how those differences are important to us, and ascribe similar feelings of significance and importance to anyone else who is different from us. Especially, we can learn to be sensitive to differences in etiquette, values, traditions, and communication styles and to be flexible in our interactions with others.

We can learn not to prejudge others simply because they are different from us. And we can learn to confront prejudice in our associates' behaviors. Name-calling and inappropriate uses of humor hurt everyone, and they are never necessary or useful.

We can learn the rules of another person's culture. We can work to increase our own flexibility and adaptability, and we can learn to use language without giving offense. Finally, we can learn to give and get feedback often.

And if we learn these things, our lives will change. The workplace will become more accommodating and welcoming. Productivity will increase, and so will the work group's cohesiveness.

12. Thiederman, op. cit., p. 37.
13. United States Census Bureau, data from 1990 census, reported in *The Chronicle of Higher Education* Web site. Figures cover people 5 years old and older who "sometimes or always" speak a language other than English at home.

NOTES ....

1. United Nations Population Division, *World Population Prospects 1990* (United Nations, New York, 1991), pp. 226–233.
2. Daisy Kabagarama, *Breaking the Ice: A Guide to Understanding People from Other Cultures* (Boston, Allyn and Bacon, 1993), p. 10.
3. American Council on Education, "Minority Changes Hold Major Implications for US" (*Higher Education and National Affairs*, 1984), p. 8.
4. Sondra Thiederman, *Bridging Cultural Barriers for Corporate Success: How to Manage the Multicultural Work Force* (New York, Lexington Books, Macmillan, 1991), p. 2.
5. Michael S. Hanna and James W. Gibson, *Public Speaking for Personal Success* (Dubuque, Iowa, Wm. C. Brown Publishers, 1992), p. 209, and adapted from Katharine Hull Kappas, "A Study of Humor in Children's Books," M.A. thesis, University of Chicago, 1965, pp. 53–56. Used by permission.
6. F. R. Kluckhohn and F. L. Strodtbeck, *Variations in Value Orientations* (Evanston, IL, Row, Patterson, & Co., 1961).
7. Thiederman, op cit., p. 82.
8. M. K. Ho, "Cross-cultural Family Counseling," in *Family Therapy with Ethnic Minorities* (Newbury Park, Calif., Sage, 1987), p. 232.
9. After H. Ned Seelye and Alan Seelye-James, *Culture Clash* (Lincolnwood, Ill., NTC Business Books, 1995), p. 38.
10. For a charming and lucid explanation of this cultural difference, see Raymonde Carroll, *Cultural Misunderstandings: The French-American Experience,* trans. Carol Volk (Chicago, University of Chicago Press, 1987), pp. 72–76.
11. After Donald Wing Sue and David Sue, *Counseling the Culturally Different: Theory and Practice* (New York, Wiley, 1990), p. 67.

RECOMMENDED READINGS ....

Raymonde Carroll. *Cultural Misunderstandings: The French-American Experience.* Trans. Carol Volk. Chicago, University of Chicago Press, 1987.

Carley H. Dodd. *Dynamics of Intercultural Communication,* 4th ed. Dubuque, Iowa, Wm. C. Brown Publishers, 1995.

William B. Gudykunst, Lea P. Stewart, and Stella Ting-Toomey, eds. *Communication, Culture, and Organizational Processes.* Beverly Hills, Calif., Sage, 1985.

William B. Gudykunst and Young Yun Kim. *Communicating With Strangers: An Approach to Intercultural Communication.* Reading, Mass., Addison-Wesley, 1984.

H. Ned Seelye and Alan Seelye-James. *Culture Clash.* Lincolnwood, Ill., NTC Business Books, 1995.

Fons Trompenaars. *Riding the Waves of Culture: Understanding Diversity in Global Business.* New York, Irwin, 1994.

DISCUSSION QUESTIONS......................

1. Studies suggest that Japanese children, on average, like school more than children from other nations. Using your own experience as a schoolchild, how would you account for this finding? Thinking of your childhood, what parts of school did you particularly like? What parts did you particularly dislike?
2. Select a copy of a weekly newsmagazine, such as *Time* or *U.S. News and World Report,* and find in it a report on something that occurred in another country. Examine this report to see if U.S.

cultural assumptions have influenced the presentation of the news in any way.

3. Agree with your classmates to watch a natural history show such as *National Geographic Explorer* on television. Does the show suggest or point to the relationship between nature and man?

4. Find an ad in a magazine that relies on images from nature. What do you think the advertiser wants you to believe about the relationship between the product or company and the environment? Why?

5. Interview a student of a culture different from yours concerning his or her attitudes and values as listed in Exhibit 4.7. Come to class prepared to report your findings.

INTERNET ACTIVITY . . . .

1. Open one of these search engines: Infoseek Guide (http://guide.infoseek.com/) or Altavista Search (http://www.altavista.digital.com/).
   Type these key words: *managing diversity*. You will get about 100,000 "hits," but the first ten or so should be very productive. Pretend you are the new manager of a highly diverse division of your organization. You have many ethnic minority people, you have an even distribution of men and women, and some are old and some are young. Spend several minutes looking for answers to this question: "What are the major issues involved in managing diversity?" Compare and contrast your findings from this research with the issues raised in this chapter, and prepare to discuss your findings with your classmates.

PART II
Basic Considerations: Foundations for Communication in Organizations

Who we think we are and who we think others are constitute the most basic considerations in all communication events. Your sense of self, and your self-confidence, control the choices you make to interact with others and how you perceive other people's behavior. They tell you what to listen to and which nonverbal messages to interpret and which to ignore. They inform the interpretations you will make of all that incoming information. And, finally, they control how you act upon and react to the incoming information.

What we experience in every face-to-face communication event, and in most mediated communication encounters, consists of verbal and nonverbal messages. So Part II includes three chapters dealing with these basic considerations. Chapter 5 is about perception and listening. Chapter 6 is about nonverbal communication. They constitute the most basic considerations in interpersonal communication.

Technology is becoming more and more important to organizational life. Not one of us escapes its impact. Understanding technology and using it effectively are two important concerns of Chapter 7.

CHAPTER 5

Perception and Listening

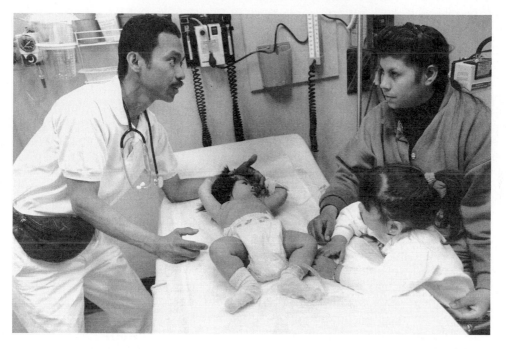

Upon completion of this chapter, you should be able to:

1. Explain how perception is governed by selectivity, subjectivity, and thought processes.
2. Explain how selectivity in perception is both a hindrance and a benefit.
3. Describe how subjectivity may distort perception.
4. Explain how the mind manipulates structure, meaning, and causality to distort perception.
5. State and explain how perceptual sets, implicit personality theory, the leniency effect, and the halo effect influence our ability to perceive another person.
6. Explain the components of the listening process: sensing, attending, understanding, and remembering.
7. Describe potential difficulties that you might encounter with sensing.
8. Cite five difficulties that might be encountered in attending.
9. Cite four factors that might interfere with understanding.
10. Explain what is meant by a forgetting curve.

11. Indicate the importance of working hard at listening.

12. Explain and demonstrate the skill of active listening.

13. Discuss the need to check out inferences while listening.

*I*magine that you are the night manager of a stereo equipment store. The two people who work for you are competent salespeople, but they do not really understand the operation. You worked in sales for a similar retail outlet for two years and recently took this position as night manager. You believe you are doing a good job, but you're not sure exactly what impression your boss has of you. Now a problem has arisen. A new shipment of stereo receivers has come in, and you've been asked to unpack several and price them. These sets look like a model you already stock, which is currently on special for $249, but the new model has several new features and will retail for $450. Just before you go to dinner, you leave a note for Phil, who is waiting on a customer: "Unpack two or three of the new sets and set them on the shelf." You intend to price them on your return and to get them on the sales floor in anticipation of a full-page advertisement in the morning newspaper. You return to find that Phil has not only unpacked the new sets but put them out front and sold two of them at the $249 sale price. This will cost the company about $400.

If you react at all like most people do, your first thought after the initial shock might be, "How could this happen to me?" Next you may wonder, "How will I explain this one to the boss?" When you say, "This went wrong," your supervisor may hear, "I am inept." You hope your boss will not conclude you are inept—this is your first opportunity to manage people, and you want and need his recommendation. This situation presents some perceptual problems. Our discussion of perception and related issues should give you some help in answering these two questions: "How could this happen?" and "How do I explain it to the boss?"

In this chapter we will take a close look at how perception works and what that means to you. Ultimately, the goal is to help you to perceive yourself and others more accurately and to approach phenomena and events in your world with greater confidence and accuracy. Especially, we want you to become more aware of misperceptions that can cause pitfalls in your interactions with others.

Your listening skills will help you to manage perceptual problems. To listen actively and empathically is to get and give feedback, to verify the inferences you are drawing, and to correct and control errors. The greater the skills you have in this area, the fewer perceptual problems you are likely to have.

NATURE OF PERCEPTION

In any communication situation individuals are exposed to a variety of potential messages. The things they see, hear, touch, smell, and taste all have a potential for communicating. Some of these sensations are taken into your body through the senses, registered in the brain, and processed into a meaningful message. Other stimuli are not allowed to register in the brain. To understand how it is that some stimuli register and others do not, you need to understand the nature of the perceptual process.

Perception is governed by three basic factors: selectivity, subjectivity, and structure. *Selectivity* means we make choices when we attend to available stimuli; *subjectivity* refers to the fact that we relate what we perceive to similar experiences we have had; and *structure* means that we impose patterns, meaning, and causality on the stimuli we take in and register in our brain. These three factors do not act independently. Instead they work together in various combinations. Take a minute to study Exhibit 5.1. What kind of person is pictured? Please stop reading and examine the sketch.

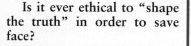

Is it ever ethical to "shape the truth" in order to save face?

You may say the person in the picture is *either* an old woman with a big nose *or* a young woman, looking off to your left, with a very little nose. Or you may see that both are actually in the picture. If you saw the old woman and another person said that this was a picture of a young girl, how would you respond? Would you politely explain how the person is wrong? The point of these questions is that each of us has faith in *our own* perceptions.

Actually, you chose certain stimuli coming from the sketch and structured what you saw in a meaningful way; you applied your experience in perceiving sketches to help you to make sense of the picture. Another person will do the same things you did and may come up with a different conclusion.

The purpose of this illustration and the material that follows is twofold: We hope to help you understand some of the difficulties encountered *any time*

**Exhibit 5.1
THE CHANGING LADY**

SOURCE: E. G. Boring used this figure in his classic experiments conducted during the early 1900s.

you perceive, and we hope you will therefore be motivated to check the accuracy of your perception when checking is practical. Now let's examine perception more closely.

Perception Is Alive

We know that the perception process involves the perceivers in creating the world in which they live. We participate *actively* in perceiving, creating, and experiencing the world. We know also that perception works *inductively*. That is, we generate whole images of things and people based upon the observation of their parts. For example, when you see a man wearing a tie and coat walking toward you, you "know" that the tie goes around his neck and that the coat's fabric wraps around his back. If you "see" two books, as in Exhibit 5.2, one upon the other, you have to generate the whole image out of the parts.

Perception Is Selective

We cannot possibly attend to the vast number of stimuli acting upon us. For example, are you aware that your left foot completely fills your shoe? Is there a clock ticking nearby? When we call your attention to these things, they come to your awareness. Otherwise, you filter them out; you elect not to attend to them.

The problem of selectivity is difficult to overcome. We find sometimes that even a concerted effort may not overcome it. For example, how many F's are in the sentence below? Count them carefully.

FINISHED FILES ARE THE RESULT
OF YEARS OF SCIENTIFIC
STUDY COMBINED WITH THE
EXPERIENCE OF MANY YEARS
OF EXPERTS.*

Exhibit 5.2

---

*Used by permission of the Pacific Institute, Inc., Seattle, Washington, Jack Fitterer, President.

We find that the F's in the longer words are often selected to be counted. The F's in such words as *of* are often unnoticed. This happens despite the fact that people are asked to count carefully. There are seven F's—did you count them all?

This selection process serves a useful purpose. Imagine yourself in a typical entry-level office in a large company. You may be in a big room with several desks and partitions to give privacy. Activity and noise levels will be high. Because you practice selectivity, you are able to filter out the noise when necessary.

Even though selectivity produces great benefits by allowing us to filter out irrelevant noise, it can also create problems. Sometimes we filter out relevant information. Especially susceptible to this filtering process are nonverbal cues, which may have less *intensity* than verbal messages. Intense stimuli are more readily selected. For example, in your position as night manager at the stereo shop, had you underlined the words *new sets* in your note to Phil, he might have realized that he was unpacking a new product. You would have increased the intensity of that stimulus. So the first thing we can say about perception is that *we actively engage in selective perception.*

Perception Is Subjective

A second component of the perceptual process causes us to select some stimuli from our environment and reject others. Our experience is subjective; we choose what we see as important in a particular situation. *Experience is personal.* To illustrate this notion to yourself, try this experiment. After you have listened to a lecture or taken notes at an important meeting, compare what you have on your paper with what others have written. Do you notice differences? If so, you have experienced subjective perception. Your unique past experience will cause you to perceive in a certain way. In the stereo retail store example you may have asked Phil to unpack and put merchandise out on the *front shelves* before. If so, that may be what he thought you said in your note. His past experience led him to conclude that that was what you meant. Moreover, his experience with the merchandise may have led him to conclude that the new sets were merely more of the same sale stock. Perhaps he filtered out the qualities of the new sets that would have allowed him to differentiate.[1] This matter of subjective perception gives rise to the notion that people always have a good reason for doing what they do.

Perception Is Structured

After you perceive, you manipulate the information in your mind to give it structure, meaning, and causality. We all have a tendency to take incomplete bits of information about people and form a whole person—we go beyond what we know. Solomon Asch demonstrated how easily people do this nearly fifty years ago.[2] The subjects in his experiment wrote *paragraphs* about a person, given a list of adjectives that represented opposing traits of the person.

Not only do we need to imagine the "whole person," we need to view as *meaningful* the stimuli we receive. Thus, if your note to Phil had read, "Unpack, shelve," Phil would have added enough of his own ideas to make sense out of it. Later if you had asked him what you said in your note, he might have replied, "You told me to unpack the receivers and put them out front with the rest of the stock." Phil let his experience fill in the gaps.

We also need to connect things by *causality*. People do things for reasons. There are causes for our behavior, and there are causes for the actions of others.[3] When we observe or participate in communication, we take pieces of information we have selected and weigh them against our experience to assign causality. Since our ability to perceive is limited, we are likely to do some filling in and thereby open our understanding to error. We project ourselves into situations and ascribe motives.

For example, suppose you had been meeting a member of the opposite sex in a lounge area after 10 A.M. English class. For the past two days, in a change of routine, this person has passed right on through the area. What is the meaning of that behavior? We believe that you would take it to mean something and might also fill in the details. Thus you would be attributing causality.

Given what we have said about perception—that it is an *active* process, highly *selective,* and utterly *subjective*—we come to the inevitable conclusion that you will never perceive anything as completely as it occurs.

The problem of inaccurate perception is compounded when we try to observe something as complex as a person. If we want to improve our ability to communicate, it makes sense to understand some of the perceptual problems that can arise.

PERCEIVING OTHERS . . . .

Many of the difficulties encountered in person perception can be ascribed to four mental processing errors: (1) perceptual sets, (2) implicit personality theory, (3) the leniency effect, and (4) the halo effect.

Perceptual Sets

Have you ever believed beforehand that you would not like a person you were to meet, and then didn't? Have you ever expected to do poorly on an exam, and then did? Have you ever anticipated an exciting weekend and then experienced it? These outcomes might be attributed to the fact that you expected them. A *perceptual set* is a strong expectation that forces you to perceive something as you had expected it to be. For example, if you go looking for a particular book on your bookshelf, you are likely to find it. You were "set" to find its remembered size and color and, perhaps, its general location.

Perceptual set also applies to your experience of persons and events. For example, if you are subconsciously looking for evidence that another person is angry with you, you are likely to find that evidence in the person's behavior. If you attend a meeting that you believe will be controversial, you are likely to find evidence of the controversy.

Leticia Babcock, a 26-year-old engineer in her first management position, reported such a case of perceptual set to a seminar on organizational communication. Her position placed her in a supervisory role over seven people, one of whom, a man named Will, had been working at the plant in the same job for nearly twenty years. She was, herself, a second-generation employee at the plant; her father had worked there. Her dad and Will had known each other since she was a little girl, so Leticia had some misgivings about being Will's supervisor.

Because a change in engineering design had changed the performance requirements on Will's job, it became Leticia's responsibility to teach Will a new procedure. When she approached Will, she "picked up on" what she reported as "his hesitance and reluctance." "I thought Will was mad because we'd changed his job, and I was sure he was going to be my first problem." But things worked out, and she later had an opportunity to report her feelings to Will in a social context. "Heck, Lettie," said Will. "I wasn't mad or anything. I was just thinking about how fine it is that I've known my new boss since she was a little girl."

> We know it's possible for leaders to "provide set" as a means of controlling other people's perceptions. Are there any ethical implications attached to this fact? Explain.

You can see that perceptual set can create difficulties. Preconceived expectations may be positive or negative, and either may be incorrect. For example, a student who entered a company in Dallas shortly after graduating reported that her boss believed that all entry-level people were only marginally competent. This perceptual set caused the boss to focus on difficulties and to ignore successes. The boss probably believed his perceptions were accurate, but his orientation caused the new graduate considerable discomfort during her probationary period.

The principle behind this kind of perceptual distortion is that when people expect to observe something, they are apt to pick it out of whatever they observe, ignoring and discounting contradictory information. Perhaps entry-level employees *are* somewhat incompetent in comparison with more experienced people. But they gain experience and skill with each passing day on the job. And surely they know something—otherwise, why would anyone want to hire them? The boss was treating competence as though it were *static*, when it ought to be seen as a *dynamic*.[4]

Think for a moment about someone you met recently. Everybody has the potential for both friendly and unfriendly, positive and negative behaviors. If you *focused* on one or the other, you were apt to allow it to register more strongly on your consciousness; you may have come to see what you expected to see.

A department chairman reported his first meeting with the new head of another department—someone who had been "brought in from outside."

> I thought the guy was arrogant and aloof. He didn't have much to say. He didn't do any small talk. He stayed in his office, and he rarely would even go out with the gang to have lunch. So, of course, I didn't like him.

> Later, after I got to know him, I found out that Zack is shy. But more than that, he was new on his job, and he wanted to make a good impression. So he was being careful. Also, he's a gentle guy, and he wanted to be sure that he didn't offend anyone.

Implicit Personality Theory

Now imagine yourself again as the new night manager at the stereo shop, looking over performance evaluations of the employees. You come to one for Marty that describes her as experienced, informed, and skilled. Try to imagine her if you can.

If you have an image in your head, see if you can fill in these blanks about Marty. She is also _____, _____, and _____.

If you could fill in these blanks, did you use any words like unfriendly, meek, hesitant, or passive? Our guess is that you did not. *Implicit personality theory* is an idea about the way we think of people as possessing traits and skills that fit together. It suggests that we see some traits as fitting together and others as not. To the extent that we ignore or discount those traits of an individual that do not seem to fit, we distort our perception of that person.

Of course, this phenomenon may not be a problem. There is no harm in experiencing Marty positively until her behavior shows you otherwise. But there can be problems. For example, we all know people who are competent at doing tasks but incompetent at interpersonal communication.

Our point is that, in the process of perceiving, we actively construct schema of reality. That is, we create meaning and add to it what comes to us from the world through our senses. The world inside ourselves is not a copy of the world outside ourselves.[5] Be aware of this tendency as you evaluate people. If you understand that there is a tendency to distort reality—either positively or negatively—you may be able to guard against it.

Leniency Effect

The *leniency effect* is a perceptual difficulty that sometimes serves a useful purpose in our efforts to meet new people. It occurs when we attach importance or significance to traits we think of as positive and too little significance or importance to traits that we think of as negative.[6] Can you remember when you met somebody for the first time? We assume that the person sent messages about both positive and negative characteristics for you to perceive. Did the person make a positive or negative impression on you? If you answer somewhat positive or quite positive, you *may* be experiencing the leniency effect. Research has disclosed that this tendency is so strong in a few folks that they perceive another person positively in the face of almost totally negative and damaging information.[7]

The fact that we have the tendency to perceptual leniency is not always a problem. When we perceive a person for the first time, we really do have many facts with which to form an impression. A tendency to emphasize the positive increases the likelihood that we will be open to a second encounter and more data.

In other situations, such as those in which we are evaluating another's performance, the leniency effect may be damaging. We are not suggesting that you overemphasize the negative, but, to give a fair appraisal of a person's performance, you must at least be aware that the leniency effect is common.

Halo Effect

The *halo effect* occurs when we observe a person being competent in one area and assume that the person is competent in other areas. For example, as night manager in the stereo shop, you might have a talk with the sales representative from a record company. This sales representative might talk at length about the technical merits of the new stereophonic tuner soon to appear. Would you assume because he knows the record business that he understands electronics? He may or may not, but if you make this assumption without checking it out, you could be a victim of the perceptual error called the "halo effect."

In truth, you know that a good scholar is not necessarily a good teacher. Some very fine thinkers lack a sense of performance in the classroom. Similarly, just because a person is a fine first-line supervisor, that does not guarantee that the person will be a skillful manager. Administrative detail does not require the same talents as personal leadership.

. . . . **PERCEPTUAL PROBLEMS IN WORK SETTINGS**

Perhaps the best-known study of perceptual problems in the workplace was carried out by Rensis Likert.[8] He reported substantial disagreement between subordinates' and supervisors' perceptions and understanding of work problems. Supervisors appear to have considerably more confidence in their view than subordinates have in the supervisor's view. Likert reported that 34 percent of the employees surveyed said their supervisor understood their problems well, but 95 percent of the supervisors said they understood the problems of their employees well. Likert asked this same question of these supervisors and their immediate superiors: 51 percent of the supervisors said that their immediate supervisor knew their problems well, while 90 percent of the immediate supervisors (people at the general foreman level) believed they understood the problems of their subordinates (the foremen who worked for them) well.

Clearly, perceptual difficulties cause problems in organizations. In fact, research demonstrates that they are particularly troublesome when the perceptual disagreement is over role. Differences here can affect both production and employee morale. If an employee is not clear about what he or she is expected to do, that person's level of production falls. The production of others who depend on that person also falls. This decreased production is likely to lead to a low performance appraisal score and consequently low morale. The employee may even feel betrayed when he or she eventually becomes aware of the expectations of the supervisor. The fact that perceptual ambiguity leads to this sort of problem is well-documented in the research literature. Research by W. Clay Hamner and Henry L. Tosi, John M. Ivancevich and James H. Donnelly, and D. W. Organ and C. N. Green[9] suggests that perceptual ambiguity between supervisors and subordinates with respect to role can lead to anxiety, dissatisfaction, and lack of interest in the job.

Effective perception is essential to effective listening. In fact, the perceptual process forms the first two steps in the listening process—sensing and attending. Perception is the mechanism through which we secure the data we use in the listening process. But there is more to listening than perception. Let's turn to an examination of the listening process and listening skills.

THE LISTENING PROCESS . . . .

Don, a student who went to work for a large retail sales company, reported an experience he had that pointed out the importance of good listening. Don's boss, Kathy, invited him to go to lunch one Thursday afternoon. Don accepted. He knew that lunch with Kathy, without the usual lunch group, would be a good opportunity to get to know her better. Kathy had been working closely with Don on material for the annual report, and they had just polished the final draft. Don figured that this was sort of a celebration of their hard work. Don also knew that he had been working hard since he joined the company a year ago and figured the invitation might also be a sign of recognition.

Kathy knew that Don was ready for promotion, and she was, in fact, grooming him for promotion. Kathy wanted to know Don a little better before she made her recommendation. She thought, too, that this luncheon would be a good opportunity to see how he might react to the idea of moving up.

After they had finished lunch, Kathy leaned forward slightly and said to Don, "The company may promote you soon, I think. Over the past several months, I've been trying to prepare you to handle day-to-day management problems. What do you think about a new assignment?"

Don just sat there for a minute. Well, actually it just seemed like a minute. It was only a few seconds.

Kathy continued. "I'm guessing that you're pleased and perhaps caught a little bit by surprise at this idea of promotion. My first promotion caught me a bit by surprise, too. I'm going to need an assistant since Phyllis is to be transferred."

Don admitted that he was both surprised and pleased that she had such confidence in him. He was about to say more, but it was clear that Kathy had more to say, so he just paused to listen.

Kathy moved on to talk about the annual report. "I'm really glad that we got the annual report out. It's the best work on this report that I've seen in years!" The single most difficult problem in doing that report each year is coordination. You know, each of the parts has to follow a format. After I've met with everyone and carefully explained how each part must be, I always discover that someone didn't listen. Then the report is delayed while that person goes back and rewrites. For me the most bothersome day-to-day problem in managing people is with those who don't listen. Some people cannot be promoted because they have such chronic listening problems."

Kathy paused for a moment, so Don empathized with her concern about the listening problem. "That really is a problem. Maybe some of our people need to learn how to improve their listening. Do you think some training would help?"

Kathy liked the idea. In fact, she put Don in charge of talking to the training department about a suitable training program in listening.

Kathy is right in her understanding of the importance of listening. Poor listening creates problems; good listening contributes to productivity. Tom Peters, business consultant and coauthor of *In Search of Excellence* and *A Passion for Excellence,* is quoted as offering this advice: Find out what the customers really care about, and then act. Listening—that's the key. Listening is an important issue for all workers, from supervisors down to and including entry-level personnel.[10]

These are some of the considerations that led us to include material on listening behavior in this book. In this section we introduce the major components of the listening process and discuss the problems that can arise with each of these components. We also offer some recommendations on how to develop listening skills.

> One of the ethical principles underlying this book is "do no harm." Could failure to develop one's listening skills be considered unethical? Under what circumstances can *omission* create ethical issues in the same fashion that *commission* sometimes does?

Components of the Listening Process

Had Kathy gone on to explain her frustration with how people listened she would have told how she had to explain three times to one employee how to display overtime data. Examine the model of the listening process in Exhibit 5.3. Where in the listening process do you suppose the breakdown occurred? Of course, we cannot tell without being able to examine the situation firsthand, but we believe the model should be helpful in deciding where the breakdown could have occurred.

The model divides listening into four component parts—sensing, attending, understanding, and remembering. Let's take a closer look at each of these processes before considering associated problems, including noise.

Sensing

Sensing is the act of receiving stimuli through the five senses. It is not necessarily a conscious act. For example, any sound wave that has sufficient intensity

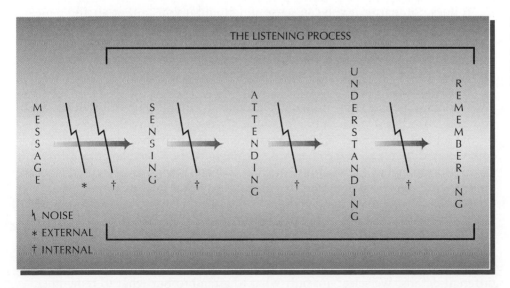

Exhibit 5.3
COMPONENTS OF THE LISTENING PROCESS

to reach the ear may be heard. You may ask, then, why you are unable to hear the ticking of the clock when you are working. We would answer that, in fact, you can hear the clock. The sound had sufficient intensity to reach your ear but is blocked by the second major element of the listening process: attending.

Attending

You may not be selecting the particular stimuli—the tick of the clock—to be part of your consciousness. We refer to this as not *attending*. You recall that we introduced the idea of selective perception earlier in this Chapter (page 100). Put that material into the context of listening. Theoretically, you are able to sense and attend to thousands of stimuli at a time, but you cannot attend to all of them. Therefore, you select the ones that are important to you and ignore the others.

All of us have failed to notice footsteps as someone entered the room because we were paying attention to a book we were reading. We filtered them out. But suppose the footsteps were those of your boss, who had needed to talk with you; you would have filtered out an important sound. Filtering of this kind can also happen when you are listening to someone. You may filter out important pieces of information.

Understanding

The third component is *understanding*, which can be defined as interpreting and evaluating what comes in through the senses. This step is so important that one writer has based his whole model of the listening process on it. Blaine Goss presents an information-processing model of listening in which he suggests: signal processing (understanding the segments and structures of what we hear) → literal processing (understanding the meaning and simple implications of what we hear) → reflective processing (understanding a deeper meaning through critical analysis and coming to appreciate what we hear).[11] Thus understanding is an important part of the listening process.

It does not matter if you can sense and attend if you cannot attribute meaning. When you understand messages, you pick up meanings similar to those intended by the person speaking. You may understand even *more* than other people intend to communicate by observing nonverbal clues (see Chapter 6).

Remembering

For many people, remembering is the most difficult part of listening. Have you ever introduced yourself to a person, only to forget the other person's name by the end of the conversation? Most of us have had this experience. If it is sometimes difficult to remember a name, imagine how much more difficult it can be to remember detailed instructions. *Remembering* suggests that you are able to store information in your brain and recall that information later.

Remembering, like attending, is selective. To illustrate this idea to yourself, talk with someone about a movie you both have seen. You may discover that you have remembered the things most interesting and useful to you and have forgotten others. Your friend will have remembered what he or she found interesting. Comparing notes, you'll probably discover that you have remembered different details. We select not only what to attend to but what to remember.

Any or all of the four components—sensing, attending, understanding, and re-membering—can dysfunction. We will discuss the problems that can arise and then introduce techniques to overcome them. We organize the material in this way because the components are closely related to one another, and sometimes problems overlap. The final section will offer techniques to help overcome these blocks to good listening.

Larry R. Smeltzer and Kittie W. Watson found that listening habits can be improved both through understanding and an incentive to change. You can help yourself become a better listener if, as you read about these problems associated with listening, you think about times you have experienced them.[12]

Problems with Sensing

For our purposes we will say that there are two problems related to sensing: physical impairment and external noise. Obviously, not being able to sense ade-quately makes it hard for the listener. Perhaps a competent professional can aid the impairment. Then, you can train yourself to take maximum advantage of your sensing ability.

The second problem is *noise,* or interference. Everyone who has ever at-tended movies can recall the experience of someone nearby talking or joking loudly. The talk made it more difficult to hear accurately. Talking is not necessar-ily the only kind of noise; the sounds of people passing by or of word processing equipment are other examples. Other factors that can interfere with your atten-tion like inadequate light that may impair your sight can also be "noise."

For some people, impairment of senses and unwanted noise can affect the listening process at the same time. For example, a person with normal stereo-phonic hearing can select which ear to use to attend. If there is a source of un-wanted noise between that person and another, the listener can "tune out" the side with the noise and focus on the other side. People with hearing in only one ear have to take in all sound-based information through that ear. They have no choice about how to use their hearing apparatus. A television set between a lis-tener with one good ear and the source of speech can directly affect communi-cation.

Problems with Attending

Attending difficulties are more numerous than sensing problems. Five aspects of attention inhibit listening.

Selective Perception and Attending

We have said that people perceive and attend *selectively.* On the basis of our past experience we select what in the present situation is worth perceiving and attending. If the situation is similar enough, then we may select appropriately.

But no two situations are identical. Because things are always changing, we nearly always need to adjust our sense of what to attend to. For some people, an awareness of the fact that things always change is enough to cause them to sift carefully.

Poor Attending Habits

Ralph Nichols and L. A. Stevens cite three poor attending habits.[13] Some people *fake attention.* They sit as if they were listening carefully but are in fact thinking about something else. The habit of taking "mental vacations" makes it harder for them to listen.

A second poor attending habit is to *avoid difficult listening.* People who do not expose themselves to difficult listening situations do not gain practice in attending to difficult material.

The third is to *listen only for facts.* This kind of attending may cause the listener to miss important cues. Tone of voice and variations in the rate of speaking are two factors that often reveal a great deal. People who have trained themselves to listen for and jot down the facts may miss these nonverbal cues and thereby misunderstand the message.

Listener Attitudes and Needs That Interfere

Attitude will have a significant impact on how people attend to a message. For example, if you did not like your boss or did not trust his or her judgment, then you might not listen carefully. If you were *forced* by your company to attend a seminar, your attitude might get in the way of listening. Status can be a related problem. If you think it is inappropriate for your workers to offer you advice, you may pay less attention when they do. This same attitude-perception mechanism works when a person tries to listen to a coworker who has a different perspective on how to do a job. This person avoids listening to the other's view.

A strong need to hear a message in a particular way may cause people to attend to certain parts of the message and ignore others. People attend to stimuli that satisfy their needs.[14] We often hear what we *think* was said because our needs and values cause us to ignore disconfirming stimuli.[15]

Students frequently tell us of employment interviewing experiences. One student reported the following: "I experienced a distortion problem while interviewing for a job at a national convention. I thought the position was just the job for me. Later I talked to a friend who had interviewed for the same position, who said, 'I thought you were not interested in any job that promised a *temporary contract.*' I was told the position was temporary, but had allowed the attractiveness of the job description to capture my attention!"

Low Intensity of the Message

Some messages may be presented in such an unenthusiastic way that they are difficult to attend. You may have discovered how difficult it is to listen when an instructor drones on. You cannot increase the intensity of that lecture, but you are not doomed to listening failure. Nichols suggests that deciding early in the listening task that you have some use for the material will help you attend.[16] Active listening, discussed in the last section of this chapter, will also help.

Too Long a Message

Donald Campbell found that the longer the message, the greater a person's information loss.[17] People have a natural tendency to shorten, simplify, and eliminate detail when listening to a long message. In addition, people tend to drop the middle of a long message. It is easy to remember the first and last parts of the message but difficult to remember the middle.

Problems with Understanding

Understanding and agreement are not the same. Some people say they don't understand when actually they understand fully, but don't agree. This is confusing to the speaker. We define *understanding* to mean interpreting and evaluating words in the way the speaker intended them to be interpreted and evaluated. Problems of understanding can be attributed to four factors, as follows.

Different Fields of Experience

We know what words mean from our experience with them. The total of your remembered past experiences comprises your field of experience. Your experience with the words we are writing here will be relevant to your interpretation. For example, if you have read another author's definition and discussion of the concept "field of experience" and it differs from this one, you may be having trouble understanding this passage. Similarly, the degree of difference between your own and your boss's experiences may one day be reflected in the degree of understanding (or misunderstanding) you share.

Inability to Empathize

Because of different fields of experience, on almost every issue people are likely to hold different values. Your ability to empathize with another person is closely related to the fit of your value system and that of the other person. Sometimes our differing orientations make it difficult to see each other's way of looking at a situation. Sometimes it is hard even to imagine another way of viewing a particular situation. A frequent result is that people spend time mentally criticizing another person's view, constructing arguments to refute his or her ideas, and *not listening*.

Empathizing is an activity in which participants attempt to put themselves in another's mental and situational framework. One person tries to look at the situation from the other's viewpoint. By its nature, empathy requires an active mental commitment to what is being said. A greater commitment results in greater understanding.

Poor Use of Feedback

Almost everyone has stopped at a service station to ask for directions. What can we do if we want to be sure we understand the directions? One technique is to repeat the directions back to the person and ask for correction of errors. Why don't we do this when we receive other information? Perhaps the answer is that feedback takes time and we believe we already understand.

Mental Sets

The fourth problem related to understanding is alluded to by such terms as "close-minded," "overly critical," and "polarized viewpoint." Mental sets such as these cause listeners to assume that they know what is "right" and prevent them from understanding another's view. We are certainly not saying that you should not have opinions. You need to believe, however, that others also have something to say. Unless you can put your opinion aside, you may not hear theirs.

Problems with Remembering

How long will you remember what you have heard? Tony Buzan has suggested that you will forget 80 percent of the details in just twenty-four hours.[18] The curve that he plotted is based on data he collected from students who had memorized word lists (Exhibit 5.4). Buzan discovered that we are not 100 percent efficient at remembering even when we have just completed the task. Notice there is a rise just after the task is completed because the mind keeps working and making connections. Our remembering is more efficient for a short period after we've completed a learning task than it is *during* the task. Researchers have been aware of this forgetting curve for over a century. Herman Ebbinghaus did basic research with forgetting in 1885.[19] Compare the Ebbinghaus curve with Buzan's. *Notice that the negative acceleration of the retention curve seems to be the general rule.* The important phenomenon is that both researchers reported the relatively rapid drop we experience in remembering.

The next section explores what we can do to overcome these various sensing, attending, understanding, and remembering difficulties.

**Exhibit 5.4
FORGETTING
CURVES**

SOURCE: Adapted from *Use Both Sides of Your Brain* by Tony Buzan. Copyright © 1983 by Tony Buzan. (New York, Dutton, 1976).

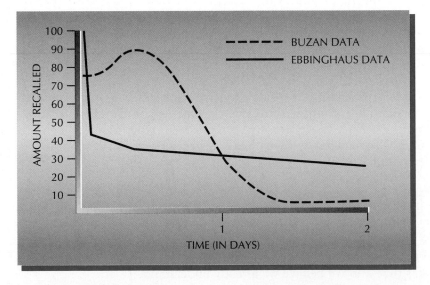

Recall the conversation between Kathy and Don at the restaurant. Don wisely suggested training in listening as one solution to Kathy's problem. Listening is a communication skill just as talking is, and it can be improved by learning and practicing. Some writers present long lists of dos and don'ts about effective listening, but we choose not to do so. We believe you are more likely to improve your listening if you learn a few techniques. Here are five suggestions.

Listening Requires Effort

Becoming a better listener requires a determination to make the effort to understand and remember the speaker's message. You should make an effort to get the main points and the information you need from the speaker's message.

For example, suppose you are working at your desk when the secretary brings in a memo that she tells you is "important." Working hard at listening could mean, in this case, overcoming your resistance to discovering why the secretary said the memo was important. You might be in the middle of trying to solve some problems for your unit. You might have a prior experience similar to this one—the secretary has thought things were important but you didn't think so. Perhaps the important part of the memo—that is, what the secretary thought made it important—is not self-evident; the importance might lie in what you are supposed to do with it. All these considerations could be called noise, the noise you must be able to overcome. So discipline and hard work are essential to good listening.

Take another example. A message seems to you to be routine information. You tune in, and then tune out, assuming you have received the message. But this time the boss has changed a procedure. Wouldn't you be embarrassed to explain you just did not make an effort to listen? What might the boss assume about your competence? Wouldn't the boss be a bit miffed?

Paraphrase the Content

Two areas of difficulty in the listening process, as we saw in the last section, are attending and understanding. The technique of paraphrasing will do double duty: it will help you to attend more carefully and help you to know if you understand. When *paraphrasing the content,* a technique also called *active listening,* you repeat back to the speaker what you believe the person said. Thus you are forced to concentrate on what is being said. Paraphrasing is not parroting but putting what you have heard into your own words. When you do this, the speaker hears your interpretation of what was said and can correct your understanding; by paraphrasing, you'll know if you understand. You can continue if you do; you can be corrected if you don't.

You may think that paraphrasing everything the other person says would drive anybody mad. You are right. Paraphrasing is a technique to be used when the information being given is particularly important to you or the organization, is complex or involves several steps, and involves a problem and the person has come to you for help. You must also have the time to exert the needed effort. Routine talk and information sharing do not usually require this special attention. If you learn to use it properly, paraphrasing is a powerful listening technique.

You may also argue that paraphrasing seems artificial. We think that the artificial sound of the talk will disappear if you practice its use. One reason paraphrasing sounds this way is that people use the same words to lead into active listening every time. They may say something like, "What I hear you saying is. . . ." This is a perfectly good lead-in, but if overused it causes the conversation to sound artificial. Learn a variety of ways of saying, "I want to feed back what you've said."

There are major benefits to active listening. We feel good about ourselves when we find that someone is interested in what we say. We believe that the other person cares about us because he or she has taken time to listen. We feel more confident that that person will be able to do the task. We assume that the listener is a person of good will and understands the task. We have more confidence in his or her willingness to do the task. All these things strengthen our relationship.

Check Out Your Inferences

Listening is more than just hearing what was said directly because it is often difficult for people to say directly what they are feeling, needing, or wanting. Thus a useful listening technique is to verify your inferences when you are unsure of the speaker's meaning. A piece of research reveals that effective managers ask questions when listening to subordinates. In a half-hour conversation, some ask literally hundreds.[20] This skill requires a high degree of selectivity in responding to the other person's talk. Inferences about negative feelings, for example, ought to be carefully weighed before responding. In this regard, plan and practice saying, "What I'm *guessing* you mean [feel, need, or want] is. . . ." Otherwise, the usefulness of the check-out technique will be limited. Incidentally, many of the opportunities you will have to check out your inferences are under circumstances in which there are relatively few negatives. People generally spend their working days in situations where relationships are either positive or neutral. If the situation becomes negatively loaded, the check-out technique serves a double purpose by not only allowing better understanding but also slowing down the talk, giving participants time to think.

Suppose your boss says, "Things are really getting busy. How is your work load now? It seems as though I don't have enough hours to get everything done." How might you respond? What could you check out? You could say, "It sounds like you are experiencing overload, Stan. Would you like me to help in some way?" You could also ignore the possibility that the boss wants more than to let you know how busy he is, but we think it is better to check out the implied message.

Remember that it is very hard for many people to communicate about their feelings associated with the content of their talk. When an underlying feeling is clearly evident, it is probably better to respond to it. Carl Rogers suggests that responding to the obvious feeling facilitates the expression of related feelings and helps both the *listener and the speaker* understand the surrounding feelings and assumptions, needs, or other thoughts.[21]

We cannot tell you with certainty when it would be appropriate to respond to the feelings. You must consider the context. It is often appropriate if a person comes to you for help or when you are carrying out performance appraisal interviews. We will say more about performance appraisal and counseling in Chapter 10.

Empathize with the Speaker

A most useful listening technique is *empathizing*. This allows you to understand another's frame of reference. Empathic listening involves suspending evaluation. When a listener imposes a frame of reference on another person, there exists a tendency to evaluate. Learning to withhold evaluation is a necessary discipline for empathic listeners. Evaluative listening is a deliberative activity and therefore different from empathic listening. Charles Kelly drew this distinction clearly in his comprehensive research on listening:

> The difference between empathic listening and deliberative [evaluative] listening is primarily motivational. Both listeners seek the same objective: accurate understanding of communication from another. . . . The empathic listener lets his understanding of the speaker determine his modes of evaluation, which are automatic; the deliberative listener's understanding of the speaker is filtered through his predetermined modes of selective listening, and he actually spends less time as a communication receiver. The empathic listener is more apt to be a consistent listener, and is less prone to his own or other distractions.[22]

The deliberative listener pursues an evaluative orientation from the start. In contrast, the empathic listener tries to withhold evaluation long enough to understand the other's view.

A person who works for an advertising firm has a favorite story he is willing to tell close friends, although he is a bit embarrassed by it now. It illustrates the four skills we have discussed in the past few pages. Near the end of the first year with the company, José noticed several events that caused him sleepless nights. He noticed that his name had been left out of the latest departmental and company telephone directory. Also, Sally, his boss, had scribbled a note to alert him to expect a move to a "temporary office down the hall." He also noticed that Sally had seemed irritable whenever he had had occasion to talk to her. José's sleepless nights were spent trying to figure out what all this might mean. Was he about to be transferred? Was he goofing up enough to be fired? He was worried. Finally he screwed up his courage and approached Sally.

"Can I see you for a moment? I need to talk."

Sally had noticed that José's productivity had dropped some recently and was concerned. She accepted his offer to talk.

José continued. "You know that I want to do well and that I try to do the work I'm assigned. I wonder what you think about how I'm doing."

Sally noticed that José's expression and voice signaled that he was perhaps a bit anxious and concerned. She decided that she ought to work hard at listening, use active listening, check out his feelings, and understand his point of view—the four listening skills we presented above.

"I understand that you want to do a good job and that you want me to know you're a hard worker," Sally said. "You look a little anxious about this. Could you tell me how you're feeling right now?"

José explained. "I haven't really had a great deal of feedback lately and I want to do well."

"So you haven't heard enough about how you're doing. I want all the people who work for me to know how they're doing." Sally knit her brow as she traveled back through time. "I remember how I felt when I was in my first job. It's important to know what the boss thinks. Can you tell me more about the problem?"

"I think I can. Mostly, I feel anxious, worried. This is my first real job."

Sally carried the questioning further. "Is there anything that I did that led you to feel so anxious and worried?"

"Well, this might seem a bit silly," José explained, "but you told me that I was going to be moved to the small office down the hall. And then my name didn't even appear in the company or the departmental telephone book. And then it seemed as if you might be angry with me—at least it seemed like you came around less to see how I was doing."

Sally checked out what she thought she heard. "I want to be sure I understand you. You were concerned about the upcoming move to the office down the hall. You noticed that your name was omitted from the telephone directory. You also noticed that I didn't seem to come around as much as I used to do to check on how you were doing. You thought that this might have something to do with how well you were doing your job?"

José confirmed Sally's inference.

"I see how you might have drawn that conclusion," Sally continued. "I also see how you'd feel anxious and worried. You're doing fine. Remember that I agreed with your assessment of your work when we did our six-month performance review. I can explain each of these things that bothered you. Let me do that now."

Sally used good listening skills. She worked hard at listening. She used active listening. She checked out her inferences and fed back the feelings as well as the content. She empathized with José by trying to get into his way of looking at the situation. In addition to the four components of the listening process listed earlier, the fifth suggestion, remembering what was said, helped Sally and José have a successful communication.

Work on Remembering

It is possible to prevent the *sharp* drop in the amount of content remembered after an exchange, but not to prevent some drop. Three techniques aid memory: (1) organization, (2) repetition, and (3) association.[23]

In his useful book, *Use Both Sides of Your Brain,* Tony Buzan suggests ways to intervene in the forgetting process. Study his graph of the forgetting curve pictured in Exhibit 5.5. He suggests that you take notes while listening, if possible. If it is not, then make some notes within about ten minutes after listening. Afterward, reorganize the notes and add detail. Do this within about ten minutes after having listened. Buzan suggests both a review (repetition) and an organizing session. This may be enough for most listening.

If the content of your listening is something you will need to remember over an extended period of time, you may want to practice recalling ideas. Practice sessions should be different from the first review session. Write all that you can remember. Compare your writing with your own notes. Then relearn what you have forgotten. Space these practice sessions, as the figure suggests, at twenty-four hours, one week, one month, six months, and so on (if necessary). This kind of practice permits interruption of the forgetting curve.

We also suggest you rely on note taking for recollection of details and on association to remember the broad concepts. Some general principles of note taking seem to apply:

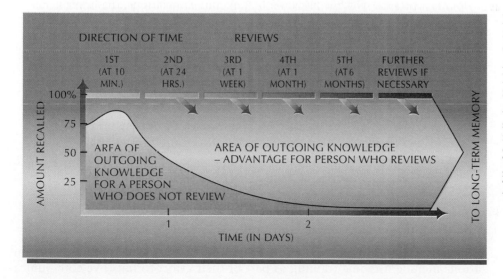

Exhibit 5.5 SPACING ORGANIZING AND PRACTICE SESSIONS TO AID MEMORY

SOURCE: Adapted from *Use Both Sides of Your Brain* by Tony Buzan. Copyright © 1983 by Tony Buzan. (New York, Dutton, 1976).

1. *Discover the speaker's organizational pattern if there is one.*
2. *Keep precise notes.* Note taking can get in the way of listening. Use either key words or key phrases. Later, fill in enough detail to be sure of complete information recall.
3. *Develop a personal shorthand for common words and terms.* Perhaps you have begun to study logic and have become aware of a repeating pattern called a "categorical syllogism." The pattern includes a general statement (All men are mortal), a particular statement (Mike is a man), and a necessary conclusion derived from the two statements (Therefore, Mike is mortal.) You may also have discovered that the symbol for "therefore" in geometric proofs is a triangle of dots ($\therefore$). This is a useful mathematical shorthand that can be used as a very convenient personal shorthand. Thus, the categorical syllogism stated above can be noted:

   Men die.

   M = Man.

   $\therefore$ M will die.

4. *Review and rewrite your notes within about ten minutes after you complete the listening activity.* Buzan contends that this takes advantage of the peak of remembering. The mind continues to make associations and linkages for a short period after you complete the listening task.[24]

Some very important advantages follow from the practice of note taking, note reorganizing, and review. Reviewing things you wish to remember aids your memory by establishing stored material that can be used for associations and linkages. Buzan succinctly presents this idea:

> Failure to review is . . . bad for general memory [general knowledge]. If each new piece of information is neglected, it will not remain at a conscious level, and will not be available to form new memory connections. As memory is a process which is based on linking and associations, the fewer items there are in the recall store, the less the possibility for new items to be registered and connected.

> On the opposite side of this coin, the advantages for the person who *does* review are enormous. The more he maintains his current body of knowledge, the more he will be able to absorb and handle. When he studies, the expanding amount of knowledge at his command will enable him to digest new knowledge far more easily, each new piece of information being absorbed in the context of his existing store of relevant information.[25]

Try these techniques. They help *improve* memory, and they will also help you to begin forming habits that will pay off.

A Parting Plea

We want to make a plea for working at improving your listening. Many organizations include listening training as part of their effort to improve communication. American Telephone and Telegraph, 3M, General Electric, and Dun and Bradstreet are all organizations that understand the need for listening training.[26] Other organizations spend thousands on training, yet do not provide anything on listening.[27] We encourage you to take the suggestions offered here and make it a personal goal to improve your listening.

SUMMARY ....

We hope that you now have a healthy skepticism about your ability to perceive events accurately. It is normal behavior to perceive selectively and to be subjective as you bring your experience to bear on events. These mechanisms allow you to concentrate, to filter out irrelevant data, and to assign meaning to what you are perceiving. As you perceive a phenomenon in your environment, you also impose structure, meaning, and causality. We noted that these are all useful, though they also produce problems.

We talked about perceiving others as an interesting but difficult process. Although all of us need to be reasonably accurate in predicting another's behavior, perceptual difficulties often stand in the way. You may find yourself acting in light of a perceptual set, generalizing from a few personality traits, emphasizing the positive traits more than the negative ones, and/or imagining that a person's superior ability in one area gives the person expertise in a related area. Recognizing these difficulties is one way of improving perception.

Our discussion of listening began with a description of the four components of the listening process: sensing, attending, understanding, and remembering. Each of these presents a potential area of difficulty for a listener. If your sensing mechanisms are faulty, you will not receive the message. If you are distracted and do not attend, you will not know what was said. If you do not understand, you may assume one message when the speaker means another. If you cannot remember the message that you processed, your whole listening effort is wasted.

As a result of not listening carefully, your boss and those who work with you may draw conclusions about your competence that you do not want them to make.

We discussed problems associated with each of these areas. Sensing problems may be related to actual defects in the mechanisms or to noise from the environment. Attending problems emerge from a greater range of difficulties. These include selective perception, poor attending habits, the listener's attitudes and needs, low-intensity messages, and messages that are too long. Difficulties related to understanding can be attributed to four sources: different fields of experience, inability to empathize, poor use of feedback, and various mental sets. Finally, as forgetting curves demonstrate, people forget much detail unless they are careful to remember. We concluded that important listening skills must be practiced if they are to be acquired, and we suggested how to do that:

1. Work hard at listening.
2. Paraphrase the content.
3. Check out inferences.
4. Empathize.
5. Work at remembering by taking notes, drawing associations, and reviewing often.

NOTES ....

1. For an excellent survey of the research regarding perception, see Stephen B. Klein, *Learning: Principles and Applications* (New York, McGraw-Hill, 1987), pp. 222–233.
2. Solomon E. Asch, "Forming Impressions of Personality," *Journal of Abnormal and Social Psychology*, 41 (1946):258–290.

3. R. Tagiuri, "Person Perception," in *The Handbook of Social Psychology,* vol. 3, *The Individual in a Social Context,* Gardner Lindzey and Elliot Aronson, eds. (Reading, Mass., Addison-Wesley, 1969), pp. 395–449.

4. Michael Argyle, *Social Interaction* (Chicago, Aldine, 1969), pp. 151–152.

5. See Susan T. Fishe and Shelley E. Taylor, *Social Cognition* (New York, McGraw-Hill, 1991), Chapter 6.

6. Tagiuri, op. cit., pp. 408–418.

7. Gerald L. Wilson, "Trusting and Self-Disclosure in Dyads," Ph.D. diss., University of Wisconsin, 1979.

8. Rensis Likert, *New Patterns of Management* (New York, McGraw-Hill, 1961), p. 52.

9. W. Clay Hamner and Henry L. Tosi, "Relationship of Role Conflict and Role Ambiguity to Job Involvement Measures," *Journal of Applied Psychology,* **59** (1974):497–499; John M. Ivancevich and James H. Donnelly, "A Study of Role Clarity and Need for Clarity for Three Occupational Groups," *Academy of Management Journal,* **17** (1974):28–35; D. W. Organ and C. N. Green, "The Perceived Purposefulness of Job Behavior: Antecedents and Consequences," *Academy of Management Journal,* **17** (1974): 69–78.

10. J. Beels, "It's Time to Get Back to the Basics," *Industrial Finishing* (May 1987):28.

11. Blaine Goss, "Listening as Information Processing," *Communication Quarterly,* **30** (Fall 1982):304–307.

12. Larry R. Smeltzer and Kittie W. Watson, "Listening: An Empirical Comparison of Discussion Length and Level of Incentive," *Central States Speech Journal,* **35** (Fall 1984):166–170.

13. Ralph Nichols and L. A. Stevens, *Are You Listening?* (New York, McGraw-Hill, 1957).

14. Lee Thayer, *Communication and Communication Systems* (Homewood, Ill., Irwin, 1968), pp. 51–53.

15. Ibid., pp. 53–54.

16. Ralph Nichols, "Listening Is a 10 Part Skill," *Nation's Business,* **45** (1957):56–60.

17. Donald Campbell, "Systematic Error on the Part of Human Links in Communication Systems," *Information and Control,* **1** (1958):334–369.

18. Tony Buzan, *Use Both Sides of Your Brain* (New York, Dutton, 1976), pp. 49–50.

19. Herman Ebbinghaus, *Über das Gedachtnis: Untersuchungen der experimentelen Psychologie* (Leipzig, Dancker & Humbolt, 1885). Interest in researching this phenomenon has begun to pick up in the past few years in relation to split-brain studies and their offshoots. In all the research we know about, the retention curves look about the same as the two we present.

20. S. Zurier, "Strictly for Salesmen," *Industrial Distribution* (August 1987):47.

21. Carl Rogers, "Releasing Expression," in *Counseling and Psychotherapy* (Boston, Houghton Mifflin, 1942).

22. Charles Kelly, "Empathic Listening," in Robert Cathcart and Larry Samovar, eds. *Small Group Communication: A Reader* (Dubuque, Brown, 1984), p. 297.

23. James E. Deese, *The Psychology of Learning,* 2d ed. (New York, McGraw-Hill, 1958), pp. 237–248.

24. Buzan, op cit., p. 55.

25. Ibid., p. 57.

26. A. D. Wolvin and C. G. Coakley, "A Survey of the Status of Listening Training in Some Fortune 500 Companies," *Communication Education* (1991):152–165.

27. J. Procter, "Haven't You Heard a Word I Have Said: Getting Managers to Listen," *IEEE Transactions on Professional Communication,* **37** (1994).

RECOMMENDED READINGS ....

Judi Brownell. *Building Active Listening Skills.* Englewood Cliffs, N.J., Prentice-Hall, 1986. This book, which focuses on active listening, will be helpful to those who wish to increase their skill in this area.

Kenneth E. Boulding. *The Image: Knowledge in Life and Society.* Ann Arbor, University of Michigan Press, 1956. An image of a person is composed of the sum of what he or she thinks and knows. Boulding suggests that images change through communication and feedback.

Blaine Goss. *Processing Communication.* Belmont, Calif., Wadsworth, 1982. This textbook begins its treatment of processing with three chapters that include discussion of perception.

Albert Hastorf, David Schneider, and Judith Polefka. *Person Perception*. Reading, Mass., Addison-Wesley, 1970. Reviews the research in the field to 1970.

Charles M. Kelly. "Empathic Listening." In Robert S. Cathcart and Larry A. Samovar, eds., *Small Group Communication: A Reader*. Dubuque, Brown, 1984, pp. 296–304. This essay was the first to present a carefully drawn distinction between deliberative and empathic listening.

Carl R. Rogers and Richard E. Farson. "Active Listening." In Richard Huseman, Cal Logue, and Dwight Freshley, eds., *Readings in Interpersonal and Organizational Communication*, 3d ed., pp. 561–576, Boston, Holbrook, 1977. An insightful discussion of the listening process.

Andrew D. Wolvin and Carolyn G. Coakley. *Listening*, 4th ed. Dubuque, Brown, 1992. This textbook was written to explain the complexities of the listening process. It also seeks to help improve an individual's listening skills.

DISCUSSION QUESTIONS ....

1. Select one class member to be the focus of attention. Then, with all the other class members working privately, write down on a piece of paper bits of information that attract your attention. You might focus on dress, posture, grooming details, gestures, looks, and the like. Now try to find five adjectives that describe the *person*. Compare the adjectives with the information you listed. Have you gone beyond the data you listed in the selection of adjectives? Compare your findings with those of others in the class.

2. Focus your attention on your professor, and write down five adjectives about him or her. How were you able to derive those adjectives? On what data have you based them? Try to ex-plain your selection in terms of perceptual set, implicit personality theory, the leniency effect, or the halo effect.

3. Suppose you have an employee working for you who seems skilled and who you believe has potential, but who lacks confidence. What steps would you take to help improve his or her self-confidence?

4. Sort through your experiences over the past twenty-four hours and try to identify difficult listening situations. What factors contributed to the difficulty in listening that you experienced? You might wish to use the components of the listening process as a convenient way to organize your analysis.

5. On the chalkboard, compile a list of listening difficulties identified by class members. As a group, suggest at least one or two strategies for overcoming each difficulty, and indicate why you think they will work.

6. Working with a partner in your class, practice active listening skills. Take turns making a statement about something important that has happened over the past day or so. Be sure to give each other something to work with. For example, "It was really hard getting out of bed this morning. I heard the buzzer, and just couldn't seem to get started. Then I stubbed my toe on the foot of the bed, and about the time I got to the bathroom door my sister cut in front of me and slammed the door in my face. And the dog had apparently asked to get out, but no one heard it. He'd soiled the rug in front of the door. . . ." At the end of the exercise, each of you should judge whether the other has engaged in empathic listening or deliberative listening. Be able to explain the difference.

INTERNET ACTIVITIES ....

1. Suppose you wanted to contract some training on the subjects of perception and listening. Use the Internet to locate at least five vendors for this training. How much information can you glean from the Internet, and what kinds of information did you need that you could not find? Bring your notes to class for comparison and contrast with your classmates' notes.

2. If you type the word *listening* into the search bar of Altavista Search (http://www.altavista/digital.com/), what do you find? Explore both musical paths and language paths until you are confident you can participate actively in a classroom discussion of the Internet's resources on these topics.

3. When we listen to each other in a conference we have both visual and auditory cues that aren't available on the Internet. What are the implications for organizations which increasingly use the World Wide Web as a means of communication?

CHAPTER 6

Language and Nonverbal Communication

Upon completion of this chapter, you should be able to:

1. Describe and explain how verbal and nonverbal communication are related in a "package" of messages.
2. Describe how language creates reality and how it carries meaning.
3. Specify and explain six ways in which to use language well.
4. Identify and explain four uses of nonverbal communication.
5. Describe the relationship between volume of space and status.
6. Suggest the kinds of messages a person conveys with his or her use of time and space.
7. Explain the significance of touching, eye contact, and physical appearance.
8. Determine appropriate dress for various work situations.

When two people talk, they exchange messages, negotiate, and share meanings and understanding. Indeed, when people talk they define themselves as humans through their use of signs and symbols. These symbols are always either verbal or nonverbal. Thus we use two major message systems. These systems are so intimately tied together that separating them out for the purposes of this discussion is both awkward and difficult. Consider: You are reading these words, so you are processing the verbal system. However, you may also be "hearing" the voice buried in the language, and certainly you are responding to the message of typeface, the message of font size, and the message of white space. You undoubtedly have noticed if someone came before you marking the words with a highlighter or a pencil. All those marks are part of the nonverbal package that permeates this book.

When we talk we wrap up our words with other nonverbal messages—the messages of vocal tone and quality, the message of posture, the messages of facial expression, the messages of space and time, and the like. These nonverbal messages flow smoothly together and occur simultaneously with the sentences. They are a part of speech, and they control in large measure how you interpret what another person means. To communicate effectively, then, you must understand and develop skills in the use of both verbal and nonverbal message systems.

THE LANGUAGE SYSTEM ....

What Is Language?

You could say that language is a system of signs and symbols. It is governed by rules—called syntax and grammar—for the use of those signs and symbols. Language allows human beings to produce messages about the things and events going on within themselves and about things and events beyond their immediate presence and their immediate time.

Human languages all have certain specific characteristics that set them off from other creatures' communication systems. (1) Human languages are arbitrary. This means that the relationship between a word and the thing the word represents or stands for is completely arbitrary. Except for the conventions of English, we might just as easily have called this book you are holding a "toad." It would make as much sense, except for the conventions of English. (2) Human language is always productive. That is, the number of sentences and the number of ideas we can create in language is unlimited. Each expression of an idea can be original—plus, we can write a sentence that you may never have heard or read before, and so long as we conform to the rules governing the use of English, you can understand it. We can also create a sentence that is completely "off the wall," but you know English, so you can, in some sense, understand it. For example: "My computer jumped off the desk, ran to the tree and ate the chicken perched on the lowest limb." Reading this sentence, you might well think that its author had gone nuts, but you could make out the sense of the sentence nevertheless. (3) All human languages are discreet. That is, the distinctions we can make among the sounds become distinctions of meaning as well. *Cat* means something different from *hat*, which means something different from *bat* because of this feature of discreteness in language. (4) Human languages always have a measure of duality. That is, all human languages have two levels of organization. The sounds are well organized, plus the meanings are well organized.

But so what? What difference does any of this discussion about language make to a reader studying communication in business and professional settings? It is these features of the language that allow us to communicate using the languages we know. With language we create reality. With language we convey meaning.

How Does Language Create Reality?

The words and phrases we use create reality. What is outside a person exists, of course, but human beings can't know it or communicate about it—and thus it doesn't become meaningful or real—without language. Language carries three kinds of meaning: denotative, connotative, and relational. What we believe, what we trust in, what we depend on and feel right about constitutes our truth. Our truth may not agree with someone else's notions at all! Any controversial issue is controversial because people do not create the same reality from the raw materials of language. For example, your ideas about the appropriate role of government in regulating business depend entirely upon the reality inside you. There is no "truth" outside yourself quite like your image. There is no "truth" out there that exactly matches up with the meanings you have in your head.

How Does Language Carry Meaning?

Each of the three kinds of meaning—denotative, connotative, and relational—influences every communication event in your life.

Denotative Meaning

Denotative meaning is a shared understanding. The definitions in a dictionary point to such shared, denotative meanings. Denotation, then, is the reality that members of a speech community generally accept when they use a word. All words have denotative value. If they did not, we could not talk with each other. But not everyone understands the meanings we have for a word. For example, some words are highly technical jargon known only by a few specialists, some are slang, and some are specific to a particular locality or a particular workplace. If someone says, "Let's go to a movie," you know what the person wants to do because you share the denotative meanings of a speech community. If someone asks you to "evacuate the CS_2 from the second line," you might not quite know what he wants.

Connotative Meaning

Connotative meaning is the affective value of a word—that is, the emotional association you bring to it. Any word can carry emotional implications. For example, the word *mother* will undoubtedly be emotionally loaded for you. It involves, as all connotation involves, a degree of positive or negative value. It involves, as all connotation involves, a power dimension, such as light-heavy, or strong-weak, or hard-soft. And it involves, as all connotation involves, a movement dimension such as hot-cold, fast-slow, active-passive.[1]

Relational Meaning

The relational meaning of language identifies and defines how people orient to each other when they talk. Some people "talk down" to others, for example. Some people build you up. You usually know which is which, and you respond to the other person's definition of your relationship with him or her.

To illustrate this important idea, suppose you encounter a racist joke in the workplace. Almost certainly you will decide the speaker is racist. You have assigned relational meaning to the speaker's use of language. Similarly, if someone seems sexist to you, that perception is almost certainly a function of the speaker's language choices. You can tell if a speaker seems prejudiced against the elderly people, against gay and lesbian people, and against people who use crutches or canes, glasses or hearing aids, etc. All these "truths" go on inside you because of the relational meanings in the language system.

How Can Language Be Used Most Effectively?

Thus, language can create problems if it is not used skillfully. On the other hand, language can also be a very powerful asset to the skillful speaker. The question arises, How can language be used most effectively? We offer six broad categories of advice we believe can make a difference to you. In each category we suggest a number of ways you can improve your use of language.

Use Appropriate Language

Language is appropriate when it doesn't offend. Language is appropriate when it is free from sexism, racism, and the like. And, to the extent possible, good communicators try to avoid trite expressions and clichés, for these tired phrases render language usage inappropriate in most cases.

To avoid insensitive and sexist language, try to focus on the person rather than on some irrelevant feature of the person. Do not imply anything negative, and avoid euphemisms that might insult another person. Exhibit 6.1 displays several examples you will find helpful.

Exhibit 6.1 EXAMPLES OF APPROPRIATE AND INAPPROPRIATE LANGUAGE USAGE

Insensitive	Better	Sexist	Better
The deaf person	The person	Businessman	Executive, manager, leader
The woman doctor	The doctor	Fireman	Firefighter
The mentally retarded man	The man	Foreman	Supervisor
The black lawyer	The lawyer	Manpower	Workers, work force, labor force
The old woman	The woman	Policeman	Police officer

Avoid Trite Expressions

Trite expressions are expressions that have been overused and worn out. A trite expression was likely vibrant speech when it first occurred, but because it found favor with so many people it became extremely common and thus quite dull. Trite expressions can make you seem ignorant, unoriginal, and sometimes shallow. Exhibit 6.2 lists several examples of trite expression. You can think of many others. They never strengthen your image; they damage it.

Use Simple Language

The simpler and more direct and active your language usage, the more likely you are to be understood. Everyone knows this fact, but we sometimes lose sight of it. Who knows why we sometimes allow ourselves to be tempted to toss in an 85-cent word when a nickel word will do. Of course, you should know some 85-centers, but you should think hard before you use them. If the person you're communicating with doesn't know the word, you risk his or her misunderstanding, and in addition, you risk your image in that person's head. Why say *accompany* when you mean *go with*? Why say *utilize* when you mean *use*? Why say *pursuant to* when you mean *following*? Exhibit 6.3 displays some fancy words and simpler ways to say them.

Use Clear Language

Clear language says something. Clear language drives the listener forward. It is specific and powerful. Exhibit 6.4 provides examples.

Use Vivid Language

Vivid language captures the imagination of the listener and creates images in his or her head. It is specific and clear. Specific talk—language that gives real names, colors, numbers—provides the materials with which listeners can build images. Compare these two examples. Both are grammatically correct, but the first is not specific. The second is far more vivid.

1. "The man tried to open the valve, and when he turned the handle the pipe burst and he was injured."
2. "On the second shift last night, Mac Voguel tried to open a high-pressure valve that was frozen. After five minutes of struggling he managed a

Exhibit 6.2 EXAMPLES OF TRITE EXPRESSIONS	
Over the hill	Crack of dawn
Cool as a cucumber	Spring chicken
Make a long story short	Signed, sealed, delivered
Sick as a dog	Open-and-shut case
Rat race	Trump-tight argument
Flat as a pancake	Pretty as a picture

Exhibit 6.3	SIMPLER WORDS AND PHRASES		
Why say . . .	When you mean . . .	Why say . . .	When you mean . . .
Attached herewith	Here's	Necessitate	Cause
At the present time	Now	Promulgate	Announce
Feasible	Can be done	Recapitulate	Sum up
Inasmuch as	Since	Subsequently	After, later, then

quarter-turn, but that apparently cracked the housing. When the pipe burst the concussion blew Mr. Voguel back so hard that he hit a wall about ten feet behind him and broke two ribs."

The second version tells a story. You can imagine the scene because the speaker has provided details.

Use Action Language

One way to use action language is to let the subject of your sentences perform the action of the verbs. Use the active voice. Here are some examples:

Active: The CEO gave me a personal tour of the home office.
Passive: I was given a personal tour of the home office by the CEO.
Active: Jackson drew up the schedule.
Passive: The schedule was drawn up by Jackson.
Active: The foreman saw the safety violation.
Passive: The safety violation was seen by the foreman.

As you can tell from these examples, passive voice often includes forms of the verb "to be," such as *is, am, are, was,* and *will be.* Action language usually means short sentences, time words, and interrupted rhythms. When you put all this together with the active voice, your talk seems compelling and magnetic. People want to listen. Your words draw them in.

Exhibit 6.4	"SAY-NOTHING" WORDS	
Say-Nothing Words	Example	Better
A lot	I need a lot of money.	I need $50,000.
Kind of	This is kind of a difficult problem.	This is a difficult problem.
I think that	I think that this will solve the problem.	This will solve the problem.
Very	He is a very powerful person.	He is a powerful person.
	This is a very beautiful view.	This is a beautiful view.
Sort of	This idea is sort of problematic.	This idea is problematic.

Your words have impact in direct proportion to how your listeners interpret them. Recall that communication events always involve both words and a nonverbal package of signs and symbols that tell people how to interpret the words. The nonverbal components are so important in most contexts that people will often believe nonverbal messages before they will accept a direct statement! Thus it seems important to study the nonverbal message system as an equal and essential part of our interactions.

....**THE NONVERBAL SYSTEM**

What Are Nonverbal Messages?

It is difficult, if not impossible, to separate verbal from nonverbal messages. Communications scholars have pondered this problem for years. Frank Dance, for example, pointed out that part of the difficulty in defining nonverbal communication arises from the fact that the signals *are* nonverbal, while a definition is clearly a verbal activity.[2] Randall Harrison and Mark Knapp show that some nonverbal communication may not even be intended as communication at all.[3] Some scholars have tried to simplify the range of their study by ruling out of bounds any nonverbal behaviors that are not intentional. We define *nonverbal messages* as those communications that are not spoken or written words. This definition includes all messages that have an impact.

Senior students bring us many stories of their trials and tribulations in job seeking. Here is one that points to the importance of nonverbal communication. Keith was being interviewed by a woman named Deborah. It was vitally important to him to receive a job offer from the company. If you have participated in an interview for an important job, you know he felt nervous. As Keith entered the room, Deborah offered him a seat and sat right next to him. He felt uncomfortable. He believed it was important to maintain eye contact but found that was difficult. Deborah looked off into the distance much of the time and frequently leaned away. Near the end of the interview Deborah was looking over the top of her glasses at him. Keith also noticed that she just stood up when she wanted to signal the end of the interview. Keith automatically stood up too, Deborah shook his hand, and he was out of her office before he realized the interview was over. In going over the events, Keith felt uneasy about the whole thing. He thought he had done well but wasn't sure. Using our definition of nonverbal messages—communications that are not spoken or written words and that have an impact—we would conclude that Deborah communicated nonverbally to Keith in the employment interview.

Uses of Nonverbal Communication

We think nonverbal messages serve four primary purposes: reinforcement, modification, substitution, and regulation.

Consider Keith in the interview situation we described above. As he entered the office, he reached out and gave Deborah a warm handshake and a smile and said, "I'm really happy to be here and pleased that you could take time to talk to me today." In this case the nonverbal messages—the pleasant handshake and smile—*reinforced* the verbal greeting.

Suppose, however, that Keith had had an anxious look and a shaky voice and had offered no handshake at all. Had this been the case, nonverbal communication would have *modified* the verbal message by contradicting it. Do you think the verbal or nonverbal would have been believed here? Or suppose that Deborah had talked to Keith about how interesting she found his résumé, but all the while she was watching the events going on outside her window. Keith would have had reason to disbelieve her verbal message.

A third use of nonverbal communication is *substitution:* it takes the place of verbal acts. When Deborah concluded that she had enough information and that Keith had had an opportunity to ask enough questions, she just stood up and shook Keith's hand. He guessed that she had concluded the interview, although she did not say so verbally. Her actions served as a substitute for the words.

Finally, nonverbal behavior can *regulate* behavior. Deborah may have placed one chair in an obvious place so that Keith would understand that he was to take that seat. She may also have controlled his behavior by giving cues when she wanted him to talk. Perhaps she did this by remaining silent. Perhaps she used a falling intonation at the end of a sentence to signal she wanted him to talk.

Nonverbal Codes

If you spend a moment thinking about each of these four uses of nonverbal messages, you will see that the messages can be conveyed in various ways. Besides obvious body movements, for example, placement of Keith's chair and other furniture about her office represents use of space as a nonverbal message system. Nonverbal message systems are referred to as *codes*. There are several general types of codes: environmental, temporal, and person-oriented.

Environmental Codes

Spatial messages should concern you when you work in an organizational setting. Ignoring them can affect the behavior of the people you work with. Three examples from the research literature illustrate our point.

Abraham Maslow and Norbett Mintz placed people in one of three kinds of rooms and asked them to rate a group of photographs of faces. One group occupied an "ugly" room (which looked like a janitor's closet); one group occupied an "average" room (a professor's office); and one group was placed in a "beautiful" room (a conference room). All other factors were kept constant. Those in the beautiful room rated the photos significantly higher than those in the ugly room. The beautiful room also produced more positive feelings than did the ugly room, which actually produced negative feelings.[4]

Researchers in Munich studying the effect of color on IQ test scores of children found further evidence of the effect of environment as a message code. Children who described their testing room as beautiful (blue, yellow, yellow-green, or orange rooms) scored twelve points higher than those who described their testing room as ugly (white, black, or brown rooms).[5]

Exhibit 6.5   COLOR IN THE ENVIRONMENT: MOODS CREATED AND SYMBOLIC MESSAGES

Color	Moods	Symbolic Meanings
Red	Hot, affectionate, angry, defiant, contrary, hostile, full of vitality, calm, tender	Happiness, lust, intimacy, love, restlessness, agitation, royalty, rage, sin, blood
Blue	Cool, pleasant, leisurely, distant, infinite, secure, transcendent, calm, tender	Dignity, sadness, tenderness, truth
Yellow	Unpleasant, exciting, hostile, cheerful, joyful, jovial	Superficial glamor, sun, light, wisdom, masculinity, royalty (in China), age (in Greece), prostitution (in Italy), famine (in Egypt)
Orange	Unpleasant, exciting, disturbed, distressed, upset, defiant, contrary, hostile, stimulating	Sun, fruitfulness, harvest, thoughtfulness
Purple	Depressed, sad, dignified, stately	Wisdom, victory, pomp, wealth, humility, tragedy
Green	Cool, pleasant, leisurely, in control	Security, peace, jealousy, hate, aggressiveness, calm
Black	Sad, intense, anxiety, fear, despondent, dejected, melancholy, unhappy	Darkness, power, mastery, protection, decay, mystery, wisdom, death, atonement
Brown	Sad, not tender, despondent, dejected, melancholy, unhappy	Melancholy, protection, autumn, decay, humility, atonement
White	Joy, lightness, neutral, cold	Solemnity, purity, femininity, humility, joy, light, innocence, fidelity, cowardice

SOURCE: J. K. Burgoon and T. J. Saine, *The Unspoken Dialogue: An Introduction to Nonverbal Communication* (Boston, Houghton Mifflin, 1978), p. 110. Reprinted with permission.

Color.   Judee Burgoon and Tom Saine[6] developed Exhibit 6.5 for their book, *The Unspoken Dialogue: An Introduction to Nonverbal Communication*. It shows how colors in the environment affect our moods and our understanding. It explains why fast-food chains use lively oranges, yellows, and reds, and why the cool, tranquilizing blues and greens and the earth tones of navy, burgundy, and chocolate are used in airliners. It explains why black, navy, charcoal, wine, and so on are considered "power colors."

Researchers on crowding—another spatial element—used census data to identify high-density population areas. They discovered higher-than-normal difficulties with physical and mental health in these locations.[7] A different study revealed attitude differences between students subjected to crowding and others who were not. Students in high-density dormitories developed more negative impressions of the

Can you imagine any un-
ethical uses of space at work?

warmth and friendliness of other residents in their buildings and of the dorm itself than did those in low-density dorms.[8]

In looking at environmental codes, it is helpful to differentiate several features and discuss them separately. We will explore volume of space, objects in the environment, light intensity, personal space, and arranging office space.

Volume of space. One environmental feature with significant message impact is *volume of space.* For example, casual observation will tell you that high ceiling rooms foster concentrations of people, as in bank lobbies, large hotels, and the like, while low ceilings cause people to spread out. That may be why recently built libraries are designed with lower ceilings.

Similarly, we can verify by observation how design of sidewalks, green lawns, and the size and shape of atriums affect the boundaries and mark the beginnings of space. Corporate officials know such design features are important to an organization's overall image.

To illustrate, when International Paper Company moved its corporate offices to Memphis from New York, the company moved into an office tower in a beautifully landscaped park, complete with artificial lake, carefully planned garden, enormous lobbies, and the like. The whole structure is clad in green and black marble, highly polished chrome, and glass, softened by the architect with rounded corners and curved lines at some of the windows.

But how might you use this information? If you were an interviewer, you could conduct a selection interview in the closetlike interviewing space provided by the personnel office, in a private, rather comfortable lounge space, or in your office. Assume that each of these places is equally private and well furnished. A small space is likely to be perceived as confining, an office as less confining and more businesslike, and the lounge as more expansive and informal. Generally, you would want to pick the office so the interviewees would perceive the communication to be businesslike, but would not feel confined. Do not assume, however, that you would always want your office as the interview site. Another place might sometimes serve your purposes better. It might relax the interviewee, for instance, if you moved from your office to a private portion of the company cafeteria for coffee.

So the volume of space affects the perception of communication. It is also used as an index of status and power within the organization. Research by N. M. Henley, Albert Mehrabian, and Marc Riess and Barry Schlenker shows that the space prerogatives of powerful individuals include (1) larger personal spaces (e.g., in offices and homes); (2) more freedom of movement in and control of other people's spaces; and (3) the taking of positions that give them more prominence when seated.[9] Your personal experience will confirm this research. Take a walk through any department in your college or university. You will be able to observe status differences by noticing the space differences. This relationship between power and space is so prevalent in our society that Schlenker commented:

The rich live on palatial estates; the poor are crowded into slums. Dominant street gangs in cities claim the best and biggest "turf." People with high status even take up more space with their signatures than those of low status. The relationship between space and power is salient even for young children, who build forts and clubhouses and defend them from invasion from unwanted outsiders.[10]

Objects in the environment.   The second feature of the environment that communicates is the *objects* within the space. One suggestion we made earlier relates to this: Do not keep your desk in a mess. A feature of Maslow and Mintz's ugly room was that it was a mess. People around you may draw conclusions about your work habits from looking at your desk. Judee Burgoon and Thomas Saine report that "lack of orderliness can cause people to feel anxious or frustrated. Conversely, an aesthetically pleasing arrangement may entice people to linger."[11]

The objects within an office communicate. Researchers have found that including aesthetic objects, such as paintings, wall hangings, and potted plants, significantly increase the perception of the occupant's authoritativeness and trustworthiness. They also found that the presence of professionally related items, such as award plaques and a professional-looking library, added to this perception.[12]

Furniture can also send messages about willingness to communicate. People who wish to discourage communication can use desks as barriers. One manager we know actually had all the chairs except his own removed from his office. He wanted those who came in to take care of their business and get out. Furniture, even in lounge areas, can be placed to discourage communication. Robert Sommer studied an attractive lounge in the women's ward of a state hospital which was rarely used for communication. He found that the seating was arranged so the room was easiest to clean; chairs were set around the perimeter in neat rows and in the middle facing away from each other. He changed the seating so that chairs faced each other, and people began to use the lounge to talk.[13]

Often seating arrangements focus attention on a leader and enhance the perception of that person's power. Marvin Shaw reported that seating arrangements affect the amount of communication, who talks to whom, how much each person talks, and who seems to dominate the group. Those who occupy central places tend to dominate, while those who are seated on the periphery are often left out or are infrequent participants.[14] The shape of a table influences these power seating arrangements. Research confirms what you may have discovered through experience: the end position of a rectangular table is associated with power. We find that:

1. People usually save the head spot for the highest-status member of the group.[15] Also, the high-status member will often take the head spot if given the opportunity to do so.[16]
2. People who are given the head spot through random assignment report that they often feel more like a leader than when assigned a side position.[17]
3. People assigned the head position talk and are talked to more than others.[18] They are also seen by group members as more talkative, dominant, self-confident, persuasive, and intelligent than people seated on the sides.[19]

People who wish to indicate willingness to cooperate or confront can do so by taking the appropriate seat. In his book *Power!*, Michael Korda noted that the chairman of the board takes the head of the table. The next most important person, the president or chief executive officer, takes the seat on the side, to the chairman's immediate right. Korda commented:

> If the latter [the CEO] sits at the opposite end of the table (playing "mother," so to speak, in dining-table terms) he not only has the sun in his eyes [the table is arranged so that the window is usually to the chairman's back], but is almost always placing himself in an adversary position vis-à-vis the chairman.[20]

This observation is supported by Sommer, who associated face-to-face arrangements with confrontation and side-by-side arrangements with cooperation.[21] Conversations are often associated with corner-to-corner or across-table arrangements of people on the sides. You can manage a communication to some extent by allowing the other person to sit first and then taking a position that reflects your purpose.

Your organization will have some cultural expectations about objects and their arrangement. If you are a long-time member of the organization, you will undoubtedly recognize some of these expectations. If you are a new member, you will want to look around. What kinds of objects do the successful members collect in their offices? How are their offices arranged? What kinds of desks and other objects give cues to a person's place in the organization? Compare the offices of successful people at various levels of the organization and make use of what you find.

Light intensity.   A third factor is *light intensity*. Soft, low light seems to facilitate social talking, while brighter, more intense light facilitates task-oriented communication. But some caution is in order. If you turn the light too low, you may create an atmosphere that is too informal for a work area. If the light is too bright, it may cause fatigue and a desire to escape.[22]

Personal space.   Finally, people use *personal space* as a type of environmental manipulation. People in most societies reserve special space around them as private. You may be aware of an uncomfortable feeling when someone moves too close. But we do let some people come very close to us and do not feel uncomfortable. This bubblelike private space shrinks and expands depending on the relationship. Edward T. Hall, a prominent anthropologist, noticed this difference and labeled the close space "intimate distance." He found that for most Americans, intimate distance extends to eighteen inches and is reserved for conveying secret information and very close relationships. Extending out from there to a distance of four feet is space used for normal, informal social conversations, termed "personal-casual distance."[23]

Both business transactions and those of a less personal nature are carried on at a "social-consultative" distance of from four to twelve feet. Hall divided the social-consultative space into near and far phases. The near phase is used to present a personal image. The far phase begins at about six and one-half feet and may be used to keep people of lower power at a distance. In fact, Mehrabian reported that low-status people typically choose to remain at a distance from a more powerful person.[24]

"Public distance" is used for public address and communication outside of buildings. In the near phase it extends from twelve to twenty-five feet. The far phase begins at twenty-five feet. Details of Mehrabian's scheme are presented in Exhibit 6.6.

The main implication to be drawn from this discussion of space is that people will be most comfortable if they are allowed to keep the appropriate distance for the kind of communication in which they are engaged.

Arranging office space. In the case of Keith's interview, he was uneasy because Deborah's office arrangement caused him to sit too close. Be sure as you arrange your office and space that the chairs and desks are placed to allow for comfortable business communication. A wise thing to do is to allow for use of both the near and far social-consultative distance. If you have enough room and furniture, you can do this. If you do not, arrange your furniture so that you can come out from behind your desk when you need to *and* allow chairs to be at about five and one-half feet. If this is not possible because of a small office, set the chairs at an angle between 45 and 90 degrees so that somewhat less eye contact can be appropriately maintained. This gives the illusion of greater distance.

One very clear application of this information on space and environment is in the arrangement of office space. The way the people in an office arrange furniture can dramatically affect communication. One of our students presented us with a good example of the significance of furniture arrangement in a business office. The secretaries in this particular business were permitted to arrange the furniture in the central office any way they wanted. One day the student noticed a dramatic change. The office had been changed from the arrangement shown on the left in Exhibit 6.7 to the arrangement on the right.

When the student quizzed the secretaries about the change, they explained: "Too many people have been milling around. We put the desk in front of the door to stop people before they can get in. We ask them what they want. They tell us. We take care of it. They go away." They continued, "We moved the other things to discourage people from waking through so much. The path is not as easy for them as it used to be." You can easily see what they are talking about.

You can arrange your office so as to control the perception of power and formality, thereby making the conversation easier or harder for the visitor. Most entry-level college graduates have little space with which to work. But even a small narrow office can allow you to exercise some control. In Exhibit 6.8 Michael Korda shows three possible arrangements. All three are alike in that they use the desk as a barrier. But the middle and last arrangements are more powerful than the first in that they allow for direct eye contact and force the visitor to look into the sunlight of the window. The second arrangement gives the visitor much of the space, putting the office owner's back up against the wall. The third office is the most powerfully arranged. Moving the desk forward reserves most of the office space for the occupant while giving very little space to the visitor.

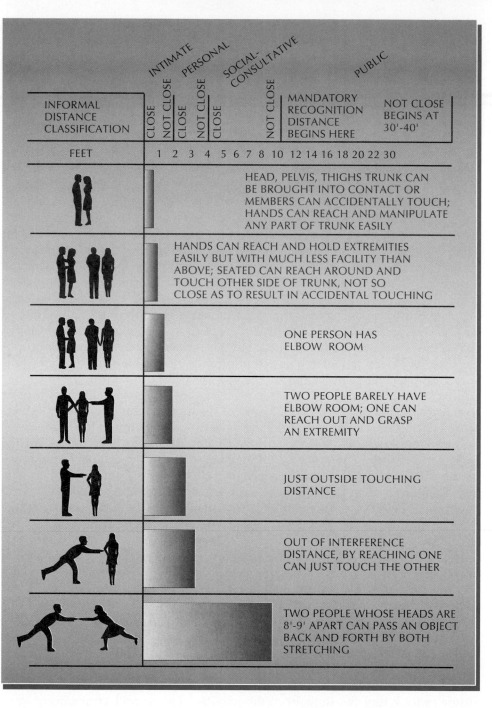

Exhibit 6.6 HALL'S CATEGORIES FOR THE USE OF SPACE*

*In this chart the kinesthetic portion has been illustrated with sketches to indicate visually how these distances are set.

SOURCE: E. T. Hall, "Proxemics," *Current Anthropology,* 9 (1968):93. © 1968 by the University of Chicago. Reprinted by permission.

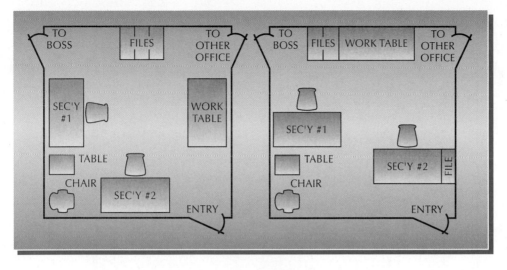

Exhibit 6.7
TWO
ARRANGE-
MENTS OF
THE SAME
OFFICE

You will have more space and more furniture to arrange as you move up in the organization. This, of course, provides more options—you can have both a formal and informal work area. Korda suggests the power implications of these areas: the formal work area is a high-pressure area; the informal work area is a semisocial area.[25] These areas can be used to accentuate or minimize power. Exhibit 6.9 presents an office with various positions designated by the letters *A* through *E*. Can you identify the more powerful positions available to a visitor in this office?

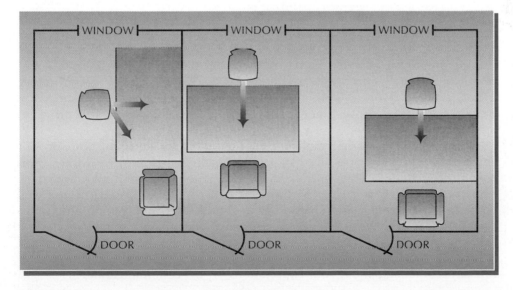

Exhibit 6.8
THREE OFFICE
ARRANGE-
MENTS

SOURCE: Michael Korda, *Power! How to Get It, How to Use It* (New York, Random House, 1975), p. 196. Used by permission.

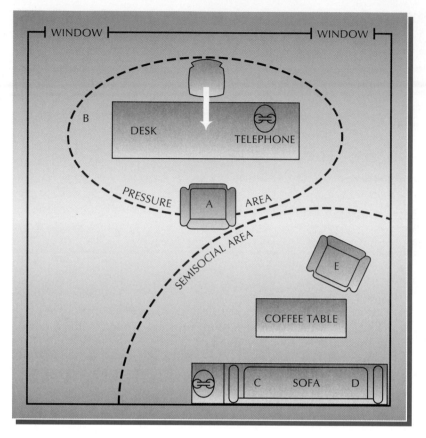

Exhibit 6.9 FURNITURE ARRANGE- MENT IN A MEDIUM-SIZE OFFICE

SOURCE: Michael Korda, *Power! How to Get It, How to Use It* (New York, Random House, 1975), p. 199. Used by permission.

We think the visitor's power positions are represented by *B* and *C*. *B* is powerful because it allows the visitor to get close to the office owner. It allows some violation of that person's space. In addition, the visitor may actually use that portion of the person's desk as if it were his or her own. Position *C* is also powerful because it cuts off the telephone. It also forces the office owner to take either position *D* or *E*. This is an especially powerful move, particularly if weighty business is to be conducted, as it does not allow the office owner to hide behind any barriers.

Consider the nonverbal implications of the arrangement of furniture in your entry-level office. Suppose you have a ten-foot by ten-foot office with a standard desk, a filing cabinet, a desk chair, a chair for a visitor, and a bookcase. Will you put the desk facing the wall? Or will you put your back to the wall with the desk facing out? What advantages and disadvantages do you see to each arrangement? Will you place the visitor's chair so that the desk acts as a barrier? Or will you place it in some position that will provide more openness? Where will the bookcase and filing cabinet be placed? Your placement of furniture says something about your expectations for the communication.

Temporal Codes

Edward T. Hall pointed out cultural differences in the use of time. For example, he reported that the Navajo Indians understand the starting time of ceremonial events to be *when the necessary preparations are made.* They would not be able to tell you a "clock time." He also reported that businesspeople in some South American countries begin their business appointments thirty minutes or more beyond what we would normally expect. Contrast this with a standard North American business appointment. If you arrive within five minutes you are "right on time." If you arrive ten minutes late, you may have to explain yourself. If you are going to be fifteen or more minutes late, you'd better call ahead!

In the world of business and organizations in American culture, time is often viewed as a commodity. We make time. We buy time. We save time. We spend time. Time is like money! In this society your ability to manage time, to create schedules and follow them, and to arrive at the appointed place at the designated time will be noticed.

If you live in a culture like this, you should get practice in scheduling events and following these schedules. Further, you should work toward on-time habits. We believe that these behaviors become habits, and that if you don't have these habits established before you take your first fulltime job, they will be difficult to establish, and your use of time may be perceived as erratic.

Your management of these space and time arrangements creates powerful messages about who you are and how you operate. We pointed out how you might use each of these message systems effectively. The cues you give with your face and body offer you even more opportunities to convey the nonverbal messages that you want to get across. You might call some of these small behaviors "micropolitical cues."[26]

Person-Oriented Codes

Nonverbal messages that are related directly to the individual person include touch, face and body language, and physical appearance. All these can serve as powerful communicators, but touching is probably most powerful. Barbara Bate[27] and Judy Cornelia Pearson[28] have provided excellent and thorough discussions of gender differences in nonverbal communication for Americans. These differences seem especially relevant in a society in which women are an increasingly important percentage of the work force. Exhibit 6.10 provides an overview of expectations placed on women because of gender ideals. Exhibits 6.11 through 6.16 cite specific research that located differences between men and women in how we use space, eye contact, facial, posture, and gestural cues, and touch.

Touching. *Touching* involves moving into another's space and making body contact. The impact of touching is so vital that there is evidence that touch deprivation in infants can be damaging to development and growth. The film *Second Chance* reports the case of a 22-month-old girl who weighed fifteen pounds and was unable to walk. An average child of this age weighs about twenty-five pounds. Her mother touched the child only to change her diaper

Exhibit 6.10   NONVERBAL BEHAVIOR EXPECTATIONS RELATED TO
GENDER IDEALS*

Nonverbal Location	Gender Ideal	
	Feminine	Masculine
Voice	Higher pitch	Lower pitch
	Varied intonation	Sometimes monotone
	Softer on average	Louder on average
Body	Arms and legs crossed	Arms and legs stretched
	Enclosed appearance	Open appearance
	Head tilted	Head erect
	Clothing decorative	Clothing uniform
	May initiate hugs with either sex	Initiate touch of female in work or social settings
Face	Frequent smiles	Rare facial animation
	Watch while listening	Look away often as speaker or listener
Environment	Claim limited space	Claim large personal space
	Use color and objects to to convey mood	Use color and objects to show power

*The title of this table suggests *expectations,* not *behaviors,* because we know more about gender-based cues people expect than about how often they are used.

SOURCE: From Barbara Bate, *Communication and the Sexes* (New York, Harper & Row, 1988), p. 58. Reprinted by permission of the publisher.

and prop a bottle in her mouth. When a substitute mother began to hold her, she cried, but sustained touch and cuddling eventually produced a dramatic reversal of the child's stunted physical and emotional growth. When we become adults, touching is transformed into the more societally accepted verbal stroking. Thus, when we are physically touched by another in the context of a work situation, it takes on unusual significance.

Erving Goffman reports that high-status people have the prerogative to initiate touching of those below them, yet low-power people do not usually touch a superior without an invitation.[69] Barry Schlenker suggests that the power of touch seems to come from the fact that it can be viewed as an invasion of one's space.[70] Korda provides an example of how President Lyndon Johnson used touch as a show of power. The president would "squeeze his subordinates' knees, punch them, stab his finger in their stomach, and generally use every physical means to show just who had power."[71] We are confident that much of President Johnson's touching behavior would not have been accepted if he had been merely Mr. Johnson.

Hand shaking can be an appropriate and useful touching behavior in an organizational environment. It may also connote power, as may placing a hand on

Exhibit 6.11   PROXEMIC DIFFERENCES OF WOMEN AND MEN

Female Behavior	Male Behavior
Women are approached more closely.[29]	Men are approached less closely.
Women approach others more closely.[30]	Men approach others less closely.
Women discriminate more about whom they approach.[31]	Men discriminate less about whom they approach.
Women's approach creates less anxiety.	Men's approach creates more anxiety.[32]
Women prefer to interact side by side.[33]	Men prefer to interact face-to-face.
Women are least comfortable with side-by-side invasions.[34]	Men are least comfortable with frontal invasions.[35]
Women are more likely to be placed on the side of a rectangular table.[36]	Men are more likely to be placed at the head of a rectangular table.[37]
High self-concept women approach others more closely than do low self-concept women, and than men of high or low self-concepts.[38]	High self-concept men approach others more closely than low self-concept men, but not as closely as high self-concept women.
Sociability and status of females has no effect on the amount of space they are given.[39]	Unsociable, low-status males are given more room than sociable, high-status males and than all women.
Women stand farther away from people who are speaking loudly.[40]	Men maintain the same distance away from people who are speaking loudly or softly.
Women respond as easily in close quarters as in larger spaces.	Men respond less in crowded conditions than in larger spaces.[41]
Women flee more quickly when invasion is accompanied by talk.[42]	Men flee more quickly when invasion is not accompanied by talk.
Women have less territory.[43]	Men have more territory.

SOURCE: Judy Cornelia Pearson, *Gender and Communication* (Dubuque, Iowa, Brown, 1985).

Exhibit 6.12   KINESIC (EYE CONTACT) DIFFERENCES OF WOMEN AND MEN

Female Behavior	Male Behavior
Women establish more eye contact than do men.[44]	Men establish less eye contact than do women.
Women engage in a higher percentage of mutual looking than do men.[45]	Males engage in more mutual eye gazing as they age.[46]
Women avert their gaze more than do men.[47]	Men engage in staring behavior rather than in gaze aversion.
Women appear to value eye contact more than do men.[48]	Men do not appear to be disturbed by people who do not watch them.

SOURCE: Judy Cornelia Pearson, *Gender and Communication* (Dubuque, Iowa, Brown, 1985).

Exhibit 6.13   KINESIC (FACIAL EXPRESSION) DIFFERENCES OF WOMEN AND MEN

Female Behavior	Male Behavior
Women use more facial expression and are more expressive than are men.[49]	Men use less facial expression and are less expressive than women.
Women are better at conveying emotions than are men.[50]	Men do not convey their emotions through their faces.
Women demonstrate superior recognition memory of their own facial expressions.[51]	Men do not recall their own facial expressions.
Women smile more than men.[52]	Men smile less than women.
Women are more apt to return smiles when someone smiles at them.[53]	Men are less likely to return a smile than are women.
Women are more attracted to others who smile.[54]	Men are not more attracted to others who smile.

SOURCE: Judy Cornelia Pearson, *Gender and Communication* (Dubuque, Iowa, Brown, 1985).

a subordinate's shoulder. While pats often connote friendliness or playfulness, strokes often connote sexual desire.[72] In general the wisest course you can take in the matter of touching is just to avoid it altogether in the world of work. Beyond a simple handshake, it's just too risky. In recent years the courts have made clear that sexual harassment is forbidden. (See Chapter 8 for a discussion of sexual harassment.) Since people can misconstrue the meaning of touch and other nonverbal messages, it is best to remain circumspect at all times.

Exhibit 6.14   KINESIC (POSTURE AND BEARING) DIFFERENCES OF WOMEN AND MEN

Female Behavior	Male Behavior
Women tend to hold their legs more closely together.	Men tend to have their legs apart at a 10- to 15-degree angle.
Women maintain their arms close to their body.	Men hold their arms about 5 to 10 degrees away from their bodies.
Women rely on more closed body positions.	Men rely on more open body positions.[55]
Women tend to engage in less body lean.	Men tend to engage in more backward lean.[56]
Women walk with their pelvis rolled slightly forward.	Men walk with their entire pelvis rolled slightly back.
Women present their entire body from their neck to their ankles as a moving entity when they walk.[57]	Men move their arms independently and exhibit a slight twist of their rib cage.

SOURCE: Judy Cornelia Pearson, *Gender and Communication* (Dubuque, Iowa, Brown, 1985).

Exhibit 6.15   KINESIC (GESTURAL) DIFFERENCES IN WOMEN AND MEN

Female Behavior	Male Behavior
Women use fewer gestures than do men. Women discriminate in their use of gestures as they use fewer gestures with other women and more with men.[58]	Men use more gestures than women. Men do not discriminate between male and female partners in their use of gestures.
Women tend to keep their hands down on the arms of a chair more than do men.[59]	Men rarely keep their hands down on the arms of a chair.
Women use fewer one-handed gestures and arm movements.[60]	Men use more one-handed gestures and arm movements.
Women play with their hair or clothing, place their hands in their lap, and tap their hands more frequently than do men.[61]	Men use sweeping hand gestures, stretching the hands, cracking the knuckles, pointing, and using arms to lift the body from a chair or table more frequently.
Women tend to cross their legs at the knees or cross their ankles with their knees slightly apart.[62]	Men tend to sit with their legs apart or with their legs stretched out in front of them and their ankles crossed.
Women tap their hands.	Men exhibit greater leg and foot movement including tapping their feet.[63]

SOURCE: Judy Cornelia Pearson, *Gender and Communication* (Dubuque, Iowa, Brown, 1985).

Exhibit 6.16   TACTILE DIFFERENCES BETWEEN WOMEN AND MEN

Female Behavior	Male Behavior
Women touch others less than men do.	Men touch others more than women do.[64]
Women are touched more by others.[65]	Men are touched less than women.
Women value touching more than do men.[66]	Men do not value touch as much as women.
Women distinguish between touching behavior which indicates warmth and touching behavior which suggests sexual intent.	Men do not make distinctions between various kinds of touch.[67]
Women view touch as an expressive behavior which demonstrates warmth and affiliation.	Men generally view touch as an instrumental behavior leading to sexual activity, or as behavior which is childish, indicative of dependency and a lack of manliness.[68]

SOURCE: Judy Cornelia Pearson, *Gender and Communication* (Dubuque, Iowa, Brown, 1985).

> Under what circumstances is it ethically okay to touch someone else at work? When is it not okay to touch someone, what ethical principles constrain you from touching?

Facial and eye behavior.   Of all the bodily cues observed in interactions, the face seems to exert a special influence.[73] Facial cues are important indicators of an individual's orientation. In fact, we know a personnel manager in a major manufacturing firm who viewed them as so important that he refused to hire anyone who would not look him in the eye. He had decided he could not trust those applicants, regardless of qualifications and past records. Dale Leathers reviewed the research literature about facial cues, concluding that the face is enormously communicative:

1. The face communicates *evaluative* judgments through pleasant and unpleasant expressions that suggest whether the communicator sees the current object of his attention as good or bad.
2. The face communicates *interest* or *disinterest* in other people or in the surrounding environment.
3. The face communicates *intensity* and hence degree of involvement in the situation.
4. The face communicates the amount of *control* the individual has over his or her own expressions.
5. The face communicates the factor of *understanding* or lack of it.[74]

If you have tried to describe someone's facial expressions and their meanings, you know it is hard. Paul Ekman and Wallace Friesen attempted to make this task easier by systematizing the description. They divided the face into three regions: region I, the brows and forehead; region II, the eyes, eyelids, and bridge of the nose; and region III, the cheeks, nose, mouth, chin, and jaw.[75]

Once they had a method of classifying, they (along with S. S. Tomkins)[76] were able to discover which emotions are conveyed by the various regions. They found that *disgust* was conveyed by the cheeks/mouth area, *fear* by the eyes/eyelids, *sadness* by the brows/forehead and eyes/eyelids, *happiness* by the cheeks/mouth and eyes/eyelids, *anger* by both cheeks/mouth and brows/forehead, and *surprise* by any of the three.

Power, another variable researchers investigate, seems to be conveyed by eyebrows and/or eye contact. Caroline Keating and associates linked raised eyebrows with surprise, fear, and retreat, indicating lack of power. Lowering the eyebrows suggests aggression and dominance. A direct and steady gaze is an almost universal symbol of high status and power or an attempt to assert such power. To stare in this way is a privilege of high status.[77]

Low-status people are not expected to sustain direct eye contact with superiors. In fact, when another person is unwilling to look us in the eye, we may infer that he or she is embarrassed, appeased, or submissive. A study that compared looking down with looking straight ahead found that those who looked ahead were perceived as more alert, secure, active, and receptive than those who did not.[78]

We would not want to give an uneven picture of what eye contact means. Several studies have demonstrated the prerogative of high-status, powerful people to regulate their own behavior. One study showed that the higher the status, the less the expectation that the high-status person ought to look at the other person. The lower the status and the less powerful the person, the more time that individual will spend looking at the powerful members—especially while listening.[79] In another study Ralph Exline and his associates found that ROTC cadet officers who spent more time looking at subordinates (a lower-status activity) received the lowest leadership performance ratings.[80] These two studies suggest that a high-status person establishes dominance through stares and direct gaze, but shifts to a much less attentive pattern once this relationship is established. But use of these kinds of status-differentiating behaviors can affect the climate of an interaction. Martin Remland suggests that low-status nonverbal communication by a superior is seen as an indication that the person is more considerate than one who engages in high-status nonverbal communication.[81]

The smile is another powerful nonverbal facial expression. Research indicates that smiling behavior is associated with success in sales and perception of intelligence.[82] But the smile used at a socially inappropriate moment is associated with deception, as the face at rest does not normally display a smile.[83]

This information may be useful to you in at least two ways—on condition you hold your conclusions tentative and keep your behavior contextually appropriate. First, you may wish to assess the power and status relationships among people. Knowledge of nonverbal power signals will surely be of value. Second, in some relationships you may be able to use this knowledge to advance your status. For example, a task group composed of individuals from different departments but with equal status will always have to determine its own status relationships, as a necessary condition for its members to be satisfied and happy. It might be in your interest—if you are upwardly mobile—to emerge as a high-status member in successful work groups. Knowledge of eye-contact behavior can give you an edge in this situation without jeopardizing your position in your own department and without in any way harming the group. Indeed, your emergence in a high status position may benefit the group and be the central reason the group is successful.

Physical appearance and dress. If a man were to stand in your doorway without speaking a word, you would soon come to some conclusions. For example, you would be able to tell almost immediately whether or not you would like to talk with him. Most people believe they can know various things about another merely by observing the person's physical appearance. Although it may not be a surprise, a number of researchers have shown that people assume a great deal by observation of appearance. Those who are physically attractive are seen as more sexual, personable, persuasive, popular, happy, kind, interesting, confident, sociable, serious, outgoing, and so on. They are expected to be happier in their marriages, to have better jobs, to live more fulfilling lives.[84] A person's appearance would tell you whether to approach or avoid him or her. If a man were wearing a well-tailored navy blue pinstripe suit and had well-groomed hair, you would be more likely to approach him than if he were wearing dirty and torn clothes and badly needed a haircut.

So physical appearance affects the influence a person may have on others. People with a pleasant appearance (as judged by those around them) have greater social power, influence, and credibility. Research shows that people make an effort to follow the lead, conform to the wishes, and believe the statements of individuals who are perceived as physically attractive.[85] The pleasing person not only will be more influential but probably better liked than one who is unattractive.[86]

Before you modestly conclude that there is no use competing in the physical attractiveness area, realize that attractiveness, like other attributes, falls into a bell-shaped curve. There is a great deal you can do to present a pleasant appearance. In fact, we believe that being too handsome or beautiful may actually present some liabilities for people in the world of work. We'll give you two bits of advice about physical attractiveness: pay attention to the appearance of your body, and pay attention to the way you dress.

The way you take care of your body influences the way it looks and the impression you leave with others. You may not be able to control your body type, but most people can control such things as weight and physical fitness. These attributes are viewed by people in our society as a measure of your personality *because* you have control over them. You certainly can control whether or not you and your clothes appear clean and fresh.

We believe that you can help build the image you want not only through proper diet and physical fitness but also through dress. There are no unbending rules to help you make decisions about dress: the work situation, the profession, and those around you all help determine what is acceptable. To compound the uncertainties even further, all of us know people who ignore dress standards and are still relatively successful.

Notions about what is appropriate dress have been changing. For example, IBM had long insisted that its employees wear a dark suit and white shirt. Then in 1993, Louis Gerstner, IBM's new chairman, made a public appearance in a blue shirt. This was a signal that the standard had changed, and employees got the message. Some job sites found workers on the job without a suit and tie. A spokesperson for IBM explained the new standard: "You try to dress like your customers do."[87]

In spite of all the ambiguities, common sense can help determine what you should wear in a work situation. Two standards can guide you: first, look at what other people are wearing; and second, read what those who have studied the subject have said. Look at your colleagues in the workplace and see how those in a position just above your current job dress. Then see if there are some common elements in the way the successful ones dress. You have a clue if there are commonalities.

SUMMARY . . . .

In this chapter we talked about the impact of nonverbal elements on the image you create within an organization. We have defined nonverbal communication as communication that is not composed of spoken or written words. Next, we discussed uses of nonverbal communication. It reinforces, modifies, and regulates the verbal aspects of your communication as well as substituting for them.

Certain environmental factors influence

communication. These include attractiveness of the surroundings, color, and crowding. We considered allocation of space as a message system as well. We discussed volume of space and its implications regarding power. Central seating locations can also signal leadership in groups. In addition, personal space is important. Business affairs, for example, are best conducted in the social-consultative space that ranges from four to twelve feet.

We suggested next that management and use of time will speak of your efficiency. Following that, we indicated that touching behavior involves personal space and thus can serve a valuable function if carried out appropriately. We presented data about facial and eye behavior that data indicate the face can express various feelings as well as dominance. Finally, we reviewed research about physical appearance and dress. We found that attractive, well-dressed people seem to be more successful than others not considered as beautiful or well-attired. We concluded with recommendations for appropriate attire in business situations.

NOTES . . . .

1. This idea was first introduced by Charles E. Osgood in his essay, "The Nature of Measurement of Meaning," *Psychological Bulletin*, **49** (1952):197–237. See also the classic work by Charles E. Osgood, George Suci, and Percy Tannenbaum, *The Measurement of Meaning* (Urbana, Ill., University of Illinois Press, 1957).

2. Frank Dance, "Toward a Theory of Human Communication," in *Human Communication Theory*, Frank Dance, ed. (New York, Holt, Rinehart & Winston, 1967), p. 290.

3. Randall P. Harrison and Mark L. Knapp, "Toward an Understanding of Nonverbal Communication Systems," *Journal of Communication*, 22, no. 4 (1972):339–352.

4. Abraham H. Maslow and Norbett L. Mintz, "Effects of Esthetic Surroundings: 1. Initial Effects of Three Esthetic Conditions upon Perceiving 'Energy' and 'Well-being' in Faces," *Journal of Psychology*, 41 (1956):247–254.

5. "Blue Is Beautiful," *Time*, September 17, 1973, p. 66.

6. Judee K. Burgoon and Thomas J. Saine, *The Unspoken Dialogue: An Introduction to Nonverbal Communication* (Boston, Houghton Mifflin, 1978), p. 110.

7. A. H. Esser, *Behavior and Environment* (New York, Plenum, 1971); René Dubos, *Man Adapting* (New Haven, Yale University Press, 1965), pp. 100–109; D. Stokols, "A Social-Psychological Model of Human Crowding Phenomena," *Journal of the American Institute of Planners*, **38** (1972):72–84.

8. Andrew Baum and S. Valins, "Residential Environments: Group Size and Crowding," *Proceedings of the American Psychological Association* (1973), pp. 211–212.

9. N. M. Henley, *Body Politics: Power, Sex, and Nonverbal Communication* (Englewood Cliffs, N.J., Prentice Hall, 1977); Albert Mehrabian, *Silent Messages: Implicit Communication of Emotions and Attitudes*, 2d ed. (Belmont, Calif., Wadsworth, 1981); Marc Riess and Barry R. Schlenker, "Attitude Change and Responsibility Avoidance as Modes of Dilemma Resolution in Forced Compliance Settings," *Journal of Personality and Social Psychology*, **35** (1977):21–30.

10. Barry R. Schlenker, *Impression Management* (Monterey, Calif., Brooks/Cole, 1980), p. 247.

11. Burgoon and Saine, op. cit., p. 107.

12. Edward W. Miles and Dale G. Leathers, "The Impact of Aesthetic and Professionally Related Objects on Credibility in the Office Setting," *Southern Speech Communication Journal*, **49** (1984):361–379.

13. Robert Sommer, *Personal Space* (Englewood Cliffs, N.J., Prentice Hall, 1969).

14. Marvin E. Shaw, *Group Dynamics: The Psychology of Small Group Behavior*, 3d ed. (New York, McGraw-Hill, 1981).

15. D. F. Lott and Robert Somer, "Seating Arrangements and Status," *Journal of Personality and Social Psychology*, **7** (1967):90–94.

16. F. L. Strodtbeck and L. H. Hook, "The Social Dimensions of a Twelve-Man Jury Table," *Sociometry*, 24 (1961):297–315.

17. L. T. Howells and S. W. Becker, "Seating Arrangement and Leadership Emergence," *Journal of Abnormal and Social Psychology*, **64** (1962):148–150.

18. P. A. Hare and B. F. Bales, "Seating Position and Small Group Interaction," *Sociometry,* **26** (1963):480–486.

19. R. J. Pellegrini, "Some Effects of Seating Position on Social Perception," *Psychological Reports,* **28** (1971):887–893.

20. Michael Korda, *Power! How to Get It, How to Use It* (New York, Random House, 1975), p. 236.

21. Sommer, op cit.

22. Burgoon and Saine, op. cit.

23. E. T. Hall, *The Silent Language* (Garden City, N.Y., Doubleday, 1959). All references to Hall in the following pages are from this work.

24. Mehrabian, op. cit.

25. Korda, op. cit., p. 199.

26. See Nancy Henley, *Body Politics: Power, Sex, and Nonverbal Communication* (Englewood Cliffs, N.J., Prentice-Hall/Spectrum, 1977).

27. Barbara Bate, *Communication and the Sexes* (New York, Harper & Row, 1988).

28. Judy Cornelia Pearson, *Gender and Communication* (Dubuque, Iowa, Brown, 1985).

29. Gloria Leventhal and Michelle Matturo, "Differential Effects of Spatial Crowding and Sex on Behavior," *Perceptual Motor Skills,* **51** (1980):111–119; Billy A. Barios, Claire L. Corbitt, J. Philip, and Jeff S. Topping, "Effects of Social Stigma on Interpersonal Distance," *The Psychological Record,* **26** (1976):343–348.

30. Aubrey B. Fisher, "Differential Effects of Sexual Composition and Interactional Context on Interaction Patterns in Dyads," *Human Communication Research,* **9** (1983):225–238; Robert Sommer, "Studies in Personal Space," *Sociometry,* **22** (1959):247–260; Martin Giesen and Harry A. McClaren, "Discussion, Distance and Sex: Changes in Impressions and Attraction During Small Group Interaction," *Sociometry,* **39** (1976):60–70; Michael Argyle and Janet Dean, "Eye Contact, Distance and Affiliation," *Sociometry,* **28** (1965):289–304.

31. Michael A. Dosey and Murray Meisels, "Personal Space and Self-Protection," *Journal of Personality and Social Psychology,* **11** (1969):93–97.

32. Paul R. Bleda and Sharon Estee Bleda, "Effects of Sex and Smoking on Reactions to Spatial Invasion at a Shopping Mall," *The Journal of Social Psychology,* **104** (1978):311–312.

33. Gloria Leventhal, Marsha Lipshultz, and Anthony Chiodo, "Sex and Setting Effects on Seating Arrangement," *The Journal of Psychology,* **100** (1978):21–26.

34. Miles Patterson, Sherry Mullens, and Jeanne Romano, "Compensatory Reactions to Spatial Intrusion," *Sociometry,* **34** (1971):114–121.

35. Jeffery David Fisher and Donn Byrne, "Too Close for Comfort: Sex Differences in Response to Invasions of Personal Space," *Journal of Personality and Social Psychology,* **31** (1975):15–21.

36. D. B. Roger and R. L. Reid, "Small Group Ecology Revisited—Personal Space and Role Differentiation," *British Journal of Social and Clinical Psychology,* **17** (1978):43–46.

37. Dale F. Lott and Robert Sommer, "Seating Arrangements and Status," *Journal of Personality and Social Psychology,* **7** (1967):90–95.

38. Lois O. Stratton, Dennis J. Tekippe, and Grad L. Flick, "Personal Space and Self-Concept," *Sociometry,* **36** (1973):424–429.

39. Michele Andrisia Wittig and Paul Skolnick, "Sex Differences in Personal Space," *Sex Roles,* **4** (1978):493–503.

40. J. Guthrie Ford, Robert E. Cramer, and Gayle Owens, "A Paralinguistic Consideration of Proxemic Behavior," *Perceptual and Motor Skills,* **45** (1977):487–493.

41. Frank Prerost, "The Effects of High Spatial Density on Humor Appreciation: Age and Sex Differences," *Social Behavior and Personality,* **8** (1980):239–244.

42. Eric Sundstrom and Mary G. Sundstrom, "Personal Space Invasions: What Happens When the Invader Asks Permission?" *Environmental Psychology and Nonverbal Behavior* (Winter 1977):76–82; Denise Polit and Marianne LaFrance, "Sex Differences in Reaction to Spatial Invasion," *The Journal of Social Psychology,* **102** (1977):59–60.

43. Irene Hanson Frieze, "Nonverbal Aspects of Femininity and Masculinity Which Perpetuate Sex-Role Stereotypes," paper presented at the Eastern Psychological Association, 1974.

44. S. Thayer and W. Schiff, "Eye-Contact, Facial Expression, and the Experience of Time," *The Journal of Social Psychology* (1975):117–124; Zick Rubin, "Measurement of Romantic Love," *Journal of Personality and Social Psychology,*

16 (1970):265–273; Phoebe C. Ellsworth, J. Merrill Carlsmith, and Alexander Henson, "The Stare as a Stimulus to Flight in Human Subjects: A Series of Field Experiments," *Journal of Personality and Social Psychology,* **21** (1972):302–311; Rosalind D. Muirhead and Morton Goldman, "Mutual Eye Contact as Affected by Seating Position, Sex, and Age," *The Journal of Social Psychology,* **109** (1979):201–206; Phoebe C. Ellsworth and Linda M. Ludwig, "Visual Behavior in Social Interaction," *Journal of Communication,* **22** (1972):375–403.

45. Ralph Exline, David Gray, and Dorothy Shuette, "Visual Behavior in Dyads as Affected by Interview Content and Sex of Respondent," *Journal of Personality and Social Psychology,* **1** (1965):201–209.

46. Rosalind D. Muirhead and Morton Goldman, "Mutual Eye Contact as Affected by Seating Position, Sex, and Age," *The Journal of Social Psychology,* **109** (1979):201–206.

47. K. Dierks-Stewart, "Sex Differences in Nonverbal Communication: An Alternative Perspective" in Cynthia L. Berryman and Virginia A. Eman, eds., *Communication, Language and Sex: Proceedings of the First Conference* (Rowley, Mass., Newbury House, 1979), pp. 112–121.

48. Chris L. Kleinke, Armando A. Bustos, Frederick F. Meeker, and Richard A. Staneski, "Effects of Self-Attributed and Other Attributed Gaze on Interpersonal Evaluations Between Males and Females," *Journal of Experimental Social Psychology,* **9** (1973): 154–163; Michael Argyle, Jansur Lalljee, and Mark Cook, "The Effects of Visibility on Interaction in a Dyad," *Human Relations,* **21** (1968):3–17.

49. Albert Mehrabian, *Nonverbal Communication* (Chicago, Aldine-Atherton, 1972); Ross Buck, Robert E. Miller, and William F. Caul, "Sex, Personality, and Physiological Variables in the Communication of Affect Via Facial Expression," *Journal of Personality and Social Psychology,* **17** (1971):314–318.

50. Allen Schiffenbauer and Amy Babineau, "Sex Role Stereotypes and the Spontaneous Attribution of Emotion," *Journal of Research in Personality,* **10** (1976):137–145.

51. Daniel A. Yarmey, "Through the Looking Glass: Sex Differences in Memory for Self-Facial Poses," *Journal of Research in Personality,* **13** (1979):450–459.

52. Michael Argyle, *Bodily Communication* (New York, International Universities Press, 1975); K. Dierks-Stewart, "The Effects of Protracted Invasion on an Individual's Action Territory," unpublished master's thesis, Bowling Green State University, 1976; Susan J. Frances, "Sex Differences in Nonverbal Behavior," *Sex Roles,* **5** (1979):519–535; Mary B. Parlee, "Women Smile Less for Success," *Psychology Today,* **12** (1979):16.

53. Nancy Henley and Barrie Thorne, "Womanspeak and Manspeak: Sex Differences and Sexism in Communication, Verbal and Nonverbal," from Alice Sargent, ed., *Beyond Sex Roles* (St. Paul, Minn., West, 1977).

54. Sing Lau, "The Effect of Smiling on Personal Perception," *The Journal of Social Psychology,* **117** (1982):63–67.

55. Elizabeth Aries, "Verbal and Nonverbal Behavior in Single-Sex and Mixed-Sex Groups," *Psychological Reports,* **51** (1982):127–134.

56. Ibid.

57. Ray L. Birdwhistell, "Masculinity and Femininity as Display," in *Kinesics and Context,* by Ray L. Birdwhistell (Philadelphia, University of Pennsylvania Press, 1970).

58. P. Peterson, "An Investigation of Sex Differences in Regard to Nonverbal Body Gestures," *Proceedings of the Speech Communication Association Summer Conference,* Austin, 1975.

59. Ibid.

60. Robert Shuter, "A Study of Nonverbal Communication Among Jews and Protestants," *The Journal of Social Psychology,* **109** (1979):31–41.

61. Peterson, op. cit.

62. Ibid.

63. Ibid.

64. Nancy M. Henley, *Body Politics: Power, Sex and Nonverbal Communication* (Englewood Cliffs, N.J., Prentice Hall, 1977); Nancy M. Henley, "The Politics of Touch," from Phillip Brown, ed., *Radical Psychology* (New York, Harper & Row, 1973), pp. 421–433.

65. David W. Austin, "Nonverbal Cues Influencing Client and Nonclient Perception of Counselors," unpublished doctoral dissertation, University of Wyoming, 1973; Henley, *Body Politics,* op. cit; Henley, "The Politics of Touch," op. cit.

66. Jeffrey D. Fisher, M. Rytting, and R. Heslin, "Hands Touching Hands: Affective and Evaluative Affects in Interpersonal Touch," *Sociometry,* **39** (1976):416–421.

67. Dawn Druley, Dan Cassriel, and March H. Hollendar, "A Cuddler's Guide to Love," *Self Magazine* (May 1980):96–100.

68. Ibid.

69. Erving Goffman, *Interactional Ritual* (Garden City, N.Y., Doubleday/Anchor, 1967).

70. Schlenker, op. cit.

71. Korda, *Power!,* p. 268.

72. Tuan Nguyen, Richard Heslin, and Michele L. Nguyen, "The Meanings of Touch: Sex Differences," *Journal of Communication,* **25** (1975):92–103.

73. See Ralph V. Exline, "Visual Interaction: The Glances of Power and Preference," in J. K. Cole, ed., *Nebraska Symposium on Motivation* (Lincoln, University of Nebraska Press, 1971); Mehrabian, *Silent Messages.*

74. Dale G. Leathers, *Nonverbal Communication Systems* (Boston, Allyn & Bacon, 1976), pp. 33–34.

75. Paul Ekman and Wallace V. Friesen, "Nonverbal Leakage and Clues to Deception," *Psychiatry,* **32** (1969):88–106.

76. S. S. Tomkins, *Affect, Imagery, Consciousness* (New York, Springer, 1962).

77. Caroline F. Keating, Allan Mazur, and Marshall H. Segall, "Facial Gestures Which Influence the Perception of Status," *Sociometry,* **40** (1977):374–376.

78. James W. Tankard, "Effects of Eye Position on Person Perception," *Perceptual and Motor Skills,* **31** (1970):883–893.

79. Exline, "Visual Interaction: The Glances of Power and Preference," op. cit.

80. R. V. Exline, S. L. Ellyson, and B. E. Long, "Visual Behavior as an Aspect of Power Role Relationships," in *Nonverbal Communication of Aggression,* Patricia Plimer, Lester Krames, and Thomas Alloway, eds. (New York, Plenum, 1975).

81. Martin S. Remland, "Leadership Impressions and Nonverbal Communication in a Superior-Subordinate Interaction," paper presented at Speech Communication Association annual meeting, Louisville, Ky., 1982.

82. D. J. Moore, "To Trust, Perchance to Buy," *Psychology Today,* **16** (1982):50–54; Sing Lau, "The Effect of Smiling on Person Perception," *Journal of Social Psychology,* **117** (1982):63–67.

83. Mark. E. Comandena, "Nonverbal Correlates of Deception: A Contextual Analysis," paper presented at Speech Communication Association annual meeting, Louisville, Ky., 1982.

84. See Keith Gibbins, "Communication Aspects of Women's Clothes and Their Relation to Fashionability," *British Journal of Social and Clinical Psychology,* **8** (1964):301–312; Ellen Berscheid and Elaine Walster, "Physical Attractiveness," in *Advances in Experimental Social Psychology,* 7, Leonard Berkowitz, ed. (New York, Academic Press, 1974); C. L. Kleinke, *First Impressions: The Psychology of Encountering Others* (Englewood Cliffs, N.J., Prentice Hall, 1975).

85. Judson Mills and Elliot Aronson, "Opinion Change as a Function of the Communicator's Attractiveness and Desire to Influence," *Journal of Personality and Social Psychology* (1965):173–177; Harold Sigall and Elliot Aronson, "Liking for an Evaluator as a Function of Her Physical Attractiveness and Nature of the Evaluations," *Journal of Experimental Social Psychology,* **5** (1969):93–100; Robin N. Widgery and Bullock Webster, "The Effects of Physical Attractiveness upon Perceived Initial Credibility," *Michigan Speech Journal,* **4** (1969):9–15; Harold Sigal, Richard Page, and Ann C. Brown, "Effort Expenditure as a Function of Evaluation and Evaluator Attractiveness," *Representative Research in Social Psychology,* **2** (1971):19–25.

86. Berscheid and Walster, "Physical Attractiveness," op. cit.

87. J. Matthews, "In Offices across America, Attire Is Changing," *Washington Post* (January 31, 1994):26.

RECOMMENDED READINGS . . . .

Barbara Bate. *Communication and the Sexes.* Prospect Heights, Ill., Waveland, 1992.

Mark L. Hickson and Don W. Stacks. *NVC: Nonverbal Communication: Studies and Applications,* 3d ed. Dubuque, Iowa, Brown, 1993.

Mark L. Knapp. *Essentials of Nonverbal Communication.* New York, Holt, Rinehart & Winston, 1980. A brief and well-researched textbook on nonverbal communication.

Loretta A. Malandro and Larry L. Barker. *Nonverbal Communication,* 2d ed. Reading, Mass., Addison-Wesley, 1988. A well-researched book on nonverbal communication.

Virginia P. Richmond and James C. Mc-Croskey, *Nonverbal Communication in Interpersonal Relations.* Boston, Allyn and Bacon, 1995. These scholars provide specific applications of nonverbal communication to the interpersonal setting.

DISCUSSION QUESTIONS ....

1. Go into three offices and look closely at the layout of space, artifacts, lighting, decor, and the like. After each visit, answer the following questions:
   a. What is the person who uses the office like?
   b. What does this person do to facilitate or inhibit communication with others in the office?
   c. What status cues do you find in the office? Are those signals there on purpose or by accident?
2. Assume that one of the offices you visited for question 1 is yours. How would you arrange that office to:
   a. enhance your credibility?
   b. facilitate communication?
   c. inhibit communication?
   d. equalize status differences?
3. How would you decide what to wear to an important employment interview? How would you decide what to wear during your first day at work on a new job?

INTERNET ACTIVITIES ....

1. Suppose three new employees come to work in your department. Each speaks excellent English as a second language. One is from Japan, the second is from Saudi Arabia, the third is from Argentina. They are all entry-level employees, and all are in their mid-twenties. Would these facts influence how you interact with them? In particular terms, what can you find out from the Internet to guide you?
2. Given the same three employees, see what you can learn from the Internet about appropriate social distance. Use this chart to guide your note-taking, then bring your findings to class for comparison and contrast with the work of other students.

	Male, 25 years old	Female, 25 years old	Male, 60 years old	Female, 60 years old
Japanese Male				
Saudi Arabian male				
Argentinean male				
Japanese female				
Saudi Arabian female				
Argentinean female				

CHAPTER 7

Technology in the Workplace
Karen A. Burton

OBJECTIVES

Upon completion of this chapter, you should be able to:

1. Describe some characteristics of communication technologies.
2. List some communication technologies used in the workplace today.
3. Explain how technologies support electronic meetings and groups.
4. Discuss how the Internet has changed communication for organizations.
5. Given an example of how communication technologies are converging today.
6. Discuss how communication technologies influence organizations.

TELECOMMUTING AT DIGITAL EQUIPMENT

Karen Burton is a sales executive with Digital Equipment. Her team is responsible for $20 million in sales a year to a global chemical account. On a typical workday, Karen brings her coffee from the kitchen down the hall into her office.

152

She is barefoot and wearing shorts and a T-shirt. She opens her laptop, checks her calendar, and sets an alarm for a teleconference at 9 A.M. Noting a visit to a customer coming up in two weeks, she sends an electronic mail request to her travel service. Scanning the email, there is a message from her nephew, Dan: "Aunt Karen, I can't wait to go to New Orleans. . . ." She smiles and sends off a quick reply. Another email notifies her that a video conference for all employees is scheduled for 3 P.M. that day. The president of the company will announce an important new Internet product, and product engineers will demonstrate it in action. A tone lets her know that a fax is being received by her laptop, and soon the laser printer is printing her trip itinerary for her approval.

The phone rings. "Hello George, you sound like you're in a hurry. How can I help you?"

"Karen," George says, sounding harried, "I hate to ask this type of question, but what does Digital have comparable to a Compaq Proliant server? I need it right away."

While Karen is talking to George, she connects to the Internet and Compaq's home page. Looking at the product specifications, she clicks on Digital's Web IR (an Intranet information retrieval system), finds a similar product, and downloads the information to her laptop.

"Is this what you need, George?" She then clicks on a quotation system and tells him the prices of the Digital products. "And the delivery will be next day. George, I am sending you a quotation as we speak. I'll also include a detailed brochure on your new Digital computer. Would you rather get this by fax or email?"

Later Karen changes into business casual attire, tucks the laptop in her briefcase, and drives into town to a business conference outlet. She gives the attendant the code for her conference and settles down to participate in the training program.

After the product introduction ceremony, there is a phone number on the screen for a question-and-answer session with the product engineering team. "This is Mike, with Digital in UK. When will this product be shipping in Europe?" On the drive home, Karen checks her voicemail using her cellular phone and then returns phone calls.

Just another workday!

Digital Equipment is a technology company with $15 billion in sales and more than 50,000 employees worldwide. At Digital, work is something you do, not a place you go. In 1996, over 3,000 Digital employees were telecommuters, working from home, at customer sites, or on the road. "Most telecommuters feel their quality of life has improved, along with their productivity and job satisfaction," reports A. B. Blocker, manager of Digital's telecommuting program and a longtime telecommuter.[1]

Digital's telecommuting program has realized significant cost savings through reduced office space, reduced administrative support, and reduced spending on environmental compliance (each physical office or building in the United States must meet a variety of local, state, and federal regulations). There are some disadvantages. Finding space and quiet in the home, time spent traveling to business centers, and isolation from the support systems of an office environment can be hurdles. The benefits are flexible work hours, elimination of the stress and wasted time associated with commuting, and use of the technology tools that Digital provides for telecommuters.

Digital is not alone. In 1996, Business Research Group found that more than 3 million large and midsize companies offered telecommuting as an option to their employees.[2]

Telecommuting is possible because technologies enable work anytime, anyplace. Technology in the workplace affects how we communicate, the work we do, and the shape of organizations. In this chapter we discuss the rapidly changing world of communication technologies.

RAPIDLY CHANGING COMMUNICATION TECHNOLOGY ....

Developments in communication technology happen so rapidly that, by the time you read this sentence, all the specific technologies described in this chapter may be obsolete. Over the last twenty years, three important developments have transformed how we communicate in the workplace. First is the ability to create, store, process, and transmit any type of information in *digital* format. Second is the ever-increasing *speed* with which technology enables us to store, process, and transmit digital information. Third is the exponential *reduction of size and cost* of new technology. Digital technology has changed the nature of messages people use. People send and receive video, sound, and photographs, as well as text and graphics, literally at the speed of light. These three developments have begun to transform organizations and the nature of work.

All this rapid development leaves some people breathless. They feel they cannot possibly keep up. It helps to remember two things in this fast-paced environment: First, change is constant. Rather than trying to keep up with all the developments, find an organizing framework that can help you select an appropriate technology to communicate a particular message at a given time. Second, communication technologies are only tools—they cannot replace basic communication skills. The goal of this chapter is to provide you with an organizing framework, an overview of communication technologies in the workplace, and an understanding of the impacts of communication technologies on organizations.

CATEGORIZING COMMUNICATION TECHNOLOGIES ....

Communication technologies can be categorized (or organized) by their characteristics. We introduce four: (1) time and place; (2) interactivity; (3) one-to-one, one-to-many, or many-to-many orientation; and (4) person or subject. These characteristics can help us evaluate and select an appropriate technology for a given communication task.

Exhibit 7.1	COMMUNICATION TECHNOLOGY ACROSS TIME AND PLACE		
		TIME	
		Same	Different
PLACE	Same	Face to face meeting Slide show tools Electronic meeting aids	Answering machine Information Kiosk Groupware
	Different	Telephone Teleconferencing Videoconferencing On-line Chat	Voice mail Electronic mail CD-ROM Internet

Time and Place

Communication tools allow us to communicate across time and place[3] (see Exhibit 7.1). Face-to-face meetings happen in the same time and same place. Telephone conversations happen at the same time, but the communicators may be across the street or on the other side of the world. An information kiosk in an airport gives the same information to many people at different times, but in the same place. Electronic mail and voicemail allow us to communicate with others at their convenience—in different times and different places.

Interactivity

Another characteristic of communication technologies is the degree to which they are interactive. *Interactive* means "acting or capable of acting on each other." A face-to-face conversation is the most highly interactive form of communication. The telephone allows people to talk to each other in real time, but body language is lost. Voicemail is not interactive—it is a one-way communication. It may lead to an interactive call back—but only if you leave your number! Electronic mail (email) is more interactive than voice mail because it automatically includes a return address. Messages are quickly exchanged.

Electronic documents can be interactive. A book on CD-ROM allows you to act on it by following your own path through the book, selecting a video clip, or reading the text. Internet documents are even more interactive. You can search for an article, link to the sources, send electronic mail to the author, read comments from other readers, or post a question of your own. Printed books and articles are not at all interactive: you cannot easily communicate with the author, sources, or other readers.

One-to-One, One-to-Many, or Many-to-Many Orientation

Communication technologies enable one-to-one, one-to-many, or many-to-many communication. Basic telephone service is an example of a one-to-one communication technology. Teleconferencing connects many to many. Electronic mail distribution lists send the same message to a list of people and thus are a form of one-to-many communication. If you subscribe to some Internet newsgroups, every member receives all the messages you post and you receive all the messages other members post. A newsgroup is a many-to-many communication tool.

Person or Subject

Some communication technologies, such as the telephone and electronic mail, require you to know the unique phone number or address of the person you want to contact. Other technologies allow you to search for an interesting subject and to post a message. For example, Bulletin Board Services and Internet newsgroups are organized by subject. This allows anyone with interest in or expertise on a subject to participate without having to know exactly where or whom to contact.

In summary, though communication technologies are changing at an ever-accelerating rate, these four characteristics are a constant organizing framework. Technologies can help you span time and place differences, communicate interactively or while disconnected, reach one or many people, and find information by subject or by person. Understanding these characteristics will guide you to select the appropriate communication tool to relay a message or find the information you need and will help you be a skilled business communicator.

COMMUNICATION TECHNOLOGY IN BUSINESS AND PROFESSIONAL SETTINGS ....

Here we examine five general classes of communication technologies in the workplace, as shown in Exhibit 7.2: spoken, written, group communication, productivity tools, and information navigation tools. Along the way, we use

Exhibit 7.2 CLASSES OF COMMUNICATION TECHNOLOGIES				
Spoken	Written	Group	Productivity	Navigation
Telephone	Word Processing	Email	Calendar	Organizational Data
Cellular	Publishing	Video text	Address Book	Public databases
Pager	Facsimile	Bulletin Boards	"To Do" List	Executive Information
Voicemail	Viewers	Groupware	Personal Digital	System (EIS)
Voice Input	Browsers	Slide show	Assistant (PDA)	Intelligent Agents
Voice Command	Hypermedia	Teleconference	Contact Manager	"Spiders" or search agents
Voice Query	CD-ROM	Videoconference		
		Decision support		

some new terms. Each new word is defined either in the text or in the glossary on pages 176–177.

Spoken or Voice Technologies

The oldest and most universal communication technology used today is the *telephone,* developed in 1876. It has taken over 100 years to achieve worldwide telephone service. What is most extraordinary about this achievement is that the wires, fiber-optic cables, satellites, switches, and many other kinds of necessary equipment are invisible to us. We take for granted that we can pick up the telephone and within seconds speak to just about anyone, anywhere in the world.

New developments in voice communication have given us a host of new features, such as call forwarding and call waiting. Wireless technologies, like *cellular phones,* have extended our ability to talk to others while driving our car or sitting out by the pool. If you don't carry a phone, a *pager* can contact you, deliver electronic mail, provide voice messaging, and allow you to type a quick reply. The pager will call the sender back and speak the text to him or her without your having to find a phone.

Voicemail (a computerized phone answering system) stores voice messages as digital files to save and forward. Voicemail reduces "telephone tag," a frustrating exchange of telephone messages. However, voicemail can also inhibit communication. You may have experienced the frustration of not being able to reach a "real person." Voicemail can be very effective in relaying information that does not require discussion. When you are connected to someone's voicemail, always leave complete information including your name, your number, and a message. If you have voicemail, keep your voicemail greeting brief and up-to-date.

Interactive voice response allows companies to route incoming calls using voice menus. Interactive voice response systems provide 24-hour access to information (such as checking account balances) and reduce labor cost for answering and routing calls. However, according to John Goodman, president of Technical Assistance Research Programs, the downside is "the minute a customer gets voice mail, you take a 10-percent hit in customer satisfaction."[4] Organizations should give the caller an option to speak to someone and limit menu choices to no more than four.

Today's voice tools allow us to speak text into word processors (*voice input*) and command a computer to do simple functions (*voice command*). Voice command is essential when users need to have their hands or eyes busy on another task. When you are driving, you can tell your cellular phone to "call home." Manufacturing operators need to drive forklifts while they input inventory changes into shipping computers. Automated voice attendants eliminate the need for a receptionist at a business office to direct calls and have reduced the need for directory assistance operators.

Voice query allows you to retrieve information. For example, you can call a stock quoting service, ask for the appropriate stock exchange (New York, NASDAQ, or Toronto), name one of 2,000 companies, and hear an up-to-date stock quote in seconds. In Orlando, Florida, the American Automobile Association (AAA) offers voice direction-finding instructions. The caller speaks two telephone numbers to indicate starting point and destination. The system calculates the shortest distance and speaks driving instructions. This service is not feasible using live operators, since the computer creates new instructions instantly for each request.[5]

Voice technologies will soon revolutionize the way we use computers. Voice command will lead to the most important voice technology of all—*natural language computer interface.* Access to all kinds of digital information will be as simple as talking to a communication device. It will likely be too small to allow keyboard or even touch input. Soon, when we can speak to our computers, the digital world will be as universally accessible as the telephone is today.[6]

Written Communication Technology

Document creation and publishing are the most commonly used communication technologies in the workplace. *Word processors* create, edit, print, and store electronic documents. Dozens of word processors are available, such as Microsoft *Word,* Lotus *AmiPro,* and Claris *Works.* Word processors offer many options for creating a document, including typing on a keyboard, speaking, scanning a page, or even handwriting. Once a document is created, word processors provide almost unlimited editing capabilities, from simply moving a sentence to checking spelling and grammar. Users can create *multimedia* documents by combining text with graphics, images, video, and sound. Finally, word processors print and store documents electronically. Note that while word processors can deliver a polished, professional document, they cannot write a well-crafted message. *Message* or *massage* are both correct to the spellchecker; a person must provide the context and content.

Desktop publishing is more sophisticated than word processing. Publishing tools require more skill to use and more time to learn. They provide advanced layout features such as multiple columns per page, wrapping text around graphics, and preparation of electronic output for high-speed, full-color printing presses. These tools were once available only to highly skilled layout designers. Now these sophisticated tools and a personal computer make publishing accessible to many more people. At the same time, such tools have raised our expectations. We expect fast, polished results.

Today the differences between desktop publishing and word processing have blurred because the sophistication of word processors has advanced so rapidly. Generally, word processing is appropriate for most business communication and small publishing jobs. Desktop publishing works better for designing newsletters, manuals, and any document that requires hard-copy distribution or needs the polish of full-color printing.

Document sharing software allows people with different word processors, desktop publishers, or even types of computers to share the same documents. For example, Adobe developed *portable document format* (pdf) to view or print finished documents without having the programs that created them. For example, say an artist creates a polished brochure on a Macintosh computer using a desktop publishing tool. The brochure is sent as a "pdf" file along with the *Acrobat* viewer. A salesperson with a Windows notebook computer can download the brochure, view it, and print it using only the *Acrobat* viewer. The Adobe *Acrobat* viewer is a free program that works on many computers.

On the Internet a free program called a *web browser* allows many types of computers to view documents, images, video, and sound, even though they may have been created in different countries or on different systems using many different software programs. This is possible because of the Internet standards. There are many document sharing tools available today. As standards are widely adopted, electronic document sharing between organizations with vastly different communication technologies is fast becoming reality.

Another publishing concept, *hypertext,* creates interactive documents. When you last read a book, did you turn to Chapter 1 and read the entire book sequentially, page one, page two, and so on? We guess not. We guess you followed your own path through the pages. You probably scanned the table of contents, flipped to a chapter that interested you, then looked up a note at the end of a chapter. With hypertext, you follow "links" (usually highlighted or underlined words) through the text in this same way. *Hypermedia* simply extends this concept to include all kinds of digital information, just like multimedia documents. These technologies form the basis for interactive training software, CD-ROM publishing, and the Internet World Wide Web (WWW). The world of publishing will never be the same as a result.

Multimedia requires large amounts of storage, especially for video, images, and sound. CD-ROM (Compact Disc, Read Only Memory) has made multimedia affordable. The first interactive multimedia CD-ROM—Grolier's Electronic Encyclopedia—was not available until 1987.[7] In 1994, only two thousand titles were available. By 1996, over 10,000 titles were on the market and almost every personal computer sold included a CD-ROM.[8] Today a CD-ROM can store 600 MB (megabytes, or million bytes) or 250,000 pages of text and costs about $7.[9] Issuing software programs and documentation on CD-ROM reduces the costs of publishing and distribution. Businesses distribute manuals, literature, and interactive training inexpensively using CD-ROM. Microsoft's *Encarta Encyclopedia* is on one CD-ROM containing 9 million words of text, 8 hours of sound, 7,000 photographs and illustrations, 800 maps, 250 interactive charts and tables, and 100 animation and video clips—and costs less than $100.[10] CD-ROM is predicted to have ten times the storage and cost even less in the future.[11]

Communicating between Groups: Networked Technologies

For groups of people in an organization to communicate electronically requires a device (such as a computer or telephone) and a *network*, the connections between the devices. Within a building or a campus, a "local area network" (LAN) using wire or optical fiber can provide from 10 Mbps (million bits per second) to 1,000 Mbps. "Wide area networks" (WANs) connect across town or across the world.

Sometimes new Internet users, called "newbys," make mistakes that produce very insulting responses from others on the network. These insults are called "flames." Is it ethical for more experienced users to "flame newbys" as a way of teaching them?

The most universal WAN is the telephone network. Dialing up over the telephone network, 36 Kbps (thousand bits per second) was the fastest speed available at the beginning of 1997. To transfer a complex image could take 10 minutes at 36 Kbps, compared to just seconds at 1,000 Mbps over a LAN.

The rapid advancements of multimedia technology have pushed network providers to increase their WAN transmission capability. Telephone companies now offer Integrated Services Digital Network (ISDN), a digital telephone connection. ISDN carries voice, data, or video over copper or fiber lines with speeds up to 56 Kbps—six to ten times faster than standard telephone lines. Cable companies are developing and testing cable modems with up to 350 times faster speeds (10 to 27 Mbps).[12] Note that these speeds are still relatively slow compared to 1,000 Mbps LANs.

Organizations create their own private WANs. Commercial networks, such as America Online, Prodigy, and Compuserv, are WANs that sell access time to organizations and individuals. Public access WANs include the telephone network, cable television, and the Internet. There is a convergence of networking technologies going on today. High-speed networks will connect us all with virtually unlimited digital service in the future.

Electronic Mail

The communication technology that has driven organizations to build networks and the most widely used network application is *electronic mail*. Electronic mail (email) allows you to send and receive messages over a network. Most large organizations have their own "secure" networks for electronic mail. The Internet acts as the Interorganizational network for many businesses and individuals to exchange electronic mail. More than 25 billion email messages were sent in 1995.[13] A conservative estimate is that by 1998, 150 million people will use email.[14]

Electronic mail typically has forms for addressing mail and a simple text editor to create messages. Features include address books (Exhibit 7.3), nicknames, and distribution lists. Folders store and organize messages. New mail goes into an "Inbox" folder. Messages you have sent go into an "Outbox" folder. Almost any digital file can be sent as an attachment to the electronic mail message. There are many electronic mail software programs available for the personal computer, including Lotus *ccMail* and Microsoft *Mail*. Internet browsers include a mail feature. Commercial services such as *America Online* offer electronic mail.

Organizations use email differently depending on their culture, policies, and resources. With more people working from home or telecommuting, some companies are encouraging their employees to socialize via email and the Internet in order to provide a setting for the kind of innovation that results from casual encounters in the office with coworkers. Verifone, for example, gives every member of each mobile worker's family their own email address.[15]

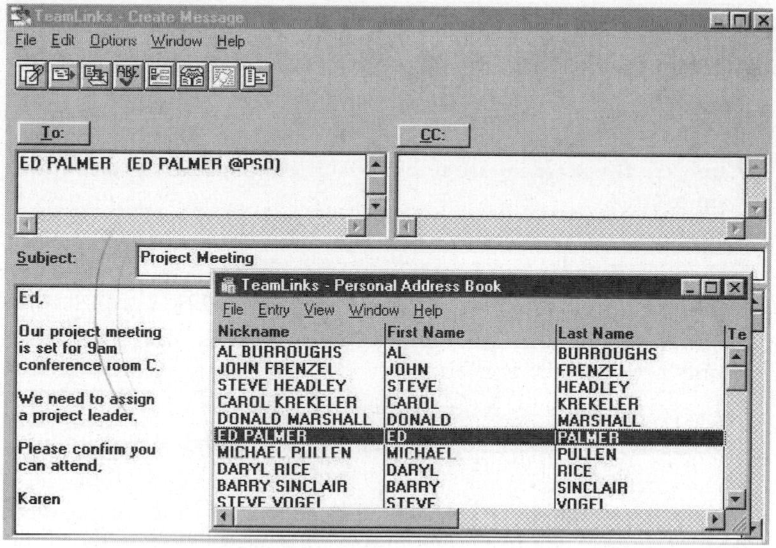

Exhibit 7.3
DRAG AND
DROP TO
ADDRESS
ELECTRONIC
MAIL.

Electronic mail is rapidly replacing written memos and letters. Email can encourage collaboration, streamline communication, and distribute work to remote workers.[16] However, you still need good writing skills to communicate effectively via email. A 1996 study found that 65 percent of email messages failed to communicate their meaning the first time.[17] Exhibit 7.4 lists some basic rules of email etiquette.

Sharing Information over Networks

Both telephone and electronic mail are directed to a person. Other tools, like videotext and groupware, share information by subject. You do not have to know an address, the name of a person, or where to locate the information.

Today's work-group computing tools evolved from text sharing tools such as videotext and bulletin board systems. *Videotext* distributes information from a computer to an inexpensive, text-only terminal over a network. The largest videotext project, *Minitel* in France, is a consumer service operating since the early 1980s with over 8 million home users today. Minitel replaced telephone directories with small, free text terminals, then expanded to thousands of services, including train schedules and catalogs.[18] Organizations adopt videotext to publish electronically, in one place, frequently used documents, such as personnel policies, product descriptions, or operating instructions.

Videotext is a one-to-many communication tool. The software requires specialized knowledge to create and store documents on a large computer. Everyone in the organization uses the most current version of a document. This saves publishing and distribution costs. Document updates happen more often than would be feasible in print. Since access is by subject, anyone can find a particular document easily. These wonderful applications are already being replaced by

---

Exhibit 7.4   EMAIL ETIQUETTE

These "rules of etiquette" will help you be a good email citizen:

1. Treat email as seriously as other business communication.

   Put everything into the first paragraph. Readers want and need to scan their email quickly. If your ideas are to be considered they must be clear, straightforward, and up front.

2. Don't contribute to email overload.

   Be brief. Email is no place to write expansive letters. Think of email messages as brief memos. If you must send a long written work, attach it to the email memo.

   Never flood your receiver with written materials. Don't "reply to all" if you really only need to reply to the sender.

3. Be specific and action-oriented in your subject line.

4. Don't use ALL CAPS. They're hard to read and they mean "shout."

5. Remember: Email is not private. Although email feels almost like talk, and even though you can touch the "delete" button at any time, email never really goes away. Email is more like publishing than like talking on the phone, because email messages remain in the computers (sent from and received by). Plus, the receiver can forward an email message to the world. Resist using language you would not want to defend. Be uniformly courteous and careful.

6. Give negative feedback or discuss conflicts in person—not via email.

---

groupware and Internet technologies, however, because the newer technologies are easier to use and less expensive to maintain.

Bulletin boards (BBS) are similar to videotext in that they offer a central information store organized by subject. However, bulletin boards are a more interactive, many-to-many technology. Readers can post questions and add comments of their own. Bulletin boards are ideal for providing product service and support or for sharing interest in a topic. For example, a product support bulletin board service lists frequently asked questions (FAQs). Users search by keyword for a particular problem. They see postings of answers by experts, as well as the comments and experiences of other users. A newsgroup is a similar tool on the Internet. By the time you read this chapter, a web page or groupware tool may already have become the standard for providing shared information, replacing videotext and bulletin board services.

Groupware technology combines the information sharing of videotext or bulletin board services with the messaging capabilities of electronic mail. Organizations use these tools to automate business processes. Using *Lotus Notes,* for example, participants share information by subject, route messages, and fill out forms. Suppose many different people participate in writing a proposal to build a new manufacturing facility. Engineers will design it, purchasing agents will get pricing from vendors, accountants will analyze the costs, and management will weigh the expected output of the facility against the total cost. Each of these people will participate in a Notes conference called "Build New Plant," posting their part of the information, posing questions, and checking on progress even though they may be in different cities. Once the proposal is complete, a Notes application routes a form with the final project numbers for electronic approval. When they build the manufacturing facility, engineers and construction managers will update progress against the "Project Status" conference.

Meetings

Work groups spend a great deal of their time in meetings. No wonder so many communication tools are available to facilitate meetings and help teams accomplish their tasks. Presentation software and spreadsheet graphics provide visual aids. Other tools such as teleconferencing, videoconferencing, and electronic whiteboards make meetings possible when groups cannot be face-to-face. Process tools, such as decision support, guide groups to better results. Group participants who use these tools report more creativity, greater productivity, increased efficiency,[19] higher membership satisfaction, and greater desire to use the tools in the future.[20]

Presentation tools, such as Microsoft *PowerPoint* or Harvard *Business Graphics*, allow you to design, create, and present exciting visual aids. (You may wish to refer to Chapter 15 for a discussion of visual aids as supporting material. When speakers use presentation software, the effect on the audience can be very powerful. Indeed, Pearson, Folshke, Paulson, and Burggraf[21] found that visual materials improve retention, clarity, and audience interest levels and that speakers using them appear to be more credible than speakers who don't use them.

Slide show software allows you to work from an outline, create speaker notes, time your presentation, and use transition effects. High-impact colors, graphics, clip art, audio and video clips, and even animation add excitement to presentations. Special effects should reinforce your message, not overwhelm the viewer. Today presentation tools are the norm for professional presentations.

Spreadsheet tools, such as Microsoft *Excel*, Lotus *1-2-3*, or Borland *Quatro Pro*, allow you to reduce large amounts of numerical data into a graphical presentation format. These tools excel for explaining financial results or analyzing a series of numerical reports. A presentation tool may incorporate a spreadsheet graphic.

Even if you cannot meet face-to-face, prepare visuals for electronic meetings using presentation tools. Ensure that each participant will have the presentation ahead of time. Prepare for a teleconference by sending the presentation through electronic mail or in hard copy format. Plan to share the presentation over the videoconferencing network.

Teleconferencing allows people to hold meetings over the telephone, even though they may be in many different places. For a small monthly charge, individuals can connect two other people on the telephone for impromptu meetings. Organizations use teleconferencing services to connect small groups or hundreds of people by calling a special number at an assigned time. For example, one company's sales managers from across the country have a teleconference each Friday afternoon at 4 P.M. to review sales that week and to answer questions about their business. A laptop support group offers a teleconference each week, to give a brief talk and answer questions from salespeople.

Teleconferences can be quickly arranged and are inexpensive. For large groups, it is important to have an agenda and a moderator for the call to facilitate taking turns. Teleconferencing has its limitations, however. Only one person can speak at a time. Also, you lose the nonverbal feedback that is available when you meet with group members in person. Visuals are difficult to incorporate, especially with large groups. Because of these limitations, teleconferencing is most effective for single-issue discussions and well-structured informational meetings.

Video conferencing allows you to see as well as hear over the network. Meetings held this way are generally better organized and more productive than teleconferences.[22] Today, special video conferencing rooms provide two-way interactive video of participants, two-way whiteboards, and shared presentation visuals. (Incidentally, AT&T first introduced this concept at the 1964 New York World's Fair.) Using this technology, organizations can save enormous amounts of money and time required for travel. Studies show that 75 percent of business travel is to attend meetings.[23]

With high-speed networks and powerful personal computers, some people now videoconference right at their desks. A tiny camera is built in to the PC monitor to allow the person you are in contact with to see you, and you see the other person in a window on the PC monitor. White Pine's *CU-SeeMe* software (Exhibit 7.5) enables multi-user video conferencing, shares and annotates documents, and offers a chat feature (for users with a connection under 100 Kbps). Someday we may all use a videophone, just as we use a telephone today.

Electronic whiteboards, such as the Xerox *Liveboard,* extend video conferencing to shared handwritten and electronic information. *Liveboard* looks like a whiteboard such as those found in classrooms and conference rooms. It is a self-contained unit that includes a personal computer, an electronic pen, a key-

**Exhibit 7.5
VIDEO-
CONFERENC-
ING ON A
PERSONAL
COMPUTER**

board, and a mouse. A *Liveboard* unit at each location of a video conference allows participants to all see the same displayed information. The board can display any information that you could display on a personal computer, such as presentation visuals, spreadsheets, or computer graphics. Participants can also write on the whiteboard using an electronic pen.[24] Whiteboard technology allows people to record the product of their conversations and decision-making meetings for future use. At the touch of a button, the board prints a copy of the display or stores the entire conference on the computer. Using this technology, anyone who could not "make" the meeting can "review it" later.

Some people are worried that as we delegate more and more to computers we will forget basic skills. Rogers calls this outcome "deskilling." Do you think business organizations should compensate for deskilling the work force by providing workers with education? Would that compromise the American education system?

Virtual reality is emerging as a potential alternative to video conferencing. Virtual reality uses computer graphics to simulate a meeting place. Participants see each other as graphical images on the computer. Each participant wears a headset that allows him or her to view the three-dimensional "meeting room" and see the images of other participants. Some systems show a three-dimensional image on a screen; more advanced systems project a holographic image of the participant in the room.

Virtual reality can show body language and provide awareness of eye contact, cues often lost in videoconferencing. Presentations can include three-dimensional graphics. For example, a construction progress meeting could include a walk-through of the proposed building design. However, virtual reality is expensive and the current technology requires bulky equipment.

Video conferencing and virtual reality technologies provide the visual cues and body language of a face-to-face meeting. *Decision support systems* eliminate undesirable interpersonal communication cues from the meeting process. For example, a group can hold a brainstorming session with each participant typing comments on a computer screen. The system projects these comments for the whole group to view without showing who created each comment. This frees people to be more open and focus on the quality of the ideas, rather than on the individual. Some people might hesitate to disagree with their boss or a friend in a face-to-face meeting. Using decision support allows everyone to freely express their opinions, and better decision making can result.

In summary, technologies that support groups include networks, electronic mail, information sharing tools, and meeting facilitation tools. Organizations are assigning work to task teams, self-managing teams, and departmental work groups. These technologies improve productivity, increase collaboration, and streamline communication in today's workplace.

Productivity Tools

Personal productivity tools include personal organizers, personal digital assistants, and contact managers. These tools are standard in nearly all workplaces today. They replace the desktop calendar, Rolodex or address book, phone book, "to do" list, and many other paper tools.

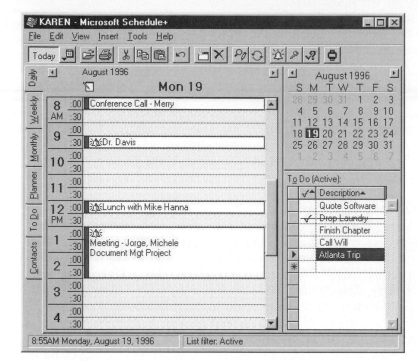

Exhibit 7.6
VIEW OF A
CALENDAR
AND "TO DO"
LIST

Personal organizer software is an electronic version of the calendar, "to do" list, and address book (Exhibit 7.6). Using these tools, such as Lotus *Organizer,* Microsoft *Schedule+,* and Starfish *Sidekick,* you can track meetings and appointments, view your schedule by day, week, month, or year, prioritize a "to do" list, and update your address book. You can set an alarm to remind you of a meeting, and you can share your calendar with others.

A *personal digital assistant* (PDA) is a specialized palm-size (or smaller) computer that includes personal organizer software and other features, such as wireless networking, electronic mail, paging, handwriting recognition, and Internet access. PDAs are low-cost and portable. They must limit storage and applications to achieve miniature size and low cost. In 1996, Texas Instruments' Personal Organizer weighs 4.8 ounces and costs $150. The Apple MessagePad weighs less than 1 pound and costs $800. At Disney World in Florida, workers do customer surveys using Apple MessagePads and a special pen to fill in answers on the handheld screen.[25] Companies like UPS use special PDAs to reduce delivery paperwork and capture customer signatures electronically. Other applications automate paper-intensive jobs in retail, customer service, and health care.

Contact managers integrate a database of contacts (like a detailed address book) with other tools found in personal organizers. Contact managers keep a history of activities, write reports about how you've used your time, create form letters, process electronic mail, and even dial the telephone. Salespeople, lawyers, and accountants were the first to use popular contact managers, like

Symantec's *ACT!* Many organizations standardize on the personal organizer or contact manager employees use, so they can share schedules and reporting.[26]

Today offices still have phone books and fax (facsimile) machines. A *fax* machine transmits the image of a document over the telephone lines. Fax machines are inexpensive, use the telephone network, and can transmit any hard-copy document. Personal computers with fax programs can exchange documents with people who don't have a computer. However, fax is only an interim technology for document sharing. When personal computers and networks become as universally available as the telephone is today, fax, along with paper calendars and phone books, will be obsolete.

Navigating through Information

Organizations must manage large amounts of *internal* information about their business, such as product specifications, service descriptions, operating instructions, financial results, and personnel records. To keep current on their industry, they use *external* information services, such as *Dun & Bradstreet* for credit ratings on vendors and customers, *Dialog* for market research, and *Nexus/Lexis* for news and legal publications. Retrieval services, such as *Individual First!* or *Profound*, scan thousands of daily news articles selecting those that match a user profile and keywords related to an industry, then send a summary via electronic mail. For example, if you work for a chemical company as a computer programmer, you could receive any articles about new developments in computers as well as news about your company and your company's competitors.

Executive information systems (EIS) summarize large amounts of information, represent it graphically, and allow many different views. For example, Phillips Petroleum developed an executive information system to set the price of gasoline based on the global supply of oil, refining capacity of their plants, and customer demand. The effect of this technology was to decentralize decision making. Pricing decisions previously made by senior managers, with input from staffs of analysts, are now made by local terminal managers using the EIS system and taking into account local competitors' prices.[27]

How will you keep up with all this information? *Intelligent agents* allow you to filter, prioritize, and customize information. For example, an electronic mail agent automatically files incoming mail into folders by criteria that you select. Messages from your boss might go into "Read Immediately." A message with the subject phrase "Project Beta" might go into a folder by that name. If you get a copy (or cc) of a message being sent to someone else, it might go into a "Read Later" folder.

Agent technology learns from your habits, subscribes you to interest groups that match your profile, automatically deletes junk mail, and summarizes information for you. An example is an Internet tool called *PointCast*. *PointCast* displays a steady news feed of headlines on your computer screen based on your preferences. You can click on any headline to retrieve the full news story. The software and the service are free; they are supported by intermittent advertising spots.[28] Another well-known intelligent agent called *Firefly* helps to find movies and music that you might like by learning about you and comparing your likes and dislikes with those of other users.[29]

THE INTERNET . . . .

> *If the Internet continues to become as widely deployed at the rate it's going today, in five to 10 years all telecommunication will . . . be based on what the Internet (then) becomes. The Internet is going to evolve into a two-way, real-time communication system for data . . . (developing) in 10 years as the phone did in 100 years.*[30]

Jim Clark, CEO, Netscape, in a Luxembourg address, July, 1996

The *Internet* (the "Net") is a collection of *inter*connected *net*works that make up a worldwide information utility. The Internet evolved from a 1969 Department of Defense project called ARPANET. Initially it was four computers linked by a network. By 1995, there were over 5 million computers participating. The National Science Foundation subsidizes and maintains the core network today. Universities, research institutions, and organizations connect their networks to the Net. Individuals access the Internet through local Internet service providers and commercial networks such as America Online, Prodigy, and Compuserv. Just like our interstate highway system, the Internet belongs to all of us since our tax dollars built it. And just like our interstate system, it is always congested and under construction!

With the introduction of the *World Wide Web (WWW)* in 1992, businesses and individuals began to use the Internet in exponentially growing numbers, adding a million users each month by 1995. The WWW is an easy-to-use, graphical interface to the Internet that requires a personal computer and a software program called a "web browser." The web browser is a software program on your desktop designed to display web pages with many types of digital information—text, images, graphics, photos, animation, video, and sound. The National Center for Supercomputing Applications (NCSA) developed the first web browser, *Mosaic,* and freely distributed it. Today there are many web browsers, such as Netscape *Navigator* and Microsoft's *Internet Explorer.*

You can find virtually anything and everything by searching the Net. For example, a search on "Japan" would turn up a virtual tour of Tokyo, today's yen conversion factor, live pictures of Japanese sights, satellite photos of the Japanese islands, a map of Tokyo subways, and much more. To find this information, you simply access any one of the many powerful search engines available to you on the Internet (such as *AltaVista,* shown in Exhibit 7.7) and enter the keyword (in this case, "Japan"). In seconds, you will receive back a list of all Internet sites that mention Japan. The list is your link to those sites, which you can visit with a click of your mouse. The advent of free and easy-to-use search engines and web browsers has made billions of pages of Internet information accessible to the general public.

The Net allows many different types of computers to share many different types of information using Internet standards. These tools are inexpensive and easy to use. Organizations are adopting these same tools to distribute internal information. When a company creates a private network using the standards and software tools used on the Internet, it is called an *Intranet*.

> The Internet developed in an unregulated environment. No coherent policy exists regarding privacy, security, intellectual property rights, pornography, and access. Should the Internet be regulated? If so, by whom?

The Internet connects business-owned private networks with universities, research groups, and other companies—their customers and suppliers—and with millions of individuals. Unprecedented interorganizational communication has changed how organizations do business. Individuals can compete with global companies by marketing or publishing on the Internet. The very nature of marketing and publishing is changing right before our eyes on the Net.

For more information about the Internet, see Internet Sources and Internet Activities at the end of this chapter.

CONVERGING TECHNOLOGIES

One trend that you may have already discerned as you read about these communication technologies is that they are converging. Word processors and desktop publishers both incorporate multimedia. Devices like BellSouth's Simon, for example, can combine a cellular phone and a PDA. Nearly every tool described here—from a word processor to a PDA—incorporates some type of Internet access. Radio comes over the Internet and radio shows advertise Internet home pages. Soon we may have all these technologies in the wallet-sized single information device predicted by Bill Gates, CEO of Microsoft, in his 1995 book *The Road Ahead*.[31]

Exhibit 7.7
SEARCHING THE INTERNET USING ALTAVISTA

ALTAVISTA Search OnSite Knowledge | Advanced | Simple | Private eXtension Products | Help

Search [the Web ▼] and Display the Results [in Standard Form ▼]

["communication technologies"] [Submit]

Tip: To get an exact match count, go to Advanced Search and select **Display the Results as a Count only**

Word count: communication technologies: about 8000

Documents 1-10 of about 7000 matching some of the query terms, best matches first.

Alló Communication Technologies, Inc.
Both speed and productivity are a must for today's business environments: the ability to

COMMUNICATION TECHNOLOGY IN ORGANIZATIONS . . . .

There can be no doubt about the influence of technology on organizations. Communication technologies enable organizations to do business. The use of technology, in turn, has an impact on the organization, its culture, its structure, and ultimately, its success in meeting its goals.

Selecting the Right Technology

Organizations use technologies to perform tasks that relate to their business goals.[32] Communication technology, like any other business investment, is carefully selected and justified. To select the right communication tool, you must weigh the cost to prepare and distribute a message against the benefits of that message and the social context.

Selecting the right technology requires attention to five factors: message, audience, context, time, and cost versus benefit.

Message

First, consider the message. Are you providing information, seeking to persuade, or setting out a course of action? Presentation software might be effective for a marketing message, but spreadsheet software might be more effective for a discussion of financial results. Graphics and images more effectively relay a complicated message than does text alone. Note that if a message is complex, requires negotiation, or deals with controversial subjects, most people prefer to communicate face-to-face.[33]

Careful consideration of the optimal form and "packaging" of messages is well worth the time it takes. Managers who can select appropriate technology for a message have longer tenure, higher positions, and better performance reviews.[34]

Audience

Who will be your audience and what are their expectations? Is the message to one person or to a group? Will the audience be in the same time and place, the same time but a different place, or in different times and places? The more you know about your audience, the more effective you can be.

Context

The context of your message includes formal and informal policies, legal considerations, and the social environment. Most organizations have policies about how to use communication technologies appropriately. Some of these policies are explicit and published, while others are informal and learned through experience. Most companies restrict the distribution of trade secrets, personnel information, or anything that is "company confidential." Other policies are as simple as using courtesy and appropriate language.

Be aware that electronic mail and voicemail, while they may seem private, are open to review by the communication service provider. If you are working in an organization, that means that the organization has the right to review your messages. Email and other forms of electronic communication are protected under the Electronic Communication Privacy Act of 1986, which prohibits a third party (for example, the government, the police, or an individual) from accessing your electronic communication without consent or a search warrant. Legally, however, sending a communication via email is the equivalent of sending a postcard in that neither has the same protection as a first class letter.[35] Consider any electronic document as thoughtfully as you would approach its hard-copy equivalent. Also, keep in mind that using the delete function on a computer to remove a document does not mean the document can no longer be retrieved.

> Organizations adopt technologies to increase productivity and decrease costs. The result is often loss of jobs. What obligations, if any, do organizations have toward the people whose jobs disappear? Should the government become involved in the problem?

The social environment of an organization influences the use of technologies. Coworkers' attitudes, past experiences and skills, ease of access, training, reliability, individual differences such as personality, and constraints of time, place, and cost are all social factors that influence how we use communication technology.[36] Sitkin, Sutcliffe, and Barrios-Choplin found that certain communication technologies may have symbolic meaning in an organization. For example, a face-to-face meeting may symbolize caring, whereas a written document may indicate authority.[37]

Time

Is the message time-sensitive? When does the message need to be delivered? (The answer should not always be, "Yesterday!")

One of the effects of communication technologies is the ability to deliver almost immediate responses to requests. However, taking the time to carefully prepare your messages and responses can make you more effective. Also, anytime you write a message when you're upset, set it aside and reread (and edit) it later before sending it.[38]

Cost versus Benefit

Weigh the cost and time required to use a communication tool against the value, longevity, and requirements of the message. For example, if you were preparing to brief your team on this month's work results, you could use a presentation tool on your personal computer. However, if you were creating a new product introduction to be used by your company's sales force for the next three months, you could justify the time and expense to use desktop publishing, produce a full-color layout, and have it distributed on CD-ROM.

The Impact of Communication Technologies on Organizations

Every day we read or hear about new innovation in technology: change bombards us. For organizations, as for individuals, technology has both expected and unexpected impacts. Most of these impacts are positive, but some are not. In this section we touch on the way technology affects productivity, the distribution of

> Some people believe we need safeguards to ensure that the poor are not excluded from employment opportunities, voter education, and medical care conducted on the Internet. Does everyone have a right to access the Internet?

work, competitive advantage, information inequality, information overload, security and privacy, and job skills requirements.

Productivity and Employment

Organizations usually adopt technologies to achieve an increase in productivity. As a result, some jobs are lost and new skills are needed. In 1994, Federal Express implemented a web page to allow 12,000 customers a day to track their own packages over the Internet instead of calling a customer service representative. In so doing, they not only met their goal of servicing customer inquiries faster and more efficiently, but they also saved an estimated $2 million.[39] Inquiries now take fewer customer service representatives, but the technology requires more people with skills in computer programming, graphic design, and networks.

Distributed and Centralized Work

Communication technologies distribute work closer to customers—to the home, in our cars, or just about anywhere. Distributed work reduces commuting traffic and lowers costs for office space. Employees work more flexible hours, fitting work into family life. The downside of this scenario is that work is everywhere. Some people feel they cannot get away from their work. They suffer stress and feel isolated. Organizations lose informal communication channels, the "chats around the watercooler," that spark innovative new ideas. Managers worry about what workers are doing, although studies have shown that telecommuters are more productive at home than they were when they worked in the office.[40]

The same technology that allows us to distribute work also makes it practical to centralize some work. Large companies that once had local offices in cities across the country can now create centralized telemarketing centers to sell their products more cost-effectively. Using overnight delivery, products ship from a central warehouse to anywhere in the country. Customers get fast response, 24-hour service, and products that cost less. The downside to centralization is that local offices are closed and jobs are lost.

Competitive Advantage versus Risk

Every organization must decide when to adopt a communication technology. Everett M. Rogers developed a "diffusion of innovation" theory that describes how individuals and organizations adopt technologies.[41] Early adopters of a new technology pay a higher price and take more risks. The upside is they may gain a competitive advantage. When a technology is well-established, the costs and risks are less but so are the opportunities for benefits. You may have experienced this yourself: "Do I buy a personal computer now or wait until the price goes down?"

Information Inequality

Almost fifty years after the telephone was invented, Congress passed the Communication Act of 1934 granting AT&T protection from antitrust actions in return for a promise to provide universal phone service to everyone.[42] Does everyone have a right to a personal computer and access to the Internet? What about Third World countries that do not have the advantage of our technologies? Are we creating a world of information have and have-nots? We have to consider a whole new set of ethical issues.

Information Overload

You may have experienced information overload as you read this chapter! The author certainly struggled with a daily deluge of new information while writing it. With so much information available to us, how do we keep up? The pace of technology will continually force us to learn new skills or be left behind. Yet, organizations already worry about how much time people spend reading email or "surfing the Net." Intelligent agents may help us soon, but information overload is a real issue today.

> Organizations promote responsible use of their networks through policies and user identification and by reserving the right to monitor electronic communication. On the Internet, people can elect to communicate anonymously. Some people believe that anonymity has led to Internet abuses. Should anonymity be allowed?

Security and Privacy

The need to protect the security and privacy of information on computers and networks concerns government and industry. Organizations try to develop secure, private networks with "firewalls" that protect them from access by others on the unregulated Net. Encryption technologies have been developed to protect information. Government and industry debate whether or not these should be government-controlled or privately owned. The Internet evolved in an unregulated environment where freedom to share information is highly valued. However, concerns about fraud and pornography have prompted Congress to consider regulation. Our legal system has not kept up with our technology.

Job Skills Needed

Some people worry that as we delegate more and more tasks to computers, we will not develop basic skills and that there will be more technology-aided low-paying jobs for unskilled workers. Rogers described this as "a process of job simplification by means of computer technology so that less skilled, lower-paid workers can be substituted for more-educated, higher-paid employees."[43] An example can be found in the fast-food industry. Cash registers picture food items on the keys and make change automatically. Employees need not be able to read, memorize prices, or make change, as they did in the past. The result is low-paying, low-skill jobs with no future. A similar process happens in the professional world. Architects use computer-aided design (CAD) systems in place of basic drafting. Finance professionals use spreadsheets to create amortization schedules. Jobs requiring basic skills, such as drafting and loan clerking, are fewer. At the same time, professionals are challenged to acquire even greater technology skills to stay competitive.

Your success as a communicator, as a researcher, or as a businessperson depends on using the new communication technologies. Basic computer skills are essential. Learn to select appropriate tools and to apply communication principles, rather than attempting to know everything about technology.

SUMMARY . . . .

Communication technologies will continue to change rapidly, but these tools cannot replace basic communication skills. Technologies can help you span time-and-place differences, communicate interactively or disconnected, reach one or many people, and find information by subject or by person. What they cannot do is replace the ingenuity of the human user.

The telephone is the oldest and most universal communication technology today. Voice technologies include voicemail, voice command and input, and voice query. Natural language may someday be the preferred computer interface. Document creation and publishing are the most commonly used communication technologies in the workplace. Technologies to support groups include networks, electronic mail, information sharing tools, and meeting facilitation tools. Productivity tools replace paper calendars, address books, and "to do" lists. Filing cabinets and manuals are being replaced by databases that we must learn to navigate with the help of agents.

The Internet is a worldwide information utility that has made interorganizational and individual communication possible at unprecedented levels. It has also revolutionized publishing. The World Wide Web has made the Internet easy to use, prompting millions of individuals to participate and organizations to adopt Intranets for distributing information.

Communication technologies are selected based on their ability to meet business goals. To select a technology, you should consider the message, audience, context, time, and cost versus benefit. Communication technologies have both expected and unexpected, positive and negative impacts on organizations. You will need to continue to learn about technologies throughout your career to stay competitive in this fast-changing world.

NOTES . . . .

1. "Home Alone? It's Working Out," *Digital Today,* August 15, 1996.

2. Mary Beth Marklein, "Telecommuters Gain Momentum," *USA Today* (June 18, 1996), p. 6E.

3. This model has been widely used in the literature. See R. Johansen et al., *Leading Business Teams* (Reading, Mass., Addison-Wesley, 1991). See also P. Lloyd, ed., *Groupware in the 21st Century: Computer Supported Cooperative Working toward the Millennium,* (Westport, Conn., Praeger Publishers, 1994), p. 34. Marie E. Flatley used the model to organize her pamphlet *Teaching Electronic Communication: Technology for the Digital Age,* (Little Rock, Delta Pi Epsilon, 1996). Apple Computer uses it as a means of planning and thinking about its product development.

4. C. Scanlon, "Pluses and Pitfalls in Voice Mail," *Nations Business,* (May 1996), p. 57R.

5. J. A. Oberteuffer, "Commercial Applications of Speech Interface Technology: An Industry at the Threshold," *Proceedings of National Academy of Sciences USA* **92** (October 1995):10007–10010.

6. N. Negroponte, *Being Digital* (New York, Vintage Books, 1995), p. 148.

7. A. E. Grant, *Communication Technology Update* (Newton, Mass., Butterworth-Heineman, 1994), p. 180.

8. N. Negroponte, op. cit., p. 68.

9. Blank CD-ROM media prices range from $6.50 to $7.50; information from *PC Today,* **10** (July 1996):176.

10. Bill Gates, *The Road Ahead,* (New York, Penguin Books, 1995), p. 117.

11. Negroponte, op. cit.

12. D. J. Lynch, "Speedier Access: Cable and Phone Companies Compete," *Information Week,* June 16, 1996, p. 4E.

13. N. Burns, "E-mail beyond the LAN," *PC Magazine,* **14,** no. 8 (April 25, 1995):102–105.

14. A. Palermo and D. Johnson, "Electronic Mail Software Market Review and Forecast, 1993–1998," IDC Report 9568.

15. F. Becker, "One Line, Off Limits?" *Mobile Office,* July 1996, p. 34.

16. T. McCollum, "The Case for E-mail," *Nations Business,* **84,** no. 5 (May 1996):61–63.

17. "E-mail Not a Communication Cure-all," *Information Week,* July 15, 1996, p. 86.

18. W. Dizard, *Old Media, New Media: Mass Communication in the Information Age* (White Plains, N.Y., Longman, 1994), p. 13.

19. M. E. Kranz and V. I. Sessna, "Meeting Make-overs," *PC Magazine,* June 14, 1994, pp. 205–212.

20. B. N. O'Connor and M. Bronner, "Facilitation Curriculum Development: The Role of Electronic Meeting Systems," *NABTE Review,* **22** (1995):5–9.

21. M. Pearson, J. Folshke, D. Paulson, and C. Burggraf, "The Relationship between Student Preconceptions of the Multimedia Classroom and Student Learning Styles," ERIC Document 374 482.

22. M. Desmond, "Video Conferencing: Coast to Coast and Face-to-Face," *PC World,* March 1994, pp. 177–186.

23. C. Egido, "Teleconferencing as a Technology to Support Cooperative Work: Its Possibilities and Limitations," in *Intellectual Teamwork* (Hillsdale, N.J., Lawrence Erlbaum Associates, 1990), p. 355.

24. T. Smart, "Beyond Talk and Chalk," *Business Week,* June 7, 1993, p. 54.

25. J. Gambon, "PDAs in the Palm of Your Hand," *Information Week,* July 22, 1996, p. 46.

26. J. Swenson, "PIMS: Not So Personal," *Information Week,* August 5, 1996, pp. 66–68.

27. P. Lloyd, ed., *Groupware in the 21st Century: Computer Supported Cooperative Working toward the Millennium* (Westport, Conn., Praeger Publishers, 1994), p. 112.

28. "The PointCast Network," *PC Today,* **10,** no. 7 (July 1996):34.

29. J. R. Harrow, "The Rapidly Changing Face of Computing," *Digital Equipment,* July 15, 1996.

30. Source for this is Reuters, as reported in Harrow, op. cit.

31. Gates, op. cit., pp. 74–75.

32. J. Fulk and C. Steinfeld, eds., *Organizations and Communication Technology* (Newbury Park, Calif., Sage, 1990), p. 51.

33. K. A. Burton, "Communication Technology Use in Organizations: Effects of Personality Type and Dispersed Work Groups," Masters Thesis, University of Southern Alabama, May 1996.

34. R. H. Lengel and R. L. Daft, "Selection of Communication Media as an Executive Skill," *Academy of Management Journal,* **11,** no. 3 (1988): 225–232.

35. R. Posch, "E-mail and Voice Mail: Basic Legal Issues for Corporate Management," *Direct Marketing,* 54–56.

36. Fulk and Steinfeld, op. cit., p. 127.

37. S. Sitkin, K. Sutcliffe, and J. Barrios-Choplin, "A Dual Capacity Model of Communication Media Choice in Organizations," *Human Communication Research,* 18(4), pp. 563–568.

38. R. Ross, J. Abernathy, J. Bertolucci, and L. McLaughlin, "With E-mail Image Is Everything," *PC World,* **12,** no. 10, p. 57(20).

39. A. Cortese, "Special Report: Here Comes the Intranet," *Business Week,* February 26, 1996, p. 77.

40. "Home Alone? It's Working Out," op. cit.

41. E. M. Rogers, *Communication Technology: The New Media in Society* (New York, The Free Press, 1986), pp. 116–150.

42. A. E. Grant, ed., *Communication Technology Update* (Newton, Mass., Butterworth-Heineman), p. 322.

43. Rogers, op. cit., pp. 239–240.

RECOMMENDED READINGS ....

To read about the latest communication technology developments, consult current issues of *PC World, Mobile Office, Information Week,* and *Popular Science.*

Wilson Dizard. *Old Media, New Media.* White Plains, N.Y., Longman, 1994. This book provides an overview of how we got where we are today.

Nicholas Negroponte. *Being Digital.* New York, Vintage Books, 1995. This book offers a view of the future.

INTERNET SOURCES ....

Brendan P. Kehoe. *Zen and the Art of the Internet: A Beginner's Guide.* Upper Saddle River, N.J., Prentice Hall, 1996.

Ed Krol. *Whole Internet User's Guide and Catalog.* Sebastopol, Calif., O'Reilly & Associates, 1992.

Internet Sites:

The Internet and its origins

- Internet Society Home Page: http://www.isoc.org
- The World Wide Web Consortium: http://www.w3.org

- EFF's Extended Guide to the Internet: http://www.nova.edu/Inter-Links Searching the Internet
- AltaVista Search Engine: http://www.altavista.com
- Commercial Sites Index: http://www.directory.net

DISCUSSION QUESTIONS . . . .

1. Consider how the characteristics of communication technologies would help you to decide whether to use the telephone, leave a voicemail message, or send an electronic mail message in the following situations:
   a. To get approval for vacation
   b. To ask a colleague to agree to help you on a project
   c. To let a coworker know that a meeting was canceled
   d. To distribute minutes of a meeting
2. You are a new manager at a company that uses many communication technologies. Your boss has asked you to evaluate and recommend a video conferencing system to reduce travel costs and improve productivity. Describe what technologies you will evaluate and the criteria to select the right technology. What features will you recommend and why?
3. Discuss the impact of the Internet on business communication. What are the benefits to business? What problems does the Internet present to business?

TECHNOLOGY GLOSSARY . . . .

BBS (Bulletin Board Services) An information store by subject where readers can post questions and comments over a network

CD-ROM *Compact Disc, Read Only Memory*

Cellular telephone Wireless telephone

Chat A computer-based real-time conversation

DSS (decision support system) A software/hardware system that filters out interpersonal cues to promote better group decision making

Desktop publishing A sophisticated word processor that provides advanced layout features

EIS (executive information system) System for summarizing large amounts of information to help with decision making

Email (electronic mail) A software program that allows you to send and receive messages over a network

Facsimile (fax) A transmission of an image of a document

Fiber-optic network A network that uses light waves over a glass or plastic cable to transmit information

Groupware A system that combines information sharing by subject with messaging capabilities

Hypertext A document publishing technique that allows readers to nonsequentially follow links through the text. Hypermedia includes text, graphics, images, video, and sound.

Information kiosk A computer display that gives information; for example, a traveler's guide in an airport

Intelligent agents A software tool that filters, prioritizes, and customizes information

Interactivity Tools or electronic documents that are capable of acting on each other; see *hypertext*

Internet A collection of "interconnected" networks that make up a worldwide information utility. The core network is subsidized and maintained by the National Science Foundation

ISDN (Integrated Services Digital Network) A digital telephone connection that can carry voice, data, or video

Kbps Thousand bits per second

LAN (local area network) A network within a building or campus, using wire or fiber-optic cable

Mbps Million bits per second

Network Connections between computers

Newsgroup An information-sharing software program. Users subscribe to a subject of interest and post and receive messages about that subject. See also *BBS*

Pager A small device that notifies you when someone is trying to call

PDA (Personal Digital Assistant) A small, inexpensive specialized computer

Search engines   Software tools that allow you to search large databases or networks. For example, AltaVista is a search engine (or "spider") that allows you to search over 30 million pages on the Internet

Telecommuter   Someone who works from home, from a customer site, or while traveling

Teleconference   A voice connection for two or more people

Video conference   A video and voice connection for two or more people

Videotext   An information repository using inexpensive, text-only terminals over a network

Viewer   Software program that allows document sharing

Voice command   Instruct a computer to do simple functions (by speaking commands)

Voice input   Tools that allow us to speak text into computers

Voicemail   A computerized phone answering system that stores voice messages as digital files

Voice query   Retrieve information (through speaking commands)

WAN (Wide Area Network)   A network across town or the world, using wire, fiber-optic cable, satellites, and other devices

Whiteboard   A computer-based board shared by two or more people over a net

Word processing   A software tool to create, edit, print, and store electronic documents

WWW (World Wide Web)   A graphical interface to the Internet

INTERNET ACTIVITIES . . . .

1. You have been asked by management to discover, then make recommendations for purchase of, the best-quality mid-price-range package of computer equipment for a twenty-five-station training center. You are to present your findings to a committee in the form of a proposal. This is an exciting opportunity for you, but there is a catch—the committee is going to meet at 8:00 A.M. tomorrow. Working alone, use the Internet resources you can find to come up with this proposal, jot down your notes, and come to the meeting! Remember that you must be prepared to justify your recommendations to management.

2. Suppose you own fifty shares of Intel stock and fifty shares of Microsoft stock. Use the Internet to discover what your stock is worth, then explain to the class how you found the information.

3. Your boss asks you, "Who published Nicholas Negroponte's book, *Being Digital,* and when?" You respond, "I don't know, but I'll look it up and get back to you within the hour." The library is already closed, so you can't call there for help. All you have is the Internet. How do you answer, and how did you find the answer?

PART III
Organizational Contexts: Interpersonal

*I*nterpersonal communication is in many respects the lifeblood of organizational life. Two-person communication events, such as superior-subordinate communication or interviewer-interviewee communication, make up many of an organization's important activities. These activities include both task and relationship dimensions as is explained in Chapter 8. The messages sent and received in these dimensions will determine how successfully interpersonal communication is accomplished. Your understanding of power, language use, supportiveness, and conflict management will increase the skill with which you can manage these communications. Chapters 8 and 9 address these issues.

A special application of interpersonal communication occurs in an interview. Three general types of interviews are important to all professionals: those that provide entry into the organization, those that seek information, and those that address performance. Chapter 10 is about the interviews you will experience on the job. First, you will learn about basic types of interviews. This leads to information applicable to all interviews: approaches, structure, and the questioning process. The most important interview of your career is the performance appraisal interview. You will learn about the goals of this interview as well as a variety of ways to approach it. You will also learn about information gathering and other specialized interviews in this chapter. Chapter 11 is about the communication event of hiring and being hired. You will come to understand how the organization's culture imposes itself upon the employment process. This leads to a discussion of important issues related to the hiring process: application letters, résumés, and the interview itself.

CHAPTER 8

Interpersonal Communication

OBJECTIVES

Upon completion of this chapter, you should be able to:

1. Describe the major features of a relationship.
2. Understand and be able to use the language skills of personalizing, recognizing inferences, and expressing feelings, wants, and needs.
3. Recognize and be able to use in your communication Gibb's components of a supportive climate.
4. Understand issues related to sexual harassment and the options available for managing them.

Communicating with other people (in business and organizational settings) can be difficult. Perplexing questions sometimes seem to defy the most skillful individuals. How do you manage difficult people? What communication skills are involved in building your personal credibility? How should you behave in the game of office politics? What communication skills will make a difference in a sales event? Are there any public relations implications in interpersonal contexts? If so, what are they, and how should you manage them? And what about motivation? Is there something you can learn to do that will motivate top performers? How about those performers who are really slacking off? Are there things you can learn to do that will help you position yourself for promotion?

Clearly, these questions are about interpersonal communication as it occurs throughout the workday to everyone in every organization.

If you follow Charles through a typical workday, you will see him talking to other supervisors, coworkers, and staff. The success of his talking with them—that is, his success in his job—is a direct result of his communication skill. Imagine this communication event involving Charles and his boss, Henry.

HENRY: Charles, have you finished those performance appraisals? They're due tomorrow.

CHARLES: (Realizing that he hasn't, Charles replies in a somewhat whiny tone.) Gosh, Henry, I've had so much to do. I don't know what to say.

HENRY: (He assumes a folded-arms position, stares directly at Charles, and raises his voice.) Get those finished by the end of the day! (Henry then walks away before Charles can reply.)

Charles knew that this communication did not turn out well for him, that his credibility was at stake; he wanted to do better next time. So that evening he began talking to himself: "What happened this time? What did I do to cause this? How can I avoid this kind of thing next time? What can I do to manage situations like this better?"

First, of course, Charles might have avoided part of the problem through better time management. Aside from this, Charles could have enhanced his credibility and probably gotten a more favorable outcome if he had communicated differently.

Understanding how relationships develop and what is involved in them is essential to your success in interpersonal communication. Learning how to understand relationships brings great satisfaction, of course. It also brings greater success. Although it is difficult to be certain, we think most—perhaps 75 percent or more—of all the trouble and conflict that people experience in their personal and professional lives occurs as the result of some relational problem.[1]

TASK AND RELATIONSHIP COMMUNICATION . . . .

Every communication event includes two dimensions. The *task dimension* refers to the objects, phenomena, people, and events that occur outside of ourselves. For example, if someone asks you, "Please take my car, go to the store, and buy two reams of high-quality typing paper," you know exactly what to do. That is because you understand the task dimension of communication.

At the same moment, every communication event includes a relationship dimension. The *relationship dimension* refers to messages about the particular relationship between source and receiver. In the "take my car" example, you would certainly monitor the sentence to see if the other person was putting you up or down. You would decide whether the other person's definition of your relationship was appropriate. If so, you would not be offended, but if not, you undoubtedly would be offended.

If the statement were a request, the speaker might say, "I don't want to inconvenience you, but I need a favor. Would you be willing to . . .?" You would know instantly that the speaker was making a request. Thus you would know that the speaker was putting you up, and putting himself into the subordinate position the request requires. You would also know if the speaker were taking a superior position. So you can tell the participants' definition of a relationship by monitoring the talk.

The interesting thing about relationships is that they are always in the present, and they are always inside the individuals! If you think about it for a moment, you will realize that, although you can think about the future and remember the past, you always live in the present moment. This idea is called the *absolute present,* and it is very important to our interpersonal communication.

Because you live in the present, your relationships are present-tense phenomena. That is because your relationships with other people exist inside of you. Think about your relationship with one of your parents. As you do this, you will realize that your thinking about your mother or father is going on right now.

You may be able to remember what happened yesterday between you and your parent. You may be able to anticipate what will occur tomorrow. But you are doing both those things inside yourself today. Indeed, there is nothing outside yourself that you might call your relationship with your parent. Relationships always exist inside the people who have them.

Thus, relationships are always *personal.* They exist in the present moment, and inside yourself. They exist in what you are saying to yourself about the other person, and about yourself in relationship to the other person.

The task dimension of communication includes such things as topics, objects, processes, and the like. For example, if someone says to you, "Would you be willing to represent the company at a meeting in Washington, D.C., next Thursday?" you would understand that he was asking you to make a trip. You know what the request involves in the task dimension. You will also understand there is a relationship message implied in the sentence.

The person asking you is your supervisor. He has the authority to make the request, and to expect you will comply. He has the budget to afford your expenses. He has knowledge of your training and ability, and believes that you can represent the company well. All these things are known to you and to him. Notice he really isn't giving a command. He understands you can choose to say no and he is not in a position to make a demand. (A demand might be, "Go to Washington next Thursday and attend this meeting. Here are your tickets.") Your response to the request will depend on how you put all those variables together in your mind. Your eagerness or reluctance to comply with it will depend on your understanding of the relationship dimension of your supervisor's request.

. . . .**FEATURES OF RELATIONSHIPS**

Understanding several features of relationships will allow you to communicate better in them. Relationships include some level of attraction, are internal, are always present, include expectations, and have some level of importance.

Attraction

A *relationship* can be understood as being some level of *attraction* between two or more people. (Note that we are not necessarily referring to sexual attraction here.) Thus when you disclose your thoughts and feelings to another person, an impression is formed that leads to some degree of attraction.

Another way to express this idea is to say that all relationships include the liking/disliking component, and this liking/disliking is based on the *image* that you have of the other person. Each of us carries certain mental pictures of others we know. To illustrate this idea, you can work with your own experiences.

On a piece of paper, write the name of someone you know. Then quickly jot down several features of the individual's personality. Begin with the phrase "The person is . . ." Now place a plus sign (+) next to the personality features that you usually like, and place a minus sign (−) next to the personality features that you usually do not like. Place a checkmark (✓) next to those personality features you neither like nor dislike.

If you were able to complete this exercise, you did so introspectively. *You* created the image of the other person, and *you* listed the features of personality that you attributed to him or her. *You* assigned the liking/disliking to those personality features. The other person may not even be aware you have been thinking about the exercise.

Liking is an important component of relationships in the working world, too. If someone likes you well enough to take you under her wing, to show you the ropes, to become your mentor, that can make a difference in your success.

People like each other, are attracted to each other, for a variety of reasons. A large part of interpersonal attraction flows from the way people talk. We tend to like people who support and confirm us and to pull away from and defend ourselves from people who are judgmental, controlling, and aggressive.

Internality

We have already mentioned this second feature of relationships. They are *always internal*. They exist inside people, in the way they think about each other and what they want from each other. They exist in what people are saying to themselves about each other. A relationship is not a material thing between you and another person. Rather, the relationship is in your mind and in the other person's mind.

This is a highly useful idea because it puts you in control of this important relational component. If you are committing an error as you talk to yourself about the other person, and if the other person is committing an error as he or she thinks about you, those errors will surely affect the interactions you have. But you can also change the way you talk to yourselves about each other!

To illustrate this useful idea, try to imagine the intimate relationship that exists between an editor and an author. For the relationship to work, the author must risk exposing thoughts and feelings to the editor. Sometimes those things will be private. Sometimes they will be sensitive. Sometimes they will be incomplete, foggy, incorrect, or ill-conceived. The editor, too, is exposed. The way the editor responds to the author's work says much about the editor's knowledge, expertise, experience, and professionalism. It is a risky, intimate relationship.

Notice that the relationship exists in the head of each of them, in the images and feelings and wants each has in regard to the other. The artifacts of that relationship—the author's manuscript and the editor's marginal comments—are not the relationship.

Now suppose that the editor has in mind an image of the author that says, "This author is angry, hostile, and uncooperative." That image will certainly affect all interactions with the author. For instance, as the author approaches, the editor is likely to withdraw. If the author says, "That section goes better where I had it before," the editor is likely to hear that statement as angry and uncooperative.

The author's side of the relationship is equally subjective and subject to errors. Suppose the author observes the editor's withdrawing behavior. The author may decide, "This editor is aloof and condescending and doesn't look me in the eye. The editor probably isn't interested in the project and thinks my work is fundamentally weak." If the editor writes in the margin, "Example needed here," the author may very well take that to mean, "This is a bad piece of writing."

Suppose they meet to discuss their project. The author walks up to the editor, who withdraws. The author judges the withdrawal as evidence of aloofness and condescension and either backs off or advances. The editor interprets these behaviors as angry and hostile and withdraws again.

You can see that this cycle of events can be damaging to both the editor and the author. Certainly, misinterpretations can make a difference to the success of their writing project. But the fact that the relationship is in their heads liberates the editor and the author. They can choose to talk with each other about their relationship. And they can make changes that put themselves in control of the relationship. They do not have to perpetuate the problems they are creating because the relationship is inside each of them, not between them.

The Absolute Present

A third feature of relationships is that they are *always in the present*. Because relationships are internal things, existing in people's minds, they are time-bound. What happened yesterday is gone forever. You remember yesterday's events in the present, inside your head. The recollections become part of your images of the other person, part of your relationship. They are stored (in the present) in language.

This idea is liberating. It means you are free, forever, of trying to take back something that happened in the past. Since that is clearly impossible, if you un-

> The idea that relationships exist in the absolute present disconcerts some people because they think it's unrealistic. What do you think? And can you find any ethical implications flowing from the principle?

derstand this principle of the "absolute now" you will never waste time trying to do it. Instead, understanding this feature of a relationship, you will make contracts for the future.

We can refer once again to the editor and the author to illustrate the value of this principle. Suppose the author says to the editor, "You told me to make those changes. I made them. Now you want me to change the material again."

The editor can go into the past tense (a function of language, but not possible in real time) and try to defend herself, or she can stay in the present and make contracts for the future. "Yes, I did that. Now I think I was wrong. What I'd like is for you to add some real-life examples to the chapter." This statement gives the author the choice to rewrite, and thus to do what the editor wants, or not. Their negotiations can go somewhere so long as they keep out of the past. And it is their choice to make contracts rather than engage in recriminations.

Perhaps one more example will make these last two ideas clear. Suppose Roger walks up to May Beth one afternoon just after lunch and says, "Sometimes you make me so mad I want to scream. I hear you told the vice-president I was goofing off on the job. That's a dirty lie, and I want you to take it back." Roger's statement creates these problems:

1. He represents his impressions of what happened as true, and as May Beth's fault.
2. He demands that May Beth perform an impossible feat—that she take back the past.

May Beth has no choice but to stay in the present. She can't take back the past. Further, she is not responsible for what Roger has done with the facts. Because she knows her relationship with Roger is inside herself and inside Roger, she can work with the concepts they have of the relationship to bring them into line. She might say, "I'm sorry you're angry." This statement acknowledges Roger's anger but does not accept responsibility for it. Rather, it returns the responsibility for Roger's anger back to Roger. "I guess you must be talking about a conversation I had with the vice-president this morning. What do you think I said?" This statement acknowledges to Roger that she did in fact speak with the vice-president and offers additional information: the conversation took place this morning. Notice the last sentence: May Beth checks out what Roger thinks she said. She doesn't pretend to be able to read Roger's mind or to know what went on in Roger's past. She asks.

ROGER: You told him I was goofing off, and I resent it.
MAY BETH: That's not true. He asked me when you arrived this morning, and I told him I thought it was about nine-thirty. I said nothing about goofing off. In fact, I didn't make any judgments about your arrival time at all.

Because May Beth understands that relationships are internal to the parties in the relationship, she knows their interpretations of life events affecting the relationship are likely to be different. In addition, because she understands relationships are always in the present, she does not hook into Roger's demand that she take something back. Her awareness of these two principles allows her to try to correct Roger's misunderstanding and avoid unnecessary conflict.

Expectations

Relationships also involve *expectations*. The expectations humans have of one another are critical to their relationships, and talk about expectations is important.

For example, perhaps you show a business report you prepared to a friend. You ask this person to read over a particular section. A reaction like "Gosh, that's really great" could prompt two responses. If what was wanted was a compliment, then the statement would seem appropriate. But if what was expected was some constructive criticism, then the statement would be disappointing. What really counts in this example is the *expectation* you have of the friend. Is it fair for you to be satisfied or dissatisfied with the response unless you make your expectations known to the other from the outset? Probably not. In fact, talk about our relationships ought to reflect the expectations we have.

Go back, in your head, to the individual you described earlier. You developed a pretty clear image of that individual and identified the characteristics in that image that were positive and not positive. That is, you identified the characteristics of liking/disliking for the other. Now focus on your expectations for that relationship. What, for instance, do you expect to be that individual's behavior toward you when you meet after a separation—say, at an airport?

What you expect from another person usually depends on the role you have taken on for yourself and on the role you have assigned to the other person. Your expectations of your boss, for example, will almost certainly be centered on his or her behaviors in the *role* of boss. You believe that the boss will behave as bosses are "supposed" to behave toward subordinates. This expectation may include such things as task assignment ("Please organize a report for the upcoming meeting") or performance appraisal ("I think your consistent effort has paid off for the company, and I want it to pay off for you. I'm raising your salary"). In sum, you expect the boss to behave in ways that are consistent with your image of boss.

This idea is an important one, too. Imagine the possibilities for trouble if you assume a set of role behaviors but the other person doesn't know what they are! For instance, in most business organizations, a person who is in marketing is assumed to be involved in sales or advertising. That understanding implies a good many related behaviors. A person in research and development is assumed to be involved in the work of inventing and developing new or improved products. The implied set of behaviors is far removed from the typical notion of marketing.

In the American banking industry, however, the role behaviors of a person in bank marketing are more closely related to the research and development group than to the advertising and sales group. A bank marketing expert is supposed to develop new or improved services that the bank can offer to its customers and to help the local branches find ways to make those new or improved services fit into

> Can you name some of the questions of ethics your authors may be referring to in this paragraph?

the bank's operations. Thus, if you assume a bank marketer is a salesperson, and if you expect salesperson-like behavior, you will be disappointed.

We will argue that expectations, based on role assignment and role taking, are often at fault when people come into conflict. Being clear on what the expectations are can make a difference in the quality of a person's working day.

Importance

A final characteristic of all relationships is that they have a degree of importance. We make inferences about this matter of importance, and we act on those inferences. How important is the other person to us? How important is the other to our aspirations and goals? How important are we to the other? Far more complex than these difficult questions are questions we have about how important the other person is in relation to third parties in the organization. We play out a game of office politics on the basis of our inferences about this very complex and difficult reality.

To illustrate this idea, suppose that you are a newly hired member of the corporate auditing department. Your department does "full-scope audits." That is, your department examines not only the books in each facility but all of the company's records, looking for ways to explain the financial accounts and checking to determine that each manager in each facility is conforming to company policy.

The auditing department is one of the best places for you to work, since you want to move up in the company on a fast track. You know that a couple of years doing full-scope audits is the quickest way for you to learn your company's business. But that also creates a problem.

As auditor, your job is to look for procedural exceptions and violations, which can be threatening to the managers. And you know that a manager won't forget it was you who cited a gross miscalculation. Thus, if you aspire to move into the plant where the manager is employed, the importance of your relationship with the manager may influence your behavior.

Questions of ethics aside, you can see that in this situation you would be confronted with the question of the *importance* of your relationship and also the relative importance of your relationships with the plant manager and the audit manager.

To make the situation even more complex, suppose you do the right thing. You determine to write up the violation. *How* you write up the violation is a subjective thing, and an important one. Now, suppose the plant manager is a friend of your supervisor's boss. They have been with the same company for twenty years. They play golf together on weekends. They send their children to the same college, and they drove together to that college to visit them three weekends ago. Here we have a second level of importance. You will surely struggle with that report, since you believe the relationship between your supervisor's boss and the plant manager is important.

So far we have said that all relationships have certain characteristic features that are important to your success in interpersonal communication. One feature is attraction, or liking/disliking. The attraction is based on an image you carry in your head. The second feature is that relationships are internal. That is, they are the product of an individual's thinking and feeling processes. A third feature of relationships is that they are in the present. In the present tense we experience our emotions and our wants and expectations. In the present tense we assign and take on roles, and we learn to demand certain behaviors from each other on the basis of that role assigning and role taking. Finally, all relationships feature some assessment of the importance of the relationships.

....**INTERPERSONAL CONCERNS**

Now that you have some understanding of the basic features of interpersonal relationships and how they fit together, you are ready to consider three interpersonal concerns. These are central to managing and maintaining interpersonal relationships within business and professional settings.

One interpersonal problem you will encounter flows from *language use*. How you use language will have a profound effect on your ability to manage and maintain relationships. We will make suggestions that will help you better use language to achieve your aims. Our second area of concern is with the maintenance of a *supportive communication climate*. You will want to be supportive in the face of circumstances that may seem to call for the opposite sort of behavior, defensiveness. Supportiveness is a key facilitator of self-disclosure and trust and therefore is central to managing and maintaining your relationships. The final problem area you must deal with is *sexual harassment* within the work environment. We do not want to believe it exists, but unfortunately, it does, and many of us will come into contact with it.

Let's take a closer look now at each of these three concerns and how to cope with them.

Expressing Wants, Needs, and Feelings

Language is the basis of all that we do and is therefore related to each topic in this book. But there are some specific skills that will help you be clearer about your wants, needs, and feelings in a variety of situations.

Much of what we believe about language is embodied in a short book by Herb Hess and Charles Tucker, *Talking about Relationships*. The authors argue that it is important to examine language use because "to a large extent every person is a prisoner of the language he has learned."[2] We learn ways to talk to others that do not allow us to express our wants, needs, and feelings clearly. This limits us because our inability to express these things keeps others from knowing what they are, and we experience frustration in our relationships. There are some relatively easy ways to change your language to express emotions and needs more clearly.

Language use causes problems in our communication in the work situation. A student of ours who owns a small business complained about his frustration when he presented an idea to his employees. He said they "have a problem understanding the [his] ideas and accepting them. They become defensive when I approach them about this lack of understanding."

Assume you are the employee and this person is your boss. Assume further that you have heard his presentation of a new marketing plan and you believe there are problems with the approach. The boss says to you, "The problem is you don't understand what I'm trying to tell you. Most people would approach marketing our product this way. I believe strongly that if you listen more carefully, you will understand. Try it my way; it will work." How would you feel in response to this approach? Might you become frustrated, anxious, angry?

Now consider different language that the boss might have used. Suppose the boss said, "I'm feeling frustrated and notice that you look puzzled. I think you may not understand me. The approach I've suggested to marketing this product seems sound to me. I'm wondering if I'm not being clear or if something else is happening here?" (The communication could at this point take several different directions.) How would you feel about the situation now? We believe you might feel better about the boss. Language does make a difference.

Personalizing Language

One difference between these two language samples is that the first sample tried to shift responsibility for the boss's problem onto you, whereas in the second sample he acknowledges his responsibility. We call this difference *personalizing,* an idea based on the notion that our relationships are always internal to ourselves, and that they exist in the language we use to talk about them to ourselves.

Consider the language: "The problem you're having is. . . . Most people would approach marketing this product this way." Who was having the problem? Did the boss need to "gang up" on you by giving the ownership of the idea to "most people"? If you feel frustration, or if you have ever experienced anger in similar situations, it may be because the talk is characterized by blame (*you* are the problem) and an attempt to overwhelm (in case you don't believe this, you should know that most people oppose you). Two skills help avoid this difficulty.

Skill 1: Explicitly signify that I (the speaker) am the one possessing the feelings, wants, and beliefs when that is what I mean.
Skill 2: Refrain from holding others responsible for what is going on.[3]

The boss might say instead, "I'm feeling frustrated because it seems that I'm not being clear. The approach I've suggested to marketing this product seems sound to me." Notice that this use of language incorporates the skills suggested above.

We have found it helpful to give practice in identifying personalized statements. Before you continue reading, test your understanding of this idea. Circle the numbers of the following statements that you believe to be personalized:

1. You make me angry.
2. You don't respect me.

3. I want you to give me the report by five o'clock.
4. It's not fair for you to leave work fifteen minutes early.
5. I'd like you to pick up the letter Charlie has for me when you're down in purchasing.

Compare your response to someone else's. We believe statements 3 and 5 are personalized. Statement 1, "You make me angry,"puts the responsibility for the anger on the other person. The speaker, and not the other person, is feeling the anger. This shifting of responsibility may cause the other person to become defensive. If you do not want the person to become angry, then personalize the statement by saying, "I'm angry."

Statement 2, "You don't respect me," is not personalized and is a blaming statement. Another way to express this feeling is: "I feel angry when you don't seem to treat my ideas seriously." (The last part of this sentence would necessarily vary with whatever inference the person drew from the situation: "I feel angry when . . ." "I feel angry because . . .") It may take courage to say you are experiencing an emotional response and you are guessing about the other's motives.

Finally, the statement "It's not fair for you to leave work fifteen minutes early" is not personalized. This language puts the lack of fairness on some generalized other person. The language implies that the matter of fairness is *intrinsic* to the situation and that everyone shares the same value system. A more direct alternative is: "I feel frustrated when you leave work fifteen minutes early. This means more work for me and puts me behind schedule." In each of these cases, personalizing reduces the blaming activity. Reduced blaming, in turn, decreases the likelihood of defensiveness and increases the likelihood the other person will be open to talk about the issue. In addition, reporting the inferences and making the situation more open increase the possibility of understanding and a more accurate response.

Recognizing Inferences

A second problem with the language used by the boss is that inferences were spoken as facts. Consider the sentence "The problem you're having is understanding what I'm trying to tell you." The boss is guessing about what is going on. His employees may understand what he is saying but disagree. They know that the boss is wrong, but he does not know it. If the boss would recognize his inference and allow for other possibilities, the conflict might be better managed.

The boss might have said, "I'm feeling frustrated and notice that you look puzzled. I think you may not understand me. I'm wondering if I'm not being clear, or if something else is happening here?" The difference between this and the earlier sentence comes in part from the boss's recognizing that he was speaking an inference and choosing to check it out.

Two skills help avoid confusing observations and guesses:

Skill 1: State observations first, then inference(s).
Skill 2: Check out your inferences with the other person.[4]

Take a moment to check your understanding of the difference between inferences and observations. Circle the numbers of statements that are inferences.

1. The sun will rise tomorrow.
2. Pete will meet Sue at two o'clock in the company cafeteria.
3. John cannot finish the report since there is not enough time.
4. Juan spent two hours talking to the boss.
5. Phil was trying to influence the boss and secure a larger raise.

Three of these sentences are inferences. Observations are things you can see; inferences are conclusions *based on* observation. You cannot see things that are in the future. Neither can you see motivations. Sentences 1 and 2 are inferences because they address future events. Although the sentence "The sun will rise tomorrow" is a highly probable guess, it is still an inference because it refers to a future event. In the case of sentence 5, the assumption is that Phil was trying to influence the boss because of some observations that were made. You would be right in calling the communication an observation only if you actually heard Phil say that he wanted a larger raise.

Drawing inferences about other people without checking them out can lead to problems. You will inevitably be wrong sometimes, and you can get into trouble when you make wrong guesses. Your actions will be wiser if you talk about your observations and inferences in order to check their accuracy.

Expressing Feelings

When you communicate with another person, you are doing two things: (1) thinking about the issue, and (2) feeling something with respect to the issue and the other person. Thus, if you are to understand others and respond appropriately, you must know how the others are feeling about the issue. This helps you to talk to them.

Expressing feelings can be difficult and inappropriate. There are times when others may take advantage if you allow them to know how you feel. For example, you may try not to let another person know you are angry. There are times when others might take advantage of you if they knew what you were thinking, so you do not tell them. People withhold feelings more often than thoughts. Such discrimination against talking about feelings can be counterproductive.

Remember the boss's statement, "I'm feeling frustrated and notice you look puzzled." The boss was wise to verbalize the feeling and to attempt to check out the guess about them. To verbalize feelings is to maintain a cooperative climate. Wrong guesses about them often create resentment and reduce cooperation. We urge you to report your feelings when the activity is cooperative and the person is supportive of you. Here are some skills that will be helpful:

Skill 1: Learn to disclose your feelings in proportion to the intimacy of the relationship.
Skill 2: Personalize disclosures.
Skill 3: Time your disclosures. (Sometimes people are not ready to hear about your frustration.)

Skill 4: Report feelings as clearly as you can.

Skill 5: Report before explaining. (Reporting causes you to focus on the feeling more directly.)[5]

> Some people use strong, often profane or vulgar language to express themselves when they are excited, angry, or otherwise aroused. Other people are sometimes offended by such language—even to the point of responding in kind. *Why* does this kind of language usage offend some people? What are the ethical issues involved?

Some people think they express a clear feeling when they do not. One of the problems is expressing a "head" feeling. We mean "believe" but say "feel." For example, "I feel that you don't want to go to the meeting." This is a belief, not a feeling. Say "believe" if that is what you mean. The second problem is of a different type—the vague, or fuzzy, feeling. It is not helpful to say "I'm feeling pretty strongly that . . ." when "I am disappointed . . ." gives the listener a more accurate picture. The final problem with statements of feeling comes when we report past feelings as though they were present. When we do this, we are not in touch with the feeling. Rather, we are *thinking* about it. In such cases it would be more accurate to say something like "When this happens, I usually feel. . . ."

See if you can pick out the clear expressions of feelings from this list:

1. I feel that we are not communicating.
2. I feel discouraged when I hear you talk like that.
3. I feel hopeful about the new secretary we hired.
4. I'm terrified of flying.
5. I'm interested in doing well in business.

Statement 2 seems a direct expression of feeling. Each of the others has certain problems. Statement 1 refers to a belief, not a feeling. Statements 3 and 5 are head feelings because they describe cognitive activity. Because statement 4 is out of context, it is difficult to tell whether it is a clear statement of feelings. If you and your boss are talking in your office and you say, "I'm terrified of flying," then that would be a statement of past feelings and would not qualify as consistent with a system that assumes feelings exist in the present. But if you and your boss are 30,000 feet above Kansas and you are shaking with fear, then "I'm terrified of flying" would represent a true, present-tense feeling.

Expressing Wants and Needs

Finally, be clear about what you want. The other person cannot meet your needs without knowing what they are. If most of what you want in relation to your work is reasonable, and if what you want has the potential to further your goals and those of the organization, then being clear is important to both you and the organization. That increases the likelihood that your wants will be satisfied.

What makes communication about wants unclear? The problem is often twofold. First, we do not state *specifically* what we want. When the boss said, "The problem is not listening carefully to what's being said," he was only *implying* that what he wanted was more careful listening. Second, we do not state our wants in terms of specific actions the other person can take. If the boss had said, "I'd like you to say back to me what you believe I've told you," his statement would have been far clearer and easier to understand.

These five skills will help you express wants clearly:

Skill 1: Say what you want to *do* rather than what you want to feel. You may want to feel something, but it is better to state the behavior that will result in the feeling.

Skill 2: State the wanted behavior explicitly.

Skill 3: Specify a time for doing instead of leaving the time indefinite.

Skill 4: Say what you want rather than what you don't want. This skill does not necessarily enhance clarity, but it often avoids defensiveness.

Skill 5: State your wants in terms of actions that you can control. Instead of saying "I want you to listen more carefully," say "I want to be able to say this in language that will be clear to you."[6]

To see if you understand how to use these skills, evaluate the following list and then compare your evaluation with ours:

1. I plan to work late tonight.
2. I hope to enjoy myself at the company picnic.
3. I don't want my boss to be angry about the late report.
4. I want to be an upwardly mobile person.
5. Please do not read further until you have evaluated these sentences.

Statement 1 is clear and it specifies a time. Statements 2 and 4 do not state the want in terms of specific behavior. If the speakers could say what they want to do, their wants would stand more of a chance of being realized. Although statement 3 puts the want in negative terms, it does specify what behavior is wanted from the other person. It would be wiser to specify what the speaker will do to avoid the boss's anger or else what action he or she wants from the boss, rather than which feeling the speaker doesn't want. Statement 5 says what isn't wanted from the other person rather than what is.

Supportive Communication

Being defensive is much easier than being supportive. But why is this the case?

Consider the statement "You make me angry!" You almost certainly believe this to be true when you utter it. In reality, though, you *choose* to be angry. At this point someone may argue, "There is no choice involved! If someone does something that causes me to become angry, that person *makes* me angry." We say, "Not true." All of us are in control of our feelings if we want to be in control. Suppose your boss said things that might have been answered with anger, but you chose to keep cool. If you can remember a single situation such as this, then you must conclude that you have choices about your behavior. You have the choice to be supportive. Circumstances do not necessarily *dictate* defensive behavior.

Supportive and Defensive Communication

We want to be clear about what we mean by *defensive behavior* and *supportive behavior.* In this context we mean any behavior, but especially communication behavior, that either reflects or causes feelings of defensiveness on one hand or feelings of assurance and support on the other. If you behave in such a way that another person feels she has to defend herself, you have behaved defensively. If you feel under attack and defend yourself, that, too, is defensive behavior. On the other hand, if, as the result of a communication event, a person feels accepted and confirmed, or acts in a way that causes someone to feel accepted and confirmed, then that behavior is supportive.

Have you ever tried to cause another person to be angry when he or she refused to become so? It can be pretty tough to make someone angry if the person refuses. Unwillingness to participate in an argument suggests that the person is trying to control the situation. The person will not fight because he or she doesn't want to. From our perspective, that person is controlling the relationship by controlling his or her behavior. That is precisely what you can do, too, by remaining supportive.

Assume for the moment that you do choose to behave defensively. You must assume that the other person will respond likewise only if he or she chooses to do so. Since anger is a very common response to anger from another, it is reasonable to suppose it *will* be chosen. Now consider the consequences of what you have created. When you become defensive—say, angry—do you start thinking about what you will say next? If you are thinking of your next argument, are you at the same time really listening to the other person? Perhaps you become more rigid in your position. Perhaps you try to control the situation. Perhaps you try to think of ways to win—to lash out, get even, hurt the other—and tell the individual you do not care how he or she feels.

You can begin to understand why the matter of choice is so important when you consider what happens when you are feeling defensive:

1. You stop listening and begin thinking about what you will say next.
2. You become rigid in your position.
3. You try to find some way to get even or lash out.
4. You regret that you let things get out of hand if the relationship is important to you.

How would you feel about coming to work tomorrow if you let your emotions get out of control in an argument with your boss? This kind of interpersonal problem can be avoided if you learn the skills of supportive communication behavior.

We are going to attempt to create some defensiveness-producing talk to illustrate what it sounds like. See if you can listen objectively. The speaker is your boss. You have come into her office to discuss an idea for a project. You have just presented your idea. She responds:

> Your plan is totally bankrupt! I can't imagine that you could have wasted your time on such a foolish idea. I'm sure that you'll learn in time what it takes; you're a bright person. What you need to do is get some practical experience. I know what you ought to do. I have some projects that I've worked on. I have a few minutes tomorrow—how about coming in and I'll

> Have you ever expressed yourself in strong, perhaps verbally violent language? Did this expression have any impact on the other person? Did it matter?

show you the plans for a few of the projects I created. I'm sure you can figure out how to do it when you see what I've done!

How do you feel now? If you have ever experienced language like this you undoubtedly prepared to defend yourself. You felt attacked. (We overdid the strength of the message for emphasis.) Try the same message cast in less intense language:

Your plan is not the best. I hope you didn't spend too much time on it. Given a little time, you'll be able to polish your ideas. Practical experience will help. I can give you some help by showing you what I've done. I'm sure you can learn how to write a better plan by seeing a successful one.

You might not feel as angry in the face of this less threatening language, but you would probably still feel defensive because the statements are cast in defensiveness-producing language.

Jack Gibb's classic essay, "Defensive Communication," suggests that defensive behavior is "that behavior which occurs when an individual perceives threat or anticipates threat."

Besides talking about the topic, he thinks about how he appears to others, how he may be seen more favorably, how he may win, dominate, impress, or escape punishment, and/or how he may avoid or mitigate a perceived or an anticipated attack.

Such inner feelings and outward acts tend to create defensive postures in others; and, if unchecked, the ensuing *circular response* becomes increasingly destructive. Defensive behavior, in short, engenders defensive listening, and this in turn produces postural, facial, and verbal cues which raise the defensive level of the original communicator.[7]

Gibb believes, as we do, that defensiveness-producing behaviors involve an attempt to win, dominate, impress, or escape punishment. Further, he says that defensive behavior causes an "ensuing circular response [that] becomes increasingly destructive [lashing-out behavior?]."

Ethical guidelines for interpersonal communication

To communicate ethically on an interpersonal level, keep three guidelines in mind:

1. Show respect for the other person. Lying and distortion of facts and figures are not ethical behaviors.

2. Show respect for the other person's ideas even if your ideas differ. To accomplish this, maintain an attitude of equality. Try to minimize differences in ability, status, power, and intellectual prowess.

3. Encourage the other person to make free choices. Refrain from extreme emotional appeals. Don't manipulate—manipulation restricts the other person's choices. Moreover, manipulative behavior is ethically questionable interpersonal behavior.

How to Communicate Supportively

What, then, is the solution to the problem of choosing defensiveness-producing communication? Gibb produced the six pairs of behaviors exhibited in Exhibit 8.1 to answer this question.[8]

On the basis of that table, we classify the communication behavior of the boss in the example on the previous page like this:

Exhibit 8.1 CATEGORIES OF BEHAVIOR THAT GENERATE OR REDUCE DEFENSIVENESS

Behavior That Generates Defensiveness	Behavior That Reduces Defensiveness
Evaluation: Judgments or assessments of another that imply the other's "not okayness"	*Description:* Statements or questions that confirm the other as okay, and that treat the other's ideas and his image and self-concept with respect
Control: Behaviors that attempt to manipulate others—to impose upon them a point of view or attitude or some behavioral restraint	*Problem orientation:* Behaviors that make clear to the other that you wish to collaborate in defining a a mutual problem and seek its solution; cooperation, not competition in approach to others
Neutrality: Behaviors that show little or no concern for others, and that treat the other as a *thing,* capable only of functions, rather than as a person capable of choices and emotions	*Empathy:* Behaviors that show an attempt to identify with the other's thinking and feeling, and that show respect for the other's value-belief system and affirm his human dignity
Superiority: Behaviors that expressly state or imply a "one up" position and that discount the other; behaviors that state or imply "I'm okay but you're not okay"	*Equality:* Behaviors that expressly state or assume "I'm okay and you're okay, too"; behaviors that minimize differences in status, ability, power, and the like
Certainty: Behaviors that show rigid commitment to a point of view, and that suggest or imply that the other's ideas are wrong if they don't conform to that point of view; behaviors that create a win-lose definition of the situation	*Provisionalism:* Shows of one's own willingness to be tentative, to suggest that additional information might result in change of mind; behaviors that show willingness to cooperate in problem solving and that create a win-win definition of the situation
Strategy: To preplan a goal, then manipulate the other into believing he or she is making the decision; to imply caring that does not exist	*Spontaneity:* Straightforward, candid expressions of one's own attitudes, beliefs, and feelings

SOURCE: Adapted from Jack R. Gibb, "Defensive Communication," *Journal of Communication* (September 1961):142–145. Reprinted by permission of the International Communication Association.

Evaluation: Your plan is totally bankrupt!

Evaluation, superiority, certainty: I can't imagine that you could have wasted your time on such a foolish idea.

Certainty, superiority, evaluation: I'm sure that you'll learn in time what it takes; you're a bright person.

Certainty, control: What you need to do is to get some practical experience.

Certainty, control: I know what you ought to do.

Superiority, neutrality, strategy: I have some projects that I've worked on. I have a few minutes tomorrow—how about coming in and I'll show you the plans for a few of the projects I created. [Note that this is not a question.]

Certainty, superiority: I'm sure you can figure out how to do it when you see what I've done!

Now imagine a different presentation of the same message and the same content.

> I notice that your marketing plan favors the placement of new bank machines in six locations around the city. I'm wondering how you selected the locations and if others were considered. [Reply.] I believe you like to study all angles of an issue, so I'm wondering if you might like to treat these ideas as tentative and sit down and talk about each. I remember how tough it was and still is for me to check all possibilities. I'm willing to share some ideas that might be useful.

We believe that this third version is more supportive than the first and that it would be interpreted as supportive if the history of the relationship was supportive. Examine the talk with respect to Gibb's categories:

Description: I notice that your marketing plan favors the placement of bank machines in six locations around the city. I'm wondering how you selected the locations and if others were considered.

Problem orientation, equality, provisionalism: I believe you like to study all angles of an issue, so I'm wondering if you might like to treat these ideas as tentative and sit down and talk about each.

Empathy: I remember how tough it was and still is for me to check all possibilities.

Provisionalism: I'm willing to share some ideas that might be useful.

Defensiveness and supportiveness are important feelings that can define a relationship. Their importance lies not only in making us feel good but in affecting our ability to coordinate our efforts with those of others at work. The negative effects of defensiveness on our ability to communicate and coordinate activity are enormous. But what are the effects of supportiveness? Gibb summarizes these succinctly:

> The more "supportive" or defensive-reductive the climate the less the receiver reads into the communication distorted loadings which arise from projections of his own anxieties, motives, and concerns. *As defenses are re-*

duced, the receivers become better able to concentrate upon the structure, the content, and the cognitive meanings of the message.[9]

We urge you to practice supportive behavior. We want you to see for yourself its remarkable effects. You may be able to control the other person's defensiveness by your supportive behavior if that person values your relationship.

We have argued in this section that you must be able to understand and cope with interpersonal problems if you are to be successful in business and organizational settings. Thus far, we have talked about two problematic areas: language use and supportive behavior. We now turn to a discussion of a final area of concern: sexual harassment.

> Under what circumstances can a person safely and ethically approach a colleague at work with a sexual interest? Be as specific as you can in answering this ethical question.

Sexual Harassment

Unfortunately, sexual harassment occurs with surprising frequency in the workplace. It is one of the more difficult interpersonal communication problems to address because incidents of sexual harassment always involve a power play.

Sexual harassment refers to any unsolicited and unwelcome contact that has a sexual basis. In 1980, the Equal Employment Opportunity Commission (EEOC) identified sexual harassment as a kind of sex discrimination under Title VII of the Civil Rights Act of 1964.[10] Sexual harassment is especially heinous because it creates an uncomfortable work environment for the target of the harassment. This harassment creates uneasy, hostile, offensive, and intimidating working conditions that interfere with the victim's ability to do the job. Sexual harassment creates job dissatisfaction. Sexual harassment is against the law.

Sexual harassment takes many forms. It can be one action or several actions directed against a group or against an individual. It can be directed by a group or by an individual. It often takes the form of sex-oriented verbal kidding, smutty jokes, wolf whistles, comments about a person's physical appearance, questions about a person's private life, displays of sexually explicit pictures, and belittlement based on sex role stereotyping. Deliberate physical contact, such as pinching and patting, brushing, hugging, touching, kissing, and the like, also constitutes sexual harassment. But the most common form of sexual harassment is a *quid pro quo*—a direct request for sexual favors in return for keeping a job or getting a promotion.

Incidents of sexual harassment should never occur in the workplace, but they too often do. And victims can be either male or female. Victims don't like the treatment; they are certainly not flattered by it. Rather, they are offended, yet they often hesitate to report it when it occurs. Why?

Sometimes victims are afraid a complaint will jeopardize their careers. Sometimes they believe their situation is unique, that harassment doesn't happen to others. They may feel inferior and helpless. They sometimes worry that the situation may worsen if they inform. They may believe it is unprofessional to inform on an assailant. Victims sometimes fear that others will believe they asked to be harassed. Victims have reported they fear their peers or superiors will respond with adverse treatment toward them. Sometimes, even, victims attempt to protect their assailants, trying not to get them into trouble. And, too often, the workplace doesn't have suitable grievance procedures, or the victim doesn't know what the procedures are or how to use them.

Sexual harassment is everyone's business, however. Employers have a duty to maintain a harassment-free working environment for all employees. They are culpable under the law, even if they do not know their employees are harassing others.

S. G. Bingham looked at communication strategies that might be used to deal with sexual harassment in the workplace.[11] Bingham pointed out that people who are harassed are faced with multiple communication goals. Their desire to do something about the harassment may compete with the goal of keeping their jobs and the goal of saving face. Thus, Bingham concludes that there is no ideal way to manage harassment. Although direct, assertive confrontation is often the best strategy, there are times when another strategy, like dealing with the harasser in an empathic manner, might be used.

So, if you are a victim, what should you do? We offer these suggestions:

1. *Tell the assailant directly that the behavior is not welcome.* The EEOC has taken the position that if the victim participates in the conduct—for example, laughing at and sharing sex-loaded stories and jokes—the individual is presumed to welcome the conduct. To overcome this presumption, you must tell the harasser that the conduct is not welcome.

2. *Be sure of your grounds.* The more severe the behavior the less pervasive the conduct needs to be in order to qualify as a hostile working environment. A single rape qualifies. A single invitation to dinner or a date does not. A single incidence of unwelcome touching of intimate body areas is grounds for legal action. A single incidence of sexual flirtation or off-color language that is merely annoying would not establish a hostile environment. Be sure of your grounds.

3. *Remember that you are not alone.* You may feel responsible for what is happening to you. You may be thinking, "I should be able to control this." You may believe that you're alone, that no one will understand what you are going through. But you are not alone! Other people have probably been harassed by the same assailant. They understand—and care about—what you are going through. Further, most people in the workplace are well-intended. For moral reasons, as well as for legal reasons, they do not want to tolerate sexual harassment. Remember that you are not alone.

4. *Complain to the appropriate person.* If a colleague or coworker is attempting to victimize you, report it to your immediate supervisor. If your immediate supervisor is harassing you, report it to his or her immediate supervisor. Ask about the procedures for reporting sexual harassment at the employee personnel or human resources office. Ask a labor union representative how

to report. Complain to the appropriate person. Do not allow yourself to be victimized.

SUMMARY

Every communication event includes both a task dimension (about things and topics outside oneself) and a relationship dimension (about feelings, wants and expectations, and so on). Relationships exist in role assigning and role taking—in what people say to themselves about their relationship. Also, relationships exist in the present and at no other time. These two facts account for almost everything we think about when people mention interpersonal communication. Interpersonal attraction provides an obvious example because it flows from identification. Similarly, what we expect and the importance we attach to it flow from inside ourselves. And because this is so, everything we need in order to manage a relationship is available to us in that moment, provided we have the skills we need to take advantage of it.

Learning to express wants, needs, and feelings constitutes an important portion of the necessary skills. In addition, we need to learn how to personalize—to make clear in our choice of language that we're taking responsibility for our own feelings, judgments, and inferences. These skills, while easy to talk about, are sometimes very difficult to assimilate. They pay off, however, in greatly enhanced ability to manage relationships, so they are skills worth learning and practicing. Much of this chapter described in detail how to acquire these skills.

In addition, this chapter compares and contrasts behaviors that produce defensiveness in others and behaviors that reduce defensiveness in others. To be able to choose which behaviors you will exhibit is obviously an important set of skills for relationship management. For if, by accident or by intention, you cause someone to feel defensive, that person's ability to listen to you or to negotiate with you shuts down as he or she shifts to a new agenda of saving face.

We describe sexual harassment as a separate issue because it is one of the most difficult of all interpersonal communication events to manage. Sexual harassment is pervasive, but it never has to happen and it is never acceptable. If you are a victim, you can confront it—and you should.

NOTES

1. For an in-depth treatment of these interpersonal concerns, see Gerald L. Wilson, Allan M. Hantz, and Michael S. Hanna, *Interpersonal Growth Through Communication,* 2d ed. (Dubuque, Iowa, Brown, 1988).
2. Herbert J. Hess and Charles O. Tucker, *Talking about Relationships,* 2d ed. (Prospect Heights, Ill., Waveland Press, 1980), p. 1.
3. Ibid., p. 14.
4. Ibid., p. 26.
5. Ibid., pp. 39–43.
6. Ibid., pp. 56–58.
7. Jack R. Gibb, "Defensive Communication," *Journal of Communication,* **2** (September 1961):141 (italics added).
8. Support for a number of Gibb's elements has been found. See William F. Eadie, "Defensive Communication Revisited: A Critical Examination of Gibb's Theory," *Southern Speech Communication Journal,* **47** (Winter 1982):163–177.
9. Gibb, op. cit., p. 142 (italics added).
10. *Federal Register,* 1980, p. 25025.
11. S. G. Bingham, "Communication Strategies for Managing Sexual Harassment in Organizations: Understanding Message Options and Their Effect," *Journal of Applied Communication Research,* **19** (1991):88–115.

RECOMMENDED READINGS . . . .

Irwin Altman and Dalmas A. Taylor, *Social Penetration: The Development of Interpersonal Relationships.* New York, Holt, Rinehart & Winston, 1973. This study develops an interesting and useful model of how interpersonal relationships develop.

Eric Berne, *Games People Play: The Psychology of Human Relationships.* New York, Grove Press, 1964. This book examines the way people sometimes use games as substitutes for honest, direct communication.

Jack Gibb. "Defensive Communication." *Journal of Communication,* **2** (September 1961):141–148. This article presents Gibb's supportive and defensive classifications in detail.

H. Lloyd Goodall, Jr. "The Interpersonal Situation." In *Human Communication: Creating Reality.* Dubuque, Iowa, Brown, 1983, pp. 139–166. This chapter presents the interpersonal communication situation as an opportunity to create, manage, and maintain rewarding relationships. It emphasizes the mutuality of relationships.

Philip M. Podsakoff. "Determinants of a Supervisor's Use of Rewards and Punishment: A Literature Review and Suggestions for Further Research." *Organizational Behavior and Human Performance,* **29** (1982):58–83. This essay will be of interest to those who find the topic of power intriguing. The work includes a review of some unpublished work.

Gerald L. Wilson, Alan M. Hantz, and Michael S. Hanna. *Interpersonal Growth through Communication.* Dubuque, Iowa, Brown, 1995. This book, as the title suggests, focuses on maintaining and nurturing interpersonal relationships through attention to communication skills.

DISCUSSION QUESTIONS . . . .

1. Suppose that you are a supervisor. A new employee has just stepped through the door to report for his first day of work. What kinds of things can you do to create a climate in which the new employee will feel free to ask you questions? How can you facilitate the development of your relationship with the employee? Be as specific as you can.

2. If you were the new employee in the situation described in question 1, what would you do to contribute to the appropriate climate? What would you do to develop an appropriate relationship with the supervisor?

3. Elect three members of your class to spend ten minutes role-playing the following situation before the class. (Be sure to take notes while the class members are playing the roles.)
   Role 1: Boss. Age 52. Middle-class, self-made man. Very religious.
   Role 2: Employee. Age 22. Overworked.
   Situation: Employee has worked until 7 P.M. for the past three days. Boss asks employee to stay again tonight. It is the employee's first wedding anniversary and she has an important date with her husband. She emphatically tells the boss no.

   Now, as a class, analyze the conversation, using the following questions for guidance:
   a. Did you find evidence of personalizing? Did you find instances in which the participants might have done better to personalize their language?
   b. What evidence do you have that the participants drew inferences from the talk?
   c. Did the participants have difficulty separating observations from inferences? Did this cause any trouble?
   d. Were the participants able to express their feelings clearly? How did the climate affect self-expression?
   e. Were the participants descriptive or evaluative? Did they take a problem orientation?
   f. Did you see any evidence of attempts to control?
   g. Were there any incidences of strategizing, superiority, certainty, or neutrality? What suggestions would you make to the participants to help them improve their communications?
   h. Assess the general communication climate. Was it defensive or supportive? And to what extent?
   i. What kind of strategies did those involved use to manage the conflict? Were they successful? Why?

INTERNET ACTIVITIES ....

1. One of the people who wrote this book is Mike Hanna. What does he require of students in his course, CA 211, Interpersonal Communication, to get an A grade? How do you know? Does he answer his email? How do you know? What else could you find out about him? How did you find it?

2. If you didn't already own this book and only knew the title, but you wanted to study the table of contents so that you could make a decision whether to buy it, where would you look on the Internet?

3. Is it interpersonal communication when you order a garment from Lands' End online? (http://www.Landsend.com/) Prepare to defend your answer in a discussion with your classmates.

CHAPTER 9

Conflict Management

OBJECTIVES ....

Upon completion of this chapter, you should be able to:

1. Define the term *conflict* and tell the difference between interpersonal and intrapersonal conflict.
2. Compare and contrast *win-lose, lose-lose,* and *win-win* responses to conflict, and categorize forcing, withdrawal, silencing, smoothing, compromise, and negotiation and bargaining according to these categories of response.
3. Describe how to analyze a conflict, using either Filley's model or Lulofs's model.
4. Name, describe, and explain the six structural components of a conflict, and suggest six ways to tell if an organization is experiencing conflict.
5. Tell how to plan the goals for a conflict episode in both the task and relationship dimensions of communication.
6. Explain how to identify the issues in a conflict.
7. Describe four principles that control the exercise of power in organizations, name and describe the bases of power that reside inside individuals and in-

side organizations, then explain how to determine whether to force a conflict or to negotiate it.

8. Define *trust, uncertainty,* and *face* and describe the implications of these definitions for successful analysis of the structure of a conflict.

9. Specify the four-step agenda for negotiating in the task dimension and the three-step agenda for negotiating in the relationship dimension.

10. Describe the four levels of involvement for a third-party intervention and how to determine which level is appropriate for a given conflict intervention, and explain how to determine if you are the right person to perform a third-party intervention.

*C*onflict is inevitable. It's neither good nor bad; it simply *is*. In business and professional contexts, in corporations and organizations, conflict is not only inevitable, it is also frequent! It follows from this argument (conflict is inevitable and frequent) that conflict must serve important interpersonal and organizational purposes. So, whether we like it or not, we must learn to analyze and, where appropriate, intervene in a broad range of conflict situations.

In this chapter we lay out the most common forms of interpersonal and organizational conflicts, and we suggest appropriate interventions that appear to flow from a communication perspective. Our purpose is to help you to identify and analyze conflict so that you will know what choices you can—or should—make under the circumstances of a particular conflict episode.

WHAT IS CONFLICT?

Conflict is so pervasive in our society that a desktop dictionary may offer as many as a dozen separate meanings for the term. To be in conflict is to be on a literal or psychological collision course with someone else; to be at variance or in opposition to another. Common understanding of conflict involves some element of clash, so much so that people may use a warfare metaphor to describe their understanding. In their minds conflict goes beyond mere quarrel or controversy—it is a battle. Conflict implies incompatibility and antagonism. Nevertheless, even though most people in U.S. society think of their conflicts in negative terms, conflict serves important purposes.

Definitions

The word *conflict*, and the words we use to define it, set up so powerful an image that people often do not know how to handle themselves in conflict situations. Conflict is pervasive. Conflict is inevitable. It happens between people, between groups, and in organizations. Conflict causes us to marshal our power and energy and to focus carefully on other people. What's needed is a clear definition.

We like Joyce Hocker and William Wilmot's[1] definition of interpersonal conflict, first published in 1978: "Interpersonal conflict is an expressed struggle

> Under what conditions or circumstances might expansion or escalation of a conflict be ethical?

between interdependent parties over perceived limited resources, scarce rewards, incompatible goals, or interference." By this definition, interpersonal conflict does not exist until it is expressed. It exists between people who need each other in some way. And the problem is perception, which may or may not be accurate. By Hocker and Wilmot's definition, the conflict parties must perceive they have incompatible goals, seek some scarce reward, want more of some resource than is available, or believe that the other person is interfering with them.

This definition can be extended to organizational contexts. Cathy Costantino and Christina Merchant do so in *Designing Conflict Management Systems: A Guide to Creating Productive and Healthy Organizations*: "In the organizational context, conflict is an expression of dissatisfaction or disagreement with an interaction, process, product, or service." They add that the dissatisfaction can result from many factors. They list (1) differing expectations, (2) competing goals, (3) conflicting interests, (4) confusing communications, and (5) unsatisfactory interpersonal relations.[2] Thus, conflicts can occur in interpersonal, group, and organizational contexts.

After reviewing the massive literature on conflict and its properties, Roxane Salyer Lulofs concluded that "conflict occurs in situations in which (1) the people are interdependent; (2) the people perceive that they seek different outcomes or they favor different means to the same ends; and/or (3) the people perceive that the other is interfering with their pursuit of scarce rewards or resources (such as money, time, affection, status, power, etc.)."[3] Conflicts can also occur in either the task or relationship dimensions of communication.

Conflict Can Be Productive or Destructive

Although U.S. society generally dislikes conflict and experiences it as negative behavior, conflict can be productive *or* destructive. Conflicts are productive when they produce outcomes that participants are satisfied with. When individuals think they have gained as a result of their conflicts, when they feel good about the balance in their relationship between cooperation and competition, their conflicts are productive. In other words, productive conflicts serve productive purposes. In contrast, conflicts are destructive when people expand and escalate them; that is, when conflict participants lose sight of their original goals and replace those goals with something else, such as "winning" the contest or hurting the other participant. If the outcome of a conflict doesn't allow the participants to see benefits for themselves or their organization, you can be sure that the conflict was destructive.

By these definitions, an additional conclusion seems warranted. Conflict is not a product. It is a process. When conflict occurs within organizations, it points to member unhappiness or dissatisfaction. It is not some isolated thing that can be manipulated or controlled. It flows from human interaction, and it shows up in many ways.

Scholars have studied conflicts at five separate levels: intrapersonal, interpersonal, organizational, interorganizational, and international. Here we are interested in the first three.

Intrapersonal Conflict

The most intimate level of conflict, intrapersonal conflict, occurs *within* people. Psychologists label three principal kinds of intrapersonal conflict: approach-approach, approach-avoidance, and avoidance-avoidance. They are presented in Exhibit 9.1.

Interpersonal Conflict

Interpersonal conflict occurs in two types. In one type, the conflict is between individuals. You might, for example, come into conflict with one of your colleagues because you believe she is trying for the promotion you want. In the other type of interpersonal conflict, the conflict is between an individual and a group. For example, a newly arrived employee may discover that her initiatives for change place her in conflict with other members of her work group.

Organizational Conflict

Organizational conflict occurs when internal groups, such as separate departments, work groups, or *ad hoc* decision-making bodies, come into conflict. It also occurs when *group functions* come into conflict. For example, the market-

Exhibit 9.1 THE PRINCIPAL KINDS OF INTRAPERSONAL CONFLICT		
Kind	Description	Example
Approach-approach	The person must choose between two equally attractive but mutually exclusive goals.	The new car buyer's choice between the Ford Crown Victoria and the Chevy Impala
Approach-avoidance	The person must choose an attractive goal plus its undesirable consequence.	A really good job offer that would mean moving to a different city
Avoidance-avoidance	The person must choose between an undesirable goal or its undesirable consequence.	Choosing to work late on three consecutive nights rather than attend an important meeting ill-prepared.

ing group of a large organization (which performs advertising and sales functions) might well create problems for the production group (responsible for design and manufacturing functions) by selling more units than the production group can build.

Organizations can find themselves in conflict with other organizations, too. For example, a state might make very great concessions (tax waivers, deep discounts in the price of state-owned land, special training "deals") to attract a large chemical firm, then discover that the chemical plant's emissions into the air and water do not meet state or federal environmental quality standards. The company wants to comply but also wants to keep costs low. The state wants the company to make a profit in order to provide jobs and, in the long haul, to contribute to the tax base. The federal government wants the company to meet emission standards. Interorganizational conflicts can be very complex.

From management's point of view, learning to identify the early stages of organizational conflict may determine whether or not managers can respond appropriately to it or design an appropriate intervention. Exhibit 9.2 displays some of the manifestations of conflict managers can look for.

Exhibit 9.2 SOME MANIFESTATIONS OF ORGANIZATIONAL CONFLICT[4]	
Competition	When individuals and groups begin to compete instead of cooperate with each other, conflict may be a problem. Of course, not every competition is conflict. However, if the individual or group goal of winning becomes more important than the organization's goals (productivity, stability, growth, etc.) then conflict definitely is a problem.
Dispute	Visible manifestations of organizational conflict, disputes include grievances, complaints, lawsuits, disciplinary actions, and the like.
Inefficiency and lack of productivity	When work is deliberately delayed and output is deliberately decreased, you can be sure organizational conflict exists. When usually happy and productive employees refuse to participate as part of a team, you've found organizational conflict.
Low morale	Unhappiness and low morale are often the result of hidden conflict. Low morale may show up as inefficiency, loss of motivation, or low energy levels.
Sabotage	When someone deliberately interferes with production by attempting to damage the organization or its processes, such as, for example, someone deliberately contaminating raw materials during a labor dispute, you have clear evidence of organizational conflict.
Withholding information	The flow of information *is* the organization. If someone disrupts the flow of information or withholds it altogether, you have evidence of distrust, frustration with the status hierarchy, and the like. In many cases information is power, and thus withholding it is a power play in organizational conflict.

. . . .**CAUSES OF AND RESPONSES TO CONFLICTS**

People in leadership positions in an organization must be able to do more than merely identify the manifestations of conflict. In order to work out an intervention—in order to manage the conflict situation appropriately—they must understand it. What caused it? How is it structured? What, if anything, should be done about it?

> Under what conditions, if ever, should departments or other subgroups in an organization engage in competition? What are the ethical considerations you took into account as you arrived at your answer?

Common Causes of Conflicts

Recall the key terms of Hocker and Wilmot's definition of interpersonal conflict: *expression, interdependence,* and *perception.* The most common causes of conflict in the workplace center on these features. Exhibit 9.3 illustrates fifteen common causes of conflict and shows how interdependence and perception are involved. Remember, the parties need each other, the issues are as much about the parties' perceptions as they are about the facts, and the parties have many choices about how they can express themselves.

How Individuals and Organizations Respond to Conflict

The range of options for responding to conflict depends upon how the people involved orient themselves. If they take a "win-lose" orientation, the most likely choice is to fight. If they take a "lose-lose" orientation, they may avoid the conflict or run from it or accommodate themselves. If they take a "win-win" orientation they are likely to look for ways to make the most of it.

These orientations (win-lose, lose-lose, win-win) are easy to understand when people are distanced from the conflict but are very difficult to choose from while in the throes of a conflict. If a person adopts a win-lose orientation, then he or she will think of self and other as antagonists. In order for one to win, the other must lose. Team sports illustrate this orientation. In order for the Steelers to win, the Dolphins must lose. No one is happy if the game ends in a tie. But the problem is that business is not a game, and employees are not involved in team sport. If one department wins and another department loses, then each department has lets its own goals take precedence over the organization's goals. From the perspective of the company, departments who engage in such a win-lose contest damage the organization.

Sometimes people take a lose-lose orientation that damages everyone involved. "If I'm (or we're) going down, then I'm (or we're) not going down alone."

A third option is available—the option we prefer in most cases. Rather than fight or flee, people in organizations can negotiate with each other. When people take a win-win orientation they look for ways to secure a better deal for everyone. Their conflicts are productive and morale is usually higher.

When organizations and groups decide to fight, it often appears as arrogance or bullying rather than blatant fighting. For example, it is arrogant for a company, through its spokesperson, to belittle and diminish its employees or its publics: "You know that the union is always out for its own selfish ends rather than for the greater good of all." "How can the banks expect to stay in business

Exhibit 9.3   SOME COMMON CAUSES OF CONFLICT

Element in the Definition	Common Cause	Example
Expressed struggle	1. Communication problems	1. A highly qualified Dutch engineer is passed over for promotion by a U.S. manager because he "doesn't try to sell himself." The engineer, of course, was acting modestly and waiting for the manager to bring the subject to personal qualities.
	2. Personal dislike or distrust	2. Mary doesn't tell Ellen important information she learned in a conversation with one of the employees because she doesn't trust Ellen to use the information wisely.
	3. Organizational communication system dysfunction	3. Two managers arrive at different and contradicting decisions because they used different data bases.
	4. Role specialization	4. A highly trained computer programmer cannot persuade his supervisor to invest in software that he knows will make his work more efficient and more effective because the supervisor doesn't have the technical knowledge to see the value of his proposal.
Interdependent people	5. Contract violations	5. William doesn't get a raise he thinks he deserves. He has worked many overtime hours and thus helped the company to achieve its productivity goals.
	6. Role conflicts	6. Nancy, a first-line supervisor, is expected by management to be their representative to labor, and by labor to represent their interests to management. In another example, if Nancy's daughter gets sick, Nancy's role as parent may interfere with her role as supervisor.
	7. Status disagreements	7. When the company moved to a new facility, Max found his new office to be significantly smaller than Imran's new office, even though Max has worked for the company longer and they have the same title.
Perceived scarce rewards	8. Competition for rewards	8. The sales department had decided to give a new car to the top sales representative, and the two best reps have decided they want to own it.

(Exhibit 9.3 continued from page 210)

Perceived limited resources	9. Competition for resources	9. The division manager has a fixed budget for the three departments under his umbrella. Two can just get by on their allocations for the year, but the third wants a significant increase in order to purchase much-needed equipment.
Perceived incompatible goals	10. Functional conflicts	10. Marketing (advertising and sales) wants to close on contracts that exceed by half what the production group can manufacture.
	11. Conflicts of values	11. Marketing values speed in manufacturing and sales; the production group values high quality much more than speed.
	12. Goal differences	12. The physician wants to keep patients in the hospital a little longer because her goal is to secure patient health; hospital administration wants to empty the beds as rapidly as possible to reduce costs and increase income.
	13. Environmental pressures	13. The company must keep its costs down to make a profit for its investors and is therefore willing to operate at the margins of state and federal standards, but the state and federal regulating agencies understand those standards as minimums and are pressuring the company to clean up its act.
Perceived interference	14. Hierarchy problems	14. Members of the executive group believe they listen carefully to subordinates; middle managers don't think they listen at all.
	15. Interpersonal relationships	15. Haygood intensely dislikes Williamson, and the feeling is mutual. Now they find they're required to work together.

if the government regulators are so rigid we cannot make good management decisions?" "Why is it the state's business that we occasionally leak a little more toxin into the atmosphere? Overall we're well within the standards."

Individuals can be every bit as subtle when they decide to fight or flee, although they don't always choose subtlety. The most common fight-or-flight strategies—every one a win-lose or lose-lose strategy—are forcing, withdrawal, and smoothing. Notice that fight-or-flight strategies can be very effective techniques for managing conflict in the short term.

Forcing refers to the use of power to cause another individual to comply. Each individual tries to get "one up" on the other. Whoever succeeds wins, and the other loses. Thus, forcing is a win-lose response. As you will see, there are occasions that call for forcing as the conflict management strategy of choice.

Withdrawal is a strategy of retreating from conflicts. If you want to discuss an issue, for example, but your colleague keeps avoiding you, he wins and you lose. You didn't get what you wanted, but he did. Thus, withdrawal is also a win-lose response to conflict.

Silencing someone means exercising power in such a way that the person stops talking. The most obvious example would be for a high-power individual to say or imply "Shut up!" to a lower-power person. Silencing is a win-lose conflict management strategy because the person who has been silenced does not get to deal with the conflict issues.

Smoothing refers to playing down conflicts. It happens, for example, when you emphasize the positive, common interests between you and the other, but avoid issues that might cause trouble. Because smoothing things over doesn't really allow people to deal with the issues that produced conflict, it is a lose-lose response. Both parties continue to bear the burden of unresolved and unmanaged differences.

Compromise does not fall neatly into either the fight or the flight strategies. Rather, compromise looks for a position in which each party gives and gets a little, splitting the difference if possible. Some people think of compromise as win-win. Others think of compromise as lose-lose. We think compromise falls into both categories because each party in a conflict gains some of what they want, but have to give up a little in order to gain it. Because there are elements of win-win, it is common to hear people place a very high value on compromise. Indeed, compromise often seems the solution of choice when conflicts occur. But there's a better way.

Negotiation and bargaining is the only true win-win response to conflict in organizations. In this approach the parties attempt to resolve their differences to their mutual benefit. Of course, negotiation may well involve elements of compromise, but the focus of this method is not on the middle ground.

ANALYZING CONFLICT SITUATIONS ....

Conflicts do not occur suddenly, materializing out of nothing and for no reason. Rather, conflict is a process. It often has no clear beginning or ending. So much is this the case that people must organize, or "punctuate," their conflicts in an effort to understand them. *Punctuation* in this context is the arbitrary act of deciding where an event begins and where it ends.

To illustrate, remember the two children engaged in conflict mentioned in Chapter 1:

ELLEN: "Mamma, mamma! Susan hit me."
MOM: "Susan, did you hit Ellen?"
SUSAN: "Yes, but that's because she wouldn't give me my toy."
ELLEN: "But you wouldn't give me back my book."

Notice how both Ellen and Susan attempt to place an arbitrary beginning on their conflict episode. For Ellen, the conflict began when Susan would not give her the toy. Susan, on the other hand, begins the conflict when Ellen would not give back her book. According to Kenneth Thomas,[5] a *process model* focuses on the sequence of events within a conflict episode. In contrast, a *structural model* focuses on the conditions that shape a conflict. To understand a conflict episode, we must understand as much as possible about both processes and structures.

Conflict As Process

Alan C. Filley[6] presents a process model of conflict that presumes each conflict episode within a relationship sets the stage for future conflicts. In this model, shown in Exhibit 9.4, conflict episodes begin with a conflict aftermath. *Conflict aftermath* is the sum of all our experiences of conflict in the relationship, plus our other conflicts as well. It includes what we think and how we feel about those conflicts—for example, estimates of what worked and what did not work to help us attain our goals.

Latent conflict is any area of our lives we feel strongly enough about that we might be willing to fight about. For example, you might be willing to do conflict over your political views or over some part of your value system; and you might be willing to do conflict if you think someone is mistreating your friend or shortchanging you in some way.

In Filley's model, *felt conflict* refers to what is going on inside you. In Exhibit 9.1, presented earlier in this chapter, the conflicts that belong in this category are approach-approach, approach avoidance, and avoidance avoidance conflicts. *Perceived conflict* refers to one's personal, on-the-spot analysis and in-

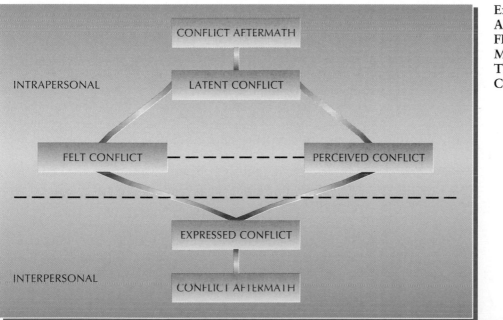

Exhibit 9.4
ALAN C.
FILLEY'S
MODEL OF IN-
TERPERSONAL
CONFLICT

How might a person express his or her conflict appropriately when emotions are running strong?

terpretation of the conflict episode as it is occurring. It refers to how you see or understand the event.

In Filley's model, a dotted line marks the threshold between intrapersonal and interpersonal events, making the point that interpersonal conflict does not exist until it is expressed. *Expressed conflict* is the first level of interpersonal conflict in Filley's model. It consists of the verbal and nonverbal messages used to manifest the conflict to others.

Thus it is possible to analyze conflicts as process. It may be as useful in some cases, however, to view conflicts as structure, thus to focus attention upon the component parts of the structure.

Conflict As Structure

General system theory argues that a system is the sum total of all the component parts of a thing, plus all the relationships among the component parts, tied together so tightly that any change anywhere in the system changes the entire system. This idea suggests a conceptual schema for the structure of a conflict. One reasonable analysis of the structure lists six component parts of a conflict: (1) goals, (2) issues related to those goals, (3) power within and around the conflicting parties, (4) uncertainty about issues, goals, and power, (5) trust, and (6) face. These six components, plus all the relationships among them, constitute the structure of a conflict.

Goals.

One way to understand the term goal is as an intention behind a decision or action. For example, you might decide to buy a late-model used car. You go to the car lot, find something to your liking, and enter into negotiations with the salesperson. Your decisions and actions (buy a late-model used car; go to the lot; identify a car that meets your specifications; enter into negotiations) all flow from your goal of securing dependable transportation. A conflict goal, then, is what you want to achieve or accomplish from a conflict.

Suppose you decide to engage in conflict behavior. What do you want to accomplish from doing the conflict? Whatever it is, the decision to engage in conflict flows from some intention on your part. And, too, the other person's decision to engage in conflict behavior flows from his or her goals. We believe that people often decide to engage in conflict behavior without a *clear* notion of what they want to accomplish; however, conflict can be more productive if people take the time to plan their goals.

Planning goals in the task dimension.   Recall that every communication event occurs in two dimensions: a task dimension, which is about objects, phenomena, and events; and a relationship dimension, which is about feelings, wants, intentions, and so forth. Planning conflict goals in the task dimension implies a five-step analysis:

1. Focus on interests, not positions. What do you want to accomplish? What do you want to change?
2. Write the goals in terms of the other person's behaviors. What do you want the other person to do? When? And how will you know that he or she has done it?
3. Name the resources you control that you could use as currency in the negotiation.
4. Sort out your goals into two categories: "absolutely must have" and "can live without."
5. Examine your list of goals to eliminate any goal that is not obtainable.

> **Is it appropriate, or ethical, to engage in conflicts when you don't know what you want to accomplish from the conflict?**

Planning goals in the relationship dimension.   You can also plan goals in the relationship dimension. This planning implies a three-step analysis:

1. Think beyond the other person to the value and welfare of your relationship with him or her. For example, you might be very angry with your colleague, but you need him and are interdependent with him. What do you want to change in the nature of the relationship per se?
2. Think beyond the present moment to your future needs from the relationship. For example, right now you may not need or value your interdependence with the other person, but you might value that interdependence next week or next month.
3. List ways to do a conflict with the other person and still maintain your relationship, and to maintain the other person's trust in you or your group or organization.

Face-saving goals.   As you will soon see, face-saving behavior is very important to successful conflict management and negotiation. Face-saving goals imply a three step analysis:

1. List several ways to maintain or restore your own self-image during and after a conflict episode.
2. List several ways to maintain or restore the other person's self-image during and after a conflict episode.
3. Identify several ways to attack the other person's self-image, and list in writing any conditions that may require such an attack.

Issues

A goal is what a participant seeks to accomplish. An *issue* is the focal point of a conflict, the question to be settled. An issue defines the conflict for most people. Issues point to the incompatibilities that give rise to conflicts. Issues typically can be analyzed by casting them in the form of yes-or-no questions.

Based on a review of the literature on conflict issues, Lulofs[7] lists five basic kinds of incompatibilities around which conflict issues revolve: (1) control over material resources, (2) personal desires for things to be or occur in a certain way, (3)) disagreements over how things ought to be or occur, (4) disagreements over relationship definitions, and (5) disagreements over what constitutes real-

Exhibit 9.5 SOME CONFLICT ISSUES FLOW FROM INCOMPATIBILITIES	
Source of Incompatibility	Sample Issues
Control over material resources	"Do I have final decision-making authority over this budget or don't I?"
	"Is this computer here for my exclusive use? Or must I share it with two other people?"
Personal desires for things to be or occur in a certain way	"Will you appoint me to the position of Division Manager?"
Disagreements over how things ought to be or occur	"Shall we agree, then, to a policy that all desktop computers will be Windows 95 machines?"
Disagreements over relationship definitions	"Am I the boss, or not?"
	"Do you work for me or not?"
	"Does John have any say over what I do at work, or how I do it?"
Disagreements over what constitutes reality	"Can we do this thing legally?"
	"Does this emission standard safeguard our employees and our community?"

ity. These five categories provide a way to organize conflict issues. Exhibit 9.5 illustrates such issues.

Power

A massive literature exists that attempts to define power.[8] For our purposes, understand the term *power* to mean one person's ability to bring sufficient force upon another to change his or her behavior. In an organizational context, power refers to the person's ability to affect how things work out. You might be able, for example, to influence how things come out by exercising your clout in the organization. You might also be very well-connected outside the organization and thus be able to bring a good deal of pressure to bear that is independent of your relationship to the organization. These two differences are evident in the frequently heard story of the son-in-law who got his job because of his wife's influence on her father, the CEO, but who rose quickly through the ranks in the organization because he had talent, tenacity, and credibility. Thus, there are at least two distinct arenas from which power flows: power flows from outside the organization and power flows from within it.

Power from outside the organization.   Mintzberg[9] identified five means of external influence upon organizations and arranged them roughly to form a continuum from the most general, least direct means through the most focused and directly personal means of influencing an organization. He lists:

1. *Social norms,* including all the rules and ethics within which the organization must function—the environment or atmosphere of generally accepted standards of behavior. These are informal, but they constrain the organization and its members nonetheless. For example, the police are expected to inform the members of a family that one of its members was killed in an automobile wreck before it informs the newspapers.
2. *Formal constraints,* such as a court of law or regulatory agencies might impose. Examples: Sexual harassment is illegal as well as immoral. OSHA requires companies to train employees about the fire hazards on their jobs.
3. *Pressure campaigns,* such as an environmental group might mount to pressure a food packing plant to treat its effluent water more thoroughly. Another example would be the Green Peace organization's campaign to obstruct the harvesting of whales in the Pacific Ocean by placing its ship in the way of the whaling vessels and by chaining its members to the intake apparatus of such vessels.
4. *Direct controls,* such as securing a seat on an organization's board of directors for a representative of one's group. When people organize to elect a representative to the school board, for example, they hope to exercise direct control on the school system's decision making.
5. *Direct access,* such as securing a seat on the board of directors for oneself as a personal, focused, formal means of influencing the board or the organization the board oversees.

These five means of influence are external to an organization. They are available to anyone who has or can tap into the external power coalitions that surround an organization.

Power in organizations.   Power can be exercised as behavior control or fate control. Behavior control occurs when someone uses social power to exercise restraint or direction over another person's choices of behavior. Fate control occurs when someone uses power to predetermine the outcome of events in another person's life in a way that is unavoidable by that person. For example, if someone should stand on a bridge tossing rocks onto the cars passing underneath, damage to the cars, and perhaps the people, would fall into the category of fate control. No one in the car would even know the villain was on the bridge until it was too late to do anything to prevent the damage.

In this book we're interested in the exercise of power as behavior control. Power within an organization is perceived as the influence one person has over another, and it is based in dependency. Thus it is interpersonal. To the extent that someone is dependent on you, and perceives that dependency, you have power in the relationship. Power, then, is not something one actually *has*; it is part of the relationship between two people. If I perceive you as powerful, then in our relationship, you have power. In that process of perceiving, I give you the power.

> **Can you think of an ethical example of exercising power as fate control?**

Interpersonal power is reciprocal. That is, two people must share it as a function of their interdependence. I extend power to you, but I also draw power from you. To illustrate, a professor and her students are engaged in a relationship by reason that they know each other; share the classroom, the syllabus, and the educational goals of a course; and so on. The professor and the students also share power in reciprocity.

Finally, there is a sense in which it is wise to think of power as though it were money in a checking account. If you were to write check after check you might draw your checking account down to zero. At that point you would be bankrupt. Just as people have checking accounts, it is possible to imagine that each individual in an organization has a power account, and each power attempt by the power agent costs him or her something. That is, each power attempt draws down the power account in exactly the same fashion that writing a check draws down a checking account. Keep these three ideas (power is a function of relationship, is therefore reciprocal, and can be depleted) in mind as you consider what follows.

Although others have addressed interpersonal, or social power, J. R. P. French and B. H. Raven[10] provided one of the clearest discussions. Their work was published nearly forty years ago, but it remains an extremely useful model for studying power. French and Raven identified five categories of power: coercive, reward, legitimate, referent, and expert.

Coercive power is often associated with force. It is about choices. If a power holder takes away another's choices or the other's perception that she has choices, then the power play is coercive. A boss who says "Get back to work or you're fired!" is engaging in coercion. A manager who uses his position to require subordinates to do his bidding against their will is coercing them if he leaves them without the perception they have a choice. The decision to use coercive power is most effective when it is directed at specific people, and especially when it is not carried out. In general, although it may be very effective, we do not recommend the use of coercive power because the risk is so great. Coercion can create martyrs, and the legitimacy of a coercive power play may be challenged. Certainly it has the potential to cause negative feelings and thus may stimulate powerful conflicts.

Reward power flows from one person's ability to control what others value. To the extent that a manager can control something his workers value, he has reward power in relationship to them. Notice that reward power is reciprocal. Professors, for example, control grades, the nature of the course syllabus, the attendance policy, and so on. The students, in return, control the feedback that flows directly to the professor about his or her success in teaching, about his or her self-concept as a teacher, and the like. In addition, students can sometimes indirectly influence rewards a teacher receives by reporting positively (or negatively) on the teacher's performance in the classroom.

Legitimate power derives from being assigned a role within an organization. If you have the position of supervisor you draw power from your employees because they believe you have a legitimate right to supervise them. Some legitimate power descends upon individuals from above, by appointment; some flows to them from their peers by election.

Referent power results when one person identifies with another. The stronger the identification, the greater the referent power. To illustrate, if your friend reports that he is in conflict with someone you have never met, you might very well take the side of your friend. If you do so, you do so on faith in your friend's ability to tell everything as it occurred (referent power) and because you like him (also referent power).

Expert power completes the list. To the extent that one person knows something or has information that another person needs or wants, then the first has expert power over the second. Expert power is generally limited to one area of knowledge, and attempts at influence in areas other than the power agent's expertise may very well reduce the agent's influence in his area of expertise.[11] The wisdom to be drawn from this research is never to represent yourself as an expert when you don't know what you're talking about!

Power, then, is part of the structure of conflict. It can be used wisely or it can be abused. It is a property of the social relationship between power agents. Exercise of power incurs certain costs. Power agents control in two ways—fate control and behavior control. Finally, power is usable only to the extent that the power agent is not hurt by using it. That is, if a power agent thinks his exercise of power will damage himself, and if he wants to avoid the damage, then he can't use his power.

Trust

Trust is about belief in, or reliance upon, the strength, ability, and integrity of others. To trust is to believe that the other person is honest and has one's best interest at heart. Thus, *to trust* means to believe that we can predict another's behavior because we perceive the other as both honest and benevolent toward us.[12] If you trust someone you expect that he or she will honor the social contract that exists between you. If you perceive a violation of any part of the contract, you are likely to feel betrayed. And if the perceived violation seems significant enough, you are likely to engage in conflict behavior with the other.

To illustrate: If you trust your immediate supervisor you do not expect him to lie about you as he represents you to his immediate superior. For him to do so would violate your understanding of the social contract that exists between him and you. But if for some reason you knew he *had* lied in such a situation, and more particularly, lied in such a way as to discredit you, you would be likely to do conflict with him. Or let's say you don't know for sure but merely suspect that your supervisor has lied about you. Your uncertainty, by itself, could be enough to cause conflict.

Uncertainty

Uncertainty means the quality or state of being indefinite, unpredictable. It points to a lack of confidence, to hesitance, no doubt about whether trust in another individual is misplaced.[13] When we're uncertain about another person's attitudes and beliefs, or when we're uncertain about the extent to which we can

> Could you make the argument that the study of organizational communication is ethical, inherently, and failure to study organizational communication is inherently unethical? Why or why not?

predict the other person's behavior, we become vigilant. We monitor ourselves and other people's behaviors[14]—we observe their verbal and nonverbal communication—and we draw inferences on the basis of those observations. If we conclude, correctly or incorrectly, that there has been a violation of the social contract or contracts that exist between us, we feel betrayed.[15] If our conclusions about others or about our contracts with them are incorrect, then the only way we have of managing the situation is to communicate so as to reduce our uncertainty.

And if a relationship is to continue, then the only chance it has of doing so is if the parties can continually renew and update their information about each other, about themselves, and about their social, contractual relationships.[16] They can only do that by communicating with each other.

To follow through on the previous example, suppose you suspect your immediate supervisor has misrepresented you, to your detriment, in a conversation with his boss. You are uncertain; you do not know for sure, but you suspect he has lied. What a powerful set of conclusions you are likely to draw! He doesn't have your well-being at heart. It now appears he no longer understands the nature of your agreements with him as you understand them, and as you thought he did. You begin to reevaluate your relationship with him, and you begin to wonder if he is trustworthy.

In the workplace we have all kinds of social contracts that have never been written down. To illustrate, Robinson and Rousseau[17] identified ten commonly perceived violations of the psychological contracts at work. They estimated, on the basis of the frequency reported to them, a rank-order in which such violations are believed by employees to occur: (1) Training, or rather, absence of or discrepancies in training, was at the top of the list. (2) Issues of compensation—of discrepancies between what was promised and what was realized—came next. (3) Promotion and advancement came third, followed by (4) the nature of the job and (5) the degree of job security a person could expect.

The second five included (6) feedback and reviews that seemed inadequate when compared with what was promised, and (7) management's refusal or neglect in asking for input or giving notice of changes. (8) Failure of the management to give as much responsibility and challenge as promised came next, followed by (9) misrepresentation of the knowledge, working style, and reputation of the people already working in the organization. (10) An "other" category of unfulfilled promises that did not fit into the other nine categories rounded out the list.

Whether the employees' perceptions were correct or not is irrelevant to the damage those perceptions caused to their relationships in the workplace. Moreover, it seems clear to us that in every case, better organizational communication was called for in order to reduce the uncertainty in the minds of those individuals who felt betrayed.

Face

The concept of "face" is not exclusively an oriental notion. Erving Goffman's[18] classic work made it clear that everyone has an image of themselves and that they work hard to maintain that image, that face, when they talk with others. Moreover, people generally cooperate with each other in this matter. But if face is threatened, especially in conflict situations, people may drop whatever else they are doing and go to work trying to save face. Attacks on face, then, whether intentional or inadvertent, seem especially threatening. Certainly, face must be considered part of the structure of conflicts.

Brown and Levison[19] believe people have two kinds of face needs: (1) they need and want to be liked and respected by others who are important to them, and (2) they want and need to be free from constraints and impositions. If we begin to pick up messages from people who are important to us that we are not liked and respected, or that others are about to impose constraints and impositions upon us, then we may well begin to defend our faces rather than attempt to understand and solve problems.

As a final follow-through on the example of your supervisor's misrepresenting you to his superior: It is easy to see many issues in this situation strong enough to trigger face work. Does the perceived lie mean that your supervisor no longer likes or respects you? Do you now have to either address or live with a change in the impression your supervisor's boss has of you? Does your supervisor's lie mean that the higher-ups may start placing limits and controls on you? If so, what kinds, and when, and can they be lived with? Thus you are uncertain, and you may consider the possibility, at least, of making a move to save face. Conflict behavior may very well come next.

CONFLICT INTERVENTIONS

When conflict exists, it also brings with it two choices. One of these is to leave it alone in hopes that it will solve or resolve itself. Sometimes, for example, it is wiser to let people work things out for themselves. To illustrate with a domestic example, wise parents often let their children work out their own conflicts rather than intervene. Wise managers, too, must consider this possibility when conflicts occur within their spans of control. And, of course, if you are in conflict with someone else, the possibility exists that to do nothing is the wisest choice. Another choice is to attempt to address the conflict directly.

Direct Conflict Intervention

Lulofs argues that people would be far better off if they would only "do conflict" when "true conflict" exists. She suggests that much of what passes for true conflict is pseudo conflict, false conflict, unrealistic conflict, or misplaced conflict. She presents a set of questions in a flow diagram to help sort out true conflicts from the other kinds. Exhibit 9.6 shows her model for diagnosing conflicts.[20] Using this model you can begin your analysis of a conflict by asking yourself if you and the other person seek different outcomes or different means to an end, or whether the other person is interfering with your goals. If you get a "no" answer you don't have a conflict, so there is no reason to do conflict. If you get a "yes" answer you go on to the next question, following the flow until

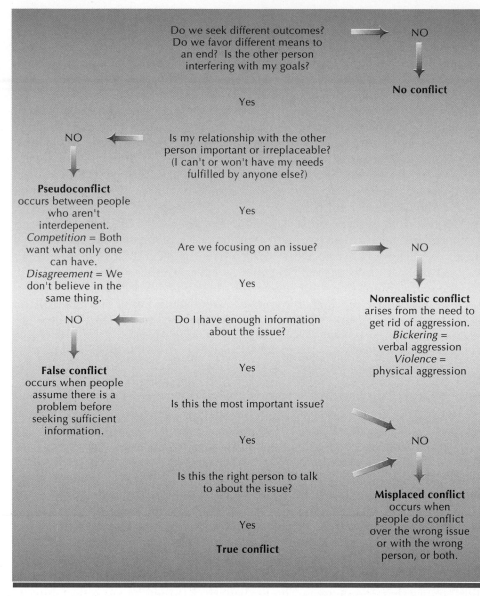

Exhibit 9.6 LULOFS'S MODEL FOR DIAGNOSING A CONFLICT

SOURCE: From Roxane Salyer Lulofs, *Conflict: From Theory to Action* (Scottsdale, Ariz., Gorsuch Scarisbrick, 1994), p. 38. Reprinted with permission.

you come to true conflict. Only then, according to Lulofs's model, does it make sense to engage in conflict behavior.

Notice, however, that the model does not leave room for doubt. What if you don't know for sure how to answer one of the questions? In this case you must talk with the person. You can't read another person's mind; the only thing you have left if you want to know his or her thoughts is talk. You must ask the other person. And the other person has the same problem. He or she can't read your mind and thus must ask you what you're thinking and feeling in order to know. (Notice, again, when we're in conflict, trust comes into play. If you are uncertain whether you trust the other person, or if the other person is uncertain whether to trust you, you may find yourself in trouble.)

Preliminaries to Negotiation and Bargaining

How, then, should you "do conflict"? We have already asserted that it is possible to take a win-win orientation to conflict management. In the case of important, ongoing relationships a win-win approach offers the greatest opportunity for a satisfactory outcome. Remember, interpersonal conflict exists between interdependent people—people who need each other. Yet, given these assertions, you might question why managers would want to employ any other conflict management strategy. More careful thought will tell you that some circumstances decrease the chance that a win-win strategy can succeed. Thus a particular situation might require you to force an issue rather than negotiate it. Over fifteen years ago, Eleanor Phillips and Ric Cheston[21] reported that these are two of the most common approaches to conflict management, but that the success of the choice was related to the type of conflict. They listed five conditions that would help someone choose between forcing and negotiating. Exhibit 9.7 displays the situational indicators that appear to be most helpful.

The left-hand column identifies the indicators. The middle and right-hand columns tell you what choice to make within that indicator's range. For example, suppose you are the manager in a situation controlled by both federal regulations and corporate policy. Let us say that an employee has repeatedly entered a confined space without taking the safety precautions designed to save his life.

Under "Conflict issue" you discover there is no goal agreement. Rather, there is a single best way required by corporate policy and federal law. There is no room for negotiation. The only and best choice is to use power to force the situation. Further, it is clearly a case of subordinate discipline. For some reason the employee chooses to disregard procedures that have the goal of protecting his safety. Under the rubric "Power relationships" you can locate a clear superior-subordinate, unequal power relationship. And under "Potential for recurrence" you discover the situation might involve changing by task or it might involve removal or transfer of personnel. Thus you can see that there are many reasons why a person might choose to force an issue rather than negotiate it. However, in a larger number of cases, negotiation and bargaining is the preferred conflict management practice.

Negotiation and Bargaining

In Chapter 8 we suggested that our relationships exist only inside ourselves—in what we're saying to ourselves, in role assignment, and in role taking. We also said that every communication event includes both a task dimension and a relationship dimension. To the extent this claim is true, the practice of ne-

Exhibit 9.7   CHOOSING A CONFLICT MANAGEMENT METHOD

Indicator	Negotiate If the Situation Involves:	Force the Situation When It Involves:
Conflict issue	Goal agreement	"One best way"
	Joint working relationship	Conflict of values
	Good communication	Scarce resources
		Subordinate discipline
Power relationships	Peers, equal power	Superior-subordinate
	Coalition	Unequal political power
	No power issue exists	Control of resources
Existing procedures	Review committee	Arbitration
	Objective criteria are agreed	Adjudication
	Equal representation of involved parties	No agreed-upon criteria
		Unequal representation of parties
Climate	Trust, regard for others	Personal antagonism
	Open-mindedness	History of forcing
	History of cooperation	Continuing and bitter conflict
	No history of conflict	Strong adversary relationship
	Group goals oriented to organizational goals	
Potential for recurrence of conflict	Conflict inherent in the structure of the situation	Changing by task or removal or transfer of personnel
	Need for ongoing conflict management	

gotiation and bargaining also occurs in both the task and relationship dimensions of communication.

In the task dimension.   One of the best-selling little books published in the early 1980s carried the title *Getting to Yes: Negotiating Agreement Without Giving In.*[22] It came out of the Harvard University Law School Negotiation Project. The purpose was to try to identify the best way for people to deal with their differences without ending up in a bitter fight. The result is five pieces of advice, each of which bears some elaboration.

1. *Don't bargain over positions.* Doing so is inefficient, it threatens the relationship, and it produces unwise decisions. To illustrate, a labor union representative and a management representative might be negotiating who provides safety shoes—the company or the employees. They are bargaining over position if they lock into a conversation like: "Management!" "No! Labor!" Instead, they could fall back, find the area of agreement (both want

to keep workers safe), and then negotiate a means by which they can accomplish that goal.

2. *Separate the people from the problem.* Assume that the people, both parties in a conflict, are concerned about the substance of the controversy and also about the relationship that exists between them. Treat the person on the "other side" with respect and dignity. Listen empathically; try to understand that person's concerns. Realize that that person has a stake in the problem just as surely as you do. With this in mind, make it clear that you value the other person, and that the problem to be negotiated lies outside the person or your relationship with the person.

3. *Seek options that produce benefits for both parties.* Withhold criticism until you have had a chance to explore as many options as you can create. Don't assume that your situation is a zero-sum (win-lose) situation. Rather, try to accept that the other person's problem is also your problem, just as surely as you know that your problem is the other person's problem.

Gary Karrass[23] argues that the one best way to produce benefits for both parties is always to ask for something in return for every concession. Consider how you might negotiate something in return for a reduction in price:

Price versus volume: "I can take $50.00 less per unit if you double the number of units you order." "I can produce a single multimedia training title for about $10,000. However, if you will agree up front to take ten titles, I can save enough to give them to you for $8,500 each."

Price versus a longer commitment: "I'll take 9 percent commission on this real estate transaction if you agree to give me an exclusive listing on your next three properties." "I'll give you a better rate if you'll agree to a fifteen-year mortgage instead of ten."

Price versus additional items: "If you buy all the computers from us we'll shave $150 from the unit price." "Give us the maintenance contract on both your buildings and we'll reduce the price by 12 percent."

Price versus better terms: "Pay half now and half on delivery and we'll shave 8 percent off the price." "If you'll put off payment until after January 1 we'll pass the tax savings along to you in the form of a discounted price."

Price versus anything you or the other person values: Approaching the situation in this way will allow you to find a better deal for both parties. What the other person wants does not necessarily have to have monetary value. Indeed, if William Schutz's FIRO theory is correct, what people want most is inclusion, control, and affection.[24] Always ask for something in return for concessions.

4. *Agree on the objective criteria you will apply when making the decision:* If you can come to agreement on which criteria you will use to judge the quality of your agreements you will have come a long way toward successful conflict management. When both parties in a conflict can agree on the fairness of such standards, or the fairness of procedures, they are far more likely to accept and support the outcomes of a conflict episode. For example, a husband and wife might have many different ideas for taking their family vaca-

tion together. To choose among them the couple might agree that cost, time, and safety are fair and reasonable criteria. The vacation must be affordable and within the planned budget, and it must be possible for all family members to go during the time frame and to accomplish what they wish to accomplish. Finally, the option selected must secure every family member's safety as far as possible. (For example, the husband and wife might decide that one of the children is too young to safety go scuba diving.)

What we've said so far, then, is that negotiation and bargaining strategies offer an excellent opportunity for effective conflict management when the problem at issue is in the task dimension of communication. As often as not, however, the problem lies in the relationship dimension.

In the relationship dimension. In conflict episodes, in which much of the conflict revolves around feelings and wants, the skills we described in Chapter 8 seem especially relevant. In particular, we want to review three pieces of advice:

1. *Come to the present tense; stay in the present tense.* Remember that your conflict exists right now, in the moment. The skill is to use language that makes this clear. Instead of "You betrayed me yesterday," say, "I am aware of the betrayal." No one can take back a mistake once they've made it. However, people can agree about how they will behave in the future, so it makes sense to focus attention on the here and now—to talk about feelings and wants you are experiencing in the moment.

2. *Talk about yourself, not about the other negotiator.* Recall that each of us is responsible for our own nervous system. In Chapter 8 we described how to accept responsibility, in language, for our own attitudes, feelings, beliefs, wants, and so on. Rather than saying "You make me mad," say, "I am angry." Rather than "You are wrong," say, "I don't see the situation that way." Rather than "You're a liar," say, "I don't trust that sentence." The more you talk about yourself the less the other person has to defend his or her face and the more likely that person is to remain open to negotiation and problem solving.

3. *Talk about feelings and wants of both conflict participants.* In Chapter 8 we urged you to learn the skills involved in talking about your feelings, wants, and needs. Our point at this moment is that feelings and wants are always involved in a conflict. One of the most effective conflict management strategies is to bring feelings and wants up to the level of talk. Remember, no one can read your mind, so people cannot know what you're thinking unless you tell them. It follows that you cannot read another person's mind, either. The only way you can know what other people are thinking or feeling is for them to tell you.

Third-Party Conflict Interventions

In the workplace people often have to decide if they want to become involved in conflicts between other people that do not directly involve them personally. For example, it is not uncommon for a supervisor to have to step between two of her workers. It is not uncommon for managers to have to intervene in conflicts between individuals or between whole departments of employees. Thus, learning to understand and to manage third-party conflict interventions seems an important kind of communication skill in business and professional settings.

By *third-party intervention* we mean a situation in which one person—a neutral who is not involved in the conflict—acts to help conflicted parties to manage their conflict. In U.S. society third-party interventions distribute along a continuum that describes the amount of legal and binding control the intervener has in imposing a decision upon the conflicted parties. Exhibit 9.8 shows that continuum.

The decision about whether to serve in a third-party capacity, and in which capacity, is not an easy one. When—and under what circumstances—should a third-party intervene?

Exhibit 9.8 A CONTINUUM OF THIRD-PARTY INTERVENTIONS			
Least Intervener Authority and Control			Greatest Intervener Authority and Control
Conciliation	Mediation	Arbitration	Adjudication
An informal, flexible feelings-based intervention that seeks to help parties stabilize their relationship. Conciliation leaves the decision-making control to the conflicting parties. This intervention takes time and should be used early and proactively.	A mediator focuses primarily on the problem, not on the relationship between the conflicting parties. The mediator's role is somewhat formal but remains flexible in terms of the specific strategies and processes used to work to resolve a specific problem.	In arbitration, each side presents its position and the arbitrator decides for the conflicting parties. The decision is controlled by the third party (arbitrator), but it may not be binding. Arbitration is efficient and much to be preferred in most cases over a court case.	An adjudicator, such as a judge, for example, makes a legally binding decision in order to solve a legal problem. This third-party intervention is a very formal process that works best when what's needed is a final, binding decision to end the conflict in progress. It should be seen as a last resort, and it cannot work in a conflict over values.

- If the decision is urgent and the sides are polarized, a third-party intervention is needed.
- If the conflict is complex and beyond the conflicting parties' abilities to deal with it, a third-party intervention is needed.
- If the conflicting parties do not trust each other, a third-party intervention is needed.
- If the conflicting parties do not want to solve or resolve the conflict, a third-party intervention is needed.

How involved should a third-party be, and how much control should a third-party exercise? After reviewing a very large body of research about the matter, Joseph Folger and Marshall Scott Poole[25] identified six conditions that can influence the decision making:

1. If there isn't much time and a solution is needed right away or if the group or organization's survival is at risk, then a highly authoritative style of intervention is called for.
2. If the conflict is long-standing and the lines between sides are clearly drawn, and if the sides don't think they can solve the problem themselves, then a highly authoritative style of intervention is called for.
3. If the conflict is acrimonious and highly charged, then a highly authoritative style of intervention is called for; as the acrimony eases, then a less authoritative style may work better.
4. A third party will be successful in adopting an authoritative style of intervention to the extent he or she is seen by both conflicting parties as credible and legitimate.
5. The greater the communication skills of the conflicting parties the less the requirement for an authoritative style of intervention.
6. What the group expects determines the most appropriate initial style of third-party intervention. However, once the third-party establishes credibility with the conflicting parties, he or she can deviate from the group's expectations and still function effectively.

Finally, it seems evident that a decision to participate as a third-party intervener requires some confidence that you are the right choice for the job. Do not make the mistake of entering into a third-party role unless you are confident that you are, indeed, the best choice available. The costs of failure are too high to make such an error. Some questions come to mind that will help make this determination:

1. Are the conflicting parties truly ready for a third-party intervention? What evidence do you have to support your conclusion?
2. Are you sure that the conflicting parties have requested help?
3. How do you know that the conflicting parties want you, personally, to help—as opposed to, say, asking you to secure someone else to help?
4. Are you skillful enough? Do you have the knowledge, interpersonal negotiation skills, and so on to help them? Or can you help them best by referring them to another person?

5. Are you available and flexible enough to help the conflicting parties? Are you free from bias? Or, are you committed to one of the parties, grinding an ax, or unable to help because of time, position, and the like?

6. Can you say "no" with equal confidence to both the sides in a conflict? If not, you may be too involved in the conflict to be helpful as a third-party intervener.

> Given this description and discussion of third-party interventions, what are the ethical implications involved in the decision to perform a third-party intervention?

SUMMARY

Conflict is common in organizations. It can be usefully defined as an *expressed* struggle between *interdependent people* over *perceptions*. The key terms, italicized here, point to the most common causes of organizational conflict. Conflict can be productive if the conflict participants are satisfied with the outcomes, but destructive if they are not. The goal in business and professional settings is to make conflict work for the organization. People and organizations often respond to conflict by adopting a win-lose orientation, and sometimes this choice may be the wisest. In other situations it makes sense to adopt a win-win approach. Forcing, withdrawal, silencing, and smoothing are win-lose strategies. Compromise is both win-win and lose-lose, since it involves giving up part of what one wants in order to secure another part. Negotiation and bargaining is the only win-win response to organizational conflict.

Conflict can be analyzed as process and as structure. When you think of it as flowing through time you are thinking in process terms. When you think about the component parts you are thinking of structure. Both analytical approaches offer insights that will allow you to understand a conflict situation and decide what to do about it.

Conflict interventions can be direct and third-party interventions. Both kinds of interventions should be designed on the basis of sound analysis and planning.

NOTES

1. Joyce L. Hocker and William W. Wilmot, *Interpersonal Conflict* (Dubuque, Iowa, Brown, 1978).

2. Cathy A. Costantino and Christina Sickles Merchant, *Designing Conflict Management Systems: A Guide to Creating Productive and Healthy Organizations* (San Francisco, Jossey-Bass Publishers, 1996), p. 4.

3. Roxane Salyer Lulofs, *Conflict: From Theory to Action* (Scottsdale, Ariz., Gorsuch Scarisbrick, 1994), p. 12.

4. After Costantino and Merchant, op. cit., p. 6.

5. Kenneth Thomas, "Conflict and Conflict Management," in *The Handbook of Industrial and Organizational Psychology*, M. D. Dunnett, ed., (Chicago, Rand McNally, 1976), p. 889.

6. Alan C. Filley, *Interpersonal Conflict Resolution* (Glenview, Ill., Scott, Foresman, 1975), p. 8. The model presented in this text is a slight revision of Filley's original.

7. Lulofs, op. cit., p. 164.

8. For an excellent review and summary of that literature see Charles R. Berger, "Power, Dominance and Social Interaction" in *Handbook of Interpersonal Communication*, 2d ed., Mark L. Knapp and Gerald R. Miller, eds., (Thousand Oaks, Calif., Sage, 1994), pp. 450–507.

9. Henry L. Mintzberg, *Power In and Around Organizations* (Englewood Cliffs, N.J., Prentice Hall, 1983), pp. 48–49.

10. J. R. P. French and B. H. Raven, "The Bases of Social Power," in *Studies in Social Power*, Dorwin Cartwright, ed. (Ann Arbor, Mich., Institute for Social Research, 1959), pp. 150–167.

11. Ibid., p. 164.

12. John G. Holmes and John K. Rempel, "Trust in Close Relationships" in *Close Relationships*, Clyde Hendrick, ed. (Newbury Park, Calif., Sage, 1989), pp. 187–220.

13. Perhaps the most lucid presentation of the ideas surrounding uncertainty appears in Charles R. Berger and James J. Bradac, *Language and Social Knowledge: Uncertainty in Interpersonal Relations* (London, Edward Arnold Publishers, 1982). See, particularly, Chapter 1, Uncertainty

and the Nature of Interpersonal Communication, and Chapter 2, Uncertainty Reduction and the Generation of Social Knowledge.

14. See Mark Snyder and Jeffry A. Simpson, "Orientations Toward Romantic Relationships," in *Intimate Relationships: Development, Dynamics, and Deterioration,* Daniel Perlman and Steve Duck, eds., (Newbury Park, Calif., Sage, 1987), pp. 45–62, and see especially pp. 46–47.

15. See Denise M. Rousseau, *Psychological Contracts in Organizations: Understanding Written and Unwritten Agreements* (Thousand Oaks, Calif., Sage, 1995), Chapter 4, pp. 90–110.

16. Berger and Bradac, op. cit., p. 13.

17. S. L. Robinson and D. M. Rousseau, "Violating the Psychological Contract: Not the Exception but the Norm," *Journal of Organizational Behavior,* May, 1994, pp. 245–259.

18. This discussion is based on the benchmark work by Erving Goffman, *The Presentation of Self in Everyday Life* (Garden City, N.Y., Doubleday, 1959). See also "On Face Work," in *Interaction Ritual,* Erving Goffman, ed. (New York, Anchor Books, 1967), pp. 5–45. See also Howard Giles and Richard L. Street, Jr., "Communicator Characteristics and Behavior" under the rubric "The Social Psychology of Impression Management" in *Handbook of Interpersonal Communication,* 2d ed. Mark L. Knapp and Gerald R. Miller, eds. (Thousand Oaks, Calif., Sage, 1994), pp. 132–134.

19. Penelope Brown and Stephen Levinson, *Politeness: Some Universals in Language Usage* (Cambridge, Cambridge University Press, 1987).

20. Lulofs, op. cit., p. 38, used with permission.

21. Eleanor Phillips and Ric Cheston, "Conflict Resolution: What Works?" © 1979 by the Regents of the University of California. Reprinted from *California Management Review,* volume XXI, no. 4., p. 82, by permission of the Regents.

22. Roger Fisher and William Ury, *Getting to Yes: Negotiating Agreement Without Giving In* (New York, Penguin Books, 1981).

23. Gary Karrass, *Negotiate to Close: How to Make More Successful Deals* (New York, Simon & Schuster, 1985), pp. 161–169.

24. William C. Schutz, *FIRO: A Three-dimensional Theory of Interpersonal Behavior* (New York, Holt, Rinehart & Winston, 1958).

25. Joseph Folger and Marshall Scott Poole, *Working Through Conflict* (Glenview, Ill., Scott, Foresman, 1984), p. 191.

RECOMMENDED READINGS . . . .

Dudley D. Cahn, ed. *Conflict in Personal Relationships.* Hillsdale, N.J., Lawrence Erlbaum Associates, 1994. This anthology of essays focuses on interpersonal relationships of all kinds, but especially in the world of work.

Cathy A. Costantino and Christina Sickles Merchant. *Designing Conflict Management Systems: A Guide to Creating Productive and Healthy Organizations.* San Francisco, Jossey-Bass Publishers, 1996. A very practical, direct, and easy-to-follow book that is, nevertheless, very well grounded in research. The book is about conflicts in business organizations that result from change.

Roxane Salyer Lulofs. *Conflict: From Theory to Action.* Scottsdale, Ariz., Gorsuch Scarisbrick, 1994. This is one of the most thoroughly researched and well-grounded sources of information available about conflicts of all kinds. Not an easy read, but worth the trouble.

Willem F. G. Mastenbroek. *Conflict Management and Organizational Development.* New York, Wiley, 1993. This excellent book provides a logical, concise, up-to-date treatment from the human resources/organizational development perspective.

DISCUSSION QUESTIONS . . . .

1. Examine the business section of your local newspaper or a national daily newspaper for news of conflicts that may have emerged. Share these with a small group of classmates, then, working as a group, determine if you can analyze the conflicts according to either Filley's or Lulofs's models.

2. The front page of nearly every newspaper displays news of interpersonal conflicts. Agree with two or three classmates to become knowledgeable about one such conflict, then present your analysis to the class. Do you think conflicts that

make news might have been managed using principles discussed in this chapter?

3. To learn about the kinds of conflicts that occur most often in small businesses, conduct a small research project. Working with a few classmates, develop a brief telephone questionnaire using the materials from this chapter as your guide, then have each group member phone at least five executives or managers from different small businesses to conduct the survey. Tabulate the results and bring your findings to class. What are the conflict issues in and around small businesses? What did your group learn from the exercise?

INTERNET ACTIVITIES ....

1. Use Infoseek Guide (http://guide.infoseek.com/) *or* AltaVista Search (http://www.altavista.digital.com/) to discover if anyone on the World Wide Web offers third-party conflict intervention services on a consulting basis to corporations. Is someone near your town offering such services? Suppose your CEO directs you to locate "a reputable consulting firm" to provide this service. How would you go about evaluating the reputation of the service provider? Could you make this evaluation using the Internet?

2. You would like to improve your negotiation and bargaining skills because you have decided to buy a new car. Take it as a given that the dealer will sell you a car if he can make $1,000 over costs. You are considering a Toyota Camry, a Ford Taurus, and a Honda Accord. You want the car to come with power windows, a sunroof, leather upholstery, and a really good stereo system. What's the bargaining range you should stay within? One of the search engines will help you find current prices. If it's still on the Web, try The Car Czar (http://www.carczar.com/choices.htm).

CHAPTER 10

Interviewing and Interviews: On the Job

OBJECTIVES ....

Upon completion of this chapter, you should be able to:

1. Cite the specific purposes interviews serve in organizations.
2. Establish a purpose, select and schedule questions, and plan an interview in order to achieve a predetermined goal.
3. Cite the specific purposes of a performance appraisal interview.
4. Identify several strategies likely to produce a positive performance appraisal climate.

5. Explain the techniques critical to employee-centered problem solving.
6. Create and implement a plan to conduct an employee-centered appraisal interview.
7. Develop and implement a plan for participating, as an employee, in an appraisal interview.

M ark and Sandra Sanford are entrepreneurs. In addition to holding full-time jobs, they maintain a business devoted to publishing a business directory. However, when you ask them, as we did, what they do for a living, you do not hear about their full-time jobs or their own small business. Instead they both respond, in unison and with confidence, that they are in the "informational interviewing business."

They explain that informational interviewing is one of the most important occupations in America's service-related economy. They point out that every business is only as profitable as the information gathered to provide a factual and interpretive basis for decision making, problem solving, and strategic planning. Persons who are skilled in locating and eliciting information are therefore highly valued.

Phil Williams, a senior at an eastern university, was heavily into the process of interviewing. Using the university's placement service, he had scheduled three interviews for the day. The last offered the most promising career opportunity. The interview had been with a well-established firm that was large enough to give him the opportunity to move up quickly in the organization. Phil was confident after the interview because he believed that he had made a good impression. He also had worked hard in school and knew that his credentials were very competitive. The interview reinforced his excitement about taking a job with the firm. The interviewer, the same man who would be his supervisor, seemed impressive and personable. Phil could actually imagine working for this man who behaved so competently during the interview. Phil was offered the job, and he accepted it. Interviews can be exciting for the interviewee if the interviewer understands his or her role and performs it well.

You may not have had much reason to think about the role of the interviewer or interviewee because most of us have not had extensive experience with these roles. Yet, these skills are most important for you to acquire.

This chapter begins with a discussion of the kinds of interviews found in organizations. Next, information is provided to help you prepare for interviews. Finally, we discuss performance appraisal, one of the most important kinds of organizational interviewing. Chapter 11 concludes our presentation of interviews with a full treatment of selection interviews.

TYPES OF INTERVIEWS

Interviews in organizations have six general purposes: (1) selecting members, (2) appraising performance, (3) in-depth information gathering, (4) collecting survey information, (5) problem solving, and (6) persuasion.

Selection Interview

Our students seem especially interested in the selection interview because they have apprehensions about the process. This type of interview is conducted for the purpose of making a decision about the interviewee's qualifications for membership in some program, group, or organization. Because of its "either/ or" decision outcome, the selection interview tends to be a highly planned, narrowly purposeful activity that separates it from all other interviewing types and formats. For that reason, we've devoted the next full chapter (Chapter 11) to it.

Performance Appraisal Interview

The performance appraisal is the tool by which you and your work will be evaluated. Thus, skill in this type of interview is one of the most essential skills an employee of any company can master, regardless of position, occupation, or profession.

Unlike selection interviews, there is seldom an either/or decision in appraisal interviews. Instead, the performance appraisal interview tends to focus on encouraging the employee and solving performance difficulties. As many authorities have pointed out, the performance appraisal is the chief communication mechanism by which organizations either improve or fail.[1]

You can transfer performance appraisal skills into any interpersonal setting where attitudes, values, beliefs, and behavior are issues. Performance appraisal skills are also useful when you help others solve problems.

In-depth Information Gathering Interview

The in-depth information gathering interview is used by newspaper and television reporters, radio personalities, academic researchers, popular authors, technical writers, advertising and marketing specialists, actors and directors, and organizational consultants and trainers. This kind of interview is designed *to acquire information about a subject, process, or person.* It is characterized by asking and answering both planned and spontaneous questions. When done well, it has the smooth flow of informal, intelligent conversation.

One of the attractive features of mastering the in-depth information gathering interview is that its skills transfer nicely to interpersonal conversations with new acquaintances, friends, and colleagues. Learning how to ask questions during this type of interview is a skill that you can practice every day in a variety of settings.

Survey Interview

Collecting survey data, such as buying habits, attitudes toward a new zoning policy, thoughts and feelings about a national problem, is a very specialized skill. The characteristics of a survey interview are essentially similar to an in-depth information gathering interview, with two differences. First, the survey interview generally lasts a shorter time. Second, it is usually accompanied by some paper-and-pencil instrument for recording responses to brief preplanned, pretested questions.

If you plan to pursue a career in marketing, advertising, or public relations, these interviewing skills will form a valuable part of your education. You will use them often on the job. If your career plans do not include these professions, the skills acquired will still be valuable because they will help you evaluate the quality of surveys conducted by others.

> Can you imagine any kinds of questions or questioning that would strain communication ethics? Is it ethical to attempt to lead people to feel and act in a preplanned way?

Counseling/Problem-Solving Interview

Interviews can be used to make a decision about a course of action. When the intent of the interviewer is to work through some difficulty with an interviewee, it is a problem-solving interview situation.

Counselors and supervisors use problem-solving interviews to help employees overcome work and personal problems. Nonprofit agencies use them to determine ways to acquire funding for programs. Health care professionals use them to deal productively with patients and clients. Managers use them to prevent problems from interrupting work and to reach deadlines.

Clearly, skills used in problem-solving interviews can be applied in many situations. They are useful as reasoning and motivating tools, as ways to overcome conflict, and as ways to negotiate outcomes. Problem solving is one of the contemporary hallmarks of a well-educated, communicatively competent individual.

Persuasive Interview

In a persuasive interview the interviewer tries to exert influence over the interviewee. The interviewer attempts to lead the interviewee to think, feel, and act in a preplanned way.

Selling is one of the most common persuasive interviews. Over 6 million people in the United States work in sales. Beyond selling products, many of us sell ideas. We persuade our bosses to do things that we think will make our work more productive. We persuade friends, parents, children, and colleagues to help us with our projects. Recruiters persuade candidates to take jobs. Health care professionals persuade their patients and clients to follow prescribed advice. Our world is filled with opportunities to use persuasive interviews.

. . . . **GENERAL APPROACHES TO INTERVIEWS**

Interviews may take either a directive or nondirective approach or some combination of these. Using a *directive approach,* the interviewer begins by establishing the purpose of the interview. A directive interviewer generally controls the interview by structuring the event and by asking nearly all the questions. In contrast, using a *nondirective approach,* the interviewer turns over control of the interview to the interviewee. For example, a supervisor, Linda, may perceive that the interviewee, George, needs to vent some dissatisfaction in an appraisal

> Can an interviewer go too far in psychologically preparing an interviewee to respond to questions? If so, what are the ethical limits?

interview before productive discussion can take place. Linda might begin with, "I sense that you may have some things you want to say to me, George. Why don't you begin?"

In spite of the fact that the interviewee is allowed to control the interview, the interviewer has a reason for calling the interview and that usually means the interviewer influences to some degree the direction the interview will take.

The purpose of the interview will usually determine the approach. A directive approach may be used for in-depth probing, survey, employment/selection, and persuasive interviews. A nondirective approach is useful for some counseling, performance appraisal, and problem-solving interviews.

BEGINNING THE INTERVIEW . . . .

Organizational research studies,[2] as well as practical experience, show that there are three interrelated goals for the opening of an interview:

1. To make the interviewee feel welcomed and relaxed.
2. To provide the interviewee with a sense of purpose.
3. To preview some of the major topics to be covered.

You will want to help the interviewee feel welcomed and relaxed. People generally perform better when they are not experiencing too much tension. The opening of an interview should provide a climate that allows participants to relax.

How is this goal accomplished? While the answer to this question depends largely on the personalities of the individuals involved, in general, it is easier for an interviewee to feel comfortable if the interviewer is relaxed. It is advisable, of course, for both parties to be well prepared for the interview.

Nonverbal cues such as a smile, a friendly facial expression, eye contact, a firm handshake, or open gestures set the tone. Introduce yourself. Greet the other person by name if possible. A polite inquiry such as, "How is it going today for you?" will help establish the relationship.

The second major goal of an effective opening should be to provide a sense of purpose and direction. This is primarily the responsibility of the interviewer, who must, early on, state the purpose of the interview and try to provide any additional information relevant to that purpose. For instance, during employment interviews the interviewer often will establish the purpose early on by describing the company and the job description and by explaining in general terms what type of employee is being sought. During an appraisal interview the supervisor might establish the purpose by explaining the policies concerning performance appraisals and by letting the interviewee know how she or he plans to proceed. During in-depth informational interviews the purpose should be stated clearly and directly soon after greetings have been made. Any questions about uses of the information should be answered. During survey and problem-solving interviews, the purpose should be followed by an explanation of how the interview will proceed.

The third major goal of an interview opening should be to preview the internal divisions of the interview. This allows the interviewer to understand the structure for his or her questions and will help the interviewee see the direction the interview will take. Previews serve as markers for people and therefore should make use of numerical references (e.g., first, second, third) and key words that will be easily recalled (e.g., education, work experience, future goals). Limit the number of markers in the preview to between two and four for easy recall.

....**DEVELOPING THE PATTERN OF QUESTIONING**

The opening of the interview establishes rapport, suggests the purpose, and describes the topics to be pursued. In this section we will describe two interrelated concerns about interview questions: (1) organization and (2) structure.

Selecting a Pattern of Organization

These four basic patterns of organization are used to guide topic development:

1. *Topical pattern.* This pattern is based on the assumption that an interviewer wants to explore more than one area. We suggest you limit the number of topics to five or fewer and order them logically.

    The topic pattern is also widely used in performance appraisal interviews. The supervisor has a list of topics (performance categories) such as attitude toward work, relationship with others, willingness to work overtime, performance of established duties, and training needs. Because there are a variety of topics, the topical pattern is appropriate.

2. *Time.* Chronology is useful in a wide range of interviews, both as a general organizing device and as a way to pursue a subunit of questioning. An interviewer can organize topics by dates. So, for example, a person in a computer firm interviewing a development expert for a technical document might use the time sequence to develop questions concerning a product development and implementation cycle.

    The time pattern is useful in an employment interview. The interviewer might begin with high school education, move to early work experience, then take up college education, and so forth. Thus, the topics of the interview are arranged chronologically. Each topic can also be patterned chronologically.

3. *Cause to effect.* The idea of this sequence is to discuss causes prior to effects and then to link causes to effects. When an effect is very dramatic, the cause-effect order may be reversed with good results.

    For example, let's assume you are the supervisor of a manufacturing operation that has experienced a work slowdown. You are interviewing workers about the situation to find out what is causing the problem. You would briefly describe the slowdown and then pursue questions related to causes. After the causes have been identified, you pursue the effects these causes are creating and then link causes to effects.

4. *Problem/solution.* The problem-solving structure is appropriate, as its name implies, for problem-solving interviews. The goal is to help the interviewee overcome a problem by naming its causes and effects. Problem/solution is also useful as a subunit structure for information gathering, employment, performance appraisal, and persuasive interviews.

The problem-solving structure supposes that identification of a problem and how it is defined will lead to a solution. When using this structure, it is helpful to divide the body of your interview into a discussion of the problem and a discussion of the solution. Then, link the solution sequence to the problem sequence. Sometimes the problem, its significance, and solutions are developed in a series of interviews.

These four strategies suggest the available ways of planning for the developmental questioning sequence of the body of an interview.

Determining the Kind of Structure Needed

Structure can be characterized by the terms *nonscheduled, moderately scheduled, highly scheduled*, and *standardized*. The term *schedule* is used by interviewers to denote the list of questions to be used.

Nonscheduled

A nonscheduled interview has no preplanned questions. The interviewer may have a general goal for the interview but has not written out specific questions. Thus, the interview is guided by a series of topics that may or may not be written. As a result, the interviewer has nearly complete freedom in phrasing and posing questions. This style of interview is useful when not much is known about the interviewee or that person's grasp of a topic.

Moderately Scheduled

A moderately scheduled interview contains major topics along with possible probing or secondary questions for each. (Secondary or probing questions are addressed on page 243.) It is one of the most often used interviewing formats. It saves preparation time, and its flexibility encourages a positive relational climate. That is, it encourages interviewees to be open, to elaborate on answers given, and to provide important details and examples.

Employment interviewers use this format in all phases of the selection process. Appraisal, problem-solving, and persuasive interviews can benefit from this approach. In-depth interviewers find the method especially helpful too.

However attractive this approach may seem, there are times when a less flexible schedule is needed.

Highly Scheduled

A highly scheduled interview contains all the questions, including those to be used for probing, ordered and worded as they will be asked. This approach is recommended for screening interviews when, for example, the group or organization wants to compare qualifications of candidates. Tightly controlled or stringent conditions may mandate such interviews. For example, when an organization is involved with regulative agencies, questions must be tightly monitored. Follow-up or probing questions may also need to be specified. The screening interview is generally followed by a callback interview that can be more flexible.

Highly Scheduled, Standardized

The highly scheduled, standardized interview is used on occasions where there is a need to quantify answers. This format is used for surveys and in some health care interviews. It provides not only questions worded as they will be asked but also optional answers. The purpose of a survey interview is to determine how a sample population responds to the same series of carefully worded questions.

The choice of which interviewing schedule to use should be based on the particular demands of the situation. Exhibit 10.1 provides a summary.

....**CONCLUDING THE INTERVIEW**

The conclusion of an interview also requires structure. The goals for an interview closing are similar to those of an opening.

There are three important aims that govern the closing phase in most interviews. First, the interviewer should review the major topics and the responses given to them. This procedure allows modification or changes in answers if necessary. Second, the interviewer should provide opportunity to add information that may have been left out. Valuable additional information can be obtained by asking a simple question: "Is there anything else we need to discuss regarding [name the topic or purpose] that you would like to bring up?"

Third, formally end the interview. An announcement that the interview is over takes the form of a simple "thank you," a handshake, and walking the interviewee out of the office.

Exhibit 10.1 SUMMARY OF STRUCTURAL CHOICES FOR INTERVIEWS	
Context	Appropriate Type of Format
Screening/recruitment	Highly scheduled
Employment	Moderately scheduled
Appraisal	Moderately scheduled
Survey	Highly scheduled, standardized
Problem-solving	Moderately scheduled
In-depth information gathering	Moderately scheduled or highly scheduled
Persuasive	Moderately scheduled

THE QUESTIONING PROCESS . . . .

A skilled interviewer needs a thorough understanding of open and closed questions, of primary and secondary questions, and when to use each.

Open Questions

An *open question* asks for broad, general information. A reporter might say, "Tell me about your inventions." The purpose of an open question is to allow the respondent freedom to answer in his or her own way. Open questions generally produce a great deal of information, organized by the interviewee's own thought process. It is possible to control how much freedom you give a respondent by using one of two different types of open questions: highly open and moderately open.

Highly Open Questions

A *highly open question* suggests a general topic area but allows almost complete freedom of response. An example: "Tell me about yourself." A survey question might be, "What has been your experience with our call-waiting service?" The engineering department head might ask an employee to describe his performance. All of these are highly open because of the freedom of response they allow.

Moderately Open Questions

A *moderately open question* is used to produce a less lengthy and more focused answer. Instead of "Tell me about yourself," a recruiter might say, "Tell me why you chose to go to school at Northern Illinois University." Instead of "What has been your experience with our call-waiting service," the interviewer might ask, "How have you responded to the interruption by our call-waiting signal?"

Here are some guidelines that will help you decide how to ask open questions.

When to Use Open Questions

1. When you want to relax the interviewee, and when the question is easy to answer. (Often an interview will begin with such a question.)
2. When you want to discover what the interviewee thinks is important.
3. When you want to evaluate the communication skills of the interviewee.
4. When you want to evaluate what the interviewee knows.
5. When you are interested in the interviewee's values or feelings.
6. When you wish to open a new area of questioning and intend to follow up with questions prompted by the information the interviewee provides.

Remember, since the respondent has greater control when you use an open question, that person may not choose to talk about the information you want. You may have to take control by asking more specific questions. Also realize that it is difficult to code and tabulate, or record, the kind of information received from an open question. Juan Blackwell, an interviewer from a personnel department, was investigating employee complaints. He said, "Millie, you have been working for us for twenty years and we value your opinion. Tell me, do you know of any problems in the plant?" Then Millie began. Ten minutes later she stopped.

> At what point does control become an ethical problem? What options can you imagine for an *interviewee* under such circumstances?

Open questions sometimes present problems in interviews where different interviewers will be collecting information for comparison. Different interviewers may not record enough information from different, or even the same, questions to make comparisons. Even if each interviewer does an adequate job of recording, they may not all select the same kind of information. It is best to use a standard interview schedule if you are using more than one interviewer.

Closed Questions

A *closed question* narrows response options to a specific area, so it gives the interviewer more focus on specific information wanted. A law-enforcement officer used a series of closed questions in an on-the-job interview with a driver he stopped.

OFFICER: Good afternoon, sir. Do you know the speed limit on this street?
DRIVER: I believe it is 40.
OFFICER: The limit here is 35. Did you see the speed limit sign in the last block?
DRIVER: No, I didn't.
OFFICER: How fast do you think you were going?
DRIVER: Between 40 and 45.
OFFICER: I clocked you at 47.

Moderately Closed Questions
A *moderately closed question* asks the respondent to supply a particular piece of information. For example, a marketing representative asked a consumer, "What other brands of toothpaste have you tried?" A sales representative asked, "How many computers are in operation in your department?"

Highly Closed Questions
A *highly closed question* implies a very limited response or supplies a short list of responses from which the respondent selects. You will find this type of question in multiple-choice examinations. The highly closed question is most appropriate for surveys. Here is an example of two highly closed questions:

What is your yearly salary?
_____ Under $5,000   _____ $20,001 to $30,000
_____ $5,000 to $10,000   _____ $30,001 to $40,000
_____ $10,001 to $20,000   _____ Over $40,000

Which of these is the most important as you look at a prospective employer?

_____ Growth industry   _____ Responsibility/challenge

_____ National reputation   _____ Location of facility

Another format for a highly closed question is a *rating scale*. Here is an example of this kind of scale using "satisfied" and "dissatisfied" as endpoints.

On a scale of 1 to 5, with 1 being very satisfied and 5 being very dissatisfied, how satisfied are you with your job?

Satisfied   1   2   3   4   5   Dissatisfied

A third format for a highly closed question asks the interviewee to *rank order* a series of responses. For example,

Rank order these in order of importance with respect to your work.

_____ Challenge   _____ Opportunity for advancement

_____ Job security   _____ Opportunity to be involved

A final type of highly closed question is the *bipolar* question. Such questions limit the respondent to one of two answers. For example, a nurse might ask, "Do you think you can continue working if I give you some Tylenol?"

This type of question assumes that there is no middle ground. The question, "Do you think that inflation will be higher or lower next year?" assumes the answer is not "about the same."

So closed questions provide distinct advantages when you use them effectively, but they can also create problems because of the information you collect. Most of the problems associated with closed questions are related to the control exerted by the question. First, the controlled nature of the responses makes it easy for an interviewee who does not know about a topic to fake understanding. It does not necessarily take any knowledge of the topic to say yes or no, to agree or disagree.

Second, the limited nature of these responses does not allow the respondent to reveal some information that might affect the results. That is, the interviewee may wish to volunteer information but has no convenient way to do so.

Third, there is not much opportunity to build rapport when closed questions comprise the major part of an interview. Lack of response freedom and response flexibility can be frustrating for the interviewee. The respondent may end up thinking the interviewer is the focus of the interview and the interviewer does not care about how the questions are answered.

Finally, closed questions do not allow the interviewer to assess how the interviewee is feeling. Both verbal and nonverbal cues are limited.

When to Use Closed Questions

There are five guidelines to keep in mind when you use closed questions:

1. When you want to have control over both the questions and the answers.
2. When you need specific information and the time for interviews is short.
3. When you are administering multiple interviews and ease of coding, tabulating, analyzing, and replicating are important.
4. When you are not particularly interested in "why" and when the feelings behind the interviewee's answer are not important.
5. When you think the interviewers you will use in multiple interviews are not particularly skilled.

Primary and Secondary Questions

The *primary* designation is given to any question that initiates a new line of inquiry. A primary question makes sense when taken by itself. For example, a physician said, "Tell me about the pain in your arm." This was a primary question. When she asked, "How often does it bother you?" she asked a secondary question.

Secondary questions derive their significance from the function they perform in the sequence of questions. *Secondary questions* follow primary questions; they are questions that probe deeper. There are four kinds of secondary (probing) questions, which are designated by the word *probe*.

The Elaboration Probe

An *elaboration probe* is used to encourage a respondent to provide additional information. Here are two examples:

A selection interviewer, in response to the interviewee's statement, "I had trouble with my boss," said, "Tell me more about that."
A supervisor who discovered during a performance appraisal interview that a coworker was distracting the interviewee asked, "What else is there to this?"

"What happened next?" "Go on." "Is there more to say about this?" are all examples of elaboration probes.

Clarification Probe

A *clarification probe* seeks further information when a respondent gives a vague answer. An exit interview provides an example.

INTERVIEWER: Tell me why you want to leave your position.
INTERVIEWEE: Well, it has to do with pace. The pace is too much for me.
INTERVIEWER: I don't understand what you mean by pace. Would you say more?

Sometimes an answer is clear, but you want to know the feeling or attitude represented. You might attempt to get at the feeling as this interviewer did:

INTERVIEWER: Tell me why you want to leave your position.
INTERVIEWEE: It has to do with my relationship with my supervisor. I feel held back.
INTERVIEWER: Why do you say "held back"?

Other examples abound:

In a performance appraisal interview, the interviewer responded, "You say you think your work is average. What do you mean by 'average work'?"

A candidate for a secretarial job was asked, "What do you mean by 'I get upset when my boss pressures me'?"

A supervisor asked her employee about a recent argument with a coworker: "Why did you react that way?"

Reflective Probe

The *reflective probe* (also called a "mirror question") feeds back what the interviewee said, to gain clarification. It is also used to check the accuracy of a statement.

A salesperson used this internal summary with a customer who was buying prizes for use in a safety campaign.

> Okay, George, let's review the plan. You want 300 key rings with the company logo for employees who have not had an accident during the last quarter. Then you want 100 wooden plaques with the logo and the inscription, "Six-Month Safety Club." Finally, you want three dozen lightweight jackets in forest green with the logo on the front right for those who have had an accident-free year?

The reflective probe may also be used to check the interviewer's understanding of a response to a primary question.

EMPLOYEE: I think I've been on time to work lately.
SUPERVISOR: So, you haven't been late in the past three months?
EMPLOYEE: That's right.

Clearinghouse Probe

The interviewer asks a *clearinghouse question* to allow a respondent to tell anything that might remain unsaid.

One journalist we know typically closes her interviews with a clearinghouse statement along these lines: "I appreciate all the information you have given me about the services you provide for the deaf. Is there anything else you would like me to know about deafness that would be of interest to the community?

Now we turn to the performance appraisal context for an in-depth look at how to plan, carry out, and participate in this important interview.

THE PERFORMANCE APPRAISAL INTERVIEW ....

Suppose that midway through this course your instructor called your name and asked to speak to you, saying, "It's midterm and I've decided to give oral evaluations so students will have the opportunity to know how they are doing and how to improve where necessary. When can you come by my office so that we can talk?" If your experience is like ours, your initial response to this proposition is likely to be a mild anxiety reaction. The thought of being appraised often produces anxiety, stress, and sometimes defensiveness. Much of your self-concept is invested in being a student. Check out how this notion applies to you by filling in these blanks.

> When I seriously think about sitting across from my professor and talking about my effort in this course, I feel _____, _____, and _____.

While we cannot predict your answer, we are concerned that a performance appraisal has the potential for producing anxiety.

Research bares this notion that performance appraisals are anxiety-producing and are avoided when possible. Investigators C. O. Longenecker, H. P. Sims, and D. A. Gioia note that nearly every executive dreads performance appraisals at some time or other. They hate both giving them and getting them.[3] Further, there are some good grounds for these feelings. Evidence suggests that appraisals are often not the straightforward assessment they ought to be. T. A. Judge and G. R. Ferris found that performance appraisals are influenced by the supervisor's liking of the subordinate as well as similarity in demographic features.[4] The appraisal process can even be a "political" activity. One supervisor remarked, "I will use the review process to do what is best for my people and my division. . . ." Accurately describing an employee's performance is really not as important as generating ratings that keep things cooking.[5]

The irony in this situation is that the appraisal interview can and ought to produce a different effect. Accept, for a moment, that people do identify with their work. Part of that identification will necessarily reside in their ability to do the work with which they identify. Consequently, most people want to do well. The appraisal process ought to help them do well.

You can see, too, the logic in the notion that supervisors also want people to do well. Supervisors have a goal—to make the maximum contribution their section can make to the organization. If the performance appraisal system is working properly, it ought to accomplish this goal without distorting subordinate appraisals.

It follows that performance appraisals ought to help the individual employee do well, allow the supervisor to do well, and ultimately, cause the organization to do well. We think these objectives can be achieved and that subordinates can come away from the process feeling OK about themselves if performance appraisals are carried out effectively.

This section focuses on the elements of an effective appraisal interview and offers practical suggestions for preparing for and conducting these interviews. We describe some commonly accepted goals for appraisal interviews and then compare these with some of the approaches in use. Next, we present our approach—the employee-centered problem-solving interview—in three parts: discussion of the climate, presentation of effective techniques, and suggestions about the format of the interview.[6] Finally, we discuss how you can do better in a performance appraisal interview.

Goals for Performance Appraisal Interviews

Andrew Domico, who works for a large paper manufacturing company in Mobile, Alabama, was recently promoted. Apparently he had not realized that his promotion would also bring him the responsibility for talking with the seven people he supervised about their performance on the job. Like many supervisors, Andy felt uneasy about the task, and for a long time he had been avoiding the inevitable. When he could no longer put off the appraisal interviews, he came to us for advice. We suggested that he begin by listing as many goals as he could think of for these interviews.

Appraisal interviews are performed to achieve a number of purposes:[7]

1. To help the employee to do the job better.
2. To give the employee a clear picture of how well he or she is doing.
3. To build stronger, closer relationships with the employee.
4. To develop practical plans for improvement.
5. To recognize employee accomplishments.
6. To communicate the need for improvement.
7. To counsel and provide help.
8. To discover what employees are thinking.
9. To let the employee know what is expected.
10. To set objectives for future performance.
11. To warn or threaten.
12. To reveal the employee's ideas, feelings, and/or problems.
13. To discover the aspirations of the employee.
14. To determine training needs.

Although some of these objectives (for example, threatening) might not always be desirable, most of them are usually appropriate. Because this is so, the work of the supervisor is both difficult and complicated. The number of goals and the fact that some of them further the employee's development while others further only the aims of the organization complicate the performance appraisal task still further.

The Employee-Centered Problem-Solving Interview

Three things are important for a successful performance appraisal interview: a favorable climate, appropriate techniques, and the necessary structure.

Climate

Andy will have created a positive climate if his employee (1) achieves a high level of participation in the interview, (2) does not feel defensive, and (3) feels supported.

A significant body of research concludes that, in general, the more employees participate in the appraisal process, the more satisfied they are with the appraisal interview *and* the supervisor.[8] An interview in which the employee does most of the talking is probably employee-centered. Such an interview also appears to increase the employee's commitment to carrying out the goals discussed, but "airtime" measures might be misleading.[9] If during much of the time the employee is giving defensive reactions, these objectives might not be met.[10]

Andy can reduce defensive behavior by avoiding activities that promote defensiveness. Two researchers have reasoned that because employees are generally apprehensive about being appraised, reduction of the number of negative criticisms and removal of the discussion of salary from the appraisal can reduce defensiveness.[11] Beyond this, be sure to practice effective conflict management, as discussed in Chapter 9.

Andy can also use supportive behavior. W. F. Nemeroff and Kenneth Wexley found that supportive appraisal behavior (taking the attitude of helper, treating the appraisee as equal, showing respect for the appraisee) yielded more satisfaction with respect to the session and with the supervisor.[12] In addition, Gary Latham and Lise Saari found that supportive behavior resulted in higher goals being set.[13]

Techniques

Here are several important techniques that Bill needs to practice to be successful:

Give the employee a worksheet before the interview that allows the person to think about performance issues. Ronald Burke and his associates found that doing this was associated with a positive outcome.[14] A worksheet might include these questions:

1. What are your duties and responsibilities?
2. What are the problems you encounter on the job?
3. What is the quality of your performance with respect to your duties?
4. How do you see your work in comparison to others in similar positions?

The chief advantage of this procedure is that it gives the employee an opportunity to prepare and therefore to be more active in the interview.

Encourage rather than praise. Herbert Meyer, Emanual Kay, and John French discovered that praise had little effect on the outcome of a performance appraisal.[15] Richard Farson suggested that praise can have negative outcomes and often causes defensiveness.[16] Praise may be viewed by the appraisee as threatening—a statement of superiority. Further, Farson notes that praise may increase the distance between the supervisor and employee and also decrease contact between the two. Meyer and his associates concluded in their essay in the *Harvard Business Review* that praise was not useful "because it was regarded as the sandwich which surrounds the raw meat."[17]

Encouragement is a desirable alternative to praise. As a supervisor, you can be sensitive to employees' areas of accomplishment and affirm their sense of pride in what they have done well. When the employee is reviewing areas of strength, you can acknowledge these. For example, you might say, "You seem pleased by the way you handled that." Or when the employee mentions an accomplishment, you can say, "I appreciate what you did." Although the source of the compliment is the supervisor, the recognition has come from the employee. Thus the possibility of interpreting a remark as manipulative is lessened.

Listen actively and feed back the employee's important ideas.   Active listening is an interpersonal skill in which the listener paraphrases what is heard and feeds it back to the speaker. Paraphrasing is casting what you have heard in your own words; it is not parroting. The employee is encouraged by paraphrase because it makes clear that the supervisor listened well enough to understand. The technique also provides the employee an opportunity to correct any faulty impressions. You may want to review the discussion on active listening in Chapter 5.

Keep the interview employee-centered.   The focus of the interview should be on the *employee's* reasoning, analysis, and solutions, when possible. Suppose you say to an employee, "I noticed that you've been late to work the past two days. I want you to get up earlier in the morning so that you can get here on time!" This is clearly not focused on his or her reasoning or analysis or solutions. Another way of saying this is, "I noticed that you've been late to work the past two days. I'm wondering what the problem is and if there is something either you or I can do to solve it." This presents the problem from the employee's view and is therefore likely to cause less resentment. This approach has been shown to yield better performance.[18]

Do not criticize too much.   Giving few instead of many criticisms produces less defensiveness and a greater chance of your employee's achieving improvement.[19] Research found that those areas of the job that were most criticized were the ones in which least improvement was made. When similar areas received less criticism, more improvement was noted. Likewise, the overall number of criticisms was positively correlated with the number of defensive reactions by the employee.[20]

When you do discuss areas where improvement is needed, Jack Gibb's advice about maintaining a supportive climate, summarized in Exhibit 10.2, seems sensible.[21] You will be more successful if you are able to be supportive of the other person.

Discuss salary in an interview that is separate from the performance appraisal interview.   If you talk about salary in an appraisal interview, you may destroy the frame of mind to discuss improvements.[22] The salary interview should come *after* the formal performance appraisal interview. If a salary discussion precedes the interview, the latter may turn into a session where your employee seeks to justify a greater increase or find out why you gave only a limited one. It may also increase the employee's tension. Your goal is to improve the employee's productivity, happiness, and self-worth; it is *not* to debate salary or justify yourself.

Exhibit 10.2 DOS AND DON'TS IN APPRAISAL INTERVIEWS	
Dos	**Don'ts**
Describe the employee's behavior.	Evaluate.
Share the discussion of the problem, soliciting the employee's ideas and suggestions.	Give advice.
Be straightforward in reporting your feelings and in structuring the interview.	Be manipulative and appear to employ some secret strategy.
Put yourself in the place of the employee—empathize.	Appear neutral and unconcerned.
Project a sense of equality.	Pull rank or act superior.
Remain open to new ideas and be tentative in your suggestions.	Maintain rigid positions with respect to your ideas; exhibit defensiveness-arousing uncertainty.

Establish specific goals and performance objectives.   There is clear evidence that *setting specific goals is very important to improvement.*[23] Meyer, Kay, and French discovered that setting specific goals for improvement yielded twice as much improvement as did talking of general goals or criticizing without any goal discussion.[24] For example, it is more likely that workers will increase production if you jointly set goals. It is better to say, "We agree, then, that you will try to increase your production to 150 units a day by the end of the next month" than to say, "We agree, then, that you will increase your production." Both of these represent goals, but the first will motivate the employee more.

Establish regular checkpoints to review employee progress toward the goals.   Appraisal systems that do not emphasize periodic checking on goal accomplishment *do not serve to motivate the employee.* Alva Kindall and James Gatza include this as one of the important steps, suggesting that there are often logical checking points in the completion of a project, or other company-imposed reporting dates.[25] Since each organization is different in this regard, we are unable to suggest a universally applicable periodic schedule. We think, however, that either the supervisor or the employee should initiate the suggestion that such a schedule be agreed upon. We cannot think of a situation in which the suggestion, if initiated by an employee, would be seen as negative.

Conduct interviews at least twice a year.   Waiting a year to talk again about an employee's performance has drawbacks. People forget objectives and commitments over a long period. In addition, situations can change. Old goals may no longer be applicable.[26] So we think it is well to conduct at least two appraisal interviews each year, and perhaps more.

> Given these findings from research, could lack of frequent performance appraisals be considered unethical?

Be consistent in your style. Try to achieve consistency between your usual interaction style and the employee-centered style you use in the appraisal interview. If you do not practice a problem-solving, coaching orientation in day-to-day activities, this style will seem insincere in the interview. Meyer and his associates suggest that you talk regularly with the employee about the job and play the role of helper rather than judge in the process of problem resolution.[27] This concept of helper is consistent with the role of the supervisor in the employee-centered appraisal interview.

Frank J. Landy and his associates suggest that several of these appraisal techniques work together to create a sense of fairness and accuracy.[28] In a questionnaire administered to 356 employees of a large manufacturing firm, the employees identified frequency of evaluation, identification of goals to eliminate weaknesses, and supervisor's knowledge of a subordinate's level of performance and duties as being related to their perceptions of the fairness and accuracy of the performance evaluation.

Structure of the Plan

The likelihood of the supervisor's being successful without some clear plan and approach in mind seems doubtful. We offer the following plan as one likely to achieve the goals of an appraisal interview.

Ask the employee to prepare for the interview. The employee could profit by spending some time considering these four questions prior to the actual interview:

1. What are my important job duties and responsibilities?
2. What are the major problems I encounter on the job?
3. How does my job performance meet the job goals and duties?
4. How does my performance compare to that of others doing similar work?

Establish or reestablish goals related to the specific job. Ask the employee:

1. What things does a person in this job need to do to be successful?
2. What do you think are the most difficult parts of your job?
3. What are the less difficult parts of your job?

Have the employee analyze performance. A study by Ronald J. Burke and his associates found that subordinates who were encouraged to talk about their ideas were more likely than those who weren't to see their supervisors as helpful, constructive, and willing to assist them in resolving job problems.[29]

Ask the employee:

1. Which of the activities you listed do you think you were most successful with? Least successful with?
2. Would you take each of the difficult and less difficult parts of your job that you listed and talk with me about how you see yourself handling each?

If the employee has missed a key issue, an appropriate response might be: "I have been thinking about what is important in a job like yours and have been wondering if [you name it] might also be important. What do you think?" (Employee talks.) Then, "How well do you see yourself doing this duty?"

Summarize any difficulties with performance that came out of the analysis. Examine your findings. Summarize the difficulties you've identified. Then explore alternative solutions with the employee through brainstorming. You might say, "You have listed these difficulties—_____, _____, and _____. I'm wondering what you think you might do to overcome [name the difficulty]."

Give some suggestions if the employee is unable to make any. You might say: "I have thought some about the difficulties you suggest. I can think of a solution or two that might be helpful. I wonder what you think of each of these." You can then reveal the tentative ideas.

Assist the employee in selecting a solution. In this step you review the ways the employee has suggested that the problem might be resolved. Then ask: "Which of these ideas do you think are best? Which are most reasonable?"

Attempt to get the employee to consider the outcome of the selected solution. The employee needs to know what it will take to do whatever he or she has agreed to. This important step is a transition to the next step, goal setting. It also may lead to the selection of a different solution. The employee may discover the favored solution is not practical or workable. Ask: "What are the likely results if you do [describe the solution]?"

Establish new goals and obtain the employee's commitment. Goal setting is a very important part of the plan. Remember these goals must be accepted by the employee if maximum motivation is to come from the goal setting. A goal is more likely to be accomplished when it is perceived to be under a person's control.[30] Notice that the goal-setting question is followed by the questions that seek to gain commitment to them. The three questions you will want to ask are (1) "What have you decided to do?" (2) "When will you do it?" and (3) (if the interviewee has not improved after previous appraisals) "What shall I do if you don't do what you say you will do?"

Plan for training if it appears to be the solution. You should keep training in mind as you conduct performance appraisal interviews. Sometimes employees do not know how to do certain aspects of the job as well as they should. This may become evident as they tell you about steps toward achieving a particular goal. Motivation alone will not solve a performance problem if there is also a training problem.

Plan with the employee for follow-up. Determine how you will know when the employee has met the goal and when it would be appropriate to check on goal accomplishment. The employee can help. Ask: "How will you know when you have achieved these goals? When shall we get back together to see how you are doing?"

Let the employee know you will help.   The employee is likely to feel supported if you offer help. In a recent study, Gary Blau found that such an offer is especially important when the task is complex or ambiguous.[31] You have greater expertise, power, and control, and it may be comforting to the employee to know that you are available if needed. You might say, "Be sure to let me know if I can help you achieve these goals."

Keep in mind the main rationale for employee-centered problem solving is employee self-development. Each time employees move through this sequence, they learn to solve work problems.

A Successful Evaluation System

Your organization may not have set procedures that you are asked to follow. Here we present the evaluation procedure used by McCormack & Dodge, a fast-growing computer software company in Huntsville, Alabama, as an example of a system that follows an employee-centered philosophy. Exhibit 10.3 reproduces their rating instructions. A study of this exhibit can help you draw maximum benefit from an evaluation.

Participating Effectively As the Interviewee

Suppose that you are now employed part-time as a salesperson by Retailers Unlimited. You are particularly pleased by this job as you intend to make your career retail sales. You hope to be invited to participate in their management training program upon graduation. You are required to participate in the appraisal process at Retailers even though you are part-time. Retailers believes that these interviews are a good way to keep their employees informed and motivated. The situation can best be summed up as one in which you want to do a good job and also want to be perceived as a person who has management potential.

Suppose we substitute the word *internship* for *part-time worker*. You might prefer to imagine yourself in an internship, facing a midway evaluation. Try to think about what you would do to make your interview successful. Are you able to formulate ideas about how you would approach this communication problem? Can you translate these into a specific plan? The remainder of this chapter presents a plan that you can use as your guide.

Conducting a Self-Assessment

Answer the following questions in writing and think about the implications of your answers:

1. What are my principal duties?
2. How well have I carried out each of these duties?

Exhibit 10.3   MCCORMACK & DODGE PERFORMANCE EVALUATION

The employee information and signature section across the top of the inside pages of
the evaluation form will be completed as follows:

Please print:	Signatures:	Date:
Employee Name _____	Employee _____	
Reviewing Manager _____	Manager_____	
Department/Cost Center _____	Next Level Manager_____	
Date of hire_____	Personnel _____	

Managers evaluate each performance factor on two scales. The first scale is a determination of how heavily each item should be weighted, or how important it is in
relation to all other factors. The second scale is a determination of how well the
employee performs in relation to the manager's expectations:

These performance factors are *weighted* as:

Critical: the performance factor is absolutely vital to job performance. *Each* factor
weighted as critical is unquestionably necessary to fulfilling the function of that
job. The evaluation of the employee's performance would alter significantly if the
employee did not meet the manager's expectations in those critical areas.

Important: the performance factor is very significant to job performance. Each is important, but *no one single* factor is critical to job performance. Rather, the successful performance of an individual is determined by the *overall* accomplishment
of *all* important components.

Desirable: the performance factor is included in the evaluation, not as a necessary
component to the job, but as a complementary component. It would be positive if
the individual performed at or above the manager's expectations for these factors,
but the overall impression of performance would not alter significantly if the individual did not perform well for these factors.

The performance factors are then *rated* as:

1. Exceeds expectations: the employee *consistently* and *significantly* exceeds the ex-
    pectations of performance for this factor—*unusually high level of excellence.*
2. Meets expectations: the employee demonstrates good performance for this factor.
    The manager's standards are essentially met.
    A rating of "(2) Meets expectations" does not mean average or mediocre per-
    formance. Expectation standards for performance are high and should be commu-
    nicated as such.
3. Does not meet expectations: the employee does not meet expectations of perfor-
    mance for this factor. Improvement is required.
    The Plus (+) or Minus (−) signs allow for further indication of how well each
    factor was performed.

The performance appraisal includes three categories of *performance factors:*

I. *General performance factors:* job components that apply to all positions, such as
    quality of work, organizing skills, initiative.
    (1) *Job knowledge:* depth of understanding of the content and procedures of the
        job and of the field of specialization.
    (2) *Quality of work:* thoroughness, accuracy, and completeness exhibited in
        routine assignments and special projects.

(Exhibit 10.3 continued on page 254)

(Exhibit 10.3 continued from page 253)

     (3) *Responsiveness to supervision:* timeliness of pursuing and completing tasks and objectives; acceptance of responsibility.

     (4) *Organizing skills:* planning, scheduling, coordinating tasks and assignments effectively.

     (5) *Judgment:* analyzing and evaluating situations; success in reaching correct and optimum decisions.

     (6) *Attitude:* ability and desire to cooperate with others toward the best interest of all concerned.

     (7) *Initiative:* ability to organize and develop constructive ideas; to perform new or assigned tasks in a self-directed manner.

     (8) *Self-development:* desire to improve performance and to strengthen both personal and job skills.

     (9) *Communication skills:* ability to communicate with superiors, peers, and subordinates.

    (10) *Supervisory skills* (if applicable): *Human Factors:* ability to select, motivate, and develop subordinates.

    (11) *Supervisory skills* (if applicable): *Managerial Factors:* skill in planning, organizing, controlling, and coordinating departmental activities; cost control effectiveness.

 II. *Performance to job standards:* the standard functions of the employee's job. Any individual in a particular job should be rated on the standards of the job which are taken from the job description.

III. *Performance to goals and objectives:* the goals that the manager and the employee have *previously* determined. These should be relevant to the particular employee's performance, as opposed to being generic to the job description.

Comments

The manager's comments are *required* for all factors weighted as critical and any factors that exceed or did not meet expectations. Any additional comments related to performance of an individual in each performance category are welcomed.

The purpose of the comment sections is to document for the employee *why* the manager chose to put an *X* in the box for that factor. What was going through the manager's mind when he or she decided to put an *X* in:

Exceeds expectations—What did the employee do above and beyond the expectations for the factor?

Did not meet expectations—What was not accomplished? How could the employee improve performance?

An *X* in the box simply indicates the result of the manager's decision—not the reasons why that decision was made. Neither praise (exceeds expectations) nor criticism (did not meet expectations) really alters performance. It simply makes the employee feel good or bad for a short period of time. By providing information as to *why* performance was rated as it was, an employee can understand what actions need to be continued or improved. These comments make the "performance to goals and objectives" section much easier to complete and to relate the goals and objectives to actual performance.

SOURCE: Used by permission of McCormack & Dodge Corporation, Natick, MA.

3. How does my performance compare with that of my coworkers in similar jobs?
4. What problems have I encountered on the job?
5. What are several approaches I might employ to deal with these problems?
6. Would I promote myself if I were the boss? Why? Why not?

We believe these questions cover most of the central concerns of supervisors, and they will help you anticipate what you probably will be asked. You will also find them helpful if you must evaluate others.

> This chapter has offered very specific guidelines and suggestions to help you draw people out—to get them to talk. Do you find any ethical problems involved in telling someone how to draw information from another person? How much help of this kind is too much?

Asking Informational Questions

It is generally important not to challenge or argue unless that is unavoidable. In asking questions, keep these guidelines in mind:

1. Try to get the interviewer to give you as much information as possible about your performance. If the employer is not following an employee-centered plan, you may hear evaluative comments about your performance.
2. Try to get the employer to give specific examples to illustrate what is meant, if possible.
3. Try to get specific suggestions about what you can do to improve.
4. Summarize what you think you have heard to discover if you really do understand.
5. Be prepared to discuss your performance difficulties. An interviewer following an employee centered style will try to get you to think about any problems in your performance.
6. If you think that the interviewer and you have reached similar conclusions about what you can do, check it out by restating the conclusions.
7. Ask for information and suggestions from the interviewer if the interview seems to be stalled. Avoid questions or statements that challenge. Examples of informational, as opposed to challenging, statements are given in Exhibit 10.4

You might wish to avoid challenging your employer because it is difficult to challenge without creating defensiveness. We do not believe, however, that you should avoid challenging altogether. If you think it is necessary, keep in mind Jack Gibb's supportive and defensive behavior categories. Exhibit 10.5 gives some examples of how you might use supportive categories in a conversation about your performance.

Applying the Principles of Language Use

We discussed the principles of language use in Chapter 8. The basic principles are:

1. Personalize your communication.
2. Realize when you make an inference and choose words to reflect this.
3. Clarify the fact that you are hearing an inference when that is what it is.

Exhibit 10.4   EXAMPLES OF INFORMATIONAL AND CHALLENGING STATEMENTS

Informational	Challenging
I'm wondering what I have been doing that leads you to that conclusion?	I don't see how you can say that! How do you know?
Would you describe some specific difficulties you have observed so I can know how to improve?	What do *you* want me to do?
Looking at my performance, can you suggest particular things you'd like me to do that I'm not now doing?	I'll do anything you say. You're the boss!
Sometimes people do things that irritate or frustrate others. Am I doing anything you'd like me not to do?	And I'll refrain from doing what you tell me not to do. You're the boss.

4. When it seems appropriate to report your feelings, do so precisely, before explaining and interpreting them.
5. Say explicitly what you want rather than what you do not want.
6. State your wants in terms of actions you can control.

You may want to review the material on interviews in the beginning of this chapter before you participate in a performance appraisal interview.

Exhibit 10.5   EXAMPLES OF SUPPORTIVE STATEMENTS

Category	Example
Description	From my perspective, this is what I thought I was doing.
Provisionalism	There are several ways of attacking this problem. I thought that what I did had a good chance of working even though other methods might also work. What other methods would you suggest?
Equality and problem orientation	I recognize your point of view on this issue and wonder if there is some way we can work together on this problem.
Empathy	I believe we both want to get the best product from our effort, and I am beginning to understand how difficult it is to coordinate our effort. If we can find a specific solution to this problem, it will help us achieve this optimum effort.

SUMMARY ....

We have presented basic issues of the interviewing process. The interview's opening, schedule of questions, and closing must be planned. An opening should (1) make the interviewee feel welcomed and relaxed, (2) provide the interviewee a sense of purpose, and (3) preview the major topics to be covered. Closings should (1) review the major topics and responses, (2) provide opportunity to add information that may have been omitted, and (3) formally end the interview.

The schedule of questions might be ordered by topic, time, cause to effect, or problem/solution. Questions that are planned will be more open or less open depending on the interviewer's purpose. The specificity of the questions will range from questions drawn spontaneously during the interview to specifically worded questions and response categories written prior to the interview and used as written. Follow-up questions, both planned and unplanned, will be used to add depth and clarity to the interviewee's responses. Finally, a decision must be made as to how directive the interviewer will be in carrying out the interview.

We have presented each side of the performance appraisal interview because we believe you will experience both sides in your career. The first part of our presentation centered on the role of the supervisor in conducting performance appraisal interviews. We discussed the goals and perspectives managers might have for conducting these interviews.

Next, we looked at the employee-centered problem-solving approach as a method of meeting most of the goals of the interview. In this approach it is necessary to create a climate for the interview so that the employee participates actively, does not feel defensive, and does feel supported by the supervisor.

In carrying out the employee-centered problem-solving appraisal interview, you should employ these techniques:

1. Help the employee focus on duties and performance with respect to these.

2. Encourage rather than praise.
3. Listen actively and feed back the employee's important ideas.
4. Keep the perspective employee-centered.
5. Do not criticize too much.
6. Discuss salary in an interview separate from the appraisal interview.
7. Establish specific goals and performance objectives.
8. Establish checkpoints to review the employee's progress toward goals.
9. Conduct interviews at least semiannually.
10. Be consistent in your style.

In addition, we discussed a sequence to follow in planning the performance appraisal interview that includes these steps:

1. Ask the employee to prepare for the interview by doing a self-analysis.
2. Establish or reestablish goals related to the specific job.
3. Have the employee analyze performance.
4. Summarize any performance difficulties that came out of the analysis.
5. Assist the employee in selecting a solution by reviewing the ideas.
6. Attempt to get the employee to consider outcomes of solutions.
7. Establish new goals and obtain the employee's commitment to the plan.
8. Plan for training if it appears to be the solution to the problem.
9. Plan with the employee for evaluation and follow-up.
10. Let the employee know that you will help.

Finally, we offered a plan to use when you are the interviewee:

1. Conduct a self-assessment.
2. Ask informational questions.
3. Apply the principles of language to be clear about your wants, needs, and feelings.

NOTES ....

1. H. Lloyd Goodall, Jr., Gerald L. Wilson, and Christopher L. Waagen, "The Performance Ap-

praisal Interview: An Interpretive Assessment, *The Quarterly Journal of Speech,* **72** (1986): 74–87.

2. Meryl R. Lewis, "Surprise and Sense-Making: What Newcomers Experience On Entering Unfamiliar Organizational Settings," *Administrative Science Quarterly,* **23** (1980):225–251.

3. C. O. Longenecker, H. P. Sims, and D. A. Gioia, "Behind the Mask: The Politics of Employee Appraisal," *Academy of Management Executive,* **1** (1987):183–193.

4. T. A. Judge and G. R. Ferris, "Social Contexts of Performance Evaluation Decisions," *Academy of Management Journal,* **36** (1993):80–105.

5. Longenecker, Sims, and Gioia, op. cit.

6. Gerald L. Wilson and H. Lloyd Goodall, Jr., "The Performance Appraisal Interview: A Review of the Literature with Implications for Communication Research," Southern Speech Association Meeting, Winston-Salem, N.C., April 1985. Also, see Hermine Zagat Levine, "Consensus on Performance Appraisals at Work," *Personnel* (1986):63–71.

7. Compiled from suggestions by Cal W. Downs, Wil Linkugel, and David M. Berg, *The Organizational Communicator* (New York, Harper & Row, 1977), p. 104; Felix M. Lopez, Jr., *Personnel Interviewing* (New York, McGraw-Hill, 1965), p. 148; "Performance Appraisal and Review," (Ann Arbor, Mich., The Foundation for Research on Human Behavior, 1958).

8. See Norman R. F. Maier, *The Appraisal Interview* (New York, Wiley, 1958); A. R. Solem, "Some Supervisory Problems in Appraisal Interviewing," *Personnel Administration,* **23** (1960): 27–40; M. M. Greller, "Subordinate Participation and Reactions to the Appraisal Interview," *Journal of Applied Psychology,* **60** (1975): 544–549; W. F. Nemeroff and K. N. Wexley, "Relationships between Performance Appraisal Interview Characteristics and Interview Outcomes as Perceived by Supervisors and Subordinates," paper presented at the 1977 Academy of Management Meeting, cited in R. J. Burke et al., "Characteristics of Effective Employee Performance Review and Development Interviews: Replication and Extension," *Personnel Psychology,* **31** (1978):903–905; and K. N. Wexley, J. P. Singh, and G. A. Yukl, "Subordinate Personality as a Moderator of the Effects of Participation in

Three Types of Appraisal Interviews," *Journal of Applied Psychology,* **58** (1973):54–59.

9. Maier, op. cit., pp. 1–20; Solem, op. cit., pp. 27–40; Greller, op. cit., pp. 544–549.

10. Greller, op. cit., pp. 544–549.

11. E. F. Huse and Emanuel Kay, "Increasing Management Effectiveness through Work Planning," in *The Personnel Job: A Changing World* (New York, American Management Association, 1964).

12. Nemeroff and Wexley, op. cit.

13. Gary P. Latham and Lise M. Saari, "Importance of Supportive Relationships in Goal Setting," *Journal of Applied Psychology,* **64** (1979):151–156.

14. Burke et al., op. cit., pp. 903–919.

15. Herbert H. Meyer, Emanual Kay, and John R. P. French, Jr., "Split Roles in Performance Appraisal," *Harvard Business Review,* January–February 1965, pp. 123–129.

16. Richard E. Farson, "Praise Reappraised," *Harvard Business Review,* September–October 1963, pp. 61–66.

17. Meyer, Kay, and French, op. cit., p. 127.

18. Latham and Saari, op. cit.

19. Emanuel Kay, Herbert H. Meyer, and John R. P. French, Jr., "Effects of Threat in a Performance Appraisal Interview," *Journal of Applied Psychology,* **49** (October 1965):311–317.

20. Huse and Kay, op. cit.

21. J. R. Gibb, "Defensive Communication," *Journal of Communication,* **11,** no. 3 (September 1961):141–148.

22. Meyer, Kay, and French, op. cit., pp. 124–127.

23. Feedback and goal setting have been found to be significantly related to subordinates' perception of equity and to the accuracy and clarity of information exchanged. See John M. Ivancevich, "Subordinates' Reaction to Performance Appraisal Interviews: A Test of Feedback and Goal Setting Techniques," *Journal of Applied Psychology,* **67** (1982):581–587.

24. Meyer, Kay, and French, op. cit.

25. Alva F. Kindall and James Gatza, "Positive Program for Performance Appraisal," *Harvard Business Review,* November–December 1963, p. 158.

26. Ibid.

27. Meyer, Kay, and French, op. cit.

28. Frank J. Landy, Janet Barnes-Farrell, and Jeanette N. Cleveland, "Perceived Fairness and

Accuracy of Performance Evaluation: A Follow-Up," *Journal of Applied Psychology,* 65 (1980): 355–356.

29. Ronald J. Burke, William F. Weitzel, and Tamara Weir, "Characteristics of Effective Employee Performance Review and Development Interviews: One More Time," *Psychological Reports,* 47 (1980):683–695.

30. Mirian Erez and Frederick H. Kanfer, "Role of Goal Acceptance in Goal Setting and Task Performance," *Academy of Management Review,* 8 (1983):455.

31. Gary Blau, "The Effect of Source Competence on Worker Attitudes," *Journal of Applied Communication Research,* 14 (1986):33.

RECOMMENDED READINGS ....

M. Beer. "Performance Appraisal." In J. W. Lorsch (ed.), *Handbook of Organizational Behavior.* Englewood Cliffs, N.J., Prentice Hall, 1987, pp. 286–300. This chapter is an excellent reference regarding issues of appraising performance.

Cal W. Downs, G. Paul Smeyak, and Ernest Martin. "Appraisal Interviews," "Counseling Interviews," and "Discipline Interviews." In *Professional Interviewing,* pp. 160–187, 188–207, 215–229. New York, Harper & Row, 1980. Downs and his associates offer additional material in these chapters on interviews.

William F. Eadie. "Defensive Communication Revisited: A Critical Examination of Gibb's Theory." *Southern Speech Communication Journal,* 47 (Winter 1982):163–177.

David W. Ewing, "How to Negotiate with Employees." *Harvard Business Review,* January–February 1983, pp. 103–110. This interesting essay presents a practicing manager's experience with handling complaints.

H. Lloyd Goodall, Jr., Gerald L. Wilson, and Christopher L. Waagen. "The Performance Appraisals Interview: An Interpretive Reassessment." *Quarterly Journal of Speech,* 72 (February 1986):74–87. These authors provide an interesting and useful perspective on the performance appraisal interview.

Gerald L. Wilson and H. Lloyd Goodall, Jr. *Interviewing In Context.* New York, McGraw-Hill, 1991. This book is an especially useful reference for answering specific questions about any of the topics discussed in this chapter.

DISCUSSION QUESTIONS ....

With a small group of your classmates, plan an interview appraising the performance in your class to date of (a) your professor; (b) a classmate; and (c) yourself. Then answer the following questions and share your answers with your classmates.

1. For each of the appraisals, what would be necessary to create a positive performance appraisal climate?
2. Develop suggestions for encouraging each of the individuals.
3. Does relative power and status influence the task of appraisal? How? What may be done to address power and status differences?
4. Are there any significant differences to be found in the way the professor and the classmate might prepare for an appraisal interview?

INTERNET ACTIVITIES ....

1. Do you think the many commercial employment services available on the World Wide Web are helpful? How do you determine the qualifications and quality of the advice they provide? Check out (http://www.proactive-inst.com/) for an example.
2. Suppose your annual performance appraisal review resulted in the suggestion that you take a course about interpersonal communication in interview settings. Check out your local college or university's offerings on the Internet, and make notes to share with classmates. What did you discover about the institution? Who teaches the courses? Can you take such a course online? Where? How? How much will it cost?

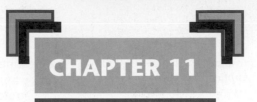

CHAPTER 11

The Selection Interview: Hiring and Being Hired for the Job

OBJECTIVES

Upon completion of this chapter, you should be able to:

1. Explain the importance of job descriptions, initial questions, EEOC guidelines, and setting to the interviewer in preparing for an interview.
2. Distinguish among legal and illegal questions that might be asked in an employment interview and formulate appropriate answers to difficult and/or illegal employment interview questions.
3. Do a preinterview informational interview.
4. Do a self-analysis of job skills.
5. Prepare a cover letter and résumé for a selection interview.
6. Research an organization to gather preemployment information.
7. Prepare for and practice typical questions asked by employment recruiters.
8. Prepare a list of questions to ask an employment recruiter.
9. Develop interviewer strategies for beginning an interview, motivating an interviewee to talk, avoiding various kinds of biases, and concluding the interview.

10. Develop interviewer methods that allow careful interpretation of data collected from an interviewee.
11. Identify the rules of behavior that should be observed during an interview.
12. Prepare a strategy for handling a group interview.

*I*magine yourself as an established professional who must interview others for your organization. Organizations like candidates to meet their upwardly mobile professionals for two reasons: (1) it is good recruiting procedure, and (2) it gives them a chance to test your judgment. If you are asked to interview, you will want a reputation for recommending the best people. The task of being the interviewer can be a challenge even for an established professional.

Perhaps you are far enough away from being established as a professional that you can't imagine being the interviewer. Instead, perhaps, you see yourself as the interviewee. For many the thought of participating in a selection interview brings a mild rush of nervous energy. This tension is related to the fact that we are being evaluated and much is at stake. But remember that the organization, too, is on display. We decide whether we want to work for an organization. There is a great deal of mystery connected with the interview process. Understanding the process and being prepared can alleviate this tension.

The first half of this chapter leads us through the process of preparing for the selection interview—both as an interviewer and interviewee. The second half describes considerations regarding the interview. These, too, are considered from the interviewer and interviewee perspectives.

....PREPARING FOR THE INTERVIEW: THE INTERVIEWER

A novice may think that the interviewer's part is easy. It is not. Many candidates have bad experiences with interviews through no fault of their own. Applicants often turn down job offers because they cannot imagine working for an organization that would use incompetent recruiters. If you work long enough for a company, you will be involved in selecting new professionals. What we say here can serve as a reference when you are called upon to conduct an employment interview.

In preparing for an interview, recruiters need to follow a certain sequence of steps, including:

1. Consulting the job description.
2. Deciding on a structure for the interview and preparing initial questions.
3. Checking Equal Employment Opportunity Commission (EEOC) guidelines.
4. Arranging the setting.

Consulting the Job Description

Many job descriptions are out-of-date or do not correspond to the job's actual duties. Do some checking. In *How Effective Executives Interview,* Walter Mahler gives a list of steps to follow for updating the specifications for executive positions.[1] With a little imagination you will be able to adapt the list that follows, which is based on his list, to your situation.

1. Do not leave updating the job description to the staff. It is your responsibility.
2. Check your list with other people who are familiar with the job.
3. Look at business or operating objectives.
4. Check to see if the position description is up-to-date.
5. Consider what factors contributed to the success and failure of present and past incumbents.
6. Analyze relevant competitors of the company. What personnel factors, if any, might give them an advantage?
7. Give attention to future changes that might occur in the job.
8. Separate critical qualifications from those that would be nice to have.

With the job description and the answers to these questions in hand, you are ready to prepare a chart of the responsibilities and qualities needed. The two-column list in Exhibit 11.1, for a departmental secretary in a university setting, is a useful model. Upon completion of the analysis, you are ready for the next steps.

Assessing Corporate Culture

The interviewer will find it easy to discover what the organization thinks about recruiting. There are likely to be some published procedures that reflect the or-

Exhibit 11.1 TWO-COLUMN JOB ANALYSIS	
Job Responsibilities	Qualities Needed
Greet people and make them feel comfortable	Articulateness, good communication skills, personableness, self-assurance
Solve problems for students and faculty	Attentiveness to detail, good judgment, ability to be convincing but not pushy, analytical mindedness
Type and reproduce handouts and tests for classroom use	Ability to pass typing test, follow a list of priorities, and be punctual
Take dictation and produce departmental correspondence	Ability to pass shorthand test, transcribe accurately, and spell and punctuate
Keep departmental records, including financial records	Honesty, mathematical accuracy
Manage interpersonal relations among departmental personnel	Liking for people, integrity, ability to be supportive, social sensitivity
Supervise student workers	Ability to organize, plan; tactfulness, good judgment

ganization's cultural expectations. Further, a person who is asked to take part in recruiting will undoubtedly have been in the organization long enough to understand what is expected. Beyond this, a recruiter will have access to those who routinely do this kind of work. If you are asked to help interview, find out what managers are looking for in a successful candidate. Ask also what causes disinterest in a candidate.

Reviewing the Résumé and Application Form

This process involves reading the applicant's letter, résumé, and application form (if your organization uses one). Look for continuity in the person's work and employment experience. Do you notice time gaps? You will want to probe these gaps to see if they are related to the way the candidate might perform. Consider the variety of reasons a person might not have been employed. A person may have been in school, been laid off, been fired, quit to take an extended vacation, been sitting around the house, been in jail, and so forth. Each of these possibilities has some potential consequence for hiring. A person may be laid off because of circumstances or perhaps because the work he was doing just wasn't that valuable. A person may have been between jobs and taken the opportunity to enrich herself, or she may have just sat around doing nothing. You will want to know what the person was doing during gaps in employment and the reasons for that choice.

> Employers sometimes receive one hundred or more applications for a single job. Occasionally they are tempted to "screen" the applicants by looking for particular features in the documents the candidates produce. For example, one interviewer automatically screens out any candidate who sends a document containing a misspelled word. Is this behavior ethical? What conditions would render it unethical?

Examine the candidate's references if they are included. Are these people in a position to observe the candidate's skills? Sometimes a candidate includes personal friends, clergy, and neighbors; these are not going to be helpful to you.

Next, check the candidate's reference letters. Most reference letters are positive—after all, who would ask a person who might reveal damaging information to write on his or her behalf? Sometimes these letters can be useful though. A middle-of-the-road letter, one that is not somewhat glowing, can be a bad sign. Notice if any of the letters speak specifically about outstanding contributions and/or past performance. Make a note of such comments, as these are areas that you may choose to pursue. For example, an interviewer for a small tool manufacturer noticed that a reference talked about a sales award. Questions were framed to probe this: "Tell me about how you came to win a sales contest." "Who was involved in the competition?" "What do you think it takes to win such an award?"

Look to see what kinds of educational experiences the person has had. Generally, this information is limited to the names of the schools and courses of study. Try to assess the quality of these programs from your organization's perspective.

Finally, check the application form, if there is one. Look here for completeness. Are all necessary blanks filled in? If not, there may be a reason for leaving a blank. Make a note of missing information in case you decide to interview the candidate later. Check also for the same kinds of information discussed above.

Structuring the Interview and Preparing Initial Questions

Generally you should work for a moderate degree of structure in your interviews, especially if you will be seeing a number of candidates. Research shows that structuring an interview will (1) force you to be more consistent, (2) cause you to talk less, and (3) allow you to achieve higher agreement with other interviewers, if you are part of a team of interviewers.[2] We think that planning topics and questions is a good idea. Cal Downs found that certain topics arise in most selection interviews.[3] Although not all were initiated by the interviewer, the topics most often covered, in order of the frequency discussed, are:

1. Job expectations
2. Academic background
3. Knowledge about job and company
4. Scholastic record
5. Work experience
6. Geographical preference
7. Interviewing for other jobs
8. Family background
9. Goals
10. Extracurricular activities
11. Strengths and/or weaknesses
12. Salary expectations

Framing questions for each topic is often difficult for an inexperienced interviewer. We recommend that you structure your interview by content area, taking advantage of the list of questions in Exhibit 11.2. Use it as a start, but tailor the questions to the job description. Also, keep in mind you may want to eliminate some of the less relevant content areas, especially if you are limited in time. And, of course, you will not necessarily want to ask all the questions in an area.

It is often useful to begin questioning in a content area by asking a broad question, such as "Tell me about your communication major." When you ask an unfocused question like this, applicants must focus and organize ideas and tell you what *they* think is important. This allows you to check their ability to analyze and organize—important communication skills you will want to evaluate. But limit the number of questions of this kind. They do not give you the specific information needed to compare candidates.

Ask some relatively easy questions early in the interview. Save the difficult questions for later, when candidates have begun to warm up to handling questions. Keep in mind that your structure has to be flexible. If a candidate is having difficulty with certain types of questions, be flexible enough to shift away from these questions. Come back to them later and try asking them in a different way.

Reviewing EEOC Guidelines

Discrimination in employment based on race, color, religion, sex, marital status, or national origin is forbidden by Title VII of the Civil Rights Act of 1964. In 1967, employment discrimination based on age was outlawed. Discrimination

Exhibit 11.2   QUESTIONS AND FOLLOW-UP QUESTIONS FOR SELECTION INTERVIEWS

I. Education

1. Why did you select your major area of study?
2. Why did you select your college/university?
3. If you were starting college again, what would you do differently? Why?
4. What subjects were most interesting? Useful? Why?
5. What subjects were least interesting? Useful? Why?
6. What classes/subjects did you do well in? Why?
7. What classes/subjects were difficult for you? Why?
8. Other than the courses you studied, what is the most important thing you learned from your college experience?
9. What did you learn from your extracurricular activities?
10. What would be your advice to an entering college student regarding participation in extracurricular activities?
11. What elective coursework did you take? Why did you select these courses?
12. What does it mean to you to have a college degree?
13. How did you finance your college education?

II. Experience

14. Describe each of your work experiences.
15. What do you see as your strengths as an employee?
16. You say that a strength you have is _____. Give me some indication, perhaps an example, that illustrates this strength.
17. Describe the employee you most enjoy working with.
18. Describe the employee you least like working with.
19. What is an ideal boss like?
20. What traits in a boss do you least like?
21. What were the best aspects of your last job?
22. What were the worst aspects of your last job?
23. What were some of your achievements in your last job?
24. What were some of the disappointments in your last job?
25. Do you see yourself as a leader/manager of people? Explain your answer.
26. What kind of work situations would you like to avoid? Why?
27. What skills are needed to be successful as a _____?
28. What are some of the pressures you've encountered in your work experience?
29. How have you worked to manage these work-related pressures?
30. In considering potential employers, what are the most important characteristics? What is *the most important*?
31. What frustrations have you encountered in your work experience? How have you handled these frustrations?

(Exhibit 11.2 continued on page 266)

(Exhibit 11.2 continued from page 265)

II. Experience (cont.)

32. What aspects of your last job were difficult for you?

33. Sometimes a work assignment requires frequent travel. How do you react to the prospect of frequent travel?

34. How would you evaluate the progress you made in your last job?

35. Do you think the progress you made in your last job is representative of your ability? Why? Why not?

36. How can a boss help an employee develop his or her capabilities?

37. What areas has your boss suggested you improve? What did you do to improve?

38. Most employees and bosses have some disagreements. What are some things that you and your boss have disagreed about?

39. What does it take to be a good leader?

III. Position and Company

40. Why did you select this company?

41. Why did you decide to apply for this particular position?

42. How do you see yourself being qualified for this position?

43. What about this position is especially attractive to you?

44. What do you see in the position that is not attractive to you?

45. Why should I hire you?

46. Tell me what you know about our company.

47. Are you willing to relocate?

IV. Self-Evaluation

48. Tell me a little bit about yourself. Describe yourself.

49. If you could relive your life, what might you do differently?

50. What do you see as your strengths? Good qualities? Talents? How do you know that you possess these? Give examples of each.

51. What do you see as your weak points? Areas for improvement? Things you have difficulty doing? What have you done to deal with these?

52. In what areas of work do you lack confidence? Explain. What are you doing about these?

53. In what areas of work are you most confident?

54. Describe a specific work problem you had. Tell what you did to solve this problem.

55. What traits or skills are most important to being successful? Why? Evaluate yourself in relation to these traits or skills.

56. What do you consider to be your greatest work achievement? Why?

57. What does it mean to you to be a self-starter? Do you see yourself as a self-starter? Explain.

58. What factors in a work situation provide motivation for you?

(Exhibit 11.2 continued on page 267)

(Exhibit 11.2 continued from page 266)

V. Goals

59. Where do you see yourself being in your profession in five years? In ten years? How did you establish these goals? What will you need to do to achieve these goals?

60. What are your salary expectations for this position? Starting salary? Salary in five years?

61. Elaborate on the career objective you presented in your résumé.

62. What has influenced you most to select your particular career goal?

VI. Military Service

63. What kind of specific responsibilities did you have in the service?

64. What traits make a successful leader in the (name branch of service)?

65. What did you learn about work from your tour of duty?

66. What traits are needed to be a successful military person?

67. What traits detract from success as a military person?

against handicapped people was attacked by the Rehabilitation Act of 1973, and again in 1990 by the Americans with Disabilities Act. In 1974, Congress provided for preference in employment and promotions for veterans of the Vietnam era by the Vietnam Era Veterans Readjustment Assistance Act.

Congress has produced this legislation and created governmental policing agencies to enforce the law in order to provide an opportunity for *all* qualified Americans to work. The principal governmental agency charged with policing the law is the EEOC. This agency has the power to bring those not in compliance to court. Thus, a series of court rulings has led to a set of guidelines and the following list of illegal areas of questioning:[4]

1. Change of name (may reveal national origin).
2. Maiden or former name of spouse (may reveal marital status).
3. Previous foreign address (may reveal national origin).
4. Birthplace of applicant, applicant's spouse, parents, or relatives (may reveal national origin).
5. Applicant's religion.
6. Applicant's complexion or color of skin
7. Applicant's citizenship or national origin.*
8. Applicant's foreign military service.
9. Name and address of relative to be notified (may reveal foreign-born parents). You can ask for *person* to be notified.
10. Applicant's arrest or conviction record—unless you can prove that it is a business necessity (particularly true of arrest record).

---

*Can ask if they have a legal right to work in the United States. This allows conformance with the Immigration Reform Act of 1987.

11. Applicant's height—unless height can be demonstrated to be a bona fide occupational qualification.

In the search for a position in marketing, a young woman reported being asked: "Do you plan to have a family? And, if so, what are your plans for caring for the children while you work?"

These questions, of course, do not in any way relate to whether the individual is qualified for the position. Moreover, they are not only impertinent but illegal. The candidate handled the question well, we thought: "If you don't mind a preface remark about the illegality of that question, then I will tell you what our plans are in that regard."

The reason we think her answer was a particularly good one is that it took all possibilities into account. She served notice that she understood the law and that she was assertive enough to deal with infractions directly in a relatively high-risk situation. She also was able to show that she was tolerant of ignorance but prepared to treat the ignorance with information. Finally, she communicated that she would answer the question because she felt it was innocent enough.

The test you should keep in mind when asking interview questions is this: "Does this information pertain to a *bona fide occupational qualification?*" In other words, does the information really tell anything about the applicant's qualifications for this job? Sometimes employers are curious about arrangements for child care, plans women may have for childbearing, marriage plans, divorces, activities related to activist groups, and the like. None of these relate *directly* to legal employment considerations and therefore they are none of the employer's business. They are very good grounds for an EEOC complaint and therefore you should avoid them. A summary of the laws with respect to equal employment is provided in Exhibit 11.3.

Keep in mind that any particular list of laws provides general guidelines. Court interpretations of the laws allow the employer to know what specific lines of questioning are illegal. Some state laws may be more restrictive than those passed by Congress. You should check with the personnel office for the most recent interpretation of the law.

Arranging the Setting

How you arrange the setting in which an interview occurs will have an impact on it. Try to arrange for privacy. We know there will be situations in which privacy is impossible, but at least stay out of the flow of traffic. You may desire some degree of formality in the setting for a variety of reasons. If you are interviewing someone who will work for you, you may wish for the formality of your office. Keep in mind that the choice to stay behind your desk will communicate something about you.

Some college recruiters recommend that an interviewer aim at informality because it will relax the candidate. If this is what you want, you might arrange for seating that is more direct and an atmosphere that is less imposing than your office. Try moving away from your desk and setting chairs so that they are fairly equal—perhaps at 90-degree angles with a coffee table in between and in-

Exhibit 11.3   FEDERAL LAWS THAT APPLY TO SELECTION INTERVIEWS AND EMPLOYMENT

Civil Rights Act (1866)

This legislation gave all persons the same contractual rights as "white citizens." It was the first law that prohibited discrimination.

Equal Pay Act (1963, 1972)

This act made it unlawful to pay different hourly rates for the same work on the basis of sex. It amended the Fair Labor Standards Act. It exempts academic, administrative, and professional employees from the overtime provisions of that act. The Wage-Hour Division of the Labor Department administers this act.

Civil Rights Act (1964, 1972)

This comprehensive act forbade employment or membership discrimination by employers, employment agencies, and unions on the basis of race, color, religion, sex, or national origin. It established the Equal Employment Opportunity Commission. (An amendment in 1972 allowed the EEOC to initiate court action to force compliance.) Provisions of this act are administered by the Office of Civil Rights of the Department of Health and Human Services and the EEOC.

Age Discrimination in Employment Act (1967, 1978)

This act makes it unlawful to discriminate against applicants or employees who are between forty and sixty-five years of age. (In 1978, this act was amended to raise the age to seventy years, but exempted employees covered by collective bargaining contracts.) Some job categories are exempted if a bona fide occupational qualification is involved. The act applies to employers with twenty or more employees. The Wage-Hour Division of the Labor Department administers the act.

Equal Employment Opportunity Act (1972)

This act amended Title VII of the 1964 act to broaden coverage and to give the EEOC authority to bring lawsuits. It also included educational institutions under Title VII. EEOC has administrative authority.

Amendments to Higher Education Act of 1965 (1972)

These amendments prohibit sex discrimination in federally assisted educational programs and allow educational institutions to fall under the Equal Pay Act. Sex discrimination provisions are enforced by the Department of Education.

Rehabilitation Act (1973)

This act mandates affirmative action to employ and promote qualified handicapped persons. It applies to federal contract holders employing fifty or more persons. Departments of Labor and Health and Human Services administer this act.

Vietnam Era Veterans Readjustment Assistance Act (1974)

Employers with government contracts of $10,000 or more must take affirmative action to employ and promote Vietnam era veterans. Enforced by Labor Department when complaints are received.

Immigration Reform and Control Act (1987)

This act prohibits discrimination on the basis of citizenship, providing an alien has a work permit and appropriate visa. Enforced by the Labor Department and Health and Human Services Department.

(Exhibit 11.3 continued on page 270)

> *(Exhibit 11.3 continued from page 269)*
>
> **Americans with Disabilities Act (1990)**
>
> This act requires equal access to employment and "reasonable accommodations" for persons with disabilities. A disability is any physical or mental impairment that substantially limits one or more major life activity. Job candidates can only be questioned about their ability to perform essential job functions. If a person indicates during the application process a need for reasonable accommodation—for example, an interpreter for a deaf person—the employer is obligated to provide it at its own expense.

> Is it possible for someone to be *overprepared* for an interview?

direct lighting. Your organization may have a suitable room that is used for this purpose. One interviewer we know often takes a candidate to the company cafeteria to have coffee.

We have looked at an employment interview from both the candidate's and the employer's point of view. The focus has been primarily on *preparation*. The second half of this chapter addresses what goes on during an employment interview.

PREPARING FOR THE INTERVIEW: THE INTERVIEWEE'S RESPONSIBILITIES ....

Consider how you planned for the last interview you had. How did you secure the interview? What did you do to get ready? Check to see how closely the following describes your preparation. If it was for a nonprofessional position, did you just put on appropriate clothing and go to the interview? If it was for a professional position, did you prepare a résumé, consider questions you might be asked, put on appropriate clothing, and go to the interview?

We recommend a six-step plan:

1. Doing preinterview informational interviewing
2. Doing a self-analysis
3. Preparing a résumé (data sheet) and cover letter
4. Researching the various organizations to which you might apply
5. Preparing and practicing for typical questions asked by employers
6. Preparing a list of questions you might ask an employer

Conducting Preinterview Informational Interviews

Interview one or two professionals who are actually working in the field of your choice. This interview ought to take place several months before you begin making appointments for interviews. Otherwise, it could be perceived as a ploy and may keep you from being considered seriously by firms where you have conducted informational interviews.

One complaint of interviewers is that college students do not have practical experience. A fact-finding interview can give you a great deal of information about what a particular field of work is like. Here are some good questions to ask the professional:

1. What is a typical day like?
2. What kinds of skills are most valuable?
3. What kinds of coursework were most valuable?
4. What are the most difficult problems that you have to face?
5. How do you manage these problems successfully?
6. What are the most rewarding parts of your job? Why?
7. What are typical starting salaries? What are salaries after five years?
8. Which are the major firms or organizations in this city who employ people in your profession?
9. What are some other job titles for people with your training?
10. What would be a reasonable career goal for a person in this position—say, in five years? in ten years?
11. What professional organizations would a person in your position join?
12. What are the main benefits of working for a company like [name the company]?

You can see the value in knowing this kind of information. Some professionals will be flattered if you ask for a short interview; others will not be willing to take the time. As an alternative, you might persuade a student group to sponsor a program during which professionals would address these questions.

Conducting a Self-Analysis

There are two areas in which analysis would be helpful as you begin to plan for an employment interview; those personal characteristics of yours that might be valuable and the preferences you have for a job and organization.

All of us have strengths that would make us good employees. The problem comes in identifying these strengths. Exhibit 11.4 presents a list of traits developed by Lois Einhorn for the Career Center at Indiana University. Rate yourself on each of these categories. Remember that careful evaluation produces the most useful results. Now take each trait you rated yourself highly on and write down a work or school example that illustrates the trait. Remember that most employers ask about your strengths. So pick two or three of your strengths and be prepared to give good examples.

Now rate your preferences in Exhibit 11.5, which lists characteristics of jobs and companies. Check the items according to their relative importance to you. Analysis of this information will help you decide which companies you'd like to interview.

Tom Reardon has discovered some interesting correlations between students' grade point average (GPA) and the organizational characteristics these students valued.[5] The lists in Exhibit 11.6 differ on the basis of whether the re-

Exhibit 11.4 INVENTORY OF PERSONAL TRAITS

Trait	Poor		Average		Excellent
	1	2	3	4	5
1. Dependable	( )	( )	( )	( )	( )
2. Honest	( )	( )	( )	( )	( )
3. Motivated	( )	( )	( )	( )	( )
4. Assertive	( )	( )	( )	( )	( )
5. Outgoing	( )	( )	( )	( )	( )
6. Persistent	( )	( )	( )	( )	( )
7. Conscientious	( )	( )	( )	( )	( )
8. Ambitious	( )	( )	( )	( )	( )
9. Punctual	( )	( )	( )	( )	( )
10. Creative	( )	( )	( )	( )	( )
11. Intelligent	( )	( )	( )	( )	( )
12. Mature	( )	( )	( )	( )	( )
13. Emotionally stable	( )	( )	( )	( )	( )
14. Enthusiastic	( )	( )	( )	( )	( )
15. Flexible	( )	( )	( )	( )	( )
16. Realistic	( )	( )	( )	( )	( )
17. Responsible	( )	( )	( )	( )	( )
18. Serious	( )	( )	( )	( )	( )
19. Pleasant	( )	( )	( )	( )	( )
20. Sincere	( )	( )	( )	( )	( )
21. Analytical	( )	( )	( )	( )	( )
22. Organized	( )	( )	( )	( )	( )
23. Having a good appearance	( )	( )	( )	( )	( )
24. Able to get along with coworkers	( )	( )	( )	( )	( )
25. Able to get along with supervisors	( )	( )	( )	( )	( )
26. Having oral communication skills	( )	( )	( )	( )	( )
27. Having written communication skills	( )	( )	( )	( )	( )
28. Having good references	( )	( )	( )	( )	( )
29. Having good school attendance	( )	( )	( )	( )	( )
30. Having good job attendance	( )	( )	( )	( )	( )
31. Willing to work long hours	( )	( )	( )	( )	( )
32. Willing to work evenings and weekends	( )	( )	( )	( )	( )
33. Willing to relocate	( )	( )	( )	( )	( )
34. Willing to travel	( )	( )	( )	( )	( )
35. Willing to commute a long distance	( )	( )	( )	( )	( )

(Exhibit 11.4 continued on page 273)

(Exhibit 11.4 continued from page 272)					
36. Willing to start at the bottom and advance according to own merit	( )	( )	( )	( )	( )
37. Able to accept criticism	( )	( )	( )	( )	( )
38. Able to motivate others	( )	( )	( )	( )	( )
39. Able to follow through on something until it is done	( )	( )	( )	( )	( )
40. Able to make good use of time	( )	( )	( )	( )	( )
41. Goal- (or achievement-) oriented	( )	( )	( )	( )	( )
42. Healthy	( )	( )	( )	( )	( )
43. Able to take initiative	( )	( )	( )	( )	( )
44. Able to follow directions	( )	( )	( )	( )	( )
45. Detail-oriented	( )	( )	( )	( )	( )
46. Able to learn quickly	( )	( )	( )	( )	( )
47. Willing to work hard	( )	( )	( )	( )	( )
48. Having moral standards	( )	( )	( )	( )	( )
49. Poised	( )	( )	( )	( )	( )
50. Having growth potential	( )	( )	( )	( )	( )
51. Others	( )	( )	( )	( )	( )

SOURCE: Adapted from Lois Einhorn, *Interviewing . . . A Job in Itself*, pp. 4–5. Used by permission of the Career Center of Indiana University.

spondents are above average or average students. We think it is interesting to see which items each category of student values.

One group of researchers speculates that the questions asked by the applicant help to reveal the person's motivation.[6] This idea supports Reardon—if high GPA people are highly motivated. Often you will be given an opportunity to ask questions, and what you ask will tell something about your personal orientation. We will return to this issue later.

Continue your analysis of your own strengths and weaknesses by asking yourself about your training and experience. This will lead to a résumé. Begin by listing the courses that relate to your designated professional goal. In which of these courses did you excel? How were your grades in these courses? Were there any special projects that allowed you to gain practical experience? Might any of your college professors be helpful to you in locating a job?

Consider your work background. If you have held a job, you are in a better position to be hired than a person who has never held a job. List all jobs you have held and the names of your supervisors. Would your supervisors describe you as a good employee? Why? What work skills did you display that might be valued by other employers? How do these skills relate to the strengths you discovered in your personal trait analysis? Have the jobs you held helped you to finance part of your education? If so, this is important to emphasize.

Exhibit 11.5 PREFERENCES IN JOB CHARACTERIZATION

	Importance		
Factors	Not Important	Average Importance	Very Important
1. Challenge	( )	( )	( )
2. Responsibility	( )	( )	( )
3. Stability of company	( )	( )	( )
4. Security of job within company	( )	( )	( )
5. Size of company	( )	( )	( )
6. Training program	( )	( )	( )
7. Initial job duties	( )	( )	( )
8. Advancement opportunities	( )	( )	( )
9. Amount of contact with coworkers	( )	( )	( )
10. Amount of contact with the public	( )	( )	( )
11. Starting salary	( )	( )	( )
12. Financial rewards "down the road"	( )	( )	( )
13. Degree of independence	( )	( )	( )
14. Opportunity to show initiative	( )	( )	( )
15. Degree of employee involvement in decision making	( )	( )	( )
16. Opportunity to be creative	( )	( )	( )
17. Type of industry	( )	( )	( )
18. Company's reputation in the industry	( )	( )	( )
19. Prestige of job within the company	( )	( )	( )
20. Degree of results seen from job	( )	( )	( )
21. Variety of duties	( )	( )	( )
22. What the boss is like	( )	( )	( )
23. What the coworkers are like	( )	( )	( )
24. Suburban or metropolitan community	( )	( )	( )
25. Hours	( )	( )	( )
26. Benefits	( )	( )	( )
27. Commuting distance involved	( )	( )	( )
28. Amount of overnight travel involved	( )	( )	( )
29. Number of moves from one city to another	( )	( )	( )
30. Facilities of office or plant	( )	( )	( )
31. Spouse's desires	( )	( )	( )
32. Others (list)	( )	( )	( )

SOURCE: From Lois Einhorn, *Interviewing . . . A Job in Itself,* p. 3. Used by permission of the Career Center of Indiana University.

Exhibit 11.6   THE TOP TEN EMPLOYER CHARACTERISTICS STUDENTS WANT

Above-Average Students (3.2 to 4.0 GPA) ($N = 325$)	Average Students (2.0 to 3.2 GPA) ($N = 443$)
*1. Employer is in a growth industry.	1. National or local reputation.
2. Potential for advancement.	2. Location of employer.
*3. Past history of growth/success.	3. Potential for advancement.
*4. Opportunity for continued education	4. Salary.
5. Salary.	5. Responsibility/challenge/freedom.
†6. National or local reputation.	6. Fringe benefits.
†7. Location of employer.	7. Prestige of working for employer.
8. Fringe benefits.	8. Employer is in a growth industry.
†9. Responsibility/challenge/freedom.	9. Past history of growth/success.
10. Prestige of working for employer.	10. Opportunity for continued education.

*Significant at .01 level

†Significant at .05 level

SOURCE: Reprinted from the Winter 1980 *Journal of Career Planning & Employment* with the permission of the College Placement Council, Inc., copyright holder.

Were you involved in any extracurricular activities? (If not, get involved now—if it is not too late). Have you invested any time in community service projects? (This is easy to do because service groups are usually looking for help.) Have you held any leadership positions in clubs or organizations? If so, list them, and anything else which might be an asset. Put everything you can think of on your worksheet. You can sort through the information on your worksheet later.

Assessing Corporate Culture

Communication events within an organization always take place within its cultural context. Selection interviews should be more productive for the applicant who is informed about the organization's culture. However, the interviewee will find the task of discovering cultural expectations somewhat difficult. Obviously, an outsider does not have access to the information that normally would be available to an insider.

One source of information consists of public documents. You should obtain a copy of the organization's annual report. What kind of business does the organization do? Does it fit any of the categories described by Deal and Kennedy that we presented in Chapter 1? Does it, for example, fit the "work hard/play hard" metaphor? If the business is one that relies heavily on direct sales to its customers, then this might be a cultural fit. Do the primary values of the culture center on customers and their needs? Success in this type of company depends on persistence. One more contact with the customer, a few more telephone calls, make this hard work. When you interview for a company where this is the over-riding cultural model, find ways to show that you believe in hard work and are persistent.

Check the organization's recruitment materials. What do the brochures tell you? Is the presentation crisp and formal? Is it friendly and chatty? Are there any stories about organizational heroes? If so, what characteristics seem to be emphasized? Look to see how the materials talk about the organization itself and its relation to its consumers. Are there themes that will tell you something about the people? If it is a manufacturing firm, for example, does it say anything about management's attitudes toward workers? Does it say anything about the company's concern for customers? Does it brag about products and how they are being received by customers? Does it suggest that it views its products as being on the cutting edge in its industry? You will undoubtedly find themes. If the organization is clearly concerned about its relationships with customers, this then provides an area for you to demonstrate your interest. If you are asked what makes for a successful company, for example, you might reply, "A company that takes time to discover its customers' needs and then acts on them." (Of course, you would expand on this response somewhat.) If the organization prides itself as one whose products are on the cutting edge, then you would be advised to study and be knowledgeable about the most recent advances in the industry.

If you know someone who is a part of the organization, you may be able to discover additional information. Pay attention to where this person's place is in the organization. Can you discover what subculture the person represents? A line worker's perception of an organization and its culture may not be as valuable to you as that of a person at some level of management—especially if you are interested in a management traineeship. Begin your questioning by asking what it is like to work in the organization. Ask also what it takes to be successful in the organization. See if the person can also tell you about some of the organization's prominent members. Ask too about the things in which the company takes pride. Finally, be sure to ask what the company looks for in a new employee. The answers to these questions will help you know what special research you need to do to be prepared and to gain a sense of how to present yourself in the interview.

Preparing a Cover Letter and Résumé

The primary purpose of a cover letter and résumé is to persuade the recruiter to grant you an interview. If you answer an advertisement in a placement bulletin or a newspaper, you will be using both the cover letter and the résumé. The cover letter is important because it gives you the opportunity to show the employer that you can write well and that you can adapt your presentation of yourself to a specific job. The résumé serves to highlight your background, education, and achievements. Its primary purpose is to cause the interviewer to want a personal interview with you.

Attention to detail in résumé preparation is important. Even such things as securing high-quality photocopies of your résumé can make a difference. One research team, Charles P. Bird and Dawn D. Puglisi, found that professionals who were asked to judge candidates were unable to ignore the fact that the résumé of a superior candidate was a poor-quality photocopy.[7]

> No one with any sense would present an outright lie in a cover letter or a résumé. However, people do try to present the strongest possible image—sometimes by leaving things out or by changing things around a bit. Do you think this behavior is ethical?

The Cover Letter

There are some rather specific conventions surrounding cover letters. Here are some of the important dos and don'ts:

1. Always send an original copy of the letter. Do not send a Xerox or a carbon copy. If you cannot type, hire a typist.
2. Address the cover letter to a real person. Do not send it to "Dear Sir or Madam." It is worth the effort and expense to call the firm and ask the receptionist for the correct name. Say, "I would like to address a letter to the person who hires people for [name the area]. Could you tell me this person's name, spell it, please, and give the person's title?"
3. Do not allow any misspelled words or excessive erasures or white-outs.
4. Follow one of the typical business letter formats. (The one we use in Exhibit 11.7 is always appropriate.)
5. Use high-quality, cotton-content paper, white or off-white. Do not use flashy colors or erasable bond.
6. Space the letter attractively on the page. Leave a little more margin at the top than at the sides; allow approximately one-inch margins on the sides. Confine the letter to one page and do not run it too close to the bottom.

Structure the letter to include at least three paragraphs. The first paragraph generally should state the purpose of the letter, the particular position for which you are applying, and how you came to know about the position. You might also tell, here, why you are interested in the particular employer, or you could start the second paragraph with this information.

The reasons you are interested in the particular position, the organization, and its products or services could begin the second paragraph. You should highlight your qualifications and explain how your academic background qualifies you to be a candidate for the position. If you have had work experience or have special qualifications, tell about these briefly and explain how they give you unique qualifications for the position. Refer the reader to the enclosed résumé that summarizes your qualifications, training, and experiences.

The third paragraph should ask for an interview and may suggest times when you are available. Repeat your telephone number in the letter and offer to provide any additional information that might be helpful in evaluating your credentials. Finally, close your letter with thanks and some statement about anticipating their future contact. Say in some way, "I look forward to hearing from you."

2000 Hillcrest Road
Mobile, Alabama 36609
February 10,19--

Mr. G. L. Rhodarty
Personnel Manager
XYZ Corporation
3000 Executive Park
Mobile, Alabama 36604

Dear Mr. Rhodarty:

Please consider my application for a position with your company. I am especially interested in XYZ Corporation because of its successful history and record of continuous growth and stability. I will be graduated in May from the University of South Alabama with a Bachelor of Arts degree in communication with an emphasis in organizational communication.

The enclosed resume will give you the pertinent facts about my education and past record of employment, which I believe qualify me for a position with your company. My particular interests lie in the areas of personnel development and training, especially human relations. The confidence I feel in handling personnel contacts has been gained from both my work experience and classes I have taken in communication and psychology. The variety of my work experience has given me the ability to adapt and relate to people easily and quickly. I am free to travel if the position warrants it, and I like to travel.

I would appreciate the opportunity to discuss employment possibilities with you personally in an interview. I believe that would enable us to discuss more fully my training and experience. I may be reached at the above address or at 334-111-2222. Thank you for your consideration of my application.

Sincerely,

John Q. Student

**Exhibit 11.7
SAMPLE
COVER
LETTER**

Exhibit 11.7 presents a cover letter. Remember that each cover letter is adapted to the particular job and should be freshly typed.

The Résumé

Imagine your résumé sandwiched in a stack of 200 others. What can you do to make it stand out as deserving of special attention? You can print your résumé on off-white paper. You can also give it some graphic appeal by using quality paper, allowing adequate margins, underlining various important parts, and the like. But beyond these considerations there are no guarantees. The average résumé in a stack of 200 will receive much less than a minute of attention. If you violate certain expectations, however, it will be rejected immediately.[8]

Exhibit 11.8   RÉSUMÉ FACTORS THAT CAUSE DISINTEREST IN CANDIDATE

Factor that Causes Disinterest	Strongly Agree	Agree	Neutral	Disagree	Strongly Disagree
Poor grammar	44%	53%	2%	1%	—
Spelling errors	27	60	11	2	—
Poor organization	18	58	21	3	—
Overpromise	15	44	35	5	1%

SOURCE: Reprinted from the Fall 1979 *Journal of Career Planning & Employment* with the permission of the College Placement Council, Inc., copyright holder.

Exhibit 11.9   EMPLOYER REACTION TO RÉSUMÉ DATA

Résumé Item	Yes, Should Appear	No	No Opinion
Career objective	66%	8%	27%
Extracurricular activities	76%	15%	9%
College(s) attended	76%	3%	20%
College grade-point average	57%	14%	29%
Specific courses taken	57%	23%	20%
Interests and hobbies	53%	11%	37%
Honors/awards	56%	9%	35%
List of references	8%	47%	45%

SOURCE: Beverly Culwell, "Employer Preferences Regarding Résumés and Application Letters," unpublished paper, School of Business, Missouri Southern State College.

We think that the best way to call attention to your résumé is to anticipate the needs of the reader. Consider that résumés serve at least three purposes: to open the door to an interview, to provide an outline for the interview, and to act as a reminder of the interview. Therefore, the following concerns are important:

1. Neatness and attention to expectations of employers
2. Information retrieval
3. Completeness of information, in a condensed form

Some important research is helpful in understanding what employers expect. A number of researchers have examined these expectations.[9] Exhibit 11.8 presents the most common causes of disinterest in the candidate; Exhibit 11.9 suggests what data employers preferred to see in the résumé; and Exhibit 11.10 addresses the issue of résumé form. You can see there is considerable agreement about the

Exhibit 11.10   AGREEMENT ON MATTERS OF FORM AND STYLE

Form and/or Style Issue	Strongly Agree	Agree	Neutral	Disagree	Strongly Disagree
Résumés should be $8^{1}/_{2}" \times 11"$	79%	15%	6%	—	—
A résumé should be a maximum of two pages long	51%	32%	8%	5%	4%
I am unlikely to pursue a candidate whose résumé is more than two pages long	10%	27%	47%	16%	—
A résumé should be only one page long	36%	30%	24%	8%	2%
I am more likely to pursue a candidate whose résumé has graphic appeal	3%	31%	42%	22%	2%

SOURCE: Reprinted from the Fall 1979 *Journal of Career Planning & Employment* with the permission of the College Placement Council, Inc., copyright holder.

causes of disinterest in candidates and about items to be included in the résumé. There is also fairly uniform agreement about the form the résumé should take.

The résumé is an information sheet. It should be designed in such a way that it gives the expected information in easy-to-read form. It should contain:

1. *Name, addresses, and telephone numbers.*
2. *Career objectives or goals.* This is usually the kind of job you are seeking.
3. *Educational background.* Degree(s), major, minor, special training, and other significant educational experiences are listed with their dates. Grade point average can be given here also. If it is not particularly impressive, omit it.
4. *Experience.* List the jobs you have had, beginning with the most recent and working backward. Include job title, name of employer, specific duties, and responsibilities. List special accomplishments.
5. *Honors.* List any special awards, recognitions, and scholarships.
6. *Activities.* Here list service clubs, preprofessional societies, other clubs, and interests. List any offices held or other leadership provided.
7. *References.* These may be given, but we recommend just saying "References furnished upon request."

Sometimes we are asked, "Should I put personal information on my résumé?" There is no "right" answer, but generally we would say no. Research shows that about 26 percent of employers expect it, but this is not a good enough reason to include it. It does add a personal touch that allows the employer to get a better picture of you. At the same time, it often includes irrelevant material that can be used for illegal discrimination. By giving birth date, you are, of course, stating your age. Height and weight are also irrelevant considerations unless you are applying for certain jobs. You will need to decide whether you want to include this information or not.

Exhibit 11.11 shows a sample résumé that reflects our suggestions. We think it is a good one and can be helpful in planning your own résumé. Exhibits

	Applicant's Name	
ADDRESSES:	<u>Home</u> 2000 Hillcrest Road Mobile, Alabama 36609 334-111-2222	<u>College</u> Smith Residence Center University of South Alabama 334-222-3333
OBJECTIVES:	My immediate objective is to obtain a position in business in the field of public relations. My long-range goal is public relations management.	
EDUCATION:	B.A., University of South Alabama, expected May 1997. <u>Major area:</u> Organizational communication and public relations. <u>Minor area:</u> Marketing	
GPA:	Overall: 3.2; Major area: 3.5; Minor area: 3.0 (4.0 scale)	
EXPERIENCE:		
1996-97	Information clerk, Smith Residence Center. Responsible for answering phone and giving information.	
1995-97	<u>Editorial Staff, Vanguard,</u> student weekly newspaper. Researched and wrote news stories and editorials, assisted in layout and design.	
Summer 1994	<u>Part-time assistant, public relations, Illinois Bell Telephone Company,</u> Dekalb. Helped to design brochures; wrote a speech for use in the high school; edited in-house newspaper.	
1993-94	<u>Part-time salesperson, Hall's Shoe Store,</u> Mobile. Sold men's and women's shoes, took departmental inventory.	
Summer 1993	<u>Lifeguard, municipal swimming pool,</u> Mobile. Taught swimming and enforced water safety programs.	
HONORS:	Dean's list for junior and senior years. Outstanding Student in Communication Arts, 1996-1997.	
ACTIVITIES:	Member, Public Relations Council of Alabama, Student Chapter, 1994-1997, and vice-president 1996-1997.	
REFERENCES:	Furnished upon request.	

Exhibit 11.11 SAMPLE RÉSUMÉ

John J. Doe
1200 Vienna Boulevard
Mobile, Alabama 36609

Telephone: (334)-222-3344

JOB OBJECTIVE: A marketing management position with a
major industrial firm.

1994-1997

EDUCATION:
University of South Alabama, Mobile, Alabama
Master of Business Administration, General Business

1981-1986

University of Alabama, Tuscaloosa, Alabama
B.S., Chemical Engineering
Treasurer of Student Chapter AIChE, 1985-1986
Worked part-time earning 50 percent of college expenses

MAJOR STRENGTHS
Technical: Capable of working with large amounts of technical data;
able to compile, interpret, and present reports using computer data as
a base. Research capabilities: have know-how in generating technical
information systematically.
Verbal and Written: Able to prepare written sales proposals in a clear,
concise manner. Able to prepare marketing brochures to convey
strong points of the product.
Managerial: Able to oversee, manage, and direct work of others. Can
develop program projects in a professional manner. Able to work with
details of a large project comfortably. Pragmatic in making judgements
or reaching conclusions about matters requiring action; able to accept
consequences of my judgement and decisions.
Marketing: Capable of assessing the needs of customers; able to
suggest ways of improving current assessments and very much
involved with problem solving.
Creative: Able to conceive new ideas, develop programs, and
institute new procedures.
Social: Have ability to relate on a continuous basis with clientele
in a social setting.

EXPERIENCE
A.B.C. Corporation
Mobile, Alabama

1993-Present

Demonstration Plant Supervisor. Direct the work of four professional
engineers gathering data for operation of the latest in Chlor-alkali
manufacturing equipment. Prepare and deliver technology
presentations to prospective licensees who visit the plant. Prepare
program objectives and coordinate plant operation with research program
conducted in Ohio. Prepare and manage both capital and operating
budgets in excess of $4 million annually. Review performance of
professional engineers annually. Compile data and interpret monthly
results in written reports to upper management.

**Exhibit 11.12
SAMPLE
RÉSUMÉ**

11.12 and 11.13 show some alternative ways of arranging information. Exhibit 11.12 is the first page of a résumé of a person who has had considerable experience. Note how he arranges his strengths so that they stand out. Exhibit 11.13 shows an emphasis on the applicant's administrative and human relations skills. This applicant is looking for a management position. As you can see by these examples, there are a number of ways to structure a résumé.

JOHN DOE
1111 ZALE AVENUE
MOBILE, ALABAMA 36691
(334) 395-6161

JOB OBJECTIVE: Entry-level management track position in personnel staffing.

EDUCATION
1993-1997 University of South Alabama, Mobile, Alabama
B.S.: Psychology, minor in Economics. GPA: 3.4 (A = 4). June 1997

SKILLS
ADMINISTRATIVE AND MANAGEMENT SKILLS
- Supervised staff, budgets, and facilities in business and nonprofit organizations.
- Directed programs for University Placement Office, planned workshops, coordinated public relations, and evaluated effectiveness.
- Attended to detail. Challenged by making systems work. Gathered sophisticated information as research assistant. Processed orders for meat company, and routed truck logistics (increasing efficiency by 20 percent).

HUMAN RELATIONS AND COMMUNICATION SKILLS

- Able to communicate in speaking and writing - clearly, concisely, and effectively.
- Attentive listener, able to help people "think out loud," reflect on experiences, identify problems, and develop solutions.
- Seasoned interviewer, skills developed as stringer for newspaper.
- Able to develop rapport quickly and easily.

EXPERIENCE
Ponder Meat Company
Mobile, Alabama
1994-1997 Assistant Manager for Inventories. Enjoyed industrial side of management by assisting in maintenance of inventories, processing orders, and directing transportation strategies.
Counselors, Inc.
Mobile, Alabama
1992-1994 Supervisor of Training. Recruited, trained, and supervised staff for program to educate high-risk students about self-management skills.
University of South Alabama
Mobile, Alabama
1991-1992 Placement Assistant. Worked part-time for several years to present "Career Orientation" workshops to students.
Mobile Press-Register
Mobile, Alabama
1990-1991 Journalist. Worked as part-time "stringer," conducting interviews, gathering facts, writing news and features. Published 50 articles.
Other Part-Time and Summer Experiences. Student intern in psychology department; tutor in English, math, and other subjects; waiter; and busboy.

INTERESTS AND ACTIVITIES
Vice-president, Senior Class in college.
Salutatorian in high school.
Active in Student Council, debate and swim teams at the University of South Alabama.

CREDENTIALS AVAILABLE UPON REQUEST

**Exhibit 11.13
SAMPLE
RÉSUMÉ**

Conducting the Job Search

At some time in the search for employment you will face the question, "Where should I begin looking for prospective employers?" This might be one of your first considerations or it might come after you have prepared credentials. There are many places for you to consider. You may be overwhelmed by the time it takes to conduct a vigorous search. But you can save time by understanding where to look for the most promising job opportunities.

The most promising source of jobs lies in the field that has the kind of job you want. When you are determined to stay in your local area, local sources are best. Exhibit 11.14 suggests local sources that may be most promising. You will want to pursue a different set of contact points if you are willing to move.

Researching the Organization

You will make a better impression than other candidates for the job if you carefully research the organization. Just as you are impressed when an interviewer takes the time to study your résumé thoroughly, employers are gratified when you have taken time to study their organization.

Organizations have been known to ask specific questions about an applicant's knowledge of their firm. One interviewer we know routinely says, "Tell me what our company's stock was selling for this morning." One of our students reported being asked by a paper company representative: "How much paper is produced in our mill across the street?" The student knew the answer because he had taken the time to read the trade journal. (He got the job too.)

There are two types of information you want to know: that which is public and that which only the employees of the organization know. Sources of public information are numerous. Consult your school's placement center; the Chamber of Commerce; the organization's annual report; *Thomas' Register of American Manufacturers; Moody's Industrial Manual; Standard and Poor's Industrial Index and Register;* Dun and Bradstreet's *Middle Market Directory, Million Dollar Directory, Reference Book; Fortune's Plant and Product Directory; US Industrial Outlook;* and *Business Index.* Also, check to see if the organization's business is the focus of a trade journal.

Here are some questions you will be able to answer from these sources:

1. Location of the organization's plants, offices, and branches
2. Age of the company and its history
3. Services the company offers or products it produces, and yearly sales
4. Growth and potential, and rank within its industry
5. Competitors in the industry
6. Information that is specific to a particular field, such as objectives, program, and funding sources for a social service agency; or circulation, affiliations with other media, competition, and growth history for a newspaper

Not surprisingly, sources of private information are not as accessible. You might get answers to some of these questions if you do informational interview-

---

Exhibit 11.14 WHERE TO SEARCH FOR JOB OPPORTUNITIES

Where to Search and Success Rates

1. Professional placement agencies (1%)
2. State placement offices (2%)
3. University placement offices (10%)
4. Professional association placement services (AMA, SCA, ASTD) (40%)
5. Relatives (25%)
6. Professional associates, former colleagues, friends (75%)
7. Former teachers (30%)
8. Newspaper and magazine advertisements (25%)
9. Mass mailing to job lists (5%)
10. Mass mailing to the *Fortune 500* lists (5%)
11. People holding a similar job (50%)
12. Personnel directors (?)
13. Leads from former employers (5%)
14. Social acquaintances (clubs, PTA, Scouts, etc.) (10%)
15. Workshops or seminars (60% long term; 15% short term)
16. Take your classes on field trips (50% long term; 1% short term)
17. Create your own (1%)
18. Write corporate officers (5%)
19. Fellow students, fraternity brothers, or sorority sisters (60%)
20. Voluntary organizations (United Fund, Community Center, etc.) (15%)
21. Gimmicks (mailing your face in chairman or president's picture, etc.) (5%)
22. Work for the local Chamber of Commerce (15%)
23. Start your own business (10%)
24. Advertise your qualifications in journals, magazines, and other publications (2%)

SOURCE: Charles J. Stewart and William B. Cash, Jr., *Interviewing: Principles and Practices*, 4th ed., p. 213. Copyright © 1985 Wm. C. Brown Publishers, Dubuque, Iowa. All rights reserved. Reprinted by permission.

---

ing. Check with alumni, friends, stockbrokers, and anyone else who might have experience with the firm. Sometimes a direct phone call to the personnel department of the company can be rewarding.

These are some questions to ask:

1. In your opinion, what kind of public image does the organization have?
2. Is there high turnover? If so, why?
3. What educational and training programs does the company have?
4. Will the organization help employees return to college for advanced study?
5. What is a realistic entry-level salary for a job in your profession?

6. What kind of benefits does the company offer?
7. What is the company's policy on transferring people to other locations?
8. What is the general work climate like?
9. Do subordinates participate in decisions?
10. What are the most serious problems faced by people in your part of the organization?
11. What is the company's stock selling for (on the day of the interview)?

You can see that some of these questions would *not* be appropriate to ask a recruiter. Yet often they are important for your future. We think doing your homework is just a common-sense thing to do, but it is also impressive to recruiters.

Preparing for and Practicing Typical Recruiter Questions

Ask people who have participated in a number of interviews if they were asked any surprise questions and they will tell you several that neither they nor you would have anticipated. For example, during a selection interview one of us reported to a dean that a graduate school friend was studying communication and the elderly. The next question from the dean was, "Why would anyone want to talk to old people anyway? They just want to be left alone." Then the dean paused for a response.

Obviously, we cannot prepare you for every question. There are, however, some very good lists of typical questions, such as the ones in Exhibit 11.15. Use these lists to prepare for unexpected questions. We suggest that you develop an answer to each question.

We recommend that you practice answering questions from the list we have provided. Videotape your answers if you can. If you cannot, at least audiotape the answers so that you can analyze both the verbal and the nonverbal content. (Ask a friend to play interviewer.) You may be surprised by what you hear. For example, taping may reveal that you are a person who chops your sentences with pauses. The interviewer may decide the excessive pauses mean you are unsure of yourself and your answers. This may merely be a habit you have acquired, but the interviewer does not know that. With a little effort you may eliminate this vocal pattern.

Then analyze your answers, keeping in mind that an organization wants to know that:

1. You have selected your profession for good reasons.
2. You have selected the organization for good reasons.
3. You are reasonably ambitious.
4. You are a hard worker.
5. You know your weaknesses and strengths.
6. You are working to correct any weaknesses.
7. You can be relied upon to do the job and to follow through.
8. You have some goals and they are reasonable.
9. You are trustworthy.
10. You like people and are likable.

Exhibit 11.15   TYPICAL INTERVIEW QUESTIONS

1. What are your long-range and short-range goals and activities? When and why did you establish these goals? How are you preparing yourself to achieve them?

2. What specific goals, other than those related to your occupation, have you established for yourself for the next ten years?

3. What do you see yourself doing five years from now?

4. What do you really want to do in life?

5. What are your long-range career objectives?

6. How do you plan to achieve your career goals?

7. What are the most important rewards you expect in your business career?

8. What do you expect to be earning in five years?

9. Why did you choose the career for which you are preparing?

10. Which is more important to you, the money or the type of job?

11. What do you consider to be your greatest strengths and weaknesses?

12. How would you describe yourself?

13. How do you think a friend or professor who knows you well would describe you?

14. What motivates you to put forth your greatest effort?

15. How has your college experience prepared you for a business career?

16. Why should I hire you?

17. What qualifications do you have that make you think that you will be successful in business?

18. How do you determine or evaluate success?

19. What do you think it takes to be successful in a company like ours?

20. In what ways do you think you can make a contribution to our company?

21. What qualities should a successful manager possess?

22. Describe the relationship that should exist between a supervisor and those reporting to him or her.

23. What two or three accomplishments have given you the most satisfaction? Why?

24. Describe your most rewarding college experience.

25. If you were hiring a graduate for this position, what qualities would you look for?

26. Why did you select your college or university?

27. What led you to choose your field or major study?

28. What college subjects did you like best? Why?

29. What college subjects did you like least? Why?

30. If you could do so, how would you plan your academic study differently? Why?

31. What changes would you make in your college or university? Why?

32. Do you have plans for continued study? An advanced degree?

(Exhibit 11.15 continued on page 288)

(Exhibit 11.15 continued from page 287)

33. Do you think that your grades are a good indication of your academic achievement?

34. What have you learned from participation in extracurricular activities?

35. In what kind of a work environment are you most comfortable?

36. How do you work under pressure?

37. In what part-time or summer jobs have you been most interested?

38. How would you describe the ideal job for you following graduation?

39. Why did you decide to seek a position with this company?

40. What do you know about our company?

41. What two or three things are most important to you in your job?

42. Are you seeking employment in a company of a certain size? Why?

43. What criteria are you using to evaluate the company for which you hope to work?

44. Do you have a geographical preference? Why?

45. Will you relocate? Does relocation bother you?

46. Are you willing to travel?

47. Are you willing to spend at least six months as a trainee?

48. Why do you think you might like to live in the community in which our company is located?

49. What major problem have you encountered and how did you deal with it?

50. What have you learned from your mistakes?

We think it would be helpful to you to add these additional, somewhat difficult questions to the list.

51. Did you do the best job you could in school? If not, why?

52. What kind of boss do you prefer? Why?

53. Describe a typical day of work at the XYZ Company for which you worked.

54. What are some of the important lessons you have learned from jobs you have held?

55. What types of books do you read? What was the last one you read?

56. What kinds of things cause you to lose your temper?

57. Are you a leader? Give an example.

58. Are you a creative person? Give an example of your creativity.

59. Are you analytical? Give an example.

60. What are the most important books in your field?

SOURCE: From *Northwestern Lindquist-Endicott Report* by Victor R. Lindquist, Northwestern University Placement Service, Evanston, Illinois. Used by permission.

11. You get along with people and will "fit" with other employees.
12. You will have the interests of the company in mind when you act.

See if your answers give evidence of some of these items. For example, telling the interviewer that you have been active in clubs and organizations will say that you probably like people. A steady work record will show that you believe in working. The fact that you have been successful in difficult courses and that you have carried out special projects in school will show that you are ambitious and probably a hard worker. The judgments recruiters make are based on their speculation about you. The decisions recruiters make are based upon what they *think* is true—although what they think may not actually be the case.

Questioning the Interviewer

What you ask the recruiter will tell much about you, although you will not always get the opportunity to ask questions. If you ask about salary, retirement, and other benefits, the recruiter may decide you are one of those people who is too concerned about what the company can do for the employee. Many recruiters view this as an inappropriate priority for a candidate. If you ask questions about things that a little research would have told you, you may be viewed negatively also.

Do ask questions that will point to your strengths, show that you have done research, and help you know when you can expect the recruiter to make a decision. You might want to ask, "Will I be involved in decisions in my department?" Or you might ask, "What kind of training and professional development opportunities are available as I progress in the organization?" Keep in mind that the recruiter may not be able to answer specific questions about your area. Here are some additional questions you might ask *if it seems appropriate.* (A note of caution: Do not ask so many questions that you appear to be quizzing the recruiter.)

1. What are some of the things that you have enjoyed most about working for XYZ Company?
2. Will there be a training program or period? If so, what can I expect?
3. If I do well in this initial position, what would be my next step?
4. Is there anything else you would find useful to have in evaluating my qualifications?
5. When might I expect to hear from you about your decision?

The question about time frame is a good one. It implies a continuing relationship with the recruiter. It also allows you to know how to follow up on the interview, and when. A call to the recruiter toward the end of the time frame may allow you to find out if the job has already gone to another candidate. Employers operate in different ways. Some may not be planning to fill a position for a month or more; others will make a decision within a couple of weeks. You want to know when you can quit worrying about a particular position. The time-frame question provides another advantage, although you don't really need to use it in this way. You may prefer a position in one company but be offered a job with another. The time-frame question provides you an opportunity to contact the first company without seeming too anxious. If you are offered your second-choice job, we think you ought to call your first-choice employer and tell the interviewer the situation. Sometimes direct assertiveness will move an organization off dead center and into your camp. Besides, what have you got to lose?

MANAGING THE INTERVIEW: THE INTERVIEWER . . . .

Beginning the Interview

Some interviewers are tempted to try to relax the applicant by several minutes of small talk. We think this is not wise. Applicants realize that recruiters make decisions early in the interview, so they may think that this behavior is some sort of ploy. Small talk also makes some interviewees nervous as they wonder when the "real" interview will begin.

We think it is better to start by orienting the applicant and then asking an easy but substantive question. There are two perspectives on orienting the interviewee. Some recruiters prefer to discuss specific job qualifications late in the interview. They believe that early information about the job allows the candidate to pitch qualifications to the job—to "manufacture" qualifications to meet the situation. Other recruiters prefer to give job specifications and details first.

We believe that potential employees are entitled to some information about the job. You may not wish to be specific early on, but at least tell the person in general terms what is involved. Presumably you want to know why candidates think that they are qualified. How can this be accomplished if you do not give at least a general job description?

Use the orientation to set the tone of the interview. Tell the interviewee how you would like to be addressed. Give some indication of how you will proceed; you might say, "I'll begin by asking some questions about your education, move to your previous employment, then to your present work situation. After that, you can ask me questions." Gary Richetto and Joseph Zima suggest that this type of orientation is particularly important in cases where the interviewee is highly anxious.[10] A good opening question is, "Tell me a little about yourself." Most people can handle this question, and it gives a perspective on what the applicant sees as important.

Motivating the Interviewee to Talk

Avoid difficult questions in the first part of the interview; they increase the tension level and may cause the candidate to say less. Also, avoid sensitive areas of questioning until later. Bypass probing of unfavorable information that may come out early in the interview. For example, if the interviewee suggests that he or she has been fired from a job, you might say, "Many people experience difficulties with employers early in their careers. Let's talk about what you did in your next job." Later in the interview you may want to come back to probe this area.

Ask questions that are both open and clear. This means trying to avoid questions that can be answered by a yes or no. Encourage the applicant to tell you more by asking, "And what happened next?"[11] Be sure that you use questions rather than statements as you attempt to motivate the interviewee, and do not constantly interrupt. Interruptive statements are a significant predictor that the interviewee will judge the interviewer as not an empathic listener. Be careful not to be concerned about short pauses. Sometimes a pause merely means that the candidate is thinking about what else ought to be said. Wait.

Probing

Sometimes the interviewee cannot be motivated to tell you all you need to know about some area of concern. In this case you will need to know how to probe for more. Probing is accomplished by asking a chain of related questions. Probing requires careful and analytical listening. (Remember the principles we described in Chapter 5.) What you ask comes from what the candidate has just told you; you usually cannot plan these questions. Suppose you asked, "What were some of your favorite courses in your major?" You might follow by asking, "Why was your study of small group communication your favorite?" You might ask further, "How do you see these experiences you cite as being related to your professional goals?" Probing will allow you to analyze both communication skill and depth of thought.

Watch for answers to questions that do not answer what you asked. Do not assume that the person is avoiding a straight answer and do not blame the applicant for misinterpreting the question. You might say, "I guess I was not clear with that question. Let me try to rephrase it." If the person does not answer you directly the second time, make a mental note to come back to the topic later.

Avoiding Biases

Bias may inadvertently slip into an interview. One source of bias may be your own questioning. You may be telegraphing the preferred answer by the way you ask the question. For example, you might say, "That is interesting, tell me more about it." Or you might say, "I think that _____ is extremely important to job success. Tell me about your experience and training in this area." You can see how revealing your biases may lead interviewees to respond as they think you would like.

Another source of bias lies in the order in which you interview candidates. Researchers have found that the quality of preceding candidates can influence a recruiter's opinion of a current candidate. For example, Kenneth Wexley and his associates found that when an average candidate was preceded by two very good candidates, the average candidate seemed to be much better than he or she actually was.[12] This effect was observed mainly for average candidates and not for very good or very poor candidates. Being aware of such a bias is your best defense against it, but we also suggest that you review your work after each series of interviews.

Time of day can be a source of bias in conducting an interview. Harvey Tschirgi and Jon Huegli discovered that a high percentage of negative decisions

Exhibit 11.16   HOUR-BY-HOUR ANALYSIS OF INTERVIEWS WITH RECORDED DECISIONS

Time of Day Interview Held	Number of Interviews	Number of Positive Decisions	Percentage of Positive Decisions	Number of Negative Decisions	Percentage of Negative Decisions
A.M.:					
9–10	22	12	55	10	45
10–11	22	14	64	8	36
11–12	12	4	33	8	67
P.M.					
12–1	4	3	75	1	25
1–2	17	9	53	8	47
2–3	23	15	65	8	35
3–4	21	13	62	8	38
4–5	15	5	33	10	67
5–6	4	1	33	2	67
Totals	140	76		63	

SOURCE: Reprinted from the Winter 1979 *Journal of Career Planning & Employment* with the permission of the College Placement Council, Inc., copyright holder.

were made just before the lunch hour and just before the end of the day.[13] Their hour-by-hour analysis, based on interviews conducted by seventeen private organizations at Ohio University, is displayed in Exhibit 11.16. Certainly it is not the case that the worst candidates always end up with interviews scheduled at these times!

Bias also creeps in when proper weight is not given to positive information. Thomas Hollmann investigated the claim that interviewers give too much weight to negative information, particularly if it comes early in the interview. He discovered that interviewers process negative information accurately, but they do not place enough weight on positive information.[14] In other words, the presence of negative information causes the recruiter to pay less attention to equally important positive information. The consequence is that interviewers let some very good candidates go. While employers cannot afford to ignore negative information, they can be aware of this processing bias.

Concluding the Interview

Keep in mind that whether you select or reject the candidate, you want the person to view your organization as attractive. The image of your company is important and you are its public relations officer in the interview. Try to end on a positive note. Do not stop the questioning with a series of difficult questions or probing of negative information. Move to an area where the candidate can experience pleasant, free-flowing conversation. Talk about the organization and why you enjoy working for it. You need to do some selling of the company in this interview, and this is a good place to say a little more about it. Mention the company's growth and image in the community. Talk about some of the company's key benefits. Do not overdo this, of course, but make your company sound like a good place to work.

Ask if there are any final questions. Then tell the candidate when you plan to make a decision. Give a time frame that encompasses a couple of weeks, but do not indicate that the person either will or will not be hired. You may think that this is the best candidate and say that, only to discover that the next candidate is even better! Or you might tell an average candidate that she or he does not have one of the important qualifications, later to discover that person is the preferred candidate.

Interpreting Interview Data

As soon as practical after the interview is complete, record your impressions. Your organization may have a form for this purpose. If not, you can make your own. Exhibit 11.17 shows a typical two-part evaluation form—the first part is a rating scale, the second a series of open questions. Use this check sheet in conjunction with the two-column job analysis you did before the interview for analysis of your data. Interpreting the data is not an easy task and is tied to the interviewer's value system. We cannot tell you what makes a good employee for a particular job; this depends on job and and situational constraints.[15] We do, however, have a few suggestions that will make the task easier.

Keep in mind the information we have presented about biases. Research about bias indicates that (1) a preceding candidate who is very good may make an average candidate look better, (2) the time of day in which you interview may bias choices, (3) the order in which you interview may cause a contrast effect, and (4) positive information may be given much less attention in the face of negative information.

Keep in mind that you may have biased the answers by the way you presented the question. Your perception of a candidate may be wrong because of bias you introduced. Be sure not to signal the appropriate response by the way you ask the question. Some candidates may be quicker than others to pick up on your cue and thus may appear to be the better candidate when they aren't.

Use several interviews for promising candidates. Often lower-level candidates get only a single interview. We think this can be a mistake. You will avoid some costly errors if you conduct several interviews. Many organizations have someone other than the initial contact conduct the second interview. The two then compare and contrast their impressions in the hope of arriving at the best applicant.

	Poor	Fair	Good	Very Good	Excellent
Preparation for the interview	_____	_____	_____	_____	_____
Attitude	_____	_____	_____	_____	_____
Level of maturity	_____	_____	_____	_____	_____
Level of motivation	_____	_____	_____	_____	_____
Self–confidence	_____	_____	_____	_____	_____
Ability to get along	_____	_____	_____	_____	_____
Communication ability	_____	_____	_____	_____	_____
Appearance	_____	_____	_____	_____	_____
Knowledge of organization	_____	_____	_____	_____	_____
Academic preparation	_____	_____	_____	_____	_____
Work experiences	_____	_____	_____	_____	_____

Answer these open–ended questions:

1. How well prepared was the applicant?
2. Describe the applicant's strengths.
3. Describe the applicant's weaknesses.
4. How does the applicant compare to the other applicants?
5. How well does the applicant's qualifications fit the organization's present and future needs?
6. What is the applicant's potential for development?
7. How well does the applicant understand what is required in this position?
8. How well does the applicant understand our organization?
9. Should we hire this person? Why? Or, why not?

**Exhibit 11.17
APPLICANT
EVALUATION
FORM**

Prior to any interviewing, make a check sheet of qualifications with space to write about each. After each interview, fill the sheet out for the candidate. This will force you to consider the same qualities for each candidate. Thus you will have a basis for comparison after you have concluded a series of interviews.

Forcing yourself to write something about each interview will also cause you to think more carefully about the candidates, but be careful not to make any marks on the person's résumé or employment application form. The EEOC has discovered that certain employers marked applications in ways that signaled discrimination for blacks, women, Hispanics, and others. Any marks on résumés or applications may be suspect if EEOC decides to examine your firm's employment files. We advise that you keep the notes you make after the interview together in a file separate from the applicant's file. Also, do not write evaluative comments *during the interview.* Write factual information and not inferences. Notes taken *during the interview* become a part of the applicant's file, and an applicant who thinks you have illegally discriminated can legally demand to see them later.

Prepare a list of specific questions for use in the second interview. Attempts to match qualifications with a job description will usually produce some areas of uncertainty. The second interview allows you to gather additional data to strengthen your inferences that the preferred candidate is the right person for the job.

....**MANAGING THE INTERVIEW: THE APPLICANT**

You may be discouraged at this point because there is much to do merely to be prepared for the interview. Employment interviewing is complex, but there exists a good deal of help. For example, Northwestern University's Placement Service lists the most frequent complaints employers make about interviewees (see Exhibit 11.18).

Exhibit 11.18   MOST FREQUENT INTERVIEWER COMPLAINTS ABOUT INTERVIEWEES

Rank	Complaint
1	Poor personality, manners; lack of poise, confidence; arrogant, egotistical, conceited
2	Poor appearance, lack of neatness, careless dress
3	Lack of enthusiasm, shows little interest, no evidence of initiative, lack of drive
4	Lack of goals and objectives, lack of ambition, poorly motivated, does not know interests, uncertain, indecisive, poor planning
5	Inability to express self well, poor oral expression, poor habits of speech
6	Unrealistic salary demands, overemphasis on money, more interested in salary than opportunity, unrealistic concerning promotion to top jobs
7	Lack of maturity, no leadership potential
8	Lack of extracurricular activities, inadequate reasons for not participating in activities
9	Failure to get information about our company, lack of preparation for the interview, inability to ask intelligent questions
10	Lack of interest in security and benefits, "what can you do for me" attitude
11	Objects to travel, unwilling to relocate

SOURCE: From *Northwestern Lindquist-Endicott Report* by Victor R. Lindquist, Northwestern University Placement Service, Evanston, Illinois. Used by permission.

These complaints can be avoided. The preparation we recommended will allow you to show that you are prepared and have appropriate interests and expectations. If you practice interviewing, you will sharpen your communication skills. Avoid giving reason for these complaints as you interview.

Asking Questions of the Interviewer

You will also want to ask some questions. We've already made a few suggestions in this regard. Ask about any special job responsibilities you might have. Ask about the organization's professional development and/or training programs. Ask about opportunities to advance with the company, assuming you do well on the job. *Do not* ask about company benefits or salary or what the company can do for you; if you are invited for a second interview, the matter of salary will be discussed. The employer will want you to know about remuneration so that you can evaluate its adequacy. Take a list of questions you have prepared, along with extra copies of your résumé, to the interview.

Combating Gender, Ethnic, and Religious Bias

In an interview, you are likely to be asked illegal questions.[16] There aren't any perfect ways to handle these questions. There is always a risk. You may choose to answer the question and forget about the fact that it may create bias. If you answer the question directly, the employer may use your answer to actually discriminate against you. Or you may politely refuse to answer. If you avoid answering the question, the employer may not hire you because you were evasive. You will want to do a quick analysis of the interviewer's motives, as best as you can determine them, to make a decision about how you want to answer.

Research shows that when most interviewees are presented with an illegal question, they answer it straightforwardly.[17] We also know that typical interviewees experience illegal questions as inappropriate even if they do not understand that the questions are illegal.[18] These two statements taken together are a bit disturbing and lead to a question. Why do people who are uncomfortable with an illegal question answer it? It seems reasonable to suppose that they believe they have no other option if they are interested in securing employment. While we do not deny that the interviewee is at a disadvantage when asked an illegal question, we do think that there are options other than answering the question directly. There are a range of options to be used as the interviewee sees fit. We present options and examples for your consideration and practice.

These strategies convey messages that range from answering the question directly to addressing the perceived concern of the interviewer to terminating the interview. These strategies are based on the work of Joann Keyton and Jeff Springston.[19] The assumption for each strategy, except the terminating strategy, is that it is used with the goal of doing the least damage to the interviewee's candidacy.

Three criteria are offered for making a decision about which strategy will work best. These are: (1) the perceived use of the information, (2) the importance of the information asked for, and (3) the desire to secure the position.

Let's examine how these strategies might be used. First, what seems to be the interviewer's intent? The primary interest here is in whether the interviewer seems to want the information to discriminate illegally. Sometimes the tone of the interview will allow you to make this judgment. Second, how important is revealing the information? Perhaps the interviewee may judge that giving the information is not particularly important or objectionable. Third, how important is securing the position? The position may be so important to the interviewee that he or she is willing to risk providing the information to be viewed as cooperative.

Exhibit 11.19 presents eight response strategies with exemplary responses. These are meant to serve as a model for you to use in practicing response strategies.

We have provided some answers that students have reported using to illustrate these strategies. The first two questions were asked of a woman who was interviewing for a school system job. The last illegal question was asked by the owner of a grocery store in Illinois. The first question:

Q: Are you married or single?
A: That's a personal question. I'd be happy to answer any questions about my qualifications.

An alternative answer:

A: If you're concerned about how my marital status might affect my staying with the school system, you should know that I am a professional and intend to continue working regardless of events in my personal life. I am single (or married).

The second question:

Q: How old are your children? Who will be babysitting with them?
A: I don't see how that information would be helpful in evaluating me as an employee, but I have children and have made arrangements for their care.

Alternative answers:

A: I'm not sure what information you want by asking these questions. Could you tell me what it is you want to know?
A: I'm not sure how these questions pertain to my qualifications. I'm, of course, willing to answer any question you'd like to ask about my training or experience.

The third question:

Q: Do you participate actively in a church?
A: My religious activities are personal. I do not mix my professional life with my personal life. I'd prefer to talk about my job qualifications.

Alternative answers:

A: I'm not sure how this question relates to my qualifications. [Then you might say,] I prefer to pass on that one. [or] I'd prefer to tell you more directly

---

**Exhibit 11.19   EXEMPLARY RESPONSES TO ILLEGAL
INTERVIEW QUESTIONS**

1. *Termination of the interview.*
   Example: "It's interesting that your company uses such questions as a basis for hiring. I expect to file a complaint with the Equal Employment Opportunity Commission because you discriminate on an illegal basis."

2. *Direct refusal.*
   Example: "I'm sorry, this is not a question that I am willing to answer."

3. *Direct refusal with reason.*
   Example: "I'm sorry, this is not a question that I am willing to answer because this information is personal."

4. *Asking how information relates to job qualification.*
   Example: "I am not sure how this question pertains to my qualifications for this job. I'd be happy to answer it if I can understand how it pertains to my qualifications."

5. *Telling that information is personal.*
   Example: "This information is personal. I don't mix my personal life with my professional life. I'd be happy to talk about my job qualifications."

6. *Acknowledging concern/asking for information.*
   Example: "I'm not sure what you want to know by asking this question. Could you tell me what it is you want to know?"

7. *Answering perceived concern.*
   Example: "I take it that your question about my plans for child care is a concern about the likelihood that I may be absent from work when they are ill. I want to assure you that I see myself as a professional person and will behave in a professionally responsible manner when they are ill."

8. *Answering the question and the perceived concern.*
   Example: "I am married. If you are concerned about how my marital status might affect my staying with the school system, I can assure you that I am a professional and intend to continue working regardless of the events in my personal life."

---

what you want to know. [You could stop here.] I'd be happy to answer questions about my training and experience.

A: [If you are sure you do not want the job and would like to put a stop to this kind of questioning, you might say,] This is a highly illegal question. It is interesting that your company uses such questions as a basis for hiring. I expect to file a complaint with the Equal Employment Opportunity Commission because you discriminate on an illegal basis. What is your name?

Sometimes an interviewer may ask an illegal question with the intent of getting at job-related information. An interviewer for an insurance company once asked about family ties. She was trying to determine social bases for finding clients and for selling insurance. If the interviewee understands the basis for what is being asked, an answer that will provide the information without giving out illegal information can be given.

There are many other illegal questions that might be asked. Remember that the answers to illegal questions asked by inexperienced interviewers may not be information used in making hiring decisions.[20] Sometimes the interviewer is just trying to be friendly and does not understand the law. You have to decide what the situation is and then formulate an answer.

> At first blush these rules of the game appear innocuous. Can you see any ethical issues or implications when you consider the rules more carefully?

Abiding by the Rules of the Game

Interviewees are often turned down for not observing the rules of behavior rather than because they do not have the qualifications. Some of the special rules you must observe and prepare for if you are to be successful are discussed below.

Be present at the appropriate time.   Plan to arrive at least fifteen minutes ahead of the time of the interview. You may want to take care of personal needs, have trouble finding the office, or get stuck in traffic. Fifteen minutes is not much time, but it's enough to handle last-minute details. Most interviewers consider promptness very important.

Dress appropriately.   Go back to Chapter 6 and review what we said about dress and physical appearance. Remember that proper hair length, appropriate use of colognes and perfumes, and other grooming are important concerns. Incidentally, we think it's good advice to remove any outside clothes—heavy coats, hats, and the like—before you enter the office for the interview.

Be friendly and responsive.   Smile. Try to show that you are enjoying the conversation. Use gestures in your conversation that are appropriately smooth and emphatic. Make sure you get the interviewer's name right and use it once or twice—Mr. Smith and not John.

Do not take over the interview.   Most interviewers expect to control the interview; let them. Also, don't interrupt the interviewer. Do not be surprised, however, if an interviewer expects you to carry the interview. Broad, general questions are often a signal of this situation.

Give more than one- or two-word answers to questions.   Most interviewers will want you to talk. Very short answers show a lack of thoroughness and may mean that you cannot carry a conversation. Give the interviewer something with which to work. On the other hand, do not drone on forever with meaningless talk.

Avoid the negative.   Do not criticize your present or past employers. Think of positive reasons for leaving. For example, tell the recruiter that you left to take a job that would allow you to grow professionally. If the situation was bad, you can mention it, but don't dwell on it or explain it in detail. Sometimes our students worry about having been fired from a position—that if the recruiter knew of the firing, it might damage their chances. Often they want to hide the fact. Our advice is that such an effort would be fruitless at best—and probably counterproductive. Lots of people get fired, and that fact suggests, or should suggest, that there is no disgrace involved. Moreover, every personnel director, and almost every interviewer, knows how to find out about a candidate's successes or failures on the job.

We would advise you not to hide a firing or dismissal. You can and should accentuate the positive side, but do not try to hide anything. The risk is too great. Suppose you hide a firing and someone in the organization discovers it later. The discovery is liable to cost your job.

Be prepared to sell yourself.   The recruiter will ask what training you have had to prepare you to do the job. Do not brag. Say that you have had some very good educational and work experiences and that you have been successful. Mention that you believe you can do the job because of a successful experience that relates to the job and then describe it.

Show an interest in the company.   Tell the employer that you want to work for the company (if you do) and why. Do not beg for a job, however. You may be asked why you selected to interview with this company. This is an opportunity to express interest. Take advantage of it.

Conform to the culture's norms if you can do so without violating your own ethic.   Common sense and simple courtesy suggest these rules:

Do not use profanity or slang, even if the interviewer does.
Do not continue talking while the interviewer is studying your résumé.
Do not try to interpret items on the résumé unless asked to do so.
Do not lie.
Do not look at your watch to keep track of the time.
Do not talk about salary in the first interview until and unless the interviewer raises the issue.
Do not appear to be too interested in telephone conversations that might take place during the interview.
Do not fiddle with hair or clothing.
Do not read papers on the interviewer's desk or pick up things on the desk.
Do not smoke.
Do not drink alcoholic beverages if, for instance, the interview takes place in a restaurant.

Take a few notes if you want.   There may be some information you will want later. Be sure it is accurate; write it down. But do so courteously. Ask, "Do you mind if I jot a note or two?" You can also write some of the questions you will ask on the same pad. When you ask when the interviewer will get in touch with you, you may want to write the information down so you will remember it.

Handling the Group Interview

A popular kind of interviewing is the *group interview*. The personnel section arranges for several candidates to be interviewed as a group. This has several advantages for the organization, though it can be unnerving for the interviewees. The purpose of such an interview seems to be very much like the technique commonly referred to as the "stress interview." The organization wants to discover how the interviewees will handle themselves in a very stressful situation, what personality characteristics will emerge (who is willing to take charge, or who is willing to be thoughtful and cautious but assertive under pressure) or how the several interviewees vie for control of the situation. While this type of interview allows for comparisons and contrasts, it is not useful, in our opinion, because it produces a kind of tension in candidates not likely to be encountered in normal working situations. If you can avoid a group interview, we recommend that you do so. If you cannot—and there are some situations in which you will not be able to—then there are some techniques you can use to manage the situation:

1. Apply the suggestions we have made in the chapters on interpersonal communication and group participation and leadership. These may help you convey the impression you are a thoughtful, take-charge person.
2. Ask the interviewer—or some representative—before the interview why the company uses this technique. Most of the time the company knows why it is using some technique; and if you can discover it, you will be that much ahead. We think the direct approach is the best to discover why a company would use the group interview technique. You might say something like, "Mr. Jones, would you mind telling me what you are attempting to discover by using this method of interviewing? It would help me greatly to know how to respond to the situation." Such a statement *is* a take-charge statement. It shows you are reflective, that you like to plan ahead, and that you are concerned about your image and like to live up to expectations. Even if the company representative declines to answer the question, you are still likely to earn some "points."
3. Prepare as you would normally prepare to answer the typical questions we suggest in the first part of the chapter.
4. Do organizational research. Many of the other candidates will not research the organization, and this will set you apart from them.
5. Listen carefully to the questions. Under these circumstances you will not want to ask that a question be repeated because you have not understood.
6. Pay close attention to what other candidates say. You may be asked to react to what they have said. If you have not been listening, then you will not be able to respond. Be sure you have paper so that you can take notes.
7. Be especially careful about the questions you ask. If you can think of an especially good question or two, be sure to word them carefully prior to the session. Write them down so that you have them ready and look for opportune moments to bring them up during the interview.

You may be able to turn a difficult situation into an advantageous one for you by following these suggestions.

SUMMARY . . . .

Selection interviews produce particular constraints on the communication process. We provided advice, based on our experience and what researchers have found, to help you know how to manage these communications.

The interviewer prepares carefully by (1) gathering information about and updating the job description, (2) deciding on the appropriate structure for the interview and initial questions, (3) reviewing EEOC guidelines to make sure no illegal questions are asked, and (4) considering and arranging the setting.

Key considerations for the interviewee are understanding the process, preparation, and practice. For the interviewee this means these six steps: (1) gathering information about the job and problems related to it through informational interviewing and library research, (2) doing a self-analysis to gain understanding of strengths and weaknesses, (3) preparing a résumé and cover letter that conform to the expectation of recruiters, (4) researching the organization by conducting interviews and library research, (5) preparing to answer employer questions by rehearsing answers to typical questions and self-criticism of taped responses, and (6) preparing a list of questions to ask an employer.

Interviewers must be concerned with techniques for conducting an employment interview. We presented strategies for motivating the interviewee, along with information about avoiding bias. We pointed out that both the beginning and ending of the interview are very important since they set the tone. They serve to relax the candidate, get the necessary information, and build a favorable image of the company. In interpreting the data the interviewer should keep in mind sources of bias. The interviewer can eliminate bias by following carefully worked-out check sheets listing the qualifications for the specific job and by conducting multiple interviews.

Interviewees ought to ask appropriate questions of the recruiter and present themselves well. They should handle illegal questions tactfully but firmly, based on the particular goal they have. They should follow the guidelines for appropriate interview behavior. Finally, they should use techniques for managing group interviews to turn them to their advantage.

NOTES . . . .

1. Walter R. Mahler, *How Effective Executives Interview* (Homewood, Ill., Dow Jones/Irwin, 1976), pp. 77–83.
2. D. P. Schwab and H. G. Heneman III, "Relationship between Interview Structure and Interviewer Reliability in an Employment Situation," *Journal of Applied Psychology,* 53 (1969): 214–217.
3. Cal W. Downs, "A Content Analysis of Twenty Selection Interviews," *Personnel Administration and Public Personnel Review,* September 1972, p. 25.
4. For further analysis of illegal questions asked in employment interviews, see Fredric M. Jablin, "Use of Discriminatory Questions in Screening Interviews," *Personnel Administrator,* 27 (1982): 41–44.
5. Thomas Reardon, "Preselection: How Students Prescreen Employers," *Journal of College Placement,* 40, no. 2 (Winter 1979):53–55.
6. Robert Gifford, Cheuk Fan Ng, and Margaret Wilkinson, "Nonverbal Cues in the Employment Interview: Links between Applicant Qualities and Interviewer Judgment," *Journal of Applied Psychology,* 70 (1985):735.
7. Charles P. Bird and Dawn D. Puglisi, "Method of Résumé Reproduction and Evaluations of Employment Suitability," *Journal of Business Communication,* 13 (1986):31–40.
8. Ibid.
9. Edward Rogers, "Elements of Efficient Job Hunting," *Journal of College Placement,* 40, no. 1 (Fall 1979):55–58; Victor R. Lindquist, *The North-Western Lindquist-Endicott Report.* The Placement Center, Northwestern University, 1988; Beverly Culwell, "Employer Preferences Regarding Résumés and Application Letters," unpublished paper, School of Business, Missouri Southern State College.

10. Gary M. Richetto and Joseph P. Zima, *Fundamentals of Interviewing* (Chicago, Science Research Associates, 1976).

11. Karen B. McComb and Fredric M. Jablin, "Verbal Correlates of Interviewer Empathic Listening and Employment Interview Outcomes," *Communication Monographs,* 51 (1984):367.

12. Kenneth N. Wexley et al., "Importance of Contrast Effects in Employment Interviews," *Journal of Applied Psychology,* 56 (1972): 45–48.

13. Harvey D. Tschirgi and Jon M. Huegli, "Monitoring the Employment Interview," *Journal of College Placement,* Winter 1979, p. 39.

14. Thomas D. Hollmann, "Employment Interviewers' Errors in Processing Positive and Negative Information," *Journal of Applied Psychology,* 56 (1972):130–134. See also Arthur A. Witkin, "Commonly Overlooked Dimensions of Employee Selection," *Personnel Journal,* 59 (1980): 573–588.

15. Donna Bogar Goodall and H. Lloyd Goodall, Jr., "The Employment Interview: A Selective Review of the Literature with Implications for Communication Research," *Communication Quarterly,* 30 (1982):116–124.

16. Jeff K. Springston and Joann Keyton, "The prevalence of potentially illegal questioning in pre-employment screening," in *Global Implications for Business Communications: Theory, Technology and Practice,* S. J. Bruno (ed.), Proceedings of the Association for Business Communication meeting (1988):247–263.

17. W. D. Siegfried and K. Wood, "Reducing College Student's Compliance with Inappropriate Interview Requests: An Educational Approach," *Journal of College Student Personnel,* 14 (1983):66–71.

18. Ibid.

19. Joann Keyton and Jeff K. Springston, "I Don't Want to Answer That! A Response Strategy Model for Potentially Discriminatory Questions," paper presented at the annual meeting of the Speech Association, San Francisco, November 1989.

20. For further counsel on answering illegal questions, see: Fredric M. Jablin and Craig D. Tengler, "Facing Discrimination in On-Campus Interviews," *Journal of College Placement,* 42 (1982):57–61.

RECOMMENDED READINGS ....

W. E. Barlow and E. Z. Hane. "A Practical Guide to the Americans with Disabilities Act," *Personnel Journal,* 71 (1992):53–60.

Richard N. Bolles, *What Color Is Your Parachute? A Practical Manual for Job Hunters and Career-Changers.* Berkeley, Calif., Ten Speed Press, 1997. This guide to job hunting is updated every year.

Cal W. Downs, G. Paul Smeyak, and Ernest Martin. "The Selection Interview" and "Selection Interviews: The Interviewee's Perspective." In *Professional Interviewing.* New York, Harper & Row, 1980, pp. 107–139, 146–159. These chapters provide detailed descriptions of the employment selection process.

John D. Drake. *Interviewing for Managers.* New York, American Management Association, 1972. This is a good book for more help in conducting interviews.

Lois J. Einhorn, Patricia Hays Bradley, and John E. Baird, Jr. *Effective Employment Interviewing.* Glenview, Ill., Scott, Foresman, 1982. Here is a book written by communication studies scholars. Its principal author worked as a professional recruiter.

Gerald L. Wilson and H. Lloyd Goodall, Jr. *Interviewing in Context.* New York, McGraw-Hill, 1991. Chapters 6 and 7 focus on the selection interview, first from the interviewer and then from the interviewee perspective.

DISCUSSION QUESTIONS ....

1. If you had the opportunity to talk with a professional in your field, what questions would you want to ask that person, and why?

2. Develop a résumé that you might use to apply for a position. If you have not had extensive working experience, don't worry about it. Just include what you can to represent yourself. Bring copies of the résumé to class to share with other members. Share résumés, then discuss these questions:

   a. What features of the résumés seem attractive to you?

b. What features seem to control eye movement and attention?

c. Were some résumés easier to use than others? What are the differences?

3. Suppose you were going to interview the person whose résumé you found most attractive. What questions would you ask that individual? How did the résumé contribute to your selection of the questions you would ask?

4. Two or three pairs of students should role-play an interview while the class observes. Then the entire class should discuss the following questions:

a. How effective were the questions asked by the interviewer and interviewee? Why do you think that?

b. How successfully did the interviewer guide the exchange? Did the interviewee have any influence on guiding the exchange? If so, how?

c. What suggestions would you make to the interviewee to improve the performance?

5. Review the questions provided in Exhibits 11.2 and 11.16. Pick out the five most difficult questions and answer them. Share your answers with the class.

6. Identify the two illegal questions you believe would be most difficult to handle. Share with the class how you might answer these.

INTERNET ACTIVITIES . . . .

1. You are going to interview for a position with an on-campus recruiter. In order to prepare you want to research the company, which you can do using the Internet. What can you find out from Moody's (http://www.moodys.com/) about your chosen company? How would that be useful?

2. Can you find any help on the World Wide Web for designing your résumé? Keep notes and report back to the class.

PART IV
Organizational Contexts:
The Group Context

We are convinced that a person who wants to succeed in complex organizations must learn to be an effective group participant. This means you must know how to identify what communication behaviors a group needs, then provide them. It also means you must learn how a group "fits" into the organization, and what that means to the group's task performance.

In Chapter 12, Small Group Communication Processes, we describe some dynamics of a group. Here we talk of "reading"

and serving a group's needs and of providing leadership when appropriate. Here we talk also about such concerns as group size, cohesiveness, productivity, and tensions and stresses and what these features of group process mean to you.

In Chapter 13, Communicating with a Group or Staff, we describe the most common kinds of group events and then give you detailed information about how to plan for those events—whether you are leader or member.

CHAPTER 12

Small Group Communication Processes

....OBJECTIVES

Upon completion of this chapter, you should be able to:

1. Explain why the size of a group is important to member participation, leadership, consensus achievement, and task performance.
2. Distinguish additive, disjunctive, and conjunctive tasks, and relate each of these to group size.
3. Describe the relationship between cohesiveness and productivity, and explain how each of these may be influenced by communication behavior.
4. Describe and explain the notions of primary and secondary tension and show how the ability to monitor tension levels in a work group may be useful.
5. Explain how trial and error affect emergence and the evolution of group norms.
6. Specify appropriate leadership behaviors that can be applied to the issues of group size and tasks, cohesiveness, productivity, tension and conflict, and roles and norms.

*T*his chapter describes, as clearly as possible, some group dynamics. We wish to provide a set of analytical tools to help you choose what to do in groups in accordance with the needs of a group. We will suggest how you might contribute leadership, noting that leadership is not the exclusive prerogative of assigned leaders.

This chapter focuses on several essential concerns: group size and tasks, cohesiveness and productivity, tension and conflict, group history, the emergence of roles and norms, and leadership. Intuition and a good deal of evidence suggest that an individual's skill in group participation is an essential ingredient in the formula for success. Groups conduct much of the business of organizations.

As a bright college graduate with a good deal of book learning about organizations, you must realize that, every time you work on a committee, you will be evaluated by other members. Often those members will be from different levels in the hierarchy and different departments in the organization. Because of the impact of your group work, we believe it is to your advantage to learn everything you can about groups.

WHY STUDY GROUPS? . . . .

There is little doubt that the study of group communication is increasingly important in business and professional organizations. Consultants are teaching seminars in group behavior that center on leadership, team building, task management, and the like. Corporate trainers are buying materials for in-house programs for executives, and for technically trained professionals who do not have management responsibility (such as engineers and chemists.) And college and university courses in group communication are becoming more and more popular each year.

Why is this emphasis upon group behavior growing? We believe the question is easily answered: More and more activities of business are conducted in groups.

It's important, then, to understand the problems that can arise from group communication. Group decisions can be better than individual decisions in many contexts. Groups bring to bear a much greater wealth of information and expertise than does an individual. And groups can be much more creative than individuals.

On the other hand, there are many tasks in which a group decision-making process is counterproductive. For example, you would not want delicate brain surgery to be the result of group decision-making. A highly trained expert handles the task better.

The question of when and to what extent to use group decision-making procedures will be addressed shortly. For now, we begin with questions of group size and group task.

GROUP SIZE AND GROUP TASKS . . . .

We think the ideal working group ranges in size from three to about twelve members who come together to discuss issues and to achieve commonly held goals. Notice that this statement includes two considerations: size and tasks.

Size

Generally, a gathering of fewer than three people is too small to call a group. The communication between two people is not confounded by numbers. They can signal how to pass the talk back and forth. They can punctuate the transaction without interference. They can express themselves according to rules they set for themselves. They are a dyad, not a group. Similarly, when the number of people in a group approaches twelve, then for reasons we will soon discuss, it is probably getting too big.

Size of a group has been related to such attributes as participation, leadership, member reaction, the ability to achieve consensus, group structure, and performance. Since the research does not clearly favor an optimum size for every group, we can describe the findings only in general terms, then suggest implications we see in that research. Thanks to a large body of literature[1] and common sense, we know that, generally speaking, the larger the group:

1. The more the variety of skills and abilities and the greater the knowledge available to it.
2. The more actual help it can call upon to accomplish its tasks.
3. The greater the opportunity for people to meet others who seem to them attractive, interesting, confirming, and desirable.
4. The more opportunities for individual anonymity.

Thus these clear advantages to large groups ought to be considered by the leadership against these disadvantages:

1. *The larger the group, the more likely that subgroups will form.* Subgroups can be damaging since they can become more important to members than the larger group. The potential for conflict is greater if subgroups form, and competition for scarce resources becomes an issue. While we have taken pains in Chapter 9 to assure you that conflict per se is not necessarily evil, the fact remains that it can be destructive. The larger the group, the greater the amount of conflict to be managed and thus the greater energy all members must devote to managing it.
2. *The larger the group, the more unequal member participation.* Leadership and decision making in larger groups go to the articulate few who tend to override the less-likely-to-participate members. Member participation is directly related to group size. If an individual is invited to a meeting because he or she has something to contribute, it follows that the group ought to hear from the member. If the size of the group inhibits the member's participation, the size of the group is dysfunctional.
3. *The larger the group, the less time for participation by each member.*
4. *The larger the group, the more likely that participation will be dominated by the talkative few, and the greater the likelihood that those few will address each other or the group as a whole rather than the ideas of a particular individual.*
5. *The larger the group, the more demands placed on the leader.*
6. *The larger the group, the more tolerance it might have for leadership takeover of group functions.* A group of six members, for example, might

very well agree that each person must contribute not only talk but action to implement group decisions. In contrast, a group of twenty might allow a leader to assign tasks to individual members or subgroups. Because this is so, an identifiable leader is far more likely to emerge in a larger group than in a smaller one. Smaller groups tend to be far more cohesive: as size increases, so does the amount of disagreement, antagonism, and, curiously, release of tension. Thus, in most cases, the larger the group, the less the tension—an inverse relationship that is very important. We will discuss this relationship in detail later in the chapter when we talk about tension and conflict.

7. *The larger the group, the greater the trouble in achieving consensus.* Sometimes (as we shall see in Chapter 13) a group *must* support a decision. Consensus, in such a case, is important. The balance between size and consensus is a significant leadership consideration. Closely related to consensus is the idea that a group's size will influence members' willingness to conform to norms, or rules. The research on this matter is equivocal, and the relationship between size and conformity is obscure. Common sense suggests that a larger group has more opportunities to pressure a member into conformity. To the extent that this is true, it is another relationship between size and the quality of group performance.

Tasks

Decisions about what size a group should be depend also on the task. I.D. Steiner identified three kinds of tasks: additive, disjunctive, and conjunctive.[2]

The more people who work on an *additive* task, the greater the output and the more effective the group's performance. In most additive tasks, however, the quality of each individual's performance is somewhat decreased.

Drive down any major highway and you find a road crew whose task is to pick up the litter. Their task is additive: the more people doing the job, the more trash collected and the more effective the cleaning. But the individual members of the group will work less effectively and efficiently than if there were fewer workers.

A *disjunctive* task is one in which the productivity of a group depends on its most competent member. Up to a point, the greater the number of members, the greater the likelihood that the group will have the expertise needed to do the task. Beyond that point, once the group has the necessary expertise, additional members do not contribute substantially to task performance.

One of the authors once volunteered to assist in the development of an equipment grant application to fund a computer laboratory. Since several colleges had programs that would benefit from the equipment grant, it made sense to pull together a group of volunteers from each of the several colleges. The group's final makeup included key individuals from the colleges of continuing education, education, and arts and sciences. Six men and women worked to describe the computer equipment needs for the lab. But when the time came to develop a budget, the group realized that not one person among its membership had the knowledge. We knew in general terms what we wanted, but we did not know which pieces of equipment to specify. The group had been stopped by a task that was beyond its best-informed member.

A *conjunctive* task is one in which the outcome depends on every person in the group performing part of the task. Performance is determined by the least efficient individual. Our language is full of references to this phenomenon: the most common is "a chain is only as strong as its weakest link."

A restaurant interiors design group is a good example of this kind of group. Each member of the design group controls a segment of the overall task. If, for example, the cabinetmaker could not complete that part of the job, everyone else had to stall until it could be done. If the kitchen designer couldn't get the stainless steel out of the plant for installation, that could mean that a stud wall could not be placed, which would mean the booths and tables could not be attached to the wall, and the plasterers, painters, and paperhangers could not apply their skills.

In addition to size and type of task, another factor with a strong effect on how groups perform is cohesiveness.

..............................COHESIVENESS, PRODUCTIVITY, AND MEMBER SATISFACTION

Cohesiveness and productivity are tied together in complex ways. In some cases, as cohesiveness increases, so does productivity. In other instances, more cohesiveness means less productivity. In still other cases, there appears to be a curvilinear relationship between cohesiveness and productivity, so that in the beginning increased cohesiveness yields increased productivity, but at some point that levels off and then more cohesiveness yields a decline in productivity.[3] But before we go further, let us define the two words.

Cohesiveness means how well the group likes itself, or the extent to which individual members want to be included in or be important to the group or their willingness to work together. Cohesiveness includes the individual member's pride and commitment to the others as well as the group's willingness to maintain itself over time.

Productivity is the yield of talk about tasks and goals. It refers to a group's ability to work, and to produce.

Exhibit 12.1 illustrates the relationship between cohesiveness and productivity. Notice that productivity runs from zero to infinity. This suggests that productivity can theoretically be increased to any feasible level.

Notice where the curve begins in the lower left corner of the figure. You will see that, while a group can have zero cohesiveness, it can still be productive. Its talk in the task dimension might yield units of productivity even though members do not have any particular liking for the group, do not identify with the group, do not especially aspire to be useful to the group, and so on.

From a leadership perspective, there is an optimum level of cohesiveness if the goal is to generate maximum productivity. If a group becomes too cohesive, it can get so involved in itself it loses sight of its tasks and goals, replacing them with other agenda items, such as joy of expression, interpersonal attraction, and

Exhibit 12.1 RELATIONSHIP BETWEEN COHESIVENESS AND PRODUCTIVITY

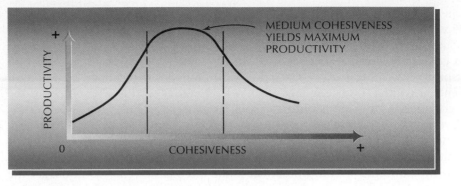

satisfaction. Informed leaders will undoubtedly monitor the cohesiveness of a group in order to sustain maximum productivity.

Important to the leadership of any group or organization are the consequences of cohesiveness: (1) maintenance of group membership, (2) influence of the group on its members, (3) participation and loyalty of group members, and (4) members' feelings of security. These consequences are most obvious when the group is voluntary, when it is just beginning, and when the tasks of the group have been approved and/or mandated by an organization.

You might wonder how a group can evolve into a cohesive unit. We believe that the most important condition is member satisfaction, about belonging to the group and about the role relationships. After examining 450 studies of what makes group members satisfied with their experiences, Richard Heslin and Dexter Dunphy identified three conditions that explain most member satisfaction: (1) the perception of progress toward group goals, (2) the perception of freedom to participate, and (3) status consensus.[4]

When people work in groups they agree to give up some of their individual sovereignty so the group process can work. They make themselves interdependent, and they assume an obligation to one another to adhere to the highest standards of ethical conduct. Some ethical standards you can follow when working in groups are:

1. Determine to do your best and participate fully.

2. Determine to behave rationally and with the group's interest in mind.

3. Make a commitment to fair play. Determine to seek, present, and explore all the ideas and evidence, whether they seem contradictory or not.

4. Determine to listen carefully, to provide feedback, to try to understand what the other person is saying, to evaluate what you have heard carefully, and to treat other members' ideas seriously.

5. Participate actively and analytically. Determine to make a contribution that will help the group succeed.

Actual progress toward a goal is relatively unimportant to members' satisfaction. The *perception of progress toward the goal,* however, is very important. Similarly, actual participation in group processes is not very significant to a member's satisfaction. What counts is that the members perceive they are free to participate. Status consensus has to do with the perception by group members that the evolving status hierarchy is "right." If everyone in the group agrees one member is the leader, for example, then that agreement constitutes status consensus. As you will see, there are many things individual group members can do to assist a group in these three important areas.

How can a leader monitor the cohesiveness of a working group? We think that a very useful way to do this is to study the levels of tension and conflict in the group.

....**TENSION AND CONFLICT**

People have speculated about tension levels in groups since group dynamics first became a field of study. Ernest Bormann separated tension into two categories: primary and secondary.[5]

Primary and Secondary Tension

Bormann called the tension a group experiences when it comes together for the first time *primary tension.* You might recall how it feels when you walk into a party and discover that you are the only person you know. That is primary tension.

You could not properly call the collection of individuals who are experiencing primary tension a group, since at that stage the individuals do not yet have a group identity. The point at which people are able to get primary tension below the level of tolerance for tension is the moment of groupness. (See Exhibit 12.2.) At that point the collection of people becomes a group.

As soon as a group reduces primary tension to a tolerable level, it is able to get to work on its tasks. If members are in a good group—that is to say, a productive one—they will interact openly and freely with one another. Sooner or later someone will introduce something that causes tension to rise. If the tension

**Exhibit 12.2
PRIMARY
TENSION AND
GROUP
FORMATION**

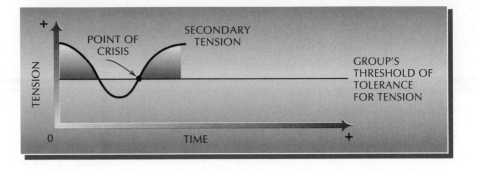

**Exhibit 12.3
A GROUP
CRISIS AND
SECONDARY
TENSION**

rises above the group's threshold of tolerance, it is called *secondary tension,* illustrated in Exhibit 12.3.

A group experiencing high levels of secondary tension will usually have difficulty working on its task. Indeed, an operational definition of secondary tension is tension so great that the group must address it; it can no longer be ignored.

Both primary and secondary tensions are natural. In fact, there can be no group that does not have some kind of tension. So tension per se is not harmful. And once primary tension is eliminated, it will not return fully. Each succeeding meeting may be characterized, at the beginning, by a little primary tension, but it never becomes as intense as it first was—unless the group membership changes.

What is especially interesting and useful about this analysis is that the tension provides a means by which to monitor what is going on in the group. If you can observe tension levels in a group across time, then perhaps you can discover what "triggers" the group, and you can time your leadership bids, contributions, persuasive appeals, tension-releasing interventions, and the like.

Usefulness of Tension and Conflict

In a working group, conflict manifests itself in the tension you can see in people's faces and postures and hear in their voice and message structures. When tension is at a tolerable level, the group can ignore conflict.

As time passes, a group evolves roles that feel right to it and rules by which the interactions are controlled. It develops some expectations about its tasks and about the kinds and frequencies of tension and conflict it can tolerate. Any change in the structure, the roles, or the rules, any change or initiatives for change in ways of doing things, introduce tension. A group learns how to function by trial and error. It does not give up its gains enthusiastically. So initiatives for change yield tension and conflict.

Yet all progress implies change. If things remain as they always have been, there may be no progress. So progress, even toward task goals, implies change, which necessarily introduces tension. A group usually does not function productively in the task dimension without tension.

To illustrate, Exhibit 12.4 shows the tension history of a work group that did not have difficulty overcoming primary tension. Members were a group

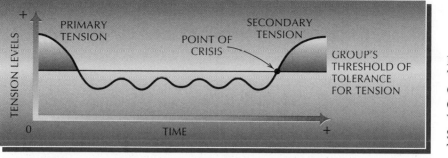

Exhibit 12.4
THE HISTORY
OF A WORK
GROUP
WITH HIGH
SECONDARY
TENSION

from early on. Notice that their first crisis occurred after a fairly apparently struggle that finally escalated beyond the limits of the group's tolerance. We might predict that this group will disband. The secondary tension is way above the group's tolerance level. Possibly one individual is causing the tension, and in that case, the deviant member might be expelled from the group. In any event, we can predict that the group will act on its tension soon. It has no other choice.

> Under what circumstances would it be ethical to create tension deliberately in a group?

Exhibit 12.5 charts a different group. This group, too, was able to overcome primary tension easily. But note that the levels of tension continue to drop. Such low levels of tension might suggest that the group was so cohesive that it allowed the social agenda to become primary. Another possibility is that the group was utterly apathetic. In that case, its members would not have invested anything of themselves in the group. Rather than introduce any controversy at all, the members might have sat there, meeting after meeting, doing nothing. If the groups in Exhibit 12.4 or 12.5 actually existed, they could not have been very productive. No group with that much or that little tension stands a chance of making much progress toward task goals.

A third hypothetical group is illustrated in Exhibit 12.6. This one has an optimum chance of being productive. The group had no difficulty eliminating primary tension. After a short period of productive work, the group experi-

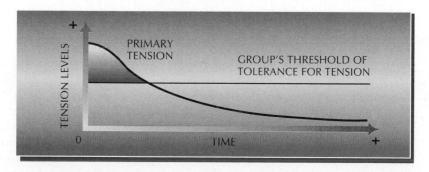

Exhibit 12.5
THE HISTORY
OF A WORK
GROUP WITH
CONTINUOUS
DIMINISHING
TENSION

Exhibit 12.6 THE HISTORY OF A WORK GROUP THAT HAS ADAPTED SUCCESSFULLY TO SECONDARY TENSION

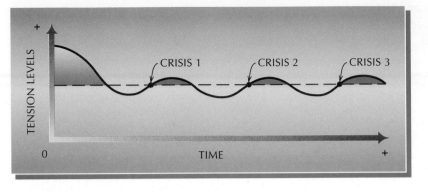

enced a crisis. Secondary tension, recall, is tension so great that the group can no longer ignore it. Thus the group would have addressed the problem causing the tension. The crisis passed, and tension levels dropped within the range the group could tolerate. Shortly afterward, the group experienced its second crisis. Again it was successful in dealing with the tension levels. A third crisis occurred and the group dealt successfully with it, too. Such a group would be ideal in a business organization, since it would develop a history of success in resolving its crises, and it would seem to have the kind of leaders and participants willing and able to accommodate changes in assumptions and procedures.

What does all this material on tension have to do with you? What are its implications for your choices of behavior? We think it implies:

1. *When tension levels are too high, talk about the source of the tension.* Stay in the present tense. Talk about yourself as much as possible. Talk about feelings, wants and expectations, and intentions. And be sure to check out the accuracy of any inferences. Try to follow Jack Gibb's advice about using language that is supportive.
2. *When tension levels are too low, talk about procedures and commitment to group goals.* Inevitably you will encounter a group that cannot seem to get anything done. It may well be that the group needs a sense of direction. When this happens, you will want to be able to focus on goals and suggest some procedures. Exhibit 12.7 will help.
3. *When tension levels are optimal, talk about the agenda.*

GROUP CULTURE

Group culture develops from the moment a group first meets, and continues to develop as the group's members relax and open up with one another and gain confidence in their ability to handle problems, exploring the limits of the group mentality and abilities and challenging each other's contributions and ideas.

According to Richard W. Brislin,[6] "A culture can be explained as an identifiable group with shared beliefs and experiences, feelings of worth and value attached to those experiences, and a shared interest in a common historical background." Brislin's definition is very helpful. It points to an identifiable group

Exhibit 12.7 GROUP DISCUSSION TECHNIQUES	
Name	Description
Brainstorming	Brainstorming is the process of generating as many ideas as possible without any attempt to evaluate the ideas as they are mentioned. Group members assign someone to take notes at a chalkboard or flipchart. For a specified period of time the members spontaneously and rapidly "toss out" ideas that are recorded as they occur at the chalkboard.
	After the ideas are recorded, the group can then approach the record in a variety of ways. For example, subgroups can rank-order the ideas; individuals might work quietly for a moment to attempt to identify the two or three best ideas; and so on.
Nominal group technique	This technique is based on two well-established assumptions: (1) People working by themselves but in the company of a group will produce more than people working privately. (2) Not everyone talks the same amount of time, so procedures may be necessary to assure that everyone participates.
	For a specified time, usually twenty minutes, group members silently write down every good idea they can think of. A master list is created from this private work, using a round-robin process in which each member, in turn, states one and only one idea.
	Discussion of the ideas is not allowed. Leader includes self in this process.
	Ideas are then clarified *but not* evaluated. Group members, working privately and on secret ballots, rank-order the ideas from the master list. The separate rankings are recorded for the group, which then engages in problem-solving discussion in an attempt to reach consensus.
Delphi technique	Group members do not meet face-to-face for this technique. Requires motivated members who can write their thoughts clearly. Technique involves four steps: (1) Participant's ideas are collected, listed, and distributed by group leader. (2) Each member develops a synthesis of the listed ideas. (3) Group leader develops an integration of the lists into a single master list, which is then sent out to members. (4) Participants vote on the issues of the master list—generally by ranking or rating—then return the votes to the leader.

whose members operate on the assumptions they share: beliefs, experiences, and the like. The members assume themselves to be members of the "in group."

Clifford Geertz[7] understands culture to be "an historically transmitted pattern of meanings embodied in symbols, a system of inherited conceptions expressed in symbolic forms. . . ." This too is a valuable definition because it points to the central importance of communication behavior.

Combine these two definitions and you come to a definition of group culture. *Group culture* is the shared history, beliefs, experiences, and pattern of meanings of an identifiable group of people. This definition focuses upon the elements that foster cohesiveness and that render one group different from another.

To illustrate how a group culture evolves, suppose two coworkers meet as a result of a special project group to which they are appointed. At first they notice each other, know that they will be working together, and consequently decide to get better acquainted. Perhaps they go to the company cafeteria for coffee. This meeting follows the rules laid out for such an event. He says something like, "I notice that you work for the marketing department. How are you liking it?" She says, "I like it fine. How is life in the sales department?" He might later say, "I really liked the point you made about marketing the new personal computer." She is likely to reply, "Thank you. I noticed you had some good ideas too. It's going to be fun to work together." Thus they stroke each other, and they stay well within the rules for social interaction. They rarely express any reservations they might have about each other.

After a while, their relationship will be on steadier ground. They will have experienced tensions and conflicts and will have gained confidence that they can address similar issues without threatening the relationship. He may say, "I think you might be more careful when you talk to Bill. You know he plays golf with the vice-president for marketing?" She takes this new bit of information, and they talk about the politics of the meeting. She also shares her feelings and ideas about him and his behavior. They learn to accommodate each other. They share private thoughts. Their relationship takes on private role definitions. They develop a history of relating to and dealing with each other.

Similarly, working groups develop a history over time. The ways members come to do things and the relationships they develop with each other make up that group's culture. If a group experiences success in managing tension, conflict, and the task, it gains a confidence that allows its members to open up. Thus the group becomes increasingly able to deal with ideas that produce tension. A way to study a group's potential for productivity, then, is to study its tensions. To the participating member or to a group leader, this ongoing analysis of the tension levels suggests, to some extent, what behaviors will be most beneficial to the group and when those behaviors will be welcome.

The group culture is also important because it embodies the rules that govern and the roles that contribute to the group. The roles that members of a group play and the norms governing their interactions are related to the success the group will have, both socially and with regard to its tasks.

THE ROLES AND NORMS OF A GROUP ....

When Jean became a manager at the telephone company, her life in the organization changed. One day her division manager asked her to represent the division on a planning committee that would reflect the interests of the entire organization. People from every branch of the organization would attend, and the group was to select its own leadership. The project promised to take the organization along paths it had not followed before. Some group members had never met. Others knew each other from other contacts in the organization; Jean herself knew two of the other members. But the group, as a unit, had no history.

This was going to be an important assignment for Jean. In preparing for the first meeting, Jean glanced through some notes she had made when she first became a supervisor. She had not, at that time, developed a sense of how to get along in groups. In frustration she had gone to a nearby town to chat with a professor of group communication she knew socially. One of the slips in Jean's file of notes was especially useful to her. It is also especially interesting to us, as it provides a convenient organizational motif for discussing the important matters of norms and roles (and their relationship to membership satisfaction in groups). Exhibit 12.8 is a reasonable facsimile of the page of notes from Jean's file. The figure clearly shows the importance of trial and error to the development of norms and roles and membership satisfaction.

Jean could recall the sound of this professor's voice across the years as she studied the sketch.

"At its most simple level," the professor said, "trial and error is a method of learning that has enormous impact on groups. Suppose I have a simple problem—say, to hammer a nail into a block of wood. I pick up the hammer, strike the nail, and the nail bends. Error. I try again. Twice I strike the nail and the nail drives deeper into the block. On the third strike, the nail bends. I try again, this time holding the hammer somewhat differently, and I swing the hammer from my elbow instead of from my wrist. The nail drives completely into the block. By a trial-and-error method I have learned the secret of driving a nail. If I try something and it is successful, I repeat the behavior. You can say I learned that behavior. If I try something and it fails, then I try something different the next time. You can say I made an error, then learned to do something differently."

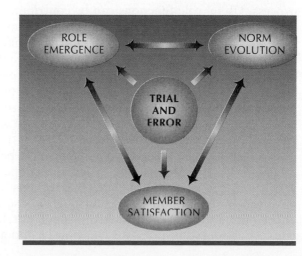

Exhibit 12.8 A SHEET FROM JEAN'S FILE ON GROUP COMMUNICATION

"But what's driving a nail got to do with my problem? I don't see what you are trying to get me to see." Jean was unimpressed by the professor's story.

"What I am working up to, Jean," said the professor, "is that you can use the same method in groups that I did in the hammer-and-nail illustration, to learn how to perform better and leave the impression you want."

Now Jean was getting interested. "Will you explain that?" she asked.

"Look. Suppose I go into a group. I don't know the members and they don't know me. We don't know what to expect. I don't know the rules of the game. They don't know whether I will help or hinder them."

Jean nodded as the professor continued. "The first thing I do is behave! I do something—even if it's only to stick out my hand and shake with the guy sitting next to me. If the trial wasn't an error, nothing negative will happen. If it *was* an error, the group will punish me in some way."

"OK," said Jean. "Then what?"

"The same thing happens over and over. I behave in some way. The group rewards or punishes my behavior. The members teach me the role I will play. In the same way, they teach me the rules they play by."

"Then you're saying that's how people get their roles in groups?" asked Jean. "It's just that simple?"

"Not quite *that* simple." The professor smiled. "You've got to contribute something. But in general, that's how it works. Timing is involved—as well as the needs of the group and your understanding of those needs. All these things are part of the magic of role and rule emergence."

What the professor had told Jean was *how* roles and rules emerge from the talk in a group. He had not told her *what* roles and rules emerge. We suggest that there are both useful and counterproductive role functions and group norms.

Role Functions

The names of roles that people play are not important—there are many roles in groups. What is important is the functions that roles contribute to the group process. Useful role functions can be contributed by any member and by more than one member. What tends to happen is that individuals, by trial and error, learn certain behaviors—such as cracking a joke to relieve tension—that seem to be useful. If the individual is reinforced for this behavior, that person may take the behavior from group to group. This explains why roles appear to be "played" by people. Exhibit 12.9 displays the important role functions that any individual can contribute to a group. You will see from this table the communication behaviors that make the difference to successful groups can be contributed by any member.

On the other hand, some communication behaviors are counterproductive to group success. An individual who is uncooperative, displays subjectivity toward both problems and people, and remains aloof and sullen would clearly have the wrong attitude. An individual whose contributions are ill-informed and whose behavior is inattentive cannot but hinder a group. An individual who evades questions, reasons fallaciously, and avoids or ignores the reasoning

Exhibit 12.9	VITAL ROLES ANY MEMBER CAN CONTRIBUTE
Function	Descriptive Communication Behavior
Task dimension leadership	Goal setting, agenda setting, procedure setting, idea seeking, evaluation seeking, summarizing, behavior monitoring and controlling, climate monitoring and setting, team building
Social dimension leadership	Summarizing, climate monitoring and setting, conflict managing, tension releasing, relationship analyzing
Critical thinking	Idea contributing, conflict instigating, idea evaluating, frequent and sometimes skeptical questioning
Information sharing	Idea contributing, information seeking, information recording, summarizing

of others cannot help the group. An individual whose language use is inadequate and who disregards the leadership of others, veers off the course of discussion, and takes the rest of the group with him or her will hinder group progress. An individual who attempts to usurp power, pretends to have knowledge, and distorts and deceives will certainly be counterproductive. We think that individuals who behave in any of these ways constitute the most difficult leadership problems for a group. The interpersonal skills required to handle such people must be well polished and well developed.

> Occasionally someone deviates from group norms just because the norm exists and is easy to identify, and because the individual feels deviant. Is this ethical behavior? Why or why not?

Group Norms

A *norm* is a behavioral expectation on which members of a group agree. Some norms are particular to certain groups, and some are generally subscribed to by whole cultures. Group norms and cultural norms may or may not be similar. For our purposes, we focus on norms that are particular to working groups. These norms develop around the procedures a group learns to follow and concern the tasks it addresses and the relationships the members develop with each other.

Since the group's norms evolve out of trial and error, a group often will be unaware of them. One thing is sure: the more cohesive the group, the more distinct and clear its norms. For example, a member of the sales force at a new car dealership in Mobile, Alabama, reports that the salesmen dress similarly even though there is no dress code. This group has developed a norm about dress.

A norm is productive if it contributes to goal attainment, counterproductive if it inhibits goal attainment. An informed observer can make the judgment about which norms are which. The question is not "What norms are counterproductive?" but rather, "How can I encourage productive norms and help change counterproductive ones?" The answer lies in skillful leadership.

LEADERSHIP IN GROUPS . . . .

In this section we will take up issues raised earlier in the chapter and consider some of the leadership communication choices you can make that might be helpful in groups. But first, you might take a look at Exhibit 12.10, which is a list of leadership activities divided into the task and social dimensions of communication. You can see that any participant can contribute the functions listed; none is the exclusive prerogative of a recognized leader.

Group Size and Tasks

Pay attention to the number of people in the group, remembering that sometimes a group will be too large for the purpose for which it was assembled. Since subgroups will probably form anyway, it is reasonable to suggest that a large group be divided into more manageable subgroups that will work independently on the task, then return to the larger group for general discussion and approval of the results. If the task is conjunctive, the optimum size for most groups would be five, six, or seven members. Recall that conjunctive tasks are those in which the members are interdependent and the success of the group depends on the level of the least competent member. Thus a smaller size provides essential controls and opportunities to compensate for the least competent member, monitor progress, and provide task-centered leadership. If the task is additive (that is, the more members, the better) then do nothing or suggest that additional members be recruited. If a task is disjunctive (with success dependent on finding an individual with expertise necessary to do the job), then suggest procedures that will identify the expertise available and tap into it. Group size is relevant here too, since in larger groups some very expert members may remain silent. Therefore, suggest that larger groups be divided into smaller task forces, which will identify the available expertise and be better able to utilize it.

Cohesiveness

Effective leadership will be aware of the relationship between cohesiveness and productivity and will build cohesiveness to an optimal point.

Member Satisfaction

This is the most important component of group cohesiveness. We said that member satisfaction depends on perceiving progress toward the task, perceiving freedom to participate, and status consensus. To assist members in perceiving progress toward goals, it is useful to restate the goals clearly and often, and to subdivide them into smaller units. When the smaller units have been accomplished, call attention to the fact. State directly that you believe the group is being productive and you are pleased with the productivity—if you are. If you are frustrated, you can reveal it, and the reasons for it, so long as you can at the same time make a constructive proposal that will assist the group to achieve its goals. Remember that the members will not be offended by this show of concern for the group's well-being, on condition that you use competent interpersonal

Exhibit 12.10   OPERATIONAL DEFINITION OF LEADERSHIP CATEGORIES

Task-Related Functional Behavior

1. *Developing orientation and defining a problem.* Diagnosing or interpreting situations or problems; describing a task or problem; identifying subproblems or specific needs; identifying initial conditions, constraints, or goals; introducing new ideas; summarizing events in a nonevaluative or nonintegrative manner.

2. *Facilitating information exchange.* Asking for factual information, clarification, or repetition; clarifying others' comments; directing communications; supporting other members' right to speak.

3. *Facilitating evaluation and analysis.* Asking for or providing evaluations or analysis concerning paths to goals or goal attainment; abstractly exploring means to goals; analyzing interrelations among variables; examining consequences of actions; statements of principles; hypothesis development and testing; reasoning, logical elaboration, or calculation.

4. *Developing plans.* Proposing plans concerning the task or interpersonal environment—procedural as well as task plans; suggesting general strategies for coping with a task, problem, or subproblem.

5. *Proposing solutions.* Proposing complete or partial solutions.

6. *Initiating behavior.* Requests for nonspecific action—for example, "Let's get started"; behaviors with an activational rather than motivational connotation—for example, behaviors focusing on overcoming inertia rather than achieving a specific end.

7. *Coordinating or directing behavior.* Requesting specific actions; indicating where or when specific behaviors are to be performed; indicating roles to be played by particular group members; assigning members to subtasks.

8. *Removing barriers or providing resources.* Explaining or showing others how to do a job or approach a problem; providing information relevant to carrying out actions; providing material resources; eliminating tasks or interpersonal obstacles.

Socioemotionally Related Leadership Behavior

9. *Enhancing task motivation.* Stressing the importance of goals; exhorting group members to work harder; making rewards contingent upon good task performance; complimenting an individual's task performance.

10. *Fulfilling nontask needs of members.* Showing concern for others as individuals; supporting their self-esteem or worth; indicating acceptance or admiration of others that is not based on their task performance; consoling others.

11. *Reducing or avoiding conflict.* Asking for preferences; seeking consensus; moderating or resolving differences; providing justifications of behavior; apologizing for behavior.

12. *Developing a positive group atmosphere.* Indicating gratitude, general satisfaction, or positive affect; complimenting group performance or output; general courtesies; friendly behavior.

SOURCE: From Robert G. Lord, "Operational Definition of Leadership Categories," *Administrative Science Quarterly*, 22 (March 1977):122. Reprinted by permission of *Administrative Science Quarterly*.

skills in the doing. The key is to speak supportively. You may wish to review Gibb's lists of defensive and supportive climates in Chapter 8 just before you act.

To help a group perceive freedom to participate, supportive behavior is also very important. But in addition it is a good idea to state directly that you wish to hear from members on issues of substance. For example, you might say something like: "I'd like to hear what Mike has to say about this idea." Or you might suggest a procedure that will cause people to say what they think, such as: "Look, I think everyone has a point of view on this. I would like to hear what each of you thinks. I'd be happy to start, if that will help. I just want to hear everyone's ideas before we decide."

To help a group achieve status consensus seems more difficult. Still, any group member can make a contribution. Suppose an individual is smarting from having lost a leadership bid in a group. You know that individual is a high-status member and could mean trouble if ignored. Assure people like this that you are confident of their contributions. Find some way to give them an important task. Take them into your confidence and make allies out of them. Especially if you emerge as a leader but even if you do not, reinforce member contributions by using "stroking behavior," a topic we address next.

Stroking

Cohesive groups grow out of positive interpersonal relationships. Thus all the material on improving interpersonal relationships applies to team building. The most critical part of this kind of positive interpersonal experience is expressions of unconditional positive regard and confirmation of the self—*strokes*. Strokes count because they do both the stroker and the recipient a lot of good. It is sometimes not so obvious that stroking contributes to the group good as well. Incidentally, nothing whatsoever in the literature says that people cannot and should not *ask* for strokes. Similarly, nothing prohibits direct talk about stroking behavior. These injunctions are buried deep in the culture, and they are counterproductive.

Group Talk

Cohesive groups have been found to talk about themselves as a unit, saying "we," "our group," and "us." Use this common appeal to groupness; it is a good leadership device. Similarly, cohesive groups recognize shared needs and goals. Thus talk about oneself ("I would like to move on to the next topic") will not be nearly so cohesiveness building as talk about the group's interests and needs ("*We* are stuck, I think. What do you think? Shall we move on? Do you think we have done enough with this topic?"). This kind of talk causes the group to make joint decisions. The greater the number of such joint decisions, the greater the likelihood that cohesiveness will increase.

Benefits to Membership

Cohesive groups believe that there are positive payoffs attached to being in the group. To build cohesiveness, wise leadership creates benefits that members get from the group, or if they already exist, makes those benefits known. Developing skill in paying off group members and causing the payoff to be perceived as tied to membership will surely build cohesiveness.

A small group of recently hired accountants at one of the "big eight" accounting firms was a most cohesive group. New accountants *wanted* to be a member of that group because they could see it provided benefits to its members: status in the larger group of accountants, sharing of insights (which helped all the members to learn more and faster), sharing of resources, and support for each other when it was needed. When new accountants became "members," their life as accountants changed dramatically. They felt good about themselves and the group; they learned far more, or felt they did; they had help over the "humps" of being new accountants.

Too Much Cohesiveness

Groups can become committed to their decisions because they want to defend the decision-making processes of their group, and not because the group's decisions are good. Indeed, it is not uncommon to hear of a group that has become so cohesive that it develops this malady. Irving L. Janis called the problem "groupthink."[8] Groups suffering from groupthink make decisions that can be without an apparent basis in reality. The members of such a group come to believe that they're unusually moral and powerful. They close their minds to views different from their own. They stereotype individuals who don't agree with them as evil, or weak, or stupid. They minimize their own doubts, and they pressure other people to conform to their point of view. The result, of course, is impaired decision making. But what can be done?

Dennis S. Gouran[9] identified three ways groups promote errors in thinking. First, groups introduce atypical information on a progressive basis. For example, a group member might describe an administrator in uncomplimentary terms, thus setting a tone and perspective for other members. Other members begin to search through their experiences with the administrator, looking for something to reinforce the uncomplimentary description. Others, still, add on to the evolving characterization.

A second way groups promote errors in their thinking is by passively accepting specialized knowledge. For example, groups will simply accept as true a statement such as, "I got this information from my doctor, and he ought to know."

Gouran identified a third way that too-cohesive groups promote errors in thinking. They construct scenarios and scripts—fantasies—that become the mind-set into which their decision making must take place. For example, a member might construct an image of what it would be like if the group's decision were adopted by management. Someone else chimes in with a comment. Soon members "understand" their fantasy as criteria against which their decisions are judged.

Janis suggested nine things that groups could do to prevent groupthink.[10]

1. The group could assign one member the role of *critical evaluator*. That person's task is to make sure possible objections are identified and introduced into the decision making.

2. Group leaders should take an impartial role rather than stating preferences and expectations.
3. Organizations should routinely set up more than one policy-planning and evaluating group to work on the same question.
4. Groups should divide into subgroups, meet separately with different chairpersons, then come together to hammer out differences.
5. Group members should discuss the group's work with trusted associates outside the group and report the associates' reactions to the group.
6. Groups should invite one or more outside experts to group meetings, on a staggered basis. These visitors should be encouraged to challenge the group's views.
7. At every meeting where policy decisions are discussed, at least one member should be assigned the role of devil's advocate.
8. When policy decisions have significant implications, a sizable block of time (perhaps an entire meeting) should be spent surveying warning signals from rivals and constructing alternative scenarios of the rivals' intentions.
9. After reaching consensus, policy-making groups should schedule a "second-chance" meeting in which members express any lingering doubts and rethink the entire issue before a final and definitive choice is made.

If you ever find yourself defending your group's decisions in the face of well-intended and thoughtful opposition, you would do well to remember that the other person always has a good reason for that position. Are you defending your position because it is better or because your group developed it? Sometimes group decisions are wrong. Do not let your sense of cohesiveness get in the way of effective decision making.

Productivity

Leadership behaviors related to productivity are as numerous as tasks and goals. The central idea running throughout them may be stated simply: Find the track; get on the track; stay on the track.

With regard to *finding the track,* if you are a wise member, you will help the group to develop a problem-solving agenda, then break the agenda into sequential units, each of which can be achieved over a brief period of time.

With regard to *getting on the track,* group leadership must pay attention to the tension levels of the group during each meeting. At the beginning of each meeting, after a group has been separated for a while, there is a period of time when members must renegotiate their relationships. This phenomenon is common to groups and must be tolerated, but, if it goes too far, it can be counterproductive. Leonard and Natalie Zunin argue persuasively that this period of time does not last more than four minutes. In fact, they claim that the tenor of the relationship for the remainder of the meeting depends on the skill with which individuals renegotiate their relationships within those first four minutes.[11]

When the tension is broken, the leader—or in the absence of a leader, any member—should restate or introduce the problem, focus group attention on the issues, and as clearly as possible state the problem in the form of a question. Discussion of procedures may be useful at this point. For example, the designated leader or any member might say something like: "The reason we're here is to begin the process of answering the question 'What, if anything, should the company do to adjust to _____?'" Then the immediate cause and background leading to the discussion should be presented. Finally: "I think it would be well to begin by trying to define the problem clearly in terms of some subquestions. Who has the problem? To what extent does the problem exist? Is the problem going to go away by itself?"

> Many organizations have "downsized" and "right-sized" to the point where employees may feel overworked and undervalued. Fewer and fewer people do more and more work. At what point does corporate emphasis on productivity become unethical?

With regard to *staying on the track,* task leadership is a matter of guiding the group's discussion of the problem. This means that the leader ought to be aware of the agenda for the task dimension and attempt to stay with that agenda.

Staying on the track includes recognizing and pointing out tangents and irrelevant talk. As leader, you can say something like: "Bill, I don't see how what you are saying relates to where we are. I think we're talking about _____. What relationship do you see?" Or, more directly, you might say something like: "That point is interesting, but it seems to me to be irrelevant to the question. Am I missing something, Joan?" Tact and skill are required because sensibilities and egos are involved, and therefore so is cohesiveness. The key is to give simple acceptance to the person who is steering the group off the track. In each of the examples above, acceptance is clearly involved in the checking questions: "What relationship do you see?" "Am I missing something, Joan?" If you practice you can develop a good many different ways of saying, politely and inoffensively, that the discussion is off the track.

Clarifying ideas and restating ideas are two important parts of leadership that every member can contribute. The tasks can be done directly, as in: "I'm unclear about what you've just said, Jill. Did you mean to suggest _____?" "You seem to be saying _____." "I want to be sure that I've understood you. May I restate that in my own words and have you OK my understanding?" Again, we suggest that you practice a variety of ways to say, "I'd like to clarify that point."

Staying on the track involves asking the right questions, too. Any member can follow the discussion, notice that the group is stuck, and then ask the right question to focus the group's attention. For example, you might say: "We seem to have talked ourselves into a box. Are we agreed that _____?" Keep in mind that good questions are the pivotal points in most problem-solving discussions. They are valued highly for that reason.

Some of the more useful kinds of questions that any participant can contribute are shown in Exhibit 12.11 with examples. The key to asking the right questions is to follow closely what is going on in the group. Thus Chapter 5, on listening, is relevant.

Staying on the right track involves developing and encouraging creativity in the group's thinking. Any member can encourage creativity by offering frequent summaries, which encourage members to consider what they have accom-

Exhibit 12.11	SOME USEFUL QUESTIONS TO KEEP A GROUP ON TRACK
Type of Question	**Example**
Questions designed to get information	Joe, what do you think about _____? Can anyone tell me what _____? Which of the alternatives seems _____? Has anyone looked into _____? Will you check that out and return with the information? Did you ask the vice-president about _____? Where can we find this information?
Questions designed to confirm agreement or understanding	Are we agreed about _____? Are we saying that _____? Have we resolved the conflict over _____? Let's see, do we understand this in the same way?
Questions designed to seek clarification	I want to be sure I am clear about your ideas. Did you say _____? You seem to be taking the position _____. Are you?
Questions designed to manage conflict	Can we set this point aside for the moment and look at _____? I think we're stuck on this point. Shall we shift gears and look at _____? Perhaps we could approach this in a different way. Are you willing to _____?
Questions designed to verify inferences	I'm guessing that you mean _____. Is that what you mean? You seem to be feeling _____. How do you feel?
Questions designed to secure participation	Mary, what do you think about _____? I would like it if we could all state our positions on this idea. Does anyone disagree? Can we adopt _____ procedures?

plished as a context for what they are currently interested in. Another way is to request time and participation from the group for developing alternative paths. Groups often come to decision points but limit themselves to either-or thinking about their choices. You can make an important leadership contribution by saying: "Look, I think we have come to a decision point." (Here, summarize briefly.) "I would like us to spend a little time generating a list of approaches we might take to the next goal, which seems to me to be _____."

Tension and Conflict

We have said that tension is inevitable in a productive group but that sometimes the tension can become so great that it threatens the group. Any member of a group can monitor tension and conflict and intervene when that seems warranted. We think that conflict management is so important that we devoted Chapter 9 to that factor. Joyce L. Hocker and William Wilmot summarize their excellent text on interpersonal conflict with a chapter on intervention principles and practices. They say that a person in conflict has three possible choices: (1) to change the behavior of the other party or parties, (2) to change the structure of the conflict, and (3) to change his or her own behavior.[12] Group members can examine their own involvement in the conflict and choose among these alternatives. But a group member can also contribute leadership by pointing out the possibilities to the group when other members are in counterproductive conflict.

For example, you could say something like this: "It seems to me that the conflict is over the approaches you two would take toward solving the problem. I'd like us to spend some time thinking of alternatives you both might accept." Or you might say, if it is the case, "I think you are fighting about something that can be changed without damaging our productivity." Then suggest a change. Or you might confront the conflict situation directly and ask for a change in behavior. "Mary, I think you are objecting on some personal ground, and Brian, you too seem to be grinding a private ax. If that is the case, would you be willing to work on that conflict in some other context?" Of course, such an approach might well be the end of your friendship, but we do not think so. In this regard, there is a common saying among effective managers: "Don't take a management job unless you're willing to make the tough decision." A person in a high executive position once interpreted that as meaning you have to be willing to fire your best friend.

Sometimes tensions build up that can be easily dispelled. Tension releasing is a useful skill, but difficult to prescribe. We can recommend, however, some leadership behaviors that experience has taught us. For one thing, when a group's tension is clearly too high, it is a good idea to suggest a break. There does not have to be a reason other than the tension. You might say something like: "I think it would be good to take a ten-minute break. Do you agree?" A tension-laden group will jump at the chance to get away from the scene for a while.

Another thing you can do to manage tension is to talk about it directly. The skills related to talking about feelings, which we discussed in Chapter 8, come into play here. You might say: "I'm feeling really tense right now. Is anyone else feeling that way? If so, I'd like to talk about that for a moment." We think that clear talk about feelings—personalized and in the present—is a good idea.

Still another way to release tension is relevant humor. This is a difficult prescription for us to make because what seems funny is so clearly context related. Still, if you have the gift of humor, you can make it an asset to groups experiencing secondary tension. Even outrageous behavior can serve to release tension, but successful outrageousness requires a particular interactive style. The risk is that the behavior might reflect negatively on the one displaying it.

A good way to deal with dysfunctional levels of tension is to shift ground. If, for instance, the tension is growing out of conflict about tasks, you might suggest that the group attend to procedures. Similarly, tension growing out of conflict about procedures might be broken if the ground is shifted to tasks. You could say something like: "I think we're stuck at this point. May I suggest that we look at this issue in a different way? What I propose is _____."

Finally, a very good way to release tension is to substitute something else for it. The most obvious substitute is affection. You might say: "Mary, I dislike what you are saying about [task] but I want you to know that my dislike doesn't extend to you personally. Let's take a moment to remind ourselves we have real regard for each other." Or you might say: "I'm aware that we're having some conflict about this, but I'd like to point out we were agreed about [something else]." Then tell the group something the other person did that merits their esteem.

Leadership opportunities in groups are frequent and varied. Any member will become more skilled with practice, and there are many opportunities to practice. Two important things needed are clear understanding of what is happening in the group and an appreciation for the present tense. Relationships are all in the present. Thus tension is a present-tense phenomenon, and the ability to manage the tension requires active, present-tense participation by the would-be leader.

Roles and Norms

Recalling that both norms (behavioral rules to which the group agrees) and roles (the behavioral patterns the individuals enact) evolve out of trial and error, you can see that observant group members can have leadership impact by providing the rewards and punishments implied in the trial-and-error method. This skill is especially useful with regard to norms. Sometimes, for example, a norm will be counterproductive, but the group will not be aware the norm has evolved. Any member, having identified such a norm, can call attention to it, express the concern that the norm is counterproductive, and then, if the group agrees, suggest an alternative procedure. For example, in one group a member said: "Look, guys. Something crazy happens in this group every time anyone comes into the room late. There's a period of joking around that gets us off the track and wastes time. I'd like us to agree that we all will make a better effort to be on time. [Then, since they agreed] To help us do that, I suggest that we agree to form a party kitty. Anyone who is late has to kick in five bucks to the kitty." The group agreed and has not had a problem with tardy members since.

Roles and norms represent a consensus of sorts and therefore may be resistant to change. Another approach to norm changing is to try to get support from other members privately, before bringing up the behavior to the group. You may notice that someone else seems to be as uncomfortable with a norm as you are, and you might talk to that individual. If the two of you can agree a change is needed, then bring it up to the group. Similarly, a role behavior that seems counterproductive can be directly addressed in private without embarrassment to the person playing the role. Sometimes this private conversation technique is all that is necessary to effect a change.

A word of caution is warranted. You may think that some behavior is counterproductive. You may be right. But you may also be wrong. Therefore, before you act, we recommend that you be as certain as you can your judgment is correct. Don't act too swiftly. Otherwise the group members are more likely to resent than to appreciate your intervention. You will know from the way they interact with you if you have gone too far or moved too soon. If that is the case, back off. You can't afford to squander your own reputation and reception in the group, even out of well-intended motives.

SUMMARY ....

This chapter has dealt with the work group. We noted that group size is important to the success of a group and therefore to the decisions you might make regarding how you will participate and the leadership you will contribute. We also tied group size to members' willingness to work together, to the ways groups distribute the amount of participation in the group, and to whether or not a group will have difficulty achieving consensus. Size, too, was related to the success of groups in reaching their goals, depending on whether the task is additive, disjunctive, or conjunctive.

Both task and social dimensions are important to group processes. Talk in the task dimension yields productivity, and talk in the social dimension yields cohesiveness. Since for most groups increasing levels of cohesiveness bring increasing productivity, we explained how each of these dimensions can be influenced by communication behavior. We introduced the idea that members can monitor the social dimension by observing evidence of tension levels as the group evolves. In addition, we showed how it is possible to use that information to influence members' perceptions that they are making progress toward their goals, that they are free to participate in the group's discussions, and that they have reached consensus on the status hierarchy. We suggested that these three things are necessary conditions to the evolution of member satisfaction.

We talked next about trial and error as fundamental to the learning processes which lead to establishment of group norms. Trial and error were also shown to be important to the process by which roles are taught in a group.

Finally, we suggested specific and appropriate leadership behaviors you can apply to the issues of group size and tasks, cohesiveness, productivity, the management of tension and conflict, and the evolution of roles and norms.

NOTES ....

1. You will probably not usually be involved in determining group size early in your career. In most organizational contexts that is a function of management. For greater information concerning group size see Donelson R. Forsyth, *An Introduction to Group Dynamics* (Monterey, Calif., Brooks/Cole, 1983), pp. 137–138, 152–155, 217–218.
2. I. D. Steiner, *Group Process and Productivity* (New York, Academic, 1972).
3. Clovis R. Shepherd, *Small Groups: Some Sociological Perspectives* (Scranton, Pa., Chandler, 1964), pp. 88–97. The curvilinear relationship is described also in B. Aubrey Fisher, *Small Group Decision Making: Communication and the Group Process* (New York: McGraw-Hill, 1980), pp. 39–44.
4. Richard Heslin and Dexter Dunphy, "The Dimensions of Member Satisfaction in Small Groups," *Human Relations,* **17** (1964):99–112.
5. Ernest G. Bormann, *Discussion and Group Methods: Theory and Practice* (New York, Harper & Row, 1969), pp. 167–173.
6. Richard W. Brislin, *Cross-Cultural Encounters: Face-to-face Interaction* (New York, Pergamon, 1981), p. 2.

7. Clifford Geertz, *The Interpretation of Cultures* (New York, Basic Books, 1973), p. 89.

8. Irving L. Janis, *Groupthink: Psychological Studies of Policy Decisions and Fiascoes,* 2d ed. (Boston, Houghton Mifflin, 1982).

9. Dennis S. Gouran, "Inferential Errors, Interaction, and Group Decision-Making," in Randy Y. Hirokawa and Marshall Scott Poole, eds., *Communication and Group Decision-Making* (Beverly Hills, Calif., Sage, 1986), pp. 93–111.

10. Irving L. Janis, op. cit., Chapter 11, pp. 260–276.

11. Leonard Zunin with Natalie Zunin, *Contact: The First Four Minutes* (New York, Ballantine, 1972).

12. Joyce L. Hocker and William W. Wilmot, *Interpersonal Conflict* (Dubuque, Iowa, Brown, 1985), pp. 157–158.

RECOMMENDED READINGS ....

John K. Brilhart and Gloria J. Galanes. *Effective Group Discussion,* 6th ed. Dubuque, Iowa, Brown & Benchmark, 1995. This textbook is especially known for its integration of theory and practice.

Donald G. Ellis and B. Aubrey Fisher. *Small Group Decision Making,* 2d ed. New York, McGraw-Hill, 1980. This is among the best textbooks on group communication. Especially useful are the chapters on decision making, conflict, and improving communication effectiveness. Included is a glossary, which the serious student will find useful since the literature on group behavior is utterly jargon-bound.

Donald R. Forsyth. *Group Dynamics,* 2d ed. Pacific Grove, Calif., Brooks/Cole, 1990. This standard reference work is a comprehensive collection of well-written essays that review and explain the enormous literature on group dynamics.

Randy Y. Hirokawa and Marshall Scott Poole, eds., *Communication and Group Decision-Making,* Beverly Hills, Calif., Sage, 1986. This is a standard reference work for any serious student of group communication. A collection of essays, it is organized according to the most critical issues in group behavior.

DISCUSSION QUESTIONS ....

1. The literature on small-group behavior makes clear that from three to eleven members constitute an ideal number. Compare and contrast a seven-member group with a fifteen-member group with respect to:
   a. Participation of the members.
   b. Leadership.
   c. Consensus achievement.
   d. Task performance.

2. Do you know of any group that is too cohesive? Why do you believe it is so? What might a participant do to influence the level of cohesiveness in order to bring it under control?

3. Do you know of any group that is not cohesive enough? Why do you believe that is so? What might a participant do to influence the level of cohesiveness in such a group?

4. The child's game of "Hot and Cold" can be used to demonstrate the power of reward and punishment in response to trial and error as group members teach each other the roles and norms of the group. Ask one member of your class to leave the room. Determine a task for the absent member to perform. Bring him or her back and, without words, using only applause and boos as your communication system, see how long it takes to teach the individual the behavior you have selected. (Example: The individual might be taught to pick up a certain piece of chalk, carry it across the room, and write something on the chalkboard.)

5. As a class, suggest ways in which members of a group might deal with unproductive norms that they find in groups to which they belong.

INTERNET ACTIVITIES ....

1. Type "group AND decision-making" in the search box of the Excite search engine (http://www.excite.com/). What help can you find for a decision-making task group? Would you recommend using the Internet for this purpose?

2. Leadership is one of the hottest topics in business and professional organizations. Can you determine who is trying to make a profit from this fact on the Internet? Record your path through the Internet, then report your findings and how you arrived at them to your class.

CHAPTER 13

Communicating with a Group or Staff

Upon completion of this chapter, you should be able to:

1. Identify at least three kinds of group events.
2. Identify and explain three important rules in planning for group meetings.
3. Enumerate and elaborate on the steps to follow in a routine decision-making meeting.
4. Select an appropriate agenda for a decision-making meeting.
5. Plan and implement participative management groups.
6. Cite the ten steps in planning a conference, distinguishing the details for handling both the task and social dimensions in each of these steps.
7. Use a conference planning check sheet to plan a conference.
8. Explain the steps to be followed in planning a regular monthly meeting, including doing homework and setting an agenda.

*I*n the first eleven chapters we looked at communication that happens inside individuals and between two individuals. But more and more, work in orga-

**Exhibit 13.1
INDIVIDUALS,
DYADS, AND
GROUPS**

As numbers increase, the principles that govern the communications of a smaller number still apply.

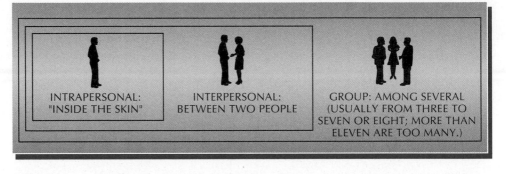

INTRAPERSONAL:
"INSIDE THE SKIN"

INTERPERSONAL:
BETWEEN TWO PEOPLE

GROUP: AMONG SEVERAL
(USUALLY FROM THREE TO
SEVEN OR EIGHT; MORE THAN
ELEVEN ARE TOO MANY.)

nizations is being carried on in groups. People gather at every level, both formally and informally, for an enormous variety of purposes. What applies to individuals and two-person communication also applies to groups. Exhibit 13.1 illustrates that all the principles germane to one individual processing communication events apply to situations in which two people work with each other. All the principles that apply to two-person communication apply also to group communication. But as the number of people increases, new notions apply. It is significantly more complicated to work in a group than it is to work with one other person.

KINDS OF GROUP EVENTS ....

In the world of work there are at least four distinct and separable group events that you will experience. The first is the *routine meeting.* For instance, the plant manager calls a regular meeting of the supervisors of the several departments. Regular Monday-morning meetings are held in almost every kind of organization. The branch managers of the largest bank in Mobile, Alabama, meet for breakfast every Tuesday morning. Most working departments hold a routine weekly meeting.

The *participative management group meeting* is a second kind of group event. Individuals meet to bring their experiences and expertise to bear on a problem that their work group identifies. For example, a product or unit supervisor might ask workers to meet voluntarily to discuss departmental problems. This group would discuss the problems and make decisions. The department would then try to implement these ideas. Such group meetings are often called quality circles.

The *project group meeting* is a third type of group. For example, a project group of restaurant designers includes an expert in kitchen design, a buyer who knows what is available in prebuilt components, an interior designer, a cabinetmaker/carpenter, and a supervisor. Group members work on more than one project at a time and may be spread throughout the city. But they also are always in close contact with one another, and they are both cohesive and productive.

A fourth group event is a *conference,* sometimes called a *sales meeting* or a *seminar.* In fact, there are many names for the special-event conference. Many companies hold an annual management conference, which lasts for several days and includes individuals from a broad geographical area. Such events are held at Scott Paper Company, International Paper Company, Monsanto, and countless other large, geographically dispersed organizations.

Each group event calls for a distinctly different treatment, and each is based on different expectations and assumptions. Before looking at the specific characteristics of each, we will discuss some common characteristics and concerns.

> The exercise of power may be found throughout this discussion of planning for and leading group meetings. At what point, if ever, does the exercise of power become abuse of power?

PLANNING FOR AND LEADING MEETINGS

Suppose you have been employed with your company for about five years. You walk into your office after lunch and find your boss, Jean, waiting patiently.

"Hi," she says. "How was lunch?"

"Pretty good, Jean. I found a Japanese restaurant that's offering an all-you-can-eat buffet."

You are warming up to telling Jean about this restaurant when she says, "We're going to have a meeting in two months, and I'd like you to be in charge."

Slowly at first, then with increasing vividness, your awareness of all the things that could go wrong begin to weigh on you. You have never run a meeting. You have no file of pointers and tips, no list of dos and don'ts.

Many things can go wrong at meetings. Thousands of meetings are held in the business community every day. Many flow smoothly and easily, but others are horrible to experience. What is the difference? We think one difference is planning.

We were once asked to go into an organization in Rockford, Illinois, to consult with management about the number of meetings they were having. They felt they really needed all of the meetings. They were extraordinarily frustrated: one of their pet complaints was that there were just too many meetings. This squandered time.

After a quick review of their problem we made a simple recommendation that they implemented. Within the week people in that organization were phoning in their appreciation. They thought we had done something wonderful. Actually, all we did was to short-circuit their penchant for calling meetings! The advice was this: Every time you call a meeting, tell all participants, in writing, (1) what you expect them to contribute to the meeting, or what you anticipate they will learn that justifies their being there; (2) what you expect them to bring, such as files, resources, expertise; and (3) what is on the agenda.

Where do you start in planning group meetings? There are three important rules.

First, *be concerned with time.* John Cragan and David Wright identify certain time constraints, which we recommend to you:[1]

1. Give advance notice of the agenda, so participants will not have to start entirely from scratch or be taken by surprise as the meeting begins, and so they can bring with them what they need for the meeting.

2. Schedule meetings at the *best time*. For routine meetings, a fixed time around which members can plan works best. For *ad hoc* (one-time) groups, the scheduled time should meet the convenience of the maximum number of participants.
3. Start and end meetings on time. This seems obvious, yet much time is wasted because it is not done.
4. Regulate participation. This means exercising control over those individuals who would like to dominate or monopolize the meeting, and allotting a certain amount of time to everyone who wants it.

The second rule is: *find out about group tradition*. Cragan and Wright offer an insight that is not so obvious. Sometimes people enter positions in which they are responsible for *continuing* already fixed meeting schedules. New department heads, for example, inherit a good many rules about how things are supposed to be done. Understanding these traditions of meeting behavior is very important.

> The tradition of the company might call for you to begin the meeting with a twenty-minute slide show that concisely and graphically displays your findings. Therefore, if you sent out a thirty-page report in advance of the meeting, and then attempted to lead a round table discussion . . . you might discover that nobody had read the report.[2]

A group's notions about "how it is supposed to be" at meetings are obviously important. Learn what the expectations are, and either live within those expectations or change them in a way that is clear and acceptable to the others.

Finding these expectations is relatively simple. Ask three individuals, "Tell me how meetings are done here. What goes on? Is there anything I ought to do or not do?" The people you should ask include your superior, a peer in another agency or branch of your organization who reports to your superior, and a secretary in a position to know. Your boss's secretary will certainly know. If you inherit a secretary from the individual who had your job before you, that person will know.

The third, and final, rule is: *understand that different meetings require different planning*. After you have done your preliminary research, are sure you really do need a meeting, and have determined what the traditions of your organization seem to be, you are ready to approach the myriad details involved in setting it up.

We think that the four kinds of group events—the routine meeting, the participative management group, the monthly work-group meeting, and the formal conference—require different kinds of planning and leadership. You will certainly be asked to assume responsibilities in these groups as you progress through your career. At the entry level you may be involved in monthly departmental meetings. You may also find yourself attending participative management groups. Later in your career you may find yourself conducting monthly meetings. Once you move beyond the entry level, you may also find yourself involved in conference preparations. Take the time, now, to address each of these group meeting contexts.

Routine Decision-Making Meetings

Routine decision-making meetings occur in so many contexts and in so many forms that they defy precise description. What we include in this term is any kind of meeting in which people draw together to achieve a goal or goals. Perhaps they share a problem and something must be done about it. Perhaps they need to touch base with each other in order to be sure they are still making a co-ordinated effort. These may be problem-solving groups. They may be *ad hoc* committees. They may be a group of people sitting down to discuss a common interest and make plans. In all these cases the meetings are typically informal. Many different terms identify this kind of group.

In this section we examine some of the things that effective leadership will include in an agenda for decision-making. But note that informal groups rarely follow a precise decision-making agenda. Thus it becomes a matter of effective participation—by both the designated leader and others—to keep these agenda items in mind and to introduce them in a timely fashion.

A number of people have adapted John Dewey's pattern for *reflective thinking* to an *ad hoc* decision-making agenda.[3] They have done so because, even though groups do not often follow the steps in sequence, nevertheless groups that do include the steps seem to have greater success, produce better decisions, and feel better about those decisions than groups that do not.

We recommend, therefore, that you keep this agenda in mind every time you engage in decision-making discussion even if you do not follow it exactly.[4]

Identify, define, and delimit the problem so that it is thoroughly understood. Too often, groups jump to solutions before they fully understand the problem they are trying to solve. Sometimes problems are enormous, so large that discussants begin without fully appreciating the nature and extent of the problem. Thus, identifying and understanding the problem is very important.

To what extent is there a problem? For whom does the problem exist? Will the problem resolve or solve itself—will it go away by itself—in time? What is giving rise to the problem? What are the threads in the causal fabric? Is the problem a result of the existing system? What are the effects of the problem on those involved? On the organization?

Establish evaluative criteria against which to test solutions. This important step cannot be overemphasized, although it is sometimes not even touched upon in texts. What can be said? A particular group must establish the criteria against which it will judge its own proposals. Still, some guidelines can be drawn that might be helpful, and there are some general questions to ask yourself.

1. Is there really a problem?
2. Will the solution proposed resolve all the various aspects of the problem?
3. Is the solution capable of being implemented within the limits of reason and practicality?
4. Will the solution be desirable?

5. Will the solution create new, more serious problems than the ones it is designed to solve?

Some other constraints that may serve as evaluative criteria are:

1. Within what *budget* must we operate?
2. Within what *time frame* must we operate?
3. Within what *personnel limitations* must we operate?
4. Within what *management restrictions* must we operate?

Seek alternatives to test. From time to time, groups work through problems and solutions only to end up bickering over the matter of how the solution "works." Participants seem unable to agree that the solution they have evolved is what they want to propose. This probably is because they have not considered enough alternatives against effectively drawn evaluative criteria.

Sometimes it is useful for groups to generate as many different ideas as possible for solutions to the various parts of a problem. The more alternatives that a group can generate the better, and one way to do this is called *brainstorming*. A group proposes numerous ideas without making judgments about the quality of the ideas. Someone writes them down, but no one finds fault with anything until the group has exhausted its ability to create alternative solutions. Ideas are not discussed as they are being proposed.

Develop a solution to implement. After the group has developed and tested a variety of solutions—perhaps finding that some parts are useful and creative and others are not—it is time for participants to pull together a single plan. That process is one of compromise and agreement growing out of careful planning of the evaluative criteria and ample generation of ideas. If all the former steps are taken, a group will not find it too difficult to agree upon some set of "planks" in a plan that will solve the problem and be reasonable, practical, and desirable. If the group has not done its work to this point, it might have trouble agreeing.

Sometimes a group might not be able to agree upon a final decision, so it takes a vote. Resorting to a vote is usually a sign of the group's not having spent enough time generating ideas. Suppose the group votes, and its vote is split more or less down the middle, say, 3 to 2. Any decision the group reaches with this kind of vote split is suspect and may not come to fruition. We recommend that someone point out that the split vote will mean trouble for the proposal and that the group ought to rethink its work.

You can monitor the stages of evolution of the group decision making and point to the problem before the issue comes to a vote. If you can consistently help a group to achieve consensus, you will soon be a valued member.

Here is an example of this sequence applied by the owners of an office complex. A group was called together to make decisions related to security in its buildings. As you read the agenda, first scan the italicized selections. Then go back and read the full text.

I. *Identify, define, and delimit the problem so that it is thoroughly understood.*
   A. *What is the nature of the problem?*
   There has been a 5 percent increase in crime in our Hillsdale Office Complex. There were three burglaries, one rape, and one case of vandalism in the past three months.
      1. *Given this statement of the problem, do we all understand what was said to be the nature of the problem?*
      Yes, we agree.
      2. *Do we understand all the terminology related to the questions?*
      What is meant by burglary?
      The breaking and entering of a premises and taking of other people's property.
      3. *What kind of decision is expected of our group? Discussion and understanding of the problem? Presentation of alternative solutions? A decision?*
      Discussion of the problem and presentation of a plan for implementation.
   B. *What harm is present in the current situation?*
      1. *What is the harm?*
      The pain and suffering of the individuals involved.
      Loss of property valued at $4,500.
      Image of the office complex as providing safe working conditions for our clients.
      2. *Who is affected?*
      The workers of the Hillsdale Complex.
      All of the officers and employees of Hillsdale Corporation, indirectly.
      3. *How serious is the harm?*
      Crime is on the increase by 150 percent.
      The loss and personal injury involved are becoming substantial.
      4. *How widespread is the harm?*
      People in nearly every building have been victims or know victims.
      Occupants of buildings not directly affected have voiced their concern.
   C. *What seems to be causing the problem?*
      1. *What factors, if removed or changed, would remove or lessen the harm?*
      Vacant offices seem to attract vandalism and crime.
      Occupants do not report suspicious people who hang around.
      Office personnel leave offices unlocked when they are out briefly during the day.
      There is an impression that security is loose.
      2. *What are the obstacles to successfully removing the causes of the harm?*
      It may be difficult if not impossible to rent all our units in these buildings.
      It may be difficult to change office workers' habits.

II. *Establish evaluative criteria against which to test solutions: What criteria should we set?*

   A. *What are the important conditions—criteria—that an effective solution must meet?*

   We cannot break any existing company policy.

   We cannot spend over $5,000, the amount allocated for this project.

   We must not approve a plan that favors particular building occupants over other occupants.

   The plan we develop should be one that can be used in other facilities we own.

   B. *Are some criteria more important to us than others? Can the criteria be rank-ordered in terms of importance?*

   Yes. We must treat all occupants equally. We cannot go over the $5,000 allocated. Company policy might be changed, but only when absolutely necessary.

III. *Seek alternatives to test.*

   A. *What available alternatives might meet the causes of this problem and alleviate the harm?*

   Install an emergency alert system tied to security.

   Increase outside lighting

   Replace locks on doors with double-bolt locks.

   Offer customers incentives to expand their use of space into vacant space.

   Hire a private security company to patrol in the evenings.

IV. *Develop a solution to implement.*

   A. *Which solution or what combination of solutions seems most likely to counter the causes of the problem?*

   Better locks would help keep criminals out.

   Elimination of empty offices would allow for more people to be around to discourage crime.

   A private professional security service would provide more reliable night protection.

   Increased outside lighting would most certainly discourage crime.

   B. *Of the solutions that seem likely to be effective, which ones meet the criteria that were set?*

   Encouraging companies to expand their building use may be unfair to some as space is not available on every floor.

   Cost is a factor. The funds available will not allow for a private security company. Perhaps the county police can be enlisted to help.

   Cost of the other items is probably within the $5,000.

   C. *Given solutions that are likely to counter the causes and meet the criteria set, what seems to be the most promising solution?*

   All the solutions seem likely to help, except encouraging existing occupants to expand into unoccupied space. Making such an offer to some and not to others may anger some and cause them to move out.

V. *What plans will we set in order to implement our solution?*
  A. *What needs to be done?*
     Turn the plan over to the complex manager for implementation.
  B. *In what order?*
     Ask her to begin with lock installation, immediately.
     Contact the county police and ask them if they can provide increased patrolling of the Hillsdale Complex.
     Seek bids on a contract for upgrading outside lighting and let the contract.
  C. *By whom?*
     The complex manager will carry out these plans and report back to us within thirty days.

Several scholars have generated alternatives to this full decision-making plan. Two alternative sequences for ordering the process that have proven useful are the ideal solution sequence and the single-question sequence.

Ideal Solution Sequence

Sometimes we encounter a problem we know can be solved by a variety of solutions. Often various groups within an organization are affected by the decision directly, so that each of these groups has its "ideal" solution. Carl Larson discussed a decision-making sequence that takes these factors into account.[5] This plan asks the group to take into account various ideal solutions the involved parties favor.

It is easy to imagine a group with such a problem. Consider a special committee that was appointed by the vice-president of a university to consider a change in the between-term break in December. Follow this outline of how the group approached the situation using the ideal solution sequence and you will see how the group took into account the views of various segments of the organization.

Larson lists these four questions in the ideal solution sequence:

I. Are we all agreed on the nature of the problem?

I. We have been called together to make recommendations as to when the winter break should be taken. Do we all agree that this is our goal? (Here the problem would be analyzed as in step IA, above: What is the nature of the problem?)

II. What would be the ideal from the point of view of all interested persons or groups involved with the problem?

II. The students want more time to work before Christmas. They would like to be out at least two weeks before Christmas. The people in the registrar's office and other administrative personnel want to have more time after Christmas. The faculty senate has passed a resolution urging this committee not to split the term. They do not want to have to come back after the break and still have to complete a term. The ideal solution from the view of all parties would be to complete the term before Christmas, returning for the new term on January 2nd.

III. What conditions within the situation could be changed so that the ideal solution might be achieved? (Here is where the group considers proposals for change. They are concerned with finding the change—the solution—that will deal most effectively with the harm. But they also might discover obstacles that cannot be changed. With this in mind, they are ready to find the best possible solution.)

III. No, that would not allow time to cover the course material. Could we start the term earlier so that it could end two weeks before Christmas? Can we change the length of the term? Yes, I think so.

IV. Of the solutions available to us, which one best approximates the ideal solution? (Groups often approach this task by trying to incorporate elements of the various groups' solutions into an ideal solution.)

IV. We could extend the term break so that students would be able to work for two weeks before Christmas. The extended break would allow administrative personnel the time they want to be with their families. It would not break up the term.

Single-Question Sequence

Carl Larson's research on group problem solving found a single-question sequence, like the ideal solution sequence, produced more choices of best alternatives than did the reflective thinking pattern.[6] This sequence helps groups to identify issues that flow from a particular problem. Once they have identified the issues, they are asked to phrase them in the form of subquestions and then to identify the best solution to the major question. A governing board used this sequence to decide about adding new programs. The questions that led the board through this procedure are these:

I. What is the single question whose answer is all the group needs to know in order to accomplish its purpose?

II. What subquestions must be answered before we can answer the single question we have formulated?

III. Do we have sufficient information to answer the subquestions confidently?
  A. If yes, answer them.
  B. If no, continue below.

IV. What are the most reasonable answers to the subquestions? (Notice that the language here asks for the "most reasonable" answers. Circumstances may be such that some issues cannot be fully resolved, and therefore the group must accept the most reasonable answer.)

V. Assuming that our answers to the subquestions are correct, what is the best solution to the problem?

I. How many programs can we provide with the 10 percent increase over our current budget?

II. What programs should be instituted? How much will each cost? What cost will we incur for personnel and equipment? What is the anticipated participation in these programs?

III. The answer is no. We continue with IV, below.

IV. We cannot agree as to which programs we should initiate next year. We did agree to poll the membership and go with some of their suggestions. The average cost of each program last year was $11,000. The miscellaneous costs associated with each program were $2,450. The receipts from membership fees increased 12 percent.

V. Assuming that these figures hold, we should be able to fund two new programs at an estimated cost of $27,000.

From here the group might move to decide how to implement its decision.

Creating an Agenda to Meet Group Needs

A decision about a particular agenda for decision making is only the beginning. A wise group leader will assess the agenda's utility for the particular situation. John K. Brilhart and Gloria J. Galanes have presented a scheme that suggests how the agendas we have presented might be modified.[7] Their ideas are found in Exhibit 13.2.

Beyond any special needs that might be presented by the characteristics of the task at hand, you should consider the characteristics of your particular group. Ask these two important questions about the group and its members to help you decide on your agenda: How long have they been working together? Do they have experience in working with this kind of task?

Exhibit 13.2 PROBLEM CHARACTERISTICS MATCHED TO AGENDA STEPS		
Problem	Problem-Solving Emphasis	Agenda Steps
1. Intrinsic interest in problem is high	1. A period of ventilation before systematic problem solving.	1. A problem-solving agenda with which the group is familiar.
2. Difficulty of problem is high.	2. Detailed problem mapping with many subquestions.	2. Problem mapping, as presented in single question format. Ideation, step III of the reflective thinking format, with brainstorming.
3. Multiple solutions to problem are possible.	3. Brainstorming or nominal group process.	3. Include a criteria step, as in step II of the reflective thinking format.
4. Cooperative requirements for solving the problem are high.	4. A criteria step, creating and ranking explicit standards.	4. Include a criteria step, as in step II of the reflective thinking format.
5. High level of acceptance of the solution is required.	5. Focus on concerns of persons affected when evaluating solutions.	5. Include step II of the ideal solution format.
6. High level of technical quality is required for a decision.	6. Focus on evaluating ideas, critical thinking; perhaps invite outside experts to group to testify.	6. A reflective thinking sequence may be most suitable.
7. Members are responsible for one or a few of the stages of problem solving.	7. Shorten agenda to include only the required steps.	7. Emphasize the steps of any sequence that will allow the group to meet its charge.

A group that has been working together for a long time often has developed its own agenda system, one that works well for that group and its members. If their system allows reasonable consideration of the problems they address, then it may be a mistake to impose an unfamiliar agenda.

But how do you know if an agenda allows reasonable consideration of the problems the group addresses? There are two tests you can apply. *First, do the decisions the group implements seem to work?* Do the decisions alleviate the harm? Are the people affected by the decisions satisfied? *Second, does the group have difficulty coming to decisions?* Some problems are difficult and very controversial. We expect groups to engage in considerable conflict about their ideas, but if a group regularly has difficulty, the difficulty may be a function of the group's agenda.

Perhaps a more careful analysis of the problem is needed. Sometimes too few solutions are considered. At other times the group members have such diverse attitudes that they need to recognize and consider the ideal solutions for the various groups involved—step II of the ideal solution sequence. Decision-making difficulties can be a function of failure to discuss criteria—especially if the problem revolves around values. The group's own agenda may need to be modified to take one of these problems into account.

Leading the Group Meeting

Initiating and maintaining discussion involve such activities as keeping the group goal-oriented, introducing new agenda items, encouraging people to talk, regulating participation, summarizing group progress, and verbalizing consensus.[8] These activities make the difference between successful and less successful groups. They are behaviors any member can contribute to the group process. Certainly every group leader should be able to perform them, and the way to learn is to practice.

Inevitably, students want to know what to say or do to accomplish the things just suggested. Some language and strategies that are useful in each of these structuring and guiding activities follow:

Keeping the group goal-oriented.

Problem: The group is digressing too much into social conversation.
Solutions: (1) Comment on the social issue and then say, "Now, let's move back to discussion of causes." (2) "I don't understand how this idea is relevant to our task. Is it? If not, we need to get back to the topic."
Problem: A member persists in an effort to digress from the agenda.
Solutions: (1) "I've noticed that we seem to keep getting off the track and haven't been making our usual progress. I'm concerned that we might not finish. I'm wondering what the group thinks about this." (2) "How is it we get sidetracked? What can we do about it?"

Introducing new agenda items.

Problem: The group is ready and needs to move on to the next item.
Solutions: (1) "So we've agreed . . . [Summarize.] Let's take up the next item." (2) "So we've agreed . . . [Summarize.] Are we ready to move on?"

Encouraging members to participate.

Problem: A member doesn't participate because of shyness or reserve.
Solutions: "Recently I was talking with [name of reticent member], who had an interesting [or useful, or insightful] comment. [Name], would you be willing to share your idea?" (Of course, you must have discussed the issue.) (2) "[Name], you heard Susan. Do you agree or wish to add to her comment?"
Problem: Members seem to be lost or distracted.
Solutions: (1) "I think it would be a good idea to take stock of where we are. [Name], will you agree that we've . . . [Summarize.]" (2) "[Name], what do you think about [the topic of discussion]?"

Regulating member participation.

Problem: A member monopolizes the interaction.
Solutions: (1) Avoid excessive eye contact with the person. Establish eye contact with others to encourage them to talk. (2) Ask group members to agree to make only one point when they get the floor. (3) Break in and say, "That's an interesting idea. Let's consider [raised topic] first, John. Then we'll come back to your other idea." (4) Approach the talker in private. Tell the person you are concerned about some of the quieter members. Ask the person to help draw them out. (5) Bring the problem up to the group. If the problem seems to persist, you may have to deal with it straightforwardly. Try to be supportive, but make sure that the group recognizes it has a problem to resolve.

Summarizing and encouraging group process.

Problem: People are caught up in the interaction and have lost track of their progress.
Solution: Say, "Let's see what we've done so far." Then summarize.
Problem: The group needs encouragement.
Solution: Point out the agreement the group has reached thus far. Congratulate the group on its progress.

Total Quality Management, Empowerment, Quality Circles, and Work Teams

Quality of products and services has become a central concern of many organizations because their products and services have to compete in the world market. Joseph M. Juran, a well-known quality consultant, talked of the critical nature of quality when he addressed a group of Japanese executives in Tokyo in 1990. He pointed out that many American firms are adopting total quality management programs that in his view are allowing them to be competitive in world markets again. He predicted that "Made in America" will again stand for world-class quality.[9]

Executives have learned that customers demand quality. If they don't get it, they will turn to competitors regardless of where they do business. Thus these same executives have instituted company-wide programs designed to achieve dramatic improvement in quality and customer satisfaction. These programs focus on all aspects of the operation. For example, these organizations have begun to seek more substantial information about who their customers are and what their needs are. Products are to be more than defect-free. They must include the features that will meet customer needs and be offered for the best possible price. But meeting the needs of external customers means also meeting the needs of internal customers—the people within the organization who are affected in some way by how work is done. Programs instituted to achieve these ends are called empowerment, quality circles, and self-directed work teams. All of these programs have three quality aims:

1. Quality planning that identifies product features and plans for delivering them without deficiencies.
2. Quality improvement by reducing or eliminating deficiencies in goods, services, or processes.
3. Quality control that maintains the achievements made through quality planning and quality improvement.

Empowerment

The term *empowerment* is used to describe an effort by those charged with the leadership of an organization to share their power with those who work for them.

Empowerment can be achieved by the supervisor's turning over specific decision making regarding some aspect of a person's work. For example, a power utility turned over to its employees decision making about how to help a customer with a problem. Allowing the employee to do this produced more creative decisions about how to help the customers than might have been laid out in standard operating procedures and thus produced more satisfied employees and customers. The only guideline that employees were given was to answer three questions about their decision: Would my supervisor approve? Would the board of directors approve? And most important, would the majority of our rate payers think this is okay? A quick example of creative solutions illustrates the amazing responses employees generated. One employee delivered fresh baked bread to a customer whose home-baked bread was ruined by a power outage. The overall quality of service to customers was dramatically improved by this act of empowerment.

The term *empower* goes beyond the meaning reflected in sharing of power. It also means to enable or permit. So anything that leadership does to allow a person to do his or her job better is enabling. On the broad level there are three practices organizational leadership can use to bolster a member's sense of efficacy. First, leadership can exercise careful control in the selection and training processes. If Yuka has the ability to do the job and is carefully trained, she is likely to have the necessary skills to do the job. Second, leadership can develop policies and culture that emphasizes empowerment. These should emphasize self-determination, collaboration over competition, high performance standards, nondiscrimination, and meritocracy. Third, organizational leaders can provide loosely committed resources at lower levels in the organization. Allocation of these resources are at the discretion of those people who are charged with the particular task. For example, one utility company gave its employees authority to determine what supplies they needed, a credit card to buy them, and authorization to personally purchase the supplies. Leadership that seeks to empower finds ways to enable or permit the subordinate to do the best possible job.

Quality Circles

A popular strategy for improving quality is to involve groups of people who are doing the work in decisions that effect quality. We know that people are generally more willing to do their jobs and make an effort to change performance when they are taken into account. One very effective way of taking subordinates into account is to talk directly with them about problems and allow them to help make decisions. Direct involvement allows individuals to agree and to make a public commitment to a decision. When that happens, subordinates are more likely to make that decision work. This principle holds whether you are dealing with an individual worker or a small group of people. We have discussed participative management strategies in relation to the individual worker in Chapter 10, Interviewing and Interviews: On the Job. Now we want to extend that discussion to the group context.

Perhaps the *quality circle* is the clearest example of a participative management group. Quality circles evolved in Japanese firms through the efforts of an American consultant, Dr. Joseph Juran, who advocated participative decision making as a method of achieving quality control. In 1961 the editors of the Japanese magazine *Quality Control* took up this idea. They believed that involving first-line supervisors in quality control would increase productivity. The result of their advocacy was a new publication called *The Foreman and QC.* Participative management groups became popular in Japan and, consequently, came to the attention of American business and industry.[10] Many firms, such as Lockheed Corporation, J. C. Penney, Uniroyal, General Motors, Firestone, Chrysler, Ampex, R. J. Reynolds, Bendix, have instituted quality circles.

How Does the Participative Management Group Work?

Participative management groups seek to improve production through employee problem solving. The supervisor of such a group delegates the authority to make decisions to the group. The members of a department *voluntarily* meet to discuss work problems and make decisions. The theory is that the employees are in the best position to know about some problems, and when they are involved in decision making, they may be more committed to the outcome. But workers usually need help to be successful participants. We think you can provide that help regardless of your organizational rank. You can help build the appropriate climate and to direct and facilitate the group effort.

The supervisor of this group serves as a guide rather than as a boss who imposes a decision. Thus this person can be in an unenviable position. Once a group recommends a course of action, the supervisor must either accept the idea or reject it and thereby demoralize the group. And when the decision is implemented, it is the supervisor who must assume responsibility for the outcome, not the employees. For this reason you, as a supervisor, should be careful in selecting the problems you turn over to a participative management group. If you don't want the answer, don't ask the question.

Recognize also that participative management may not work well in certain situations. If you ask subordinates whose egos are highly involved in an issue to solve a problem related to it, they may not be objective and flexible enough to reach a quality decision. Further, a person who is highly apprehensive about communicating or is low on assertiveness is not likely to be a productive group member. Finally, a participative management group may not be successful if no member is willing to engage in leadership behaviors. A manager can guide a group but must rely on some group member for leadership too. Otherwise the manager may have too heavy a role in the group and risk being perceived as manipulative.

How Do You Structure the Meeting?

Here is a good format for the participative management decision-making activity. We assume in what follows that you are responsible for planning a participative management meeting.

1. Discover the problems.   It seems clear that the group will have to discover the problems to be addressed before it can spend time discussing them. Ask people to bring a list of things that keep them from doing their jobs well. Combine the lists on a flipchart and ask the group to rank-order the items from most to least serious.

2. Gather the relevant data.   You and other group members need time to gather information. Ask what information group members will need in order to make a quality decision. Ask for volunteers to bring the appropriate information.

3. Discover why there is a problem.   Remember that many groups are too solution-oriented. Try to get the group to discuss the causes of problems if you can. Point out that the solution ought to remove the causes.

4. Brainstorm for solutions.   It is a good idea to get all possible solutions on the table *before* a group tries to compare the alternatives. Beyond that, brainstorming usually causes a group to consider a greater number of alternatives. Ask members to withhold their comments about the ideas until they have listed as many solutions as possible.

5. Make the decision.   After alternatives have been recorded, evaluate each idea. How does each compare with the others? Which ideas do not remove the causes? Which can be eliminated? Which ideas might be combined into a comprehensive solution? What would happen if a particular decision were implemented? Is the proposed idea practical? These are all questions your group might consider.

Conducting the Meeting

There are several important guidelines called control strategies that can help a participative management group. We think that, while guiding group activity is necessary, no one should try to impose anything on a participative management group. Here are several practical suggestions:

1. Keep the group goal-oriented.   State the purpose clearly. All members should understand the group purpose and agree that the problem is important. (This is why quality-control circles use only volunteers.) Sometimes a group gets sidetracked. If that happens, you might say something like: "It seems we are a little off the subject. Should we get back to the problem?"

2. Encourage members to be involved.   Silent members are likely to remain silent if nothing is done to encourage them. If they do no talk, the group cannot use their ideas! Do not embarrass people, but see if you can start them talking. Perhaps you might do so by establishing eye contact while asking a question. Ask a person a direct question that you know he or she can answer. Encourage participation by suggesting a procedure in which members must participate. For example, a simple suggestion might do the trick: "I'd like to hear what everyone thinks. Could we go around the group, each stating his or her view in turn?" The important thing is to try to get silent members involved and to do so as soon as possible.

3. Regulate member participation.   Some people talk too little; some talk too much. Those who tend to talk too much constitute a problem for the group. Avoid eye contact with these people. Suggest that group members limit their comments to one point at a time. Often you can enlist the aid of these verbal people privately. Tell them you have noticed that some other members are not talking as much as they might. See if they will help encourage and draw out the silent ones instead of making such long comments. We learned a technique by watching the executive director of the Central Vermont Council on Aging run such a meeting. He established, in advance, that no member would be allowed more than six minutes to present and develop an idea; then he kept careful track of the time. In the middle of a sentence he said simply: "Six minutes." The speaker was not offended, but merely ended the sentence. You might try a variation of this theme.

4. Keep a sense of organization and progress.   Summarize the group's progress frequently. You will help the group keep track of what it has accomplished, and you will also give the group a sense of progress. Incidentally, your summary will also give the group an opportunity to agree with or correct your impression. Such feedback can clear up any problems and show you are listening.

5. Promote creative and critical thinking.   Help members be creative by asking them to expand on one another's ideas. Brainstorm as a way of creating ideas. Pose some of the questions we suggested in the previous section about making decisions. Ask the group to generate its own list of critical questions for testing its decision. For example, they will most certainly want to ask, "How well does the decision remove the causes we have discovered?"

We have suggested some basic information and offered advice about participative management meetings. To supplement this brief discussion, be sure to review the chapters on listening, performance appraisal interviewing, and working in groups (Chapters 5, 10, and 12).

Self-Managed Work Teams

A self-managed work team is given the power, authority, and resources for a whole work process or segment of the process and delivers that product or service to an internal or external customer. Organizational leadership provides the resources, information, and technical assistance to do the job. It turns over to the team decisions about how to proceed, how to organize itself and delegate responsibility, and so forth. The team is truly empowered to get the job done unencumbered by the traditional hierarchy. The effectiveness to the team depends on its members' initiative, skill, and knowledge.

> Some organizational leaders control by hoarding information. Others abdicate their appropriate responsibility by providing too much information and too much freedom of choice to subordinates. What are the ethical issues involved in making the decision to have a meeting or not have a meeting?

Often the scope of the team's activity is broad—budgeting, timekeeping, quality control, monitoring inventory, assigning jobs, training other team members, adjusting to and preventing problems, knowing their customers and their expectations, producing the product or service. The organization provides initial training of members in problem solving and group dynamics. It defines the basic scope of the team's responsibility and mission. The team is free to develop its own procedures and relationships. Leadership usually emerges in the self-managed team, rather than being appointed by the organization.

Regular Monthly Meetings

In many complex organizations, groups are called together each month to conduct business in a formal meeting. Its purpose may be merely informative, in which case the meeting may well include a featured speaker or reports by group members. In some organizations the monthly meeting is primarily ceremonial: speakers make their presentations not only to give information but also to display their loyalty and solidarity to the organization.

The kind of monthly meeting of greatest interest to us is the ongoing group that meets to conduct organization business. In most universities, for example, the faculty senate is such a group. In colleges it is common for a dean to hold monthly meetings of department chairpersons. Similar examples may be found in every organization. Such a meeting can be very useful, but it may also be a waste of time and energy. Careful planning is required to make this meeting productive.

Step 1. Determine That You Need a Meeting

Each time a problem is uncovered, a judgment is needed about who should make a decision about the problem. Should it be turned over to an individual or to a group? This is a complex question with no simple answer. In fact, Victor H. Vroom and Arthur G. Jago have developed an elaborate plan for making a judgment about who should make a decision.[11] Here are some important questions to be considered in making the judgment about who should wrestle with a problem. The discussion is based on Vroom and Jago's work as well as that of others.

1. *Is there one person who is truly an expert and the group is clearly not?*
   The expert should probably make the decision.
2. *Is there a severe time constraint on making a decision?*
   Turn the problem over to an individual who possesses the needed information and expertise to make a decision. Groups usually move more slowly than individuals. If the problem is given to a group, a leader can help the group move more quickly by imposing structure and holding the discussants to the time limits.
3. *Is the problem complex?*
   A complex problem usually requires a variety of views and expertise. A group is more likely to have the needed knowledge and expertise. Turn the problem over to the group, provided there is no time constraint. If the problem is simple and noncontroversial, turn it over to an individual who has the expertise to make the decision.
4. *Is it important that the group accept the decision?*
   If the problem is such that what needs to be done is clear and the group is likely to accept the decision, turn it over to an individual. If the group has to live with the decision and/or must implement it, and especially if the issue is controversial, turn the problem over to a group that has the knowledge and expertise to make a decision.

Step 2. Do Your Homework

In the task dimension, ask yourself these questions: Do I know what I am talking about? Can I support my point of view? Have I clearly identified the issues? Do I know the extent of the problems and how they are interrelated? Am I willing to put my reputation on the line for my answers to these questions?

If you think that last question seems too dramatic, think again. Your performance in a group does put your reputation on the line. Each time you communicate you produce something by which others judge the quality of your thought. If you wish to be promoted or even maintain your current position, you must give evidence of your competence.

In the social dimension, ask yourself: Have I worked through an analysis of how the problems and issues I have identified relate to the people at the meeting? Have I done this tentatively, with an open mind and with a genuine interest in and concern for their points of view? What social norms or standards of behavior may be at play? Have I kept in mind that other people may not share my ideas about what is standard?

Step 3. Set the Agenda

Some things have been found to be true about planning and setting agendas for meetings. Groups generally work together better if they are involved in setting the agenda that governs their work; and people tend to value decisions more and support them more if they have been involved in the planning stages of the discussion. So you want to take participants into account when setting agendas.

You also need to know what *must* be accomplished and hence what must be included in the agenda. A division head, for example, who calls monthly meetings of the department heads in his or her production division wishes to accomplish certain things with the meeting. These must be reflected in the agenda.

One director of a production division in Chicago, Illinois, had an "agenda committee" that included himself and two others who were department heads. It was the committee's task to set the agenda for the monthly meeting. Their procedure always followed a predictable pattern. We recommend that regular meetings follow an agenda that is predictable and includes most or all of the following items, in some order that seems convenient and appropriate to the participants.

Call to order. Participants have a right to expect the meeting will begin and end on time. In most business organizations, "time" and "money" mean the same thing. People are often very busy and must schedule their time very carefully. Participants will want to know you will be considerate of their time.

Minutes of the last meeting. The uncorrected minutes of the last meeting should be introduced early in the meeting, and either accepted as they are or corrected, then accepted. This is important because the minutes create a record of the group's productivity and decisions regarding policy and action. The history of the group may sometimes be important to the group itself or to the rest of the organization.

This kind of record is very important. For example, most departments prepare annual reports. Your boss will prepare it primarily from the minutes of groups in the department. But more important, the department is governed in large measure by the decisions of various groups within it. That paper trace is needed for the department to know what its members are doing and to ensure that its members are within the limits of agreements made.

Announcements. A person in a position of responsibility and authority will often have last-minute announcements. Some provision should be made in the agenda format so there is time for anyone who has something to report.

Unfinished business. Unfinished business from the last meeting was important last time the group met. The agenda for the group meeting ought to include some provision for taking up that unfinished business. The group may decide that other matters are more pressing and may *not* take up all old business.

New business. The new business of a group includes ideas, proposals, and problems that it has not already addressed. The items to be included ought to be decided well in advance of the meeting. Everyone at the meeting should know that those items are coming up and should have plenty of time to prepare.

If, for example, space utilization is going to be discussed at an upcoming meeting, then you will want to examine the issues, seek the advice of colleagues, and in other ways plan for your participation in the meeting. You cannot do this if you are taken by surprise. New business is only new business in the sense that it has not been discussed at a previous meeting.

Emergency business.   Some provision ought to be made for emergency business. We think that any last-minute item that seems to the group to qualify as emergency business ought to be brought up, regardless of the agenda sequence. Let the group members know that the agenda is not to be rigidly enforced. Tell them that you would appreciate a call prior to the meeting if they know about an emergency agenda item.

Timely adjournment.   Ending a meeting on time is as important as beginning it on time. Sometimes people can miss one meeting because they are delayed in another, very important one. Leadership should encourage on-time behavior by *beginning and ending on time.*

Parliamentary Procedure

When a group is very large, it sometimes becomes difficult for the group to do its work. When that happens, formally constituted groups often turn to parliamentary procedure as a means of guaranteeing progress and of protecting the interests of the minority. The rules of procedure make it possible for the group to conduct its business in an orderly and more, rather than less, efficient manner.

We present this Table of Precedence of Parliamentary Motions (Exhibit 13.3) because we know that such a table is useful. Remember that the rules are written for the convenience of the group. Do not let adherence to the rules interfere with the group's business. If everyone in a group agrees that they want to do something, they can do it without slavishly following *Robert's Rules of Order.* There is no minority view to protect when everyone agrees!

Conferences

If you are placed in charge of an important meeting, do not be intimidated by the enormous number of details. You can use this convenient way to organize your thinking. Think in terms of the two dimensions of communication: task and social. The task dimension includes the things that must be done if the group is to be productive. The social dimension, equally important, involves the feelings, wants, and images of the people who participate. As we go through each of the steps below, you will see how using the two dimensions can be helpful.

Step 1. Decide Your Purpose
In the task dimension, identify, as clearly as possible, the general objectives you wish to accomplish. Consult with your supervisors. Learn from them what they want to accomplish. Then jot those general objectives down. Play around with organizing them into some sensible sequence.

Involve top management in the planning as early as feasible. Get their views and take them into account. This will get you around the obstacle of having to make last-minute changes because of their dissatisfaction.

In the social dimension, deciding your purpose means identifying any social concerns that *must* be taken care of. For instance, a company may have a meeting for the purpose of honoring its soon-to-retire employees. The event is almost entirely social. The concerns in the social dimension then would center around making these employees feel very important. It may be that, on such an occasion, management especially wants to honor one individual. You need to know that in advance; it will have a bearing on seating arrangement.

It sometimes happens that many of the arrangements must be made around the requirements of special participants. For instance, a special speaker may be confined to a wheelchair. Such a person cannot travel up an down staircases unassisted. You should also anticipate that the person cannot stand at a lectern and may have difficulty with electronic visual aid equipment. Arrangements should be made accordingly. Ask the speaker.

> A manager we know sometimes excludes one of her colleagues from meetings—even though his management responsibilities would suggest he should be at the meetings—because she considers him a jerk. What are the ethical questions implied by her behavior, and how would you answer them?

Sometimes an individual's schedule may require that your meeting be held on a certain date and at a specific time. To illustrate, a U.S. senator from your state will undoubtedly have a full schedule. If you want that individual to appear at your meeting you will have to accommodate that schedule.

Occasionally speakers will provide copies of their address for distribution to participants. Someone will have to make copies and see that participants receive them. Arrangements will have to be made and approved by management in order to accommodate a special speaker.

Step 2. Plan the Agenda

In the task dimension, planning the agenda involves asking questions like: What topics must be covered to accomplish the purpose? How much time is available? Can we cover everything adequately? Does the agenda need to be focused? Will focusing the agenda mean a follow-up meeting is necessary? Is that warranted? Is *this* meeting warranted?

In the social dimension, it means taking other people into account. Have I checked with and received input from the others? Have I accommodated their suggestions? Their schedules?

Keep in mind that an agenda is a plan of action. You would be wise to plan the agenda carefully. Your success in this task may make all the difference between the success and failure of the entire meeting. Since the things that are most important to all the members, topics and time, are the substance of the agenda, your care in planning an agenda may have a direct bearing on your personal success.

Step 3. Identify the Other Participants

In the task dimension, identifying the other participants involves finding out who *must* be at a conference and who *should* be. How many participants are too many? Who can be eliminated if necessary?

In the social dimension, that last question is also important. Identifying the participants involves, in part, which people will get along with each other. We suggest that, if it is feasible, you ask the key participants all the task questions

Exhibit 13.3 TABLE OF PRECEDENCE OF PARLIAMENTARY MOTIONS

Once a main motion is before the meeting, any of the following motions, when appropriate, may be made. In the following table the motions are arranged from the strongest—1—to the weakest—0. A stronger motion takes precedence over any weaker motion and becomes the business before the meeting.

Precedence Number	Interrupt Speaker?	Require a Second?	Debatable?	Vote Required?	Amendable?	Subject to Referral to Committee?	Subject to Postponement?	Subject to Reconsideration?
Privileged Motions								
1. Fix time of next meeting	No	Yes	No	Maj.	Yes[1]	No	No	No
2. Adjourn	No	Yes	No	Maj.	No	No	No	No
3. Recess	No	Yes	No	Maj.	Yes	No	No	No
4. Question of privilege	Yes	No	No	Chr.	No	No	No	No
Incidental Motions								
Incidental motions are of equal rank among themselves; they are considered in the order they are moved.								
5. Appeal decision of the chair	Yes	Yes	Yes	Maj.	No	No	Yes	Yes
5. Close nominations	No	Yes	No	2/3	Yes[1]	No	No	No
5. Division of the house	Yes	No	No	None	No	No	No	No
5. Object to consideration	Yes	No	No	2/3	No	No	No	No
5. Parliamentary inquiry	Yes	No	No	None	No	No	No	No
5. Point of order	Yes	No	No	Chr.	No	No	No	No
5. Suspension of rules	No	Yes	No	2/3	No	No	No	No
5. Request for information (Will the speaker yield for a question?)	Yes	No	No	Chr. or Speaker	No	No	No	No
5. Withdraw a motion	No	No	No	Maj.	No	No	No	No

Subsidiary Motions								
6. Postpone temporarily (lay on the table)	No	Yes	No	Maj.	No	No	No	No
7. Vote immediately (previous question)	No	Yes	No	2/3	No	No	No	No
8. Limit or extend debate	No	Yes	No	2/3	Yes	No	No	No[4]
9. Postpone to a specified time	Yes	Yes	Yes	Maj.	Yes	No	No	No[4]
10. Refer to committee	No	Yes	Yes	Maj.	Yes	No	No	No[4]
11. Refer to the committee of the whole	No	Yes	Yes	Maj.	Yes	No	No	No
12. Amend an amendment	No	Yes	Yes	Maj.	No	Yes	Yes	Yes
13. Amend	No	Yes	Yes	Maj.	Yes	Yes	Yes	Yes
14. Postpone indefinitely	No	Yes	Yes	Maj.	No	No	No	No
Main Motions								
Main motions are of equal rank among themselves. They have zero precedence since they may not be considered when any other motion is before the house.								
0. General main motion	No	Yes	Yes	Maj.	Yes	Yes	Yes	Yes
0. Reconsider	Yes	Yes	Yes	Maj.	No	No	Yes[3]	No
0. Rescind	No	Yes	Yes	2/3[2]	Yes	Yes	Yes	Yes
0. Resume consideration (take from table)	No	Yes	No	Maj.	No	No	No	No[4]
0. Set special order of business	No	Yes	Yes	2/3	Yes	No	No	Yes

[1]Although the motion is not debatable, the amendment may be debated.

[2]Only a majority is required if previous notice has been given.

[3]May be postponed to a specified time only.

[4]Motion may be renewed after a change in the parliamentary situation.

SOURCE: From *Argumentation and Debate: Critical Thinking for Reasoned Decision Making*, 6th ed., by Austin J. Freeley. © 1986 by Wadsworth, Inc. Reprinted by permission of the publisher.

357

above. (Do not ask if you really do not want their advice or if you do not trust them.) Have you accommodated their suggestions? And where have you set limitations? Have you taken care of the social and status comparison problems that might arise from the narrowing process you have applied? Sometimes it becomes important to invite high-status people for social and not task reasons.

Step 4. Select the Setting

In the task dimension, selecting the setting refers to making sure the meeting place is conducive to the purpose of the conference. Is it too large? Too small? Too formal? Too informal? Is it conveniently located? Is it attractive? Will the participants think so? Are the facilities complete? You would be amazed at the number of conferences that occur in inconvenient places and that have no restrooms, no refreshment centers, limited and poor-quality sleeping arrangements, and the like.

Perhaps you can see that the questions above can be useful *in the social dimension,* too. Be sure to get some input from the participants and to accommodate that input wherever you can. A key, here, is the perception participants have that they have influence. To use William Schutz's ideas, individuals are motivated by three things: affection, inclusion, and control.[12] You will see instantly the potential you have for satisfying participants' need in each of these areas merely by including the participants in your planning.

Sometimes participants in a large conference will wish to meet in smaller groups for a variety of purposes. Exhibit 13.4 suggests six ways to organize physical settings, with reasons why each might be chosen.

Step 5. Plan for Mechanical Details

This step has to do primarily with the *task dimension.* Preparing for audiovisual presentations, food, shipping, hotel procedures, and the like are all-important in this regard and—as you will see, by implication at least—they are important to the *social dimension* as well.[13]

Audiovisual presentations. Check the facilities before determining where to hold your meeting if you have elaborate plans for audio or visual support. It is a good idea to offer those who will make presentations a chance to rehearse with the equipment. You may not be able to manage this, but you can try.

If you do not have your own audiovisual equipment and people to run it, then you need to make arrangements for every machine, including operators and spare light bulbs. Do this at the time you secure the location.

Finally, we suggest that you try everything out before the meeting. By this we mean actually, physically, go to the facility and run through the use of every piece of machinery. Do this in the room where the presentation will be given. Without a doubt, you will find a number of small problems you need to solve.

Food. Food can be very important to the success of a meeting. Get copies of all menus available at the hotel or meeting place. Talk with the catering manager at the hotel, and ask about what to serve and when. Often the catering manager will be able to give you special prices. For example, in June on the Gulf Coast shrimp are generally plentiful and therefore relatively inexpensive. You might be able to get a special shrimp meal. Likewise, the house may have a specialty that can be made available at reduced prices. Check, also, about reductions in price for increased numbers. What might cost you one price per plate if you order twenty-five plates might be 20 percent less if you order fifty plates.

Beware of serving hors d'oeuvres. They're usually expensive, and if they're salty they tend to increase the consumption of expensive beverages, too. A waiter whose job is to serve hors d'oeuvres will pay for himself in the reduction of hors d'oeuvres costs at a large meeting (as compared to serving hors d'oeuvres buffet-style). It may be a good idea to limit the serving the hors d'oeuvres to one occasion at a conference.

Keep in mind that groups want and deserve variety. For example, in some conference rooms the coffee urn stays set up all day. In the absence of alternatives some participants drink the coffee just because it's there, and often, they consume much more than they normally would or than is good for them. Remember that bottled water, iced tea, soft drinks, juices, and the like are a welcome alternative for many people. The hospitality table might be "changed out" periodically, with hot coffee, tea, and milk, and a tray of donuts and Danish until about 10:00 A.M. Around 11:00 a refreshing light drink would be appreciated, perhaps served with a simple light snack. After lunch bring back the coffee for an hour or so, but replace it with alternative light beverages in the afternoon. You may wish to end the day with wine and cheese as a means of unwinding the participants. Of course, you would want to vary this according to how long the conference goes on.

Sometimes you will not wish to provide food, but you cannot ignore the appetites of conference goers. Your task in this case is to identify good-quality food at a variety of prices and in places near the meeting site. Participants will eat breakfast, lunch, and dinner—and often in between. They will do so even if your meeting is in progress. So make it easy and pleasant for them. Do not overlook the importance of providing each participant a sheet of paper showing your suggestions, with maps or descriptions of how to get there.

Hotel.   The importance of the hotel operation to the success of your conference cannot be overstressed. If the hotel is well run, your meeting is more likely to proceed smoothly. If the hotel is not well run, then no matter how skillfully you arrange your meeting, the chances of its success are at risk. Hotel management, or mismanagement, can make or break your careful planning. Here are some pointers that seem to us worth considering.

First, make arrangements with the hotel management so that whoever you work with in planning the meeting is on hand during the meeting. Sometimes a group will need to have its meeting on a weekend. While the meeting is on, the regular weekday hotel staff may well be off. It is possible that, unless you plan carefully, there will be no one on the premises who is familiar with your arrangements. You need to have a knowledgeable member of the hotel staff available, so check on this ahead of time.

Format called	Arrangement suggested	Reason for using	Method
Round table		To promote equality of feelings; maximize participation of all members; ensure as much spontaneity as possible.	Group discussion of problems and solutions for the purpose of making a good decision or sharing information.
Symposium		To present a variety of views in the form of short speeches or reports for the benefit of the audience.	Moderator introduces the panel; provides history of the issues at hand; presents each speaker in turn; monitors time; thanks the participants; ends the meeting with a brief charge to the audience or a summary of the issue.
Panel discussion		To conduct a semistructured discussion of issues on a topic for the benefit of an audience.	Moderator introduces the panel and problem and keeps the discussion flowing; restates often; controls (somewhat) equal and fair time allocation. Members are responsible for developing points of view and have some control of agenda.
Forum		To encourage audience participation on issues surrounding a topic.	Moderator introduces the program and speaker, who presents a brief statement and interacts with the audience. Moderator participates to encourage audience involvement. A variety of discussion formats can be used.

**Exhibit 13.4
A GUIDE FOR
PLANNING
GROUP
MEETINGS**

Checking out of a hotel seems simple enough at first glance. However, sometimes meetings run beyond the usual checkout times of hotels. Be sure to arrange for this variance from the hotel's usual policy. Set aside an hour or so in the morning and another at the lunch period during which members of your group can check out. Incidentally, almost everyone at a meeting will have not only a suitcase but probably a briefcase and perhaps some other luggage as well. Make arrangements in advance of the meeting for storage of this material

(Exhibit 13.4 continued from page 360)

| Colloquy | | To inform an audience through the use of planned questions designed to get unprepared responses from participants for the benefit of the audience. | Moderator introduces the speaker and panel of questioners, then regulates rotation and time. Sometimes summarizing, sometimes clarifying, moderator does not participate as a panelist. |
| Whole–house decision making | | To debate issues as a body, then decide, using appropriate voting methods. | Moderator regulates the discussion and debate, attempting to get maximum input from both sides in order that members of the house may cast informed votes. Parliamentary procedure is commonly used to govern the event and facilitate orderly progress. |

between the time that checkout occurs and the time the participants actually leave the hotel. No one wants to leave expensive equipment and valuable papers lying around or cart them from meeting to meeting room. The upshot of lack of planning in this regard will be that the participants will take the path of least resistance: they will leave the conference.

Finally, the closer you keep advance hotel payments to the beginning of the meeting, the better, since most of these are not refundable and you cannot always predict the future. Over time, you will save your company a good deal of money—and exercise greater influence on arrangements—if you can pattern your payment program carefully. Usually, payments to hotels and airlines are not required a long time in advance. Call around. Get an idea of what is standard in the area. Use that information to negotiate advantages for your organization.

Shipping.   Shipping is very important, especially if the meeting you call is going to be in another city, but even if it is close to home. A single undelivered package, if the contents are truly important, can make the difference between success and failure for your meeting. Here are some easy-to-follow suggestions that you will be glad you followed:

1. Double-check to be sure that every label is correctly addressed and that the address is legible. We suggest you include a correct address *inside* every package as well as on the outside.

2. Send a summary of the items you have shipped to the meeting place in advance of the meeting. Keep a copy of the summary at your office. Include a copy in one of the packages. Request a copy of such a summary from anyone who sends materials to you. Be sure that summaries arrive in advance of the shipments.
3. Make arrangements with your hotel contact to return materials to their origins following the meeting. Help the hotel be as thorough as you have been.
4. Determine, far in advance, the best way to ship. Should it go via U.S. mail? Via air freight? Via the airlines? Via bus? Should the participants bring the materials? Understand that "best" is not necessarily cheapest.

Transportation.   Typically, the responsibility for transportation lies with the participants. But think about it. If participants take a plane from their home city to Chicago and a limo from the airport to the hotel, after that they are on foot. If someone has thoughtfully made arrangements, they may be able to take a sightseeing tour. If someone has planned for their needs, they may be able to use the elevated trains for which Chicago is famous. If someone has provided them with a bus and a train schedule and a list of special bus and limousine services, they could save a bundle by not taking a taxi or renting a car. All of that kind of planning falls on you as the one who plans the meeting.

Notice, in addition, that many companies own private planes. Busy executives will appreciate a list of local airstrips for private planes or notification if the hotel or resort has an airport.

Miscellaneous.   In the final analysis, planning a meeting is an exercise in careful consideration of others. You may wish to accommodate their needs even before the needs occur to them. For instance, you probably should keep a list of the participants, including addresses and phone numbers. There are many possible uses of this list, including having it on hand for Internal Revenue Service agents; responding to requests for information by participants ("What is Joe Doe's address and phone number? You know, the representative from Du Pont?"); returning materials and property lost or misplaced during the meeting; and, perhaps most important, facilitating that all-important follow-through after the meeting.

Your planning should also include securing for each person the necessary materials. Pens, paper, agenda materials, duplicate copies, and the like are necessary and should be available to all. Remember that people are forgetful. Even if you have sent them copies, they might not have them on hand at the meeting. Provide them another copy if they need it. The success of the meeting might depend upon it. Keep in mind that you wish participants to have task concerns uppermost in their minds. The trick here is to anticipate any possible embarrassment to participants while, at the same time, you ensure that everyone has everything needed.

A large number of miscellaneous details must be taken care of. A safety officer related a story that shows how important details can be. He attended an important meeting of a government agency in Jackson, Mississippi, held in a nice hotel in that southern city. He assumed it would be a rather large meeting, but it turned out that he was wrong. The entire conference, which lasted two days, was housed in a couple of meeting rooms on the second floor. When he entered the hotel through the parking lot entrance, he thought he had found the wrong place. Looking around, he noticed only one person, clearly not a conference participant, in the lobby. He asked the desk clerk and was told: "That meeting is on the second floor, in the Jackson Room." He went to the Jackson Room. It was empty. He stopped a person walking by who appeared to be a possible participant. He turned out to be the conference director! Our view is that the director could have avoided the discomfort by doing these two things:

First, he could have *provided name badges*. They're important, even if the participants are all from the same organization. People forget names. Often they do not know each other. The name badges should be distinctive, so that participants recognize their colleagues instantly. They should be large enough that vain participants who do not wear their glasses can read them. The large clip-on type is best because it does not damage clothing. But anything is better than nothing.

Second, the conference director should have *provided directions*. "Welcome" signs and other directional information should be posted in obvious places. These contribute in two ways: they assist in the general sense of welcome that participants feel, and they help get the meeting started on time.

Step 6. Publish the Agenda with the Invitation

In the task dimension, include all information necessary for participants to prepare for the meeting. See that it suggests what materials participants should bring and what homework they should do. Be sure the agenda is couched in moderate language. It is amazing to discover how many times someone runs up a flag with language like "to debate the critical problems of" or "to discuss the political aspects of" or "to discover who is responsible for."

In the social dimension, you wish to guarantee that the participants have time to prepare. Remind them once or twice between the initial invitation and the actual conference. You can do this by phone or by note. Or you can arrange to bump into a forgetful individual in the corridor of your building and say, "Sure am looking forward to your part of the meeting Wednesday." Or you might prefer to ask your secretary to confirm the participants' plans to attend. However you do it, remind them gently and skillfully. Be sure to encourage and reward inquiry and offers of help or suggestions.

Step 7. Plan the Arrangement of Participants

In the task dimension, this can be a massive problem or a very minor one. In no case is it something to be left to chance. Seating ought to be arranged with some concern for the effect you wish it to produce. Will seating arrangements maximize participation if that is what you wish? Does the physical arrangement accommodate the camera equipment and the audience's view, when that is necessary?

There are some clear concerns in *the social dimension,* too. Especially interesting are the implications that an arrangement can have for status consensus, social comparison, interpersonal conflict, and the like. Take a minute to look at the suggestions about space as a message system found in Chapter 6.

In both task and social dimensions, try to anticipate the needs of participants, vis-à-vis the arrangement of the meeting, by imagining a run-through of the day. To give you a flavor of some of the things that can happen, at a meeting in Denver, participants sat at tables arranged in the shape of a large U, illustrated in Exhibit 13.5. The head table was used by the primary group of speakers. Those of us who were there primarily as listeners but who had some things to contribute were seated around the other tables. Suppose a person was at the position marked X. Do you think that this person would feel isolated from what was going on?

On another occasion a room was arranged as in Exhibit 13.6. You might imagine the squirming among participants who, after about an hour and a half, had to pass through the doors behind the head table in order to get to the rest rooms. The arrangement should have been reversed.

If these examples seem extreme, it is because they are. Nevertheless, they happened. If you are in charge of a meeting, you need to be concerned about this kind of detail. Someone will surely notice such slipups.

Step 8. Arrange to Meet, Greet, Identify, and Introduce Participants

In the task dimension, this means taking care in advance of any protocol requirements, making sure that where feasible each participant can identify by name and expectation every other participant. It also means being sure each participant who requests or requires it will be picked up and delivered on time

Exhibit 13.5
**AN AWKWARD
CONFERENCE
SETUP**

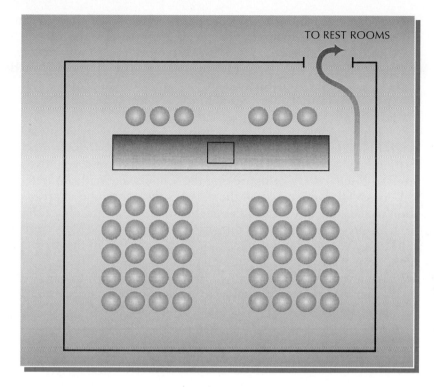

TO REST ROOMS

Exhibit 13.6
AN INCONVE-
NIENT WAY
TO THE "CON-
VENIENCES"

or knows how to make such arrangements, and each has opportunities for last-minute requests.

In the social dimension, this means causing the participants to feel like VIPs. A director of public relations once told a story about meeting a VIP at the airport near Normal, Illinois. He was in charge of meeting and greeting VIPs for his firm. The person he was meeting was obviously tired from a bumpy flight on a commuter aircraft. While driving to the hotel, he asked the VIP what his favorite drink was, then turned to other topics. When he checked the visitor into the hotel, he made arrangements for that drink to be delivered immediately to the guest's room. Five years later one of us had occasion to ask that person if he remembered the event. "Oh, yes," he said, "I'll never forget it." "One of the most welcome surprises in my life" is how he characterized the gesture.

Step 9. Begin and End on Time
In both dimensions, this means begin and end on time.

Step 10. Follow Through after the Meeting
In the task dimension, this concern focuses on agreements made during the meeting. You and others may commit yourselves to perform certain tasks. Wise leaders will gently remind others, whenever appropriate and in a planned se-

quence, of these commitments. Mention to the individuals your intention to inquire and remind them about the agreed-upon pattern, then do it.

In the social dimension, it is worth remembering that participants make a contribution, if only in coming to the meeting. They spend a good deal of time, energy, and money to be there, and they want to know and feel that their contribution is valued. Follow through with some old-fashioned stroking where that can be accomplished appropriately.

A letter to the conference participant's boss may mean more than a direct letter if the conference came off well. A president of a local firm was a master at this kind of follow-through. Following the meeting of a volunteer group, organized to discuss ways of improving the schools, he mailed a letter to each person's boss. He commented on the person's fine work and expressed his appreciation to the company. Of course, each participant heard about the compliment.

This president's generous remarks to the business leaders were important to him, too. They worked for him, too. Those involved in the project became firm supporters of the man. Do you wonder how much of the faith in him rests on his thoughtful follow-through?

For your convenience, and as a summary of what's been said so far, Exhibit 13.7 is a checklist that will help you plan a conference.

SUMMARY . . . .

This chapter has focused on the leadership decisions that must be made in planning for at least four kinds of meetings: the routine decision-making meeting, participative management group, the regular monthly meeting, and the formal conference. We noted that in planning for any meeting, it is important to observe three rules:

(1) be concerned about time, (2) discover and accommodate the group traditions that might be inherited from previous leaders, and (3) use a different approach to planning each kind of meeting.

First, we suggested that you could use a reflective thinking pattern as a task agenda in most routine decision-making meetings, although most meetings of this kind do not follow the pattern in any sequence. For each item in that agenda we made some particular suggestions about how to proceed, and provided specific questions that might improve the quality of proposals that come from these groups.

Next, we discussed participative management groups. These groups involve employees in decision making. "Quality circle" is one familiar label applied to this type of group. People who have firsthand experience with a problem have important insights into its solution. Beyond that, involvement in decision making promotes a commitment to carry out a decision. We suggested how to structure and lead a participative management meeting.

Then, we introduced a sequence that will help you plan for the regular monthly meeting. Answering four questions will help you determine how and to what extent to take other people into account and to find out whether or not to call a meeting. We also described the components that should be on the agenda of a regular monthly meeting.

Finally, we discussed ten steps and provided a checklist that will help you plan a conference. The discussion focused on the implications of each of the ten steps for the task and social dimensions of communication.

Exhibit 13.7   A CONFERENCE PLANNING CHECKLIST

1. Purpose decided?
   a. Consulted with management?
   b. Special speaker?
      (1) Identified?
      (2) Special arrangements made?
2. Task and goal thinking complete?
   a. Homework on subject complete?
   b. Issues identified?
   c. Position on issues clear and supported?
   d. How do issues relate to other participants?
3. Agenda planned?
   a. What topics must be covered?
   b. How much time available? Enough?
   c. Who needs to be consulted?
      (1) Have those people been consulted?
      (2) Have their suggestions been accommodated?
      (3) Have their schedules been accommodated?
4. Other participants identified?
   a. Who *must* be there?
   b. Who *ought* to be there?
   c. Who *may* be eliminated?
      (1) Implications?
      (2) Actions to smooth ruffled feathers?
5. Setting and location selected?
   a. Size appropriate?
   b. Formality/informality appropriate?
6. Facilities complete?
   a. Rest rooms OK?
   b. Refreshment centers OK?
   c. Acoustics OK?
   d. Seating OK?
   e. Lighting OK?
   f. Public address system OK?
   g. Sleeping arrangements OK?
   h. Food arrangements OK?
      (1) Catering manager: Name? Phone? Office hours? Location?
      (2) Catering specials?
      (3) Snack and hors d'oeuvres?
      (4) Beverages?
      (5) Restaurants nearby?
         (a) List prepared?
         (b) Maps or location finders available?

7. Hotel procedures checked out?
   a. Contact person: Name? Phone? Office hours? Location?
   b. Contact person on hand during conference?
   c. Checkout procedures?
   d. Checkout times?
   e. Storage for luggage near checkout desk?
   f. Payment schedule and procedures secured?
8. Audiovisual facilities OK?
   a. List of equipment needed?
   b. Equipment on hand?
   c. Supplemental parts on hand?
   d. Equipment functioning?
   e. Operator(s) on hand?
9. Shipping arrangements complete?
   a. Address labels accurate?
   b. Address inside each package?
   c. Summary list of shipping items?
      (1) To hotel?
      (2) From participants?
      (3) Inside one of the packages?
      (4) In file?
   d. Return arrangements made with hotel?
   e. Shipping via . . .?
   f. Hotel contact person: Name? Phone? Office hours? Location?
   g. Other contact persons?
10. Transportation arrangements complete?
    a. Airport location (private and commercial)?
    b. Airport to hotel?
    c. Available tours?
    d. Train, bus, and subway schedules?
    e. Limo service?
11. Miscellaneous arrangements identified?
    a. List of participants with addresses and phone numbers complete?
    b. Welcome posters?
    c. Direction posters?
    d. Name tags and badges?
    e. Meeting and greeting arranged?
    f. Protocol problems?

NOTES . . . .

1. John F. Cragan and David W. Wright, *Communication in Small Group Discussions: An Integrated Approach,* 4th ed. (St. Paul, West, 1995), pp. 231, 233.
2. Ibid., p. 257.
3. See J. H. McBurney and K. G. Hance, *The Principles and Methods of Discussion* (New York, Harper, 1939); and John Dewey, *How We Think* (Boston, Heath, 1910). Some controversy is beginning to surround these five steps in problem solving. One study suggests that they may not all be related to effective group decision making. Generating criteria, suggesting alternative solutions, and evaluating alternative solutions were found not to be related to effective problem solving. See Randy Y. Hirokawa, "Group Communication and Problem-Solving Effectiveness II: An Exploratory Investigation of Procedural Functions," *Western Journal of Speech Communication,* 47 (Winter 1983):59–74.
4. One research team concludes that effective group discussion is based on careful and rigorous examination of the validity of opinions and assumptions as well as careful evaluation of alternative solutions on the basis of preestablished criteria and consideration of the consequences of each alternative. Perhaps groups would produce better solutions if they more carefully followed a planned agenda. See Randy Y. Hirokawa and Roger Pace, "A Descriptive Investigation of the Possible Communication-Based Reasons for Effective and Ineffective Group Decision Making," *Communication Monographs,* 50 (1983):363–379.
5. Carl E. Larson, "Forms of Analysis and Small Group Problem-Solving," *Speech Monographs,* 36 (1969):453.
6. Ibid.
7. John K. Brilhart and Gloria J. Galanes, *Effective Group Discussion,* 8th ed. (Dubuque, Iowa, Brown & Benchmark, 1995), p. 225.
8. One researcher found that groups that spent more time engaged in these activities were judged to be more effective. See Randy Y. Hirokawa, "A Comparative Analysis of Communication Patterns within Effective and Ineffective Decision-Making Groups," *Communication Monographs,* 47 (1980):312–321.
9. Joseph M. Juran, "The Quality Imperative: Questing for the Best," *Business Week,* December 16, 1991.
10. Randy Y. Hirokawa, "Improving Intra-Organizational Communication: A Lesson from Japanese Management," *Communication Quarterly,* 30 (Winter 1982):35–40. This essay provides an interesting contrast between Japanese and American styles. It is excellent background for understanding why the concept of quality-control circles has been so successful in Japan. For practical suggestions about developing and using quality circles, see John E. Baird, Jr., and David J. Rittof, *Positive Personnel: Quality Circles Facilitator's Manual* (Prospect Heights, Ill., Waveland Press, 1983). See also John E. Baird, Jr., *Positive Personnel Practices: Quality Circles Participant's Manual* (Prospect Heights, Ill., Waveland Press, 1982), and John E. Baird, Jr., *Positive Personnel Practices: Quality Circles Leader's Manual* (Prospect Heights, Ill., Waveland Press, 1982).
11. Victor H. Vroom and Arthur G. Jago, *The New Leadership: Managing Participation in Organizations* (Englewood Cliffs, N.J., Prentice Hall, 1988), p. 220.
12. William C. Schutz, *FIRO: A Three-Dimensional Theory of Interpersonal Behavior* (New York, Holt, Rinehart & Winston, 1958).
13. Most of these ideas are the good advice of Dennis A. Stone, Director of Public Relations, Manpower, Inc., of Milwaukee, in "We're Having a Meeting and You're in Charge!" *Public Relations Journal,* 34, no. 5 (May 1978):12.

RECOMMENDED READINGS . . . .

John E. Baird, Jr. *Positive Personnel Practices: Quality Circles Leader's Manual.* Prospect Heights, Ill., Waveland Press, 1982. This book presents an in-depth treatment of participative management groups and suggestions for leading them. Included in it are suggestions for training the participants.

Ernest G. Bormann and Nancy Bormann. *Effective Small Group Communications,* 6th ed. Minneapolis, Burgess, 1996. This easy-to-read little book synthesizes the literature well and makes practical suggestions about what individuals can do in planning for group events.

John F. Cragan and David W. Wright. *Communication in Small Group Discussions: A Case Study Approach,* 4th ed. St. Paul, West, 1996. This book focuses on three kinds of group events and their leadership implications.

Linda L. Putnam. "Rethinking the Nature of Groups in Organizations." In Robert S. Cathcart and Larry A. Samovar, eds., *Small Group Communication: A Reader,* 7th ed. Dubuque, Iowa, Brown & Benchmark, 1996, pp. 51–60.

Gerald L. Wilson. *Groups in Context: Leadership and Participation in Small Groups,* 4th ed. New York, McGraw-Hill, 1996. This book focuses on a variety of group events and their leadership implications.

DISCUSSION QUESTIONS ....

1. Suppose you are about to become head of a department in a company you have recently joined. Given our injunctions that you worry about time and that you discover the group traditions, answer the following questions:
   a. How would you go about discovering group traditions?
   b. In what ways would time influence your behavior as you assume leadership in the department?
2. We have suggested that there are differences in the kinds of meetings you are likely to experi-

ence. How would those differences affect your planning and participation? How might they affect the social dimension and the task dimension of your behavior?

3. As a class, generate a list of all the group meetings that you have attended in the past month. Given the formats for group meetings we have provided, decide which formats would best facilitate the purposes of those meetings.
4. Suppose that one of your subordinates approaches you complaining that people are never ready for meetings at the appointed time. How would you respond to this situation? Do you need a group meeting? How will you take people into account?

INTERNET ACTIVITIES ....

1. In Chapter 7, Karen Burton described a number of software and hardware technologies that help organizations communicate within groups—whether in the same room or across the world. Locate five World Wide Web sites that address uses of technology to communicate with a group or staff in particularly useful or interesting ways. Write down the Internet addresses carefully, and come to class prepared to make your classmates familiar with these useful or interesting Web sites.
2. Chapter 7 describes Intranet applications for communicating with a group or staff. Can you find anything on the World Wide Web that would help managers decide whether to develop an Intranet for their company? What? Where?

PART V
Organizational Contexts:
The One-to-Many Context

Making effective presentations can contribute greatly to personal and professional career success. That effectiveness comes from mastering skills in audience analysis, developing and supporting ideas, organizing ideas, and delivering presentations. The four chapters in this part address these issues.

Chapter 14, Thinking about the Ideas and Arguments, examines the steps in preparing a presentation. The specific issues discussed include selecting a topic and purpose, audience analysis, and selecting support and evidence.

Chapter 15, Organizing the Presentation, points out the characteristics of good organization and why it is important. It completes the explanation of how to construct the presentation with help on introductions and conclusions. The chapter also tells how to select and develop visual materials.

Chapter 16, Delivering the Presentation, provides a time line for moving through the process of planning and rehearsing a presentation, delivering the presentation, and following through after the presentation.

CHAPTER 14

Thinking about the Ideas and Arguments

Upon completion of this chapter, you should be able to:

1. Explain the value of presentational speaking in business and professional contexts.
2. Select both the topic and purpose of your presentation, and then focus the speech to meet the needs of a particular audience.
3. Identify the logical and emotional arguments you need.
4. Develop and support arguments with evidence.
5. Verify that the evidence meets the test of quality.

*T*he ability to make a strong, competent, and compelling presentation is among the most needed communication skills in business and professional settings. Every day the business of business advances, or does not, on the strength of presentations. From the fairly informal talk delivered to a small decision-making group, to a training session for supervisors, to the most formal presentation before stockholders, speeches are an important way businesspeople convey information or make a point.

373

Unfortunately, not all presentations are good ones. Indeed, the workplace is rife with bad presentations—presentations that seem to wander aimlessly, bore the listeners, and have very little value to the audience. But these bad presentations never have to happen. If you can avoid the most common mistakes amateur presenters make, six of which are identified in Exhibit 14.1, you will always do well when it's your turn. This chapter will help you learn how to avoid these common mistakes and put backbone in your presentations.

GENERAL PURPOSES FOR SPEAKING . . . .

Good presentations begin with a clear understanding of what the presenter wants to accomplish. Thus it makes sense to begin this discussion of presentational speaking with an examination of general purposes. We speak in one-to-many settings to achieve one of five general aims: (1) to express ourselves, (2) to inform and teach others, (3) to persuade others, (4) to entertain others, and (5) for ceremonial purposes.

To Express Ourselves

You may have witnessed a moment in a group meeting during which one of the group members felt compelled to express himself. He may have felt strongly and so wanted to describe his feelings; he may have wanted to support or oppose an idea before the group. He just couldn't sit quietly by, even though much of what

---

Exhibit 14.1   THE SIX MOST COMMON MISTAKES AMATEUR PRESENTERS MAKE

Problem	Listener Response
1. The presentation's purpose is not clear.	*Hmmm. I wonder what this speaker wants from me?*
2. Listeners can't figure out how the speech is relevant to them.	*I wonder why I should listen to this presentation. What's in it for me?*
3. Listeners can't follow the organization of ideas easily.	*Hmmm. I can't follow this presenter's ideas, and I surely don't have time to sit here and try to figure them out.*
4. The speech is full of irrelevant or unimportant detail.	*Why is this speaker telling me all this trivial stuff?*
5. The ideas and arguments are not compelling because they aren't well-supported.	*Ho hum! This doesn't seem very interesting to me.*
6. The delivery is boring.	*This speaker doesn't seem to care; why should I? Hmmm, I wonder what will happen at the task-force meeting this afternoon? Maybe I should . . . .*

he said to the group was repetition of ideas other members had already mentioned. Such a moment illustrates the need for self-expression. People often give speeches to *express* themselves in business and professional organizations, and they should. Effective decision making depends upon it.

Notice that self-expression almost always includes additional goals, as well. To express myself may mean I want to inform or teach you something, or to persuade you to my point of view.

To Inform and Teach Others

When people attempt to add to the general fund of information so that others can make more effective decisions, they are speaking to *inform*. Sometimes they do this in a one-to-many setting. For example, you might add facts to a general decision-making discussion in order to help the group arrive at a higher-quality decision. Or you might be asked to train a group of new employees on the safety features of their jobs. Each case illustrates the general purpose to inform and teach others. Is this goal important in the workplace? Certainly so.

To Persuade Others

Any time you try to influence other people to think or feel or act differently, your selected general purpose is to *persuade*. Speechmaking with this general purpose occurs around you all the time. Every political speech, every commercial, every sales pitch, every argument in favor of or in opposition to an initiative seeks to persuade. Sometimes these attempts succeed, and sometimes they don't.

To Entertain Others

When you attempt to amuse or to relax others, when you seek to divert their attention in order to lighten a tense moment, you are trying to *entertain*. In the workplace, people who can entertain others are perceived as agreeable and are highly valued members of the organization. But speaking to entertain is not a natural act; it involves skills that might seem difficult to learn, plus a light touch and the right timing.

For Ceremonial Purposes

The ceremonies of our lives, both at work and in our personal lives, mark our important moments. People are asked to introduce visiting dignitaries, to present speakers, to give a toast, to praise others, to present an award, or to accept an award. Ceremonial speaking requires skill and grace. If you do it well you leave a very positive impression; if you don't do it well, you present an unflattering image of yourself.

IDENTIFYING AND ANALYZING YOUR AUDIENCE

Notice that for all these general purposes (to entertain, to inform, etc.), in order for speakers to succeed they must focus their attention on the audience. Presenters must meet the listeners' expectations, interests, needs, and so forth. The listeners make the decision to give speakers what they want. Thus, listeners share as much responsibility for the event as the speaker. Because this is so, presenters must know how to analyze and understand listeners. The three steps involved in coming to such an understanding are as follows: (1) identify the target audience; (2) conduct an audience analysis; then (3) draw inferences about the audience.

Identify the Target Audience

When the President of the United States comes on television to address the nation, he has a very clear purpose in mind. He wants something from his listeners, and he knows exactly who among the huge television audience can give him what he wants. He targets that subgroup and directs his arguments and persuasive appeals to that group's state of mind.

When television advertisers broadcast their commercials in a particular time slot, on a particular network, they are aiming their messages at a "target audience." They know from very careful—often expensive—research who is likely to be watching that channel at that time. They know what motivates the target group. They know what psychological appeals to use and how to use them.

Similarly, when you make a presentation, you must know what you want, and you must also know who can give you what you want. Your success will depend, in large measure, on how well you adapt your remarks to the values, attitudes, and beliefs of that target subgroup.

A skillfully prepared and delivered presentation can exercise great power for either good or evil. Here are some ethical guidelines that can help you as you prepare and deliver presentations:

1. Be candid as you reveal your thinking and feelings. Your honesty is your most valuable asset.

2. Don't make arguments or present ideas you cannot support.

3. Avoid oversimplifying complex matters.

4. Don't use emotional appeals that are insupportable in evidence or reasoning.

5. Don't pretend to be something you are not. For example, don't pretend to be an expert if you are not.

6. Let others make up their minds without manipulating them, coercing them, or misleading them.

7. Remember that preserving harmony and peace is sometimes more important than speaking your mind.

8. Choose language that accurately represents you and your vision of the truth, but do not overstate your case.

Who Is in a Position to Give You What You Want?

Anyone can give you laughter, if that's what you want. All you have to do is provoke a laugh. But not everyone can give you a decision. Suppose your presentation seeks a policy change. Who could decide to make that change? An individual? A specific group? That individual or that group of people is your target. You will have to know what issues are relevant to them and which arguments and appeals are most likely to seem compelling to them.

Can you address the individual or the members of the group directly? That is, will they be physically present in your audience? If so, then you can seek your proposed change directly. If not, then you cannot succeed with the presentation unless you change the specific purpose to something other than a direct request for the change. For example, you might ask the members of your audience to approach the target group for you—a process called "two-step flow."

What about the Other Members of the Audience?

Everyone in an audience—decision makers and people who support them—matters to a presenter. So a presenter cannot afford to ignore anyone in the audience. The trick is to design a message that moves the entire audience in the direction you want the decision makers to go while you focus most of your attention on the target subgroup (the decision makers themselves). Being individuals, audience members can—and probably will—range along a continuum from action in favor of your position to action against it.

Exhibit 14.2 illustrates a typical audience in terms of its distribution along an action continuum. Notice how the action relates to the general purposes of speech. This provides you an indication of elements to include in a presentation—on condition that you know how the audience is distributed. Suppose your analysis tells you that members of the target subgroup in this audience (0), except for one, are neutral. The one who is not neutral is more convinced than the others but is still a long way from deciding in favor of your proposal. The other people in the audience (X) are distributed as shown. Since the target subgroup is neutral, and since the bulk of the audience is either neutral or believes something other than your view, the situation calls for a speech to inform and educate.

In this case, you would want to use a light touch. The people who already believe as you do (seven members) will be pleased to hear your views support theirs. They will move toward action if you can move the decision makers toward action. However, members of the target group may feel conflicted about whether to support your idea. Certainly you could count on them to be critical

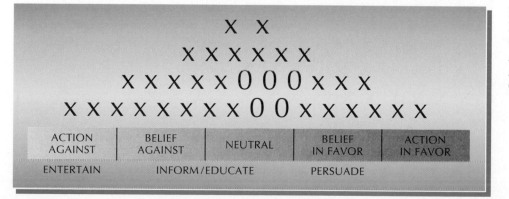

Exhibit 14.2 HYPOTHETICAL NEUTRAL AUDIENCE ON AN ACTION CONTINUUM

Consider this paragraph (in the text). Can you identify any ethical issues surrounding the advice we give? For example, do you think politicians try to remain consistent with their positions on such issues as welfare or tax reform? Do you think they should? What are the ethical questions involved?

and evaluative. Also, you could bet the target group is hearing from the ten individuals who are hostile to your position.

This presentation would seem to call for a good deal of evidence. Every controversial idea would have to be supported. The whole tone of the speech would likely go over best if you understated your arguments. Your ideas would have to seem consistent with your positions on other issues, and you would want to show how they are consistent. Moreover, the listeners could be expected to know arguments on both sides of the question, so you would have to use a both-sides approach, detailing how the other side's logic fails reasonable analysis. An audience like the one in Exhibit 14.2 will want you to reason with them.

Exhibit 14.3 illustrates a different situation. In this group, the decision makers are more spread out along the action continuum. In this example three of them already act against your point of view. Moreover, the bulk of the audience either acts against or believes against your point of view. The most supportive member of the target subgroup is undecided. In such a case you have a hostile audience. Moreover, they only need to ask their neighbors to have their views confirmed. You cannot attempt to persuade them to your point of view in this one speech. They need information, and they need it in sugar-coated doses.

It would be a mistake to try to do much more with this group than to sell yourself, then give your listeners a few facts about your subject matter. Your goals would be to build rapport and good will, to find areas of agreement, and to work to develop credibility by using sources of evidence they can accept. These are appropriate goals in the general purpose to entertain.

Exhibit 14.4 illustrates still a third hypothetical situation. Here, members of the decision-making target group already believe what you do or have already taken some action in the direction you want them to go. The situation calls for a persuasive presentation aimed at moving the three in the "belief in favor" category toward action. They will draw most of the others along with them if you can provide the bandwagon. You must provide leadership to get the desired action. Who should do what? Where, when, and how?

Exhibit 14.3 HYPOTHETICAL NEGATIVE AUDIENCE ON AN ACTION CONTINUUM

ACTION AGAINST	BELIEF AGAINST	NEUTRAL	BELIEF IN FAVOR	ACTION IN FAVOR
ENTERTAIN	INFORM/EDUCATE		PERSUADE	

A persuasive strategy for such a group would be to encourage immediate action. Try to get the group members to commit in public to action in favor of your ideas. Encourage them to discuss their views and to bring others along. Teach them and encourage them to practice answering the opposition. When they testify in support of your ideas, they persuade themselves. Finally, follow through later by keeping in contact with audience members to reinforce their commitment.

> About 400 B.C., the great philosopher Plato railed against the Sophists for teaching people to argue and persuade others. Such practices were unethical, he believed. Do you agree with Plato? Can you imagine any circumstances when a presenter could misuse logical or emotional arguments so they were no longer ethical?

Conduct an Audience Analysis

As we have seen, selecting a specific purpose and doing an audience analysis are intimately tied together. Both must proceed at the same time: analysis helps you focus your specific purpose, and your specific purpose helps you focus more clearly on the target audience. Here we describe two methods of audience analysis: direct analysis and demographic analysis.

Direct-Access Analysis

A presenter often knows many of the members in an audience well enough to contact them directly. Colleagues from work provide an obvious example. In such a case, it seems wise to ask lots of questions. What kind of information do audience members already have about your subject? How important does the subject seem to them? How do they feel about the issues surrounding the topic?

Such questions can be asked in an interview, of course, but also in written form. Exhibit 14.5 illustrates a variety of question types known to be useful in direct-access analysis. They are useful because they are easy to answer and relatively simple to tabulate. Note that any library can supply numerous references that can help you develop questionnaires.

If you have direct access to an audience, such questioning can go a long way toward building your credibility and helping you strengthen your presentation. Unfortunately, presenters do not always have direct access, and thus must draw inferences about their audiences. The most accurate inferences will be based upon careful demographic analysis.

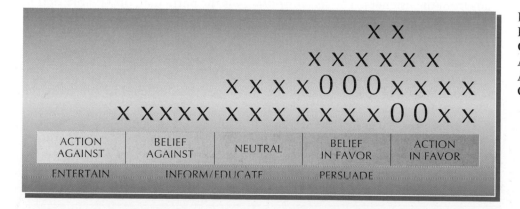

Exhibit 14.4
HYPOTHETICAL POSITIVE AUDIENCE ON AN ACTION CONTINUUM

1. Do you know which toxic materials our plant uses?
   ——— yes ——— no ——— not sure
2. Can you estimate how much toxic material our plant leaks into the environment?
   ——— yes ——— no ——— not sure
3. Is our plant more or less environmentally friendly than our competitors?
   ——— more ——— less ——— not sure
3. How much money does our plant spend on environment protection?
   large amount |___|___|___|___|___| very little
5. To what extent is the local community aware of our plant's environmental record?
   very aware |___|___|___|___|___| not at all aware
6. Do you have any comments or suggestions about our plant's environmental protection policies or history?
   _____
   _____
   _____
   _____

Exhibit 14.5 A SAMPLE QUESTIONNAIRE SHOWING USEFUL QUESTION TYPES

Demographic Analysis

Demographic analysis begins with a demographic profile of your audience. The profile describes audience members in terms of features that may influence their attitudes and beliefs about your subject. For example, age may influence opinions concerning the inclusion of a maternity clause in the group health insurance plan. People of childbearing age might be more likely to support such a clause than people who have already raised their families and now are saving for retirement. Exhibit 14.6 lists and describes some demographic features that may be relevant. Unfortunately, no perfect list exists. The presenter must determine which demographic features bear upon the topic and purpose of a speech.

DETERMINING THE SPECIFIC PURPOSE OF YOUR PRESENTATION . . . .

The general purpose of a presentation (to entertain, to inform, to persuade, etc.) tells about your broad intentions, but it doesn't specify the particular action you want from the listeners. The *specific purpose* is the particular, observable, action goal you seek from the target audience. Think in terms of observable behavior. These five guidelines will help determine the specific purpose of a presentation:

1. Write the specific purpose in a complete sentence.
2. Include both the audience and a specific behavior in the sentence.
3. Avoid figures of speech (metaphors, analogies, similes, etc.) as you write the specific purpose.
4. Double-check to assure the sentence includes only one goal—a goal that can be observed.
5. Be sure the listeners can perform the goal.

While it is perhaps the most difficult part of thinking about ideas and arguments for a presentation, determining the specific purpose is also the most impor-

Exhibit 14.6	SAMPLE LIST OF DEMOGRAPHIC FEATURES	
1. Gender	How many listeners are men? Women? What is the gender mix? What effect, if any, will gender have on member beliefs or attitudes about your subject and purpose?	*Gender might influence the choice between building a plant cafeteria versus a child care center.*
2. Age	How old are the members? What is their range of ages? How is age distributed? How is age related to your subject and purpose?	*Would age influence thinking about a mandatory early retirement policy?*
3. Education level	What is the education level of your listeners? Grade school? High school? Graduate school? Do they have a special type of educational background? How does education level relate to your subject and purpose?	*Could you use the same evidence and arguments on a group of college graduates that you used on a group of high school dropouts?*
4. Political affiliation	Are listeners primarily of one political party? Do they identify with a particular "clique" within your organization? Do they represent all elements of the political spectrum? How strongly do they hold their views? How does political affiliation relate to your subject and purpose?	*Do Republicans and Democrats see eye-to-eye on the appropriate role of government?*
5. Socioeconomic status	Do your listeners have money? Status? Is theirs a majority or minority economic and social situation? How might their status in this regard influence their attitudes, beliefs, and actions about your subject and purpose?	*Might socioeconomic status influence thinking about a proposal to save money by reducing health care coverage for employees?*
6. Religious affiliation	Are the members religious? How strongly committed? What is their religious affiliation? Do they support all the tenets of their denomination? How does religious affiliation relate to your subject and purpose?	*Would Christian fundamentalists agree with atheists about having the company health plan pay for abortions?*
7. Ethnic identification	What is the racial and ethnic composition of your audience? Is that identification relevant to your subject and purpose?	*Chapter 4 describes many differences in cultural values. Would Hispanics agree to English as an official language?*
8. Occupation	What do your listeners do? How much experience do they possess? Is their work related to your subject and purpose?	*People's jobs provide them with specialized information and experiences.*

(Exhibit 14.6 continued on page 382)

(Exhibit 14.6 continued from page 381)		
9. Organizational memberships	Are the audience members active in social, professional, or service organizations? Are they "joiners"? Does the audience's organizational memberships influence their thinking about your subject and purpose.	*Memberships in organizations tell you a lot about a person's interests. Plus, people join because they share values and goals with other members.*

tant. If you know specifically what you want to accomplish (who will do what, when, and how), everything else falls into place. Two examples will illustrate why.

Not specific: I want my listeners to know the standard operating procedures for starting the CS_2 recovery plant.
Better: I want my listeners to name the steps in sequence for starting the CS_2 recovery plant according to standard operating procedures.

Not specific: I want my listeners to volunteer for the American Red Cross blood drive being held in the plant next Wednesday.
Better: I want my listeners to give blood during the American Red Cross blood drive being held in the plant next Wednesday.

In the first example you cannot be sure what "to know" means. The sentence does not call out an observable behavior. A presentation designed to teach listeners "to know" the standard operating procedures would inevitably be out of focus. The better example states exactly what is wanted: "to name the steps in sequence." The better (more specific) purpose would help the presenter focus on the listeners rather than on the operating procedures. He or she would make every effort to help the listeners remember the steps, perhaps by inventing a mnemonic device or by drilling the listeners for rote memory.

The second example seems vague, too. What does "volunteer" mean? Does it mean to serve cookies and juice to donors? Does it mean to take names or make telephone calls? How would the presenter prepare? By extolling the virtues of volunteerism? The better statement of purpose specifies who will do what, and when; thus the presenter has a clear focus and will make it easy for the listeners to know what is wanted of them. Such a speech is much easier to develop, too, because the statement of specific purpose focuses attention on the audience rather than on the subject matter.

Recall the problem of identifying the right target group. You must seek (specify) a goal you can hope to get! If the audience members do not include individuals who can deliver what you ask for, asking is futile. That's why having a specific purpose (who will do what, when, why, where, and how) is so important. Another example will illustrate this point. Suppose the audience for a presentation is as illustrated in Exhibit 14.7. Suppose, further, that the presenter is an engineer making a request for project funding. The audience of thirty-five

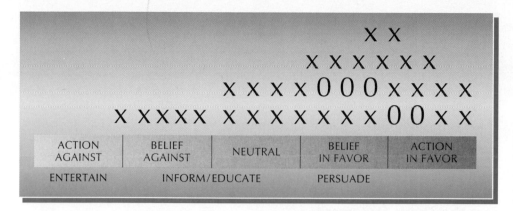

Exhibit 14.7
HYPOTHETI-
CAL POSITIVE
AUDIENCE ON
AN ACTION
CONTINUUM

members includes other engineers, a couple of financial people, one attorney, the plant manager, and four members of the plant manager's top executives. How important precise wording of the specific purpose becomes!

Not specific: I want my audience to fund my proposal.
Better: I want the executive group to agree to fund my proposal during today's meeting.

The audience cannot fund the proposal. That decision is in the hands of the plant manager and the top executives. The lawyers, engineers, and financial people can advise, but they cannot make the decision. Only five of these people are hostile to the idea. Eight more are neutral. The presenter had better focus attention on the members of the executive subgroup in the audience. Only one of them will have to move into the action column; two others have already decided to vote in favor.

Develop the Thesis Statement

A *thesis statement* occurs early in a presentation. It includes the most important point or purpose. It tells the target group what the presenter wants (who will do what, when, where, etc.). Think of the specific purpose as prior planning and the *thesis statement* as something you actually say in the speech.

Thesis statements matter a lot to a presenter's success, and so wise presenters think them through carefully, and plant them firmly in mind. If the statement is vague, the listeners may not know what to do, or even that they are expected to do anything. If the statement is vague, the target group may not experience any urgency about the matter. If the statement is vague, the listeners may be confused about when they are supposed to act. Exhibit 14.8 illustrates these problems by comparing vague and clearer thesis statements. Thus a clear statement must point to the main idea the speaker is trying to deliver, and make clear to target-group members what they are supposed to do.

Exhibit 14.8 SAMPLE THESIS STATEMENTS		
Specific Purpose	Vague	Clearer
I want the executive group to fund my proposal during today's meeting.	"Today I'm asking you to fund this proposal."	"Ladies and gentlemen of the executive committee, today I am asking you for $27,500 so that I can . . . ."
I want my partners to to agree to borrow $50,000.	"This is a good time for entrepreneurship."	"This is a good time for us to borrow venture capital."

Test the Thesis Statement

How can a presenter tell if the thesis statement is clear enough? Three questions will guide this thinking:

1. Is the thesis statement expressed in one simple, declarative sentence (not a question)?
2. Does the thesis statement summarize the purpose and main ideas of the presentation?
3. Does the thesis statement state or imply who will do what, when?

LOCATING THE LOGICAL ARGUMENTS . . . .

Having determined what you want from the target audience and having made sure you understand what makes that target audience tick, it's time to marshall the arguments. Ask yourself: What arguments and evidence seem most likely to move my target group to feel what I want, think what I want, behave as I want?

From the listeners' point of view you must answer these three questions: (1) What are you trying to tell me? (2) How do you know? (3) What difference does it make to me? The answers to these questions are arguments.

Factual Arguments

A *factual argument* says that something is. Factual arguments can be reduced to declarative sentences. They often use some form of the verb *to be*. Thus, a factual argument is a knowledge claim. Whoever makes the statement claims to know something: "This is a Chevrolet." "That is a logical conclusion." "This tractor was run without oil in the crank case." "Jackson is a thief." "Wilson was late to work." "Abbasi will be nominated in tomorrow's meeting."

Some factual arguments, of course, do not use forms of the verb *to be*. To illustrate, Exhibit 14.9 shows part of the story Tim Dahlberg, an Associated Press Sports Writer, put on the Internet following David Reid's final boxing match in the Summer Olympics. Reid won the gold medal.

The story is full of examples. The headline is a factual argument. "Reid's Dramatic Punch Gives U.S. Boxing Gold." The line "It wasn't" is a factual ar-

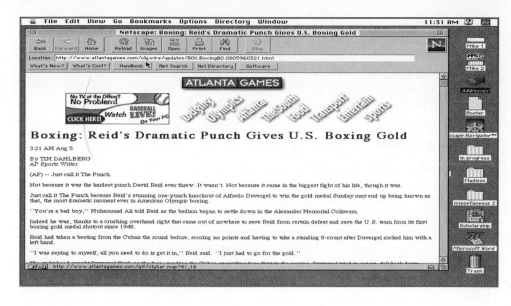

Exhibit 14.9
SPORTS STORY
ON THE
INTERNET

gument. The argument that Reid's punch "may end up being known as that, the most dramatic moment ever in American Olympic boxing" is a factual argument. Mohammed Ali's comment—"You're a bad boy"—is a factual argument. In every case, what's needed to establish a factual argument is evidence.

Values Arguments

Values arguments claim that something is good, or right, or better, or more powerful. Indeed, any claim that evaluates an object, phenomenon, or event is a values argument.

Everyday discourse is full of values arguments: "This idea seems right for us." "Our product is better than our competitor's." "My candidate is the best person for the job." "You have made a mess of things." "There's just not enough collateral in this deal for the bank to run the risk." A presenter must support values arguments by establishing a set of criteria that target listeners will agree to, then applying them, one by one, to the argument. To illustrate, consider what the speaker would have to do to establish his argument, "There's just not enough collateral in this deal for the bank to run the risk." Suppose he is one of a five-member loan committee. The customer who applied for the loan is a longtime customer of the bank, well-connected in the community and personal friends with the president of the bank. Because of personal ties to the customer, two of the members on the loan committee are inclined to make the loan; two others aren't sure. Only the speaker is hostile to the request, and only because he doesn't want to put the bank at an unacceptable risk.

To establish his position the speaker would have to define the term "enough" and the term "risk." He would have to convince the loan committee members that his notion of "how much" is correct. He would have to cause them to put their obligation to the bank's stockholders above their personal and professional connections and feelings. To do these things the speaker would need both arguments and evidence to win his position in that committee. Thus, while factual arguments rest on the weight of evidence alone, values arguments require carefully drawn factual arguments plus evidence as well.

Policy Arguments

Policy arguments always seek change of some kind. They are characterized most often by statements that someone should do something. The key terms in a policy argument are *should* and *ought:* for example, "We should approve this loan application."

For the speaker to carry this argument she would have to have a good many reasons plus a good deal of evidence. One way to think about policy arguments is to list a series of so-called stock issues. These *stock issues* (an *issue* is always a question with a "yes" or "no" answer) are so important that the wrong answer on any one of them is enough to end the meeting! The requirement to prove all the right things is sometimes called the burden of proof. It always falls to the person making a policy argument to accept the burden of proof. Exhibit 14.10 lists the stock issues and applies them to the loan committee example.

Exhibit 14.10 THE STOCK ISSUES OF A POLICY ARGUMENT	
Stock Issue	**Example**
1. Does a harm flow from our current ways of doing things?	*What harm—what problems, if any—would accrue to the bank if we deny this loan?*
2. Is the problem relevant?	*Who would be harmed? Who would have the problem?*
3. Is the problem serious?	*How serious would the harm or problem be? Is that serious enough to require us to make this loan?*
4. Is the problem or harm inherent?	*Is the harm a part of what we do now?*
5. Is it reasonable?	*Will our making the loan solve or resolve the problem? Will it remove the harm or lessen it significantly?*
6. Is it practical?	*Do we have the means necessary? Can we afford to make the loan?*
7. Is it desirable?	*Do we want to make this loan? Are there any ethical constraints? Is it consistent with our purposes?*
8. Will it create new or more serious problems?	*Are there any other constraints we should consider?*

To review: Every presenter who proposes a change of any kind must accept the burden of proof. This means the presenter must carefully work out all the logical and emotional arguments, then support them with enough evidence to appeal to the target audience group.

....LOCATING THE EMOTIONAL ARGUMENTS

Persuasion won't result from a presentation that has only logical arguments to offer. Listeners must be able not only to relate to the logic but also to feel something about the arguments. Aristotle believed a persuader could develop, control, and use three kinds of "artistic" proofs. These artistic proofs included *ethos,* meaning the kind of person a persuader is (including education, honesty, reputation, and delivery skills); *logos,* meaning "appeals to the rational intellect"; and *pathos,* meaning "appeals to the passions or to the will" (emotional proofs). Most of what we've said so far about the process of proving rests squarely on Aristotle's notions of *logos.*

In the 1970s, a fellow named Tony Schwartz introduced the notion that persuasion is not something we do to others; rather, it is something we do to ourselves. He called his idea an "evoked recall model" of persuasion.[1] The idea of the evoked recall model is to present images and information with which a target group can *identify.* If the persuader can present the right image, the target group will make a connection to something inside themselves. For example, a tire company's television advertisement showed a woman driving alone, at night, in a rainstorm. The woman, obviously worried, was leaning forward, trying to see out the windshield of her car as she drove along the deserted street. An announcer asked: "Why would you buy anything less than the very best when there's so much riding on your tires?"

The evoked recall model generated a good deal of motivation research that provided information concerning what causes people to act. That research and earlier work centered on what has been called *the hidden persuaders.*[2] Eight such hidden persuaders have been identified. Exhibit 14.11 names, describes, and provides an example of each of the hidden persuaders. Each is a powerful emotional appeal. In combination they can compel a target group of listeners to act, on condition that the presenter includes the right logical arguments and evidence (*logos*) and also establishes himself or herself as credible (*ethos*).

Once you have identified the logical and emotional arguments, the next step is to support those arguments with enough evidence to make them compelling.

....SUPPORTING THE ARGUMENTS WITH EVIDENCE

Evidence always comes in the form of statements. *Evidence* refers to any informative statement that, because it is believed by a listener (or reader), can be used as a means for gaining the listener's support.[3] Evidence does not exist outside the context of a *statement* about the evidence. A fact without a statement about it does not inform or persuade. It follows that unless the source of the statement seems credible to the listeners, the evidence will not be credible.

Exhibit 14.11	THE HIDDEN PERSUADERS		
Strategy	Evoked Recall	Appeal	Example
1. Need for emotional security	We have learned to fear, to experience emotional distress and insecurity.	Do what I ask, buy my product, etc., and you will feel secure.	Ad shows woman driving alone at night through the rain. "Buy our brand because there's so much riding on your tires."
2. Need for reassurance of worth	People often feel personally unimportant, and "not OK."	This product, compliance with this request, will make you worthy.	Announcer tells you to buy an expensive hair dressing "because you're worth it."
3. Need for ego gratification	Need for attention beyond mere reassurance of worth.	Do what I ask and you'll be seen as very important.	Ad tells you it's time for you to buy a luxury car to show others how successful you are.
4. Need for creative outlets	Need and desire to build and create things.	Compliance with request, purchase of product, etc., will let you be creative.	The entire "do-it-yourself" industry depends upon appeals to the need for creative outlets. Cookbooks are sold with this appeal.
5. Need for love objects	Need for outlets of affection and loving feelings.	If you do what I ask you will fill the gap in your life.	Ads use images of babies and puppies to evoke affectionate feelings.
6. Need for a sense of power	Children grow up feeling powerless. The society teaches us to need and strive for power.	Comply with request, buy this product, etc., and you will feel powerful.	Ad for a pickup truck shows it climbing a steep hill or going easily over rough countryside.
7. Need for roots	Our mobility has caused us to lose our sense of place. We feel displaced.	This product, service request will give you a sense of place. It will help you feel rooted.	*Old-time* lemonade. Political call for *a return to traditional values.* Restaurant that advertises *good old-fashioned home cooking like grandma used to make.* Resort advertises *escape to a slower time* while showing happy people walking near a barn.
8. Need for immortality	Death is the deepest taboo in our society. Our culture teaches us life must go on, even after death.	Compliance will extend your life in some important way.	Ads for hair coloring, ads for plastic surgery to remove wrinkles, and the entire life insurance business rest on this need.

Four kinds of evidence occur most frequently in business presentations: (1) testimony, (2) definition and explanation, (3) statistics, and (4) examples. Each can be very powerful in support of arguments, but only if the sources from which you draw them are credible.

Testimony

Testimony involves using someone else's words as evidence for your own argument. Direct quotation provides an obvious example, but you can also paraphrase what a person has said. Testimony comes from experts sometimes, but it can also come from laypeople and, occasionally, from one's own experience.

> Would it ever be ethically responsible in a business presentation to build up the reputation of a source of evidence (as political parties and advertisers often do) as a means of strengthening testimony? Suppose you believe with all your heart that the testimony is correct, but you think the source may not be strong enough to carry the argument. Would that justify exaggerating the source's reputation?

Expert Testimony

Expert testimony comes from a qualified, usually prominent person who is generally regarded as an expert in the area of his or her testimony. The source of the testimony must either be known to the listeners and trusted by them as highly knowledgeable or else hold a credentialed position that will lend credibility to the testimony.

For example, all the members of the audience might know Wayde Wilson holds the position of comptroller in the organization. His position would render Mr. Wilson's testimony credible support for an argument about the organization's financial picture. In contrast, one of the production line supervisors would be more credible as a source of evidence about something having to do with the day-to-day running of the line. The audience would probably be unwilling to accept either of these sources as credible to testify about environmental pollution caused by an accidental spill of toxic materials in the train yard.

Lay Testimony

Lay testimony is testimony from "on the street." A person who saw what happened but has no special expertise in the technical aspects of what she saw would provide "lay" testimony because she is not an expert. She could provide very powerful testimony, nevertheless. For example, a frontline supervisor at a local conveyor-belt roller manufacturer watched in shock as one of the hourly workers deliberately threw a brick into the gearbox of a machine. By the time she could collect herself enough to shout a warning, the damage was done. Her lay testimony—she saw the man throw the brick—was pivotal in the company's decision to fire the employee. It was also pivotal in a court trial about a year later, when the fired employee attempted to prove to the court that the company had fired him because of his age and race.

Personal Testimony

The various categories of personal testimony overlap because people are not easy to pigeonhole. Personal testimony is "first person" testimony. The presenter says, in effect, "I was there, I saw, this is my experience. . . ." Such "I've been there" testimony can be very powerful supporting material. To illustrate: A management trainee in a local chemical company had only recently graduated from college when he was invited to sit with the engineering planning committee as it began the process of upgrading its chemical treatment facility. The plant is a huge place full of pipes and pumps that cover nearly an acre of ground.

Once the chemical has been treated, it must be pumped to a different facility in order to be used in the production process. Thus the treatment plant is connected to the production plant by a maze of pipes and pumps, too.

To the young engineer the visual effect was "like a plate of spaghetti." He successfully argued for a series of labeled arrows so operators and engineers could tell at a glance which pipes carried what chemicals in which directions. This photograph shows some of those labels, placed there because a young man used personal testimony effectively.

In summary, presenters can use three sources of testimony to support arguments: expert testimony (from individuals who are credentialed or acknowledged to know, and who are well-regarded by the listeners), lay testimony (from ordinary individuals who have "been there and done that", and personal (first person) testimony. In every case, testimony must be perceived by the listeners as consistent—consistent with the testimony of other experts, consistent with the source's other statements, consistent with what the listeners already believe, and inherently consistent. In addition, listeners must believe the source of testimony has no preconceived or biased ideas about the subject.

Definition and Explanation

Definition and explanation are useful for clarifying other ideas in a presentation. A presenter must take every opportunity to make his or her presentation clear and sensible to the listeners. Every important term should be defined in words the target listeners understand. Both technical terms (terms only a specialist would understand) and familiar terms (that carry different connotative meanings or convey different things to different people) must be defined and explained.

**Exhibit 14.12
ARROWS AND LABELS SHOWING THE KEROSENE FLOW IN A CHEMICAL PLANT**

For example, here is a sentence recorded during a meeting of paper mill employees. The speaker casually tossed around technical terms assuming everyone in the group knew what he meant. We have italicized each term we think he might have defined or explained to help make his presentation more clear and sensible.

> How would you feel if you found out someone had invented statistics in order to persuade you, and as a result you made the decision she wanted you to make? Do you think presenters ever invent statistics? Is it ever ethical to do so?

> I have analyzed the *polyethylene-coated milk-carton stock* smoothness test results to determine the relationship between *proto-testing* and *product-testing*. Plus, I wanted to find out what variables are involved in causing the *smoothness differences* between Friday's run and Monday's run.

Statistics

Statistics summarize a large number of individual cases. Instead of saying something like "John and Marge and Kim and Soo and Dasha and Carlos and Roberta and Masato and . . .," a presenter summarizes with a statement like "Fourteen of our fifteen frontline supervisors are ready to support the shift change."

Statistics occur every day, in almost every conversation. Try to hear a speaker saying: "According to *USA Today,* children make up half the chronic poor." "James McDougal, one of the President's business partners in Arkansas, faces up to 84 years in prison and $4-and-a-half million in fines." "As many as 95 percent of American business organizations are expected to be using the Internet by the end of this decade."

Statistics can have a powerful effect on an audience if the statistics seem credible and if they don't confuse the listeners. To use statistics well, most presenters round off numbers—for example, saying "half a million" instead of $489,897.88." Presenters who wish to be effective are careful to use truly representative statistics, and they explain what the statistics mean to the listeners. For example, in a speech about supply and demand, a presenter said: "This number is so large we can't imagine it." He went on to say: "Think of it this way: There is a car that works in the United States for every man, woman, and child living here." Thus he explained what the large number meant.

Wise presenters often use visual aids to help explain the statistics they use. Graphs and charts, tables of numbers, and the like must usually be seen as well as heard in order to have the greatest impact on an audience.

Examples

Another kind of evidence, examples, lend powerful support to any presentation. Indeed, the value of examples can hardly be overemphasized. Examples give life and color and illustration to ideas. Examples clarify abstractions and bring specific situations into focus. So powerful are examples that speech teachers often call them the engines that drive the presentation.

Examples can be drawn from events that actually happened and from imagination. An example can be one of a number of things, taken to show the char-

> **What conditions render an invented example ethical or unethical?**

acter of the whole. A pattern or a model can provide an example. (A person can be a role model, for instance.)

To be effective, examples should seem typical to the listeners and truly representative of events or situations. In addition, a presenter should offer enough examples to establish the argument. Examples should be recent enough that they do not seem like ancient history. They must seem up-to-date and reflect the times.

TESTING THE QUALITY OF THE EVIDENCE

Listeners depend on presenters to offer credible evidence, but people in business and the professions have also learned a healthy skepticism. They want to believe the evidence you present, but they're also very likely to test it. They will do so by applying these questions (either consciously or unconsciously):

1. Is the presenter an honest and competent person?
2. Has the presenter given enough evidence to make the point believable?
3. Is the evidence consistent?
4. Is the evidence verifiable?
5. Is the source of evidence competent to give it?
6. Is the source of evidence biased or prejudiced?
7. Is the evidence up-to-date?

SUMMARY

Each presenter must go through a predictable sequence of events when thinking about ideas and arguments. It begins with selecting the topic and general purpose of the presentation, then moves immediately to audience analysis. Analyzing the audience means coming to know its members and makeup well enough to tie arguments and evidence together and make them credible to the target group or subgroup. Moreover, audience analysis and topic selection are intimately connected. We can begin by thinking, "I want to persuade my listeners," but we cannot make the purpose specific until we have some understanding of the particular interests and needs, attitudes, and prior opinions of the people who hear us and who must give us the goal we seek with the presentation.

Begin an audience analysis by identifying the target group. Who can give the response you want? Audience analysis can be direct, as when the speaker asks questions directly of the audience members. As often, however, audience analysis is a process of discovering the relevant demographic features of a group, then drawing inferences about how the group is likely to respond to the presentation's arguments and evidence based upon those features.

Determining a specific, action-oriented purpose and turning that into a thesis statement is the next step. Once this step is accomplished it becomes relatively easy to locate arguments and evidence that will carry the thesis. The arguments turn out to be about facts, values, and policies—each type of which requires special consideration on the part of the presenter. The arguments must be supported with testimony, definition and explanation, statistics, and examples in sufficient number, and of sufficient quality, to seem compelling.

NOTES

1. Tony Schwartz, *The Responsive Chord* (Garden City, N.Y., Anchor Press/Doubleday, 1973); Tony Schwartz, *Media: The Second God* (New York, Random House, 1981).

2. Vance Packard, *The Hidden Persuaders* (New York, Pocket Books, 1964).

3. This definition is based on the classic work of Douglas Ehninger and Wayne Brockriede, *Decision by Debate* (New York, Dodd, Mead & Company, 1963), p. 110.

RECOMMENDED READINGS ....

Michael S. Hanna and James W. Gibson. *Public Speaking for Personal Success,* 4th ed. Dubuque, Iowa, Brown & Benchmark, 1995; see, especially, Chapter 4, "Selecting and Narrowing Your Topic," Chapter 5, "Audience Analysis," and Chapter 6, "Supporting Ideas with Argument and Evidence."

Herbert W. Simons. *Persuasion: Understanding, Practice and Analysis,* 2d ed. New York, Random House, 1986. This classic work describes the process of persuasion using very clear, well-illustrated narratives.

DISCUSSION QUESTIONS ....

1. What kinds of argument and evidence, and how much, would be necessary to support a presentation that:
   a. seeks to persuade your classmates voluntarily to take on an additional ten-page term paper assignment?
   b. seeks to persuade your classmates to contribute $10 to the department in which your course is being offered?
   c. argues that your classmates should pay a $15 computer laboratory and technology fee for every course they take?
   d. asks your classmates to give blood at the local Red Cross blood bank?

2. Evidence exists in sentences. How would you evaluate the following evidence, and why?
   a. "According to Demi Moore, acupuncture is a medical miracle."
   b. "We know from Chronicles 7:14 that only God can save America now."
   c. "Budweiser is the best-selling beer in the world."
   d. "Ted Jacobs of the American Tobacco Institute says there is no evidence that ambient smoke is dangerous to the health of a non-smoker."
   e. "Dr. James Kostinger, Director of Research, Pittsburgh Academy of Forensic Medicine, says smoking marijuana may cure cancer."
   f. "Many pen experts here and abroad consider the Mont Blanc Diplomat to be the finest pen ever made."
   g. "Recent reports show Anacin's pain reliever is doctors' #1 choice."
   h. "Our tests indicate you have glaucoma."
   i. "Everyone knows Kennedy stole the 1960 election."
   j. "Dr. Joyce Brothers declared that the American girl kisses an average of seventy-nine men before getting married."
   k. "Carlton Cigarettes are lowest in 'tar' among all the major brands."
   l. "Only 34/10,000 of 1 percent of American handguns are involved in homicides."
   m. "I'll tell you how the laws got so screwed up in this country. Supreme Court Justice Felix Frankfurter was a member of the ninety-six communist front organization."
   n. "In a 1997 New Orleans test, 46 of 100 beer drinkers who 'regularly drank Budweiser' preferred an unmarked mug of Strohs Light."
   o. "Anacin has 800 milligrams of pain reliever, while Bayer and Bufferin have only 650."
   p. "We know 73 percent of Americans cheat on their federal income tax."

INTERNET ACTIVITIES ....

1. Type the words *public speaking* in the search box of the Yahoo! search engine (http://search.yahoo.com). You will find about thirty-five "hits." How would you characterize these Web sites?

2. Type the words *visual aids* onto the search box at AltaVista Search (http://www.altavista.digital.com/). Bring your impressions and notes to the class for review.

CHAPTER 15

Organizing the Presentation

OBJECTIVES ···

Upon completion of this chapter, you should be able to:

1. Explain why good organization is important.
2. Explain the characteristics of good organization.
3. Organize a speech by time, space, problem-solution, cause-effect, natural topic divisions, and the motivated sequence.
4. Specify the functions of an introduction and a conclusion.

5. Decide what parts of a presentation need visual support.
6. Decide what kind of visual material will work best for a particular presentation.
7. Design a visual aids program.
8. Develop the visual aids program.
9. Pull all the parts together into a credible and convincing presentation.

*R*ecall from the last chapter that one of the six most common mistakes amateur speakers make is poor organization of ideas. If ideas are organized poorly, listeners can't follow a speaker's argument. Note that audience members have to take what a presenter gives, at the time the presenter gives it. They have no time to compare and contrast ideas as readers do. They can't reorganize the presenter's ideas to suit their own best learning patterns. Listeners depend on the presenter to select all the evidence and all the arguments—and to arrange the arguments and evidence into a pattern that they can follow easily.

If a presenter fails to accept this obligation to organize carefully, listeners go away. They stop listening and they stop trying to understand. Sometimes they literally get to their feet and walk out of the room. Clearly, a presenter cannot succeed under those circumstances. However, it is not difficult to learn organization skills for presentational speaking.

....FOLLOW THE CHARACTERISTICS OF GOOD ORGANIZATION

In order to learn good organization skills for presentational speaking, all you have to do is follow the characteristics of good organization: (1) Good organization is clear and simple. (2) Good organization limits the number of main points. (3) Good organization flows logically from point to point.

Clear and Simple Approach

When something is *clear* it is sharply defined, distinct, easily seen and understood. It is without ambiguity and therefore entirely comprehensible. When something is *simple* it is readily understood (and remembered) because it lacks complication. Thus, the criterion that good speech organization is clear and simple implies a straightforward, uncomplicated, obvious approach.

As an example, here are two definitions of *sexual harassment*. Which do you think is easier to understand—the simple definition or the more complicated definition?

> Sexual harassment means unwelcome sexual advances, requests for sexual favors, and other verbal or physical conduct of a sexual nature, when submission to or rejection of this conduct explicitly or implicitly affects an individual's employment; unreasonably interferes with an individual's work performance; or creates an intimidating, hostile, or offensive work environment.[1]

Sexual harassment in the workplace is a problem that is pervasive, insidious and not easily cured. By its nature, it involves the most embarrassing and intimate of details. It involves persons in positions of power (usually men) doing and saying offensive things, usually to women under their dominion. These factors make coming forward with complaints of sexual harassment a stressful task.[2]

Even the first, simpler definition seems more difficult to understand than the definition offered by a lawyer recently: "Sexual harassment is unwanted sexual attention."

In an outline, keeping things clear and simple means using a direct, say-what-you-mean approach. Use simple language, and limit the number of main points.

Limited Number of Main Points

Presenters often try to do too much. They include more ideas than they can possibly develop; they create a complicated organizational structure; they include multiple arguments and subpoints. But the best organization avoids such complexity. Remember that you just can't develop a complex argument in a few minutes. Consider these two sample outlines. The first is a poor example because it's too complex. The second is much better because the speaker elected to focus attention on just one idea.

Poor Example

I. Sexual harassment has a long history in American business and industry.
   A. It has been going on since the industrial revolution, at least.
   B. It was outlawed with Title VII of the Civil Rights Act of 1964.
   C. It was first defined in the 1980s, when the EEOC, under Title VII, formulated guidelines to define sexual harassment.
II. Sexual harassment is bad for business and bad for businesspeople.
   A. Last year, sexual harassment claims increased by 200 percent.
   B. Last year, judgments, not including attorney fees, averaged about $200,000.
   C. Something like 90 percent of all sexual harassment claims are justified.
III. No one has to be a victim of sexual harassment, and no one has to victimize others.
   A. No one has to be a victim of sexual harassment.
   B. No one has to victimize others.

Better Example

I. Sexual harassment is bad for business.
   A. Last year, sexual harassment claims increased by 200 percent.
   B. Last year, judgments, not including attorney fees, averaged about $200,000.
   C. Sexual harassment damages everyone in the workplace.

Effective presenters don't try to develop many lines of analysis in a single speech. Too many ideas confuse listeners. By the time the speaker gets to the fourth or fifth main argument, the audience has forgotten the first! Moreover, a presenter just can't develop that many ideas in a limited amount of time.

> Politicians sometimes deliberately create confusion in order to avoid issues or to hide their true positions on issues. Similarly, business organizations sometimes deliberately attempt to confuse issues—for example, in the case of a massive toxic chemical leak. Do you think this is ethical behavior?

Logical Flow

Effective organization of ideas flows logically from one point to the next. Each subpoint provides an explanation in support of the main idea. For example, in the better example outline, in the previous section, each of the three subpoints gives a reason why sexual harassment is bad for business.

Logical development increases both understanding and retention in the listeners' minds. The target audience can see, immediately, where the speaker is trying to take them, and they will find it easier to come along. Here is a sample outline that flows logically from point to point. Notice how each idea leads to the next.

Specific Purpose: I want my audience to invest in Fidelity Contrafund.
Thesis Statement: The best mutual fund investment we can make right now is Fidelity Contrafund.[3]

I. Fidelity Contrafund has had a high return rate for a long time.
  A. Both Morningstar and Valueline guides include Fidelity Contrafund among their lists of the ten best total returns since 1986.
  B. Fidelity Contrafund has enjoyed a higher-than-average annual growth rate, on average, for ten years.
    1. The annual fifteen-year return was 16.6 percent.
    2. The annual ten-year return was 18.7 percent.
    3. The annual five-year return was 20.5 percent.
    4. The annual three-year return was 16.1 percent.
    5. Last year's return was 23.1 percent.
II. Fidelity Contrafund has been a low-risk investment for a long time.
  A. According to the Morningstar guide, Fidelity Contrafund is lowest in risk among the top ten best-returning mutual funds.
  B. Morningstar rates the fund as being 20 percent less risky than average.
  C. The fund has finished in the top quarter of the growth-fund category in seven of the past eight years.
III. Fidelity Contrafund has excellent long-term prospects.
  A. In ten years the fund has grown from $84 million to $19 billion in assets.
  B. The fund has grown sixty times larger under the same management.
  C. Two experts believe the long-range prospects are excellent.
    1. Eric Kobren of *Fidelity Insight* says . . .
    2. Jack Bowers of *Fidelity Monitor* says . . .

In this example outline the ideas flow logically. The listeners should invest in Fidelity Contrafund for three reasons, each stated clearly and simply.

Predictable Pattern

The structure of a presentation depends almost entirely on what the speaker is trying to accomplish and the context in which the presentation is to be given. Thus there is no single correct way to organize ideas in a presentation. However, six patterns of organization have stood up to hard use over many years: (1) time, (2) space, (3) problem/solution, (4) cause and effect, (5) natural topic divisions, and (6) the motivated sequence. They have been used so often because they work well to hold ideas together. They work because the listeners are accustomed to thinking in these patterned ways.

Time

To organize by time means to arrange ideas according to a sequence of events. You can organize by time in any direction: then to now, now to then, first to last, last to first, etc. Thus, organization by time (sometimes called chronological order) is one of the most frequently used organizational patterns.

During the presidential campaign of 1996, the Republican candidate for president was former Senator Bob Dole of Kansas. The Democratic candidate was the incumbent, President Bill Clinton. Dole's campaign developed a Web site that, among other things, offered a time line of Mr. Dole's career. Part of it is presented here as a way to illustrate organization by time:

January 11, 1995

Pushed the Congressional Accountability Act through the Senate, requiring members of Congress to live under the same laws as the American people

February 21, 1995

Introduced the Snowe-Dole Child Support Enforcement Act designed to improve and expand existing child support enforcement measures

April 10, 1995

Announced his intent to run for President of the United States

July 25, 1995

Pushed the first comprehensive lobbying reform legislation in 45 years through the Senate.

July 27, 1995

Introduced the Equal Opportunity Act

September 19, 1995

Led passage of sweeping welfare reform plan (Clinton vetoed)

October 18, 1995

Authored the "Dole GI Bill"

December 22, 1995

Led welfare reform plan to passage—vetoed by Clinton

December 22, 1995

Became the longest serving Republican Leader in Senate history

---

March 27, 1996

Engineered the passage of line-item veto in the Senate, enabling future Presidents to delete costly pork-barrel spending measures from bills

May 9, 1996

Pushed "Megan's Law" through the Senate, protecting America's children from convicted sex offenders

May 15, 1996

Announced resignation from Senate

June 6, 1996

Came within a single vote of passing the Balanced Budget Amendment

June 11, 1996

Bob Dole resigned from the Senate

August 15, 1996

Will become the Republican Party's nominee for President of the United States of America

Since people so commonly organize their own thoughts and discourse by time, you can easily help them follow your ideas by using this pattern—on condition, of course, that the subject matter suggests it. Chronological order—arrangement by time—provides listeners with a useful structure to help them keep track of and anticipate your ideas. Thus, it also helps them pay attention.

Space

Presenters often use spatial relationships to organize their ideas because, like time, space is a natural part of human cognition. We often think in terms of spatial relationships, such as top to bottom, east to west, side to side. For example, a visual aid showing the overall ground plan of the production plant invites the presenter to organize ideas about the plant layout using a spatial pattern, and it helps the listeners remember the key areas.

An employee from DelMonte International Fruits used the map of Costa Rica shown in Exhibit 15.1 to show where the company plantations lie in relation to the principal city, San Jose. The map is primitive, but it was an effective visual aid because it is simple yet detailed enough to allow the speaker to show where the plantations lie.

Problem/Solution

People often think in terms of problems and solutions. Because they do, a problem/solution sequence of ideas works well as a way to organize the ideas in a presentation. Sooner or later, a presenter will almost certainly have to use it. To review, the problem/solution sequence looks something like this:

Specific purpose: I want my target audience to change something.
Thesis statement: It is time to change (something).

**Exhibit 15.1
MAP OF
COSTA RICA**

   I. A problem exists that requires us to change something. (because)
      A. The problem is serious. (because)
         1. Evidence
         2. Evidence
      B. The problem is inherent in what we currently do. (because)
         1. Evidence
         2. Evidence
      C. The problem won't resolve itself—we must resolve it. (because)
         1. Evidence
         2. Evidence
  II. This proposal will solve the problem. (etc.)

The problem/solution sequence can flow backward, and sometimes that pattern makes greatest sense. Typically, if the problem is very simple and the solution is complex, it makes sense to put the problem first. However, if the solution is very simple and the problem complex, it might be more sensible to state the solution first. For example, a presenter might say:

> We should raze the old warehouse building for three reasons. First, it is a safety hazard. Second, just standing there empty, the building costs this company close to half a million dollars every year. Finally, we need the space for expansion of the dry wall plant. I'd like to take each of these ideas up in turn. . . .

Cause and Effect

The cause-to-effect pattern helps a target audience to understand that certain conditions are responsible for a result. The pattern is useful for organizing a presentation when your argument is that eliminating the cause will change the effect or eliminate it, too. To illustrate, suppose the effect you wish to remove is wasted storage space. What is causing the waste? Why, the company has been keeping 300 tons of paper in the warehouse that it can't sell for market price. If the company would off-load the paper—even at 50 percent below cost—you could use the wasted storage space to warehouse your new product at a savings of 35 percent. This savings would provide a rate of return of three years against the loss on the stored paper.

Like problem/solution patterns, a cause-and-effect pattern can flow in different ways. Moreover, most big effects flow from multiple causes, not a single cause. A presenter using cause and effect will probably want to identify several causes or else qualify remarks in some way: "Of course, many causes contribute to this effect, but the one we can do something about with greatest impact is . . . ."

Natural Topic Divisions

A very common way to organize ideas flows naturally from physical or conceptual features. For example, a tree suggests natural divisions: roots, trunk, branches, and leaves. Similarly, the human body suggests many natural divisions, one of which would include skin, muscle, organs, blood, and bones.

We can think of natural divisions of a topic like leadership, too. For example, a definition might suggest natural divisions: "Leadership is ability to influence a group in order to help it meet its goals." One natural division of this definition would include *ability*, then *influence*, then *group*, and finally *goals*. You can imagine how a trainer could use these natural divisions when teaching a brief unit on leadership:

> Ladies and gentlemen, there are four important parts to effective leadership that you can learn. The first is ability. You can learn how to provide leadership—it's not magic. The second is influence. You can learn how to influence, how to persuade, how to compel, how to encourage and how to empower others. The third is . . . .

Motivated Sequence

Half a century ago a man named Alan H. Monroe described an organizational pattern that works well for business presentations because, like the other patterns described here, it is consistent with the way people think. This pattern is especially useful when your purpose is to persuade. The motivated sequence has five steps: (1) attention, (2) need, (3) satisfaction, (4) visualization, and (5) action.

Attention. The purpose of the attention step is to gain the interest of the target receivers. You hope their response will be "I want to listen to this person" or "I want to read this material."

Need. The need step describes a problem or demonstrates a need to know. You hope the receiver will respond with "Something needs to be done," or "I need this information," or "My group needs to hear this message."

Communicators sometimes create the impression that a change is needed, even when it is not, in order to gain some benefit from the change. Moreover, companies sometimes build planned obsolescence into their products in order to create a need for change. Can you identify the ethical issues involved in these two facts?

Satisfaction. The satisfaction step presents a solution to some problem, thus meeting the need presented in the previous step. You want the listeners to think, "This is what I should believe," or "Yes, this is what we should do," or "This information helps me understand and is therefore useful."

Visualization. The visualization step attempts to show either the consequences of doing something or the consequences of *not* doing it. The target listeners should say to themselves, "Yes, I can see myself in a better situation if we do this," or "If this proposal is not adopted I can see myself in a worse situation."

Action. The action step asks for approval or action. The aim is to get the listener to act. "I will do what you suggest," or "I believe you," or "I feel so strongly about this that I will do something about it" are all desirable outcomes from the action step. Exhibit 15.2 illustrates an outline for a presentation that follows the motivated sequence.

LET EACH PART DO WHAT IT MUST . . . .

In the best presentations, every part of the speech serves a particular set of functions. If the presenter violates listener expectations about these functions, the speech suffers. Indeed, some presentations have been ruined because the speaker did not think through how to begin and end a speech, or how the introduction and the conclusion should be tied to the body. Every presentation should have these three parts: introduction, body, and conclusion. And in every case, the presenter should take care to get the most out of each part.

Introduction

An introduction has three functions. The first is to gather attention. An audience cannot listen to you if they're not paying attention to you. The second goal of an introduction is to state the purpose. You tell the target group the position you are going to take—or ask them to take—and the action you would like from them. We have already discussed this statement of purpose, calling it the thesis statement. The third goal is to preview what is coming so the target listeners can chart the ideas in the presentation. The fourth goal of an introduction is to make your ideas seem important to the listeners.

Here is a simple introduction that follows a four-step sequence to accomplish these goals.

Step 1. Greet the listeners. "Good afternoon, ladies and gentlemen."

Step 2. Introduce yourself and say something pleasant. "My name is Tametra Jackson, and I am very pleased to have this opportunity to talk with you today."

Step 3. State your topic. "Today I would like to talk with you about the number 3 power turbine at the Mattingly plant."

Exhibit 15.2   OUTLINE FOLLOWING THE MOTIVATED SEQUENCE

Attention Step

I. Office politics is the only game in which the person who doesn't play will always lose.
   A. The feud between Henry Ford and Lee Iacocca illustrates this point.

Need Step

I. At any level, anyone who says "I'm not political" is probably in trouble.
   A. People must know the dynamics of office politics to survive.
   B. People must be ready with strategic offense or defense in order to survive.

II. Office politics is an inescapable reality of organizational life.
   A. People in an organization contribute.
      1. Executives sometimes protect themselves at any price.
      2. Some people are empire builders.
      3. Indecisive managers create power vacuums.
   B. Events in the life of an organization contribute.
      1. Organizational restructuring contributes.
      2. Difficult company finances contribute.
      3. A tight communication policy contributes.
      4. Favoritism contributes.

Satisfaction Step

I. Three tools will increase your chance of survival.
   A. A reliable track record in the company is necessary.
      1. Know your stuff.
      2. Perform well.
      3. Avoid complacency in office politics.
   B. A communication network is essential.
      1. Stay plugged in to the formal network.
      2. Stay plugged in to the informal network.
      3. Don't depend on newsletters, memos, etc.
   C. Good working relationships are critical.
      1. Relationships are a source of power.
      2. Relationships are the key to information access.
      3. Networks are built on need, respect, trust, obligation, and friendship.

Visualization Step

I. Learning to work efficiently and to communicate effectively will help you form alliances that are mutually beneficial.
   A. You will find colleagues who are supportive of you.
   B. Your subordinates will admire and respect you.
   C. Your superiors will value you.

Action Step

I. Your success in office politics is up to you.
   A. Put an extra effort into helping others.
   B. Put an extra effort into your own career.

SOURCE: Based on "Playing Political Games," *Working Smart: The Executive Advisory Service from Learning International,* 3 (June 1986):1.

Step 4. Make the topic important to the target listeners. "It is giving us trouble beyond normal and acceptable levels, and it's costing us money."

The simple one-two-three-four pattern illustrated here will work nicely every time you have to make a presentation. It is direct, clear, and above all, simple. It works well because it helps the listeners accept your message. It works because it helps the target listeners to see the large view, then to organize your ideas in your own minds.

Body

The body of a presentation lays out the main arguments and supporting materials. It is the heart of any presentation, and the place where most of your attention should be placed. In Chapter 14 we discussed the process of proving a point of view. That entire chapter is about the body of a presentation.

Conclusion

The purpose of a conclusion, in general, is to provide a sense of completeness. Specifically, however, the purpose of the conclusion depends on the nature of your presentation. For example, you might wish to provide a final, motivated impetus to your speech, or to focus the target listeners' thinking and feelings on some key point of the speech. You might want the listeners to determine to learn more, or you might want them to act. Our advice about how to conclude a business presentation is simple. There are two steps:

Step 1. Summarize.
Step 2. Provide a "kicker."

A *summary* is a simple restatement. A *kicker* is a final, upbeat ending in which the presenter asks listeners to focus on the main ideas of the speech. To illustrate, Sheila Whitman used this summary in a presentation to about a dozen managers meeting in the conference room at their plant. Notice how, as a kicker, she skillfully asked the listeners to decide in her favor that afternoon:

> So what have I told you? Basically, I have said two things. First, we've got to bring the problem of adding odor to the gas supply under control so our employees will always be able to detect a gas leak. That's essential for their safety and because an explosion could be a catastrophe for our plant. And second, I have told you there is an easy way to solve the problem—one that will work and that is easily affordable.
>
> But, ladies and gentlemen, the decision is a management decision. You are the only ones who can authorize this change. I urge you not to wait. Authorize this proposal in your meeting this afternoon. Thank you.

A kicker can take almost any form—apt quotation, a reference to the introduction, a startling fact, a reference to occasion or surroundings, and the like. It has only one purpose—to rivet the target listeners' on the goal of the presentation.

. . . . .SUPPORT THE PRESENTATION WITH VISUAL MATERIALS

So far we have discussed the matter of organizing ideas in a presentation. We've argued that organization is important because the listeners can't give you what you want unless they can follow your presentation. But good organization serves another purpose, too. The better your organization, the easier it is for you to deliver your presentation. However, even the most powerful arguments and evidence, tied together with the strongest organizational pattern, sometimes will not be enough to move a target group toward action. It seems axiomatic that people need to see as well as hear ideas if they are going to identify with them. Thus, it makes sense for a presenter to support the organizational structure of a presentation with visual materials. This approach entails four steps: (1) decide what needs visual support, (2) decide what kinds of visual materials will work best, (3) design a visual aids program, and (4) develop the visual aids.

Decide What Needs Visual Support

Exhibit 15.3 lists six important uses of visual materials. Given the reasons for using visual aids in that list, we cannot think of a single time that a business presentation would not be strengthened by a well-designed visual program. But *what* ideas and arguments should you support with visual materials? Our advice is to keep your focus on the target listeners. What will make it easiest for them to give you what you want? Visual materials are helpful for showing problems, solutions, and benefits. Visual materials make processes and procedures clearer, and they help listeners follow steps in a sequence.

Show problems. *Show* problems as well as tell about them. In order for a listener to care about a problem he or she must identify with it. Since you often cannot bring the person to the problem, it makes sense to bring the problem to the person. One way to do this is to show it. Show it in terms that the listeners can understand and relate to.

For example, if the target listeners are financial people they will be able to relate to the numbers and figures of a proposal better if you show them the information as well as tell them. Similarly, some things just cannot be described

---

Exhibit 15.3   SIX USES OF VISUAL MATERIALS
1. To simplify complex ideas
2. To help listeners follow the organization of ideas
3. To control listener attention
4. To clarify abstraction
5. To assist listener memory
6. To assist presenter memory

You can imagine a presenter exaggerating a problem with visual materials. For example, camera angle, center of focus, and the like can create the impression that a problem is more severe than it actually is. At what point, or under what circumstances, would such an exaggeration become an ethical problem?

with words. An unsightly building, or a rust problem, or a badly undercut stream bank can be better and more easily shown than described in words. Show problems so the listeners will understand and identify with them.

Show solutions and benefits. Remember that the target listeners must understand and relate to the key ideas in your presentation if they are going to act upon them. Visual aids enhance the persuasive power of a presentation and involve listeners emotionally; people have to see in order to believe.

To illustrate, one speaker was able to generate over $100,000 in contributions, in part by showing how the money would benefit the community. Using a series of photographic slides, he showed a parcel of waterfront property. The land was overgrown; there was a ruined building. Street gangs were using the place to buy and sell drugs. The police had assigned additional surveillance on the place because of problems there. Then he showed an architect's renderings, in several views, of his development proposal—to build an Explorium and Omnimax theater on the spot. He showed a plan view of this location in relation to other landmarks in the city. The overall effect was powerful, and the speech succeeded dramatically in generating funds for the project.

Show processes, procedures, and steps in sequence. Visual aids help people follow the steps in sequences and to understand processes. This is a basic premise that underlies nearly all CD-ROM training materials. For example, Huls America, a large petrochemical plant near Mobile, Alabama, uses CD-ROM technology to train its employees to be safe at work. The training is required by the Occupational Safety and Health Administration of every industry in the land. The agency requires every manufacturer to train every employee every year on all the safety features of their jobs, plus to prove they did it and to prove the employees learned it! This enormous training requirement lends itself well to the use of computer technology. Huls' approach to the problem, and one shared by many employers, has included development of CD-ROM training programs on issues such as how workers can protect their hearing, how they can be safe from fire, how they can work safely in confined spaces, and so on.

To provide a further illustration, all petrochemical employees must learn to fill out, to read, and to explain a standard "Material Safety Data Sheet." Part of the training requires workers to actually fill out a sample sheet. Trainers distribute a sample to each employee, then project a copy onto a large screen. Step-by-step the trainers and the workers go through the process of filling out the form—a learning task that would be very difficult without the visual aid.

Decide What Kind of Visual Material Will Work Best

Anything that can be seen can be used as visual supporting material. An object, an article of clothing, a drawing, and printed letters, for example, all qualify as possible visual aids. So how does a presenter go about deciding what kinds of visual materials will work best for a particular presentation? The process of deciding begins with knowing the specific purpose of the presentation. Once that is determined, the rest should fall into place without difficulty. As a general rule of thumb, any three-dimensional object that is small enough to handle is probably too small to be seen. We recommend, therefore, that presenters consider using photographs or drawings of such objects instead. Exhibit 15.4 provides a detailed evaluation of common visual aids. Some general considerations follow.

Identify the key ideas.   The key ideas must be made memorable. It might be wise—especially if the key ideas are likely to be new to the listeners—to use visual materials to help the target listeners follow. From the listener's perspective, what ideas are likely to be difficult to grasp and thus require visual support?

Develop a first rough plan.   Using an outline of the presentation or note cards that carry the ideas and supporting arguments and evidence, decide which ideas must be supported visually and which kinds of visual materials are likely to be most helpful.

Draw rough thumbnail sketches.   Lay out a series of small sketches, one for each visual aid. Imagine giving the presentation with the visuals in mind. Do you need any new ones? Can you eliminate any? Exhibit 15.5 shows how one presenter developed rough thumbnail sketches. This series of thumbnail sketches could easily have been produced by hand. However, many presenters use such computer software as Aldus *Persuasion,* Microsoft *PowerPoint,* and *Harvard Graphics* to develop thumbnail sketches. The programs all have a design feature that allows presenters a good deal of flexibility, but you do not have to be an artist to use them. Each includes, also, a large range of "templates" designed and programmed in advance and packaged with the software.

Evaluate the Visual Aids Program

Go through the presentation again, examining whether or not each visual aid you have planned actually works to help the listeners follow the speech and identify with the arguments and evidence. If you are using computer software to produce the visual program, print out the "slides" on paper, then practice the presentation using these mock-ups as you go. Do any of the visual images require revision? Do you need any additional visual images? Can you eliminate any visual images?

Some other questions to consider as you evaluate your visual aids program: Will the visual materials you have in mind be convenient to use? Will final visual materials be worth the cost of developing and producing them? Will the visual aids program lend power to the speaker and the speech—or will the visual aids program weaken the speech?

Exhibit 15.4   SELECTING THE RIGHT VISUAL MEDIUM TO SUPPORT A PRESENTATION

Equipment	Pros	Cons	Comments
Flip charts, chalkboards, and Velcro-felt boards	Short lead time; easy and informal; inexpensive; no dependence on mechanical or electrical gear	Easily compromised by a presenter who doesn't know how to use them; appropriate only for small groups	You can write as you go, and so these are good for stimulating and recording audience-speaker interaction.
Overhead projector, 35mm slides	Professional tone; good for illustrating complex material; can be seen by large audiences	Require more planning; more difficult to prepare; quality depends on graphic and photographic skills; slide projectors require a darkened room, not good for maintaining control of an audience	Presentation software has made it easy to develop overhead transparencies. Plus, computer software has made it possible to create an overhead transparency of a photograph. Overhead projection unit may be the ultimate presentation tool—especially when combined with presentation software.
Videotape	High impact; good for large audiences	Very expensive—as much as $1,500 per minute of finished video; difficult to prepare and difficult to find well-prepared material	Videotape is effective for illustrating human-interest stories. Cameras are getting easier to use and less expensive, and video-capture capabilities for computers are becoming more readily available.
Computer-generated visual materials	Depending on software package, can be very easy to prepare; lend a professional tone; illustrations are capable of animation; can include full-motion video and full interactivity	Steep learning curve if presenter wants to be the developer; subject to technical problems, especially when combined with the Internet and the WWW; assumes availability of a fairly powerful computer	High-tech presentations are impressive and compelling. Some good software: 1. Microsoft PowerPoint 2. Aldus Persuasion 3. Claris Works 4. Gold Disk Astound Very high-end development programs include: 1. Macromedia Director 2. Oracle Media Objects 3. Macromedia Authorware

Develop the Visual Aids Program

Once you have evaluated the visual aids program, the final step is to develop it as you will use it in the presentation. Remember that you do not have to spend a lot of money to develop a useful visual aids program. Anything that can be

Exhibit 15.5 ONE PRESENTER'S THUMBNAIL SKETCHES

seen can be used as visual material. Some excellent presenters use overhead projectors and transparencies made using a computer. Others hook up their computers directly to a full-color projection system. Some excellent presentations are made using nothing more sophisticated than flipcharts and felt-tip markers. Space does not allow a full treatment of two-dimensional design principles.

SUMMARY

Good organization is clear and simple, it limits the number of main points, and it flows logically from point to point. To organize a presentation, follow a predictable pattern, such as time, space, problem-solution, cause-effect, natural topics division, or the motivated sequence (attention, need, satisfaction, visualization, and action). Each part of a presentation must do its part. The introduction has four functions: (1) to gather attention, (2) to state the purpose, (3) to preview what is coming, and (4) to make the ideas important to the listeners. The body lays out the main arguments and supporting materials. The conclusion should provide a sense of completeness and finality and should end with a "kicker" that lends a final, motivated impetus to the speech.

Presentations usually need visual support so that listeners can see as well as hear the ideas. Six considerations help in deciding what needs visual support: (1) simplify complexity, (2) help listeners follow, (3) control listener attention, (4) clarify abstractions, (5) assist listener memory, and (6) assist presenter memory. Use visual materials to show problems, solutions and benefits, processes, procedures, and steps in a sequence. In deciding what kind of visual materials to use, identify the key ideas, develop a rough plan, and draw rough thumbnail sketches. Evaluate the planned visual aids program by determining if any additions, corrections, or deletions may be needed. Also, evaluate the planned program by applying three criteria: the cost of the visuals versus the benefits, the convenience of use, and the communication power of the program. When these considerations have been completed, a presenter is ready to develop the final visual aids program.

NOTES

1. http://coyote.csusm.edu/class_schedule–f95/sexual_harassment.html
2. http://rampages.onramp.net/~collier/sexhar.htm

3. The ideas and data for this example were drawn from James K. Glassman, "Finding the Fund That Tops Them All," *The Washington Post,* Sunday, August 18, 1996, p. H1, and used with permission of James K. Glassman.

RECOMMENDED READINGS ....

Michael S. Hanna and James W. Gibson. *Public Speaking for Personal Success,* 4th ed. Dubuque, Iowa, Brown & Benchmark, 1995. This book includes two chapters on organizing and outlining ideas, and also a lengthy chapter on supporting ideas visually.

We recommend, as well, that you browse through *Publish* magazine, and any number of other popular computer-user magazines that may be found in the news section of your neighborhood supermarket. *Personal Computing, MacWorld,* and many others provide information about developing and using visual materials.

DISCUSSION QUESTIONS ....

1. As an audience member, would you rather get technical information orally, in writing, or in both forms? What difference would these options make? Under what conditions do you prefer oral channels to written channels of communication?

2. If a TV set is available to your class, view a few minutes of commercial television with the sound turned off. In what ways has the producer or director used visuals to communicate with you? What lessons did you learn from this exercise?

3. Suppose you must present materials you believe are not intrinsically interesting. What can you do to hold the target receivers' attention?

4. A simple in-class exercise will help you study the various patterns of organization. Working with one or two other class members, induce some pain in your hand by slapping it hard against a tabletop. Try to describe the experience of the pain. After each of you has made the attempt, discuss ways in which your description might be organized—by time, space, problem to solution, cause to effect, natural division by topics, or motivated sequence. Which would be the most effective method of description? Why?

5. Agree with one or two other class members to attend one of the many speechmaking events available on campus or in the community. Examine the speaker's use—or lack of use—of visual supporting materials. Can you imagine ways for the speaker to have strengthened his or her presentation with visual aids? Later, be specific as you present your findings to the class.

INTERNET ACTIVITIES ....

1. Select any topic for a presentation. Visit the World Wide Web Virtual Library (http://www.w3.org/pub/DataSources/bySubject/Overview.html). List at least ten resources directly related to your topic. Share your findings with your classmates.

2. The Internet is full of help—and free software—for people who have trouble organizing ideas. What do you make of what you find at "SquareNote" (http://sqn.com/sqn5.html)?

CHAPTER 16

Delivering the Presentation

Upon completion of this chapter, you should be able to:

1. Select appropriately from four delivery styles: (1) reading from a manuscript, (2) memorization, (3) impromptu, and (4) extemporaneous.
2. Make and use appropriate speaking notes.
3. Explain the importance of checking equipment and the physical setting.
4. Explain what to do and what not to do while waiting to speak.
5. Respond skillfully when you are introduced.
6. Describe how to follow through after a presentation.

One of us recently attended an international conference of highly placed executives from the pulp and paper industry. The purpose of the meeting was to share ideas about how technological advances could strengthen the pulp and paper industry, generally, and to help the participants (who came from all over the world) to cement their relationships and to develop their networks. Between sessions one of the participants was heard to ask: "Are you enjoying the conference?"

"Ugh!" came the reply. "Let's talk about something more pleasant."

"Why? I thought you'd be enjoying the conference."

"Well, these guys clearly know what they're talking about, but the presentations are so bad I can hardly bear to sit in there."

The disgruntled executive was describing the central focus of a three-day meeting. About two hundred people sat in a large hotel ballroom, darkened so photographs could be projected onto a large, rear-projection screen. They listened as presenters read lengthy technical papers from manuscripts. At best these conditions might be bearable. Although the presenters cared about being understood and they clearly understood their materials, the problem was that these individuals did not understand how important delivery skills are to the success of a presentation.

Exhibit 16.1 displays a sequence of events through time that all presentations must follow. It suggests what a presenter must do, and it also suggests the organization of this chapter.

WHAT TO DO BEFORE THE PRESENTATION . . . .

If you are ready to think about the actual presentation you have long since begun the process of planning and rehearsing. Now you are ready to consider the delivery of the presentation.

Choose the Method of Delivery

A presentation ought to sound as though it were occurring to you for the very first time, rather than sounding rehearsed. Your best chance to appear spontaneous rests on careful preparation. How you go about preparing may range from actually scripting the speech and committing it to memory, through mak-

Exhibit 16.1
TIME LINE FOR DELIVERING A FORMAL PRESENTA-TION

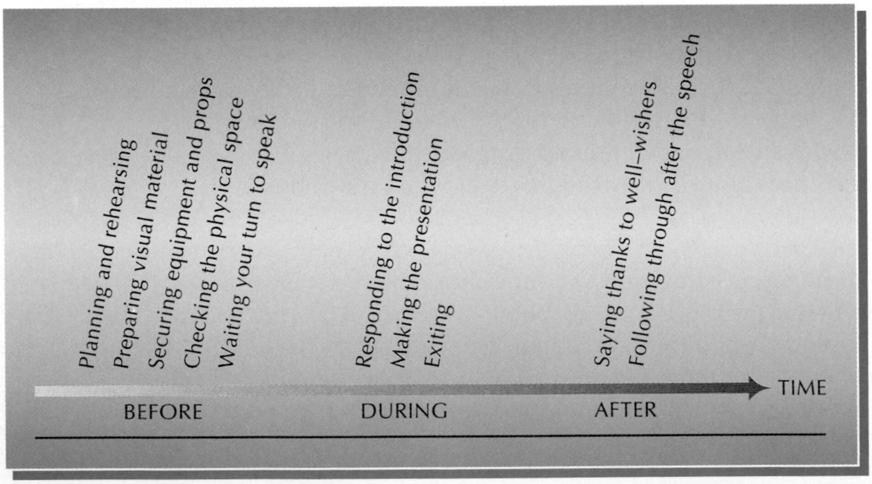

ing and following a close outline, to speaking from brief, precise notes. Some speakers use carefully sequenced visual aids as notes. In every case, the decisions you make about the style of delivery are too important to leave to chance.

Reading from a Manuscript

The idea of reading from a manuscript sometimes tempts speakers because a manuscript offers certain advantages over memorization and avoids most of the pitfalls. A manuscript might help if:

1. You must weigh each nuance of language.
2. You must present all the material in a particular sequence.
3. You must cue a technical assistant.
4. Company policy, official position, bank balances, or other matters rest on the exact use of language.
5. You read well aloud.

If one or more of these conditions requires it, and if you are satisfied that you read aloud easily and well, then write out a manuscript. We advise against manuscript reading for most presentations, however. For one thing, reading diminishes your appearance of spontaneity. Unless you are very skilled you may spend more time looking at the manuscript than at the audience. In addition, reading tends to sound mechanical.

Another compelling reason to avoid reading is that you lose opportunities to take advantage of events as they unfold in an audience. A person frowns, another nods off to sleep, still another turns to whisper to a neighbor. These cues tell you something, but only if you are not committed to a manuscript can you take advantage of them. Exhibit 16.2 summarizes the problems associated with reading from a manuscript.

If you must read, let these procedures guide you:

1. Read through the speech many times aloud. Make it sound as though this speech were occurring to you for the first time, every time.
2. Read the presentation to colleagues, friends, and neighbors, and pay attention to the feedback they give you.

Exhibit 16.2 PROBLEMS WITH READING FROM A MANUSCRIPT	
Problem	Reason
Eye contact with listeners is restricted.	Presenter concentrates more on manuscript than on listeners to be sure every word of the manuscript is spoken.
The presentation seems stilted.	Spoken language is and sounds different from written language.
Presenter appears uncertain and "wooden."	Speaker feels committed to the words of the manuscript and is fearful of deviating from the written text.

Speech writers are commonly used by executives, politicians, etc. The speech writers usually have broad permissions about the choice of language, arguments, and evidence they put into the mouths of their employers. At what point, if any, would this practice become ethically troublesome?

3. Understand every statement in the presentation—especially if, as sometimes happens, you did not personally write the speech. Sometimes audience members ask questions!
4. Rehearse with props and visual aids, far in advance of the actual presentation. If possible, videotape or audiotape yourself and study the presentation carefully. Does it sound "canned"? Or does it sound appropriately spontaneous?
5. Are visuals coordinated with the script?
6. Are you comfortable?

Memorization

The advantages of memorization are that you can choose each nuance of language carefully and you are able to time your presentation, including the placement of visual materials and other attention-getters, precisely. A memorized speech also allows you to cue others who may be helping you, such as a television production director or a lighting or special-effects assistant. And you will guarantee that you have said just what needs to be said—nothing more and nothing less.

The disadvantages of memorization seem to us to outweigh the advantages, however. When you memorize you risk that your memory will fail. What could be more painful for an audience than that awkward silence that leaves the speaker stranded with nothing to say? Exhibit 16.3 summarizes the advantages and disadvantages of memorization.

One of us once served in a consulting capacity to a candidate for mayor. The candidate was well-qualified to serve in office, but he was not an effective speaker. During the campaign he was invited to speak to one of the local knife-and-fork service clubs following lunch on a Wednesday. "I'll memorize this one," he said. "It'll be a lot better than using a manuscript." We could not persuade him otherwise. It will not surprise you that the affair ended in a mini-

Exhibit 16.3 ADVANTAGES AND DISADVANTAGES OF MEMORIZING	
Advantages	Disadvantages
1. Presenter chooses exact wording.	1. Presenter must remember the script.
2. Timing is exact.	2. Speech may sound memorized because of lack of vocal variety, emphasis, etc.
3. Presenter knows exactly what to say.	3. Memorization discourages interaction with listeners.
4. Sequence of ideas is precisely controlled.	4. Memorization may increase presenter apprehension about the speech.
5. Subtleties and nuances can be carefully prepared and worded.	5. Loss of flexibility in idea development or adaptation.

disaster for the candidate. About half way through the speech he lost his place, stumbled, and pushed the panic button. A kindly soul in the audience asked him a question to which he would certainly have a response. The rest of the presentation was directed by members of the listening audience, and the candidate never did get to make his most important position known to that group.

Impromptu Speaking

Impromptu speaking means speaking "off the cuff"—that is, making a speech without preparation. It's rarely a good idea, even when some high-ranking person asks you to do it. If you are asked to speak about something you do not know about, decline—politely but firmly. You might say, "I appreciate your interest in my views, but I just don't know enough about this subject to make a contribution. I would value hearing other points of view, of course."

Sometimes you simply can't avoid speaking on the spur of the moment. If you know the subject area but have not prepared to speak, here are some simple techniques you can use to help you through. First, take a moment to organize your thoughts. Consider saying something like "I'll be pleased to speak about this point, but I would like to take a moment to organize my thoughts." No one will be offended by a brief moment of silence while you are planning your remarks, so long as you don't take too long. Make a couple of notes to yourself. Is there a simple sentence that presents your position? Do you have a position? You may discover that you understand the problem but have not thoroughly thought through the solution to the problem. Search until you find your main idea. Do not launch into an impromptu speech without it! Organize around a simple, redundant pattern of ideas. Trust your knowledge to fill out the details. Start by telling listeners what you're going to tell them. Develop your ideas, then summarize. Recall the simple one-two-three-four introduction (Chapter 15) and use it. End with a summary and a "kicker."

Extemporaneous Speaking

The word *extemporaneous* refers to a planned speaking style that does not necessitate committing the word-for-word progression of ideas to memory but which does require the speakers to plan ideas and supporting materials carefully. An extemporaneous speaker is not concerned with the precise language of the speech. Ideas are paramount. Exhibit 16.4 suggests five pointers on using notes.

A speaker using the extemporaneous method has most of the advantages of memorized speaking and manuscript speaking, with none of the disadvantages. The presenter is likely to sound conversational and direct, and remains free to play off the audience.

Practice the Presentation

Every skill improves with practice. Thus, if you want your presentation to flow smoothly and successfully, you must practice. Begin practicing just as soon as you begin thinking about the presentation. Talk through the main ideas, and practice with the visual materials.

Exhibit 16.4   POINTERS ON USING NOTES

1. *The fewer notes, the better,* except for directly quoted materials and statistical information.
2. *Use stiff (not flimsy) paper.* No one is impressed when a presenter rattles a sheet of typing paper full of notes in front of an audience. Some presenters prefer to place a speaking outline inside a file folder.
3. *Design notes for quick information retrieval* A word or two for each idea would be much easier to use than a full sentence or paragraph.
4. *Use meta-notes as well as substantive notes.* Meta-notes are notes about the notes—for example, to cue your use of a transparency or to mention the exact location of materials you're planning to quote from a text. (See Exhibit 16.5)
5. *Use visual materials as notes.*

Talk Through the Main Ideas

The most valuable kind of practice occurs when you are formulating your ideas and supporting materials. When you say something aloud you hear the voice and you get some idea of the logic of the argument. From the first point in your planning up until the moment you are introduced, it pays to talk through the main ideas. This does not mean committing the ideas to memory. Rather, it suggests that you should speak the ideas out loud, in as many forms as you can, until you have the ideas, but not necessarily a particular sequence of words, in your head.

Practice with a Manuscript

If you determine to develop and use a manuscript, read the manuscript aloud many times before the actual presentation. You must be familiar with the pronunciation and meaning of every word if you are to sound convincing. Try to *sound* spontaneous. You do not want your delivery to call attention to itself. Tape yourself; if you discover a problem, go back and talk through the manuscript again.

Especially with manuscript speaking, presenters sometimes have difficulty working with visual materials. As you practice, actually touch and use every property and switch, and every visual aid. Place meta-notes in the margins of your manuscript to help you remember your plan (see Exhibit 16.5).

An engineer reported her failure to plan in this way. She was invited to New York to present her plant's restructuring plan to the CEO and his top-rank officers. She was naturally worried and felt nervous; she wanted to do a good job, and the presentation was an opportunity for her to advance her career. She wrote out every word, read through the manuscript often, and went to the meeting. About halfway through the presentation she realized she had forgotten to use her carefully prepared visual aids! "I was so embarrassed," she said, "I wanted to climb under the lectern and hide." Happily for her, the CEO and his executive group were in a mood to be generous. The CEO asked her to review

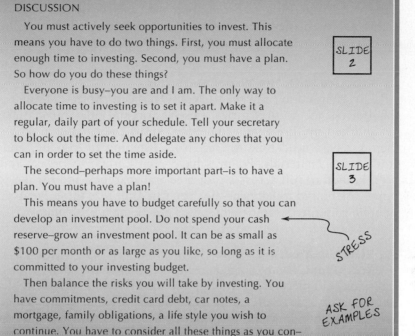

Exhibit 16.5
SAMPLE
MANUSCRIPT
WITH
META-NOTES

the transparencies, then complete the speech. As it ultimately came out, she never did go back to the manuscript. She used her visual aids package as notes, and because she was so well-prepared, she delivered the rest of the presentation extemporaneously. Don't miss the important points of this engineer's story: (1) She needed to touch every switch, and she needed to practice with her visual materials; (2) she chose manuscript delivery for the wrong reason (she wanted a crutch), and as it worked out, she didn't even need the crutch.

Practice Memorized Delivery

Speakers giving memorized presentations are often fearful they will forget what comes next. Moreover, the presentations of these speakers often *sound* memorized. If you must give a presentation from memory, about the only thing you can do is practice, practice, and then practice some more, until you are absolutely sure you will not lose your way. A well-designed visual aids package can help you stay on track, as we have already suggested.

Practice Extemporaneous Delivery

Extemporaneous delivery is planned, but the speaker has minimal notes. The secret of this kind of delivery is to prepare so carefully that one or two words on a note card for each point are all you will need in order to follow your plan. Practice with the notes each time you go over the ideas and arguments. Take advantage of the freedom notes give you to interact with the listeners. A glance at well-made notes—cards, a file folder, or an overhead slide—should be all you need.

Practice with the Visual Materials

Flip charts don't flip themselves. Overhead projectors don't aim and focus themselves, nor do they turn themselves on and off. Transparencies sometimes get shuffled up. Presenters sometimes know their material so well they forget their listeners need time to shift from listening to looking, and then time to study visual materials. Pointers have been known to break, and pencils have been known to roll across a projected transparency and off the projector. Such things are bound to happen—but you can minimize these events if you practice. Exhibit 16.6 offers some pointers for practicing a presentation.

Visit the Meeting Room

You cannot assume someone else has checked and double-checked the physical space. Go there; walk through the speech if you are able to do so. Try every switch, every piece of equipment. Where are the chairs in relation to the speaker's stand? If it is a long, narrow room, consider using a public address system, maybe with a cordless microphone so you can move about a little.

When you arrive, identify and locate the individual who can help with problems you might discover. Tell the person you are planning to do a walk-through and you will come back in time for any needed corrections to be made. Ask where the person can be found if you have any questions—or, better yet,

---

Exhibit 16.6   POINTERS FOR PRACTICING A PRESENTATION

1. Keep practice sessions brief and flexible. Go over the speech two or three times during early practice sessions. Try not to memorize any part of the speech. Experiment with notes and with the way you have organized your ideas. This is the best time to make any changes you might desire.

2. Practice in different settings and contexts. Practice while driving to work. Practice while taking a shower. Practice for your dog. Try to present the ideas, at least, to one or more close friends. Borrow the company video camera and practice before it. This will give you an idea of changes you might wish to make.

3. Practice with visual aids and mechanical equipment.

4. Practice until you are comfortable with your ideas and language and with the organization and structure of all the parts of the presentation. Then, when you are comfortable, stop practicing. This should occur a day or two before the presentation is to be delivered. The time provides you a little "distance" from the presentation, a chance to "unwind," and an opportunity to make any little last-minute changes.

take the person with you as you check the physical setup. Do you like the location of the overhead projector? Do you feel comfortable with the height of the microphone? Do you feel restricted by the lectern? Does the aisle between the speaker's stand and the first row feel like a gulf between you and the listeners? What should you do about these problems, if anything?

Behave Appropriately While Waiting to Speak

Should you get there early? Just on time? And what should you do when you get there?

Speakers must always manage the impression they leave with listeners. Thus it makes sense to think in terms of that impression as a means of determining what to do while you are waiting to speak. Try to arrive about ten minutes before the event is to begin. (Skip the cocktails.) Remember, people begin forming their impression of you as soon as they see you. Sometimes the host will want to make a few hurried introductions, or give you some last-minute instructions, or ask last-minute questions about you or your topic. It pays, therefore, to make yourself available early (but not *too* early).

If you will speak after a luncheon or dinner, then during the meal you should eat. Chat with the individuals near you. Be pleasant. *Do not work on your presentation during the meal.* During the introductions and other speeches after the meal, look at and listen to the speaker. Participate as you want your audience to participate with you. To do otherwise calls attention to yourself and leaves an unflattering impression.

. . . . **WHAT TO DO DURING THE PRESENTATION**

When You Are Introduced

When you are introduced, take the stage. Rise quietly, but with confidence. Walk to the lectern confidently, even if you don't feel confident. Don't shuffle papers or fiddle with the microphone. The audience wants to feel that you are confident and credible, that you know what you are talking about and you wish to communicate with them. Respond to the introduction quickly and politely, but not at length. Unless you have built a response into the speech, resist the temptation to elaborate on what the introducer has said. Merely say something like, "Thank you, Bob, for that generous introduction." Pause a moment to let your audience shift into a listening mode, then begin. "Good evening, ladies and gentlemen . . . ."

During the Delivery

Not surprisingly, the part of presentational speaking people fear most is actually standing before the audience and talking. Indeed, the number one fear in the United States is giving a speech. A few easy-to-follow pointers might help (see Exhibit 16.7), but we're aware there exists a risk in making suggestions. Prescriptions about voice and articulation, for example, or about standing still, moving around, gesturing, and so forth tend to assume each speaker is like every other.

Obviously, you are unique. When you speak, try to be yourself; let your own personality show. Do not pretend to be someone else or to hide what you are feeling. Let them see and know you as you really are. Beyond that, the advice we offer here may or may not apply to your situation. Nevertheless we offer five suggestions: (1) Speak up and slow down. (2) Stand still, or move for a reason. (3) Keep the microphone out of your mouth. (4) Stand beside, not in front of, your visual aids. (5) Resist fidgeting.

Speak up and slow down.   Unless a public address system is available, the listeners will depend upon you to make yourself heard. The larger the audience the greater the floor noise it generates. There are only two ways to overcome that noise. You must speak up, and you must slow down. Be sure the target listeners can hear you, and be sure they cannot misunderstand you.

Stand still, or move for a reason.   Presenters sometimes get so involved in what they are saying and how they are feeling that they begin to pace aimlessly back and forth. The audience always notices aimless and purposeless movement, which signals that the speaker is uncomfortable. Stand still, or move for a reason. Standing still may feel awkward to you, but it will look natural to the listeners. If you move, let your movement work for you. For example, if you wish to emphasize a point, move. If you wish to provide a transitional cue, move. If you want to create a special effect, move. But unless you have some reason for moving, stand still.

Keep the microphone out of your mouth.   A formal speaking situation often includes a microphone and public address system. Presenters unaccustomed to using a microphone often stoop over, get their mouths too close to the equipment, and blur the speech sounds together in the process. A microphone is a sensitive instrument. It will pick up what you are saying, so long as you stay within its range. If you can, check out the microphone ahead of time. Find out how far away you can go from it and then, during the presentation, just ignore it.

Stand beside, not in front of, your visual aids.   You may have seen presenters who turn their backs on an audience, write on the flip chart, and actually stand between their audiences and what they were writing. This behavior leaves a poor impression and says that the speaker is ill-prepared and not very skillful.

To avoid giving this kind of impression, have your visual materials prepared in advance. Stand beside each visual while you refer to it, then put it out of sight when you're not using it. If you are using an overhead projector, point to items on the transparency by placing a sharpened pencil on the slide that casts a shadow on the screen. *Do not* point at the transparency with a finger. *Do not* hold the pencil like a fencing foil, thrusting at the overhead transparency—this produces a distracting, rapidly moving shadow on the screen.

Resist fidgeting. Some behaviors—such as arranging articles of clothing, scratching, plucking at lint, brushing dandruff from your shoulders, and so on—you would never do consciously unless you were alone and in private. Curiously, some speakers do these things while they are making a presentation. Resist. Such behavior leaves an impression with the listeners that the speaker is weak and insecure.

HOW TO FOLLOW THROUGH AFTER THE PRESENTATION

Some presenters seem to think a speech is over when they utter their last sentence. However, just as the presentation actually begins when the listeners first take you into account, it does not end until the listeners move their attention away from you and onto someone or something else. Thus it makes sense to learn a few exit techniques.

Exit for Effect

That awkward pause after the last sentence, while the speaker fumbles for something to do, can be an uncomfortable moment for the listeners. They want a presentation to end with a sense of finality and direction. Following your summary and a kicker, pause. Stand quietly for a moment, then say "Thank you" and quietly sit down. If you have to move from the speaker's stand to your chair, do that with dispatch, confidently and without casual eye contact with audience members. The listeners need this time for their own purposes. They will applaud. At the same time, they will begin a flurry of evaluative comments

---

Exhibit 16.7   POINTERS ABOUT DELIVERING A PRESENTATION

1. Try to sound spontaneous.
2. Select a style of delivery to fit your needs and the listeners' needs.
3. Do not speak impromptu if you can avoid it.
4. Plan and design your notes carefully.
5. Plan and design visual materials carefully.
6. Consider your body and style of dress each to be a type of visual aid.
7. Secure and practice with equipment and props.
8. Check the physical space in which a presentation is to be delivered.
9. Consider the impression you are leaving with listeners from the first moment to the last.
10. Speak up, speak at an appropriate rate, and speak distinctly.
11. Stand still, or move for a reason.
12. Do not fidget.
13. Plan your exit.
14. Follow up after the presentation.

to each other about your speech and about you. Thus they naturally direct their attention away from you and onto each other for a brief moment. You can tell all this is happening because you can see and hear it. If it is convenient to do, and if circumstances allow it, exit during that flurry.

Say Thanks to Well-Wishers

We do not recommend hanging around the lectern or head table waiting for people in the audience to come up to congratulate you on your speech. However, people frequently do want to shake hands and talk to a speaker. You can and should keep yourself available for this activity by slowly but deliberately moving into the transition from one activity to the next. For example, in most cases the host or hostess will wish to shake your hand. Thank the individual and begin to move rather slowly with him or her toward the exit, if that is where you are going. Thus, if no one walks up to you, you are not left standing. If someone does walk up to you, pause to acknowledge the well-wishers. Often, following a business report, one presenter sits and another begins to speak. In this case you may have no chance to visit with well-wishers. Don't worry about it. You can reestablish contact with key people during the follow-up.

Do Appropriate Follow-up

You had a clear goal in mind when you planned and presented your ideas. You knew the specific action you wanted from the target audience. The task of accomplishing that goal does not end when you end your presentation. Follow-up is needed.

Follow-up seeks to collect information you can use next time you make a presentation. It also can be used to provide input to the people who asked you to make the presentation in the first place. Plan a way to determine if you got your ideas across to your key listeners, and how well your presentation was received. You may wish to consider a written evaluation form, especially if your presentation was a training program. Be sure you plan the questionnaire before you give the presentation. If you take this approach, it might be wise to ask someone else to administer the instrument for you. So far as possible, be sure your questionnaire does not lead the respondents into saying what you want them to say! Exhibit 16.8 illustrates an actual questionnaire used as follow-up to a two-hour training presentation. You can adapt it to almost any application, of course.

Making yourself available after the presentation to talk with people from the audience is another way to follow up, but it is not as reliable as a questionnaire. Another way to follow up is to observe the target listeners. Did they do what you asked them to do? For example, if your goal was to persuade the target subgroup to fund a proposal, and they fund it, then you know you succeeded.

If you promised to get back to an audience member—one who asked a question you couldn't answer, for example—do it, and do it soon. Your credibility is at stake with the individual and perhaps with people she knows.

Title: _____ Date: _____ Location: _____

Please answer the following questions by circling your response and providing comments where appropriate.

1. Overall, how would you evaluate this presentation?

    1   2   3   4   5   6   7   8   9   10

  Not   Somewhat   Valuable   Very

valuable at all   valuable   valuable

2. Overall, how effective was this session at building your skills in:

   A. Preparing for a presentation:

    1   2   3   4   5   6   7   8   9   10

  Not   Somewhat   Effective   Very

effective at all   effective   effective

   B. Organizing a presentation:

    1   2   3   4   5   6   7   8   9   10

  Not   Somewhat   Effective   Very

effective at all   effective   effective

   C. Developing visual aids:

    1   2   3   4   5   6   7   8   9   10

  Not   Somewhat   Effective   Very

effective at all   effective   effective

   D. Delivering a presentation:

    1   2   3   4   5   6   7   8   9   10

  Not   Somewhat   Effective   Very

effective at all   effective   effective

3. How appropriate was the length of the program?

    1   2   3   4   5   6   7   8   9   10

  Too short   Just right   Too long

4. How effective was the pacing of the program?

    1   2   3   4   5   6   7   8   9   10

  Too slow   Just right   Too fast

5. How well did the program keep your interest?

    1   2   3   4   5   6   7   8   9   10

  Little or no   Some   Interested   Very

  interest   interest   interested

6. How useful was the information presented?

    1   2   3   4   5   6   7   8   9   10

  Not useful   Somewhat   Useful   Very

  at all   useful   useful

7. What specifically did you like about the program?

_____

_____

_____

8. What would make this a better program?

_____

_____

_____

9. What suggestions, if any, would you make to help the presenter improve performance?

_____

_____

_____

**Exhibit 16.8
SAMPLE
FOLLOW-UP
EVALUATION
FORM**

A week or two following the presentation—or sooner if circumstances suggest—remind the target audience of your key idea. A phone call or a follow-up memo that reminds the receivers of your presentation will often nudge them into doing what you request.

To illustrate, consider this report from a restaurant designer, which highlights the importance of follow-up. The letter was written before computer-assisted design was available to restaurant designers, but the idea and the motivation behind it are as valuable now as then.

> I will never forget the first time I attended a sales meeting. A very skillful fellow who represented a refrigerator company made a sales presentation to the people at the restaurant design firm. By the end of his presentation I was convinced there were many advantages to specifying his brand of refrigerators, even though they were a bit higher priced than the competition. I was convinced about their quality and space-saving features. I was convinced they looked good and would complement any installation.

> What the salesperson wanted me to do was specify his equipment in my layouts. About a week after the presentation I got a letter from him. It said something like: "I was happy to meet you. Your work is attractive. Your designs are skillful. You are a nice person." In other words, the letter confirmed me. In the process, it also confirmed the salesman in my mind. More important to the point, though, he included a plastic template in his letter. I could quickly draw his equipment into my designs on a one-quarter-inch scale by tracing that template. It saved me something like ten minutes of drawing time, and who knows how much research time, whenever one of my layouts called for a refrigerator. All I had to do was grab that template. I could draw his refrigerators perfectly, every time—and the model number for each model was embossed on the template. You bet I started using a lot of his refrigerators in my designs.

Only your imagination limits *how* you follow through. A letter with a template worked well for one salesman. A phone call might work as well for you, or an email message. Follow up to provide your target audience as much help as you can to do what you have asked them to do.

SUMMARY . . . .

A time line for delivering a formal presentation suggests what a presenter must do before, during, and after the speaking event. Before the presentation you must choose among manuscript, memorization, impromptu, and extemporaneous delivery styles. Each of these styles carries both advantages and disadvantages, but the best advice for business and professional speaking is to use the extemporaneous style.

Practice makes a difference to a speaker's success no matter what delivery style is chosen. We recommend talking through the main ideas many times, beginning from the first moment a presentation is being planned. The practice should include, also, deliberate use and manipulation of every visual aid, every piece of equipment and every property to be used in the presentation.

Presenters should visit the meeting room prior to a speech in order to gain comfort about seating arrangements, the public address system (if present), and other considerations. While waiting to make the presentation, speakers should keep in mind what impression they wish to give their target listeners. This advice guides such things as when to arrive, whether to take a cocktail, how to "take the stage," and such matters of delivery as speaking distinctly, loudly, and slowly enough so that everyone can hear. A speaker should stand still, or move for a reason; stand beside, not in front of, visual materials; and stay an appropriate distance from the microphone.

An exit may be as important as an entrance on the effect a speech has with target listeners. Speakers should think about how to exit a presentation and how to follow through after the presentation has been delivered.

RECOMMENDED READINGS ....

Every basic public speaking text offers advice about delivery skills. Some include materials on voice and diction, how to stand, gestures, and the like. Others teach appropriate uses of overhead projectors, flip charts, the chalk board, and other aids. See, for example:

George L. Grice and John F. Skinner. *Mastering Public Speaking,* 2d ed. Boston, Allyn and Bacon, 1995.

Michael S. Hanna and James W. Gibson. *Public Speaking for Personal Success,* 4th ed. Dubuque, Iowa, Brown & Benchmark, 1995.

Clella Jaffee. *Public Speaking: A Cultural Perspective.* Belmont, Calif., Wadsworth, 1995.

John J. Makay, *Public Speaking: Theory into Practice,* 2d ed. Fort Worth, Harcourt Brace, 1995.

DISCUSSION QUESTIONS ....

1. Working with a group of classmates, see if you can name ten prominent public speakers, living or dead. Who is or was the most effective? What method of delivery did the person use, and why do you think he or she used it? What are or were the speaker's speaking strengths and weaknesses? Present your group's thinking to the class.
2. With one or two classmates, discuss what speaking behaviors you remember most clearly about your favorite high school teacher. Did the behaviors add or detract from the teacher's presentation style? Were the behaviors verbal or nonverbal? Why do you remember them so well? What learning can you draw for your own presentational speaking?
3. Examine the opening moments of your favorite television program. Analyze *how* the program opens and why the program director opens it that way. What impression does the opening give? Bring your notes to a classroom discussion.

INTERNET ACTIVITIES ....

1. Enter the Lycos search engine (http://www.lycos.com/) and type "delivering a presentation." You'll get nearly 12,000 "hits." What three hits on the first two pages seemed most helpful to you? Why?
2. Open Minnesota Western's Web site (http://minnwest.com/aboutminnwest.html). Click on the hot link *help you make educated and informed presentation decisions.* Enjoy. Come to class prepared to discuss in detail what you found.

EPILOGUE

Together we have come a long way from the first few pages of this book. Right now we are thinking that we have given you so much advice and so many suggestions that you may be feeling somewhat overloaded. It is one thing for us to say, "Communicate more effectively—here is how." It is quite another for you to take the suggestions that are pertinent to your own life and incorporate them into your own behavior. We can tell you what constitutes effective communication, but we cannot cause you to communicate more effectively. You have to do that for yourself.

But you *can* do it! You can choose to behave in any way you wish. You can determine that whatever your past has been—and you cannot change that—starting now, you will behave differently.

For a number of years it was common to see displayed on walls of offices and classrooms and sometimes in people's homes a poster that read "Today is the first day of the rest of your life." The poster was popular because the idea was, and still is, potent. When you take that first step away from the place you are right now, you are taking the first step into your own future. Where you walk is up to you.

We hope you enjoy your future as much as we have enjoyed working with you.

TROUBLESHOOTING THE ORGANIZATION

Most professionals we know keep a library of reference works to help them resolve the problems they encounter in the world of work. Sooner or later they encounter communication problems. We want this book to be helpful as a tool for working with the common communication problems that occur in all complex organizations.

Many texts written for the college classroom do not lend themselves well to use as a reference for solutions to problems. For example, a typical index—like the one at the end of this book—presents a fairly thorough list of key words. But that kind of index is not a very helpful problem-solving reference because it is not problem-specific. Thus you have to sort through many sections of a book to find answers to specific questions. Our solution was to develop this troubleshooting guide.

The guide poses more than one hundred of the most common questions people in organizations ask about communication problems. We have indexed these problems in a way that refers you to the locations in the book where solutions are suggested.

HOW TO USE THIS PROBLEM-SOLVING INDEX ....

1. Verbalize the problem you are experiencing.
2. Look for key words that describe the nature of the problem. Key words are listed alphabetically in the directory that follows.
3. Locate these key words in the problem-solution index.
4. Find a question close to the one you are asking, and turn to the indicated sections for the answer.
5. If the key words are not listed here, consult the index in the back of the book.

DIRECTORY

Problem Category and Question(s)	Location of Solution
A	
Argument	
What can I do to hone my argumentation skill?	384–392
Attending	
I find that even though I hear and remember what the boss has said, I have not gotten it straight. What might be the problem?	98–105, 108–113
What can I do to help my employees (or boss) be more accurate in perceiving what I say?	189–194
B	
No entries	
C	
Climate	
Employees seem to dread our performance appraisal interviews. Why?	216–221, 244–249
There seems to be quite a lot of tension lately. Why might this be the case?	37–41, 189–201
When I talk to the boss, I feel tense. What might be wrong? What can I do?	189–194, 212–229
When I get into an argument, it seems to escalate.	205–214
Cohesiveness	
Many of our meetings are not very productive. Is there anything I can do?	246–252, 318–331
I've noticed that some groups seem to be too social—they never get much done. Why is this the case? What can be done about the problem?	322–331
The members of my group do not seem to enjoy one another; the group does not pull together. What is wrong? What can I do?	322–331
Communication channels	
I worry about the grapevine. Should I? Since I cannot stop its use, how can I make it work for me?	36–37
Communication does not seem to flow as the organizational chart says it ought to flow. What is wrong?	30–37
I often puzzle about what is the best method for transmitting messages and to whom they ought to go. What do I need to consider to help me decide?	31–37

Problem Category and Question(s)	Location of Solution
Communication perspective	
How can I treat a problem from a communication perspective?	4–6
Competence	
The boss complains that I do not do things the way I should. (This means the way he wants me to do them.) What are some possible sources of this problem?	98–102, 189–194
I am not getting promoted and others are. What might be the problem?	105–106, 129–139, 145–146, 205–214, 216–221
What are some questions I can ask to evaluate a presenter?	384
Conference planning	
I must plan a conference. What do I do first? Next?	354–355, 358–367
Conflict	
My group has a member who picks fights. Is there something I can do?	221–229
My group has a member who is always challenging other people's ideas. Can I put a stop to this? Should I put a stop to it?	51–54, 320–321, 330–331
I have to work on a committee with a person who does not get along with others. How can I handle this situation?	216–221, 194–199
There seems to be quite a lot of tension lately. Why might this be the case?	37–41, 212–229
When I get into an argument, it seems to escalate.	205–216
I've just goofed. If I tell the boss, he'll be mad. If I don't tell the boss, the company will lose money. How can I manage this kind of conflict?	189–194, 212–229
I'd like a raise, but I'm afraid to ask for one. What can I do?	189–194
Joan and Pete are having trouble getting along. What do I do?	189–205, 212–229, 326–330
Competition is destroying my work group. I think it will soon become open warfare. What could I do?	212–229, 322–331
I need to manage this conflict successfully. Should I force a decision or should I confront these people and do problem solving?	221–229
Some groups I have known about seem to fight all the time. Others seem not to fight at all. Is there some way of knowing what is healthy for a group?	313–316, 326–331

Problem Category and Question(s)	Location of Solution
Coordinating information	
I am sometimes surprised when my boss wants to be kept informed about my efforts on the XYZ Interdepartmental Committee. Why would she care?	25–31, 39, 41–43
Why all this fuss about coordinating with other units? This stuff doesn't really concern them.	25–31, 39, 41–43
Coworker communication	
I often want reasonable things from my coworkers but they do not comply.	189–194
Credibility	
I am not sure that others will believe me. What can I do?	129–146, 379–380
I'm not getting promoted and others are. What might be the problem?	105–106, 129–139, 145–146, 189–194, 205–216
Culture	
I am joining a new organization. What do I need to look at to gain a sense of how they do things there?	13–16, 275–276, 318–321
I am going to be doing some job interviewing. How can I assess the cultural expectations of organizations for these interviews?	262–263, 275–276

D

Decision making	
We need to have a meeting to decide _____. What is important to remember about decision-making meetings?	337–346
Diversity	
I want more background on issues of diversity. Where can I find it?	72–80, 85–89
Might I somehow be reflecting biases in my communication? Are there standards I should know?	80–85
Can you give me some hints about how to better deal with issues of diversity at work?	89–92
Dress	
I'm going to start work at XYZ, and I want to know how I should dress.	145–146
I'm going to have an employment interview and want to know how to dress.	145–146, 299

Problem Category and Question(s)	Location of Solution
E	
Employee development	
I have an employee who has a poor self-concept. What can I do to help?	60–65
Ethics	
I've been assigned to a committee charged with developing a code of ethics.	16–19
What is ethical communication:	
In interpersonal situations?	16–19
In group situations?	16–19
In public speaking situations?	16–19
There is a lot of game playing where I work. Is it ethical?	16–19
Evidence	
I have an important presentation that relies on persuading people to adopt my view. What do I need to know about evidence?	384–392
How can I be more thorough in documenting my reports?	384–392
Expressing feelings	
I find it difficult to let the other person know how I'm feeling.	192–193
Expressing wants and needs	
I often want reasonable things from my coworkers, but they do not comply.	36–37, 189–194
I find it difficult to talk about my wants and needs.	189–194
F	
No entries	
G	
Giving instructions	
People do not seem to do what I ask them to do. Why? What can I do?	109–117, 395–402, 406–409
Goals	
There seems to be quite a lot of tension lately. Why might this be the case?	37–41, 313–316, 328–330
Grapevine	
I worry about the grapevine. Should I? Since I can't stop its use, how can I make it work for me?	36–37

Problem Category and Question(s)	Location of Solution
Group failure	
When I'm in charge of a group, I want to be sure it is successful. What are some of the common reasons that groups fail?	311–319, 320–321, 335–336
Group formation	
I have noticed that I'm nervous when I have to participate in a group. Why is this? Am I normal?	313–316, 328–330
I have just been given my first big promotion and have been asked to head up a special project group. Are there any special considerations I should give to group size?	308–311
Group leadership	
I must lead a group. What do I need to consider in my planning?	335–354
Group participation	
I have to work on a committee with a person who does not get along with other people. How can I handle this situation?	216–229
The members of my group do not seem to enjoy one another; the group does not pull together. What's wrong? What can I do?	322–331
Group productivity	
Many of our meetings are not very productive. Is there anything I can do?	318–331, 335–354
Group size	
I have just been given my first big promotion and have been asked to head up a special project group. Are there any special considerations I should give to group size?	308–311
H	
Hearing	
I have a hearing problem. I know that I cannot hear as well as other folks. What can I do to compensate?	108, 190–111, 113–115
I	
Ideational conflict	
My group has a member who is always challenging other people's ideas. Can I put a stop to this? Should I put a stop to it?	51–54, 320–321
Impression management	
I am going to start work at XYZ, and I want to make a good impression on my boss. What can I do?	105–106

Problem Category and Question(s)	Location of Solution
Inference problems	
When I am straightforward about the facts of a situation, the other person does not seem to understand these facts. We argue a lot.	113–118, 189–194, 216–219
Interpersonal conflict	
John and Pete are having trouble getting along. What do I do?	194–199, 221–229
Competition is destroying my work group. I think it will soon become open warfare. What could I do?	221–229, 322–331
I need to manage this conflict successfully. Should I force a decision or should I confront these people and do problem solving?	221–229, 322–331
Interviewing: Appraisal	
I am always nervous about my performance during an appraisal. How can I prepare for my performance appraisal interview?	252, 255–256
Employees seem to dread our performance appraisal interviews. Why?	244–247
I want to come up with some alternatives to our current appraisal interview system. What are some alternatives?	246–254
I must conduct performance appraisal interviews. What do I need to do to prepare?	246–254
Interviewing: Selection	
I need to prepare for questions I might be asked in a selection interview. What are some typical questions?	264–268, 286–289
What are the important considerations with respect to the *form* of my résumé?	276–283
I have been asked illegal questions in an employment interview. How can I answer these questions?	264, 267–268, 296–299
I'm concerned about hiring the best people. I know that the interviewer may bias the selection process. What are some biases to watch out for in the interview?	102–106, 291–292
How do I prepare an effective cover letter?	277–278
I'm concerned about what I might be asked in an employment interview. What are some typical questions?	264–268, 286–289
I must do employment interviewing for my company. What do I need to do to prepare?	261–270

Problem Category and Question(s)	Location of Solution
What are my options (strategies) for answering illegal employment interview questions?	264, 267–268, 296–299
What are some productive sources of job announcements?	284–285
I am going to have an employment interview and want to know how to dress.	145–146, 169–170, 299
How do I prepare a résumé? What can I leave out? What should I include?	276–283

J
No entries

K
No entries

L
Language use

I often want reasonable things from my coworkers but they do not comply.	36–37, 189–194
When I am straightforward about the facts of a situation, the other person does not seem to understand these facts. We argue a lot.	113–118, 189–194
I find it difficult to talk about my wants and needs.	189–190
I find it difficult to let the other person know how I am feeling.	192–193
How can I use language more effectively?	124–129

Leadership

I must plan a conference. What do I do?	354, 355–367
I must lead a group. What do I need to consider in my planning?	337–367
The boss is going on vacation and I will be in charge of the department's monthly meeting. What do I do first? Next?	337–346, 356–357
We need to have a meeting to decide _____. What is important to remember about decision-making meetings?	337–346
Many of our meetings are not very productive. Is there anything I can do?	318–331, 335–354
I've noticed that some groups seem to be too social—they never get much done. Why is this the case? What can be done about the problem?	325–328

Problem Category and Question(s)	Location of Solution
I have a large group meeting to lead. What might I do to keep an orderly flow?	354, 356–357
I have a meeting with some controversial issues. How can I ensure each side gets a fair hearing?	354, 356–357
I have an employee who is disruptive. What's wrong?	37–41, 244–256
I am not getting promoted and others are. What might be the problem?	105–106, 129–139, 145–146, 189–194, 205–216, 221–229
My group has a member who picks fights. Is there something I can do?	221–229
I have to work on a committee with a person who does not get along with other people. How can I handle this situation?	194–216, 216–221
Members of my group do not seem to enjoy one another; the group does not pull together. What is wrong? What can I do?	322–331
Employees seem to dread our performance appraisal interviews. Why?	194–216, 244–247
There seems to be quite a lot of tension lately. Why might this be the case?	37–41, 189–201
I need to develop my ability to use power. What are some of the sources of power I should know about?	216–221
What can I do to help my employees (or boss) be more accurate in perceiving what I say?	98–102, 109–112, 189–194
I often feel powerless. What can I do to get more power?	216–221
How can I assess the power structure in my department?	216–221
Why all this fuss about coordinating with other units? This stuff doesn't really concern them.	25–31, 39, 41–43
I think my boss has leadership problems, but I am not sure what the source of the problems might be. I would like to understand better so I can avoid these difficulties.	37–41, 65–67
Some people seem to want more structure; others seem to want less. What should I do?	57–60
I am anticipating the first meeting of XYZ group next week. I would like to be selected to lead this group. What can I do?	335-346
Competition is destroying my work group. I think it will soon become open warfare. What could I do?	205–216, 322–331

Problem Category and Question(s)	Location of Solution
Listening	
The boss complains that I do not do things the way I should. (This means the way he wants me to do them.) What are some possible sources of this problem?	98–102, 189–194
I have a hearing problem. I know that I cannot hear as well as other folks. What can I do to compensate?	108, 109–111, 113–115
When I attend the Monday-morning meeting, I cannot remember what was said. I often need to recall this information. What might I do?	117–118
M	
Monthly meeting planning	
The boss is going on vacation and I am to be in charge of the department's monthly meeting. What do I do first? Next?	335–346
N	
Networks: Communication	
I often puzzle about what is the best method for transmitting messages and to whom they ought to go. What do I need to consider to help me decide?	31–37
I am sometimes surprised when my boss wants to be kept informed about my efforts on the XYZ Interdepartmental Committee. Why would she care?	25–31
Networks: Formal	
Communication does not seem to flow as the organizational chart says it ought to flow. What is wrong?	31–37
Networks: Informal	
I worry about the grapevine. Should I? Since I cannot stop its use, how can I make it work for me?	36–37
Nonverbal communication	
I am going to start work at XYZ, and I want to know how I should dress.	145–146
I am going to move into a new office. How should I manage space?	129–139
I am anticipating the first meeting of XYZ group next week. I would like to be selected to lead this group. What can I do?	205–216, 322–331
I'm considering colors for my office. What do we know about how colors might affect communication?	130–132

Problem Category and Question(s)	Location of Solution
George lost me in the first few sentences. When I make my presentation, I would like to do much better. What are some good ways of beginning?	402, 404
I want my speech before the XYZ Club to be remembered. How can I use a conclusion to help the audience to remember?	404
Last time I gave a speech, the audience could not follow me. How can I avoid this problem?	395–404
So I have a speech to make. What should be my goal? How do I know what I want from my audience?	374–380
When I get up to present my report, how will I hold people's attention? What can I do?	391–392, 405–409, 415–417, 419–421
Writing the presentational speech is easy for me. I really feel anxious about presenting it. What can I do to ensure success?	373–424
I have never done much with visuals when I talk to a group. I know I should use them, but I do not know how. What are some suggestions?	405–409

Primary tension in groups

I have noticed that I am nervous when I have to participate in a group. Why is this? Am I normal?	313–316

Q
No entries

R
Relationship problems

I have to work on a committee with a person who does not get along with others. How can I handle this situation?	216–229
When I talk to the boss, I feel tense. What might be wrong? What can I do?	194–199, 212–229
I would like to develop closer relationships with a few of my coworkers. How do I start?	113–114, 194–199

Remembering

When I attend the Monday-morning meeting, I cannot remember what was said. I often need to recall this information. What might I do?	117–118

Roles in groups

My group is having problems completing the tasks. Might this be a role problem? What are some of the essential roles?	320–331

Problem Category and Question(s)	Location of Solution
S	
Secondary tension in groups	
Some groups seem to fight all the time. Others seem not to fight at all. Is there some way of knowing what is healthy for a group?	326–331
Self-concept	
I have an employee who has a poor self-concept. What can I do to help?	60–65
Self-confidence	
I am not getting promoted and others are. What might be the problem?	105–106, 129–139, 145–146, 189–194, 221–229
Social dimension	
I have noticed that some groups seem to be too social—they never get much done. Why is this the case? What can be done about the problem?	322–326
My group has a member who picks fights. Is there something I can do?	205–216
Space management	
I am going to move into a new office. How should I manage space?	129–139
Superior-subordinate communication	
People do not seem to do what I ask them to do. Why? What can I do?	109–117, 395–402, 406–409
I have an employee who has a poor self-concept. What can I do to help?	60–65
The boss complains that I do not do things the way I should. (This means the way he wants me to do them.) What are some possible sources of this problem?	100–102, 189–194
When I talk to the boss, I feel tense. What might be wrong? What can I do?	212–229
Systems analysis	
I am sometimes surprised when my boss wants to be kept informed about my efforts on the XYZ Interdepartmental Committee. Why would she care?	25–31
Why all this fuss about coordinating with other units? This stuff does not really concern them.	25–31

Problem Category and Question(s)	Location of Solution

T
Task, social dimensions

My group is having problems completing the task. Might this be a role problem? What are some of the essential roles?	320–331
Many of our meetings are not very productive. Is there anything I can do?	318–370, 335–354

Technology

I've gotten the impression that machines are a way of life in most organizations. What communication problems does that create?	171–173
I'm anticipating an opportunity to recommend upgrading electronic technology where I work. What should I know to guide my thinking?	152–157
I'm wondering if electronic technology can increase my personal productivity at work. What is available to help?	165–167
I sometimes have trouble navigating through the Internet. What do I need to know?	167–169
How can I most effectively use networked electronic technologies?	159–165

Tension level

The group I am in is often very tense. What can I do to reduce tension?	313–316, 328–330, 335–354
I have noticed that I am nervous when I have to participate in a group. Why is this? Am I normal?	313–316, 328–330

Time

How can I manage time better?	105–106, 139, 335–336

Topic analysis

I have to go to a meeting and talk about our department. How will I know what to say?	375–384

U
Understanding

The boss complains that I do not do things the way I should. (This means the way he wants me to do them.) What are some possible sources of this problem?	98–102, 189–194

Problem Category and Question(s)	Location of Solution
V *Visuals*	
I have never done much with visuals when I talk to a group. I know I should use them, but I do not know how. What are some suggestions?	405–409
X, Y, Z *No entries*	

APPENDIX: WRITING IN BUSINESS AND PROFESSIONAL SETTINGS

Good writing, like all other communication, gets the effect you want. Indeed, some say the only true measure of good writing is the effect it produces in the targeted reader. We believe the relationship that exists between reader and writer should control nearly all the decisions you make about what and how you write. What follows is a checklist that lists and describes the basic principles of good writing in business and professional settings.

I. I HAVE IDENTIFIED AND WRITTEN TO A SPECIFIC READER OR A SPECIFIC GROUP OF READERS. ....

You should know, and use, a receiver's name and position. You should know and adapt to the target reader's expectations, interests, feelings, images, intentions, and the like. The purpose of your written work is to connect with the target reader's mind. Provide all the information the reader needs in order to give you the decision you want. Check every assumption you make about the reader. (See pages 375–379 for a more detailed discussion of audience analysis.)

II. I HAVE A SINGLE, CLEARLY SPECIFIED PURPOSE IN MIND FOR THIS WRITTEN WORK. ....

Can you write out the specific purpose of your writing (letter, memo, report, etc.) in a single sentence? If not, you are not clear about what you want to accomplish. If so, put it in the introduction to make it easy for the reader to find. In a report, make the specific purpose clear by including a freestanding side heading.

Be sure, also, that every paragraph and every sentence drives toward the specific purpose. Drop anything that is irrelevant to that purpose.

III. I HAVE DOUBLE-CHECKED TO ASSURE THAT I HAVE FOLLOWED EACH OF THESE TEN PRINCIPLES OF CLEAR WRITING.

1. *Use short sentences, on average*.

2. *Write simple rather than complex sentences and structures*.

Each of the following statements can be made simpler, clearer, and more concise. We'll fix one, then you fix the others. Compare your thinking with a classmate's.

    a. Their ~~amazingly uniform~~ commitment to the ~~attitude that the most important part of the overall training effort was the~~ development of leadership skills surprised the members ~~of the selection sub-committee of the board.~~

Analysis:

When you encounter a long introductory clause ending with "that," strike it all.

Consider whether you can begin the sentence with the next word.

Determine what the key subject actually is! In this case it is *their commitment.*

Isolate the prepositional phrases.

Cast the sentence in the active voice—let the subject do the action of the verb.

The revised sentence reads: "Their commitment to the development of leadership skills surprised the members."

b. Prior to the conductance of the exams, trainee-owned materials should be removed from the immediate surroundings by either asking the learners to remove them, or by asking a particular class member or an assistant to assist in this important task.

c. Due to the many choices of development applications available in the market today, it is believed that engineers and programmers should utilize selection techniques that will guarantee the maximum amount of compatibility from computer platform to computer platform, and from user to user.

d. On August 11-12, Industrial Hygiene conducted a noise survey at Jackson Liquid Packaging to assess employee exposures throughout the facility and determine the continued need for sound enclosures at the sealers. Exposures are consistent with respective sound level measures, with the exception of the exposures of 97.9 and 97.6 dBa, respectively, for Mr. Roberto Gutierrez, assistant converter operator.

3. *Use words the reader knows.*

A reader does not usually have the time or inclination to look up words she does not know. Don't use them. Big words and fancy phrases actually weaken your prose. Rather, use simple, often one-syllable words. They make your writing clearer and your ideas easier to understand. Here are some examples; you can think of hundreds more.

Instead of	Try	Instead of	Try
accompany	go with	in lieu of	instead of
accomplish	do	in the near future	soon, Friday
accordingly	so	magnitude	size
advantageous	helpful	methodology	method
approximately	about	operational	working
as a means of	to	optimum	best
ascertain	find out	parameters	limits
attempt	try	personnel	people, workers

benefit	help	prioritize	rank
constitutes	is, makes up	provided that	if
designate	name, appoint	recapitulate	sum up
due to the fact that	because	remuneration	pay, $400
equitable	fair	state-of-the-art	latest
expeditious	quick, fast	terminate	end, stop
feasible	workable	therein	there
finalize	finish, complete	this department	we
impacted	hit, affected	with reference to	about
inasmuch as	since	witnessed	saw

4. Eliminate unnecessary words.

Here is an example taken from a training class. A human relations professional wrote the original; we made the changes. Most of the verbiage was unnecessary, and it weakened the idea.

~~An employee's behavior may be considered~~ appropriate / *behavior formality* ~~if, in every case, he or she establishes his or her credibility as consistently operating within the parameters of both written conduct policies and personal good taste. The degree of appropriateness, however, is~~ depend / *s* ~~ent up~~ on the context in which it / *occurs* ~~is exhibited.~~ A ~~formal~~ performance appraisal review ~~situation, in which the employee and his or her supervisor discuss his or her performance, for~~ / *provides an* example, ~~calls for a more formal behavioral pattern than might be exhibited in the lunchroom.~~

Editorial language such as *very* (~~very~~ *beautiful*) and most words that end with *ly* (~~greatly~~ *exceeded our expectations*) are candidates for elimination on grounds they don't add anything.

Eliminate needless repetition. Notice how much clearer these sentences are with the repetitions eliminated.

Up-to-date, ~~state of the art~~ computers are at every desk.
~~At the present time~~ we are considering three options.
~~As a matter of concern,~~ our committee is worried about adhering to every requirement.
We should plan ~~in advance~~ for a worst-case scenario.
The group's ~~consensus of~~ opinion was that the building should be razed.
~~In my opinion I think~~ the new flow design is too complex.
She didn't come in to work until 8:45 A.M. on Friday ~~morning~~.

5. Write action verbs where possible.

Action verbs do something. Action verbs drive and move the reader along. The problem verbs usually come in forms of *to be. Is, was, were, am, are*—such words show state of being, not action. When you write, let somebody do something.

Passive	Active
The results were reported. . . .	We reported the results. . . .
The decision has been supported by the board.	The board supported the decision.
The production floor will be inspected by Mr. Jackson.	Mr. Jackson will inspect the production floor.
The new safety standards were enforced by the safety committee.	The safety committee enforced the new standards.
A complete reorganization of the spinning floor was requested by the plant manager.	The plant manager requested a complete reorganization of the spinning floor.

Sometimes it's better to write sentences in the passive voice. Passive voice may be better when the action is more important to the reader than who did it. (*It was a landslide victory for the challenger.*) Passive voice is better when you don't know who did the action of the verb. (*The action was taken yesterday.*) When you don't want to name the performer, passive voice is better. (*I'm sorry, Charlie, but a decision was made to let you go.*) And finally, passive voice is much stronger when you state a knowledge claim. (*A is a better choice than B.*)

6. *Write the way you talk.*

For some reason, especially when writing letters and memos, some otherwise well-rounded, healthy individuals try to get fancy. The result is called "Letterese." It never strengthens the letters and memos.

Don't write . . .	If you say . . .
Your letter of the 14th has been received and its content duly noted . . .	I read your July 14 letter.
Thanking you in advance . . .	
Enclosed please find . . .	Here is . . .
I am cognizant of . . .	I understand . . .
In reference to . . .	About . . .
I regret to advise you that . . .	
We beg to remind . . .	Do you remember . . .
Wherein you state . . .	You said . . .
In due course . . .	Soon; Next week on Wednesday . . .
Please be advised . . .	
This is to inform you that . . .	
This will acknowledge . . .	I have your letter . . .
This writer . . .	I . . .

7. *Excite the reader's imagination with specifics.*

Specific details—real names, real numbers, colors—provide a reader the materials with which to create images in the mind. Concreteness (the use of specific language) makes a piece of writing far more interesting. Here are some examples.

Abstract, general language	Concrete, specific language
a significant gain	a 92% gain
a lot of money	$118,750
a labor-saving device	a tractor that does the work of 35 men
a good attendance record	She only missed one day's work in seven years.
a worker	Patrician Klenklen
in due course	within three years

Now, can you improve the following sentence by adding real names, real numbers, and colors?

His new worker argued that in due course the company would realize a significant gain in efficiency by investing a lot of money in a labor-saving device.

The sentence reads more easily and is more interesting when it is rewritten:

His new worker, Patrician Klenklen, argued that, within three years, the company would realize a 92% gain in efficiency by investing $118,750 in a tractor that does the work of 35 men.

8. *Tie what you write to your reader's experiences.*

The idea is to capture the reader's mind; to compel the reader to give you the response you want. The reader won't do it if what you write is not tied to the reader's experiences. To illustrate, engineers often have to write reports requesting money. In the pulp and paper industry the amounts of money they request can seem staggering. One engineer displayed a program proposal in which she asked for over as million dollars. Compare a few of her sentences as she wrote them and after she corrected them. Every one of her corrections was designed to tie her arguments to the readers' experiences. In this case, the proposal was addressed to the mill manager and the cabinet-rank staff.

We need the money for two reasons. First, we cannot accomplish our work on the new schedule without a significant upgrade of our equipment. Second, the Environmental Protection Agency will not allow us to continue to vent [a toxin], and we can't avoid venting it unless we change out our exhaust treatment equipment.

The writer was complaining. Her arguments focused readers' attention on her interests and concerns. We suggested she focus the readers' attention on their interests and concerns. Here's how she revised the argument:

The requested budget will allow [Company Name] to meet two of its most important goals. First, it will fund a significant upgrade in equipment and thus make it possible to meet the newly revised production schedule without having to hire new employees. Second, and equally important, the budget will allow us to change out our exhaust treatment equipment, thus to meet the Environmental Protection Agency directive dated August 27th.

9. *Use variety in sentence length, phrasing, and style.*

When everything begins to seem the same, people lose interest. Boredom sets in because nothing new is presented to capture and hold the readers' attention. This fact argues strongly that you must enrich your writing with variety. Use variety in sentence length and phrasing. Vary the approach. Vary the "look," even, of what you write.

Good writers use seven techniques to secure and hold reader attention.

Strategy	Description	How to do it
Concreteness	See Item #7 above	See Item #7 above
Suspense	Creating a state of mental uncertainty or excitement by withholding the outcome or decision from the reader.	Withhold closure of an idea until the last minute. Tell a story, but withhold the name or the outcome. Present the opposing arguments first, then overcome them with your own. Arrange thoughts in order of ascending power.
Activity	Introducing the concept and feeling of movement through the use of language.	Describe the movement of living people and inanimate objects. Help the readers see what happened or will happen.
Antagonism	Expressing opposition of forces, principles, or tendencies.	Place opposing view in juxtaposition to each other. Show the reader how the forces or principles are opposed, and the likely consequences of the antagonism. Then restore reader equilibrium with your proposal or idea.
Humor	Finding the fun in a situation or event.	Be careful; it is difficult to use humor. The best comes from clever comparison, or a witty turn of phrase, some incongruous application of a quotation. Turn the humor on yourself—never on the reader. Never use humor to diminish anyone.
Reference to experience	Reference to what the reader knows and values.	Refer to the reader's direct experience when giving examples or illustrations. Use local and familiar examples the reader is likely to know, or refer to the reader's vicarious experience. For example, use a movie you know the reader has seen as a way of illustrating your idea. Associate the new with something the reader already knows and values.
Self-interest	Direct or implied suggestion the reader will benefit personally from paying attention.	Write directly to the reader (e.g., *Where will you find a better profit margin?*) Point to the reader's personal world view and value system.

10. *Write to communicate, not to impress the reader.*

Try to become single-minded when you write. Call your specific purpose to mind and write it down. Call your specific target reader or readers to mind and hold them in mind as you write. Communicate *with* them, not at them. And resist the temptation to overwhelm the reader with long, convoluted sentences, arcane language, and the like. Written ideas cannot produce the effect you want if they are not read or understood.

IV. I HAVE ORGANIZED EVERY SECTION OF THIS WORK FOLLOWING THE SIMPLE PRINCIPLE "TELL 'EM WHAT YOU'RE GOING TO TELL 'EM, TELL 'EM, THEN TELL 'EM WHAT YOU TOLD 'EM." ....

Check the abstract.
Check the introduction.
Check the main segments of the body.
Check the conclusion.

V. I HAVE TRIED TO MAKE THE DOCUMENT ATTRACTIVE. ....

Break up the blocks of gray and surround them with white space. Use plenty of indentation, side headings, enumeration, and bullets. The human eye just won't look at a gray block for any length of time. Readers see the first few sentences, then drop to the next paragraph. If you want them to read your ideas, you must accommodate this tendency to skip over gray patches. How? Break up the paragraphs.

It's a mindless rule, but a good one nevertheless, to keep each paragraph to within about three inches—and be sure to make some much shorter. To illustrate the wisdom of this three-inch rule, here is an example found on the desk of a paper mill manager. The original looked exactly like this: all caps, single spaced, one-letter indentation, Courier font. It seems unreadable.

1. DATABASE DESCRIPTION
THE MAXIMUM NUMBER OF DATABASES IS EIGHT. EACH IS DIVIDED INTO SEPARATE FILES. FOR EXAMPLE, IN MANSFIELD IN THE POWER DATABASE THE FILES ARE: PB01, PB02, RB01, RBIN, FWTR, EVAP, PMIN, AND CALC; IN THE PAPER DATABASE THE FILES ARE: MCH1, M1IN, M1MX, MCH2, M2IN, AND M2MX; AND IN THE PULP DATABASE THE FILES ARE: PDIG, WSHR, PDIN, HDIG, CDIG, HDIN, SCHM, CAUS, AND LKIN. THE VALUES OF THE PROCESS VARIABLES FOR A GIVEN AREA (EXCEPT CALC) ARE STORED EVERY FIFTEEN MINUTES (96 FIFTEEN MINUTE RECORDS EVERY DAY FOR EACH PROCESS VARIABLE) IN THE FILE CORRESPONDING TO THAT AREA (EX: PB01 CORRESPONDS TO THE NO. 1 POWER BOILER). THE VALUES OF CALCULATIONS MADE EVERY FIFTEEN MINUTES AND STORED IN THE POWER DATABASE ARE WRITTEN TO THE FILE, CALC.

FOR REPORT PURPOSES POINTS FROM THE CALC FILE WILL BE REFERRED TO AS CALCULATED POINTS.

Consideration for the reader's needs, judicious use of white space, and a little time produced the revision that follows. Regardless of what you may think of the substance of this highly technical message, you will surely agree that the revised version is easier to read.

    I. Database Description

The maximum number of databases is eight. Each is divided into separate files. In Mansfield, for example—

    In the **Power Database,** the files are PB01, PB02, RB01, MCH2, M2IN, and M2MX.

    In the **Paper Database,** the files are MCH1, M1IN, M1MX, MCH2, M2IN, and M2MX.

    In the **Pulp Database,** the files are PDIG, WSHR, PDIN, HDIG, CDIG, HDIN, SCHM, CAUS, and LKIN.

    The values of the process variables for a given area (except CALC) are stored every fifteen minutes (96 fifteen-minute records every day for each process variable) in the file corresponding to that area. (For example, PB01 corresponds to the No. 1 power boiler.)

    The values of calculations made every fifteen minutes and stored in the power database are written to the file CALC.

    For report purposes, points from the CALC file will be referred to as calculated points.

VI. I HAVE USED PUNCTUATION TO CLARIFY MY MEANING. . . . .

The greatest problems with punctuation occur when you have to choose between one mark and another, or none at all. As a general rule—and it won't apply in every case—punctuate your writing so that the reader hears your natural pauses. Here is a little chart that will help.

Sentence Ends		Comments
Period	.	Use to end statements and after abbreviations. (Exception: Write abbreviations the way you say them. UCLA doesn't carry periods. US Postal Service state abbreviations don't carry periods.)
Question mark	?	Use after direct questions, but not after indirect questions. Examples: *How old are you?* but *He asked me how old you are.*
Exclamation point	!	Use to indicate very strong stress. Sometimes called a "screamer." It's better to let your prose carry the force of your ideas. Use very rarely.

Internal Punctuation

Comma	,	The most common mark. Use it to separate words and phrases. In technical writing, help the reader hear vocal pauses.
Semicolon	;	A semicolon can't figure out if it's a period or a comma. It separates parts of a sentence of equal rank. Unless you are very confident it's better to use a comma or a period. A general rule of thumb: a dozen semicolons should last you the rest of your life.
Colon	:	Marks anticipation. Use a colon to set up quotations, lists, and a long series. Rather than setting up a long series in a single sentence, consider an indented, bullet-marked list.
Parentheses	( )	Use to set off explanations that aren't part of a sentence but are important to it.
Dash	—	A separation mark that is stronger than a comma. Use dashes conservatively. A comma or a period will almost always be better.
Quotation marks	" "	Use to enclose direct quotations from another source and to indicate spoken language.

How you use punctuation marks depends on where you want to place the emphasis. Here are four correctly punctuated examples. Rewriting the sentences would improve them, but keep your focus on the punctuation rather than the sentence structure.

Open, casual writing without any punctuation.	One factor which at first seems unimportant to new members of the team but later turns out to be important is how much time they require to learn the computer system.
Parentheses tell the reader "this material is not very important—you can skip over it if you want."	One factor which at first seems unimportant to new members of the team (but later turns out to be important) is how much time they require to learn the computer system.
Commas set the phrase *off*, too, but you still read it.	One factor which at first seems unimportant to new members of the team, but later turns out to be important, is how much time they require to learn the computer system.
Dashes make you stop to think about the phrase.	One factor which at first seems unimportant to new members of the team—but later turns out to be important—is how much time they require to learn the computer system.

INDEX